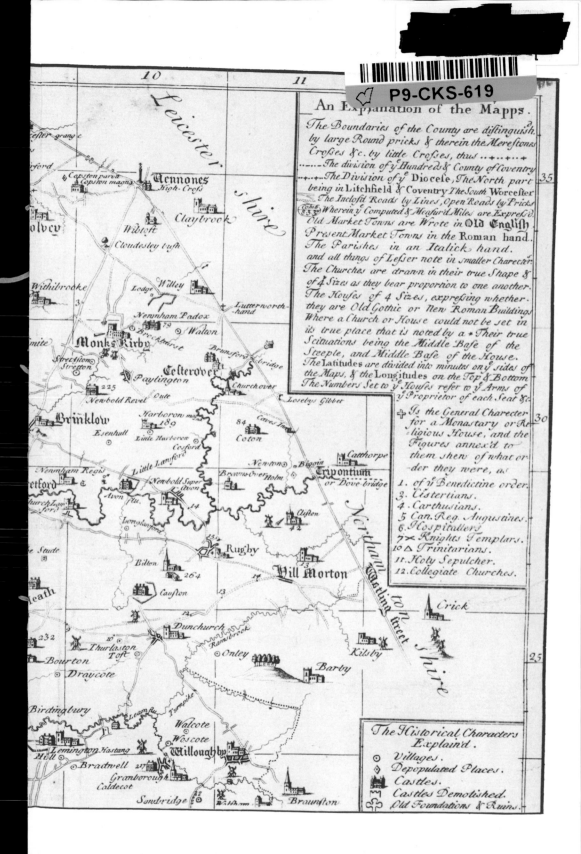

Malory

Malory

THE KNIGHT WHO BECAME
KING ARTHUR'S CHRONICLER

Christina Hardyment

HarperCollins*Publishers*
OCM 62732846

HarperCollins books may be purchased for educational, business, or
sales promotional use. For information, please write: Special Markets
Department, HarperCollins Publishers, 10 East 53rd Street, New York,
NY 10022.

First published in Great Britain in 2005 by HarperCollins Publishers.

FIRST EDITION

Maps and family trees by Les Robinson

Library of Congress Cataloging-in-Publication Data
Hardyment, Christina.
    Malory : the knight who became King Arthur's chronicler /
Christina Hardyment.—1st ed.
        p. cm.
    Includes bibliographical references and index.
    ISBN-10: 0-06-620981-1
    ISBN-13: 978-0-06-620981-4
    1. Malory, Thomas, Sir, 15th cent. 2. Great Britain—
History—Lancaster and York, 1399–1485—Biography. 3. Authors,
English—Middle English, 1100–1500—Biography. 4. Knights and
knighthood—England—Biography. 5. Arthurian romances—
Authorship. I. Title.
PR2045.H37 2006
823'.2—dc22
    [B]   2005058532

06 07 08 09 10   RRD   10 9 8 7 6 5 4 3 2 1

For Ian

CONTENTS

MALORY TIME LINE   xi

MAPS   xviii

PREFACE   1

INTRODUCTION: The Puzzle   9

The *Morte Darthur* Briefly Drawn   23

1 The Baptism Bell   39

2 Childhood   59

3 Apprenticeship in Chivalry   74

4 Taking the Adventure   86

5 Agincourt and After   104

6 The Conquest of Normandy   114

7 Winning Worship   132

8 Captains Courageous   155

9 Defending Christendom   172

10 Battling in Bayonne   191

11 Malory at Home   202

12 The Camelot Years   218

13 Misrule Doth Rise   242

14 Knight Reformer   257

15 Nemesis   273

16 Ravisher of Women?   292

17 'In No Wise Guilty'   313

18 At War with the Law   331

19 Knight Prisoner   344

20 A Powerful Patron   358

21 This Sun of York   376

22 Princepleaser   395

23 The Secret Agent   416

24 Lancaster's Champion   441

25 A Good End   460

ABBREVIATIONS   483

ENDNOTES   485

BIBLIOGRAPHY   585

LIST OF ILLUSTRATIONS   605

INDEX   609

Herein may be seen noble chivalry, courtesy, humanity, friendliness, hardiness, love, friendship, cowardice, murder, hate, virtue, and sin ... And for to pass the time this book shall be pleasant to read in, but for to give faith and belief that all is true that is contained herein, ye be at your liberty.

Caxton's Preface to Sir Thomas Malory's *Morte Darthur*

The past is a great darkness, and filled with echoes.

Margaret Atwood, *The Handmaid's Tale*

TIME LINE SHOWING EVENTS IN
SIR THOMAS MALORY'S LIFE INTERLACED
WITH CONTEMPORARY POLITICAL EVENTS

1399 Approximate date of Thomas Malory's birth

Henry IV of Lancaster usurps the throne from Richard II

1400 John Malory, Thomas's father, imprisoned in the Tower of London

Richard II dies in Pontefract Castle, probably murdered

1406 John Malory recorded as lord of Newbold Revel

1408 Richard Beauchamp, Earl of Warwick, goes to Jerusalem

1413 *Henry IV dies, succeeded by son, Henry V*

1414 Thomas Malory recorded as in the service of Beauchamp in Calais

1415 *25 October: Battle of Agincourt*

1418 Thomas Malory in France in the service of Richard, Earl of Codnor

1420 *Henry V marries Catherine of Valois, daughter of Charles VI, and is recognised as the heir to the French throne*

1421 *Birth of their son Henry, in English eyes heir to the thrones of England and France*

1422 *Death of Henry V. The infant Henry VI's realm is ruled on his behalf by a Regency Council led by his brothers John, Duke of Bedford, and Humfrey, Duke of Gloucester*

1424 A Malory recorded as Captain of Gisors

Birth of Harry Beauchamp, future Duke of Warwick

1425 Birth of Anne Beauchamp, future Countess of Warwick

1429 *April: Joan of Arc inspires the Dauphin and relieves the siege of Orléans*

17 July: The Dauphin crowned as Charles VII, King of France, at Rheims

November: Henry VI crowned at Westminster

1431 *30 May*: *Joan of Arc burnt as a heretic by the English in Rouen*

20 September: Thomas Malory witnesses a settlement in Buckinghamshire

December: Harry Beauchamp accompanies his father to Henry VI's coronation as King of France in Paris

1433/4 Death of John Malory

1435 Sir Robert Malory, Prior of the English Knights Hospitallers, sets out for Rhodes. It is likely that his nephew Thomas was with him.

1436 *Charles VII regains Paris from the English*

1439 Thomas Malory, esquire, witnesses a settlement for his first cousin Sir Philip Chetwynd, and probably accompanies him to Aquitaine

Death of Sir Richard Beauchamp, Earl of Warwick. Succession of his fourteen-year-old son Harry to the earldom. Thomas Malory certainly in his service later, and likely to have entered it after returning from Aquitaine.

1441 Sir Thomas Malory given a grant by the Vicar of Ansty (first record of him as a knight)

1443 Malory and Eustace Burnaby accused of insulting, wounding, imprisoning and robbing Thomas Smith of Spratton, Northamptonshire

1444 Henry VI makes Harry Beauchamp the first Duke of Warwick

1445 *Henry VI marries Margaret of Anjou*

1445–6 Sir Thomas Malory returned as MP for Warwickshire

1446 Death (?murder) of Harry, Duke of Warwick; the Beauchamp estates fall to his baby daughter Anne. Malory included in a list of payments to his retainers.

1447 Death (?murder) of Humfrey, Duke of Gloucester

1447/8 Birth of Malory's son and future heir, Robert

1448 *February*: *Maine surrendered to France*

1449 Death of the infant Countess of Warwick. The earldom passes to Richard Neville, husband of Harry Beauchamp's sister Anne.

1449   *29 October*: Rouen surrendered to France

November: Thomas Malory returned as MP for Great Bedwyn

1450   *4 January*: Date when Malory is later alleged to have ambushed Humphrey, Duke of Buckingham, in the woods of Coombe Abbey, Warwickshire

15 April: *Defeat of the English at Formigny*

2 May: *Murder of John de la Pole, Duke of Suffolk*

June: *Jack Cade's Rebellion*

23 May: Date when Malory is later alleged to have raped Joan Smith of Monks Kirby

31 May: Date when Malory is later alleged to have extorted money from two residents of Monks Kirby

6 August: Date when Malory is later alleged to have raped Joan Smith again, this time in Coventry, and abducted her to Barwell

12 August: *Fall of Cherbourg: 'We have now not a foot of land in Normandy'*

31 August: Date when Malory is later alleged to have extorted money from a third resident of Monks Kirby

November: Thomas Malory returned as MP for Wareham

1451   *15 March*: Second warrant issued for the arrest of Sir Thomas Malory

4 June: Date when Malory is later alleged to have stolen seven cows, two calves, 335 sheep and a cart worth £22 at Cosford, Warwickshire

13 July: Warrant issued for the arrest of Sir Thomas Malory

20 July: Date when Malory is later alleged to have stolen six does and committed damage worth £500 in the deer park of Caluden, which is rented by Buckingham from the Duke of Norfolk

25 July: Buckingham, with sixty men-at-arms, arrives at Newbold Revel to arrest Malory. Malory is committed at Coventry and imprisoned in Coleshill, the house of the Sheriff of Warwickshire, Sir William Mountford.

27 July: Malory escapes from Coleshill by swimming the moat and returns to Newbold Revel

1451   *23 August*: Malory charged at Nuneaton with all the alleged crimes listed above. The case is moved to London and Malory spends the next year in various London prisons without his case being tried.

1452   *21 October*: Malory bailed for three months

1453   *26 March*: Order for Malory's re-arrest

17 July: Defeat of the English at Battle of Châtillon and death of John Talbot, Earl of Shrewsbury, and his son, results in the total loss of Aquitaine

1 August: Henry VI falls into a catatonic stupor

6 October: Malory once more in prison

13 October: Margaret of Anjou gives birth to Edward of Lancaster

1454   *27 March: Richard, Duke of York appointed Protector of the Realm*

8 May: Malory bailed for six months

16 May: Duke of York, as Constable of England, takes an army north to quell rebels

16 October: Malory arrested for feloniously sheltering horse thieves and imprisoned in Colchester Castle; he fights his way out two weeks later

14 November: Malory appears at King's Bench, Westminster, and is once more committed to prison

1455   *19 May*: Malory moved to the Tower of London. He is shuffled in and out of several prisons for the next two and a half years.

22 May: Yorkists gain control of Henry VI after First Battle of St Albans. This is the first skirmish in the long struggle between York and Lancaster known as the 'Wars of the Roses'.

1457   *19 October*: Malory bailed out of prison by the Earl of Warwick's uncle, William Neville, Lord Fauconberg, Deputy Keeper of Calais

1457/8   Death of Malory's son, Thomas Malory, junior

1459   *23 September: Yorkists rout the royal forces at Battle of Blore Heath*

20 November: Parliament condemns Yorkists as traitors

1460   *10 July: Yorkists capture Henry VI at Battle of Northampton; Duke of Buckingham killed*

1460   22 July: Yorkists capture London and take the Tower of London; Yorkist supporters, probably including Malory, released from the city's prisons

30 December: Duke of York killed at Battle of Wakefield

1461   *January*: Abbot of Coombe summoned to appear at King's Bench. At around this time, prosecution of Malory suspended *sine die* (indefinitely).

2 February: York's son Edward, Earl of March, victorious at Battle of Mortimer's Cross

17 February: Yorkists defeated and Henry VI rescued by Margaret of Anjou's forces in Second Battle of St Albans

4 March: Edward, Earl of March, assumes crown as Edward IV

29 March: Total defeat of Lancastrians at Battle of Towton; exile of Henry VI and Margaret of Anjou

1462   *24 October*: General pardon for Sir Thomas Malory entered on Edward IV's first pardon roll

October/November: Malory arranges marriage settlement of his son Robert

October: Malory listed as on campaign with the Earl of Warwick against rebels in the north of England

1464   *15 May: Battle of Hexham routs Lancastrians*

12 September: Malory witnesses a marriage settlement for John Feilding and Helen Walsh

1465   *June: Capture of Henry VI in Ribblesdale and his imprisonment in the Tower of London*

1466/7: Birth of Malory's son and eventual heir, Nicholas

1468   *20 June: Sir Thomas Cook and other London worthies accused of treasonous intrigues*

14 July: Malory is one of fifteen Lancastrian rebels excluded by name from Edward IV's second pardon

1469   *4 March–3 March 1470*: Malory dated the completion of his 'whole book of King Arthur' to this year

20 April: Malory signs as a witness to a deathbed declaration made in Newgate Prison

1469   *26 July*: *Warwick captures Edward IV at the Battle of Edgecote*

November: *Edward IV restored to power and forgives Warwick*

1470   *22 February*: Malory is one of six Lancastrian rebels excluded from Edward IV's third general pardon

14 March: *Lancastrians defeated at Battle of 'Lose-cote Field' in Lincolnshire. Warwick and Edward's brother Clarence accused of treason: they escape to France.*

3 May: A pardon sent by Edward IV to the garrison of Calais excludes Malory and five others

22 July: *Betrothal of Margaret of Anjou's son, Edward of Lancaster, and Anne, daughter of the Earl of Warwick*

13 September: *Landing in Devon, Warwick and Clarence invade England and take London: Edward IV flees to Burgundy*

7 October: *Henry VI restored to the throne*

1471   *12 March*: Death of Sir Thomas Malory according to his recorded *inquisition post mortem*, perhaps a way of avoiding confiscation of his lands

14 March: *Edward IV lands at Ravenspur in Yorkshire*

14 March: Death of Sir Thomas Malory according to his epitaph in Greyfriars Church, London

14 April: *Edward IV defeats the Lancastrians at the Battle of Barnet; Warwick is killed*

4 May: *Prince Edward of Lancaster killed at Battle of Tewkesbury*

21/22 May: *Margaret of Anjou captured. Henry VI murdered in the Tower of London.*

1485   William Caxton publishes Sir Thomas Malory's *Birth, Life and Acts of King* Arthur, *of his noble* knights *of the* Round Table, *their marvellous Enquests and Adventures; th'Achieving of the* Sangreal, *and in the end the dolorous Death and Departing out of the World of them All*

MAPS

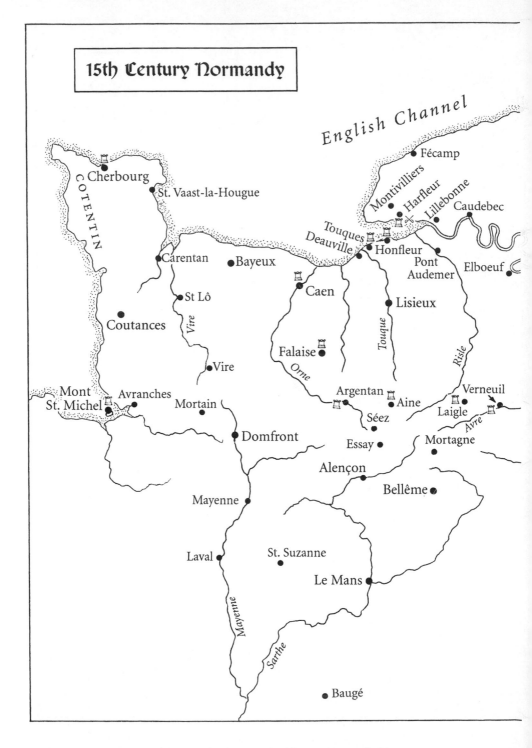

15th Century Normandy

English Channel

COTENTIN

Cherbourg
St. Vaast-la-Hougue
Carentan
Bayeux
St Lô
Coutances
Vire
Vire
Mont St. Michel
Avranches
Mortain
Domfront
Mayenne
Laval
St. Suzanne
Mayenne
Sarthe
Le Mans
Baugé

Fécamp
Montivilliers
Harfleur
Lillebonne
Caudebec
Touques
Deauville
Honfleur
Pont Audemer
Elboeuf
Caen
Lisieux
Touque
Risle
Falaise
Orne
Argentan
Aine
Verneuil
Séez
Laigle
Avre
Essay
Mortagne
Alençon
Bellême

Map of Normandy, showing significant towns and cities
during the English conquest 1417–50.

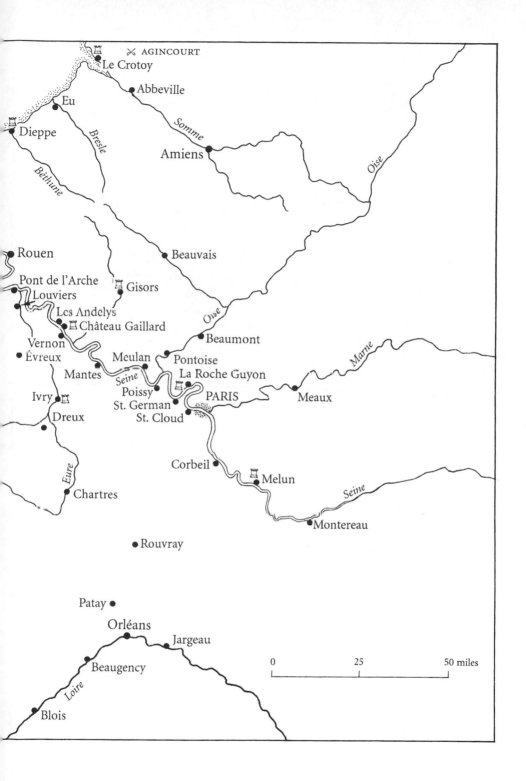

✂ AGINCOURT
Le Crotoy
Abbeville
Eu
Dieppe
Bresle
Somme
Amiens
Oise
Béthune
Rouen
Beauvais
Pont de l'Arche
Louviers
Gisors
Les Andelys
Château Gaillard
Oise
Vernon
Évreux
Beaumont
Marne
Meulan
Pontoise
Mantes
Seine
La Roche Guyon
Ivry
Poissy
St. German
PARIS
Meaux
Dreux
St. Cloud
Eure
Corbeil
Melun
Chartres
Seine
Montereau
Rouvray
Patay
Orléans
Jargeau
0   25   50 miles
Beaugency
Loire
Blois

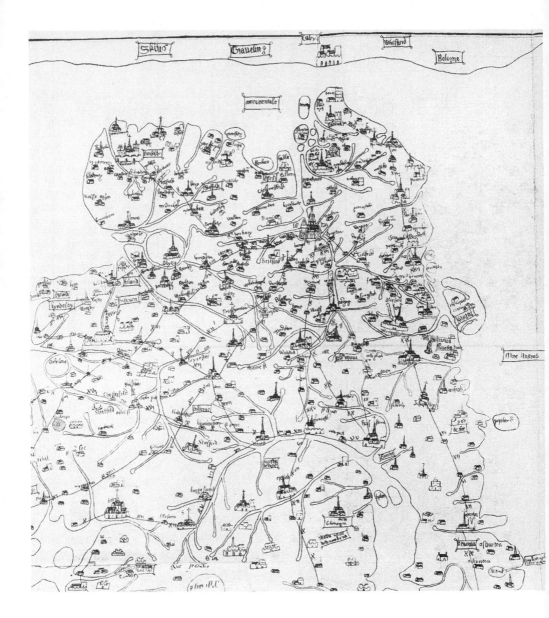

The late fourteenth-century Gough Map tilts our usual view of England onto its side and emphasises rivers as thoroughfares, rather than roads. The inclusion of the coast of France and Flanders shows how intimately connected the English then felt to their mainland territories of Calais (centre, top) and its environs.

PREFACE

Conjecture, unverified supposition, guesswork, surmise, suspicion, rough guess, shrewd idea, speculation, shot in the dark

Roget's *Thesaurus*

Fools rush in, where wise men never go.

Elvis Presley, adapting (probably unknowingly) Alexander Pope

I first read Sir Thomas Malory's *Morte Darthur* when I was a student in the 1960s. I bought it in one of the prettiest and most accessible of its many editions, the set of three slim morocco-bound pocket volumes published at the turn of the century by J. M. Dent in the Temple Classics series. It cost me three shillings on David's second-hand bookstall in Cambridge market. I bought it because I'd been reading T. H. White's *The Once and Future King*, a four-part novel about Arthur which pays constant affectionate tribute to Malory; its first and best-known part is *The Sword in the Stone*. The sound and spirit of Malory's voice have reverberated in my head ever since, and I still love his combination of high ideals and realistic acceptance of the limitations of 'sinful man' and 'sinful lady'.

It wasn't until I decided to include Malory in a book which explored the places in which writers lived and set their stories that I discovered how little was known for certain about him, and that what had come to light suggested he was an incorrigibly violent criminal who had spent most of his life in prison. But the more I looked into what was known, the more it seemed to me that unfounded assumptions had been made about motives and guilt, and that very few of his disparagers knew much about the social circumstances of his life and the realities of medieval politics and law. I didn't either, but I decided to find out, and to write a biography that would be

1

worthy of Malory, if possible clearing his name. I also wanted people to realise that his timeless book is not a remote, literary Everest but accessible, inspiring and touchingly human. I gave myself two years.

Five years on, I still feel I could dig deeper. It has been a far more difficult task than I anticipated when I first set out with courage high and heart aglow. The wise scholars who shook their heads sadly at my presumption were absolutely right to do so. My book, stuffed to the brim with conjectures, breaks a great many scholarly conventions, and I am well aware that it is as much an imagined life as a true biography. It differs materially from the entry for the author of the *Morte Darthur* in the new *Dictionary of National Biography*. But it is the first book to make the puzzling evidence that we have about Malory's life match the character of the author of the *Morte Darthur*, and the first to set him convincingly in the social and political world of his age.

Following up the scattered clues to Malory's doings was a journey of discovery which led me to medieval glories in England, France, Italy and Greece: the ruins of castles at Hanley, Castle Bytham and Fotheringhay; remote country churches splendid with Templar gargoyles; delicately carved tombs of time-polished alabaster; iridescent coats of arms in stained-glass windows; the ancient streets of Sandwich and Rouen; the formidable castles of Caen, Falaise and Gisors; Hospitaller houses in Rome and the walled citadel of Rhodes, where the Malory coat of arms can still be seen on the Inn of the English. Research into medieval records, even when puzzling over all but illegible handwriting, medieval Latin abbreviations and arcane legal terms, has been infinitely seductive. I was lucky enough to be able to do much of it in the gold-grey twilight of Oxford University's Duke Humfrey's Library, a painted cave of a room finished only a decade or so after Malory's death, where rows of leather-bound books rise to an intricately carved ceiling above long oak desks. I have no doubt that more discoveries will be made about Malory, and I hope that I have pointed the way towards some of them. But it is time to pass on my charts to the next explorer.

The endnotes contain a mixture of straightforward references, explanations of unfamiliar concepts, evidence for new assertions, and potentially relevant coincidences and associations. They are intended to inform those unfamiliar with the period and cite sources for the benefit of specialists, to be enjoyed by those who like the what-ifs of history, and to be useful pointers for those who want to take the quest for the truth about Malory's life further.

All quotations from the *Morte Darthur* (which for convenience on occasion I abbreviate to Malory's *Arthur* or the *Morte*) except phrases unique to the Winchester manuscript (see page 12) are in the modernised English of A. W. Pollard's 1900 retelling of Caxton's printed edition. This is the most accessible to the interested lay reader, even though not the most correct in scholarly terms. Besides being available second-hand in a two-volume Everyman edition and for a bargain price from Wordsworth Classics, it was superbly reprinted in 2000 by Cassell, sensitively edited by John Matthews and given magical illustrations by Anne-Marie Ferguson.

I have consulted many experts on different aspects of Malory's life and times. Professor P. J. C. Field, the greatest living authority on Malory, has been especially encouraging and supportive. Greg O'Malley's thesis and letters illuminated the world of the medieval Knights Hospitaller. Anne Sutton has been most helpful, both in personal communications and in her editorship of that unique journal, *The Ricardian*. James Ross and Tom Griffith helped me to decipher manuscripts. Dr Benjamin Thompson advised me on church matters and Nicholas Orme on hunting and children's upbringing. Dr Christine Carpenter robustly advised me against such a speculative project ('Who cares who he was anyway?'), but also shared her unparalleled knowledge of fifteenth-century Warwickshire by the loan of part of her early research work into the county. All the researchers at the History of Parliament Research Trust in Woburn Square who are working on the 1422–1504 volume of biographies of Members of Parliament contributed expertise generously (Dr Linda Clark (L. S. C.), Dr Matthew Davies (M. P. D.), Dr David Grummitt (D. I. G.), Dr Hannes Kleineke (H. W. K.), Dr Charles Moreton (C. E. M.) and Dr Simon Payling (S. J. P.)) My thanks too go to Gill Coleridge and Lucy Luck of Rogers, Coleridge, White, Michael Fishwick and his team at HarperCollins (Jane Birkett, Caroline

Hotblack, Annabel Wright, Becky Glibbery and Kate Hyde) and my indexer Sandra Raphael. Finally, my thanks go out in abundance to those who read and constructively criticised various drafts of the book: Linda Clark, P. J. C. Field, Hugh Griffith, Michael Hicks, Greg O'Malley, Anne Sutton and Ian Howlett, who also nobly accepted the ghost knight who has lurked in my life for five years. From first to last, Martin Meredith was a vital touchstone, judicious with criticism and generous with encouragement. Any merit it has owes much to all these; its inevitable shortcomings are all my own work.

Christina Hardyment
Oxford, 2005

GENEAOLOGY OF
THE HOUSES OF LANCASTER,
YORK AND BEAUFORT

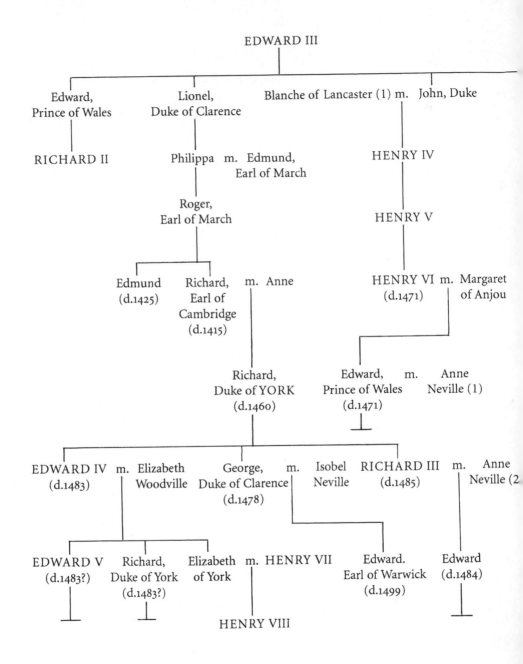

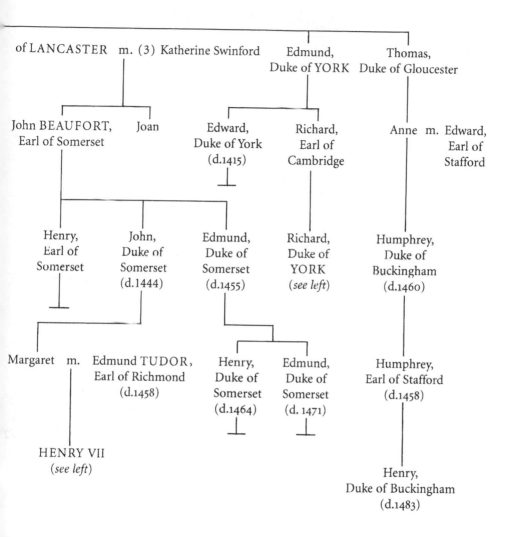

of LANCASTER   m. (3) Katherine Swinford   Edmund,   Thomas,
                                            Duke of YORK   Duke of Gloucester

John BEAUFORT,   Joan   Edward,   Richard,   Anne   m. Edward,
Earl of Somerset   Duke of York   Earl of   Earl of
                                  (d.1415)   Cambridge   Stafford

Henry,   John,   Edmund,   Richard,   Humphrey,
Earl of   Duke of   Duke of   Duke of   Duke of
Somerset   Somerset   Somerset   YORK   Buckingham
                  (d.1444)   (d.1455)   (see left)   (d.1460)

Margaret   m.   Edmund TUDOR,   Henry,   Edmund,   Humphrey,
                Earl of Richmond   Duke of   Duke of   Earl of Stafford
                (d.1458)   Somerset   Somerset   (d.1458)
                                   (d.1464)   (d. 1471)

HENRY VII   Henry,
(see left)   Duke of Buckingham
                                                                    (d.1483)

The Puzzle

It befell in the days of Uther Pendragon, when he was king of all England, and so reigned, that there was a mighty duke in Cornwall that held war against him long time. And the duke was called the Duke of Tintagil. And so by means King Uther sent for this duke, charging him to bring his wife with him, for she was called a fair lady, and a passing wise, and her name was called Igraine.

Malory, 'The Tale of King Arthur'

o understand why Sir Thomas Malory's 300,000-word history of King Arthur and his knights has been reprinted so frequently since William Caxton chose to publish it in 1485, go back and read the quotation above, the opening lines of Malory's book, aloud. The words sing off the page. Through the centuries they have been heard, either spoken or in the mind's ear, by millions of people. *Le Morte Darthur* is our most enduring national epic, written in an English we can still enjoy today – a language that had only just come of age and replaced the French once automatically spoken by the educated classes. Its full magnificent title is *The Birth, Life and Acts of King Arthur, of his noble Knights of the Round Table, their marvellous Enquests and Adventures; th'Achieving of the Sangreal, and in the end the dolorous Death and Departing out of the World of them All.* However, Caxton elected to call it simply *Le Morte Darthur*, and this ungrammatical but romantic title is in general use today. The book was instantly popular. Henry VII named his first-born son Arthur in 1487; Henry VIII arranged a Camelot-style tournament called the Field of the Cloth of Gold for King Francis I of France in 1520. Malory was admired by the Elizabethan playboy-poet Edmund

Spenser, the seventeenth-century Puritan John Milton, Queen Victoria's adored poet laureate Lord Tennyson and the artisan-craftsman William Morris.

Twentieth-century lovers of *Le Morte Darthur* are equally diverse. T. E. Lawrence kept a copy in his saddlebag during the Arab Revolt as solace from the horrors of war. C. S. Lewis thought Malory's writing was 'as musical, as forthright, as poignant, as was ever heard in England'. Raymond Chandler's Philip Marlowe was originally called Philip Malory. John Steinbeck spent months of his life in England exploring Arthurian locations and living in a medieval cottage in Somerset rewriting Malory with a biro refill stuck into a goose quill. T. H. White wrote his own Arthurian epic *The Once and Future King* as a homage to Malory: it inspired the musical *Camelot*, and Walt Disney made a cartoon of the first part of it, *The Sword in the Stone*.

Malory's influence extends far beyond readers of his book. Without him King Arthur, Gawaine, Lancelot and Guinevere, Galahad and Perceval, Tristram and Isolde would be archaic shadows. The reality and immediacy he gave to the world of the 'once and future king' have made them iconic figures, and Tintagel, Glastonbury and Winchester are places of pilgrimage for millions of visitors from all over the world. The Arthurian concepts of Camelot, the Round Table and the Holy Grail are international archetypes used in poems, novels, comic books, music, paintings, computer games and films with astonishing regularity.

Yet the reality of the man who gave their stories enduring life has been lost in a shadowland of surmise, speculation and denial for more than five centuries. Contemporaries referred often enough to Chaucer in the fourteenth century and Shakespeare in the sixteenth. Fifteenth-century writers' pens are dry on the subject of Malory as a writer, although a mid-sixteenth-century biographical dictionary describes him memorably as a man 'of heroic and magnanimous temperament' who 'easily outshone the scholars of his time'. His very identity was uncertain until 1895, when an American scholar, G. T. Kitteridge, suggested that he might have been Sir Thomas Malory of Newbold Revel, a substantial manor seven miles east of Coventry.

Until the 1920s, all that would-be biographers had unearthed about this Warwickshire knight fitted a devotee of chivalry nicely. His name appeared on a 1414 list of men-at-arms mustered to serve in Calais, which had been captured from the French by Edward III in 1347, and in 1445 he had sat in Parliament as knight of the shire for Warwickshire. His tombstone in Greyfriars Church, near Newgate in London, announced him to be a 'valiant knight' who died on 14 March 1471. Then, in 1928, a resourceful American scholar called Edward Hicks, who had been burrowing deep into unsorted archives in London's Public Record Office, published a life of Malory based on his discovery of a long and partially burned record of a court held at Nuneaton in 1451. It revealed that Sir Thomas Malory of Newbold Revel had been accused of an appalling catalogue of crimes. He had, it said, ambushed the Duke of Buckingham with intent to murder, broken out of jail, made a violent and destructive raid on the Abbey of Coombe, extorted valuables from local villagers and rustled three hundred sheep from a neighbour's estate. Worst of all, he had committed rape not once, but twice. The pimpled sheepskin parchment on which these devastating indictments against Malory were written in cramped, almost illegible handwriting had survived unnoticed for centuries among an obscure and much-damaged collection of miscellaneous legal papers. A search of other legal records by other scholars, notably A. C. Baugh, found several more misdemeanours and debts, evidence of Malory's committal to a variety of prisons, and no record of his release. To cap it all, Sir Thomas Malory's name appeared in the very short list of incorrigibly obdurate criminals whom Edward IV refused to pardon in 1468 and 1470, nearly twenty years after the original indictment.

How could a man who composed one of the most warmly human and nobly intended books of all time break every law in the book of chivalry? Authors have often had criminal careers, but not ones which clashed so violently with the spirit of their writings. Disappointed admirers of the *Morte* began to look for other candidates for authorship. They came up with two more Thomas Malorys: one from Papworth St Agnes, near Cambridge, the other from Hutton Conyers, in Yorkshire. But although superficially ingenious cases were made for each of them, closer examination has made them unconvincing.

Moreover, neither were knights and both were far more obscure than Sir Thomas Malory of Newbold Revel.

Another discovery, ten years later, altered the shape of Malory studies for ever. In 1934, Walter Oakeshott, a junior English master in one of England's oldest schools, Winchester College, asked if he could look through the medieval manuscripts in the safe of the Fellows' Library for interesting bindings. The safe was located in the college's inner sanctum: the bedroom of the High Master. The last time a medievalist had been allowed in, he had shyly pointed out that the Master's bedside rug was a priceless square of tapestry, part of a hanging showing the arms of ancient kings of England, including Arthur, which had been woven in Arras for the occasion of the christening of Prince Arthur, Henry VII's oldest son, in Winchester Cathedral in 1486.

The bindings were disappointing, but on opening one fat quarto-size handwritten volume, Oakeshott found it was peppered with proper names written in red: Sir Lancelot, Sir Bors, Sir Kay, Sir Lamorak – unmistakably, Arthur's knights. Its first and last eight pages were missing, but after comparing it to a printed edition of *Morte Darthur*, he realised that it was undoubtedly a manuscript version of Malory's famous book. Watermarks on its paper dated it to the 1470s – a decade before Caxton set it up on his press at Westminster. Scholars soon realised that it also held exciting clues to Malory's identity in the explanatory tailpieces, known as 'explicits', which ended sections of the text. Several of these contained personal references. Seventy pages into the manuscript, at the end of the first series of tales telling how King Arthur established his rule over Britain, were the words: 'This book was drawn by a knight prisoner Sir Thomas Malleorré, that God send him soon recover'. About seventy pages further on, another explicit asked 'all that readeth this tale to pray for him who this wrote that God send him good deliverance soon and hastily. Amen.'

The year 1993 saw the publication of Professor Peter Field's meticulously researched study, *The Life and Times of Sir Thomas Malory*. Carefully rehearsing the evidence for and against rival candidates, he proved beyond reasonable doubt that Sir Thomas Malory of Newbold Revel was indeed the author of the *Morte Darthur*. He also rejected the idea that Malory spent twenty years of his life in prison, and speculates that his repeated exception from pardon in the late 1460s implied a quite different kind of criminal activity: treason, a crime of which a great many fifteenth-century gentlemen were accused during the three troubled decades of strife and civil war between the rival noble houses of York and Lancaster. He concluded that Malory was probably an ally of Sir Richard Neville, Earl of Warwick, a man so powerful during what were later called the Wars of the Roses that he has been nicknamed 'Warwick the Kingmaker'. However, Field also argued that Malory was unlikely to have been the Thomas Malory who went to Calais as a man-at-arms in 1414 because that would mean that he was at least seventy in 1469 when he recorded that he had completed his 'whole book' of Arthur, too advanced an age, Field thinks, to write so splendidly. He suggests instead that the Sir Thomas Malory who wrote the *Morte Darthur* was born in about 1415–18, and came of age just before 1439, when he witnessed a document for his first cousin.

Despite Field's valiant efforts to restore Malory's good name, the damage to his reputation caused by the Nuneaton indictment in the popular imagination remains enormous. Although Malory was never brought to trial to answer its accusations, he has generally been assumed to have been guilty as charged. Modern references to him typically include such perjoratives as 'tearaway' or 'misfit', 'progress-ively unhinged', 'a common criminal'. He is seen as a man with an 'individual tendency towards violent behaviour' who 'went badly off the rails from 1450' and 'put his whole family under a cloud until nearly the end of the century': in sum, he was as mad, bad and dangerous to know as Lord Byron.

Moreover, Field's proposed new birth date for Malory leaves us with more, not fewer puzzles. The long and knowledgeably detailed descriptions of battles and military strategy in the *Morte Darthur* are those of an experienced soldier. The man who penned them must have lived a life that taught him unforgettable lessons about chivalry and loyalty, love and war. The obvious place to acquire such experi-ence was in France, for after his unexpected triumph at Agincourt in

1415, Henry V and his brothers went on to conquer the whole of Normandy and Maine. But Field's Malory is a mere child during Henry V's wars in France, and a boy in England in the 1420s, a time when any knight worth his salt was abroad establishing a reputation for prowess and 'worship'. If he was indeed born in about 1415–18, we have to ignore a great many mentions of Thomas Malorys in the medieval records between 1400 and 1431.

The issue of age also affects interpretation of the shocking crimes of which Malory was accused in 1451. For a headstrong man in his thirties to ambush, rob, pillage, poach and rape is one thing. Such acts require much more explanation if they were carried out by a mature knight and family man with a hitherto spotless record. Because of Field's new birth date for Malory, the *Morte* is now being interpreted as atonement for a wild youth – though why the thoroughly pleasurable occupation of translating French romances enticingly stuffed with 'manslaughter and bold bawdry' should be regarded as a penance is unclear.

We need not blench at the idea of Sir Thomas Malory being seventy or so when he finished revising his great book. The fact that the average age at death in the fifteenth century was forty-five for men and forty for women (childbirth was a dangerous undertaking) does not mean that everyone who survived into their sixties was doddery or senile. Those who lasted for their allotted biblical span or more were often just as able and energetic as their counterparts today. Henry Lord FitzHugh was sixty-three when he fought beside Henry V at Agincourt; he was still captain of Falaise in 1422, aged seventy. John Talbot, Earl of Shrewsbury, 'the most strenuous and audacious' of all the English commanders in France, was about sixty-seven when he was cut down at Châtillon in 1453. John, Lord Wenlock was one of England's most cunning diplomats when he was in his sixties. He was seventy when his skull was smashed with an axe at the Battle of Tewkesbury in 1471.

Today writers continue to work until late in life, and medieval authors did so too. The poet John Gower was sixty-five when he finished *Confessio Amantis*, his diverting romp through the seven deadly sins (with especial emphasis on lust). He wrote a history justifying Henry IV's coronation in 1399 when he was seventy-four, and died at the age of eighty-three. The translator and bibliophile John Shirley, whose life is an interesting parallel to Malory's, was ninety when he died in 1456. The rhyming chronicler John Hardyng was born in 1378; he was still active and adding to his chronicle when he was eighty-seven. Sir John Fortescue, the most eminent judge of the age, wrote his famous treatise on the laws of England, *De Laudibus Legum Angliae*, between 1468 and 1471, when he was almost eighty. Age is frequently a spur to creativity. The message of Thomas Dormandy's *Old Masters: Great Artists in Old Age* is that the approach of death brings with it a new urgency, a powerful shift in the inner forces that impel men and women to create; also a liberation from former constraints that can result in an artistic freedom greater than ever before. This certainly fits Sir Thomas Malory as my biography will present him. The last two books of his history of Arthur could easily have been written when he was in his sixties; they are fine examples of what Dormandy calls 'late flowerings [which] bear witness to human creativity at its most indestructible and at its most sublime'. Like Thomas Hardy and W. B. Yeats, Malory saved the best till last.

Field's richly detailed research has been a major inspiration and invaluable resource for me in writing this book. But as a distinguished academic, he has to observe a scholarly caution, and his book makes Malory's life more, not less mystifying. It does not explain the emergence of a clever, forceful writer who evidently had ideals for which he was willing to risk his life, a man whom the Lancastrian King Henry VI feared enough to imprison without trial for almost a decade, and who was one of a tiny handful of men excluded from pardon by Henry's usurping Yorkist successor, Edward IV. To achieve this, Malory's birth needs to be returned to around 1400, and what we know about his apparently criminal actions examined in the context of medieval legal practice and the troubled political world of the fifteenth century. Whether or not he was guilty of rape must be squarely faced. And a convincing explanation for his disgrace in the late 1460s must be found.

This has only recently become possible. The fifteenth century has long been a poor relation in English history – a stretch of chaos between Chaucer's celebrated *Canterbury Tales* of the 1390s and the glories of the Tudor dynasty in the sixteenth century. This view owed much to Shakespeare's eight brilliant but inaccurate history plays: *Richard II*, *Henry IV Parts I and II*, *Henry V*, *Henry VI Parts I, II* and *III*, and *Richard III*. Nor can it be denied that three of those five kings were murdered and the other two sickened and met untimely deaths, as did Edward IV, the hidden star of *Henry VI Part III*.

But in the last fifty years the extent to which the success of the Tudors was built on solid foundations laid during the reigns of the Lancastrian and Yorkist kings gradually has been recognised. Interest in the century is now intense, and books and articles on all its aspects are pouring off the presses. It is coming into focus as an exciting and eventful age in which England held more land in France than the French King, the English language came into its own, a permanent navy was established and palatial private residences with romantic names like 'Plaisaunce' and 'Joyeux Repos' were built. New interpretations of legal records are beginning to make it clear that the notorious violence of the times has been exaggerated, and that many legal accusations were false. Although battles were indeed fought on English soil, the 'Wars of the Roses' were not like the sustained, deeply ideological hostilities between the Puritans and the Royalists in the seventeenth century. During the thirty-five years of conflict, there were only around 482 days of fighting. Although England had a population of two million, 600,000 of them men of fighting age, no more than 50,000 soldiers took part at any one time. Usually campaigns were brief, involved small numbers of soldiers and were suspended during the winter. Loyalties were constantly shifting, and assigning people neatly into Lancastrian or Yorkist camps is misleading.

The country's economy was buoyant even after the notorious depletion of royal wealth during Henry VI's reign and a decade of civil war. Bohemian visitors to England in 1464 reported that the royal Treasury in the Tower of London 'exceeded the anciently famed wealth of Croesus and Midas', and described the kingdom as 'surpassingly rich in gold and silver'. No fewer than four hundred goldsmiths in London were said to be constantly busy. The travellers also mentioned the great flocks of sheep, the silver, copper, tin and lead mines, and (ruefully) 'a liquor called Alsepir' (ale-beer).

Most of the wealth of country squires like the Malorys came from sales of corn and wool, profits from pasturing other men's cattle and sheep, or, increasingly often, rents from land or indeed from whole manors. The incomes of the landed gentry varied dramatically. Of the 7,000 who could claim gentry status, only around 2,000 admitted to the minimum income of £20 which was required of Justices of the Peace in 1439. About 180 of the gentry had incomes averaging approximately £200 a year. Another 750 had incomes between £40 and £100. There were around fifty heads of noble families in 1436, a handful of whom were immensely wealthy, with incomes as high as £7,000 a year, and half of whom had incomes of less than £400 a year. It was a small world, in which men and women of rank mostly knew each other personally or by repute.

Parliament was an even more exclusive club. No more than forty magnates customarily received a summons to the House of Lords, where they sat with about the same number of 'lords spiritual' – churchmen who were often closely related to them. England's 37 counties sent 74 knights of the shire to the House of Commons, and the 85 towns sent some 170 burgesses. Armigerous lineage was highly rated, but there was much mutually profitable intermingling of landed gentlemen and the merchant community. Nobles, knights and squires often had mercantile interests of one sort or another: a stake in a textile business in Coventry, or in a Bristol cargo from the East, a connection with one or other of the London guilds. The balance of trade was at this time in England's favour, and London merchants were enormously wealthy. Around a third of London aldermen in the late fifteenth century married into county families, as did their daughters.

Although the economy had now recovered from the reduction of the population by around a third by the Black Death of 1348–9, plague still cursed the age, with major outbreaks in 1407, 1434, 1464, 1471 and 1479. The prospect of untimely death intensified religiosity. More churches were built or rebuilt in the fifteenth century than in any other except the nineteenth. Every square inch of their windows, walls, ceilings, woodwork and even floors was exuberantly decorated; the Bohemian travellers described them as 'builded of gold and set forth with jewels'. Chantry chapels were added to house the tombs of the great, roomy enough to accommodate choirs paid to sing thousands of requiem masses to ease the passage of over-worldly Christian souls through purgatory. Pilgrimage shrines such as Walsingham, Bridlington, Hailes Abbey and Canterbury were fabulously well endowed with treasures: it is not surprising that Henry VIII cast avaricious eyes upon them a century later. Clerics were often wealthy men, younger sons of gentlemen whose lifestyle differed little from that of their brothers. But there were also ascetics who strove for spiritual perfection and wrote inspiring exhortations to their human flocks. Most influential of all was the Oxford academic John Wycliffe (c.1330–84). His doctrines of the literal truth of the Bible, men's predestined path to heaven or hell, the need for sinful clergy to be removed from their livings, and the laity's right to read Christian texts in English, were condemned by the Catholic Church, but many pious laymen agreed with him. For much of his life he lived at Lutterworth, just east of Newbold Revel. His followers, who came from all ranks of society, were known as 'Lollards' and much persecuted.

This life of Malory is a portrait of a man who was intimately involved in the social and political realities of his times. He spends his formative years among such heroic figures as King Henry V, the famously chivalric 13th Earl of Warwick, Sir Richard Beauchamp, the romantic and hot-headed Duke Humfrey of Gloucester, and Joan of Arc. He is among the youngest members of the English invasion force that gathers in 1415 to besiege Harfleur and triumph at Agincourt. By the time he is twenty, he has witnessed both Henry V's conquest of Normandy and his tragically premature death, and he remains on campaign in France for another decade. In 1435 he sails with his Knight Hospitaller uncle, Robert Malory, to protect the Hospitaller headquarters in Rhodes from the Turks, and he fights in Aquitaine in 1441. He is a mature knight in the 1440s, who sits in Parliament on several occasions and is hopeful that the young King Henry VI and his beautiful French queen will re-establish English rule in Normandy and Aquitaine.

When corruption at court destroys his chosen liege lords, self-interested courtiers dominate the young King and Queen, and lawyers assert that justice is the province of the courts, not of knights, it seems to Malory that the truly chivalrous life is under threat. He takes up the banner of reform, only to fall foul of a powerful nobleman who dominates both the royal household and the Midland shires where the Malory estates lie. His support for radical elements in Parliament leads to remorseless legal persecution and repeated spells of imprisonment. Only the infamous blood feuds known as the Wars of the Roses bring him freedom in 1460 but, although he enjoys a few years as a respected elder statesman, his conscience will not allow him to rest easy. For the King to whom he owes his chivalric allegiance has been driven from his throne by a Yorkist usurper, Edward IV. He finds himself perilously involved in conspiracies and soon suffers accordingly.

The facts that we have about the Malory family's traditions and Malory's own life fit this picture. It also accords with the spirit of the author of the *Morte Darthur*, a man for whom the ethic of chivalry which is the backbone of the book was neither nostalgia nor escape. Chivalry was the fifteenth-century equivalent of today's liberal democracy: a great ideal, to which many people paid lip service but which was by no means universally observed. Once we look around Malory rather than merely at him, we can see that he lived in a world in which knights really did go on quests, joust to gain honour and please their ladies, and ride with their 'good lord' into battle.

It was a world that was becoming prosperous enough to enjoy its leisure more. Literacy was increasing, and so was interest in reading in English, rather than Latin or French. But people did not study only religion. The English gentry loved mapping their own lineage, listening to ballads and lays, and reading histories and romances. Malory was not the only knight to tackle a translation of a much-loved story. But he wrote particularly well, in a dramatic, colloquial English that everyone could, and still can, enjoy. He was also unusually thorough in his research. It has been estimated that he read at least twenty different French romances and several early English histories in order to create his own distinctly idiosyncratic history of King Arthur and the 'noble and joyous Knights of the Round Table'. To go to such lengths suggests that he had understanding patrons, who could lend or allow him to copy books, and that he had a particularly important reader in mind. Who that person was can now only be guessed at – the first eight pages of the Winchester manuscript, which might have told us the truth about the book's genesis, are missing. Lessons for future kings seem to be intended, however, and I will argue later that Malory began to write for Henry VI's benefit, then revised all he had written for Henry's son Prince Edward.

Malory also had a larger audience in mind: all the gentlefolk of England. His purpose in writing was not only to entertain, enthral and excite his readers, but to imprint the values of chivalry, loyalty, piety and courtesy indelibly on their minds. He used the word 'joyous' in its fifteenth-century sense of 'inspiring', rather than our sense of 'cheerful'. He also wanted to drive home the idea that knights were in the last resort free agents. They were loyal friends and trustworthy servants, but they were answerable only to their own sense of honour and right-doing, a code of values based on the oath they had taken on becoming knights. Justification, not atonement, was Malory's aim. It was a goal which, at a personal level, he failed to achieve. The future lay with the crooked lawyers who tied him up in a web of accusations in 1451, from which it took him almost a decade to struggle free. The growing strength of the legal process proved destructive to Malory's personal career, but it would be turned by the Tudors into their greatest source of strength, giving them more control than any other monarchs had had over their unruly subjects. Chivalric trust was replaced by legal terror. Henry VII's declared purpose was described by a contemporary as 'having many persons in danger at his pleasure', and great nobles with royal blood were more likely to find themselves in the Tower of London than honoured as kinsmen.

But the *Morte Darthur* has preserved Malory's ideals through five centuries, surfacing most vigorously when championed by Sir Walter Scott, Tennyson and the Pre-Raphaelites in the nineteenth century. It is still inspiring individuals to trust their own understanding of truth and loyalty, to right wrongs and defeat evil. The real reason for its extraordinary popularity is that it is one of the most enduring of all guides to proud independence of mind. Although keeping faith with one's liege lord is of prime importance, defiance, not submission, is the Arthurian knight's reaction to unjust treatment. What Malory's presentation of Lancelot's actions illustrates above all is the right of the just man to take the law into his own hands if he felt that that was the only way in which justice could be obtained. The *Morte Darthur* is the primer of the legendary 'English individualism'.

The *Morte Darthur*
Briefly Drawn

All that evening I sat by my fire at the Warwick Arms, steeped in a dream of the olden time, while the rain beat upon the windows, and the wind roared about the eaves and corners. From time to time I dipped into old Sir Thomas Malory's enchanting book, and fed at its rich feast of prodigies and adventures, breathed in the fragrance of its obsolete names, and dreamed again. Midnight being come at length, I read another tale, for a night-cap.

Mark Twain, *A Connecticut Yankee at King Arthur's Court* (1889)

The following short summary of the *Morte Darthur* is intended both to tempt new readers to approach it and remind aficionados of its delights. Setting out to read the whole of the wild sea of stories which Malory wrote can seem a daunting venture. His book fills between 800 and 1,000 pages, depending on which edition you choose. Some of the adventures are told at inordinate length, others shrugged off in a line. There is barely a chapter without a joust, far too many severed heads (often those of damsels), and very few satisfactory love affairs. Digressions are frequent, characters innumerable and confusingly similar in name – Sir Galahad, Sir Galagars, Sir Gahalantine, and Sir Galahalt the High Prince, King Pelles, Sir Pelleas, Sir Pellounes, Sir Palomides and Sir Pellinore, Sir Plaine de Amoure and Sir Plaine de Force, Sir Gromore Somir Joure and Sir Grummore Grummursum. Many of them are only mentioned once. Some are killed only to turn up again later.

It is easier to enjoy and make sense of the *Morte* if you know that there is method both in the way that Malory's tales were 'briefly drawn out of the French', and in the way he decided to edit, add to, and rearrange them. The spine of the stories is King Arthur's life. But Arthur is neither the book's real subject nor its true hero. Nor is any attempt made to reconstruct the sixth-century times in which most medieval historians believe Arthur reigned. What Malory is really interested in is the message for his own age in the ways in which Arthur's knights can either uphold the realm or threaten it; and its hero is unmistakably Sir Lancelot, the greatest and most thoughtful – though not the most perfect – of its knights.

William Caxton, who published the *Morte* in 1485, edited Malory's text into twenty-one separate books, each subdivided into short chapters. The informative headings to the five hundred or so chapters run in total to nearly 6,000 words, and appear together at the beginning of the book as 'The Table or Rubrics of the content of chapters'. They sound enticing – a random selection offers 'How Sir Uwain rode with the damosel of sixty year of age . . . How Sir Lancelot at the request of a lady recovered a falcon, by which he was deceived . . . How Sir Bleoberis demanded the fairest lady in King Mark's court, whom he took away, and how he was fought with . . . How Sir Tristram at a tournament bare the shield that Morgan le Fay delivered to him'. But they give little idea of the shape of the whole book. For this, Eugène Vinaver's edition of the manuscript discovered in the Winchester College library is a better guide. He divided the text into eight, using its 'explicits' as cues. These explanatory remarks were either written by Malory himself or by the two scribes who wrote the manuscript, and most of them do not exist in Caxton's printing. Some of Vinaver's divisions are short; one is extremely long. Within the parts there are groups of distinct tales, which digress from the main subject of the section.

5 'The Tale of King Arthur' (140 pages)

The story begins with illicit love: King Uther Pendragon's obsession with Igraine, wife of the Duke of Cornwall. Then comes Arthur's conception at Tintagel, his secret fostering and his surprise accession to the throne after pulling a magical sword from a stone. Arthur fights rebels on the fringes of his realm and proves himself in individual combat against over-mighty subjects, helped by Merlin's advice and magic. Margawse, the wife of King Lot of Orkney, comes to court with her four young sons, Gawaine, Gaheris, Agravaine and Gareth, and seduces Arthur. What he does not know is that she is his half-sister, one of Igraine's three daughters by the Duke of Cornwall. She bears Arthur a son, Mordred, and Merlin warns Arthur that this incestuous act will be his doom.

Between wars and jousts, hints of the future feats of such paladins as Tristram and Lancelot, and the odd imprisonment by sorceresses like Morgan le Fay (also a daughter of Igraine) comes the mysterious tale of Balin and Balan. An important prequel to the Grail quest, it explains how Pelles, the Fisher King, receives the 'dolorous stroke' that transforms his kingdom into a wasteland.

Marriage brings Arthur not just Guinevere, but the Round Table, which is presented to him by Guinevere's father, complete with a hundred of the hundred and fifty knights who could be seated around it. The gift inspires Arthur to found a prestigious chivalric order which will provide him with a loyal body of 'noble knights of worship and prowess'.

The scribe rounds off this section with the explicit that revealed that Malory was in prison either when it was written or when it was finally revised:

> Here endeth this tale, as the French book saith, from the marriage of king Uther unto king Arthur that reigned after him and did many battles.
>
> And this book endeth whereas Sir Lancelot and Sir Tristram, come to court. Who that will make any more, let him seek other books of King Arthur or of Sir Lancelot or of Sir Tristram; for this was drawn by a knight prisoner Sir Thomas Malleorré, that God send him good recover. Amen. Explicit

6 'The Tale of how Arthur became Emperor of the Romans' (20 pages in Caxton, 60 in Winchester)

In the next section, Arthur and his knights prove hugely success-ful in war, defying the demand of the 'Dictator of Rome' for tribute, hurtling into battle and conquering great tracts of Europe. Lancelot is among his commanders, but not Tristram, who has returned to Isolde's side in Cornwall. Arthur is crowned Emperor in Rome by the Pope's hand, 'and established all his lands from Rome into France'. The battles are described in graphic detail, and the magic that won Arthur the day in his French sources is replaced with convincing strategic ploys suggested by Lancelot. The importance of having reliable allies is emphasised. Even the best fighters can be outnumbered by an enemy. Equally important is giving praise when due and appropriate rewards. After Arthur has been crowned Emperor, he

> *gave lands and realms unto his servants and knights, to everych after his desert, in such wise that none complained, rich nor poor. And he gave to Sir Priamus the duchy of Lorraine; and he thanked him, and said he would serve him the days of his life; and after made dukes and earls, and made every man rich.*

Although the securing and extension of Arthur's realm are an essential prelude to Malory's story, they are only a very minor part of it. Caxton's telling fills only twenty pages. Even in the longer version of the Roman wars in the Winchester manuscript, it only takes the 'best knights of the world' sixty pages to see off the horrible hordes who have been summoned from Asia, India, Africa, Arabia and 'Europe the Large'. There is no reference to imprisonment in the manuscript explicit for this section. It says:

> *Here endeth the tale of the noble king Arthur that was Emperor himself through dignity of his hands.*
> *And here followeth after many noble tales of Sir Lancelot de Lake.*

Explicit the Noble Tale betwixt king Arthur and Lucius the Emperor of Rome.

7 'The Tale of Lancelot du Lake' (30 pages)

Next we hear about Sir Lancelot's adventures at home. A model knight, unfazed by sorceresses, and invariably successful, even when cornered naked in a tree, he sends a steady stream of conquered knights to Guinevere, but refuses to answer inquiries about his relationship with her by would-be paramours. Once again, the explicit is terse:

Explicit a noble tale of Sir Lancelot du Lake.

8 'The Tale of Sir Gareth of Orkney' (60 pages)

Twice as much space is then given to the tale of an untried young knight called Beaumains, who turns out to be both an ace at jousting and a noble of note: the younger brother of Gawaine, Gaheris and Agravane, the sons of King Lot of Orkney and Queen Margawse, King Arthur's over-amorous half-sister. The explicit at the end of this tale is an urgent cry for help:

And I pray you all that readeth this tale to pray for him that this wrote, that God send him good deliverance soon and hastily. Amen. Here endeth the tale of Sir Gareth of Orkney.

9 'The Book of Sir Tristram of Lyonesse' (430 pages)

Easily the longest, hence its description as a 'book' rather than a tale, this section of Malory's epic is the one most often heavily edited or even omitted. But to do so distorts his purpose. Malory presents a worldly, imperfect Tristram very different from Wagner's lovelorn hero. An intensely human figure, he is fond of hunting and music and feasting, and values his men friends more than his women. What matters most to him is knightly prowess, and he is more interested in catching up with Lancelot and going to tournaments than in twilit suppers with Isolde. There are long digressions which show the growing comradeship of the great knights, Lamorak, Gareth and Lancelot, and contrast their prowess with the ignoble adventures of Gawaine, Mordred and Sir Breuse Sans Pitié. Brief lives of 'young unknowns' like La Cote Male Taile, Alisander Le Orphelin and Percival draw an effective parallel between their idealism and Tristram's worldliness. King Mark, Tristram's villainous uncle, has a few chapters of notably unsuccessful adventures, and Sir Dinadan provides an amusingly cynical running critique of chivalric absurdities. There is another little trailer for the Grail quest to come. An attractive character in the book is the Saracen knight Palomides, who becomes steadily more infuriated by coming second to Tristram in both love and war, but is eventually reconciled to him, and converted to Christianity. The most important episode in the book from the point of view of Malory's main story is Lancelot's rescue of King Pelles's daughter, Elaine, 'naked as a needle' from a cauldron of boiling water. She tricks him into sleeping with her, so begetting their son Galahad. When Guinevere hears of her champion's apparent infidelity, she rejects him so utterly that he goes mad, leaping out of a window and running 'wild wood' from the court; to resurface after a long illness as the mysterious Chevalier Mal-Fet.

Either the adventures of Tristram had begun to bore Malory, or else he was short of time. For he decided to skip what is in his source the third volume of the immensely long prose romance. The explicit to this tale is less urgent, but it does include a suggestion that Malory is still in need of help; the phrase 'on all sinful' in its final line is an abbreviation of 'Thou who has mercy on all sinful souls', a standard phrase of prayer.

> Here endeth the second book of Sir Tristram de Lyonesse, which drawn was out of French by Sir Thomas Mallorré, knight, as Jesu be his help. Amen.
> But here is no rehearsal of the third book.
> But here followeth the noble tale of the Sangreal, which is called the holy vessel and the signification of the blessed blood

of our Lord Jesu Christ, which was brought into this land by Joseph of Armathea.

Therefore on all sinful, blessed Lord, have on thy knight mercy. Amen.

10 'The Tale of the Holy Grail' (90 pages)

In terms of drama, this is the high point of the book. It also puts into question all the values Malory has so far praised. For knights can only achieve the Grail by changing their ways. Most of them fail. Of the hundred and fifty knights who, after a magnificent tournament, troop away from Camelot in search of it, more than half are 'slain or destroyed', and many more wounded and crippled. Only three succeed completely, Galahad, Percival and Bors, and Galahad and Percival both chose to abandon this mortal coil and ascend into heaven. Lancelot succeeds in part, but only by promising to give up Guinevere. The explicit is a coded dedication which will be discussed later. It runs:

> *Thus endeth the tale of the Sangreal that was briefly drawn out of French – which is a tale chronicled for one of the trewest and of the holiest that is in the world – by Sir Thomas Malerorré, knight.*
>
> *O, Blessed Jesu help him through His might.*

11 'The Tale of Lancelot and Guinevere' (75 pages)

One of the most dramatic and fast-moving in the whole book, this story sees Lancelot twice rescuing Guinevere from perils – first when she is accused of trying to poison Gawaine, then when she is kidnapped by Sir Meliagaunce. It also features the sad fate of the lovelorn 'fair maid of Astolat', whom Tennyson immortalised as the Lady of Shalott, and a magnificent tournament, which Lancelot wins despite the fact that he was wounded in the buttock by a stray arrow from a 'lady archer'.

When Lancelot rescues Guinevere from Meliagaunce, his horse

is killed, and he arrives ignobly in a cart. The French romancers digressed at this point and wrote a whole volume of his adventures as the 'Chevalier de Chariot', and Malory seemed to have planned to do the same. But the book was lost or stolen and time was evidently running out. He ends this tale:

> And because I have lost the very matter of Chevalier de Chariot I depart from the tale of sir Lancelot and here I go unto the Morte Arthur, and that caused sir Agravaine. And here on the other side followeth the most piteous tale of the Morte Arthur Sans Guerdon par le chevalier Sir Thomas Malleorré, knight. Jesu, aidé lui par votre bon mercy! Amen.

12 'The Tale of the Morte Arthur' (70 pages)

If you read nothing else Malory wrote, you must read this book. The running sore of the grievances of the sons of King Lot of Orkney comes to a head with Agravaine's and Mordred's plot to incriminate Lancelot and Guinevere, forcing Arthur to face what he has long known but deliberately ignored. Lancelot escapes, but in doing so he kills thirteen knights, including Agravaine. Guinevere is condemned to burn at the stake, and when he rescues her Lancelot again deals death – this time on the unarmed Gareth and Gaheris, who he doesn't see at the foot of the stake – and takes Guinevere away to his Northumbrian fortress, Joyous Gard. Gawaine swears undying vengeance, and forces Arthur to pursue Lancelot and Guinevere to Joyous Gard. The siege is only lifted after the Pope intervenes so that Guinevere can return to Arthur without recrimination. Lancelot returns to his kingdom of Benwick (which Malory specifies as in south-west France), but Gawaine incites Arthur to take an army to attack him there. Mordred, left as Lieutenant of England, tries to abduct Guinevere, but she takes refuge in the Tower of London. Arthur returns, and in a terrible battle on Salisbury Plain, hundreds of thousands are killed – including Mordred. Arthur is mortally wounded and commands Bedivere to throw Excalibur into a lake. In response a barge appears, bearing the shady ladies who have been a leitmotif throughout the book, and takes the wounded King to Avalon to be a healed. He apparently dies – next day Bedivere meets a hermit who says that a dead corpse was brought to his chapel by 'a number of ladies' the night before. But Malory ends on a note of mystery:

> *More of the death of King Arthur could I never find, but that ladies brought him to his burials; and such one was buried there . . . Yet some men say in many parts of England that King Arthur is not dead, but had by the will of our Lord Jesu into another place; and men say that he shall come again, and he shall win the holy cross. I will not say it shall be so, but rather I will say: here in this world he changed his life. But many men say that there is written upon his tomb this verse: Hic jacet Arthurus, Rex quondam, Rexque futurus.*
> [Here lies Arthur, the once and future King]

Lancelot returns to find Guinevere in Amesbury nunnery. She rejects him because of the harm their love did to Arthur and his kingdom, and because she cannot trust him not to 'turn to the world again', and dedicates herself to prayer and the achieving of her own 'soul-heal'. Lancelot and his companions-in-arms all become monks until Lancelot too dies. At this point, in a final personal touch to a story that he has repeatedly nudged to preach a distinctly idiosyncratic message, Malory sends Sir Ector, Sir Bors, Sir Bleoberis and Sir Blamore to the Holy Land, where, as 'Sir Lancelot commanded them for to do before ever he passed out of this world, these four knights did many battles upon the miscreants or Turks. And there they died on a Good Friday, for God's sake'. The explicit to this tale is also an explicit to the entire book. Once again, it asks for deliverance. But there are some hints, which we will revisit in the penultimate chapter of this book, that Malory believes he is close to death – either because he is an old man, or because he is under threat.

> *Here is the end of the whole book of King Arthur, and of his noble knights of the Round Table, that when they were wholly*

*together there was ever an hundred and forty. And here is
the end of The Death of Arthur.*

*I pray you all, gentlemen and gentlewomen that readeth
this book of Arthur and his knights, from the beginning to
the ending, pray for me while I am on life that God send me
good deliverance. And when I am dead, I pray you all pray
for my soul. For this book was ended the ninth year of the
reign of King Edward the Fourth, by Sir Thomas Maleoré,
Knight, as Jesu help him for his great might, as he is the
servant of Jesu both day and night.*

The Messages of the Morte Darthur

Malory writes to be heard, using direct speech as often as he can. He
is confident that those who read or listen to his narrative will appreci-
ate his jokes and ironic asides as much as the detail and accuracy of
his stirring accounts of battles and tournaments, the iniquity of his
villains, the devious temptations of his sorceresses, the brave determination of his heroes, the pluck and charm of his heroines. He drew
his stories from a rich assortment of romances and chronicles, some
in alliterative Middle English verse, some in flowery French prose.
His varied sources give individual character to the various tales. But
the mind of one maker of genius unites them into a whole. C. S.
Lewis memorably likened the *Morte* to a 'cathedral of words' – added
to at different times and in different styles. This instantly satisfying
idea fits with my own sense that Malory collected and 'drew out
briefly into English' the stories all through his life, not just as a
late-life pastime while he was in prison. It is also reasonable to think
that the many individual touches he gives to his *Arthur* – digressions,
changes, added detail, insertions of the names of real English places
and people – are clues to the events and experiences of his own life.

Some of the tales Malory tells are tragic, some comic, some dramatic, some tedious, some romantic, some mysterious. Like the pieces
in a patchwork quilt, they complement each other by their differences;
together they add up to a dramatic pageant of knightly behaviour

good and bad. On several occasions three knights are arranged to contrast with each other so that lessons can be learned. The first trio to be sent on a quest are Arthur's nephew Sir Gawaine, a hot-tempered 'vengeable' man who acts before he thinks, Sir Tor, a new-made knight, and Tor's father, King Pellinore, a proven warrior and immensely strong. A similar pattern is offered when Sir Marhaus, Sir Gawaine and Sir Uwaine are each taken off into 'the country of strange adventures' for a year and a day by magical damsels of different ages. Quests are not always successfully fulfilled – Gawaine is particularly careless of women. Nor do the villains always get their just deserts: Sir Breuse sans Pitié, who specialises in trampling fallen knights under his destrier's hoofs, is never caught.

The *Morte Darthur* is, however, much more than a manual of chivalry told in magnificently high-flown language. Malory has larger themes which show his moral preoccupations. Through the labyrinthine maze of 'The Tale of Sir Tristram', he follows the thread of the destructive nature of male envy rather than Tristram's distinctly absent-minded obsession with Isolde. Loyalty is uppermost in his presentation of Sir Lancelot; the impossibility of giving it to both Arthur and Guinevere, to say nothing of Elaine, is at the root of the dilemmas that beset the man who eventually loses his premier position as 'the best knight in the world' to his own son, Galahad. Whether the way of chivalry can be resolved with Christianity is examined in the tale of the Grail quest. Malory's ingenious conclusion is that there is a place both for the unearthly perfection of Galahad and Percival, and the human strivings of Lancelot, who may not be the best knight in the world but can still, with God's good grace, perform such miracles as the healing of Sir Urry.

Malory saw Arthur and his knights as important examples – of villainy as well as of nobility, of failure as well as success, of imperfection as well as perfection. How people behave – whether they further their own interests or commit themselves to higher ideals – was important to him. He shows us heroes and villains in action, then provides asides for our benefit: 'Here men may understand that be of worship, that he was never formed that at all times might stand, but sometimes he was put to the worse by mal-fortune; and at sometime the worse knight put the better knight to a rebuke'; 'he that have a privy hurt is loth to have a shame outward'; 'ever will a coward show no mercy; and always a good man will do ever to another man as he would be done by to himself'. 'All is written for our doctrine,' wrote Caxton in his preface to the *Morte Darthur*. 'Do after the good and leave the evil, and it shall bring you to good fame and renown'. This is why Malory's characters are not archaic sixth-century figures. They are 'our noble knights of merry England', pragmatic, often errant, recognisably human men and women.

Framing the entire story are vengeful family feuds which would have struck familiar chords for Malory's contemporaries – one modern historian describes the Wars of the Roses as 'little more than a blood feud between noble families'. The Orkney clan – King Arthur's half-sister Margawse, her five sons Gawaine, Agravaine, Gaheris, Gareth and above all the incestuously-begotten Mordred, bring about the fall of Camelot just as surely as the Yorkists and the Nevilles subvert the house of Lancaster and eliminate the Beauforts. In the last two sections of his collection of tales, Malory places especial stress on the evils of such vendettas. Writing as he was in the late 1460s, he must have been well aware that the four sons of the ill-fated Duke Richard of York, Edward, Edmund, George and Richard, might be thought to parallel the four sons of the murdered King Lot of Orkney, and that their widowed mother Cecily Neville, Dowager Duchess of York, was as strong-minded and subtle a politician as Margawse, the widowed Queen of King Lot of Orkney.

So was the *Morte Darthur* meant as a political parable? Only in the very loosest sense. It would be incorrect to say that Malory saw any one fifteenth-century English king as exactly like Arthur, but references to Arthurian legends were, as this biography will show, the stuff of the times. No pageant of triumph was complete without a King Arthur blessing the proceedings, and parallels, both implicit and explicit, were frequently drawn between Arthur's exploits and contemporary happenings. There is a certain logic in viewing Henry V as like Arthur in his early years and Henry VI as the background Arthur of the long and rambling 'Book of Tristram', and indeed as the muddled, cuckolded and ill-advised Arthur of the last two books.

Interestingly, that leaves Edward IV, the King who most fancied himself as like King Arthur and most consciously modelled his court on Camelot, and in whose reign Malory completed his great work, with the role of a (successful) Mordred.

'The Portrait of his Spirit'

The way in which the *Morte Darthur* is written offers the best clues that we have to Malory's personality. Although I love Robert Louis Stevenson's bold declaration that 'A man would rather leave behind him the portrait of his spirit than the portrait of his face', it has been immensely frustrating not to have any kind of likeness of Malory. But his tough-minded, noble book does indeed provide a portrait of him: plain, faithful and true. We can hear the way he talked – brusque, direct, and with none of the wordy circumlocutions of his French sources. He comes across, first and foremost, as a great-hearted man of action, straightforward and honest, someone who went at any enemy full tilt without reflecting much on the consequences. He has a strong sense of his own worth as a knight, more than capable of righting wrongs and fighting injustice. He is interested in diversity and far from doctrinaire, realistic rather than moralistic, sympathetic to human frailties. But he was also remarkably scholarly, reading widely to construct his own unique version of Arthur's story.

His book is the fruit of deep thinking about what he read. He is a consummate storyteller, changing the interminable aural wallpaper of French romances into well-constructed and dramatic yarns with a contemporary relevance that gripped his first listeners' attention and still has a haunting enchantment today. To tell tales in such a way demands a high degree of sensitivity, an understanding of the effect of words on people achieved only through careful observation, listening and experiment, circulating the individual stories among friends and taking into account their criticisms. Studies of the Winchester manuscript show that it is punctuated to aid a narrator, and its marginalia work as a guide for such a reader. Evidently taken from whatever text the scribes were copying, they may have been made by one such friend – or even, it has been suggested, by Malory himself.

Listen to his stories read aloud, and Malory emerges as a man who loved to sit round a fire for hours with his brothers-in-arms reliving a battle blow for blow, discussing the finer points of a joust or arguing about the right approach to a fallow deer in season while swigging fine Gascon wine. When Lancelot sails for Bayonne in the south-west, Malory adds that this is 'where the wine comes from', and when Tristram and Isolde drink down the fateful love potion which they think is merely 'noble wine', they don't merely drink it, as in Malory's source, they 'laugh[ed] and made good cheer and either drank to other freely'. He likes food, giving knowledgeable details of the way the venison eaten after Lancelot's victory over Tarquin was served 'roasted, sodded [boiled] and baked'.

He is a man's man, sympathetic to male weaknesses, whether in an aside about the way an inexperienced young knight may be better on foot than on horseback, or in his casual acceptance of Tristram's chequered love-life. He is quietly but intensely romantic, and deeply interested in women, though they are something of a mystery to him. Some of his female characters are frail and pious, others clever and competent, many are frighteningly powerful and unpredictable. I imagine him a little lost for words in the bedroom, but the words he chooses when he writes about love are good simple ones, which hit the harder for their brevity.

> *And to tell the joys that were betwixt La Beale Isoud and Sir Tristram, there is no tongue can tell it, nor heart think it, nor pen write it.*

There is another kind of clue in the *Morte Darthur* as to what its author was like. More than one lover of the book has felt that Malory identifies unusually personally with one particular character. 'It is nearly always true', wrote John Steinbeck,

> *that a novelist, perhaps unconsciously, identifies himself with one chief or central character in his novel . . . Into this charac-ter he puts not only what he thinks he is but what he hopes to be. We call this spokesman the self-character . . . Now it*

seems to me that Malory's self-character would be Lancelot. All the perfections he knew went into this character, all the things of which he thought he was capable. But, being an honest man he found faults in himself, faults of vanity, faults of violence, faults even of disloyalty, and these would naturally find themselves into his dream character.

Edward Hicks ended his biography by concluding that Malory was 'shaped after the pattern of Sir Lancelot du Lake' and that 'like him, he has received double for his sins'. Vinaver agrees: 'Nowhere does Malory select his material with as little respect for the original as he showed in the Tale of Sir Lancelot'. Lancelot's outspoken opinions, hot temper, zest for life, wise judgements, foolish mistakes and melancholic reflections are, he thinks, the best evidence we have for his creator's character and personal convictions. There is undoubtedly a dramatic contrast between Malory's hero and the pretentious courtier of the French prose romance *Lancelot du Lac*, or the single-minded thug of the early English alliterative poem *Morte Arthur*.

One derivation of the name 'Malory' is 'mal-auré', which means ill-augured, or ill-fated. It may not be chance that in an original touch Malory makes Lancelot conceal his identity after he has been disgraced behind the name 'Le Chevalier Mal-fet'. A fifteenth-century Englishman indelibly scarred by the glories and miseries of love and war, of skulduggery and betrayal as well as of fidelity and glory, lies behind Lancelot. Malory eulogised him on the last page of the *Morte* as 'the courteoust knight that ever bare shield . . . the truest friend to thy lover that ever bestrode horse . . . the truest lover of a sinful man that ever loved woman . . . the kindest man that ever struck with sword . . . the meekest man and the gentlest that ever ate in hall among ladies . . . the sternest knight to . . . mortal foe that ever put spear in the rest.' This portrait of Lancelot is an important touchstone in interpreting the puzzling paradoxes that litter Malory's own life.

The Baptism Bell

*And as fast as her time came she was delivered of a fair
child, and . . . wit ye well that child was well kept and well
nourished.*

Malory, 'The Tale of King Arthur'

he oldest bell in the fine ring of eight mounted in the tower
of the church of Monks Kirby Priory, in Warwickshire, was
cast in 1390, in Worcester. It is a tangible link with the
parish's most famous resident. For at the turn of the fourteenth
century it would have been rung to summon relatives, friends and
neighbours to the baptism of Thomas, the baby son of the Malorys
of Newbold Revel. After the bellringer had finished the peal, let us
imagine him turning lookout – climbing to the top of the great red
sandstone church's tall tower. From there he had a panoramic view
over the very heart of England. Knowing who was about was essential.
These were dangerous times. Rumour had it that if Richard II had
not already been murdered in his Pontefract Castle prison, he soon
would be. But his cousin the usurping Duke of Lancaster, though
crowned Henry IV in October 1399, did not yet feel secure on the
throne. Hard-faced, hard-riding bands of armed men were scouring
the shires for 'traitors'.

To the north the lookout could see High Cross, the pinnacled
shrine that marked the meeting of the country's two most travelled
highways, Watling Street and the Fosse Way. Visible to the east were
the spires, wind-tossed banners, gilded weather-vanes and twelve turreted gates of Coventry, the fourth largest city in England and famed
for its 'Coventry Blue' cloth. Warwickshire was a fertile county, its

fields a 'green mantle so embroidered with flowers we may behold as another Eden'. The rich pastureland between the city and Monks Kirby was white with the flocks of Coombe Abbey, once famed for its piety, now sadly lax in its observances, except where profits could be made. Closer at hand were the parish's own manors and churches, each surrounded by a thatched hamlet, orchards and vegetable gardens.

Immediately to the south of Monks Kirby Priory, now a much-reduced monastic house, were the villages of Pailton, Stretton-under-Fosse and Easenhall. Settled like a mother hen in the low-lying centre of the triangle they formed was the moated manor house of Newbold Revel, its long façade reflected in the shining levels of three great fishponds. All belonged to the Malorys, the most important family in the parish. They held other manors just over the county's boundaries with Leicestershire and Northamptonshire. Thomas's father, John Malory of Newbold Revel, was well-liked; there are very few legal records showing him at odds with his tenants and neighbours, nor did he have any quarrels with the overlords of his various estates.

Although we don't know the exact date of Thomas Malory's birth, we can be sure that it was no more than a few days before his christening. The baptism of infants was never too soon at a time when immortal souls could be stolen by evil spirits for the want of a splash of holy water. The immediate atmosphere of the world into which he was born was murky, warm and richly colourful: the curtained cave of a four-poster bed in a candlelit room lined with Flemish tapestries and heated by a roaring wood fire, scented with branches of rosemary and bay. Dame Philippa Malory's female relatives, servants and friends crowded the room and cheered her on with advice, anecdotes and prayers. A nurse heated up milk scented with rose petals for the baby's first bath, and stood by as the midwife helped the sweating, crouching mother through the 'grimly throes' of birth without anaesthesia.

After being blessed, washed with a mixture of oil and salt, and swaddled tightly in protective bands, Thomas was tucked into bed with his mother, who held him to her breast and, we may imagine, 'nourished him with her own pap'. It was then believed that moral virtue – or vice – was transmitted in breast milk, so a conscientious mother, whatever her station in life, would try to suckle her own babies – especially if it was a boy, potentially an heir. News that the baby had been safely born had already been sent downstairs to the rest of the family. Outside in the courtyard an arrow was shot into the air to symbolise the boy's release from womb into world, and a short service of thanksgiving to the Blessed Virgin Mary, patroness of all births, was held in the Malorys' private chapel. Then harbingers, the family's liveried messengers, rode off 'at a wallop' to summon godparents, relatives and well-wishers to the christening.

'It is our kind to haunt arms and noble deeds'

The future historian of King Arthur came of appropriately chivalric stock. The Malorys were proud of being 'gentlemen that bear olde arms'. They had been Normans before they were Englishmen and Vikings before they were Normans. The Viking raider Rollo the Ganger became the first Duke of Normandy only a century before his descendant William shipped across the Channel to defeat Harald at the Battle of Hastings and added England to his estates. Variants on the distinctly Norse name Anketil were often given to members of the Malory family; it was anglicised to Anthony in the late fifteenth century. Besides having the ominous sense of 'maleuré', ill-augured or ill-fated, the name Malory itself could have derived from 'maillerie', a kind of mill used for beating hemp for use in the textile trade, which gave its name to such French towns as La Mailleraye-sur-Seine and La Malhoure in Brittany. Perhaps it originated as a nickname. In the Winchester manuscript, the name is spelt as both Maleorré and Malleorré; it could be that Sir Thomas personally preferred this strikingly Frenchified version of his name.

There are eleventh-century records of Malorys at Tessancourt, in the Vexin, on the Seine between Normandy and Paris. They owed allegiance to the Beaumont counts of Meulan, who invaded England in 1066 with William the Conqueror, and were rewarded with the earldom of Leicester. In 1118 an English charter signed by the Earl of

Leicester was witnessed by 'Robert Malory, son of Aschetil Malory'. Soon afterwards there was a Richard Malory on the Earl's council, and an Anschetil was in the household of the Earl's son. This Anschetil was born in 1131, knighted in 1174, and died in 1187. He became Governor of Leicester Castle, and his coat of arms was *or a lion rampant a queue fourchée gules*: a red, forked-tail lion rearing up on its hind legs against a golden background.

The Norman Malorys' first English seat was a formidable triple-moated, triple-walled stronghold at Kirkby Mallory, ten miles west of Leicester – their gallant ghosts must enjoy the fact that it was later owned by Lord Byron, and that its deer park is now the Mallory Park speedway circuit. Of the castle itself, only grass-covered ridges and ditches remain. Other manors were quickly acquired, and the family flourished over the next two centuries. Few decades went by without a Sir Anketil or a Sir Ralph or a Sir Thomas Malory distinguishing himself in battle – both abroad and in civil wars at home. Spirited, proud and headstrong, they could boast, as does Lancelot's cousin Sir Bleoberis, 'There was never none of our kin that ever was shamed in battle'. They sometimes took the law into their own hands, and were not afraid to question even the highest authority: several Malorys supported the founder of Parliament, Simon de Montfort, Earl of Leicester, against Henry III in the 1250s. But they were fiercely loyal, serving their liege lords in war, in council, in the justiciary and in household affairs. A 'Thomas Malorie' was among the 267 Knights of the Bath created on the occasion of the knighting of Edward, Prince of Wales (later Edward II) in 1306. Knighted with him were ancestors of families with whom the Malorys retained links in the fifteenth century – the Greys, the Zouches, the Bassetts and the Beauchamps. Malory coats of arms grew more elaborate, often quartered with the arms of their wives and ancestors. The lions, heraldic embodiments of courage, strength and nobility, recur time and again.

In about 1360 Sir Anketil Malory eloped with the immensely wealthy and already twice widowed Alice Bassett, 'the Lady of Dryby'. The old-fashioned and inconvenient castle at Kirkby Mallory was leased to the Abbey of Leicester, and they moved to Alice's splendid home at Castle Bytham in Lincolnshire. Sir Anketil was a fairly distant

The Malorys of Newbold Revel

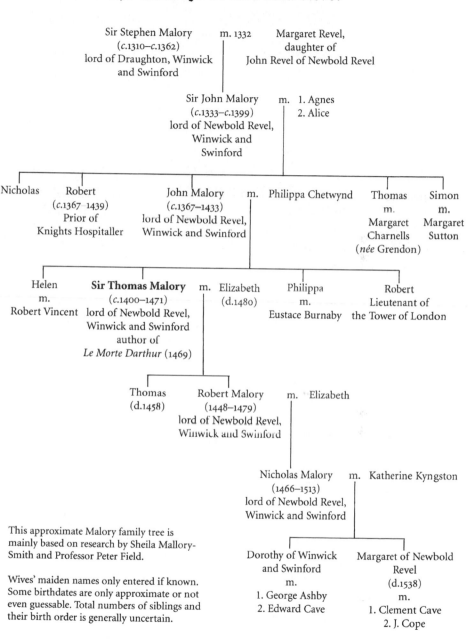

Sir Stephen Malory   m. 1332   Margaret Revel,
(*c.*1310–*c.*1362)   daughter of
lord of Draughton, Winwick   John Revel of Newbold Revel
and Swinford

Sir John Malory   m.   1. Agnes
(*c.*1333–*c.*1399)   2. Alice
lord of Newbold Revel,
Winwick and
Swinford

Nicholas   Robert   John Malory   m.   Philippa Chetwynd   Thomas   Simon
     (*c.*1367–1439)   (*c.*1367–1433)   m.   m.
       Prior of   lord of Newbold Revel,   Margaret   Margaret
Knights Hospitaller   Winwick and Swinford   Charnells   Sutton
                                                 (*née* Grendon)

Helen   **Sir Thomas Malory**   m.   Elizabeth   Philippa   Robert
m.   (*c.*1400–1471)   (d.1480)   m.   Lieutenant of
Robert Vincent   lord of Newbold Revel,   Eustace Burnaby   the Tower of London
           Winwick and Swinford
                 author of
        Le Morte Darthur (1469)

Thomas   Robert Malory   m.   Elizabeth
(d.1458)   (1448–1479)
       lord of Newbold Revel,
       Winwick and Swinford

Nicholas Malory   m.   Katherine Kyngston
(1466–1513)
lord of Newbold Revel,
Winwick and Swinford

This approximate Malory family tree is
mainly based on research by Sheila Mallory-
Smith and Professor Peter Field.

Wives' maiden names only entered if known.
Some birthdates are only approximate or not
even guessable. Total numbers of siblings and
their birth order is generally uncertain.

Dorothy of Winwick   Margaret of Newbold
and Swinford   Revel
m.   (d.1538)
1. George Ashby   m.
2. Edward Cave   1. Clement Cave
                 2. J. Cope

cousin of the Malorys of Newbold Revel, but as head of the senior branch of the family and a feoffee (a legal protector) of Tachbrook Mallory, a manor twelve miles south-west of Newbold Revel, he is likely to have called in on his journey down the Fosse Way to visit it. Interestingly, his learned kinsman William Zouche, Archbishop of York, described him as 'armiger literatus' when he named him as an executor of his will. The phrase suggests that he was unusually well-educated, with books, perhaps a substantial library, of his own. His links with the Bassetts and the Zouches, and the marriage of his daughter to the royal favourite Sir Henry Green, suggest close connections with Richard II's court, which was noted for its authors and artists. Chaucer read his stories aloud in front of the King and Queen, and finely illuminated manuscripts of such Arthurian romances as *Lancelot*, *Tristram and Isolde*, *Sir Gawain*, and *Perceval* date from these decades.

By 1400 there were eight branches of the Malory family, some eminent and some notorious, others backwoods squires and placid widows whose doings have not ruffled the surface of history. Most of their estates were in the Midlands, but they also held property in Yorkshire, Cambridgeshire, London and Kent. Medieval families took kinship seriously, and it is likely that the Malorys knew of, met and gossiped about their many cousins.

The estates built up by the Newbold Revel Malorys had been acquired by a combination of astuteness and luck in those two most uncertain of lotteries, marriage and inheritance. Originally the Malorys of Draughton, in central Northamptonshire, their first additional manor was Catthorpe, a moated and fortified house on the banks of the Avon in the extreme south-west of Leicestershire, which they held in 1232. By 1264, they also held part of the neighbouring manor of Swinford, of which the Knights Hospitallers were overlords. Bordering on their Catthorpe and Swinford holdings were lands at Shawell and Stormsworth. The four manors were linked by the River Avon. Today it is a winding willow-edged brook, but the size of the medieval bridge downstream at Lilbourne shows that in 1400 it was navigable for small craft.

Some eight miles to the south-east of the Swinford properties were the Northamptonshire lands brought into the family by Sir Simon Malory's wife, Beatrice de Boscherville, in the 1270s. They centred on the splendid manor house of Winwick and its 'messuages and appurtenances', and included its neighbouring manor West Haddon. By 1295 Sir Simon's son Sir Peter Malory also held Melcombe and Dodmerton, two Dorset manors a dozen miles west of Wareham. His wife was a Dorset heiress, but it is possible that the estates were inherited from the Malorys recorded in Dorset in 1086. Sir Peter was an eminent judge with a flamboyant coat of arms: *or three lions passant gardant sable* – three black lions rampaging across a gold ground. This was the royal arms in all but colour, perhaps granted to him in recognition of his loyal service to Edward I. As he had no children, his estates and his arms passed to his sixty-year-old elder brother Sir Roger, whose son Simon had inherited them by 1313.

It was Simon's son, Sir Stephen Malory (*c.* 1310–*c.* 1362), whose marriage brought Newbold Revel into the family. The Revels were, like the Malorys, of Norman stock. Hugh Revel (d. 1278) had been a crusader of legendary prowess, and he was one of only two Englishmen to be Grand Master of the Order of St John of Jerusalem, the Knights Hospitallers. The Malorys' acquisition of some of the Revel estates was luck rather than good management: when Sir Stephen married Margaret Revel in 1332, three brothers stood between her and inheritance. But none had heirs, and when the last of them, William Revel, died in 1383 his estates were divided between his three sisters and their descendants. 'Fenny Newbold', the neighbouring manors at Easenhall, Stretton-under-Fosse and Pailton, and land at Shawell, near Swinford, fell to Margaret's son and heir Sir John Malory, who was born soon after 1332. Only twelve miles from Winwick, and with over seven thousand acres, it made an impressive capstone to the Malory estates. Sir John now adopted a variant of the Revel arms: *ermine, a chevron gules, and a border engrailed sable,* a red chevron on a ground of ermines' tails, with a wavy black border. In time, no doubt as a homage to the Revels, Fenny Newbold was renamed Newbold Revel.

Sir John was, in all probability, Sir Thomas Malory's grandfather, though he may not have survived to see him born. In 1366 he sold

Draughton, which was inconveniently far away from the family's new estates, and bought a lifetime's interest in the estates of his cousin Sir Peter Malory of Litchborough, Northamptonshire, for himself, his wife Agnes and their son Nicholas. Sir Peter was one of the more turbulent Malorys, a bonny fighter who served the King in Ireland but who was perennially in trouble and often in debt. In 1363 he assaulted the Chief Justice. Only a personal plea from King David of Scotland and Edward III's son, the legendary Black Prince, saved him from execution. Instead he was fined £300 and sent to prison. What Sir John paid for the lifetime interest in the manor probably helped Sir Peter to settle his debt.

Sir John's extensive estates made him an important man in local affairs in the 1380s and 1390s. In 1391–2 he was Sheriff of Warwickshire and Leicestershire; in 1392–3 he was Sheriff of Northamptonshire. In 1391, when he was about sixty years old, he made a new disposition of his estates. It settled Newbold Revel and its associated lands on himself and a second wife, Alice, 'in tail'. This meant that his and Alice's children, rather than the children from his first marriage, would inherit it. But both he and Alice, who remained childless, had died by 1406. The heir was not Nicholas, who must also have died, but a younger son from Sir John's first marriage, another John Malory, who described himself as 'lord of Newbold Revel' when he witnessed a Stretton-under-Fosse deed that year.

This John Malory was our hero's father. Cadency marks on Malory of Newbold Revel shields in a window in the church of St Peter and Paul, Coleshill, nine miles from Grendon in north-west Warwickshire, suggest that he was one of five brothers. The oldest was probably the Nicholas who was described as Sir John's son in 1366. He cannot have been of age then, as his father, whose parents married in 1332, was no more than thirty-three years old at the time; he is never again recorded. As John inherited the family estates, he was probably the second son, born some time after 1366. But it is possible that he was younger than his brother Robert, born before 1375, who did not inherit because he followed Revel family tradition and joined the celibate order of Knights Hospitallers. One of the remaining brothers was Simon Malory, who married a Sutton of Chilverscoton, a manor eight miles north of Newbold Revel close to Nuneaton, and is linked with his brothers in several legal records. There is good evidence for the existence of these four brothers, but who was the fifth? If his name was Thomas, it would make sense of several records of a Thomas Malory too old to be our hero, who lived first at Catthorpe and then, after he had married a wealthy widow called Margaret Charnells, at Bramcote.

An image of John Malory survives. Stained-glass portrait windows were installed in the church of All Saints, Grendon, in about 1396 by his mother-in-law, Alice Chetwynd. The Chetwynds were a wealthy family from Staffordshire, where their main manor was Ingestre. Improving a church and filling its windows with arms and portraits of your family and of any eminent connections by marriage was a popular way of confirming possession of estates in the parish. At Stanford church, near Swinford in Leicestershire, windows showing descendants of Sir Thomas Malory and the Caves of Stanford survive in all their colourful glory, evidence of the marriage of Malory's two great-granddaughters to the Cave brothers. The Grendon windows were smashed by the Puritans. Fortunately they had been carefully copied by the seventeenth-century Warwickshire antiquarian William Dugdale.

The maker of the window at Grendon was a skilful artist, and took pains to characterise his subjects. John Malory (top left) is in full plate armour, skirted for mounted combat. He looks about thirty and has a short curly beard fringing a determined chin. Behind him is his wife Philippa Chetwynd, Thomas Malory's mother. Both are kneeling, and both are wearing the Revel arms, John on his surcoat, Philippa on her overmantle. Also pictured are Philippa's brothers Roger and Richard and their wives, her sister Margaret (bottom right) and her husband William Purefoy. Philippa's brothers and William Purefoy have boyish bobs and no beards, and they look much younger than John. Although they are also in full armour, they have no skirt-plates and their spurs are tiny in comparison with the many-pointed rowel spurs worn by John Malory. Such armour and spurs show he was an experienced soldier.

Philippa looks more mature than her sister, though both are

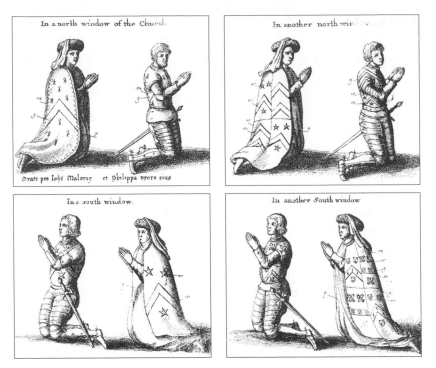

In a north window of the Church

Orate pro Iohi Malory et philippa vxore eius

In another north window

In a south window.

In another South window

beautiful, with arched eyebrows and pointed chins – in strong contrast to Helena, the hook-nosed, double-chinned wife of their older brother, and Thomasina, the bun-faced little wife of their younger brother John. Confirmation that Philippa was attractive lies in her marriage: although she would have had a dowry and held a family name of great repute, she was unlikely to inherit the Chetwynd estates. But John Malory had good prospects of his own, and could afford to marry for love and a good pedigree. For Philippa's father, Sir William Chetwynd, was both wealthier and more distinguished than Sir John Malory. Like the poet Geoffrey Chaucer, he had been an esquire of the Duke of Lancaster, John of Gaunt. He fought in Spain with Gaunt in the 1380s, and when he returned in 1389 was made Sheriff of Staffordshire.

It is likely that John and Philippa's marriage coincided with the Newbold Revel settlement made in 1391 by Sir John and that at this point the couple took up residence either in Swinford or in Winwick. When they moved to Newbold Revel is unknown, but it must have been before 1406, when John was described as John Malory of New-bold in a deed appointing him a feoffee for a man from Yelvertoft. His election as MP for Warwickshire in 1413, his appointment as Sheriff of Warwickshire and Leicestershire in 1416, and the frequent appearance of his name on commissions and as a witness to charters between 1406 and 1433, when he died, confirms the fact that he and his wife were respected local figures. They would have been personally known by most, if not all, of the county gentry families and the dozen or so peers who had interests in the county.

The Malorys were not unusual in having interests in adjacent Midlands counties. Only about six of the gentry families of Warwickshire were primarily committed to that county. And most of the noble families with interests in Warwickshire, among them the Mowbray dukes of Norfolk, the earls of Stafford and the Greys of Ruthin, had their main estates elsewhere. But there was one peer whose interests were primarily located in Warwickshire: the Earl of Warwick. The Beauchamp earls maintained a large affinity of local followers, paying many of its most eminent knights and squires annuities in exchange for their promise of allegiance 'in peace and in war'. For although in 1400 land was still legally held by 'knight service' (the old feudal commitment to fight for one's overlord in war) by now a cash payment could settle that formal obligation, and a gentleman could join the retinue of alternative, or additional, 'good lords' who would pay him a retainer for his services, and provide protection from opportunist predators who might use their influence to question legal title, grab control over a minor or an heiress, or simply seize estates by *force majeure*. When resident in the lord's household or serving him in war, a retainer received wages, maintenance and horses for himself and his servants and regular 'livery of robes'.

However, the most obvious choice as 'good lord' remained one's feudal overlord, in part because of ancient traditions of loyalty to a particular family, in part because even the most careful enfeoffing to use could be subverted by a rash of sudden deaths among feoffees and heirs, and the overlord had guardianship and marriage rights when a minor inherited. The strong sense of loyalty evident in the *Morte Darthur* is likely to have been a family trait, so it is relevant to consider who the Malorys' feudal overlords were. At this time they held Winwick of the Prior of Coventry, Swinford of the Knights Hospitallers and Newbold Revel of Thomas Holland, Earl of Kent, who was a cousin of Richard II.

It is difficult to estimate quite how wealthy the Malorys were. Medieval landowners maintained an understandable reticence as to their taxable wealth, and few comprehensive tax assessments have survived. One made in 1436 has, however, and on it the Warwickshire lands held by Philippa Malory were valued at £60, which would rank her as among the middling well-off gentry. But she was then John Malory's widow, so she may only have held part of his lands. Nor is there any record of how much tax, if any, was assessed on the family's Leicestershire and Northamptonshire estates, or of lands protected from royal taxation because they were held by the Prior of Coventry or the Knights Hospitallers. Moreover, though most of the income of the landed gentry came from land, both in the form of rents and in profits on the sales of wool and grain, many of them had industrial, commercial and mercantile interests. Coventry was famous for its dyers and weavers, and Birmingham already known for fine metal-work. Marriages were frequently made between the landed gentry and the wealthy merchant families of Bristol and London. All we can say for certain is that John and Philippa Malory managed their estates competently and lived within their means: there are no records of John being in debt. Most important of all, he handed the family estates on intact to his heir.

Godsibs and Good Lords

The most important people in the baptismal party that processed from Newbold Revel to the church porch were the three people who had undertaken to support the baby's introduction into the Christian faith. Then, as now, babies had two sponsors of their own sex and one of the opposite sex. Godsibs, as godparents were called, were chosen with care and took their responsibilities seriously. As well as making sure that their godchildren learned the fundamentals of religion and were confirmed into the Christian Church, they were to be counted on as loyal allies, perhaps generous patrons, through life. The identity of Thomas's godparents is not on record, but since a baby was almost always given the Christian name of the most important godsib, his name must provide a clue. The grandest Thomas connected with Newbold Revel was its overlord, Thomas Holland, Earl of Kent. Lords often stood as godfathers to their liegemen's children, but Holland, Richard II's nephew of the half-blood, was deeply involved in plotting against Henry IV. A safer choice would have been the dashing Sir Thomas Malory of Kirkby Mallory, not yet of age but already head of the senior branch of the family at Castle Bytham.

The parish priest met the family party in the church porch, where the first part of the ceremony, the instruction, took place. The baby was not taken into the church until any devils that might already have crept into it in its unbaptised state had been exorcised. The elaborate church porches of medieval times were designed to provide shelter for such ceremonies. The priest first made a sign of the cross on Thomas's forehead, and then asked his name, sex and baptismal state – babies thought to be on the brink of death were baptised from a flask of clean water that all midwives kept for this eventuality. No baby could be baptised twice, which is why Malory makes Merlin warn Arthur's father, King Uther Pendragon, not to have the baby boy christened before he is handed over to his foster father, Sir Ector:

> And when the child is born let it be delivered to me at yonder privy postern unchristened. So like as Merlin devised it was done. And when Sir Ector was come he made fiaunce to the king for to nourish the child like as the king desired; and there the king granted Sir Ector great rewards. Then when the lady was delivered, the king commanded two knights and two ladies to take the child, bound in a cloth of gold, and that ye deliver him to what poor man ye meet at the postern gate of the castle. So the child was delivered unto Merlin, and so he bare it forth unto Sir Ector, and made an holy man to christen him, and named him Arthur; and so Sir Ector's wife nourished him with her own pap.

51

Next, the priest put a little salt in the baby's mouth to symbolise his accession to knowledge. Finally he wetted the infant's ears and nostrils with his own powerful holy saliva and chanted an exorcism.

Then, singing cheerfully, the procession entered the gaily painted church, flooded with coloured light by its stained-glass windows. Its vast interior was chilly enough to make a tiny baby cry disconsolately, even without the salt and the spit and the strange faces and the singing. But care was taken for his comfort. Around the font to protect him from draughts stood the family's ceremonial screens, embroidered with the bold heraldic blazons of Malorys, Chetwynds and Revels, and the basin of water inside the font was padded with linen cloths. Flaming torches and flickering candles provided both warmth and distraction. Then came an unwelcome surprise: the midwife who had been cuddling him removed his shawls and handed him to the priest to be immersed in the water three times, once on each side and once on his front. Was he shocked into total silence (a bad sign, old wives said), or was his formal baptism drowned in screams? The priest was watched critically; it was thought that if 'children be well-plunged in the font, they shall be healthful in all their limbs ever after'. The entire body had be dipped into the water; incomplete immersion could lead to later weakness in the limb that stayed dry – a belief similar to the ancient legend of Achilles' heel.

After the last immersion, the senior godfather raised Thomas from the font and the priest anointed him with chrism, a sanctified mixture of oil and balsam made up annually on Maundy Thursday. Then the nurse handed the baby's chrism-cloth, a snowy-white hooded robe, to the godfather to wrap around the baby and keep the chrism in place. Once the tiny fingers of his right hand had gripped a lighted candle, Thomas Malory of Newbold Revel was a proper Christian, armed against Satan and ready to set out on his journey through life guided by God's enlightenment. The party then moved to the altar, where the godsibs professed their own faith and answered for that of the infant. They promised to protect him from peril by fire and water until he was seven, to teach him the Paternoster, Ave Maria and Creed, and to have him confirmed by the diocesan bishop.

Once the spiritual formalities were over, and hands had been ceremoniously washed, wine flavoured with spices was served to everybody in the church. Christening presents were given – gold and silver pap-dishes and cups, jewelled buckles and rings, cash, a beautifully bound psalter. Then the guests returned to Newbold Revel. The baby was taken back to his mother for a feed, then piped into his nursery by musicians and tucked up in his cradle. His nurse placed a crust of bread under the head of his mattress to keep witches away. Downstairs in the great hall there was feasting and dancing and music and tales of miracles performed by tiny babes and triumphs achieved by valiant knights.

Any gathering of kinsfolk, neighbours and friends meant talk, in discreetly lowered voices, of what was happening on the national stage. Henry IV's coronation was welcomed by most of the Warwickshire gentry, for the Dukes of Lancaster were the overlords of huge tracts of the Midlands. He promised to be a far more exciting king than the clever but lazy and unpredictable Richard II. What interested the martially-minded most was the fact that he was the first English king to be anointed at his coronation with a miraculous oil, preserved in a crystal phial enclosed in a solid gold eagle. Only just rediscovered, it had, men said, been given to St Thomas Becket by the Virgin Mary herself. She had told him that it was to anoint a future king of England who would recover the lost domains of Normandy and Aquitaine and reclaim the Holy Land from the infidels. Given the Malorys' links to the Knights Hospitallers, they would also approve the honourable treatment, and the £2,000, which Henry gave to the Emperor Manuel of Constantinople when he arrived in London in December 1400 to raise money for defence against the Turks.

John Malory is likely to have had mixed feelings about the Lancastrian usurpation. In January 1400, the Malorys' overlord Thomas Holland, Earl of Kent, joined a plot – hatched in the precincts of St Paul's Cathedral – to seize Henry IV during the Twelfth Night celebrations at Windsor. The King was tipped off and managed to escape, and within a week all the leaders of the conspiracy were dead – either lynched by furious mobs in the towns which they had tried to rally to Richard II's cause, or executed after trial. Holland was beheaded at Cirencester on 8 January. John Malory was unpopular enough with Henry IV to be imprisoned in the Tower of London on 12 February 1400. The most likely reason for his confinement in England's most secure political prison is that he was known to be a retainer of Thomas Holland, and suspected of being involved in the Twelfth Night plot. He was lucky to escape with his life. The rebellion sealed Richard II's fate. Within weeks it was announced that he had 'pined to death for very melancholy' in Pontefract Castle.

John Malory in Wales

An unusual and distinctive aspect of Malory's Arthurian history is his frequent insertion of references to Wales. These are not in his French sources, and there are so many of them that several early biographers surmised that Thomas came from Wales, or at least its borders. This theory has now been refuted, but the puzzle of the deliberately inserted Welsh references remains. Malory substitutes two named knights from north Wales, Sir Hugh of the Mountain and Sir Madok of the Mountain, for his source's anonymous 'autre chevalier de Norgales'; he also gives the King of North Wales a more prominent role in the tournament at Lonazep. In another passage, he twice puts 'the King of Wales' where his source had referred to the King of Ireland. Is there a lost version of the story, the work of a patriotic Welsh scribe? Were the references a veiled tribute to the Welsh rebels with whom Thomas would be associated in the 1460s? Or were they nostalgic memories of the way he was told the stories as a child? His father John Malory was definitely in Wales in February 1414, when he witnessed a document at Ruthin (Dyffryn Clwyd) in north-east Wales, for Reginald, Lord Grey of Ruthin. If he heard Arthurian tales told there, he might have enjoyed repeating them to his son.

He could also have been there much earlier, when there is no record of his being at home. Hundreds of Warwickshire men fought in Wales in the early 1400s. When John Malory was released from the Tower of London, he needed to make his peace with Henry IV. Serving the King in war was a sure way to win his favour, and there were plenty of opportunities for war service. Rumours that Richard II was still alive were rife, and there was deep-rooted opposition to Henry IV, especially in the North of England, where the Scots were threatening to invade, and in Wales, where the charismatic Owain Glyn Dŵr had declared himself an independent prince. After the disgrace of the Hollands, John also urgently needed the support of a local magnate. Easily the most attractive way of achieving royal favour and local support was service with the Beauchamp earls of Warwick, the most powerful nobles in the county. Warwick Castle was only fourteen miles from Newbold Revel, and John's cousin Sir Giles Malory of Litchborough, who had served in France in 1395 with John Holland, Duke of Exeter, was a valued retainer of Thomas Beauchamp, Earl of Warwick. He sat in Parliament for Northamptonshire in the Beauchamp interest in 1395, 1388 (February session), 1393 and 1394, and was steward of the household by 1397. If John Malory supported Thomas Holland in 1400 Thomas Beauchamp, who had been imprisoned for two years by Richard II, would not have looked kindly on him. But the old Earl was a broken man – he died at Warwick Castle on 8 July 1401.

His son and heir Sir Richard Beauchamp, the 13th Earl of Warwick, would have been more sympathetic. He too had mixed loyalties. He had been brought up in the cosmopolitan court of Richard and his sophisticated first queen, Anne of Bohemia, and his godparents were Richard II himself and Richard Scrope, Archbishop of York, who remained defiantly opposed to Henry IV's usurpation of the throne. However, Richard II had confiscated the Beauchamp estates and placed the heir in wardship. Once Henry of Lancaster, whose lands had also been confiscated by Richard, landed in the North in the summer of 1399, the seventeen-year-old Beauchamp rallied to his banner. Henry IV made him a Knight of Bath on the eve of his coronation in September. Tall, courteous and strikingly handsome, he would soon be renowned all over Europe for his prowess in tournaments. He continued to retain Sir Giles Malory, who once again sat for Parliament in 1401 and 1402. There could be no better 'good lord' for the Malorys of Newbold Revel.

There are no definite records of John Malory in Warwickshire until 1406, only the evidence of the Grendon window. But the fine suit of armour and businesslike spurs he is shown wearing point to him being an experienced soldier. Nothing was more profitable than fighting the King's enemies, given the equipment, skill and strength. Experienced squires and knights could earn £20 or more a year while on active service. New estates and lucrative wartime offices were granted to those who showed 'prowess', and there was always hope of plunder or ransoms. John's kinsmen had already signed up. Two lucky survivals, parchment 'muster rolls' bearing the names and ranks of men-at-arms and archers who took service under a given lord, reveal that in 1400 and 1401 a Sir Thomas Malory and a Thomas Malory esquire fought for Henry IV against the Scots in the service of Lord Grey of Codnor. Codnor had married Elizabeth Bassett, Lady Alice Malory's daughter by her first marriage, and since Sir Anketil's death in 1391 they too had lived at Castle Bytham. The Sir Thomas Malory on the roll was Anketil's oldest son, now rising twenty. The Thomas Malory esquire listed below him is most convincingly identified as the brother of his Newbold Revel cousin, John Malory.

The two campaigns curbed Scottish troublemaking effectively, and Henry turned to the much more serious problem of Wales. Owain Glyn Dŵr was supported by King Charles VI of France, whose daughter Isabel had been married to Richard II. French ships were already making raids on the English south coast and troops were massing for a landing in Wales. Worse, Glyn Dŵr had succeeded in persuading Richard II's kinsman Sir Edmund Mortimer to marry his daughter. In July 1403, he and Mortimer were joined by Harry Percy, the oldest son of the Earl of Northumberland. Percy was married to a Mortimer and was immortalised by Shakespeare as 'hare-brained Hotspur, governed by a spleen'. They planned a tripartite division of the country: Wales to Glyn Dŵr, England north of the Trent to the Percys, and England south of the Trent to Mortimer, and men were flocking to their army from all over Wales and the north of England.

Henry IV was at Nottingham, on his way north for a final settlement with the Scots, when he heard this news. He summoned the Midlands sheriffs to muster all available forces. Any able-bodied Malorys would have been among them; it did not do to ignore the King's command. With incredible speed, the King marched westwards via Lichfield. He reached Shrewsbury in time to prevent the town, which was held by his son, sixteen-year-old Prince Hal, from falling into the hands of Glyn Dŵr and Hotspur. The Earl of Warwick, Sir Richard Beauchamp, played a leading part in the battle that took place just north of Shrewsbury on 21 July. Although Glyn Dŵr evaded capture, Hotspur was defeated and killed. Beauchamp was made a Knight of the Garter two days later.

In October, Beauchamp was appointed Constable of Brecon, under the nominal command of Prince Hal. He garrisoned the castle with a hundred Warwickshire men-at-arms. No list of them survives, but the odds are that John Malory was among them; there were only about 120 gentry families in Warwickshire, and his cousin Giles Malory of Litchborough was in Beauchamp's service at this time. Beauchamp held his Brecon constableship under the general command of Grey of Codnor, who had been given a roving commission as king's lieutenant in south Wales in 1402. It is likely that the men who fought for Codnor in the Scottish wars went with him to Wales, so John Malory may have met up with his brother Thomas and his cousin Sir Thomas at Brecon. Beauchamp and his Brecon garrison came close to capturing Glyn Dŵr, who had now had himself crowned Prince of Wales, at Abergavenny, but the elusive hero escaped with only his banner, to remain a thorn in the side of the English for almost a decade.

In October 1404 Henry IV summoned Parliament to meet in Coventry, his own loyal heartland. He stayed in his palace of Kenilworth, and was royally entertained by Beauchamp at Warwick Castle. Did John Malory ride into Coventry to see the King with his little son Thomas, now about five years old, perched in front of him, clinging on to the saddlehorn? They would have seen, as a local chronicler did, a stocky, bearded man of middling height, 'well-proportioned and compact, quick and lively and of a stout courage', who scanned the bowed heads of the citizens of Coventry with small, suspicious eyes. Henry was hoping for generous loans from them, but he knew that, though outwardly loyal, they had strong Lollard leanings. And that they felt the new King had failed them by refusing to agree to Parliament's request that he raise money by curbing clerical privileges. The loans were not forthcoming, and the citizens became subtly uncooperative. 'Vittles waxed dear and lodgings strict'. Parliament was dissolved.

A year later, in May 1405, political drama seems to have come even closer to Newbold Revel. According to legend, the King's men arrived to drag the feisty nineteen-year-old Thomas Mowbray out of the sanctuary he was claiming at Monks Kirby Priory after fleeing from a failed uprising on Skipton Moor led by the Archbishop of York, Richard Scrope. They took him to Pontefract to be tried, together with Scrope and other rebels, in June. Beauchamp was one of the members of the court which found them guilty. Henry IV insisted that both men be sentenced to death. The execution of an archbishop sent almost as many ripples of horror across the country as the murder of Thomas Becket had done two hundred years earlier. Beauchamp, who was Scrope's godson, must have been appalled at the judicial murder of a priest. But he stayed loyal. Henry IV was 'the king who made him knight', and he owed him 'the faith of his body'. More importantly, he was now as close an ally of Prince Hal as Malory would make Sir Bors de Ganis an ally of Sir Lancelot du Lake. He mustered under the royal banner in Wales in the autumn, and joined the heir to the throne at the siege of Aberystwyth in 1407.

Childhood

*Small children be soft of flesh, lithe and pliant of body,
quick and light to move, and witty to learn. And they lead
their lives without thought or care. They set their hearts
only on fun, and are afraid of nothing but being beaten
with a rod; and they love an apple better than gold.*

Bartholomew Anglicus, *Concerning the Properties of Things*
(*c.* 1250)

oday the Malorys' Midlands estates seem deeply rural and
remote, but they are close to the centre of England.
Coventry, one of the busiest towns in the country, was only
seven miles away. The Lancastrian kings and queens often held court
there or in Leicester or at Kenilworth, near Warwick. Parliament met
in Coventry in 1404 and 1459, and in Leicester in 1414, 1426 and 1450.
Four of the dozen or so battles of the Wars of the Roses took place
in this part of the Midlands, and Kenilworth was an important royal
armoury. Drovers on their way from Wales to London, clothiers from
East Anglia, travellers from Yorkshire to the West Country, or from
Carlisle to London, all passed close by Winwick, Swinford and
Newbold Revel. At a leisurely pace, with stops on the way, it took the
Malorys only three days to travel the hundred miles or so to London,
Lincoln, Chester or Bristol. A rider in a hurry, with relays of fresh
horses, could get to any of these cities in one long summer's day.

The practical details Malory enjoyed adding to his tales show that
he was familiar with such travel times. When King Arthur sends the
Emperor of Rome's envoys away from his court at Carlisle to take
ship from the Kent port of Sandwich, he assumes it will take them

no more than a week, even riding only by day – as long as they don't indulge in any spying:

> *Now speed you, I counsel you, and spare not your horses,*
> *and look ye go by Watling Street and no ways else, and where*
> *night falls on you, look you there abide, be it fell or town, I*
> *take no keep; for it longeth not to aliens for to ride on nights.*
> *And may any be found a spear-length out of the way and*
> *that ye be not on the water by the sennight's end, there shall*
> *be no gold under God to pay for your ransom.*

Rightly terrified – for the Emperor's insulting demand for tribute has decided Arthur to embark on the conquest of Rome – the envoys 'spared for no horse, but hired them hackneys from town to town'. At sunset on the seventh day they reached Sandwich, where Watling Street ended, and 'so blithe were they never'.

Newbold Revel itself lies in a fertile bowl that was divided in medieval times into arable fields and strips worked by the demesne's tenants, pasture, deer park and woodland. The Smite Brook, a pretty little stream which rises in the north of the parish of Monks Kirby, meanders south-eastwards past the manor house, feeding the lake that has replaced the fishponds, then passing through the great millpool at Brinklow to Coombe Abbey, where it once filled an even more extensive range of fishponds, before joining a tributary of the Avon near Coventry.

There is no external trace of the Malorys' fifteenth-century manor house. The mansion that occupies its site is ponderously baroque with heavy sandstone window frames, swagged doorways, massive cornices and urn-topped balustrades. Victorian improvements included conservatories and a rubber-mounted dance floor in the great hall, and in the 1890s an exceptionally sporty owner added a cricket pitch, a cricketers' wing to house visiting teams, a gymnasium and a covered swimming pool. Ironically, given how much time Malory spent in captivity, his former home is now a 'school for screws': a training college run by Her Majesty's Prison Service. In the redbrick stable block, the oldest part of the house, there is a museum dedicated to 'Prisons Past, Present and Future'. On exhibition is a flogging block from Newgate, London's most ancient and notorious prison, and a place that Malory was to get to know all too well.

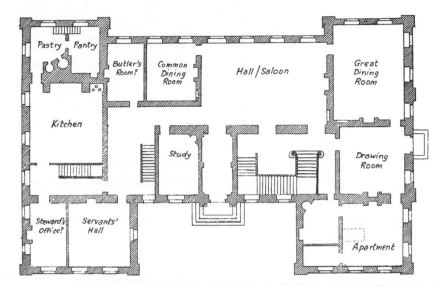

But concealed deep inside the ponderous stately home lies a secret house as snugly hidden as the kernel of a nut. It is a medieval building of generous proportions which was so solidly built that it tempted the remodellers to cheat Palladian symmetry. The shallow projecting bays of the east front are not quite the same width. The original kitchen wing was slightly narrower than the parlour wing, and this discrepancy, and the massive chimney-stack of the kitchen hearth and pastry ovens, were absorbed into the new plan to save money and effort. Another clue to the shape of the house which Thomas Malory knew as a child is the thickness of the walls that divide the staircase halls from the saloon and the room above it. Originally these were external walls and a great hall rose up through both storeys. Repair work in 1994 revealed the outline of the hall's high, steeply pitched roof on the chimney-stack wall in the upper storey.

The hidden house was very substantial, with its first storey at least built of stone and a floor plan no smaller than that of the existing house. An estate map drawn in 1703 shows it as a half-H, but it may have had more extensive side wings, or a complete courtyard in front of the house with a towered gateway entrance. An architectural historian has reconstructed a likely floor plan of the original building. He believes it had a courtyard instead of the present study, hall and grand staircase. The whole of the north side of the ground floor was devoted to the preparation and storage of food and drink. The 'pastry' was where bread and pies were made and baked. The 'surveying place' was where dishes of food were laid out so that the pages and yeoman of the household could carry them into the hall. Bread was kept in the pantry, and casks and bottles in the buttery. Small turret stairs at each side of the courtyard led to the upper chambers to the south and north. Above these there would be attics – sleeping quarters for servants and children. It is likely that the armorial window which the antiquarian and historian Sir William Dugdale copied when he visited Newbold Revel in 1637 was in the westerly parlour, where it would catch most light.

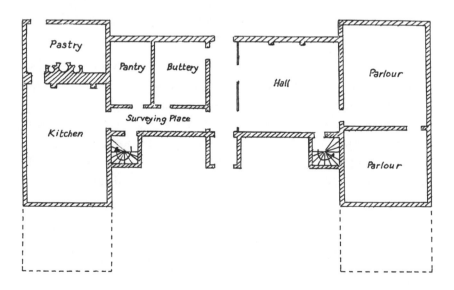

The most important person in Thomas Malory's early childhood was his nurse. The absence of records of John Malory before 1406 suggests that he was often away, and a wealthy gentlewoman like Philippa Malory was far too busy managing the affairs of the household and the family estates to take daily care of a tiny baby, however much she loved him. But nurses were not a second-best. They gave their charges more attention than their busy mothers could and were highly valued servants – bequests in medieval wills reflect the affection felt for them. They were permanent fixtures in houses blessed with many children, and comfortingly expert at caring for them.

> *The nurse is glad if the child be glad, and heavy if the child be sorry. She taketh the child up if it fall, and giveth it suck; if it weep she kisseth and lulleth it still, and gathereth the limbs, and bindeth them together, and doth cleanse and wash it when it is defiled. And for it cannot speak, the nurse lispeth and soundeth the same words to teach more easily the child . . . and she cheweth meat in her mouth and maketh it ready to the toothless child . . . and so she feedeth the child when it is an-hungered, and pleaseth the child with whispering and songs when it shall sleep, and swatheth it in sweet clothes and righteth and stretcheth out its limbs and bindeth them together with cradlebands, to keep and save the child that it have no miscrooked limbs.*

Dangers threatened small babies on every side: tainted food and water, disease, fire or attack from rats, dogs, even pigs. No more than a quarter of those born survived. A gentle born child's chances were better than most, but still slim. But all the evidence is that this made children especially precious rather than of little importance. Most medieval parents were just as attentive and affectionately accepting as modern ones.

> *All children be spotted with bad manners and think only of the present and not the future, they love plays, games, and vanity and care nothing for profit . . . They want things that are bad for them, and care more about a doll than a person . . . When they be washed, they are soon dirty again. When their mother washes and combs them, they kick and sprawl, and put out their feet and hands, and resist with all their might. They are always wanting a drink; they are no sooner out of bed, before they are crying for something to eat.*

Nursery equipment included a cradle, often a treasured family heirloom, tail-clouts (nappies) and slavering-clouts (bibs), headbands to protect the skull, swaddling bands that simulated the reassuring constriction of the womb, a basin for the daily bath already recommended as desirable, and a wood-framed and wheeled 'standing-stool' to encourage early walking. Once the child was out of petticoats and tail-clouts, its clothes were miniature versions of adult garments.

Education

For all the indulgence shown to very small children, it was taken for granted that the quickest and most effective way of transforming 'naughty babees' into gentlefolk was discipline. The Church emphasised the biblical maxim that to spare the rod was to spoil the child; it also taught that there was a special corner of hell reserved for parents who failed to apply timely chastisement, and let children grow up as 'slaves to themselves and plagues to all about them'. Parents, the late-fourteenth-century poet William Langland believed, had become over-protective as a result of the swaths of plague that had swept Europe. 'Do not please them out of reason,' he warned, 'for any power of the pestilence'. A popular later manual advised young mothers:

> *And if thy children be rebel and will not them bow low*
> *If any of them misdo, neither curse them nor blow [scold]*
> *But take a smart rod and beat them in a row*
> *Till they cry mercy and their guilt well know.*
> *Dear child, by this lore, they will love thee ever more.*

A boy who grew up in a family with as many traditions as Malory's would be taught to read and write, and to speak Latin and French. Children traditionally learned their first letters at their mother's knee, using unbreakable hornbooks engraved with alphabets and improving mottoes and maxims. They began as soon as they could lisp the letters, and had to be able to repeat what they were taught. Much of what they learned was in rhyming couplets, a very effective way of imprinting facts on the memory. Rhyme was used not just to teach children everything from arithmetic to good manners but to offer basic tips to adults on farming, housekeeping, hunting and medicine. Many such poems were written by parents for their own children and then more widely circulated.

Knowing the past history of both family and country was an important part of Malory's education. Such works were regularly read aloud, both at mealtimes and around the fire. 'The lord and knight delighteth for to hear / chronicles and stories of noble chivalry,' wrote the poet Stephen Hawes in 1509. The narrator's voice, the accompanying musical effects and the listeners' reactions (laughter, hisses and boos, tears and applause) made the experience intense and memorable. Families handed down personal mnemonics of their ancestors, added to by each generation. Rhyming historical chronicles like the one that John Hardyng finished in 1457 were full of inspiring 'mirrors and examples of times past', suitable for children and adults alike to take to heart. The single most popular history of Britain was the *Brut*, so-called because it began with the (apocryphal) arrival of Aeneas's grandson Brutus the Trojan, who supposedly founded London as New Troy. It was regularly brought up to date by 'continuers'. King Arthur was its most outstanding hero. He had been ignored in the Venerable Bede's eighth-century *Historia Eccelesiastica*, but the excavations which uncovered what was believed to be the grave of both Arthur and Guinevere at Glastonbury in 1191 may have been stimulated by his inclusion in such popular twelfth-century chronicles as that of Geoffrey of Monmouth and the *Brut*. By the fifteenth century, Arthur was generally held to be a revered hero, the only Briton among the Nine Worthies, the 'three Paynims, three Jews, and three Christian men', who were 'the most worshipfullest men of all time' and were frequently represented in civic pageants.

Malory is likely to have heard about Arthur's adventures when he was very young. The pounding rhythms and rollickingly alliterative phrases of the *Morte Arthure* have been dated to the first decade of the fifteenth century, and such a masterpiece would have been much repeated by travelling minstrels. He undoubtedly used it for his own account of King Arthur's conquest of Rome, which shows wholesale borrowings of its most memorable phrases.

Although there were some corrupt priests, monks and friars in the fifteenth century, it was a time of intense spirituality. Religion was taken deeply seriously by the laity. Hundreds of parish churches were splendidly rebuilt, and generous bequests were made for their upkeep. Malory's grandfather Sir John was given a licence in 1384 for a private oratory at Newbold Revel. This may have been a small chapel close to the house, or just an upper room with an altar at its east end. The licence suggests that the Malorys had their own chaplain. At a time when people were expected to make religious observances several times a day, beginning early in the morning, it was of course much more convenient to have a private chapel. The year in which Sir John Malory sought permission for his oratory saw the death of the most famous church reformer of the day, John Wycliffe. Wycliffe's benefice was at Lutterworth, very close to Swinford, and his supporters, nicknamed Lollards, were especially active in Coventry. Many gentry families sympathised with Wycliffe's view that the Church had become too concerned with worldly affairs, and that its insistence on holding services entirely in Latin prevented real understanding. But the close connection of both the Revels and the Malorys with the famous crusading Order of St John of Jerusalem, or Knights Hospitallers, and the evident respect Malory shows towards hermits and church rituals in the *Morte*, suggests that the family was a conventionally pious one, and would have frowned on the Lollards' heretical views on the Eucharist and predestination.

We can glean other clues about Malory's spiritual upbringing from the *Morte*. His gift for English prose suggests that he grew up in a family which owned fine books by English contemplative writers such as Mirk's *Festial*, a book of sermons, Walter Hilton's *Mixed Life*, an advice manual written especially for the lay devout, and Nicholas Love's best-selling *Mirror of the Blessed Life of Jesu Christ*. This beautiful English translation of St Bonaventura's *Meditations on the Life of Christ*, a paraphrase of the gospels, was the closest that the devout reader could get to reading the New Testament in English at a time when vernacular translations of the Bible were banned by the Church. Malory's spiritual education, begun almost as soon as he could walk, would have been tailored carefully to his understanding. 'Children have need to be fed with milk of light doctrine, and not with sad [i.e. heavy] meat of great clergy and of high contemplation,' wrote Nicholas Love in his *Mirror of Christ*. There are echoes of Love's vivid immediacy and intimate, personal touches in Malory's writing. Both often begin a subject with the companionable phrase 'Now take we . . .'; they also frequently use 'doublets', pairings of almost synonymous words.

Study and prayer were only part of childhood. Thomas must have had plenty of playmates – the children of the household and estate servants, those of neighbours, and of course his siblings. Gentry families like his own averaged six to eight children. He had at least three sisters: Isobel, Philippa and Helen, all of whom survived to marry. There were probably also brothers, and it is even possible that one or more were older than Thomas. The adventurous way of life that he chose in his twenties and thirties could signal a younger son as eager as Sir Gareth to make a name for himself.

A vivid picture of children's games at about this time is given by Malory's near contemporary, the chronicler Jean Froissart. He recalls damming brooks with tiles and floating saucers upon the water, making mud pies, cakes and tartlets and baking them in a tile oven at the edge of the fire, playing follow-my-leader, hide-and-seek and hare-and-hounds; rolling pebbles and marbles, walking on stilts, acting out charades, blowing soap bubbles from a pipe. There were also crueller pursuits. Cats and cocks were fair game for torture; wanton boys pulled wings off flies for sport. Froissart caught butterflies and tied threads to them so that 'I could make them fly where I pleased'.

Six or seven was traditionally the age when a boy passed from the care of the women of the household to that of the men. 'Let them watch from the age of five, and participate from the age of seven', directed Aristotle, still a definitive authority and much translated. The age at which formal lessons began in grammar, Latin and 'reckoning' (arithmetic) depended on aptitude; for a bright boy like Thomas Malory, it could have been as early as four. Hardyng's *Chronicle* says that children go

. . . at four year age,
To school at learn the doctrine of letters,
And after at six to have them in language,
And sit at meat seemly in all nurture.
At ten and twelve to revel is their cure,
To dance and sing, and speak of gentleness.

Thomas's family offered him inspiring mentors. His father John was, as we have seen, probably an active soldier in his youth, and was becoming an eminent local figure. His three uncles, Robert, Simon and Thomas, may also have been formative influences. Kinship loyalty is an important theme in the *Morte*. King Arthur is the uncle of the four sons of King Lot of Orkney, and when Lancelot accidentally kills Gawaine's brother and Arthur's nephew Gareth, Gawaine reminds Arthur of the fact, and the obligation it incurs, no fewer than eleven times. When Sir Ector encounters the mighty Galahad at a tournament, 'he drew him aside, and thought it no wisdom for to abide him, and also for natural love, that he was his uncle.' In other tales, uncles frequently take up arms against injustice and even sorcery. The uncle of the damsel in distress rescued by Alexander le Orphelin demolishes Morgan le Fay's macabre enchanted castle, Beau Regard. King Mark of Cornwall, who repeatedly plots the death of his nephew Tristram, is the exception who proves the rule: a wicked uncle. Malory makes Sir Percivale express disgust at the way he reneges on the loyalty expected between uncle and nephew:

Ah, fie for shame, said Sir Percivale, say ye never so more.
Are ye not uncle unto Sir Tristram, and he your nephew?

Beverley Kennedy has convincingly argued in her book *Knighthood in the Morte Darthur* that Malory deliberately presents three contrasted ways of being a knight: heroic, worldly-wise and spiritual. His uncles Thomas, Simon and Robert could be imagined to match these three types: Uncle Thomas, a veteran of Henry IV's wars against the Scots and the Welsh who fought with his nephew in France, as an heroic fighter in the best tradition of the brutal but essentially honest Gawain: 'as good a knight of his time as any is in this land';

Uncle Simon, who spent much of his later life in London, as having worldly wisdom, helping his nephew to fit into peacetime society after two decades of military service overseas; Uncle Robert as a spiritual inspiration, filling Malory's head with dreams of winning back Jerusalem, probably taking him with him to Rhodes 'to fight the miscreant Turk', and offering a model for his final hermit-like way of life, 'the servant of Jesu by day and by night'.

Teaching in schools was well adapted to children's abilities, using rhymes, riddles, word plays, woodcuts, pictures and jokes to extend vocabulary and explain meanings. Many of these have lingered in folk memory through the centuries in rhyming alphabets and nursery rhymes full of once topical allusions that seem nonsensical now. 'How many miles to Babylon?' is a distorted reference to the well-known pilgrimage shrine of Beverleyham (now Beverley) in Yorkshire, and the original rhyme asked 'Can I get there by daylight?', rather than candlelight. 'Ring-a-ring-a-roses' refers to the pomanders that were thought to protect their wearers against the plague; 'atishoo' the sneeze that signalled its onset before 'all fall down'. Thomas's first schoolmaster could have been the Malorys' own chaplain, but he might have joined a small class in a neighbour's house to be taught by the local vicar, or a chantry priest, or gone to a school in a nearby abbey such as Coombe or in Coventry itself. John Catesby, who lived close to the Malorys' manor of Winwick, sent his sons away to grammar school in the 1390s, as did Sir Edmund Stonor of Oxfordshire in the 1380s and Clement Paston of Norfolk in the 1400s.

Thomas would have known the seven-mile journey to Coventry well. Something was always happening there: fairs, markets and pageants and, most famous of all, the Corpus Christi mystery plays, a series of splendidly staged actings-out of biblical scenes and the events of Jesus Christ's life. A cast of hundreds cavorted on the great pageant wagons as they trundled through the city's streets, stopping in front of the grandest houses to act out such scenes as Noah's escape from the Flood, the Miracle of Cana or the Coming of the Magi. Every fifteenth-century king of England made a special journey at least once to Coventry to the plays and feast held on the Thursday after Trinity Sunday. The quickest way to Coventry from Newbold Revel was across country – pedestrians and horses could go more directly than wheeled traffic. To get there, Thomas and his companions followed the Smite Brook through thousands of acres of rich pastureland belonging to Coombe Abbey. They then circled the high stockade of the great deer park of Caluden – once a favourite hunting lodge of the Mowbray dukes of Norfolk, but deserted since their downfall. Next came Gosford Green, a famous tournament ground, where Thomas could pause to watch the archers at the butts and the young men practising swordplay.

The Tournament Tradition

Tournaments, great or small, were hugely popular events. They combined the attractions of the racecourse (thundering hoofs, gay silk liveries, and bookies) with those of the football ground (folk heroes and dazzling technical skills). They had their origins in northern Europe in the twelfth century and often had an Arthurian theme. At a tournament of 1278 at Hem, on the border of France and Flanders close to Tournai, knights, including Englishmen, dressed up as Arthurian characters. In the 1280s Edward I held a tournament that featured a Loathly Damsel with gigantic nose and vampire-like fangs. Edward III's tournaments were notable for their women jousters. They were 'not the best in the kingdom', but they appeared at tournaments to joust 'in diverse and wonderful male apparel'

> and thus proceeded on chosen coursers or other well-groomed horses . . . and so expended and devastated their goods, and vexed their bodies with scurrilous wantonness that . . . they neither feared God nor blushed at the chaste voice of the people.

Tournaments were much more than flamboyant exhibitionism. Entering the lists was the noble equivalent of the practice at the archery butts that was compulsory for yeomen. Riding into a mêlée knee to knee and in tight formation around the captain of their tourneying band prepared knights for riding into battle with their lord. They were 'companions-in-arms', committed to looking out for each other.

When a tournament took place at Gosford Green in the early fifteenth century, it is reasonable to imagine that the entire Malory family went to watch. They were steeped in chivalric tradition. 'It is our kind to haunt arms and noble deeds' could have been said by Thomas's father or his grandfather, though in the *Morte Darthur* the line is given to Sir Percivale and his brother Sir Aglovale. The blood of not only the Malorys but also of the warlike Boschervilles and the crusading Revels ran in young Thomas's veins. His ancestors were accustomed to serving their liege lords fearlessly, and the heroes of his *Arthur* are dedicated to such a role. Among the 267 Knights of the Bath created on the occasion of the knighting of Edward, Prince of Wales (later Edward II) in 1306 was a Thomas Malorie. His companions included William de la Zouche, Ralph Bassett, Ralph Dryby and Thomas le Grey. Members of the same families were combatants in the famous Dunstable tournament of 1334 and the prestigious north-east Midlands tourneying fraternity founded by Edward III's greatest war captain, Henry of Grosmont, Duke of Lancaster and Earl of Derby. Its foundation was directly linked to the fact that in 1337 war had been declared with France. Edward III wanted to regain the lands lost by King John over a century earlier. Campaigns were intermittent, and generally limited to the summer months. During the long truces, it was accepted chivalric practice to hold friendly jousts between champions from both countries as well as from other European states. In 1344 Edward III authorised the Duke of Lancaster's fraternity to tour Europe, and it travelled to France, Burgundy, Flanders, Italy, Bohemia and Hungary taking on all comers. After the return of the knights, they set up an annual international challenge tournament of their own in Nottinghamshire. It was held near Blyth every Whit Monday – its legacy is the name of the little village of Styrrup.

The Wembley, or perhaps Ascot, of the tournament circuit was Windsor Castle, which Froissart said had been 'built and founded by King Arthur'. In January 1344 Edward III, flushed with the success of his campaign in Brittany, sent summonses all over the country to announce a week-long tournament there. On the third day of jousting, after mass in the castle chapel, he announced that he was going to found a knightly Order of the Round Table 'of the same manner and standing as that which Lord Arthur, formerly king of England, had relinquished'. The companions of the Order would meet annually for a Whitsun-week feast. A new hall 200 feet in diameter was to be built to house an enormous circular wooden table so that all could be seated with near-equal precedence. Work began on 16 February 1344. It has been deduced from a chit for 40,000 tiles and tile-pins in the accounts of the clerk of the works that it would have been very similar to an Elizabethan theatre, with two concentric walls supporting roofed galleries and a large central open space for the table.

Events overtook the Order's foundation. When peace talks between the English and the French at Avignon broke down after Philip VI of France gave Guienne and Poitiers to his son John, Duke of Normandy, instead of returning them to England, the English began to prepare for real war. Instead of a Round Table, a smaller, more exclusive fellowship was established by 1348: the Order of the Knights of the Garter. Legend has it that it took its name from the King's gallant restoration of a blue garter to the dashing young Countess of Salisbury after it had fallen from her leg during a ball held at Calais. He reproached smirking onlookers with the words 'honi soit qui mal y pense', shame on him who thinks badly of this, and the phrase became the motto of the Order. Edward dotted garters liberally on his own clothes and bed-hangings and his personal flag-ship flew an enormous sky-blue silk banner showing St Lawrence 'powdered' with garters when he sailed to France.

Tournaments were not just practice for war. A joust could also be a duel to determine right from wrong. Anyone of knightly rank could ask to prove the justice of his cause, declaring, as Sir Tristram says to the barons of Ireland, 'Here is my body to make it good, body against body.' It did not matter who was actually the best fighter. God would see that the best man won – David beat Goliath, after all. It was an aborted joust to win justice at Thomas Malory's local tournament ground at Gosford Green that triggered Henry IV's usurpation of the throne. On 16 September 1398 Thomas Mowbray, Duke of

Norfolk, rode from Caluden to Gosford Green to joust against Henry Bolingbroke, Duke of Hereford and heir to the Duchy of Lancaster, in front of King Richard II. The stakes were high. Each had accused the other of treason. Their fellow peers had decreed that the issue should be settled by trial by combat according to the laws of chivalry. 'About the hour of prime came to the barriers of the lists the Duke of Hereford, mounted on a white courser, barded with green and blue velvet, embroidered sumptuously with swans and antelopes of goldsmiths work, armed at all points', Holinshed's *Chronicle* tells us. 'The Duke of Norfolk hovered on horseback at the entrance to the lists, his horse being barded with crimson velvet embroidered richly with lions of silver and mulberry trees.'

With more guile than good sense, Richard II stopped the duel almost before it had begun – an affront to chivalric convention that caused widespread murmurings. He sentenced both men to exile: Thomas Mowbray for life, Henry of Lancaster for nine years. Mowbray died within a year, on pilgrimage to Jerusalem. In 1399, Henry's father John of Gaunt, fourth son of Edward III and Shakespeare's 'time-honoured' Duke of Lancaster, died. Richard extended Henry's exile to life and declared the huge Lancastrian estates forfeit to the Crown. Adding such extreme injury to property to his insult to knightly etiquette was too much, especially since Henry was, if descent in the female line was disallowed, heir to Richard's throne. Within a year, Henry returned to England and claimed the crown. Backing him to the hilt were Richard, Lord Grey of Codnor, Richard Beauchamp, heir to the earldom of Warwick, Sir Ralph Bassett, Sir Humphrey Stafford and William de la Zouche, all descendants of the lords who had ridden with his ancestor Henry of Grosmont to both European tournaments and wars against the French. The background to the Gosford Green duel and its outcome show how integral to political life chivalry was for the English nobility.

Apprenticeship in Chivalry

This child will not labour for me, for anything that my
wife or I may do, but always he will be shooting or casting
darts, and glad for to see battles and to behold knights, and
always day and night he desireth of me to be made a
knight.

Malory, 'The Tale of Sir Tor'

s soon as he was old enough, Thomas Malory would have
been eager to begin his training, first as a page, and then as
an esquire. Eight or nine was not too young for a likely lad
to be sent away to a noble household to be educated in what Sir John
Fortescue called 'the urbanity and nurture of England'. The links
formed with friends made in these 'nurseries of chivalry' often lasted
for a lifetime. The grander the household the better, for it was hoped
that such promising young 'henchmen', as they were known, would
'surpass their ancestors in probity, vigour and honesty of manners,
since they will be trained in a superior and nobler household than
their parents' home'.

There is no record of where Malory learned his chivalric skills,
but Sir Richard Beauchamp's sumptuous household at Warwick
Castle would have been the ideal place for him to grow up, and he is
recorded in Beauchamp's retinue in 1414. The Beauchamp accounts
list several young boys: in 1408 the Earl's receiver paid £2 for the
lodging of a 'varlet' (i.e. valet, or page), and in 1420 £7 7s 0d was
spent on shoes, leggings, capes, lengths of green and russet cloth and
practice weapons for four youths. No names survive, but Warwick
Castle was conveniently close to Newbold Revel. Thomas's maternal

uncle William Purefoy and William Mountfort, who seems to have had kinship links of some kind with both the Chetwynds and the Malorys, were both retained by Beauchamp at this time.

Once peace settled over England, Beauchamp asked Henry IV if he could fulfil a vow to make a pilgrimage to Jerusalem. A secret reason might have been to do penance for the death of Archbishop Scrope, but he had other motives. He took with him a team of jousters to challenge knights 'both Christian and heathen' on his journey across Europe – an echo of the jaunts made by his grandfather in the 1340s and 1360s. It was a politically astute move: a way of keeping out of trouble at a time when the King and his heir were at odds. It was also an opportunity to carry out a diplomatic reconnaissance in Europe for the conquests that he and Hal dreamed of making after the death of Henry IV. Beauchamp set out early in 1408, and did not return for almost two years. His cousin Sir Baldwin Strange was in charge of his travelling household. There were sixty men-at-arms, nine grooms and six 'henchmen'. John Malory could have been one of the men-at-arms. There are no local records of him between 1407 and 1410 and the seal he used to authorise his signature on a charter towards the end of his life has three curious rounded fans which could be palm leaves on it, a sign that he made a pilgrimage to Jerusalem at some point in his life. If his son Thomas had indeed joined the Warwick Castle household by 1407, he too could have travelled with Beauchamp to France, Prussia, Lithuania, Poland, Russia, Westphalia, Germany, Italy and the Levant.

The beautifully illustrated *Pageant of the Birth, Life and Death of Richard Beauchamp, Earl of Warwick* gives stirring details of Beauchamp's adventures abroad. The book's sporting turns of phrase are uncannily similar to Malory's.

> *Entering Lombardy, [Beauchamp] was met by another herald from Sir Pandulph Malacet with a challenge to perform certain feats of arms with him at Verona, upon a day assigned for the Order of the Garter, and in the presence of Sir Galeot of Mantua; whereunto he gave his assent. And as soon as he had performed his pilgrimage to Rome, he returned to*

Verona, where he and his challenger were first to joust, next to fight with axes, afterwards with arming swords, and lastly with sharp daggers. At the day and place assigned for which exercises, came great resort of people, Sir Pandulph entering the lists with nine spears borne before him. The act of spears being ended, they fell to it with axes; in the which encounter Sir Pandulph received a sore wound on the shoulder, and had been utterly slain, but that Sir Galeot cried peace.

It is unlikely that Malory was the author, as he finished the *Morte Darthur* in 1469 and died in 1471, and the drawings in the *Pageant* are thought to date from the early 1480s. But whether he went to Jerusalem or not, he would have heard the story of the journey told and retold in Warwickshire when he was young, and he could have recounted its most memorable moments to whoever wrote the *Pageant*. He certainly knew Anne Beauchamp, by the 1470s the only remaining child of Sir Richard Beauchamp, and she was the most likely person to have commissioned its making. The *Pageant*'s title echoes the full title that Malory gave to his own book: *The Birth, Life and Acts of King Arthur and his knights of the Round Table . . . and the dolorous Death and Departing of them all*. Both works were intended to provide models of knightly conduct, virtuous lives and loyal service, and to inspire their readers to emulate the heroes whose adventures they described in stirring terms.

Beauchamp sailed from Venice for the East, arriving at Jaffa (Haifa) after six weeks at sea. In Jerusalem he visited the Holy Sepulchre and exchanged lavish gifts with one of the Turkish Sultan's lieutenants. The man disclosed that he was secretly a Christian and said that one day he would come over to England to wear the Beauchamp livery and be Marshal of the household. One of Malory's favourite characters in his 'Book of Sir Tristram' is just such a wandering paladin from the East, Sir Palomides 'the paynim' (heathen). After defeating the vile Sir Corsabrin at the tournament at Surluse, Palomides declares that he 'came into this land to be christened, and christened will I be'. Malory alters the usual account of Palomides's many gallant 'hurtlings' at the foe by having him baptised after his final defeat by Sir Tristram.

When Beauchamp returned to England, he found that Prince Hal had matured into a formidable man. The sixteenth-century chronicler Edward Hall described him as

> *of stature more than the common sort, of body lean, well-membered and strongly-made, a face beautiful, somewhat long-necked, black-haired, stout of stomach, eloquent of tongue, in martial affairs a very doctor, and of all chivalry the very Paragon. In strength and agility of body from his youth few were to him comparable: for which cause in wrestling, leaping and running no man almost durst with him resume; in casting of great iron bars and heavy stones, he excelled all men. No cold made him slothful, nor heat caused him to loiter, and when he most laboured his head was uncovered.*

The heir to the throne welcomed the Earl home by retaining him for life at the extremely generous rate of 200 marks (a mark was worth 13s 4d, two-thirds of a pound) a year; Beauchamp also gained a seat on the royal council. Henry IV was suffering from a disfiguring and painful skin disease which was seen by many as a curse upon him for the execution of Archbishop Scrope. 'From 1405 the King lost the beauty of his face,' wrote the chronicler John Capgrave. 'He was a leper, and ever fouler and fouler.' Pustules 'the size of teats' covered his face and hands, and at times he could hardly walk. He suffered a slight stroke in 1408 and had frequent fainting fits. For almost eighteen months, the royal council ruled England. But in November 1411, Henry IV became suspicious that his son wanted to depose him. Both Prince Hal and Beauchamp were sacked from the council.

For the next eighteen months they were out of favour, and spent much of their time in the Midlands. There was plenty of time for hunting and merrymaking. Prince Hal was particularly fond of the Lancastrian palace of Kenilworth, which his grandfather John of Gaunt had endowed with a banqueting hall of a size only second to that of the King at Westminster. He used his enforced leisure to begin work on a new tournament ground there, and to turn the marshes around the castle into a hundred-acre lake on which oared barges with turreted after-castles could simulate sea battles in front of a summer palace he called Pleasantmaris. Warwick Castle is only four miles from Kenilworth; Beauchamp was a regular visitor and participant in its jousts and feasts. So were other neighbouring gentry, including in all probability the Malorys.

Prince Hal was in return royally entertained at Warwick Castle. Beauchamp's youthful but already learned wife Elizabeth was the daughter and sole heir of Thomas, Lord Berkeley, an unusually intellectual peer with wide literary interests. Malory's first introduction to French versions of the Round Table legends could have been through the Beauchamps. A fabulous collection of books was donated to Bordesley Abbey, near Birmingham, by Sir Guy Beauchamp in 1306. Besides tomes on surgery, philology, lives of the saints and history, there were several romances – including a *Lancelot*, a *Grail* and a *Death of Arthur*. A condition of the gift was that they should never be sold, and Sir Guy and his heirs should always have access to them.

There is no proof that Thomas Malory served in Beauchamp's household as a boy. He could have been trained up in any of a dozen neighbouring castles and substantial manors. His father had dealings in 1407 with the Mountforts of Coleshill, close to his mother's family at Grendon, and the Astleys, whose castle was only three miles northwest of Newbold Revel, and whose daughter and heiress had just married Reginald, Lord Grey of Ruthin. Another possibility would have been service at Castle Bytham with the Greys of Codnor. As we have seen, Malorys, one of them probably Thomas's uncle, had served with Codnor in 1400 and 1401; they would do so again in 1417. Richard Grey of Codnor, now in his fifties, was Henry IV's most experienced commander, and had been effusively thanked by the 1406 Parliament for his exceptional service in the Welsh wars. In 1407 he was made Constable of Nottingham Castle and Ranger of Sherwood Forest, and in 1409 Henry IV gave him a lavish grant of 400 marks a year for life. Codnor, like Beauchamp, was a close friend of Prince Hal, and would go to Paris as his ambassador in 1413.

The Making of a Squire

Wherever he grew up, young Thomas Malory received a thorough grounding in all the chivalric arts – mental, musical and martial. Malory's earliest biographer John Bale, Bishop of Ossory, who died in 1563 and so could have talked to old men who remembered Malory, described his subject as 'outstanding from his youth for his heroic spirit and many remarkable gifts', and his competence and knowledge are evident in his writings. What exactly did he learn? Edward IV's Household Book outlined the usual education of nobly born young 'henchmen', as such boys were known. Their master had to

> show the scholars . . . to ride cleanly and surely; to draw
> them also to jousts; to learn them their harness [i.e. armour];
> to have all courtesy in words, deeds and degrees; diligently to
> keep them in rules of goings and sittings, after they be of
> honour. Moreover to teach them sundry languages, and other
> learnings virtuous, to harp, pipe, sing, dance and, with other
> honest and temperate behaviour and patience.

The master noticed what each pupil was 'most apt to learn' and let him concentrate on it, and he sat with the boys in hall to oversee their table manners and conversation. The henchmen were trained in the elaborate rituals of the chamber: dressing and undressing their lords both in armour and in ordinary clothes, sleeping on a pallet by the door ready to answer a call in the night. One medieval illumination shows squires-of-the-bedchamber attending a prince while he is relieving himself into a close stool; one is shown wiping the royal bottom. A would-be squire was expected to dress elegantly, in fine linen shirts and well-made leather shoes, with a damask or satin doublet for festive occasions, embroidered perhaps with his mentor's device. They were also taught how to serve at table and to amuse and entertain their lord and his guests at the end of the meal by dancing or 'talking of chronicles of kings and of other policies, or in piping or harping, singing or other acts martial'.

Thomas Malory was, to judge from his future career, very 'apt to learn' these latter skills. He had his own harper by 1451, and it is not far-fetched to see personal experience in the way he emphasises Sir Tristram's fondness for music. As a boy 'Tristram learned to be an harper passing all other, [so] that there was none such called in no country', he tells us. We might guess that Malory grew up into an accomplished after-dinner entertainer, reciter and singer, for when we listen to his stories read aloud, they leap into life. Good raconteurs were prized. But as 'the memory of the people is not retentive but right forgetful; when some hear long tales and histories they cannot all retain in their mind or record', so too were those who wrote down such stories.

> *Men ought to read books and gestes*
> *And histories at feasts.*
> *If writings were not made*
> *And afterwards read and recounted by clerks,*
> *Many would be the things forgotten.*

A squire was ideally as adroit intellectually as he was practically. The chronicle of the life of Sir Jacques de Lalaing said that at an early age he 'made him expert and well able to speak, understand and write in Latin and in French . . . to play chess, backgammon and other gentlemanly sports'. The rules of chess then were simpler, and it was played for intellectual reasons as well as for entertainment – it taught foresight and the ability to predict an opponent's behaviour. It is a reflection of the popularity of chess that the first book that William Caxton printed in English was *The Game and Play of Chess*, a translation of a book written by Jacques de Cessoles, a French Knight Hospitaller, in the 1330s. It was as much an allegory of social degree as a guide to how to play. But the only person who plays chess in the *Morte Darthur* is the villainous King Mark of Cornwall, a master of deviance and trickery.

Outdoor pursuits included riding, archery, swimming, tennis, boxing, running and leaping, hunting, hawking and swordsmanship. These activities would be overseen by experienced military veterans, themselves knights or squires. Malory was clearly an experienced swordsman, for his many accounts of duels are long and technically detailed. Again, he will have learned at an early age – children started practising sword-and-buckler play with wooden swords and shields from the age of five or six. Riding began on pillions behind adults, then astride a small pony. A Genoese hunting manuscript in the British Museum shows a remarkably small boy riding a pony beside his father. Each has a falcon on his wrist; slender hounds weave their way between the horses' legs. Henry IV bought a horse for his ten-year-old son John in 1399.

Handling a horse in the tiltyard was an important part of a boy's military education. Holding a lance, the rider galloped towards a tall pole with a crosspiece which had a target at one end and a padded buffer on the other. It required speed and agility to prevent the buffer knocking him out of his saddle seconds after the target was struck. But such quick reactions were essential both in tourneying and in real battles. It took practice to acquire them.

> 'By my head,' said Sir Mordred to the damosel, 'ye are greatly to blame so to rebuke him, for I warn you plainly he is a good knight, and I doubt not but he shall prove a noble knight; but as yet he may not yet sit sure on horseback, for he that shall be a good horseman it must come of usage and exercise.'

Relations between rider and horse could be close. 'Some horses suffer no man to ride on their backs but only their own lords,' wrote Bartholomew Glanville in *Medieval Lore*. 'And many horses weep when their lords be dead.' Favourite steeds were often left to close friends in wills. Malory's heroes are always on horseback, riding here, there and everywhere 'at a wallop' on their coursers, meeting damsels on fair palfreys, storming into battle on their armoured destriers. 'What is a knight but when he is on horseback?' exclaims Sir Lamorak, reproaching his brothers for allowing themselves to be unhorsed at the tournament of Surluse. 'There should no knight fight on foot but if it were for treason, or else he were driven thereto by force; therefore, brethren, sit fast on your horses, or else fight never more afore me.'

Archery was the pre-eminent outdoor sport of the time. There is a record in 1475 of wood being imported from Spain especially to make small bows for children; Henry VII gave one to his five-year-old son Arthur in 1492. All men with boys in their houses between the ages of seven and seventeen had to provide them with a bow and two arrows and bring them up to shoot. On Sundays practice was compulsory, and such tempting alternative amusements as quoits, dice, stone-casting, ball games and cock-fighting were officially banned.

The best way to exercise both riding and archery skills was by going hunting. In gentry families, men, women and children alike enjoyed riding out to hunt, and hawks and hounds were always taken along on journeys. Popular while Thomas was growing up was a long poem in which a mother explains the lore of hunting to her son. Circulating in manuscript from about 1400, it was called *Tristram* – the Arthurian hero was as fond of hunting as of harping. In bouncing couplets it explains about closed seasons, how to talk to hounds and butcher carcasses, and provides word lists of the special hunting terms applied to animals.

Malory's knights spend much of their time in pursuit of harts, boars, and such strange animals as King Pellinore's personal quest, a 'beast glatisant' that sounded like thirty pairs of hounds all giving tongue at once. Mysterious damsels turn up at King Arthur's court clutching brachet hounds and demanding that particular hinds be captured. We can deduce from the many enthusiastic references to hunting that Malory was, like Tristram, 'a great chaser' (hunter). After a passage praising Tristram for defining the terms of hunting, he can not resist butting into his own story:

> *Wherefore, as meseemeth, all gentlemen that bear old arms*
> *ought of right to honour Sir Tristram for the goodly terms*
> *that gentlemen have and use, and shall to the day of doom.*
> *'Amen' says Sir Thomas Malory!*

Boys were introduced to the complex skills and lore of hunting at the age of seven or eight, according to *The Master of Game*, a French treatise translated into English early in the fifteenth century by Edward, Duke of York, for his young cousin Henry V's 'noble and wise correction'. The book bubbles with appreciation of the joys of the sport. Early rising means that the hunter 'sees a sweet and fair morn and clear weather and bright and he heareth the song of the small birds', and staying out all day pitting wits and courage against 'the falseness and malice of the cat, the marvellous cunning of the hart and the boar that can slit a man from knee to breast and slay him all stark dead at one stroke so that he never speak thereafter'. In the evening the hunter washes his thighs and legs 'and peradventure all his body'; then spends the evening feasting and recounting the day's triumphs.

The most important thing about hunting was that it was 'the very imitation of battle'. The summary of child-rearing in Hardyng's *Chronicle* quoted earlier continues by spelling out the link between training 'lords' sons' for the chase and their military competence.

> *At fourteen years they shall to field i-sure*
> *To hunt the deer and catch an hardiness*
> *For deer to hunt and slay and see them bleed,*
> *An hardyment giveth to his courage,*
> *And also in his wit he taketh heed,*
> *Imagining to take them at avantage.*

The hunter's skills in archery, spear work, manoeuvring on horseback and quick thinking on tactics ('imagining to take them at avantage') were all as essential for war as for hunting.

In this context, swimming could also be important. Malory makes Sir Lancelot swim across the Thames in his haste to rescue Queen Guinevere, who has been kidnapped by the wicked Sir Meliagaunce, a detail not in earlier English Arthurian tellings. He was himself a good swimmer – in 1451 he escapes from imprisonment by jumping out of a window and swimming across a moat. It was a skill recommended in Vegetius's manual of military strategy and a useful one for anyone who, like Malory, fought in Normandy, where most of the battles and sieges were fought at river crossings. The River Avon runs past Warwick Castle, and we can imagine Malory jumping in, holding his nose, as some young would-be squires are drawn in a late thirteenth-century French manuscript. Little is known about how swimming was taught in medieval times, but William Horman, a fifteenth-century schoolmaster, wrote that 'children do learn to swim leaning on the rind of a tree or cork'. Water-wings, made perhaps from a pair of the inflated pig's bladders used as footballs, were also known. In 1425 a London mob in the pay of Duke Humfrey of Gloucester threatened to throw Cardinal Beaufort into the Thames 'to teach him to swim with wings' – a taunting denial of his supposedly near-angelic spiritual status. In 1531, Sir Thomas Elyot was still recommending swimming as part of a chivalric education, and the first English treatise on the subject (*De Arte Natandi*) was written by another knight, Sir Everard Digby, in the late sixteenth century.

The household chaplain would be responsible for the boys' church observances and singing practice. The ladies of the house taught them manners and respect for women. The young page in the late medieval romance *Le Petit Jehan de Saintré* is told by the elegant damsel who takes on his education to be religious, sober, temperate, peaceful and truthful.

> *Likewise be loyal of hands and mouth, and serve every man as best you may. Seek the fellowship of good men; hearken to their words and remember them. Be humble and courteous wherever you go, boasting not nor talking overmuch, neither be dumb altogether. Look to it that no lady reproach you through your default, nor any woman of whatsoever quality, and if you fall into company where men speak disworshipfully of any woman, show by gracious words that it please you not and depart.*

Mastery of the practical and intellectual skills of knighthood had to be complemented by an understanding of the chivalric code of honour that governed it: religious reverence, compassion, generosity of spirit, loyalty and dedication to justice. The best-known guide to chivalry was Ramon Lull's *Book of Knighthood and Chivalry*. At this time it was circulating only in manuscript; William Caxton printed it in 1484, the year before he printed the *Morte Darthur*. It is written in the form of an explanation of the origins and essence of chivalry given by a hermit who was once a knight to a squire who seeks to be 'adoubted knight'. Chivalry, he says, began as a way of countering wickedness by setting up truly good men to guard ordinary people against oppression.

> *It behoves the knight that by nobility and courage and by noble custom and bounty, and by the honour so great and high that he is made by his election; by his horse and by his arms be loved and redoubted by the people; and that by his love he recovers charity and learning, and by deeds recovers Verity and Justice.*

He warns the squire that a knight who merely exercised himself in arms and matters pertaining to the body without practising the virtues of chivalry was acting falsely. He must care for his lands and tenants, support his lord courageously in battle, be 'witty and discreet', maintain and defend women, administer justice and be merciful. He should certainly not be a robber himself, but should seek out robbers and traitors and punish them. He should maintain himself in appropriate state, and offer hospitality to travellers. Lechery and perjury were forbidden, and he should be humble rather than proud.

Malory's 'most pleasant jumble' of Arthurian stories illustrates this advice so thoroughly and so systematically that it is not far-fetched to suggest that Lull was one of the inspirations for his own book. That he had a profound respect for chivalry is beyond doubt. But the accusations against him made in the 1450s and 1460s seem, on the surface of things, to prove that he was 'no true knight'. Or do they, if properly understood, show that he took the tenets of chivalry much more to heart than most of his contemporaries?

Taking the Adventure

'My lord, Sir Lancelot,' said Dame Elaine, 'at this same feast of Pentecost shall your son and mine, Galahad, be made knight, for he is fully now fifteen winter old.' 'Do as ye list,' said Sir Lancelot; 'God give him grace to prove a good knight.' 'As for that,' said Dame Elaine, 'I doubt not he shall prove the best man of his kin except one.' 'Then shall he be a man good enough,' said Sir Lancelot.

Malory, 'The Tale of Isolde the Fair'

n 21 March 1413, Henry IV died, and Prince Hal, now twenty-five years old, succeeded to the English throne as Henry V. His ability, piety and warlike ambitions made him the epitome of chivalry. Beauchamp and Grey of Codnor, Malory's two most likely 'good lords', were his most trusted advisers; his three brothers John, Duke of Bedford, Thomas, Duke of Clarence, and Humfrey, Duke of Gloucester, were devotedly loyal. Despite the worst blizzard to hit England since, it was said, the days of King Lear, the coronation ceremonies began on 8 April, when Henry V conferred the Order of the Bath on fifty candidates. They had spent the previous night in the Tower, first taking a ceremonial bath and then keeping an all-night vigil in the ancient chapel of St John in the White Tower. Now they wore long green robes with narrow sleeves and great hoods. Double white silk knots with hanging tassels were fastened to their left shoulders and their robes were trimmed with miniver, the pale, silk-soft belly fur of the grey squirrel. Peace and reconciliation were the order of the day. Among the new knights were the sons of old enemies: the Earl of March and his brother Roger Mortimer, Richard Despenser and Sir John Holland, later Earl of Huntingdon. All was to be forgiven. A general pardon, an amnesty for all crimes past, would soon be offered. Not only did it wipe the slate clean for those with undiscovered crimes hanging over their heads; it raised welcome cash for the King's Treasury.

Next day, London celebrated in style. 'Gold scarlet, cotton and coloured garments paint here, with the aid of art, a new heaven'. Regardless of the snow and hail, gaudy hangings dangled from windows and banners waved from turrets and gateways as the royal procession wound its way from St Paul's Cathedral to Westminster Abbey. First came the new knights and a 'great rout of lords well-apparelled in scarlet furred with miniver', with their liveried retainers. Then came the King, his cloth-of-gold and purple robes shimmering with precious stones, his household knights splendid in surcoats. At a respectful distance came members of the city guilds, mercers and fishmongers, cutlers and drapers, armourers and butchers, sheath-makers and weavers, spurriers and skinners, glovers and tailors, wax and tallow chandlers, fruiterers and cooks, all 'adorned and decked' with the devices of their callings. Then the commons – 'an immense crowd which poured forward more thickly than the stars of heaven'.

Several Malorys could have been there: John Malory of Welton, old Sir William Malory of Walton-in-the-Wold and Tachbrook Mallory, young Sir William Malory of Papworth St Agnes, perhaps even William Malory of Hutton Conyers in Yorkshire. John Malory of Newbold Revel had more reason to be in London than any of them. A few weeks earlier, he had been elected knight of the shire for Warwickshire, and would have to be in Westminster for the opening of Henry V's first Parliament on 15 May. It is not far-fetched to imagine him bringing his family with him to stay in the Beauchamps' rambling London residence, Warwick Inn, near Newgate.

With thousands of others, the Malorys would have crowded into St Peter's, the Abbey church, to see Henry mount a high stage shimmering with hangings of cloth-of-gold. He was solemnly anointed on the head, chest, shoulders and hands with St Thomas Becket's miraculous coronation oil. Then he was presented with the sword of justice and crowned King Henry V of England and France. Next he processed to the Great Hall for the coronation feast, which on that auspicious day was 'open to all strangers and people that would come'. Sitting on a marble throne high on a dais at the upper end, he looked 'like an angel, comely and gracious'. In the galleries above him echoed the 'noise and whiffling of the waits', robed in long, brightly-coloured gowns.

As Steward of England, Beauchamp was responsible for managing the proceedings; no doubt he managed things much better than King Arthur's steward, the quarrelsome Sir Kay, who was forever offending somebody. We know Thomas Malory was in Beauchamp's service a year later; he could have attended him as he strode among the throng of guests, directing matters with a long ceremonial staff. The menu of the feast survives. Henry's stepmother Joanna of Navarre sent two paniers of best Breton lampreys, succulent eel-like fish so highly prized that only royalty was allowed to eat them. The Exchequer records also show payments to the bearers of a large pike sent by William Crosier and for two tender Sussex does from Sir John Pelham's deer park. The feast was magnificently presented in three courses, each carried through the crowds to the high table by servants on horseback. Among the most prized delicacies were blandesory (hen brawn ground with rice and milk of almonds) and flampets (fat pork and figs boiled in small ale, and then baked with cheese in a 'coffin' of egg-yolk-coloured pastry).

Between courses came exotic 'subtleties' made of spun sugar, pastry and jelly, and modelled into gilded eagles, antelopes, silvered swans with broods of cygnets. Each had loyal rhyming wishes made of hard-baked gilded pastry attached to it: 'Keep the Law / And Guard the Foi'; 'Have Pitee / On the Commonaltee'; 'Out of Court / Be banished Tort'. As for wine, the great lead-lined stone water tank in the Palace Yard was filled with it – half its taps ran with red from Gascony, the others with white Rhine wine. The start of the meal was conducted in solemn silence, but there were wild cheers when the King's champion Sir John Dymock entered on horseback dressed as St George and challenged anyone who disputed the new King's title to speak now or for ever hold their peace.

*　　*　　*

Henry V's first Parliament opened in Westminster on 15 May 1413. John Malory, his fellow knights of the shire and the two burgesses elected from every borough will have sat, as the Commons normally did, in the Abbey's great refectory. The peers sat in the Painted Chamber. The attendance was average for the time – 45 or so spiritual peers, 38 lay peers, 74 knights of the shire (two for each county), and 182 burgesses from the cities and towns. It was a relatively intimate gathering – people knew each other personally or by repute. The proceedings were opened by the King's uncle, Henry Beaufort, Bishop of Winchester and Chancellor of England, who declared that the new King would follow his revered father's foreign policy, fostering friends and fighting foes. But everyone was aware that Henry V had much more ambitious plans than his father. When they voted generous taxes for the King's needs, they had a shrewd suspicion that before long England would be at war with France.

The idea of England conquering France seems unlikely today, but in Malory's time, memories were long. The dukedom of Normandy, homeland of the conquerors of England in 1066, was still held by the King of England in 1152, when the marriage of Henry II to Elinor of Aquitaine added her huge duchy in south-west France to the English King's Continental holdings. Although King John lost Normandy to King Philip II of France in 1204, and Henry III formally ceded his claim to it, their successors never gave up hope of retrieving it. In 1337, Edward III inherited a claim to the throne of France itself from his mother Isabella, daughter of the French King Philip IV, and in 1399, he took an army to Picardy. For the rest of the century and through half of the next, the intermittent hostilities labelled by posterity 'the Hundred Years War' continued between England and France, with the great duchies of Burgundy and Brittany wavering between the English and French crowns in their alliances and allegiances. In 1346 Edward shattered the French army at Crécy and in 1347 he captured the strategically priceless stronghold of Calais, an essential bridgehead for invasion. Within sight (on a clear day) of Dover, it also allowed the English to dominate the narrows of the Channel between England and France. In 1356 his son Edward the Black Prince defeated the French at Poitiers, capturing their king, John II; the

Black Prince's son, the future Richard II, was born in Bordeaux. The 1360 Treaty of Bretigny promised the English large new territories in south-west France and an enormous ransom for King John.

But then the tide turned. Edward III did not establish a firm administrative hold on these conquests and failed to make them self-financing. By the 1370s, most of Aquitaine had resumed allegiance to France. Only Bordeaux, linked to England by its hugely profitable wine trade, clung to its old alliance with England. Richard II, Edward's ten-year-old grandson, succeeded to the throne in 1377. Once he was old enough to rule for himself, he favoured peace, and, despite the fact that King John's ransom had still not been paid in full, a twenty-eight-year truce was signed in 1398. This pacifist policy was one reason for Richard's unpopularity in England. Crossing to France on a *chevauchée*, a lightning strike by well-armed horsemen and archers in order to plunder and capture ransomable prisoners, had long been seen as an opportunity to make a quick fortune. There were still happy memories of Edward III's campaigns, when, wrote the English monk and historian Thomas Walsingham, 'there were few women who did not have something from Caen, Calais and other overseas towns; clothing, furs, bedcovers, cutlery. Tablecloths and linen, bowls in wood and silver were to be seen in every English household.'

War was also an opportunity to display chivalric prowess, a way of reliving the old romances. In 1389 Philippe de Mézières bemoaned the fact that 'God's chastisement of the sins of the Scots and the French' was attributed by the victorious English 'solely to your own valour and chivalry, drunk as you are with pride and stirred up by the stories of Lancelot and Gawain and their worldly valour'. When the Lancastrians grabbed the throne, they were well aware that renewing war with France would increase their popularity. But Henry IV was at first too hard-pressed by rebels at home and later too unwell to do much to realise such dreams – though his second son Thomas, Duke of Clarence, did make a profitable *chevauchée* into Anjou and Blois in 1412.

Now that Henry V had succeeded to the throne, he was hot for war. It was easy to find excuses for ending the truce. Royal proclamations announced that the French were 'against God and against all 'justice', keeping England's rightful possessions from her. It would ensure 'the tranquillity of kingdoms, and especially of the two kingdoms of England and France' if they were 'more coherent and united' under the English Crown. Henry intended to make the most of the civil war in France, where the Count of Armagnac and his allies were supporting the Dauphin, the heir to the French throne, against his father King Charles VI. Charles, enfeebled by wild living and now intermittently insane, was dominated by his wife Queen Isobel; they were supported by the royal dukes of Orléans and Berry. Both sides vied for the favour of the Duke of Burgundy, John the Fearless, who controlled more territory and was far wealthier than the French King, though he owed him a nominal fealty. Henry V liked the idea of winning Burgundy as an ally for England. Burgundy's realm included Brabant, in the Low Countries, an important market for English cloth. The alliance would be welcomed by London's merchants – and their moneybags were needed to pay for the war effort.

When John Malory returned to Newbold Revel after Parliament was adjourned, he would have brought news of the martial atmosphere of the capital. He himself then went to north Wales; he witnessed a document at Ruthin Castle for Reginald, Lord Grey of Ruthin, Henry V's Lieutenant in Wales, on 10 February 1414. He may have stayed there for some time; he did not sit in the Parliament which met at Leicester in April 1414, or the one which met in London in November 1414. War was now openly being called for. Ralph Neville, Earl of Westmorland, who was the King's Lieutenant in the north, advised attacking Scotland first, quoting the old adage: 'Scotland shall be tamed ere France be framed'. That idea, however, was turned on its head by Chancellor Beaufort, Bishop of Winchester. The Beauforts were descended from John of Gaunt's mistress, Katherine Swinford. Legitimised by Henry IV, though barred from inheriting the throne, they were ambitious, ruthless and as aggressively clannish as Malory makes King Arthur's nephews, the older sons of Lot of Orkney and Queen Margawse. Lacking lands of their own, the Beauforts devoted themselves to the Lancastrian kings and were generously rewarded by them.

Bishop Beaufort, half-brother of Henry IV, was the cleverest of them all, and a brilliant orator. He argued that 'he that will Scotland win, let him with France begin'. Anyone who chose to attack their poor neighbours rather than rich foreigners were 'men effeminate, more meet for a carpet than a camp, men of weak stomach desiring rather to walk in a pleasant garden than pass the seas in a tempestuous storm'.

> *If you get Scotland, you have a country barren almost of pleasure and goodness, you gain people savage, wavering and inconstant, of riches you shall have little and of poverty much. But if you get France, you shall have a country fertile, pleasant and plentiful, you shall have people, civil, witty and of good order. You shall have . . . 24 puissant duchies, 80 and odd populous counties, and an hundred and three famous bishoprics, a thousand and more fat monasteries, and parish churches 100,000 and more. This conquest is honourable, this gain is profitable, this journey is pleasant, and therefore neither to be left nor forslowed [delayed]. Vittles you shall have sufficient from Flanders, aid of men you may have daily out of England, or else to leave a competent crew in the Marches of Calais to refresh your army and to furnish still your number. Although the cost in transporting your men may be great, yet your gain shall be greater, and therefore according to the trite adage, 'he must liberally spend that will plentifully gain'.*

His counsellors' enthusiasm for war with France was music to Henry V's ears. He sent an embassy led by Codnor to France to revive all England's old claims, and express his desire to marry the King of France's youngest daughter, Catherine – on such outrageously profitable terms that he could be sure that only war would win him his bride. Another, more secret, embassy had been sent to Burgundy, to negotiate John's neutrality, perhaps even his support. He also issued orders to build new ships for the royal fleet, the foundations of a permanent national navy. He made his brother Thomas, Duke of Clarence, the first ever Admiral of England.

Thomas Malory goes to War

You grew up fast in the fifteenth century. At the age of twelve, male children were legally responsible for their actions and had to swear an oath to keep the peace. The men-at-arms called up to fight for Henry V in France in 1415 had to be 'at least 14 years of age'. Some were even younger: in 1417 the thirteen-year-old son of Sir John Cornwall swam across the Seine with his father to help him establish a crucial bridgehead at Pont d'Arche. The *Morte* itself refers to henchmen among the King's troops, warned not to blow their horns when Sir Gawaine finds that his small band is perilously close to the army of the King of Lorraine, and in attendance on Sir Priamus while he is mounting a rescue. So Thomas Malory was now capable of being a useful member of any lord's retinue. Given his enthusiasm for tournaments and warfare, he had come of age as a potential squire at exactly the right time.

On 3 February 1414, Sir Richard Beauchamp, Earl of Warwick, had been appointed Captain of Calais. It was he who would head the 'competent crew' which Bishop Beaufort had said was essential for back-up and reinforcement of any invasion force. And with him would go young Thomas Malory. According to Dugdale's *History of Warwickshire*, John Malory of Newbold Revel

> *left issue Thomas, who, in King Henry V's time, was of the retinue to Richard Beauchamp Earl of Warwick at the siege of Calais, and served there with one lance and two archers; receiving for his lance and 1 archer £20 per annum and their diet; and for the other archer 10 marks and no diet.*

Thomas himself will have been the lance. One of the archers with him was evidently more senior than the other – perhaps he too was mounted. Besides the two archers, Malory would have had a groom, at least two horses and a page.

This is the first sighting in the historical record of a Thomas Malory of the right status to be the author of the *Morte Darthur*, and it is important evidence for his age – he must have been at least fourteen to go to war as a lance attended by archers, but he need not have been much older. What better beginning to the career of the greatest of writers of chivalric romance than service with Beauchamp, who was as adept at jousting and chivalric courtesy as Tristram or Lancelot? Among the seventy-two other esquires were Warwickshire neighbours and later associates: Ralph Arderne, Ralph Green, Thomas and Richard Harcourt, William Mountford and Humphrey Stafford. Two of the squires listed, John Shirley and Richard Halsham, shared, perhaps even inspired, Malory's literary interests. Shirley, who was in his thirties, was Beauchamp's most trusted secretary; he had a substantial collection of manuscripts including verse by such poets as Geoffrey Chaucer and John Lydgate. Richard Halsham was a poet, whose verses Shirley transcribed. Also listed are four Warwickshire knights: Sir John Beauchamp, Sir William Bishopstone, Sir Ralph Bracebridge, and Sir Baldwin Strange, who probably once again organised Beauchamp's personal household arrangements.

Looked at more closely, however, Dugdale's entry turns out to be the first of the many mysteries that surround the life of Malory. There was no date on the source of his information: a list of 128 men mustered to serve with Beauchamp at Calais. But the only fifteenth-century siege of Calais was in 1436, fourteen years after the death of Henry V, when a Burgundian army surrounded it. To say that the siege of Calais was 'in King Henry V's time' would have been an extraordinary mistake for a man as familiar with the history of the fifteenth century as Dugdale. The list was definitely drawn up much earlier than 1436. We know from other sources – as did Dugdale – that Sir Baldwin Strange died in September 1416, and William Mountfort, listed as a squire, was knighted in 1415. I decided to see what Dugdale had really meant. He had the fruits of his exhaustive researches copied into stout leather-bound folio notebooks, which are now in the Bodleian Library, Oxford. They have to be read in its oldest reading room, Duke Humfrey's Library, named in honour of Henry V's youngest brother, Duke Humfrey of Gloucester, who bequeathed his books to the university in 1447. There are long oak desks in book-lined alcoves, and the golden stone, arched windows and timber-framed roof lined with painted panels of coats of arms date from the 1480s.

I opened up the notebook that contained Dugdale's list of Beauchamp's retinue and read the actual words copied out in tiny, methodical handwriting. Written, as most military records then were, in French (modernised here), the muster roll began with the words: 'C'est la retinue monsieur le Counte de Warrewyk des gens d'armes et des archiers pour sa demeure à Calais pour l'enforcement de la ville et les Marches illoeques'. 'Sa demeure' meant his stay, or residence. So the original list did not mention a siege, only the 'reinforcement of the town and its neighbouring marches'. The mystery was explained. The literal meaning of the French word 'siège' is a seat, or a place – hence the English usage 'country seat'. Dugdale was clearly using the word in this sense. That this was true was confirmed when I looked up Dugdale's entries on the other men mentioned in the roll – one or two did use the phrase 'at the siege of Calais', but most simply said that the men were in Calais 'for its reinforcement' in the time of Henry V.

Once the phantom of the siege is disposed of, Malory's experiences in Beauchamp's service can be reconstructed. The most convincing date for the muster roll is early in 1414. In January 1414 word reached England that, despite the official truce, French troops were moving into Picardy, close to Calais. On 3 February 1414 Beauchamp was formally signed up as Captain of Calais for three years. It was at this point that he went back to his native Warwickshire to recruit soldiers to take with him. Sir Baldwin Strange and John Shirley had been in charge of the Earl of Warwick's itinerant household during his European and Eastern travels. They probably also organised the Warwickshire men's march along Watling Street to Sandwich, at the mouth of the Stour estuary, where ships had been commissioned to take them across to Calais in relays. The complete journey took at least three days, probably skirting the city of London, and crossing the Thames by ferry at Westminster, or by the great bridge at Kingston. Eight-wheeled supply carts drawn by six or ten oxen trundled beside the marching men. Those who were mounted made forays into the forests to hunt for game, an enjoyable necessity on such an enterprise.

Beauchamp's harbingers rode ahead to find billets in towns along the way for those of rank. The rest spent the nights rolled up in cloaks in roadside bivouacs.

Sandwich was the most important port on the south-east coast, almost as close to Calais as Dover but with a larger and much more sheltered harbour. It commanded a short cut to the Thames estuary, the sea passage between Kent and Thanet, then an island. The drawback to Sandwich's closeness to France was that foreign raiding parties regularly crossed the Channel to pillage and plunder in England. But in 1414, with typical thoroughness, Henry V had ordered all vulnerable ports on England's south and east coasts to be similarly strengthened, and the walls of Sandwich had been reinforced. Beauchamp had a manor house at Great Mongeham, five miles south of Sandwich. Malory and his companions might have been quartered there. Nights in Sandwich itself were notoriously sleepless: news of the strength and direction of the wind was announced on a constant basis using fifes, trumpets and shouts. Sometimes weeks passed before conditions for sailing were right – the ferry boats, clumsy high-sided sailing 'coggs' and heavy-oared barges known as 'balingers', could get blown helplessly off course in rough weather.

Of all the towns that Malory's foot trod, Sandwich is the least changed. This is because, after the Stour silted up around 1500 and its quaysides were too shallow for the deeper-draught ships of Tudor times, it became, quite literally, a backwater. Its many fine medieval buildings deteriorated into slums but survived to become valued for their history, and have now been attractively restored. The streets still have names like Bowling Alley, Rope Walk, Knightrider Street and The Butts. The church is built around a massive Norman keep, from imported Caen stone. The old ramparts and freshwater conduits also survive. Walking past the Green Dragon Inn through a massive barbican to the quay beside the River Stour (now just a muddy meander), it is easy to imagine the town thronged with Henry V's men-at-arms and archers, the riverside fields full of baggage carts and grazing horses, all waiting to be taken across the Channel. Most of the boats that ferried them could carry no more than a dozen or so soldiers, with their horses, servants and equipment, at a time.

Malory's first sight of Calais would have been of a long rectangle of battlemented walls with fortified towers, some round, some square. They provided vantage points for cannon as well as rooms for the garrison. The castle, in the north-west of the town, had a great circular keep inside a double or 'curtain' wall and its own moat. Its guns dominated the harbour. The passage in from the sea was between two long breakwaters, protected by Fort Riesban, a curtain-walled round tower now incongruously topped by a German blockhouse. Today the best place to get a feel for Calais's medieval layout is the top of the tall thirteenth-century watch-tower which has miraculously survived both an eighteenth-century earthquake and the 1939–45 war. From this vantage point the vestiges of its medieval walls and towers can still be seen.

The English held about 120 square miles of land around Calais. These 'marches' extended six miles or so inland. To the east were the swampy seignories of Hammes, Mark and Oye, to the west Sangatte, Wissant and Hervelinghem, inland the higher country of Fréthun, Guines and Balinghem. There were substantial castles at Guines and Hammes, and fortified towers at Nieulay, two miles west of Calais itself, and in the other seignories. Calais, Guines and Hammes had the largest garrisons, but each of the towers had an English commander and a few men. The territory was an unwelcome bite out of the county of Picardy, a fief of the Duke of Burgundy. He was as resentful as the French about the English possession of Calais.

After it was captured by Edward III in 1347, Calais was gradually turned into a piece of England – administered from Westminster, peopled by English soldiers, merchants and their families, and part of the diocese of Canterbury. It was the most important staple, or market place, for exports of wool, leather, skins, lead and tin from England to the Continent. Maintaining its fortresses, and victualling and paying the wages of the garrison (three hundred men in peacetime and twice that number in time of war), cost thousands of pounds a year. In theory, the Exchequer paid, using money from customs and profits from the staple. In fact, few of its captains resigned their office without being owed very large amounts of money by the Crown. But the captaincy of Calais was immensely prestigious, a key political appointment. Its garrison was a highly professional standing army which decided the fate of the King of England more than once during Malory's lifetime.

For both Beauchamp and Malory, Calais held heroic echoes. When Edward III won it in 1347, Beauchamp's grandfather Thomas, 11th Earl of Warwick, was one of his commanders. At the head of the defenders was the Admiral of France, Pierre de Revel – a distant kinsman of Malory. Sir Peter Malory of Litchborough was with Edward the Black Prince when he landed at Calais in 1359. There was also a familiar face to welcome them when they arrived, Beauchamp's kinsman and deputy at Calais, Sir William Lisle. A lasting friendship with Lisle is hinted at in Malory's alteration of the name of Galahad's companion on the Grail quest from Melias de Lis to Melias de L'Isle.

Service in Calais consolidated Malory's military skills and gave him an opportunity to perfect his French. This was a time of truce, and he may well have made the most of any opportunities to explore the countryside around him, or to accompany one of the many little bands of ambassadors who rode between Calais and Paris to negotiate with both the French and the Burgundians. The marvellously detailed paintings in the *Tres Riches Heures du Duc de Berry*, which was illustrated by the Limburg brothers in the 1400s, are windows into this world. It was indeed, as Bishop Beaufort had promised the King in council, 'a country fertile, pleasant and plentiful', with 'rich cities, beautiful towns, innumerable castles', and people 'civil, witty and of good order'.

Malory would have found one embassy to Paris particularly interesting. Paris was a far grander city than London architecturally, and full of splendid churches with jewel-brilliant windows. Even then books were being sold on stalls along the banks of the Seine. Regnault de Montet, a scribe who produced many books, including two *Lancelots*, for the Duke of Berry, described how in the summer of 1414 he heard that a delegation of English ambassadors had arrived, and went to their lodgings (in the Hôtel de Bourbon) with a copy of Boethius's *Consolations of Philosophy* to see if he could sell it to them. 'What's that book under your arm?' Richard Courtenay, Bishop of Norwich, asked him as soon as he walked into the courtyard. They haggled for a while, but failed to strike a bargain, but the Bishop asked him to bring other books, including romances. Courtenay bought a Froissart, an Ovid and a *Tristan*. The Bishop came to Paris again early in 1415, and bought three more books from Regnault and twenty from an Italian trader. He looked at, but did not buy, a splendid 'Mappemonde' (map of the world), and he may have discreetly acquired other maps. The French were well aware that the English were spying out the land as well as seeking fine books. Regnault's record of these transactions only survives because he and Jean Fusoris, a maker of clocks and astronomical instruments, were arrested in September 1415 and accused of supplying Courtenay with intelligence about the French war preparations as well as books and astrolabes. Fusoris may have been guilty; Regnault was lucky enough to be freed on bail, thanks to his connections with the Duc de Berry. It is a curious little incident which has a striking parallel in Malory's own story. Late in life, in the 1460s, he and a London scrivener would also find themselves hounded as traitors suspected of aiding enemy invasion of their country.

The Twelfth Night Tourney

Although diplomatic overtures with France continued, there was no concealing Henry V's intentions. The English ambassadors had been successful in persuading Duke John of Burgundy to remain neutral if Henry pressed his claims to France. The November 1414 Parliament discussed the claims and voted extra taxes which were put towards the war effort, and Bishop Beaufort, whose Winchester see was the wealthiest in the country, lent generously of his enormous fortune. Men were ready and willing to sign up for such a glorious and profitable venture. All over England preparations were in hand. Smiths sweated at forges to make cannon, and masons carved stones for the guns and catapults. Six wing feathers were to be plucked from every goose in the country to flight the archers' arrows. Armourers turned out axes, spears, swords, armour and chain-mail. Carpenters constructed innumerable chests and casks, flat-pack siege-towers, and 'great ladders with double steps, strong enough to carry four men-at-arms'. Ships for transporting troops were commandeered in every port in the southern and eastern counties.

The French assumed that Henry's invasion would be launched from Calais. In the autumn of 1414, word came to Beauchamp at Calais that enemy troops were massing in Artois and Picardy. Nothing reveals the ceremonious and chivalric approach to war of the time better than Beauchamp's decision to make the most of the presence of all the French 'lords, knights and esquires of honour that were at that time come down into the marches of Picardy for the war' by issuing a challenge. A fortnight before Christmas, he announced 'a new point of chivalry', a series of jousts between himself and champions of France. He ordered a pavilion to be set up at the tournament ground outside Guines, on the border of the Calais marches and Picardy. In the pavilion three magnificent 'pavises' (ceremonial shields on high stands) were set up, each with a trophy attached to it. The first showed a lady standing and harping at the foot of a bed; a gold 'gratoure' (drawn in the *Beauchamp Pageant*, perhaps out of ignorance, as a grater, but the word also has the meaning of a spear tip) was tied to her sleeve. The second had a lady standing at a table 'working with pearls', with a gold gauntlet beside her. The third lady was in a garden weaving a chaplet of roses; her trophy was a golden 'poleyne' (a piece of knee armour).

Heralds were then sent to the French to say that if any knight of France 'that was born gentleman of name and arms without reproach' wanted to win the devices, he would have to fight twelve courses of spear against 'Le Chevalier Vert' for the first, fifteen strokes of the sword with 'Le Chevalier Gris' for the second, and ten courses of spears on foot without shields against 'Le Chevalier Attendant' for the third. Three French knights took up the challenge. Sir Gerald Herbaumes, 'a seemly man, accounted one of the best jousters of France', rode as Le Chevalier Rouge. Lord Hugh de Lawney appeared as 'Le Chevalier Blanche'. Lord Collard de Fiennes, a kinsman of Beauchamp through marriage, was 'Le Chevalier Noir'.

Beauchamp fought each of them on consecutive days: 6, 7 and 8 January 1415. Ostrich plumes nodded in his helm and gold gleamed from the edges of every plate of his armour. On each day his surcoat and his horse's trappings were a different colour, and he sported a different version of the Beauchamp arms. After defeating all three of the French champions, he invited them to dine with him. A great tent, festooned with the many and varied Beauchamp 'arms of old ancestry', was put up and a three-course feast laid on for the thousand or so spectators to the contest. After the final draughts of spiced wine, Beauchamp presented the French knights with splendid consolation prizes, and distributed gifts to the heralds and minstrels.

As the young Thomas Malory was in Beauchamp's service at this time, it is reasonable to imagine him witnessing this tournament and indeed recalling it when he wrote his 'Tale of Sir Gareth', an otherwise unknown story about a chivalrous young hero who summons challengers to a tournament at 'the Castle Perilous beside the Isle of Avalon'. In rapid succession he defeats the Black, the Green and the Red Knight, each time, like Beauchamp, in different-coloured armour:

> When King Agwisance of Ireland saw Sir Gareth fare so, he marvelled what knight he was, for at one time he seemed green, and another time, at his again coming, he seemed blue. And thus at every course that he rode to and fro he changed white to red and black, so that there might neither king nor knight have ready cognisance of him.

'The parallel is so close as to lead me to believe that some parts of [this tale] were written in remembrance of Beauchamp's gallant deeds,' writes Eugène Vinaver, the first editor of the Winchester manuscript. 'The noble character of the great knight who so brilliantly revived the traditions of medieval chivalry may well have suggested the topic and given him the inspiration for his life's work.' The nickname that Malory invents for Sir Gareth, a noble knight totally *sans reproche*, is Beaumains. This could have been seen by contemporaries as a tribute to Beauchamp, whose carefully lifelike tomb effigy, made by John Massingham in the 1450s, shows the 13th Earl with long, sensitive hands raised to each side of his face.

Council at Konstanz

Soon after the tournament, Beauchamp and his household, including Sir Baldwin Strange and John Shirley, left Calais for Konstanz. He was to be Henry V's chosen representative at a General Council of the Church which had been organised by Sigismund, King of Bohemia and Holy Roman Emperor. A high-minded and chivalrous man, Sigismund fought unsuccessfully against the Turks at Nicopolis in 1396. The 'infidels' were now threatening Constantinople itself, and Sigismund was determined to unite all Europe in a great crusade against them. But first the vexed question of the papal schism had to be resolved. Since 1378 the Christian Church had been divided, with one pope in Italy and another in France, at Avignon. There were now no fewer than three popes, John XXIII in Pisa, Gregory XII in Rome and Benedict XIII in Avignon.

The English embassy numbered 'three bishops, three abbots, and many notable knights, and clergy, doctors in theology and law, to the number of eight hundred horse'. Malory could have been among the attendant squires. Carrying safe-conducts, they travelled via Soissons and Metz (both places mentioned by Malory in his story of King Arthur's war against the Emperor of Rome). When they arrived in Konstanz on 21 January 1415, they lodged in 'the Painted House', close to the cathedral, where sessions of the Council met, and also convenient for the Franciscan monastery where the English discussed policy privately.

The Council had been opened by John XXIII on 5 November 1414. Its aims were to unite the Church under a single pope, reform notorious clerical abuses, and to defend the Christian faith from attack by heretics and infidels. In an innovatory move, pushed for by Beauchamp and a sign of growing national self-consciousness, voting rights were accorded to each nation instead of, as had previously happened, to individuals. But so far progress had been slow, not least because when Pope John XXIII discovered that he could not control the delegates, he fled, declaring the Council dissolved.

While the clerics argued over points of doctrine, the nobles of

Europe and their retainers turned to their favourite pastime: jousting. Beauchamp 'was challenged by and slew a great duke'. Impressed, Sigismund's Empress asked him to be her champion, and Sigismund appointed him to the prestigious office of bearer of his imperial sword. At the end of the tournament, he offered Beauchamp one of the holiest possible relics to Englishmen: the heart of their patron saint, St George. With diplomatic modesty, Beauchamp asked the Emperor to visit England and to present it to Henry V himself.

Beauchamp left well before the Council was over, but his forceful presence may have encouraged the delegates to take drastic action. Early in 1415 Pope John was captured in the Tyrol and brought back to Konstanz. Accused of a spectacular list of misdeeds, including poisoning Pope Alexander V and denying the immortality of the soul, he agreed to abdicate in exchange for being indicted only for his lesser crimes. So, Edward Gibbon tells us with relish in his *Decline and Fall of the Roman Empire*, 'the most scandalous charges were suppressed; the vicar of Christ was only accused of piracy, murder, rape, sodomy and incest'. It still took two years to heal the schism. Gregory XII resigned voluntarily in June, and Benedict was declared deposed in July 1417. In November 1417, Pope Martin V, an acceptable choice to all factions, was elected at Konstanz by the conclave of cardinals and the papacy returned to the Vatican.

Agincourt and After

*Then there was launching of great boats and small, and
full of noble men of arms; and there was much slaughter
of gentle knights, and many a full bold baron was laid full
low, on both parties.*

Malory, 'The Tale of the Morte Arthur'

eauchamp left Konstanz prematurely because war with
France was imminent. Henry V's formal announcement that
he had resolved to cross the sea to recover his rightful heritage was made on his behalf by Bishop Beaufort on 16 April 1415. The
Earl's household cavalcade travelled back to Calais, passing through
Bruges on 1 May. Beauchamp himself then crossed to England, sitting
in at meetings of the royal council on 21 and 27 May. At these sessions
decisions were taken as to who would cross to Normandy with the
King to make their names and their fortunes and who would stay to
defend England itself from attack. The King's oldest brother Thomas,
Duke of Clarence, and youngest brother Humfrey, Duke of Gloucester,
were to go with him to France; his middle brother John, Duke of
Bedford, was left in command in England. Grey of Codnor was
appointed Warden of the East Marches, to guard against any offensive
action from the Scots. This was unlikely – James I, the young King
of Scotland, was Henry's prisoner, a situation that the regent, James's
ambitious uncle the Duke of Albany, was happy to accept.

Thomas Malory's contract with Beauchamp had been for a year's
service in Calais, but with invasion in the offing, it is likely that he
signed up again; he may, like Sir Baldwin Strange and many others,
have simply stayed on in Calais. In April, 450 more men-of-war and

archers raised by Beauchamp arrived from England. The Earl himself returned on 2 August with yet more troops, to encourage the French in their belief that Henry V's threatened invasion would be launched from Calais. But he immediately slipped secretly back to England with a small bodyguard: he would be at his king's side during the invasion. Was Malory with him? We have no way of knowing.

By late July the ships that had been massing in Southampton Water for two months were filled with men. There were 2,000 knights and men-at-arms, 8,000 archers and thousands more support staff – sailors, gunners, pages, grooms, cooks, surgeons and saddlers, baggage-boys and hobelars, heralds, trumpeters and pipers, armourers and smiths. Among them was Thomas Malory's great-uncle John Chetwynd, who joined the expedition as a mounted man-at-arms with three archers on foot. On Sunday, 11 August 1415, in glorious summer weather, the English armada set sail. Henry's well-concealed aim was to establish a new English base at the mouth of the Seine by taking Harfleur, 'without exception the chief port in Normandy, and the most advantageous for carrying on . . . war in that quarter'. If all went well, he would either mount a *chevauchée* via Rouen to attack Paris, and then exit from Harfleur or Calais, or sweep south-west through Anjou and leave from the Anglophile port of Bordeaux.

The first of his ships nosed into the estuary of the Seine before dawn broke three days later. A pinnace commanded by the eighteen-year-old son of Lord Grey of Codnor was sent to find a safe place to land, and by seven o'clock a thousand men were already ashore. It took three days to disembark the whole army and its supplies and set up the siege. Henry made himself magnificently comfortable. He ate off gold plate, and listened to his minstrels inside a tent lined with a series of tapestries woven with the adventures of Sir Percival, one of the purest of King Arthur's knights.

Harfleur's walls had been strengthened and bristled with guns. It was six weeks before they were breached by the English artillery. Thousands died on both sides, of dysentery and swamp fever as well as in battle. Once the siege was over, Beauchamp and his bodyguard returned by sea to Calais, taking extra cannon in case of a counter-attack there by the French. The English fleet sailed to and fro across the Channel, taking the sick and wounded back to England and bringing much-needed supplies to Harfleur. It was typical of Henry's chivalric approach to warfare that after Harfleur fell he released sixty nobles and two hundred gentlemen prisoners on parole. They promised to bring their ransoms or their own persons to him in Calais at the feast of Martinmas on 11 October. He then sent one of his heralds to the Dauphin challenging him to single combat 'so that, sparing the many, they might bring to an end controversy respecting the rights and dominion over the kingdom'. The Dauphin was not tempted.

Henry V's forces were so depleted that his plan for a *chevauchée* deeper into France was now impossible. But merely to embark for England smacked too much of defeat, and the ships were urgently needed for the sick and wounded. He left a thousand men to defend Harfleur and set off northwards with those fit enough to march to Calais. Henry had only nine hundred men-at-arms and five thousand archers, and he knew that the French had been marshalling troops in the area for months. He gave a magniloquent justification for this apparently insane move:

> *I am possessed with a burning desire to see my territories and the places which ought to be my inheritance. Even if our enemies enlist the greatest armies, my trust is in God, and they shall not hurt my army or myself . . . I will not allow them, puffed up with pride, to rejoice in misdeeds, nor unjustly, against God, to possess my goods. They would say that through fear I have fled away, acknowledging the injustice of my cause. But I have a mind, my brave men, to encounter all dangers, rather than let them brand your King with word of ill-will. With the favour of God we will go unhurt and inviolate, and if they attempt to stop us, victorious and triumphant in all glory.*

Henry was not a foolhardy commander, and pragmatism lay behind this bombast. The best chance of survival for himself as well as his 'brave men' was to stay on land. The waters of the Channel were full of enemies, eager to grab prizes that could include a king's ransom, and the weather this late in the year was unpredictable. Calais was only 150 miles away, and Henry wanted to keep his rendez-vous with the paroled French nobles. The only major obstacle was the Somme. Henry had instructed Beauchamp to send a force from Calais to take the ford at Blanche-Tacque, close to the mouth of the river, and hold it for the English army. Three hundred men set out from Calais, but the French, whose army was at least three times the size of Henry's, were on the alert for just such an expedition. Many of the Calais men were killed or taken prisoner; the rest were forced to retreat.

Unaware that the ford was not in English hands, Henry's army slowly made its way northwards via Fécamp, Arques and Eu to Blanche-Tacque. The gory fate of the first horsemen to try the crossing revealed that the French had driven pointed stakes into the water. The ford was impassable. Henry began to trek eastwards to find a feasible point to cross the Somme without being confronted by the French army, now visible massed on the river's north bank. Fortu-nately, he had good maps, perhaps those acquired by Codnor in Paris. When his men were repelled at the strongly-garrisoned Corbie, he headed south-east instead of following the great northward bend of the river to Peronne, where the French were expecting him, and succeeded in crossing at a ford well upstream at Voyennes. At last the way to Calais was, theoretically, open. But by now the enemy army was even stronger, for Burgundy had joined the French. Heralds were sent to Henry, warning him that attack was imminent. In truth the combined Franco-Burgundian forces were in no hurry, convinced that they could not but conquer the weary English forces.

Forty-five miles from Calais, both sides drew up in battle order near a deserted village with a semi-ruined castle called Agincourt. For the first time the English appreciated the vast size of the enemy army. Hideously anonymous in snouted helms, the French soldiers stretched to the horizon like 'an innumerable horde of locusts'. Brilli-ant colour flashed from thousands of armorial surcoats; numberless banners and pennants flapped above the glittering lines. The French were rested and well-fed, their horses fresh, their armour bright and in good order, their weapons razor-sharp from the armourers' honings.

Malory, like Beauchamp, will have cursed his luck in not being part of what happened next.

> *From this day to the ending of the world,*
> *. . . it shall be remembered;*
> *We few, we happy few, we band of brothers;*
> *For he today that sheds his blood with me*
> *Shall be my brother . . .*
> *And gentlemen in England, now a-bed*
> *Shall think themselves accurs'd they were not here,*
> *And hold their manhoods cheap whiles any speaks*
> *That fought with us upon St Crispin's day.*

Shakespeare used contemporary chronicles for this speech. Henry V had been both magnificently calm and oratorically inspired. 'I would not, even if I could, increase my number by one,' he told his household steward, Sir Walter Hungerford. 'For those whom I have are the people of God . . . These humble few [will be] well able to conquer the haughty opposition of the French'.

The rest is history – and great literature. God did his stuff. Position, tactics and discipline won England the day. The French thought they could crush the English by sheer weight of numbers, but their charge was brought up short by a concealed barricade of sharpened stakes. As the leading horses crumpled against it, and the riders behind stampeded into them, the English archers, 'quick-eyed clever longbowmen [who] could hit the oystershell in the centre of the butt with the nicety of a Thames fisherman garfangling an eel', let loose a blizzard of arrows. The sheer mass of the French army now told against them. Retreat was impossible; they were 'butchered like sheep', with many suffocated in the mud of the battlefield. Two of the Duke of Burgundy's brothers were killed. So were many of the most famous knights in France, including Beauchamp's Twelfth Night tournament adversaries, Sir Gerald Herbaumes and Lord Collard de Fiennes. Hundreds more were taken prisoner, among them Charles, Duke of Orléans, and his younger brother John, nephews of King Charles VI of France. The French lost 1,400 knights and at least five thousand men-at-arms. English casualties were said to be unbelievably few, less than five hundred. Among the injured was Humfrey of Gloucester, who had 'wrought about him wonderfully' at first but had been severely wounded 'in the hams' by the Duke of Alençon.

Beauchamp was the first to greet Henry V when he arrived at Guines on Monday 28 October. We can imagine Malory among the cheering soldiers lining the streets of Calais when they entered the city the next day. After a mass in St Nicolas's Church, Henry was lodged inside the castle. He held a great feast on Halloween and then attended the usual solemn masses on All Souls' Day. It was a reminder of the thousands of recently lost souls; then and there he vowed to found a college in Oxford dedicated to their memory, and endowed to pay for prayers for their souls to be said until the glorious day of Christ's resurrection. The Fellows of All Souls' College still pray annually for the dead of Agincourt.

On 16 November Henry embarked for England, ignoring the grief-stricken Duke of Burgundy's challenge to single combat. Chivalry evidently had its limits, though Malory must have been a little disappointed by such pragmatism. The wisdom of reducing travelling by sea to a minimum was reflected in the loss of two ships in the 'boisterous' seas that arose during the crossing. But the King and his two brothers arrived safely, albeit late, at Dover. A spectacular pageant greeted Henry's entry into London on Saturday 23 November. Choirs dressed as winged cherubim and seraphim chanted Te Deums above London Bridge. The entire Fellowship of the Prophets 'with venerable white hair, in tunicles and golden copes, their heads turbaned with gold and crimson', were ranged in a pavilion above the Cornhill conduit, and released a 'great flock of sparrows and other tiny birds' as Henry came by. The twelve apostles and twelve kings of England, with King Arthur prominent among them, lined up at one end of Cheapside. At the other, beneath a canopy of clouds, was the Almighty himself in the form of a dazzling golden sun enthroned in glory and surrounded by archangels.

The Heart of Saint George

Malory probably stayed on in Calais while England celebrated. Its garrison was being enlarged, not depleted. In February 1416 Beauchamp issued an order saying that no one was to leave without special permission. France and Burgundy were treating for peace and the release on parole of the prisoners from Agincourt, but what they really wanted was revenge. French forces surrounded Harfleur and their ships patrolled the Seine estuary. The French garrisons at Boulogne and other strongholds near Calais had been strengthened, and Burgundy had over 10,000 men in the field.

On 25 April a thousand-strong cavalcade of knights clad in black surcoats sporting the grey double upright cross of the imperial Order of the Dragon jangled into the marches of Calais. They were escorting the Emperor Sigismund himself. He was trying to reconcile France and England, for he was still dreaming of taking armies from both countries with him on crusade to defend Eastern Europe from the Turks. He had just spent five weeks in Paris with King Charles and Queen Isobel, enjoying lavish banquets and discussing the possibilities of a final peace, or at least a long truce. Now he was planning to cross to England to complete his work as honest broker by persuading Henry V to agree to terms.

Beauchamp marched out of Calais to escort the Emperor into the town with a glittering escort of knights, men-at-arms and archers. At the feast held in his honour that evening, Sigismund declared that

> no Prince Christian for wisdom, nurture and manhood has such another knight as th' earl of Warwick, adding thereto that if all courtesy was lost yet might it be found again in him. And so, ever after, by the Emperor's authority [Beauchamp] was called the Father of Courtesy.

Sigismund had, as promised, brought with him the heart of Saint George. It was a priceless addition to England's relics of its patron saint – a piece of his skull and an arm bone. Ships were sent from

Dover to ferry the imperial cavalcade over to England, and Henry prepared a splendid welcome. Sigismund stayed in England for nearly four months, entertained with feasts and tournaments and presented with magnificent gifts: jewelled cups, basins of gold coins and splendidly harnessed horses. At the annual Whitsun meeting of the Knights of the Garter in the chapel of St George at Windsor on 25 May, he was made a member of the Order.

As a Garter knight, Beauchamp attended the ceremony, but he returned to Calais straight away. June saw him at the court of the Duke of Burgundy in Lille, angling for a personal meeting between the Duke, Henry V and Sigismund at Calais in October. Meanwhile the French, Scots and Bretons had massed a fleet of three hundred ships, many of them expertly manned by Genoese and Spanish sailors of fortune, to blockade Harfleur, attack Calais and invade England. Henry ordered forces to muster in Portsmouth, but by the end of June the French had ravaged Portland in Dorset and the Isle of Wight and for a short time blockaded the King's fleet in Southampton Water. Harfleur, now besieged by land and sea, was in dire straits. The English fleet set out to relieve it on 12 August, commanded by the Duke of Bedford. They reached the mouth of the Seine on the evening of 14 August, and attacked the enemy fleet immediately. Fighting went on all through the night, with many ships fired and sunk. There were terrible losses on both sides, and Bedford himself was wounded, but at last the English triumphed. Half their ships sailed on to relieve Harfleur; the rest returned to England with prisoners, prizes, which included four Genoese carracks, and the wounded.

The French attack on Harfleur and their evasive replies to the Emperor's envoys led Sigismund to declare his support for Henry V's grand vision of ousting the Valois kings from France and then leading a united Europe on crusade. Beauchamp was sent once again to Lille with news of this new agenda, but had returned to Calais by 5 September, when Sigismund and Henry arrived for rounds of talks with, first, French ambassadors and then the Duke of Burgundy himself. Henry V stayed in Calais for six weeks, with his full legal and administrative court. His usual home comforts – silks, damasks, tapestries, gold and silver plate – came with him, and huge tents of cloth of gold were erected in front of the castle, one for use as a chapel, one a banqueting hall, others for the ambassadors.

The endless negotiations must have been frustrating for the braver spirits in the Calais garrison, deprived of glory at both Harfleur and Agincourt. But an opportunity came to display the 'prowess and hardiness' on which 'hot and courageous' men like Malory prided themselves. On Thursday 24 September one of the huge Genoese carracks that had fought the English at Harfleur was sighted heading northwards to find shelter in Flanders. Beauchamp ordered the only ships available, five balingers and a 'passager', all tiny in comparison with the enormous carrack, to be armed. He himself led a crack contingent of his men on board one of them. Lord Talbot, Sir Thomas West, Sir Baldwin Strange, Sir Gilbert Umfraville and 'others prompted by manly courage', including perhaps Malory, manned the others. They shot off in pursuit of the carrack 'with what speed their sails made possible'. The carrack was out of sight before they were out of harbour, but they too had the wind in their sails. At dawn the next day the six ships caught up with the Genoese ship and threw grappling irons into her sides, although her decks were 'more than a spear's length higher than the highest of theirs'. Like hounds worrying a wild boar, the little ships took it in turns to disengage for a respite, then re-engaged time and time again until it was nearly dark.

The English were optimistic of victory, wrote the chronicler Jehan de Waurin, but 'just when our men were on the point of taking possession of the carrack they had to break off further attacks on her because of the lack of missiles and boarding ladders and weapons of offence'. A westerly wind was strengthening fearsomely, and the carrack managed to break away and continue her course for Sluys. The six smaller boats were soon tossing helplessly about in the dark in what was now a gale. It separated them from each other and drove them north-eastwards away from Calais. Somehow they all survived, beached on sandbanks, or seeing out the storm on the open sea. The same gale struck Calais, tearing in half Henry V's chapel tent and almost breaking the fastenings of the banqueting tent.

It was not until Thursday, a week after they had left, that the battered little fleet managed to return to Calais. There was sad news.

Sir Thomas West, 'an agreeable and handsome young knight', had been fatally wounded on his own ship before battle was joined, hit on the head by a huge slingstone that was being hauled up to the top-castle. Dead too was Sir Baldwin Strange, one of Beauchamp's closest friends as well as his cousin. He left Beauchamp a 'grey courser' in his will, and Beauchamp acted 'as a good lord should' by providing a pension for Lady Strange and taking one of her daughters into his Warwick Castle household.

Early in October, Henry agreed terms for a truce with the French. It was to last for five months, from 9 October 1416 to Candlemas (2 February) 1417, and to extend 'by sea, from the Pillars of Hercules [i.e. the Straits of Gibraltar] as far as the kingdom of Norway inclusive, and by land over certain specified areas in West Flanders and in Picardy as far as the Somme'. But as soon as the French ambassadors had ridden away from Calais, preparations began to receive the Duke of Burgundy himself. A deeply suspicious man, for all his title 'the Fearless', Duke John insisted on an exchange of hostages, so during three days of feasts, jousts and 'enigmatic talks', Humfrey of Gloucester kicked his heels in the nearby Burgundian town of St-Omer. What the English King and France's most powerful duke discussed can only be guessed at, but there is no doubt that Henry was planning to follow up his unexpected triumph with a second invasion of France as soon as he could muster enough strength to do so. Duke John returned to Burgundy on 8 October, but it was a week before the autumn gales eased off enough for Henry to make the storm-tossed passage to England. With him went Beauchamp, in order to attend the Parliament summoned for late October. Home too, we may guess, went Thomas Malory – released at last from an unexpectedly long but extraordinarily exciting stint of service.

The Conquest of Normandy

*And at that parliament was concluded to arrest all the
navy of the land, and to be ready within fifteen days at
Sandwich, and there [King Arthur] showed to his army
how he purposed to conquer the empire which he ought to
have of right.*

Malory, 'The Tale of King Arthur'

conic as the victory at Agincourt became, the real achievement of the 1415 campaign was the securing of Harfleur,
an essential bridgehead for Henry's planned invasion of
Normandy. To emphasise its character as a second Calais, settlers
were invited from England. Sir John Fastolf (a very able commander
who was nothing like Shakespeare's 'surfeit-swelled' ruffian) was
made its captain. In January 1417 another 900 men-at-arms and 1,500
archers were sent there. With Harfleur secured, Henry could send out
commissions to raise men for the invasion. His army mustered at
Southampton by the end of July 1417, the largest and most elaborately
equipped expeditionary force ever assembled by a medieval English
king. This time Henry V was aiming at full-scale conquest, not just
a flamboyant *chevauchée*.

Malory's experiences at Calais had clearly whetted his appetite for
war. The next mention of his name in the historical record is in
March 1418, this time in a muster roll of men who were in Normandy
under the command of Lord Grey of Codnor. This switch of allegiance
from the Beauchamp retinue, to which Malory was attached again in
later years, needs an explanation. If Malory was in France in 1418, his
name must have appeared on earlier musters. No Beauchamp musters

for this period survive, though a chronicler tells us that the Earl summoned a hundred lances and three hundred archers in 1417. But there are clues to be gleaned from the Codnor Roll, which is kept in the National Archives at Kew. It is a humble little thing, less than a foot wide. Its cover sheet is stamped 'Ex Q R [Exchequer] Ancient Miscellanea Bundle 62'. But despite its small size it holds three separate strips of parchment, all covered with names. All are muster rolls – one for the Harfleur garrison, one for a force led by Lord Willoughby, and one for men led by Grey of Codnor.

The Codnor muster is the smallest: four inches wide and about two foot long, its end torn away. The sheep of whose scraped skin it was made died nearly six hundred years ago, but the parchment is still strong and supple. The uneven side edge shows that it once had a twin. Names on muster rolls were written down twice. Then the list was 'intoothed', cut in half with zig-zag cuts, one copy for the commander, one for the Exchequer. When the commander's half was presented after the contract had been fulfilled, the clerks who paid out the soldiers' wages could match it to their own and check that no names had been illegitimately added. This particular list is small enough to be stuffed into the breast of a jerkin for safety. The black ink has faded to brown, and at one point something sharp – a dagger? an arrow? – has been stabbed through it. At the damaged end there are smudges of what looks to a romantic imagination like blood.

The top two names have extra prominence. The first is 'Le Sr de Grey de Codnor'; the second name looks like 'Mons. John de Brunby, chev [chevalier]'. It is hard to read, and no knight of that name is known. Then come fourteen names bracketed together and labelled 'squires', with a long list of archers beneath them. The second squire named is Thomas Malory de Bytham. The high position of the name and its suffix 'de Bytham' suggests that this Malory was both a commander and a senior member of the Codnors' household at Castle Bytham. The Sir Thomas Malory who had fought with Codnor in 1401 had died by 1412, so it sounds as if the man I have identified as Malory's Uncle Thomas had been promoted to constable or steward of Castle Bytham. The next name is that of Codnor's eldest son, John de Grey de Codnor, the teenager who was first ashore when Henry V invaded Harfleur. Four places further down the list of squires is a second Thomas Malory. If my reasoning is right, this is the future author of the *Morte Darthur*. Thomas Malory of Newbold Revel could once have held this list in his hands, checking that his name was recorded correctly. To earn the neat pair of strokes beside it on the muster, he would have had to show that he had all the equipment needed to earn him the daily wage of an esquire at war: bassinet helmet, armour (perhaps the very suit which his father John Malory was shown wearing in the Grendon memorial window), a lance, a short sword called a glaive, a mace and a poleaxe.

The small size of the muster, and the fact that it is dated 1 March 1418, reveal that it listed only part of Codnor's retinue. An earlier roll records that Codnor indented for a much larger force in 1417: 60 lances and 180 archers. It makes no mention of Sir John de Brunby, but does list Sir Robert Moton, who married Sir Anketil Malory's daughter Margaret, and Sir Edward Foljambe, whose son James's name comes between the two Thomas Malory esquires on the surviving roll. Also in this force was one John Hardyng, who would later write a popular rhyming chronicle of English history from pre-Arthurian times until his own age. Malory had certainly read it by the time he wrote his own Arthurian tales, as experts have found distinct signs of its influence on his writing.

It looks as if the 1418 muster roll is a combination of men from at least two different retinues. Codnor and Beauchamp often fought in company during the second invasion of France, and at times they will have needed to provide small forces to garrison captured towns or to accompany different commanders in the field. Muster rolls and the chroniclers' summaries of other retinues show that men did indeed move around in this way, with reinforcements regularly being sent out from home. It is thus reasonable to assume that Malory, and perhaps others in the list, began service in this campaign with Beauchamp, then transferred to Codnor's retinue.

The English Armada

Henry V had thought hard about the strategy of his invasion. He knew his men faced daunting obstacles. Harfleur had been a much harder nut to crack than he had foreseen. Other major cities, especially those at river crossings, had also been strongly re-fortified, and the whole of Normandy was studded with all but impregnable castles. The Seine alone had a dozen or more strung along its banks on the way to Paris. The King had studied the Roman military handbook, Vegetius's *De Re Militari*, carefully. Its advice remained, indeed remains, sound: use spies to find out your enemy's strengths and weaknesses, take the enemy by surprise when possible, starve out the besieged rather than risk your own forces in an attack, beware of pursuing a retreating enemy. Henry may have read the manual in Lord Berkeley's English translation of 1408 which updated Vegetius's account of artillery. Berkeley, who had fought against Owen Glyn Dŵr in Henry IV's campaigns, had added a paragraph on the efficacy of the 'great guns that shoot nowadays stones of so great a [weight] that no wall may withstand them, as have been shown both in the north country and [also] in the wars of Wales'.

Henry ordered the preparation of just such great guns, weighing up to 2,000 lb and mounted on carriages hauled by eight horses. Belligerently christened 'London', 'Messenger' and 'King's Daughter', they fired stone balls 2 ft in diameter and weighing 100 lb or more. Also useful were compact 'pelot-guns', which fired metal balls a few ounces in weight and could be carried two at a time on a horse. Artillery was then a Burgundian speciality. Henry hired four Burgundian master-gunners who had twenty-five gunners and fifty servitor gunners under them. Supporting the guns were siege engines little changed from Roman times: trebuchets, mangonels and mobile shelters known as 'sows' (apparently because the men's feet underneath them looked like a row of nipples). Among other siege aids were mobile wooden 'summer castles', which carried artillery and crews to operate them, and could be rolled right up to a city's walls, floating fortresses which were towed across rivers, portable bridges and mining equipment so that tunnels could be made under walls. In overall charge of the artillery was the Master of Works, Engines, Guns and Ordnance of War. In 1417, as in 1415, this was Nicholas Merbury, a near neighbour of the Malorys' Northamptonshire manor, Winwick.

It was the job of John Louth, Clerk of the Ordnance, to assemble supplies for the gunners. He was ordered to find 7,000 gunstones and 7,000 'tampions', as the wads placed between stone and charge were known. Fifty wooden yokes for oxen, each with two chains, were provided, and 320 horses to tow the wagons, with harness and extra leather for repairs. Also under Merbury's command were the mail-maker, the bowyer, the pavilioner, the sergeant-carter and sergeant-farrier, each with their own skilled teams. Army supplies included over a million goose feathers for arrows; the county sheriffs were told to amass as many again by Michaelmas. Although Henry hoped that his army would soon feed off the land, vast stores of provisions were requisitioned for immediate and emergency use. Kentish fishermen were told to fish off the Normandy coast and land their catches for the benefit of the English invaders.

Henry had taken Vegetius's advice on careful intelligence-gathering before going on campaign. One chronicle tells us that 'he got knowledge not only of what his enemies did, but of what they said and intended, so that all things to him were known, and of his devices few persons [were privy] before the thing was done'. Henry V's well-organised network of spies was complemented by an efficient messenger service that ensured continuous positive reporting on the invasion. He wrote personally to the wealthy merchants of London thanking them for their generous loans and describing English triumphs. The letters were widely circulated in England. Malory often mentions the importance of espionage in the *Morte*, aware, as the chronicler Philippe de Commines put it, that 'messenger, diplomat and spy amount to the same thing'. He describes Merlin's precautions against enemy spies – all men-of-war south of the Trent were told to carry tokens from King Arthur 'where through the king's enemies durst not ride as they did to-fore to espy'. He also explains that when King Lot's wife Margawse came 'richly beseen' to visit – and seduce –

Arthur at Caerleon, 'she was sent thither to espy the court of Arthur'.

What did it feel like to be in the second muster at Southampton? Malory would have seen many familiar faces – veterans of Harfleur and Calais, as well as comrades from Warwickshire. Estimates of the army's size vary between twelve and sixteen thousand men-at-arms and archers. Experienced in wars in Wales and on the Scottish borders, well-drilled and full of patriotic enthusiasm, Henry's forces were much more formidable than the rancour-ridden nobles, forcibly conscripted peasants and self-interested mercenaries who were half-heartedly responding to Charles VI's summons to arms. The King's brothers Clarence and Gloucester were once again prominent among the English commanders; Bedford, more reliable than either of them, was again left in England as regent.

The huge fleet set out from Southampton with 'a good and pleasant wind'. The sizes of the ships ranged from the 760-ton *Holigost*, to small merchant ships carrying only a dozen men. Henry's flagship was his father's old ship *Trinity*, once a 300-tonner but rebuilt and enlarged by Greenwich shipwrights over the last three years, using 349 oak trees, half from the royal parks, half donated by religious houses. Renamed *Trinity Royal*, she was now a 540-tonner. Lowering and raising her mighty main yard was made easier by a new invention: two massive rope-and-pulley mechanisms called 'gires'. There was a brick cooking hearth and lockable storage rooms for the butlers, pantlers, spicers, ewerers and chandlers. She had a new top-castle in the shape of a gilded copper crown, a figurehead of a painted leopard wearing a crown, and a gilded copper sceptre on top of her capstan. The whole ship was ablaze with colour – her entire external surface above the waterline was either painted or hung with painted cloths called tilts (the word is still used to describe the canvas cover of a lorry). Banners streamed from her masts and the shields of all knights aboard were hung along her deck rails. The other royal ships, *King's Chamber* and *King's Hall*, had sails embroidered with golden stars and ostrich feathers. Beauchamp's ship was equally magnificent. Embroidered on the billowing banner, forty yards long and eight yards wide, that flew from his ship's jackstaff, was a gigantic bear and ragged staff, 'powdered' with more ragged staffs.

Malory surely used his memories of that glorious departure when he describes King Arthur embarking at Sandwich with 'many galliard knights' to wreak vengeance on the tyrannical Emperor Lucius. For he adds many military and nautical details that were not in his source for this part of his story, the alliterative *Morte Arthure*.

> *Then in all haste that might be they shipped their horses and harness [armour] and all manner of ordinance [artillery] that falleth for the war, and tents and pavilions many were trussed, and so there shot from the banks many great carracks and many ships of forestage with coggs and galleys and pinnaces full noble and galiots, rowing with many oars. And thus they struck forth into the stream many sad hundreds.*

Henry kept his expedition's destination a closely guarded secret. The convoy of 1,500 ships was instructed just to follow the three royal ships. At night they were guided by a lantern at *Trinity Royal*'s masthead and the strains of the King's seventeen-strong band of minstrels and musicians. Aware that secret talks had taken place between Henry V and Burgundy, the French expected the English to land either at Calais or Harfleur, and had fortified the towns between the two English strongholds – Boulogne, Dieppe and Le Crotoy – at the mouth of the Somme. But Henry had a better plan. Rather than risk betrayal by Burgundy, he intended to sweep into the west of Normandy, using its great rivers as buffers between his army and both the Burgundian and French forces.

On 1 August, the enormous fleet approached the mouth of the River Touque, nine miles west of Honfleur, a fortress on the southern side of the Seine estuary opposite Harfleur. Today the chic seaside resorts of Deauville and Trouville-sur-Mer flank each side of the Touque, and sunbathers lie in crowded rows under gaily striped umbrellas along the foreshore where the first English soldiers landed. The garrison of Bonneville Castle, high above the little port of Touques, sent a hundred men out against them, but when an arrow from an English longbow killed their leader, they retreated. Henry gave thanks to God for his safe arrival, and dubbed forty-eight of his followers King's Knights. Then he marched upstream, occupied the town of Touques, and deployed his forces around Bonneville Castle. Within a week it had surrendered.

Making Bonneville his first new stronghold in Normandy was a good omen: the castle had been a favourite of William the Conqueror, the man from whom all English claims to Normandy originated. Today the remains of the 'Château du Guillaume le Conquérant' have been incorporated into a comfortable country house, and it is not open to the public. But you can walk to the edge of the churchyard next to it and look out to where its garrison saw the sea darkened by English sails. It is fascinating evidence of the elephantine memory and strong sense of continuity of medieval English kings that immediately after he landed at Touques, Henry V reinstituted the *Rotuli Normanniae*, the annual records of the duchy, which Duke William of Normandy had continued to keep after his conquest of England in 1066 and which were only discontinued by the English when King John finally lost Normandy in 1214.

Henry V sent Clarence south to take Lisieux, a wooden-walled town that controlled the bridge over the river used by the main road from Rouen. Then he headed for the great port of Caen, twenty-two miles to the west, a city larger and wealthier than any in England except London. The wisdom of bringing so much heavy artillery was now apparent. Caen was a heavily fortified city, its walls punctuated by towers and all but surrounded by water. The castle was begun by William the Conqueror in 1060 and finished off by his son Henry I. Today, faithfully restored after the carpet-bombing of the 1940s, its tower-studded walls and huge stone keep remain a spectacular sight.

Henry settled in for a long siege. He established his headquarters at St Stephen's Abbey, just west of the city's walls, enjoying no doubt the presence there of William the Conqueror's tomb. The River Orne was spanned using an ingenious bridge of hides, and guns and siege engines placed all around the city walls. Beauchamp's and Codnor's forces were quartered close by in the meadows beside the Abbey; we can reasonably assume that the Malorys were there as well. So too, in the retinues of Sir Walter Hungerford, the Earl of Salisbury and Sir John Cornwall, were many comrades-in-arms from the Welsh wars. The city and castle finally fell early in September 1417. When Henry's jubilant troops entered the city, Henry forbade attacks on clerics and women, but there is no doubt that there was terrible slaughter and destruction.

Legend has it that Henry himself did not stoop to plunder, and that his only trophy was a volume of French histories. Perhaps Malory acquired the first of the many 'Frensche books' he used for his Arthuriad at this point. Caen had a long tradition of learning and today bookshops still line a narrow medieval street called Rue d'Imprimeurs. The printers did not arrive until after Malory's time, of course, but before them scriveners occupied the workshops in the courtyards behind the lane's high façades. Exploring the city once order had been restored, Malory might have noticed a carving of scenes from Sir Lancelot's life sculpted at just about this time on the capital of a column in the church of St-Pierre. On one side Lancelot is shown crawling along a bridge formed by a huge sword to rescue the abducted Queen Guinevere from King Meliagaunce's castle; on another, a smiling lady is seen grasping the horn of a unicorn tame as a lapdog.

Soon after Caen fell, Bayeux, fourteen miles to the west, surrendered to Humfrey of Gloucester. Many of the surrounding strongholds followed suit, demoralised at the absence of any support from Charles VI, who was still in Rouen, and by news of the arrival of a second English army at St-Vaast-la-Hougue, on the east side of the Cotentin Peninsula. Commanded by the Earl of March, it plundered its way through the Cotentin to join Henry at Caen. Then Henry's strengthened troops swept southwards, avoiding the lofty clifftop fortress of Falaise in favour of less well-defended towns. Appalled by the news of the sack and plunder at Caen and knowing that Charles VI and his son the Dauphin were now preoccupied with defending Paris from an advancing army of Burgundians, most of the towns and strongholds of south Normandy surrendered instantly or after short sieges.

Argentan, thirty miles south of Caen, opened its gates on 6 October 1417. Built on a natural eminence and well fortified, the town was in a strategically important position on the main road to Paris. Henry V sent a force eastwards along it to secure such strongholds as Aime, Laigle and the town of Verneuil, thus protecting his forces from Dreux, a well-defended French stronghold with a large garrison. Henry stayed at Argentan until 13 October, making Codnor its captain before moving with the main army towards Alençon, twenty-five miles further south and close to the Anjou border. It, too, capitulated. The dukes of Anjou and Brittany both sued for peace, and Henry undertook not to advance further into their territory. Codnor and his retinue were doubtless grateful for some respite from the hard-driven campaigning. If the Malorys were already with him, they would have been quartered with Codnor in Argentan Castle, which had been rebuilt in 1370.

A captaincy was not merely a defensive responsibility. Once order had been established, Codnor left a skeleton garrison at Argentan and took the rest of his fighting men to join Henry's main army which was besieging Falaise. Winter was approaching. Aware that this siege was going to be a long haul, Henry ordered the pavilioner to build log huts bound with withies and roofed with turf for the men, rather than just canvas tents. As they sat round their fires all through December, they will have heard the story of how Robert the Devil, Duke of Normandy, used to look down from the castle's walls to watch Arlette, a beautiful young washerwoman, working away at the river's edge far below. Arlette became his bride, and in 1027 gave birth to a son called William, who would win the accolade of Conqueror in 1066. Falaise town surrendered on 2 January 1418, but the castle held out until February when, with its moat filled and the lower stones of its walls prised perilously loose with picks and hammers, it had no option but to surrender. After the fall of Falaise, Henry could retire to winter quarters in Caen, comfortable in the knowledge that he had now transformed the great chain of castles re-fortified by the French into protection for his own army from any attack from the east.

On other fronts, the English offensive continued. On 16 February, the day the siege of Falaise ended, Henry commissioned Humfrey of Gloucester to sweep across the Cotentin Peninsula to attack Cherbourg, another important Channel port. Codnor, with a retinue of fifty-one men-at-arms and 174 archers, was among the commanders sent with Gloucester. The Codnor muster roll which bore the name of the two Thomas Malorys was issued a month later on 18 March. It listed a much smaller number of men and must therefore be a muster of just one contingent of Codnor's retinue.

Gloucester's and Codnor's forces moved impressively rapidly, taking thirty-two castles in six weeks with very little loss of life. At Carentan, Malory would have admired the way Duke Humfrey gallantly allowed the ladies to take their jewels and personal property with them. Just after Easter, the army settled down in front of Cherbourg, which Froissart described as 'one of the strongest castles in the world'. They disposed artillery skilfully, and attacked vigorously, heaping mounds of earth higher than the city walls to enable more effective attacks, and even attempted to re-route a river. But after many casualties, they had to become resigned to a war of attrition. English ships were summoned to bring reinforcements to the siege and to blockade the port from the sea. After five months of isolation, the city surrendered on 29 September. Codnor was killed before it ended, on 1 August 1418, and the captaincy passed to Sir Walter Hungerford. Codnor's son and heir, Richard, was made bailli.

What became of Codnor's retinue, and the Malorys? It is possible that they stayed in Cherbourg, or returned to England with Codnor's son John. But it is more likely that they were among the three thousand men whom Gloucester took with him to join the King's army outside Rouen, the ultimate objective of the summer's campaigning. Rouen was the natural capital of Normandy and, in Henry V's view, 'the most notable place in France save Paris'. The siege began on 29 July, and Gloucester's forces arrived early in November. Beauchamp was already there. He had been busy, sent by Henry to negotiate with the Burgundians on 21 March, and then to invest Domfront, west of Falaise, on 2 April. Domfront had surrendered on 29 June. Gloucester was then given command of Porte St-Hilaire, a dangerous post, very close to the town and the scene of the heaviest fighting and most numerous casualties. The next gate to the south was Porte Martinville. Did Thomas Malory witness the chivalrous jousting 'à l'outrance' between its captain Laguen, Bastard of Arly, and Sir John Blount, a Staffordshire knight whose son would later be one of his feoffees?

Waurin's description of the duel shows only qualified respect for such posturings in the middle of a siege.

> *There before the barrier the two champions ran against each other with good will; but it happened that by the first blow the English knight was pierced through the body by the lance and carried off his horse, and besides was drawn by force into the town, where he soon died, which was a great pity, for he was a knight of good renown. The said Bastard was very sorry for his death, but he could do nothing else. However, he accepted 400 nobles from the friends of the deceased for giving up the body. For this thing the Bastard was greatly lauded, valued and honoured by all; but, to tell the truth, such passages of arms could profit neither the besieger nor the besieged, except for the renown of their valiant nobility.*

The siege continued, with the Burgundians' conquest of Paris making relief even more unlikely and the Rouennais reduced to eating dogs, cats, rats and even mice. Its streets full of emaciated corpses, the city finally surrendered after five months on 13 January. Beauchamp was the chief negotiator. His diplomatic skill was clearly highly prized by Henry. The King stayed in Rouen 'until the town was set in rule and governaunce'. Coins were minted bearing the words 'Henricus Rex Franciae' and work began on a grand new palace. At the Candlemas feast on 2 February, Henry wore the robes of Duke of Normandy.

Elsewhere in Normandy, Henry's other commanders were busy – Caudebec and Montvilliers surrendered to the Duke of Exeter, Honfleur to the Earl of Salisbury. Clarence advanced up the Seine. The speed with which so much of Normandy fell to the English was as great a reflection of French weakness as of English strength. Capitulation was encouraged by the generous terms which Henry offered those who surrendered, and his determination to treat the Normans with the respect due to at least potentially loyal subjects. The very first clauses in the military ordinances that ruled the behaviour of the army forbade any violence against churches, men of religion or women. Malory makes King Arthur insist that his knights swear just such an oath when he rewards them for their valour against the Emperor Lucius.

Although Englishmen were always appointed as bailiffs of conquered towns and captains of garrisons, the second-ranking post of *vicomte* and civic administration were usually left in Norman hands. The English conquest was the easier because life in Normandy before the invasion had been subject to sudden and unpredictable raids from the mercenary freebooters who ranged the country in search of spoils in the intervals of fighting in the sporadic French civil wars. Many ordinary Normans welcomed a better ordered, if subjugated, life. Being taxed, but also protected, by the English was preferable to being pillaged by brigands. 'Many people say that if the king of England be the stronger, let him be our lord, so be that we may live in peace and the quiet enjoyment of our own,' reported the chronicler of St-Denis. 'He was a prince of a high understanding and of a great will to keep justice,' wrote another contemporary, Pierre Fenin, 'wherefore the poor folk loved him above all others. For he was prone and careful to preserve the lesser folk, and to protect them from the violence and wrong that most of the nobles had done to them'.

By the end of March 1419, only five Norman fortresses remained in French hands – La Roche Guyon, Ivry, Gisors, Château Gaillard and Mont St-Michel. All were strategically sited and strongly fortified. They would only be taken by attrition. Divisions of Henry's army settled around La Roche Guyon, Ivry and Gisors. There is no clue as to where the Malorys were stationed at this time. They could have been with Beauchamp outside La Roche Guyon or with Humfrey of Gloucester at Ivry. After both had capitulated, Roche Guyon on 1 May and Ivry on 10 May, Beauchamp and Gloucester rejoined Henry. On 19 May Henry dubbed Beauchamp Count of Aumâle, which provided him with extensive estates in Normandy; in turn he undertook to maintain a retinue of ten men-at-arms and twenty mounted archers to ride out with the King for the duration of the war. Sadly there is no record of the names of the men who formed this élite royal bodyguard.

On 1 June negotiations began for a more final peace, to be sealed by the marriage of Henry V and King Charles VI's daughter Catherine.

Beauchamp acted as interpreter between Henry and Queen Isobel. On 5 July Henry sent Beauchamp to Pontoise to negotiate with the Burgundians. However, the Dauphin soon backed out. Awed at Henry's success, the Burgundians had offered to make peace with him so that they could join forces in an attack on the English. 'There may be none hope had as yet of peace,' one weary soldier wrote home. The ambassadors were 'double and false' and had made 'a fine ninny' of the English King. He ended by begging his family to 'pray for us that we may come soon out of this unlusty soldier's life into the life of England'.

Within a month, the wheel of fortune had spun again. On 26 August 1419, a meeting was arranged at Montereau between the Dauphin and his Armagnac allies and John the Fearless, Duke of Burgundy. As he rose from making his obeisance before the Dauphin, Duke John was hacked to death – revenge for his own ruthless murder of the King's brother, Duke Louis of Orléans, twelve years before. There could have been no more effective way of getting the new Duke of Burgundy (John's son Philip the Good) and King Charles VI and Queen Isobel to ally with the English against the errant heir to the throne. 'Now I shall have the lady Catherine for whom I have so longed,' Henry V exclaimed exultantly to his courtiers. But although diplomatic negotiations, again led by Beauchamp, now proceeded to more purpose, Henry had no intention of giving up the offensive.

> *He was no more weary of harness [armour] than of a light cloak. Hunger and thirst were not to him noisome. He was never afraid of a wound nor never sorrowed for the pain. He neither turned his nose from an evil savour, nor from smoke or dust would not close his eyes . . . He slept very little and that only by reason of bodily labour and unquietness of mind, from the which no small noise could wake him, insomuch that when his soldiers either sang in the nights or their minstrels played that all the camp sounded of their noise, he then slept most soundly. His courage was so constant and his heart so immutable that he cast away all fear. If any alarm*

were made by his enemies, he was first in armour and the first that would set forward.

Henry returned to Rouen briefly, then, early in September, he and Humfrey of Gloucester joined the siege of Gisors, which was in its fifth month. The town surrendered on 17 September and the castle a week later. Next to fall was Château Gaillard, Richard the Lionheart's famous 'saucy' castle, which still towers above the Seine at Les Andelys just east of Rouen.

On 5 January 1420, the Treaty of Arras made England and Burgundy firm allies. Henry undertook to treat Duke Philip as his brother so long as they both should live, and promised one of his brothers as a husband for the Duke's sister Anne. He also said he would spare no effort to pursue the Dauphin and his Armagnac accomplices. At the Twelfth Night feast next day, Henry was described as unusually merry – as well he might be. 'The English entered France through a hole in the Duke of Burgundy's skull,' lamented one French chronicler. Three months later, on 9 April 1420, the Treaty of Troyes between England and France was signed. The thirty-one-year-old Henry was to marry the nineteen-year-old Catherine and become King of France himself after the death of her father, Charles VI. Their heirs would inherit the crowns of England and France in perpetuity. The wedding was celebrated in the porch of Troyes Cathedral on 2 June. The honeymoon was spent besieging the Dauphinist stronghold of Melun. Beauchamp and his forces remained at the King's side, so, assuming that Malory had returned to his most likely liege lord, he will have seen the elegant wooden house which Henry ordered to be built near his tent for Catherine, far away enough away from the town for her 'not to be troubled by arrows'. She stayed there, 'grandly attended by dames and damsels', for four weeks of the four-month siege. 'Each day six or eight English clarions and divers other instruments played melodiously for a good hour at sunset and at daybreak'.

Melun fell on 18 November 1420, and many of the English troops were given leave to return to England. Malory describes just such an occasion when, after the conquest of Rome, the triumphant English lords, 'well-stuffed of all things', beseech King Arthur *'to release us to sport with our wives, for, worship be to Christ, this journey is well overcome'.*

'Ye say well', said the king, 'for enough is as good as a feast, for to tempt God overmuch I hold it not wisdom. And therefore make you all ready and turn we again into England.' Then there was trussing of harness with carriage full noble, and the king took his leave ... and left good governance in that noble city and all the countries ... for to ward and to keep on pain of death, that no wise his commandment be broken ... And so King Arthur passed over the sea to Sandwich haven.

Henry and Catherine themselves landed in England on 1 February 1421, borne ashore on the shoulders of the barons of the Cinque Ports and cheered by exultant crowds. Catherine's coronation took place in Westminster Abbey on 23 February. At the banquet, a fishy Lenten feast that included whale and porpoise, Beauchamp acted as Steward of England. In five years Henry V had achieved more success in France than Edward III had done in forty. Like King Arthur, Henry V could boast that 'was never king nor knights did better since God made the world'.

It is easy to imagine the impact of England's success on an ardent young squire with his head stuffed full of heroic legends like Thomas Malory. This reconstruction of his war service under Henry V goes some way towards explaining both why he chose to write about King Arthur at all, and why he was able to lend such convincing military reality to his account of King Arthur's expedition through France to Italy to conquer Lucius, the Emperor of Rome. When Malory describes diplomatic negotiations, the capture of prisoners, the setting up of ambushes, and triumphant post-battle revels, he could be describing the Lancastrian army's adventures. He adds an ambush typical of contemporary warfare to King Arthur's campaign. Sir Gawaine and Sir Bors go to parley with the Emperor, but they are well aware of his dastardly ways, and leave 'stuff of men-of-arms in a bushment'. When they are, as expected, chased by the Roman knights, they successfully lead them into the ambush and take valuable prisoners that will pay 'goods without number'. The Winchester manuscript version of this particular tale shows that Malory's first version of Arthur's European campaign was far longer than that printed by Caxton. As it is thought by many to be one of the earliest of his tales, it makes sense to see it as directly inspired by his experiences during Henry V's initial conquest of Normandy. One enterprising investigator of the relation between the times in which Malory lived and the *Morte Darthur* even sees a close parallel between the route that Henry V took through France and that which Malory makes King Arthur take when he crosses the Channel to subjugate the pride of Emperor Lucius. This is too far-fetched. There is no need to look for exact parallels between the lives and adventures of the two kings; it is enough that both were formidable warriors, immensely respected rulers and careful to observe the niceties of the chivalric code, and that Henry V's choice of the Knights of the Garter aimed to create a fellowship just as noble in purpose as King Arthur's Knights of the Round Table.

At this period of his life, Malory may have seen himself as the quintessential romantic hero. He repeatedly inserts accounts of such young men as Beaumains, Alisander le Orphelin, and La Cote Male Taile. Their idealism stands in deliberate contrast to more worldly heroes like Gawaine, Tristram and Lamorak de Galis. What they seek to do above all is to win 'worship' – a word which we now associate only with religion, though its old sense is preserved in such formal titles as 'His Worship the Lord Mayor'. An abbreviated form of 'worthwhileness', it was synonymous with esteem, honour, distinction and high repute. The high value that Malory put upon acquiring worship is reflected in the fact that he uses the word over three hundred and fifty times, in one form or another (compared to just over a hundred mentions of 'prowess'), in the course of the nine hundred or so pages of his book.

Service under Henry V could certainly have been what inspired Malory to write about King Arthur in English. For although Henry aspired to rule France, he valued his English throne the most. He placed a high value on speaking, writing and reading in English rather than in French, both in diplomatic affairs and in private life. A contemporary memorandum made by the London Brewers' Company noted that

> *Our mother-tongue, to wit the English tongue, hath in modern days begun to be honourably enlarged and adorned, for that our most excellent lord, King Henry V, hath in his letters missive and divers affairs touching his own person, more willingly chosen to declare the secrets of his will, and for the better understanding of his people, hath with a diligent mind procured the common idiom to be commended by the exercise of writing.*

Winning Worship

'Pray you that ye will tell us where we may find Sir Beaumains.' 'Fair lords,' said Sir Ironside, 'I cannot tell you, for it is full hard to find him; for such young knights as he is one, when they be in their adventures be never abiding in no place.'

Malory, 'The Tale of Beaumains'

here are very few references to Thomas Malory's activities between 1421, when he was involved in a Warwickshire law-suit, and 1439, when he witnessed a settlement for his cousin Sir Philip Chetwynd. The most convincing reason for this virtual invisibility is that he spent most of these decades in France. The conquest of Normandy between 1417 and 1420 was just the beginning of the occupation of northern France by the English. They held sway in Aquitaine for even longer. Sir John Tiptoft was in his late twenties when he was made Seneschal of the Landes, in Aquitaine, in 1408; he died in office in 1443. Thousands of men served on the Continent between 1417 and 1453, when the decisive defeat of the English at Châtillon, in Aquitaine, marked the actual, though not accepted, end of all English holdings in France except Calais. Many were granted lands of their own in Normandy and Maine, and married French girls. Others brought over wives and children, and friends and relations, from England and settled, working the land or living in towns as merchants. Running an English-style tavern in France was a favourite occupation of soldiers too old or crippled to fight. Christopher Hanson and Peter Bassett were typical of the many career soldiers of the time. Both looked after Sir John Fastolf's affairs. They spent most of the 1420s in Normandy and together wrote a chronicle of the decade. Benedicta Rowe describes it as 'a plain, soldierly account' which 'preserves something of the spirit of those who fought in the wars, a bluff delight in adventure, and very little care for the fate of non-combatants'. It is the sort of record that Malory could also have tried his hand at writing; it is certainly the approach he took to retelling Arthurian tales.

The History of Parliament Trust is now at work on the missing volume of its monumental new biographical history of all known Members of Parliament: the story of the Members who sat between 1422 and 1504. What has emerged about their lives puts Malory's apparently shocking crimes into context. 'MPs as a group . . . had an impressive record of participation in disorder and other more serious criminal activity,' observes one investigator. The researchers have also found long voids in the lives of many of their subjects, and concluded that these can be explained by absence on service in Normandy, which the English occupied more or less effectively for the next thirty years, or on campaign in other parts of France. When I trawled through the HPT's files and draft biographies, I discovered that a remarkable number of Thomas Malory's relatives, friends and neighbours spent time abroad during these decades. The glimpses we have of them are brief, but it is clear that 'haunting arms and noble deeds' was still typical of the Malorys.

Sir William Malory went to France in the retinue of Thomas Beaufort, Duke of Exeter, in 1418, and later served in that of Sir Thomas de Roos in May 1430. Thomas Arderne, a Warwickshire squire whose father Ralph Arderne's name was above that of Malory on the Beauchamp Roll in 1414, was with him. A Robert Malory is recorded in the service of Sir Richard Woodville when he returned from France in 1425; another, perhaps the same man, served under Sir John Talbot, Earl of Shrewsbury, at Château Gaillard in 1436. A John Malory and a John Walsh both went to France in March 1441 in the retinue of Sir John Cressy (whose estates were in Northamptonshire and Hertfordshire), who in turn served under Richard, Duke of York, then King's Lieutenant in France. Either the same or another John Malory, this time described as Rector of Brampton, a Knights

Hospitaller estate in Warwickshire, went to France in the retinue of John Langton in October 1444. A Richard Malory was among the mounted men mustered by Thomas Wake of Blisworth, a wealthy Northamptonshire knight, at Portsdown to cross to France in July 1443. It is not just possible but probable that Thomas Malory was also overseas in the 1420s and 1430s. Every time his name occurs in the records during these decades it is in association with men who were serving in France before or after their appearance in his company.

A cautious biographer would at this point vault two decades to the 1440s, when Malory's doings are much better documented. But to do so would leave an unsatisfactory vacuum. I like Napoleon's dictum, 'To understand a man you have to know what was happening in the world when he was twenty'. Understanding can be taken a step closer to empathy if, as well as reconstructing the relevant historical events of the world Malory certainly lived in, we sketch out a likely career for him which, though necessarily imaginary, fits the known facts. For this prolonged period of service in France explains Malory's fluency in French and wide knowledge of French romance literature, the knowledgeable way in which he describes military strategy, and what made him the confident commander and daring man of action that the records of his exploits in the 1450s show him to have been. Moreover, such adventures overseas would have made him see the politics of the 1450s and 1460s in a different perspective from younger contemporaries. Memories of Henry V and the intensely loyal commanders who surrounded him overshadowed Malory's thinking when he wrote such lines as: 'It was merry to be under such a chieftain, that would put his person in adventure as other poor knights did', 'Ever he was faithful and true of his promise', and 'If ye have need any time of my service I pray you let me have knowledge, and I shall not fail you as I am a true knight.'

The Happy Return

A record of Thomas Malory's presence in Warwickshire in June 1421 suggests that he was part of the substantial escort which left Calais on 5 March 1421 in order to bring to Warwick the 101 French prisoners who had surrendered to Beauchamp. By this time his father, John Malory, was established as an influential man in the county. The frequency with which John witnessed charters and held high office shows he was trusted by his friends and neighbours as well as by the King and Beauchamp. He had been Sheriff of Warwickshire and Leicestershire in 1416–17, and had witnessed a Swinford and Yelvertoft deed with his brother Simon in January 1417, and a Baginton deed in April 1417. Something went wrong towards the end of his term as Sheriff, however: a warrant for his arrest was issued by the Court of King's Bench in the Hilary Term of 1418. Such warrants were not unusual, and John Malory may have been expecting it: he had taken the precaution of taking out a pardon in 1417. But he evidently recovered his good name quickly. In 1419, probably as a feoffee, he conveyed part of the manor of Saddington to his cousin William Malory and in June he witnessed a deed concerning Lapworth, in Warwickshire. In October 1419 he sat as MP for Warwickshire for the second time, and in November was on a commission of array to raise local troops. In January 1420 he was asked, with others, to raise a loan in the county for the King. In February 1420 he was one of the thirteen knights and esquires in his county deemed most able to defend the realm in the King's absence. In August 1420 he witnessed two charters for Sir William Peyto of Chesterton, a manor just east of Swinford. In 1421 he witnessed two deeds for the widow of William, Lord Astley.

Thomas Malory's uncles Thomas, Simon and Robert all now lived within fifteen miles of John Malory's estates. Uncle Thomas had retired from war and settled down at Bramcote, a few miles north of Coleshill; he would die, childless, by 1428. Uncle Simon had married Margaret Sutton and settled at Chilverscoton, just south of Nuneaton. He attested the probity of the Warwickshire parliamentary election in May and December 1421 and in 1427. Uncle Robert, now a fully fledged Hospitaller knight, was preceptor of Balsall and Grafton, a group of fertile estates in north-west Warwickshire, five miles west of the royal palace of Kenilworth. He had been absent from England for much of his life. Received as a novice Hospitaller in the early 1390s, he may have travelled soon afterwards to Rhodes, the headquarters of the Order since 1312. All brother knights had to do their stint of duty in the eastern Mediterranean, guarding Rhodes itself, policing eastern waters and launching attacks on the Turks and the Egyptians. Novices could enter the Order as young as fourteen, but they were not sent out to Rhodes until they were twenty years old. We know that Sir Robert had spent at least five years in Rhodes before 1402, as there was a debate that year as to whether he or Robert Dawgeny should hold the preceptory of Hogshaw, a position which required its holder to have spent five years in Rhodes. Although both had the same seniority, Dawgeny was chosen. Both he and Sir Robert were probably then in Rhodes with the head of the English langue, Sir Walter Grendon, who is recorded visiting the Hospitaller estates in Cyprus in 1403 with the Master of the Order, Philbert de Naillac.

There are three records which refer to Thomas Malory in the early 1420s, each providing an intriguing insight into everyday medieval life. All suggest he was then of age, and all involve a family called Pulteney, who owned the Leicestershire manor of Misterton, three miles north of the Malory manor of Swinford and bordering on Shawell. They tell us that in June 1421 Thomas Malory and John Pulteney sued a man for cutting down trees in some enclosed woodland at Edgbaston just east of Birmingham, for which they were responsible as feoffees for one Thomas Middlemore, who was then serving in France. The same property may have been involved in July 1422 when Thomas Malory, Sir John Pulteney and others brought a plea of 'novel disseisin' against Richard Clodeshall of Saltley, near Edgbaston. This meant that they were complaining that Clodeshall had taken possession of a piece of property that belonged, or was enfeoffed, to them. These lawsuits sound like firm action taken by soldiers home from the wars against crooks who had profited from their absence. Finally, in 1424, Thomas Malory and Thomas Pulteney were sued by another man's executors for ten marks. It was perhaps a debt incurred while they were in France; a visit to England would have ended the protection from legal process normally accorded serving soldiers.

The Pulteney arms, joined to those of another neighbouring family, the Feildings of Newnham Paddox, are among those copied by Dugdale from an armorial window in the parlour of Newbold Revel. Sir John Pulteney was extremely wealthy, with a good deal of property in London and Hertfordshire as well as in Leicestershire. His sons Thomas and John both served, like Malory and Middlemore, in France, and his daughter Margaret was married to William Purefoy, whose mother Margaret Chetwynd was Malory's aunt. Perhaps the families were just close friends, but the message of the window may be that on one of Malory's home leaves he married a girl whose father was a Pulteney and whose mother was a Feilding. The 1424 record describes Thomas Malory as 'of Shawell'. Shawell, which bordered on Swinford, had also been inherited by the Malorys from William Revel. Thomas's father John could well have made it over to his son on the occasion of the marriage.

But Malory could have simply held Shawell as a bachelor and contented himself with flirtations with local girls. Men were in no rush to marry young, although the heirs of considerable estates were often engaged as children. Nor were women eager to become vulnerable to the perilous business of childbirth. Any young women of means could afford to be as independent in spirit as Katherine Dudley, courted by John Paston a little later in the century. His older brother was his go-between:

> As for Mistress Katherine Dudley, I have many times recommended you to her and she is nothing displeased with it. She does not mind how many gentlemen love her: she is full of love. I have spoken on your behalf, as I told her, without your knowledge. She answers me that she will have no-one these two years, and I believe her, for I think she has a life that she is well content with.

The head often ruled the heart in choosing brides. Richard Cely visited Leicester to see a girl whom his brother George was considering as a possible wife. He wrote home:

> Sir, and [if] ye be remembered, we talked together in our bed of Dalton's sister, and ye feared the conditions of father and brethren; but ye need not. I saw her, and she was at breakfast with her mother and us. She is as goodly a young woman, as fair, as well-bodied, and as sad [serious-minded] as I see any this seven year, and a good height. I pray God that it may be imprinted in your mind to set your heart there.

However, Malory's presentation of love in the Arthurian legends shows that he was too romantic to tolerate an arranged marriage. His Sir Lancelot 'loved not to be constrained to love; for love must arise of the heart, and not by no constraint'. His King Arthur agrees, with the perceptive observation that 'with many knights love is free in himself, and never will be bounden, for where he is bounden he looseth himself'. One reason for his decision not to settle down in Shawell but to continue to fight in Henry V's French wars may have been his desire to make enough money to justify a marriage for love rather than money.

Another could have been the sight of Henry V and his fair-haired young queen, of 'valorous soul' and 'fresh as the month of May'. They came to stay at Kenilworth early in March 1421 while making a tour of England which was part triumph, part thanksgiving pilgrimage to such shrines as Bridlington and Walsingham and part fund-raising campaign for Henry's next expedition to France. The Malory family could have cheered the royal couple during their state visit to Coventry on 15 March 1421. Judging by later evidence of the dates at which Malory's known sisters were married, Philippa can now be imagined as being a young lady of eighteen or so, Isobel about eleven and Helen seven. Flattering parallels between Henry V and Catherine and King Arthur and Guinevere were frequently drawn at the pageants, feasts and junketings. Henry V even expressed an interest in visiting Glastonbury to examine recently discovered relics said to be the bones of Joseph of Arimathea, the man who was believed to have brought the Holy Grail to England.

John Malory was once again elected to Parliament for Warwickshire in April 1421, and went to Westminster to take up his seat on 2 May. As Earl of Warwick, Beauchamp sat in the Lords. It was a busy but uncontroversial session; the Commons praised Henry for his triumphs and was grateful for the fact that, thanks to the generosity of his subjects as he had processed around the country, the King did not need to ask it to grant more money for the war. For Henry had raised nearly £40,000 in loans – nearly half of it from his uncle, Bishop Beaufort. The army he gathered for his return to France numbered about 1,000 knights and men-at-arms and 3,500 archers, mainly mounted.

The English forces which had remained in France had suffered a major blow three months earlier, when Henry V's brother Thomas, Duke of Clarence, who had been campaigning in Anjou in search of the Dauphin, made an impetuous surprise attack on Easter Sunday on a Franco-Scottish army ten times the size of his own which was encamped near Baugé. A thousand Englishmen were killed, including Clarence himself, and many other notable English knights, and five hundred prisoners were taken. Thomas Pulteney was a member of Clarence's retinue, and may have had to pay a ransom, but he escaped death. Grief-stricken as Henry V was at the death of his valiant, handsome brother, he reacted calmly, rightly trusting in the competence of Thomas, Lord Montagu, Earl of Salisbury, who was appointed commander-in-chief in Clarence's place, to hold the English positions until he could return. The good news was that Queen Catherine was already expecting a baby. Henry decided that she would remain in England in the care of his brother John of Bedford, until she was safely delivered.

Death in Life

The three Warwickshire records referring to Thomas Malory between 1421 and 1424 do not prove his continuous presence in England during those years. The campaigning season was normally a short summer affair. Only garrisons or besieging forces stayed in France all winter. Malory, perhaps with John Pulteney as his 'brother-in-arms', could have joined Henry V's third expeditionary force of 900 knights and men-at-arms and 3,300 archers, which set out from Dover on 10 June 1421. Alternatively, he could have gone over with the additional Beauchamp contingent raised in May 1421.

Henry V landed at Calais on 11 June. His aim was to stabilise his future realm of France by expelling the Dauphin's forces which were deployed in a wide arc around Paris, threatening communications between it and Calais and Burgundy. With the mass of the army, he headed south to relieve Chartres, which the Dauphin was besieging. Beauchamp's centre of operations was northern Normandy, where some of the most effective of the Dauphin's troops were holding several crucial fortresses and making lightning strikes from them to ravage both the marches of Calais and Burgundian territory. The three outstanding Dauphinist commanders were all professional 'free-booters' or mercenaries. Jacques d'Harcourt, who had originally fought for the English but was now in the pay of the Dauphin, was based at Le Crotoy, a stronghold at the mouth of the Somme. Etienne de Vignolles, whose nickname La Hire – 'The Fury' – was a reference to his berserker tendencies in battle, held St Riquier in Picardy. The most eminent was Sir Pothon de Saintraille, a champion jouster who had been deprived of his estates in Gascony by the English.

It would be plausible for Malory to have been in the contingent of three hundred men-at-arms from Calais who were sent to join forces with the Burgundians to attack the Dauphinist stronghold of Gamaches, on the Somme, in March 1422. They were led by Sir Ralph Butler of Sudeley, a distinguished and wealthy Warwickshire knight with strong Knights Hospitaller connections who was one of Beauchamp's right-hand men. The Burgundian commander was John of Luxembourg. In his baggage train was a young clerk, Jehan de Waurin, whose chronicles are among the most vivid records of the times, and whom Malory would have enjoyed meeting. He was the Froissart of his age – knowledgeable about war and tactics, a fervent admirer of chivalric behaviour, and on the spot during many of the incidents he recorded. In a passage describing the assault on Gamaches that echoes Malory's descriptions of Arthurian battles, he awards accolades for exceptional prowess.

> It is fit to speak of John Villain, a [Burgundian] gentleman who had that day been made a knight. He was a man of lofty stature and powerful frame, mounted on a strong horse, and wielding a very heavy axe with both hands. With this at the encounter he pushed through the greatest throng of his enemies, and having let go his bridle, he dealt such heavy blows that those he reached with fair aim could but fall to the ground to rise no more. In this condition he met Pothon de Saintraille, who, as he afterwards related, seeing the marvels that the new knight was doing, withdrew to the rear as fast as he could for fear of the axe which was dealing such heavy blows.

Such respect for a worthy adversary, especially a newly-made knight, as well as the confidence that allowed him to joke about his own retreat, was typical of the best knights of the Round Table. Sir Bleoberis and Sir Palomides knock Sir La Cote Male Taile from his saddle with their lances, but refuse to take up his challenge to continue the fight on foot. 'Wit ye well,' Malory explains, 'they are wily men of arms, and anon they know when they see a young knight by his riding, how they are sure to give him a fall from his horse or a great buffet. But for the most part they will not fight on foot with young knights, for they are wight and strongly armed.' Saintraille was captured later that day, but was quickly released in an exchange of prisoners. Malory clearly approved of him: he gratuitously puts his name into the *Morte*, a rare tribute, not once but twice. He may have been involved in his capture on this occasion. However, he had, as we shall see, a much better opportunity of getting to know Saintraille eight years later.

In October 1421 Henry V laid siege to Meaux, a crucial stronghold for communications between Paris and Burgundy. While it was under siege, news came from England that on 6 December Queen Catherine had given birth to a boy at Windsor. Lady Joan Astley, whose family estates lay five miles north of those of the Malorys in Warwickshire, was appointed as his nurse. He had been christened Henry, and his godfathers were John of Bedford and Bishop Beaufort. His godmother was Jacqueline, Countess of Holland and Hainault, a glamorous fugitive heiress who had fled to England after being forced to marry the sickly and unattractive John, Duke of Brabant, by her guardian, Duke Philip of Burgundy, who stood to inherit Brabant if John died childless. Jacqueline was much admired by Duke Humfrey of Gloucester, a lover of chivalric legends who saw her as a damsel in distress who needed a champion. He was also interested in acquiring Hainault for himself. Their increasingly amorous liaison was a diplomatic disaster at a time when England wanted to keep Burgundy as an ally. Duke Philip was already incensed that Jacqueline had been given sanctuary in England.

Meaux did not fall until 6 May 1422, fighting on until the last lance was broken and the defenders were reduced to using iron spits. Its capture had a domino effect on neighbouring castles and towns. Compiègne, Gamaches and many others sent embassies to treat with the English King. North of the Somme, Beauchamp continued his offensive, steadily reducing the strongholds held by the Dauphin's supporters between Paris and Boulogne until only Le Crotoy held out. On 22 May Queen Catherine, escorted by John of Bedford, arrived at Harfleur 'in very noble array, with a large fleet of ships full of men-at-arms and archers' in order to join Henry. The new baby, heir to the realms of England and France, remained in England in the care of Lady Astley, Jacqueline and Duke Humfrey. Bedford and Queen Catherine sailed up the Seine to Rouen, then to the palace of King Charles VI and Queen Isobel at Bois de Vincennes. Henry joined them there, and on 30 May rode beside his queen into the centre of Paris, where they held magnificent court in its great central castle, the Louvre. Beauchamp joined them there in September.

The arrival of the English fleet and the new forces would have enabled some soldiers at least to take leave in England. Such comings and goings were regular occurrences, although detailed records of who travelled, and when, are rare. It was in July 1422 that Thomas Malory, Sir John Pulteney and others brought their plea of 'novel disseisin' against Richard Clodeshall. However, they need not have been present in person to make the plea; attorneys often represented plaintiffs. Since Malory's father John now sat on the magistrates' bench as a Justice of the Peace (and would continue to do so until 1434), Thomas had a good chance of success whether he made his case in person or not.

The triumphant merrymaking in Paris was premature. The Dauphin, though down, was by no means out. He and the Duc de Touraine sortied from their base at Orléans to advance on the Burgundian stronghold of Cosne-sur-Loire. Philip of Burgundy promptly sent to Henry V for help, and Henry decided to come in force and in person. At this point, although the King's spirit was as ever willing, his flesh failed him. During the siege of Meaux he had contracted a mysterious illness – some said it was dysentery, others pleurisy, others the result of poisoning. He decided to send Bedford and Beauchamp on ahead with the English army and to follow them in a horse-drawn litter. But he soon realised that he was too weak to travel at all. He was carried back to Vincennes, where he took to his bed.

Once the Dauphin knew that the English were marching to confront him, he withdrew south of the Loire. The English exaltation was short-lived. Henry, only thirty-five years old, was dying. Bedford and Beauchamp with some of their most trusty men hastened to his bedside. Henry had time to give them his last commands for his hard-won kingdom. He asked Bedford, steady and reliable, to remain as Regent of Normandy, and told him to ask Philip of Burgundy to be Regent of France until his baby son came of age; Bedford was to take command in France himself if Philip refused. For England, he appointed Humfrey of Gloucester Protector, responsible to a Council of Regency led by their uncle, Bishop Beaufort.

Finally, Henry asked that 20,000 requiem masses be said to speed his soul's passage through purgatory. It was an unusually large number, a measure perhaps of the responsibility he felt for the deaths his campaigns had caused. Then he lamented that he had failed to fulfil his dream: to rally Christian Europe under his own banner to fight against the infidel and regain Jerusalem. His dying words were: 'Good Lord! Thou knowest that mine intent hath been, and yet is, if I might live, to re-edify the walls of Jerusalem.' It was a sincere prayer; he had been reading of the triumphs of Geoffrey of Boulogne, first European King of Jerusalem, and had sent spies to evaluate the best approach to mining the city walls. He was still waiting for their report when he died on 1 September 1422. Such a feat of pious glory would have made so many masses superfluous.

The King's embalmed body, flanked by hundreds of clerics chanting the office for the dead, was carried with sad ceremony to Rouen. It was escorted by white-robed torch-bearers and five hundred men-at-arms in black armour on black horses, with lances carried point down. From there it was taken, via Calais, to England. Behind the hearse rode his family and his household, dressed in 'vestments of wailing and tears'; behind them came the Queen and her retinue. Every night the body was laid in a church and masses said. In London it was carried through the streets to St Paul's Cathedral and then to its final resting-place, Westminster Abbey. Waurin tells us that

> *The first of the four horses which drew the chariot in which lay the king's corpse wore a collar emblazoned with the ancient arms of England; on the collar of the second horse was painted the arms of England and France quarterly, which he bore himself while living; on the collar of the third horse were painted plainly the arms of France without difference; and on the collar of the fourth horse were painted the arms which were worn while he lived in the world by the noble King Arthur, so powerful that none could conquer him; which arms were an azure shield with three golden crowns.*

It is a revealing insight into the contemporary importance of the Arthurian legend – and the degree to which Henry V was identified with King Arthur. Details of the deathbed scene and the funeral cortège were widely reported. It is tempting to see the memory of Henry's regrets at his failure to achieve Jerusalem as the reason why, in a striking variation on all other versions of the 'dolorous departing' of King Arthur and the death of Sir Lancelot, Malory sends Lancelot's kinsmen to 'establish lands' in the Holy Land and 'make many battles upon the miscreants or Turks'. He also includes an intimation of Arthur's immortality that has ever since fuelled the imaginations of all admirers of the 'once and future king':

> *Yet some men say in many parts of England that King Arthur is not dead, but [is] had by the will of our Lord Jesu in another place; and men say that he shall come again, and he shall win the holy cross. I will not say it shall be so, but rather I will say: here in this world he changed his life. But men say that there is written on his tomb this verse: Hic facet Arthurus, Rex quondam, Rexque futurus.*

The profound impact of Henry's nine-year reign was reflected in the fact that for three decades and more after his premature death, the wishes of 'the king that dead is' were repeatedly invoked as a justification for pursuing his policies. References to Henry V were explicit in such political poetics as the immensely popular *Brut* chronicle and its continuations, John Hardyng's 1450s verse chronicle of English history, and the *Libelle of English Policy* of 1436, which argued for an increase in English sea power with frequent references to the policies of 'the marvellous warrior and victorious prince King Harry the Vth'. Such references were also implicit in books written in English to laud king-led war-enterprise, such as John Lydgate's *Troy Book and Siege of Thebes*. Malory's *Morte Darthur* fits this category of encomium exactly.

So could Malory's inspiration for writing an English Arthuriad have been his experience of the reign of Henry V? That 'noble king and conqueror' had after all lined his campaign tent with hangings showing Arthurian knights, envisaged the Order of the Garter as a fellowship as close and prestigious as that of the Round Table, and interested himself in the Arthurian relics at Glastonbury. He was often likened to King Arthur, for example at the London pageant celebrating his achievements in French conquest and at his funeral. There was even a proposal that he should be added to the pantheon of great men known as the Nine Worthies. It is, however, too far-fetched to assert that there are direct parallels between Malory's *Arthur* and Henry V. Knowing nods might have been exchanged by his hearers at some passages in 'The Tale of King Arthur and the Emperor Lucius', but if Malory had wanted to write a history of his times, as Waurin did, he would have done so. He often writes like a chronicler, albeit with a sure ear for dramatic dialogue. What he puts down is straightforward rather than fanciful and, especially in the later books, unusually specific about place-names. The biographer John Bale, writing in the 1540s when memories of Thomas Malory, who died in 1471, were still fresh, confidently declared that he deserved 'the most eminent place among historians'. Interestingly Bale listed a *Collectiones Anglicas* by Malory in the first edition (1548) of his great survey of 'Illustrious British Writers', perhaps mistakenly, but perhaps because he had been told there were other books by him. The only surviving book we have that is certainly by Malory is his history of King Arthur, but that does not mean he did not write other things. Peter Field has found distinct echoes of turns of phrase in the *Morte* in the verse romance *The Wedding of Sir Gawaine and Dame Ragnell*, and has made an interesting case for Malory's authorship. He argues that although laconic, powerful and dramatically presented prose was Malory's chosen treatment for his Arthurian tales, the flair and rhythm of his writing show that he could also have written poems and ballads.

The Captain of Gisors

Despite the death of Henry V, the English continued their French offensive. Leaving Bishop Beaufort and Duke Humfrey to compete for control of the royal council which Henry V had appointed to run England, Bedford set out again for Normandy. For the next eight years he and Beauchamp, and the brilliant commanders Thomas Montagu, Earl of Salisbury, and Lord John Talbot (later Earl of

Shrewsbury), continued to extend the boundaries of English rule there and in Anjou and Maine. If Malory returned to France for the 1423 campaigning season, he could have been among the 120 men under the command of Sir Thomas Gargrave whom Beauchamp sent 'to serve the King in the retinue of John, Duke of Bedford' in 1423. Beauchamp's secretary, John Shirley, was entrusted with the wages of one knight (Gargrave), twenty-nine men-at-arms and ninety archers until the end of May 1424. Beauchamp himself remained in England, negotiating the terms of a treaty with the Scots which would see James I released after giving his promise to end Scottish aid to the French.

Gargrave joined the Burgundian knight John of Luxembourg at Guise for a combined offensive against the Dauphin's forces north of the Seine. The chronicler Jehan de Waurin was travelling with the Burgundian army. He tells us that in March 1424 Bedford went to Montdidier to mastermind operations against Compiègne, which had been retaken by the French. Bedford, he writes,

> gave orders to certain chiefs of war, both English and Burgundians, to besiege the town of Compiègne, the leader of whom was the lord of Saveuse, and with him were the bailly of Rouen, the captain of Gisors named Mallery, the lord of L'Isle-Adam, Sir Lionel de Bournouville, the lord of Crevecoeur, the lord of Thyan, and many others, who on receiving these orders, sent all around for their men with great diligence.

Since no Christian name was given for 'the captain of Gisors', there is no way of knowing if this 'Mallery' was Thomas himself, or one of his relations. Gisors was an important command. It was the capital of the Vexin, the most easterly of the eight administrative divisions ('bailli') of Normandy. Even today Gisors Castle is a spectacular sight, its vertiginous circular keep visible for miles; the remains of its turreted surrounding walls show the enormous size of the original castle. Only twenty miles north-west of Paris, Gisors controlled an important crossroads and a bridge over the River Epte. It had fallen to Henry V after a three-week siege in 1419, and he had included it in the dower of lands he gave to Queen Catherine in 1421. Sir Richard Woodville, a tried and trusted servant of Henry V, had been its first bailiff, in overall charge of administration, but he was made Seneschal of Normandy on 18 January 1421 and was now based in Rouen. For a time John Burgh acted as bailiff of Gisors, but then the official record becomes patchy.

Woodville, whose daughter would become Queen of England in 1464, knew the Malory family. His English estates were mainly in Kent, but he inherited the main family seat at Grafton (later Grafton Regis), ten miles south of Northampton, after the death of his older brother Thomas Woodville in 1434. His manor at Pattishall bordered the estates of the Litchborough Malorys, which the Malorys of New-bold Revel took over in trust for their impoverished cousins in 1366. A Robert Malory, probably the son of Simon Malory, perhaps of the Litchborough branch of the family, but certainly Thomas's kinsman, is listed among the men Woodville brought over from France and installed as garrison of the Tower of London in 1425. It could have been he who held command in Gisors in 1423, but it is also possible that Woodville placed Thomas, now in his mid-twenties and with almost ten years' experience of service in France, in charge of the castle.

Gisors was an appropriate command for a Malory. Their ancestors originated at Tessancourt, a little further north-east in the Vexin, and Boucanvilliers, a few miles to the south-east, and it was Lancastrian policy to reward successful commanders who claimed that their ancestors came over with William the Conqueror with estates in their old homeland. The family's connections with the Knights Hospitallers made it a doubly interesting captaincy for a Malory to hold. The castle of Gisors had been built by the Knights Templars, the companion order to the Knights Hospitallers. Although the Templars were disbanded in 1307, legend has it that Gisors remained true to the Templar cause and that huge quantities of Templar treasure are buried somewhere beneath it. A secret passage is said to run from the castle to Neaufles, a village two miles away. Investigations in 1963 did discover that the castle's foundations were riddled with cellars and underground passages, at least one of which must have run as far as the town, but the only hoard found dated from the late eighteenth century – hidden no doubt during the French Revolution.

The captain of a Norman fortress town had disciplinary duties as well as military ones. The Lancastrian occupation lasted for nearly thirty years, and ruled with a confusing mixture of French and English laws. Bedford was as insistent as Henry V had been that the new English subjects should be treated well, and there are many records of punishments for English soldiers who committed crimes against local people. We can hope that Malory was as fair-minded as the lords to whom King Arthur gave the estates he had won from the Emperor Lucius, ruling 'in such wise that none complained, rich nor poor'.

But a man of Malory's spirit would have preferred action in battle to civic administration. The most glorious English victory of the 1420s occurred soon after the fall of Compiègne. In June 1424, Bedford's army was drawn up outside Ivry-la-Chaussie, a seemingly impregnable castle with a combined force of 10,000 English and Burgundian troops. A messenger arrived with the news that a 14,000-strong Franco-Scottish army had captured the important border town of Verneuil by a trick. Bedford marched rapidly to Verneuil which he attacked on 16 August. Over seven thousand of the enemy were killed, including the Dauphin's most prized commanders, the Earl of Buchan and the Duke of Alençon. The Battle of Verneuil was ranked by contemporaries as an English triumph in the same league as Crécy, Poitiers and Agincourt. Although Malory may have been in Warwickshire early in 1424, when he and Thomas Pulteney were sued for ten marks by an executor, he could have returned in time to fight in the battle. If so, Verneuil would have been in his mind when he came to write of the riskiest of King Arthur's triumphs while campaigning in Europe.

> Then the king wept, and dried his eyes with a kerchief, and said, 'Your courage had near-hand destroyed you, for though ye had returned again, ye had lost no worship; for I call it folly, knights to abide when they be overmatched.' 'Nay,' said Lancelot and the others, 'for once shamed may never be recovered.'

Beauchamp was still in England when Bedford won Verneuil. He was an important member of the Regency Council, listed as attending as often as the Protector, Duke Humfrey. He also had personal business to settle. His wife Elizabeth Berkeley had died in December 1422, and his title to many of her lands was being questioned by Berkeley interests. She had borne him only daughters, and he urgently needed a son to inherit the Warwick title. On 26 November 1423 he married Isobel Despenser, a notable heiress whose vast estates compensated for the loss of some of the Berkeley lands. Among the most attractive of Isobel's possessions was Hanley Castle, overlooking the River Severn on the borders of Gloucestershire and Worcestershire just north of Tewkesbury, and she and Beauchamp were married there. On 22 March 1425 she gave birth to Harry, the longed-for male heir.

Beauchamp came out to France with six thousand more men in the autumn of 1425. This time his headquarters was a Parisian mansion, the Hôtel Jean de la Haye. If we continue to regard Malory's service under Beauchamp as the Ariadne's thread that leads us through the labyrinth of possible paths that he could have taken, we can imagine that Malory was among the Earl's Parisian household. Bedford was often in Paris too. Both Normandy and Maine were now entirely in English hands, and peace made with the Burgundians despite Duke Humfrey's marriage to Jacqueline in February 1423. Bedford had, as promised, married Burgundy's sister, Anne of Luxembourg; they were lucky enough to 'like and love each other well'. They divided their time between a new palace at Rouen, which they had romantically named Joyeux Repos, and the prettily turreted Parisian Hôtel des Tournelles. The sight of the happy couple made Beauchamp miss 'the womanhood and lusty cheer' of his own young wife. At about this time he penned a ballad and sent it to her from France.

> *I can not half the woe complain*
> *That doth my woeful heart strain*
> *With busy thought and grievous pain*
> *When I not see*
> *My fair lady whose beauty*
> *So fully presented is in me.*

Service in Beauchamp's Parisian household would have brought Malory into touch with both diplomatic and literary affairs. Beauchamp continued to be frequently employed as an ambassador and Malory's fluency in French may have made him useful on such occasions. His decision to translate French romances may also have been encouraged by the Earl who, like Henry V, favoured the English language. In 1426 Beauchamp discovered a genealogy hanging in Notre-Dame Cathedral, written in French, which showed that English kings were descended from Louis IX, commonly called Saint Louis. Realising that it was a useful piece of propaganda, he commissioned the poet John Lydgate, who was with him in France, to translate it. In the prologue to 'On the English Title to the Crown of France', Lydgate tells his readers that his work was

> . . . *the commandment*
> *Of the nobly prince and manly man,*
> *Which is so knightly and so much can,*
> *My lord of Warwick, so prudent and wise.*

In June 1425 Bedford became the legal owner of the French royal library which was housed in a tower in the Louvre. There were some eight hundred volumes, most of them collected in the fourteenth century by Charles V. One of his first acts as regent had been to order a catalogue to be made of the famous collection, but he did not actually go and look at them until 1425, when he paid Charles VI's executors rather less than the amount of the valuation for the whole library. Among the books in the collection were thirteen Arthurian texts, including two *Lancelots*, three *Grails*, a *Tristram*, two *Merlins* and what sound like contemporary compilations: 'Tristan et Lancelot et de ses faits de la Table Ronde' and 'du Saint Graal et du Tristan'. The inventory reveals that not all of the books were grand illuminated showpiece productions. One was described as 'very old and unillustrated', and one of the *Lancelots* had 'very badly formed letters'. We know that Bedford gave away or sold some books from the collection, three (including a *Grail* romance bound in with a *Death of Arthur*) to his brother Duke Humfrey. If Malory was already experimenting with translating Arthurian stories, he might have been able to acquire some of its shabbier volumes.

As Count of Aumâle, Châteaulevant and Maine, Beauchamp had extensive French estates, with castles, manors and hunting lodges to be tenanted or managed. He took part in many lucrative sieges, and a steady procession of prisoners were sent home to await ransom. His increased wealth was put to good use. He spent £500 on his London home, Warwick Inn, and Warwick Castle was provided with a magnificent new tower, a rebuilt south wing and spacious and decoratively-plastered stables. His wife's estates extended his territorial interests westwards into Gloucestershire, Staffordshire and the Welsh Marches, and he needed to make his authority felt there as well as in Warwickshire itself. Hanley Castle was rebuilt, and he began to explore the possibilities of making the Avon navigable all the way to Warwick, so that the family could travel between Hanley, on the Severn, and Warwick, on the Avon, by water.

Malory could well have made profits from the war, storing up wealth to stand him in good stead in times to come. Even if he spent most of his time in France, perhaps managing one of Beauchamp's French estates, he would certainly have returned home on occasion, either on his lord's business or his own. Now in his late twenties, we can deduce from the sort of writer he became that he was an amusing, sensitive and usefully well-educated young man, an experienced warrior who was dedicated to the ideals of chivalry.

The Giant of Mont St-Michel

Beauchamp was so successful in France that on 14 March 1426 Bedford appointed him as Captain and Lieutenant-General 'for the field' in Normandy, Anjou, Maine and the Marches of Brittany. By then England's Normandy conquests were being threatened by the Bretons, as Francis, Duke of Brittany, had thought better of alliance with the English. His brother Arthur de Richemont was high in the Dauphin's favour: he was his foremost general and Constable of France. In January 1426, Duke Francis had taken Avranches and Pontorson, important border towns between Normandy and Brittany. Beauchamp mustered men from all the English garrisons in Normandy to head westward to strengthen the border between Normandy and Brittany. If Malory was in his service, it is likely that he served in the army which retook Avranches in March and then laid siege to Pontorson. The town did not fall until early in May.

Pontorson is only six miles from the spectacular sea-girt Breton fortress of Mont-St-Michel. During the siege, Malory would have had plenty of time to explore the surrounding countryside, and collect legends about Mont-St-Michel as well as seeing for himself the only fortress never to fall during the thirty-five-year-long English occupation. He would have remembered his time there when he came to write the gory story of how King Arthur defeats the hideous giant of Mont-St-Michel. He makes King Arthur's forces land at Barfleur, near Cherbourg, which he could have passed through on campaign with Codnor.

> *Arthur . . . went forth by the crest of that hill, and saw where he sat at supper gnawing on a limb of a man, baking his broad limbs by the fire, and breechless, and three fair damosels turning three broaches whereon were broached twelve young children late born, like young birds.*

The tale had special resonance for Malory's contemporaries. The specific crime that King Arthur avenges by attacking the giant is the brutal rape and murder of the Duchess of Brittany. Henry V's stepmother Joanna of Navarre had herself once held this title. Despite the lampreys she provided for his coronation, she was never popular in England, not least because Breton pirates harassed the Cornish and Devon coasts on a regular basis. In 1419 Henry V had imprisoned her on suspicion of sorcery and confiscated her dower. Politics and economics as well as superstition lay behind the charge: Joanna had been a useful hostage for the good behaviour of her son John, now Duke of Brittany, and her substantial dower was a useful bonus for the war effort. But fear of witchcraft was universal in an age when the Devil was as real as God, and Joanna is only the first of several women of high position and power who were accused of witchcraft during Thomas Malory's lifetime. The fact that his Arthurian tales frequently feature sorceresses did not in the least lessen their credibility in the minds of those who heard them. Morgan le Fay could be thought alive and well in an age when the ancestors of a queen of England were rumoured to include the sinister fairy Melusine.

Beauchamp did not stay in the west of Normandy for long. The long-term aim of the English in France was to advance south and make the great River Loire a secure frontier for their conquests. After re-establishing control of Pontorson early in May, Beauchamp and his troops returned to Rouen, where they were congratulated by Bedford. His next assignment was the siege of Montargis, a fortified town on a northern tributary of the Loire, sixty miles south of Paris. But for once fortune did not favour him. His co-commander, the Duke of Suffolk, failed to keep adequate watch and on 5 September 1427, a French army broke the siege and relieved the town. Fifteen hundred Englishmen were killed, and the retreat to Paris was a shambles. Artillery was abandoned, as was a Warwick banner – it remained a trophy in Montargis, brought out to be jeered at on the anniversary of the battle, until 1792, when it was burned.

Captains Courageous

*She mounted her horse armed as would a man, adorned
with a doublet of rich cloth-of-gold over her breastplate;
she rode a very handsome, very proud grey courser and
displayed herself in her armour and her bearing as a captain would have done ... and in that array, with her
standard raised high and fluttering in the wind, and well-
accompanied by many noble men, she sallied forth from
the city, about four hours past midday.*

Chastellain, Chronicles

After the débâcle of Montargis, Beauchamp welcomed the
Privy Council's decision to send him back to England to
play a steadying role in the royal household by taking up the
guardianship of the young King. For Bishop Beaufort was planning to
leave England. In the hope of winning himself a cardinal's hat, he
was raising forces for holy war – a campaign in eastern Europe against
the followers of the heretic Jan Hus and the pagan Slavs of Eastern
Europe. Beauchamp was eager to spend more time on his west Midland estates with his wife and children, and to help his daughters by
Elizabeth defend their Berkeley estates from their cousin James, who
disputed their possession of the massive inheritance.

If Malory came home with Beauchamp in March 1428, he would
have been furious to hear of the high-handed action taken against
his father by William Peyto of Chesterton six months earlier. John
Malory, now in his mid-fifties, had been chosen by the local worthies
who made up the electors of the county to sit in the Commons as
MP for Warwickshire when parliamentary elections were held at
Warwick on 22 September 1427. It was his fifth election as an MP. But

William Peyto had marched into the sheriff's court with a threatening retinue at his heels a few days later and insisted on his own name being sent in, instead of John Malory's. The Under-Sheriff Edmund Coleshill, who had connections with Peyto's wife's family, the Gresleys of Drakelow, duly did so.

Peyto was only a few years older than Thomas Malory, and had been active in the war in France since 1423, when he was retained for life by Beauchamp. He had just married for the second time, and no doubt liked the idea of spending a few years at home in a position of influence. Future events make it clear that there was a long history of bad feeling between the Peytos and the Malorys; whether it stemmed from this incident or was already in existence, we have no way of knowing. It is unlikely that Peyto would have dared to threaten the election if Thomas had been at home. But when Parliament met in December 1427, it was John Malory and Sir William Mountfort who took their seats as parliamentary knights of the shire. When Beauchamp returned to Warwickshire, perhaps with Thomas Malory at his side, in March 1428, Peyto's election was voided and John Malory was reinstated. John also continued to act as a Justice of the Peace. Peyto, whose strong right arm evidently still had its uses, was placated by an increase in the retainer paid to him by Beauchamp to £20. He was appointed Sheriff for 1428–9.

Soon after this, pressure was put on John Malory to become a knight. In 1430 he is recorded as taking out a distraint of knighthood, a fine which absolved him from the duties and expenses attached to being a knight. Families entitled to coats of arms were normally required to do this if their income was over £40. Had his father's widow died, and her jointure reverted to John? Or had Thomas returned awash with French gold, so that John could extend his estates? The fact that John Malory, unlike his son Thomas, did not want to become a knight is interesting. It may have been because of age or ill-health, or because he had a large family to provide for and didn't want the added financial burdens, both social and fiscal, that knighthood entailed.

Beauchamp was formally appointed guardian to the six-year-old Henry VI in June 1428. He was to teach the little boy 'good manners, letters, languages, nurture and courtesy', and he was licensed to punish him when he behaved badly or refused to complete his lessons. The council also directed that he encourage the King to seek to do good and shun evil by recounting 'examples from history of the grace and prosperity won by virtuous kings and the disasters that overcame unrighteous rulers'. So far the young King had spent most of his boyhood in the Thames Valley, moving between such royal residences as Eltham, Westminster, Windsor and Wallingford. His public appearances were limited to the opening of parliaments, which he first did when rising two, travelling to Westminster and sitting 'with merry cheer' on his mother's lap on a portable throne, and special ceremonies at Christmas, St George's Day and Easter. In 1427 John Somerset, an able civil servant who was also a distinguished physician, was appointed as his tutor. Even at this tender age Henry VI had a reputation for extreme piety, throwing a temper tantrum when his mother wanted to travel on a Sunday. The royal council's decision to give Beauchamp authority over the young King may have been an attempt to get the boy away from his flighty mother. Queen Catherine, 'following her appetite more than her honour', had since 1425 been engaged in a passionate affair, soon a secret marriage, with her Keeper of the Wardrobe, a dashingly handsome squire called Owen ap Maredudd ap Tewdŵr. They had several children by the early 1430s, and their grandson Henry would snatch the throne from Richard III in 1485, take the crown as Henry VII, and found the royal house of Tudor.

Beauchamp did his best to introduce his young charge to manly pursuits. On Henry's seventh birthday in October 1428, he presented him with two 'little coat armours'. Later he gave him a harness trimmed with gold for his pony and a long-bladed sword 'for to learn the king to play in his tender age'. Birthdays, feast days and great festivals like Easter and Christmas were good opportunities to bring his own son Harry and the young King together, and a close friendship later developed between them. Beauchamp had other children in his direct care besides the little King and Harry: Giles, son of Duke John of Brittany, his wards Thomas Berkeley and William Harrington, and Ralph Bracebridge, whose father had died in his service in France.

Beauchamp also provided the King with a personal bodyguard of tried and tested warriors. One of these was John Chetwynd of Tixall, a cousin of Malory on his mother's side. His wife Rose, who had succeeded Joan Astley as Henry VI's nurse, remained in the royal service until February 1429. By then Chetwynd was resident Constable of Tintagel, a craggy peninsula of rock on the north coast of Cornwall, said to be the birthplace of King Arthur. If Thomas Malory had already developed an interest in Arthurian history, he may have journeyed to visit his kinsman and see the scene of Uther's magic-aided seduction of Igraine. The promontory had been fortified by the Romans, but the castle Malory would have seen was the one completely rebuilt in the 1230s for the then Earl of Cornwall and restored by Edward III's son Edward, the Black Prince, in the mid-fourteenth century. Because of its remoteness, state prisoners were occasionally confined there.

Joan of Arc

Within two years of his homecoming, Beauchamp was required to return to France and to base himself at Rouen with a substantial household. Dramatic events had been taking place. The English had recovered well from Montargis. Talbot had swept through Maine, taking Laval in March, and relieving an embattled English garrison in Le Mans, which was being ruthlessly pillaged by La Hire. In July Montagu arrived with reinforcements, captured Meung on the River Loire and then settled down to besiege Orléans itself on 12 October 1428. The stakes were high. Orléans, on the Loire directly south of Paris, was the key to access to Bourges, the Dauphin's stronghold in Touraine, to Auxerre where the Burgundian troops were stationed, and to Guienne and Bordeaux. Charles, Duke of Orléans, its natural defender, had been captured at Agincourt and was still a prisoner in England. The besieged city was held by his half-brother, John, the Bastard of Orléans. The hopes of its inhabitants rose after Montagu's death; a cannonball hit him as he was scanning the city's defences. But as heavier English artillery and more siege castles arrived, French morale sank.

Then rumours began to circulate of a peasant girl of sixteen called Joan who said that she had been sent by God to raise the siege of Orléans and crown the Dauphin at Rheims as King Charles VII. It appeared that the Dauphin had received her, that she had convinced him of the rightness of her cause, and that she had taken to the use of arms with uncanny ease. An army of French prelates and philosophers had examined her and announced that 'in Joan we find no evil but only good, humility, virginity, devotion, honesty and simplicity'.

The Dauphin was married to Marie of Anjou, daughter of the redoubtable Yolande of Aragon who, legend had it, had herself donned armour and ridden against the English at Baugé in 1421. Yolande recognised a kindred spirit in the brave and idealistic peasant girl. Her ladies-in-waiting had physically examined Joan, finding her 'a woman, and a virgin, and a maid'. It was an important test, proof that she had not had intercourse with the Devil, and so was not a sorceress, that her famous 'voices' were those of angels, not devils. It was also Yolande who financed the forces mustered to ride behind Joan to Orléans. Equipped in made-to-measure plate armour in Tours, Joan set off for Blois. She carried a banner of her own design on which was painted an image of Christ in judgement in the clouds of heaven, flanked by angels holding fleur-de-lis. On the way, she asked a man to go and fetch a sword which her 'voices' had told her was buried in a churchyard – an eerie echo of the legend of the boy Arthur pulling a sword from a stone in a churchyard.

Joan's charisma was phenomenal. She presented herself as the epitome of the holiest and purest kind of knighthood, a female Parsifal who commanded respect and reverence from everybody – even her horse. Guy de Laval, a young noble in the royal army, wrote to his mother to describe how he had seen Joan,

> *dressed entirely in white except for her head, a little axe in her hand, mount her horse, a great black charger, which reared up fiercely at the gate of her lodging and would not allow her to mount; and so she said, 'Take him to the cross' before the church down the street. There she mounted him without any resistance, as if he had been tied.*

Wherever she went, crowds pressed to touch the hem of her surcoat, or just the trappings of her newly obedient horse, and many of the best knights in France solemnly declared themselves her champions. Among them were Malory's adversaries in Picardy, Sir Pothon de Saintraille and La Hire, who apparently promised to give up his notoriously blasphemous language and to swear only 'on his baton'.

On 29 April 1429, Joan arrived at the siege of Orléans, to cheers from the French and jeers from the English. Four days later, she was the first to mount a scaling ladder against an English siege castle. Five days after that, having lost control of the city's bridge over the Loire as well as most of their siege castles, and scarcely able to credit the transformation of a demoralised enemy into an elated army united behind a banner raised by a slip of a girl, the English were forced to retreat, leaving behind them their artillery and most of their supplies and baggage. News of the victory and of the 'great miracle' of Joan herself resounded all across Europe. The English declared her to be a devil from Hell. Joan rode straight to the Dauphin, fell on her knees and clutched his legs, pleading with him to ride immediately to Rheims for his coronation. With a rare degree of decision, he agreed to do so, even though his forces would have to dislodge the English from a series of well-fortified positions in order to get there. The success of his progress along the Loire reflected his army's faith in 'La Pucelle'. The greatest victory was the Battle of Patay on 18 June 1429, when the army was led by Joan, La Hire and Sir Pothon de Saintraille. In the eyes of the French, Patay reversed the shame of Agincourt. They claimed that two thousand Englishmen were killed and only three Frenchmen. There were many valuable prisoners, most notably Talbot.

On 17 July 1429, the Dauphin was anointed with the holy oil from the sacred ampoule in the Abbey of Saint-Rémi in Rheims and crowned King Charles VII of France. The renowned *savante* Christine de Pisan came out of her eleven-year retreat from public life to publish a 448-line 'Ditié de Jehanne D'Arc' in praise of the girl-general's achievements, which had, she said, been foretold by Merlin, Bede and the Sibyl. The poet Alain Chartier, who wrote the spine-chilling 'La Belle Dame Sans Mercie', also wrote an exaltation of Joan:

O singular virgin, worthy of all glories, of all praises, of divine honours, you are the greatness of the kingdom, you are the light of the lily, you are the brilliance, you are the glory, not only of the French, but also of all Christians.

Next Joan sent a letter to the Duke of Burgundy, calling on him to make peace with the King of France so that they could defeat the English and lead a European crusade against the Turks. In this plea, and in all of her actions, Joan showed herself deeply committed to chivalric values. All through her astonishingly successful year of campaigning, she insisted on the correct rituals of respect to downfallen enemies, strict observance of holy days and regular offerings of prayers to the God with whom her angelic voices kept her so closely in touch. Her vision was uncannily like Malory's: an honourable world in which the swords of mighty and honourable knights were used in the defence of the Christian faith, the poor and the weak.

The rallying of the French behind an anointed king, emboldened and inspired by a god-sent champion, made it imperative to assert the rights of the English King of France both symbolically and by force. Although Henry VI was only eight years old, plans were made for a double coronation – one in England and one in France. This would herald a new campaign 'for the safety, defence and good governance and rule of our kingdom of France and the recovery of our rights there'. Commitment to maintaining the English conquests in France was still whole-hearted: loans and parliamentary grants to the tune of £120,000 were raised to equip and pay for troops. However, Henry VI's London coronation on 5 November 1429 was a wan affair in comparison with those of Henry IV and Henry V. For fear of the boy seeing drunkards in the streets, wine was handed out in cups instead of running in the city's fountains, and instead of a tournament a heretic was burned at the stake in Smithfield.

The arrival of the English court in France was intended to dazzle the French by an awesome display of majesty. The royal household alone numbered three hundred; it was escorted by England's greatest prelates led by Beaufort, now Cardinal of England as well as Bishop of Winchester, eight dukes and earls and thousands of men-at-arms. Among them was Thomas Malory's cousin Sir William Malory of Papworth St Agnes, Cambridgeshire, who took out letters of protection on 24 May 1430 because he was going overseas to Calais for two years with Thomas, Lord Roos. Some of the musters crossed from Southampton to Harfleur, others from Sandwich to Calais, where temporary houses had to be built for them.

Beauchamp and his household, including, we will again assume, Thomas Malory, crossed to Calais on 23 April, St George's Day. This time the Earl was accompanied by the Countess Isobel and their children, six-year-old Harry and four-year-old Anne. The Beauchamps rode straight on to Rouen to prepare quarters there for the King in its great thirteenth-century castle, Bouvreuil. Beauchamp's daughter by his first marriage, Margaret, Lady Talbot, was already resident in Bouvreuil. She was busily negotiating the ransom or exchange of her husband Sir John Talbot. But the King and his household would remain at Calais, waiting for the military situation to improve.

Then came proof positive that God was an Englishman. On 23 May 1430 Joan of Arc was captured. She had been defending her fleeing army's rearguard after a risky surprise attack against the Burgundians at Margny, near Compiègne. 'The Maid', a contemporary chronicler tells us,

> *going beyond the nature of womankind, performed a great feat and took much pain to save her company from loss, staying behind like a chief and like the most valiant member of the flock . . . An archer, a stiff and very harsh man, angry that a woman of whom one had heard so much should have surpassed so many valiant men . . . laid hold of her from the side by her cloth-of-gold doublet and pulled her from her horse flat upon the ground . . . The Burgundians and English partisans were very joyous, more than if they had taken five hundred combatants, for they did not dread or fear either captains or any other war chief as much as they had up to that day this maid.*

In July, Henry VI and his household made the journey to Rouen under heavy escort. In November, after seven months of negotiating for the best price he could get, Duke Philip of Burgundy sold Joan to the English for 10,000 *livres tournois* (about £2,500). The French King, Charles VII, swayed by advice from courtiers who had deeply resented the influence and success of the peasant girl, signally failed her. He did not offer to ransom her from Burgundy, nor, after the English had acquired her, did he suggest an exchange of Joan for Talbot.

Joan was taken to Rouen, arriving on Christmas Eve, 1430. She was imprisoned in one of the wall towers of Bouvreuil, hobbled with leg irons in a dark cell, guarded by five frequently abusive common soldiers and spied upon constantly during the five long months of her trial. Only her gaolers and inquisitors know the whole truth about Joan's treatment, but if Malory was in Beauchamp's household, quartered in the very castle in which she was imprisoned, he would have known more about it than most. Beauchamp did send his own physician to care for Joan when she fell ill but this was not necessarily the courtesy he was famed for; he was as determined as any of the English commanders that she should be tried – and found guilty. A chronicler records that Beauchamp visited Joan in her cell on Sunday 13 May with several other English nobles and two Burgundian bishops. She told them fiercely that her 'god-damned' English guards were abusing her. One of the English nobles, Humphrey Stafford, Earl of Stafford and later Duke of Buckingham, was so enraged that he began to draw his dagger out of its scabbard, intending to stab her with it, but Beauchamp grabbed his arm and stopped him. Beauchamp then ordered the guards to be changed.

The incident is the more interesting because twenty years later Buckingham, by then notorious for his harsh and vindictive disposition, was not only the most powerful noble in England but Thomas Malory's deadly enemy. The seeds of their conflict could have been laid here in Rouen when an idealistic young squire saw a loutish peer raise his weapon against a helpless girl who had shown as much prowess in battle as resolute heroines of romance like Bradamant and Alice La Beale Pilgrim. Worse may have happened: one eyewitness,

Martin Ladvenu, later testified that 'he had heard it from Joan's own mouth that an English lord entered her cell and tried to take her by force'. His purpose would have been political – the English were eager to prove that Joan was no virgin. On 30 May 1431, Joan was led into the market square where she was burned in front of a mass of English soldiery. Her executioner Maugier Leparmentier, who afterwards regarded himself as damned because he had burned a holy woman, said she called on Jesus continuously. Another eyewitness, Isambart de Pierre, recorded that

> *The words she uttered were so devout, pious, and Christian that all who watched her – and they were a great multitude – wept warm tears. Even the Cardinal of England [Beaufort] and several other Englishmen were constrained to weep and were moved to compassion.*

An English soldier who had been bringing more fuel to the fire 'stood struck in stupor as though in an ecstasy and had to be led to a tavern so that with the help of some drink he could regain his strength . . . for he had himself seen [he said], at the moment that Joan gave up her spirit, a white dove emerge from her and take flight.'

The official English line was that Joan was a sorceress and a witch. But Malory may have been more inclined to agree with William Caxton, who clearly thought that Joan should have been treated honourably, as a captured enemy captain and prisoner of war, and a ransom negotiated. 'This maid rode like a man, and was a valiant captain,' he wrote in his continuation of the history of Britain known as the *Polychronicon*. Taken in the field with many other captains,

> *she was put in prison, and there she was judged by the law to be burnt. And then she said she was with child, whereby she was respited a while; but in conclusion it was found that she was not with child, and then she was burnt in Rouen. And the other captains were put to ransom, and treated as men of war been accustomed.*

Sir Pothon de Saintraille

The most notable of the other captured captains was Sir Pothon de Saintraille. After Joan's death, the English went on the offensive, laying siege to Louviers in June 1431. Their aim was to win back the road to Rheims and crown their own King in France's holiest church. Henry VI himself remained safe in Bouvreuil Castle. But early in August news came that an attempt on Rouen itself was to be made by Saintraille. Beauchamp mustered men to make a pre-emptive counter-attack. His seven-year-old son Harry Beauchamp rode with him, in command, officially at least, of his own troop. Malory, who was later listed among young Harry's retainers, could already have been at his side, perhaps detailed to draw the boy aside during the actual battle. He would have been relieved to be in a campaign against a 'noble knight of worship', rather than witnessing the trial and execution of a witch with a disconcerting resemblance to a martyred saint.

When the English met Saintraille's forces near Beauvais on 11 August, they found that the French also had a juvenile lead: a young shepherd boy from the Cevennes whom Charles VII's advisers had insisted would be every bit as effective an inspiration as Joan of Arc. They were wrong. The French troops were scattered and both Saintraille and the shepherd boy were captured. Harry Beauchamp must have ridden back to Rouen with exultation in his heart. Saintraille was as prestigious a captive for the English as Talbot had been for the French. Saintraille received very different treatment from Joan of Arc. Although he too was imprisoned in Bouvreuil Castle, he lived in comfortable quarters and was treated with the gallant courtesy normally accorded to well-born prisoners of war. The day after he was captured, he dined at Warwick's table beside John of Luxembourg and the young Henry VI as well as the Beauchamps. At the head of the table, Margaret Talbot, well aware that Saintraille would be a highly suitable exchange for her husband, doubtless smiled at him graciously. As they dined, the corpse of the shepherd boy floated down the Seine. He had been hamstrung, sewn alive into an oxhide and thrown into the river.

English confidence in the success of their new offensive was reflected in the fact that soldiers serving in France could once more visit England without special permission from the autumn of 1431. Soon afterwards, there are records of both Thomas Malory and Thomas Pulteney in England. Pulteney is recorded at Misterton during the Michaelmas law term (9 October–28 November) and Thomas Malory witnessed a settlement by the Cheyne family, several of whose menfolk fought in France, of the manors of Quainton and Overbury in Great Missenden, Buckinghamshire on 20 September 1431.

Saintraille was escorted to Dieppe on 14 November, and stayed there for over a month while Beauchamp oversaw the coronation of the English King in Paris. Although Louviers had fallen on 28 October, Rheims was still deemed too risky to approach. Beauchamp, his countess and a retinue of fifty-three courtiers took Henry VI up the Seine to Paris in a sumptuous barge lent by the Duke of Bedford. The journey, shrouded in secrecy, took seven days. The royal entourage stayed in the Palais Royal while tailors and furriers made child-sized coronation robes. On 16 December Henry was crowned Henry II of France in the cathedral of Notre-Dame by Cardinal Beaufort. Afterwards he rode jauntily through the streets on a little white hackney under a canopy of blue cloth embroidered with golden fleur-de-lis. There were flamboyant pageants and mimes, but Paris had been close to famine only weeks earlier, and only cold meats were provided for the feasting. Jousting took place after the ceremony, but was judged feeble by one contemporary French (so perhaps biased) diarist. 'Any inhabitant of the city would have spent more to marry his daughter than the English have spent to crown their king,' he grumbled. Despite a vote of loyalty from the Paris Parlement, the mood of the city was unfriendly and the royal party returned to Rouen for Christmas. Henry VI and his household set off for Dieppe in the second week of January 1432, then travelled to Calais.

The chance survival of a book of Beauchamp's household accounts for 1431/2 reveals that four horses were acquired in Dieppe for Saintraille, his esquire and two valets and that they rode to meet Beauchamp at Abbeville on 17 January. They joined the royal party at Calais on 23 January, and embarked with them for Dover, which they reached on about 9 February. The Countess of Warwick visited Canterbury to give thanks in the cathedral for their safe return, then headed for the family's manor at Walthamstow. Beauchamp and Henry VI took carriages to Gravesend, where they boarded barges to sail up the Thames to London. The boy King made a formal entry into the city on 21 February, processing to St Paul's through streets filled with cheering crowds and splendid pageants. Beauchamp stayed at Warwick Inn for royal council meetings, then joined his wife for the journey by river and road to Warwickshire with Saintraille.

Negotiations soon began for an exchange between Saintraille and Talbot. There are records of a safeguard for Saintraille's servants to travel to France on 28 May 1432 'with regard to the liberation of Lord Talbot'. On 22 July 1432, a similar safeguard was issued for Saintraille himself to travel on parole to France with his servant Bernard de Genestaille in quest of his ransom. A man of his word, he soon returned to England, and was finally exchanged early in July 1433 for Lord Talbot and Lord Scales, who had also been captured at Patay.

In all, Saintraille stayed in England for the best part of eighteen months. What did he do to pass the time? No doubt he enjoyed the tournaments regularly held at Smithfield and Kenilworth. He may also have lingered in Beauchamp's library, nostalgically reading French romances. But he could have brought books of his own. Noblemen often had a collection of their favourite writings assembled in one volume so that they could enjoy reading, or being read to, on their travels. We know that both Henry V and the Duke of Bedford took books with them on campaign. Aware that he would have a good deal of time to while away, Sir Pothon could well have brought a contemporary Armagnac version of a *Lancelot* or a *Tristram* in the baggage carried for him by his squire and his two pages.

At some point in his life Saintraille won the respect of Thomas Malory. For in what seems to be a tribute, or just possibly a veiled thank-you for the loan of a *Tristram*, his name is twice introduced into the *Morte*. The first comes at a particularly exciting point in Sir Tristram's adventures. Tristram has been found 'naked abed' with Isolde and captured: 'And then by the assent of King Mark, and of Sir Andred, and of some of the barons, Sir Tristram was led unto a chapel that stood upon the sea rocks, there for to take his judgement'. Fury at the treachery of the knight who captured him gives Tristram the strength to wrench himself free and kill ten knights single-handed. The crowd outside the chapel surges forward. Tristram 'remembered he was naked, [fastened] the chapel door, and brake the bars of a window, and so he leapt out and fell upon the crags in the sea'. The superhero survives the fall, and three loyal knights race down to rescue him. In all known sources except for Malory their names are given as Governail, Sir Lambegus and Nicorant le Pauvre. But Malory substitutes the name 'Sentraille de Lushon' for Nicorant. Lushon is a small fief in south-west France which formed part of Saintraille's estates. Later in the *Morte Darthur*, when Malory lists the knights who try to heal Sir Urry's wound, he appears again: 'Then came Sir Hebes, Sir Morganoure, *Sir Sentraille* [my italics], sir Suppinabiles, Sir Belliance Belyaunce . . .'

Malory changes names and introduces new characters on numerous occasions in the *Morte*. There is always the possibility that he simply copied them from a source that has not survived. But Saintraille was his contemporary. He was also exactly the sort of knight that Malory most admired and, at this point at least, lived in close proximity to him in Warwickshire. Saintraille's long sojourn in England is the most likely time for a friendship to have developed between them; Malory may even have had charge of the prisoner. Such a positive tribute to a living chivalric hero suggests that there are other personal references in Malory's tales. He is certainly fond of introducing real place-names (Bamborough, Kingston, Guildford, Arundel, Winchester, and many others) into them. Given the frequency with which his contemporary, the courtier poet Sir Richard Roos, contrived to insert cryptic references to his friends and enemies into his poetry, there may be many other clues to Malory's acquaintances to be unearthed.

Six Weddings and Two Funerals

Beauchamp remained in England for five years in all. He was still officially guardian of Henry VI, but he was now spending more time on his own affairs. He did attend the Parliaments of 1433 and 1435, but his name is only occasionally listed among those present at council meetings. There are no records of Thomas Malory between 1431 and 1439, but his connections with the Beauchamps before and after these dates make it reasonable to imagine that for the first four of them Malory also stayed in England, in service to the family in Warwickshire and London. The records of the Earl's annuitants are scanty, but there are many examples of men who remained in his service after having fought for him in the French wars. Between a third and a quarter of Beauchamp's income was spent on maintaining local affinities, complex webs of favours and obligations which tied neighbours to him. Such measures were essential at a time when rights to property were constantly being challenged, either by devious legal pleadings or by the strong-arm men of a rival lord simply taking possession. Some nobles were notorious for using force to get their way, but there were remarkably few complaints against the Beauchamps. That is not to say that Sir Richard did not have enemies. One of the most aggressive, described as a 'second Jezebel' by the chronicler Adam of Usk, was his own aunt Joan, Lady Abergavenny, who disputed his possession of various lands. In 1431, Malory's father John and his uncle Simon both sat on a jury to try Joan on a charge of conspiring to assault and wound a number of men from Fillongley and Birmingham.

Thomas's father John Malory died some time between 4 December 1433, when he sealed an agreement with some Gosford tenants, and 8 June 1434, when Philippa Malory, described as his widow, was party to a marriage contract between her daughter Isobel and Edward, son of Sir Edward Doddingselles of Long Itchington, Warwickshire. Sir Edward had fought in France in Henry V's time, and was distinguished enough to be among the men of standing in the county who were required to take an oath to keep the peace in 1434. His son was

still active in France; the marriage may have been delayed by his
absence overseas – or even by John Malory's objection to it. It certainly
took place rather soon after his death. Thomas's other two sisters,
Philippa and Helen, also found husbands. Philippa, named after her
mother, had married Eustace Burneby of Watford, Northamptonshire,
by 1429. The Burnebys, whose lands bordered on Winwick, were good
family friends: John Malory witnessed a charter for Eustace's father
George Burneby in 1425, and Eustace himself was a witness to the
last surviving record of John Malory, an assignment of three rents
'of twelve pence and three capons' which he made to his Cosford
tenants on 4 December 1433. Thomas's sister Helen is recorded as the
wife of Robert Vincent of Swinford, a younger son of Richard Vincent
of Barnake, Northamptonshire, by 1440. Robert was Clerk of the
Kitchens at Warwick Castle by the early 1450s, but he may have been
there as early as 1441, when he mortgaged his Swinford manor to
Malory. Clerk of the Kitchens was a grander job than it sounds today,
one for an older man with considerable experience of how a great
household was run and a good head for figures. Soldier, squire and
household officer: all sound like respectable husbands.

After his father's death, or possibly earlier, Thomas may have
rented out the cramped and old-fashioned moated manor house at
Shawell and lived in greater style at Winwick, which was very close
to Eustace Burneby's seat at Watford. Lady Philippa remained at
Newbold Revel: she was assessed in 1436 as holding land worth £60
a year in Warwickshire. If we make the conservative guess that this
sum was the value of both Newbold Revel and the three outlying
manors of Pailton, Stretton-under-Fosse and Easenhall, it sounds like
the usual widow's dower of a third of a husband's estates. She may
also have had other assets that were protected from feudal obligations
by enfeoffment.

The Earl of Warwick's main preoccupation at this time was his
plan to marry his two children Harry and Anne to another aristocratic
brother and sister, Richard and Cecily Neville, the oldest children of
Richard Neville, Earl of Salisbury, son of the Earl of Westmorland.
The marriages would forge a double dynastic link between their
respective estates. Those of the Beauchamps were mainly in the west

and central Midlands; those of the Nevilles mainly in the north. That the Nevilles stood to gain far more from the match than the Beauchamps was reflected in the £3,000 marriage portion paid by Richard Neville for the hand of Harry Beauchamp for his daughter. Papal dispensations were required for such a match between siblings, and these were received in 1434; the actual weddings did not take place until the summer of 1436. The marriages would have a profound effect on Malory's future and, indeed, on that of England. However, in 1434 Malory was given the opportunity of embarking on a totally new adventure.

Defending Christendom

25 January 1435: Licence, by advice of the council, for Robert Malory, Prior of the Hospital of St John of Jerusalem in England, to leave the realm to fight the Sultan and his power on the summons of the master and convent of Rhodes with his brethren, household and servants

Calendar of Patent Rolls, 1435

In 1432 Thomas Malory's uncle, Sir Robert Malory, became head of the English-speaking branch, or 'langue', of the Knights Hospitallers. This prestigious office meant that he sat above all lay barons in Parliament, and was a member of the royal council; its records frequently note the presence of the 'Prior of St John'. Three priors were made Treasurers of England; their resources made them well-suited to such a position. At this time the Hospitallers were an immensely wealthy supranational organisation. Established, like the Knights Templar, during the crusading era to protect and care for pilgrims to Jerusalem, their potent military machine was financed by their extensive European estates – donated to the Order by wealthy Christians eager to win merit by supporting the continuation of the battle against the infidel. Originally based in Jerusalem itself, thanks to a generous gift of lands from the crusading hero Geoffrey of Boulogne, who conquered the city in 1099, the Hospitallers had been forced to retreat from the Levant in 1292 after the fall of Acre. By 1312 they had established themselves on Rhodes. From this strategically situated and massively fortified island citadel, they continued to protect pilgrims travelling to the Holy Land, to defend Christendom from Islamic attack, and to make lightning strikes on Turkey and Egypt. Their small but savagely effective navy, equipped with the fastest galleys afloat, became renowned. In the fifteenth century Rhodes was a busy mercantile entrepôt between East and West where Turks and Christians did business to their mutual profit, except in times of outright war.

By the 1430s there were seven langues: those of Germany, England, Spain, Italy, France, Provence and Auvergne. The English langue had responsibility for Ireland and Scotland, the Spanish for Portugal and Navarre, and the German for Scandinavia and Bohemia. Each langue was headed by a 'pilier', who lived in the langue's 'auberge' or inn in Rhodes and held *ex officio* one of the great offices of the Order. The head of the English langue was the 'Turcopilier', and he was in charge of the Order's light cavalry and responsible for the island's coastal defences. Fighting men as well as goods and funds were channelled to Rhodes from the langues' European estates. These were managed by the priors of the Order, who were supposed to go to Rhodes every five years or so to attend the Chapter-General, the Order's parliament. As a religious order, Hospitallers were subject only to the Pope, and even he usually confirmed decisions made by the Grand Master of the Order, who was elected for life and usually resided in Rhodes. The numbers of knights in residence in Rhodes at any one time fluctuated; in the 1430s there were between two and three hundred, a relatively low figure.

When he was appointed head of the English langue, Sir Robert Malory was confirmed in the possession of the commanderies of Cressing in Essex and Sandford in Oxfordshire, as well as of Balsall with Grafton, in Warwickshire. For the next three years he lived in grand style in the palatial Priory of the Order of St John at Clerkenwell, outside the city walls. Donated to the Hospitallers early in the twelfth century, Clerkenwell was one of the most extensive and luxuriously appointed houses in London, a miniature world in its own right. Five acres of gardens stretched from its windows down to the little River Wells. Around its great and small courts there were separate lodgings for the Turcopilier and the sub-Prior, the resident brethren and corrodians (pensioners who had contributed land or money to the Order), and guests, as well as a hospital, woodhouse, a slaughterhouse, a plumber's house, a laundry, and a counting (accounting) house. To the west, the Hospitallers' private deer park of St John's Wood stretched from Paddington to Hampstead; they also held the nearby Thames-side manors of Hampton Court and Sutton-at-Hone.

Like any great medieval household, the Priory had a butler, a steward, a gatekeeper, a cook, a baker, a woodreeve, squires, valets and horse-boys, a head stableman, a brewer, a cellarer, a washerwoman, a swineherd, an oxherd, a shepherd and a carter, and various pages and boys to stand in attendance and run errands. All these dependants were exempt from civil jurisdiction and subject only to the Hospitaller courts, as were the corrodians, the relatives of a Hospitaller and the tenants of his estates. So too were confraters – 'half-brothers' (who did not have to be celibate) – who were awarded their privileged status on merit or because of contributions they had made to the Order.

In 1434 Sir Robert Malory received an urgent message from Rhodes. The Hospitallers' efficient intelligence service had discovered that the Sultan of Egypt and the Sultan of Turkey were planning a potentially devastating joint attack on Rhodes. The Grand Master immediately sent envoys to all eight heads of the European divisions of the Hospitallers, asking them each to bring twenty-five fighting men to defend the island. Such a chivalric service in the cause of Christianity would undoubtedly have had a strong appeal for Sir Robert's nephew, Thomas. The defence of Rhodes was as pious an undertaking as the Knights of the Round Table's quest for the Holy Grail. There is no proof that Thomas Malory was among the knights and squires who set out with Sir Robert for Rhodes at the end of January 1435, but it would have been a natural adventure for a Malory of his age and talents to undertake. English Hospitaller knights were never a large group, and the vocation was more favoured in some families than others – those who valued prowess, spirituality and renown. A 'frater' or 'brother' knight had to be 'strong, well-formed and sound in limb' and be able to prove that he was, as Malory declares any knight of the Round Table should be, 'of gentle strain on both father's side and mother's side'. But since a Hospitaller knight took vows of celibacy and undertook to leave most, if not all, of his possessions to the Order on his death, full members of the Order were rarely oldest sons and tended to be 'gentlemen-of-arms' rather than nobles.

The Malory family's connections with the Order, direct and through marriage, were remarkably numerous, both before, during and after Sir Thomas's lifetime. Malorys granted lands to the Hospitallers at Swinford in 1279. They held their remaining lands there of the Knights, specifically of the commandery of Dingley, Northamptonshire. The Revels also gave lands at Swinford to a small commandery of the Order there in 1184, and lands at Buckby to it a little later. One of the most able and energetic of thirteenth-century Grand Masters of the Order was Hugh Revel, the only Englishman to head the whole medieval Order. Castellan of Krak des Chevaliers, and Grand Commander, Hugh became Master in 1258. He was Sir Thomas Malory's great-great-great-grand-uncle. A John Malory held the Yorkshire commandery of Newland in 1338.

In Malory's lifetime, Margaret Charnells, born Margaret Grendon, and the wife of Thomas Malory of Bramcote, was probably the niece of Walter Grendon, head of the English Hospitallers for twenty-one years from 1396 to 1417. Thomas's uncle, Simon Malory, married Margaret Sutton of Chilverscoton. The Suttons had Hospitaller traditions and, like Swinford, Chilverscoton was held of the Order. Simon Malory ended up at Clerkenwell and was buried there, perhaps a confrater, almost certainly a corrodian. A John Malory, probably Simon's or even Thomas's son, was a Knight Hospitaller by the early 1440s. He was in Rhodes during the Mameluke siege of 1444 and was there again when he was granted the commanderies of Dingley and of Battisford, Suffolk, on 21 January 1469. In 1474 he was one of the four senior knights of the Order who presented the new Prior of England Robert Multon to Edward IV, and he was buried in the Priory church. Finally, descendants of the two daughters and co-heirs of Sir Thomas's grandson Nicholas Malory, who both married Caves of Stanford, near Swinford, later became Hospitallers.

Moreover, in 1434, when the urgent demand for help arrived from the Grand Master, the English langue did not have twenty-five militarily fit Hospitaller knights to send. Most of the younger members of the Order were already in Rhodes, where the English contingent numbered about twenty. Sir William Langstrother, Commander of Quenington, Sir Robert Botill, Commander of Melchbourne and Anstey, and Sir Hugh Middleton, Commander of Beverley, signed up straight away for the journey. Each will have persuaded confraters, friends, relatives, tenants and servants to join them. The Scottish Hospitaller Sir Andrew Meldrum, Bailiff of Torpichen, brought six such companions. Two Scropes of Bolton – John and his son Henry – went with the expedition as Henry VI's ambassadors. The Scrope family's long association with the Order makes it likely that they were confraters. If Sir Robert was casting about for fighting men to make up his numbers, it would be natural to invite his nephew Thomas, tried and tested in the French wars and with a mind-set that was deeply sympathetic to the Hospitaller cause, to join the expedition. The Order, richer in assets than personnel, frequently paid suitable men-at-arms to fight for it. Like the Scropes, Thomas may have been a confrater of the Order; it was after all his overlord at Swinford.

A recurring theme of early medieval romances is that of knights joining either the Templars or the Hospitallers – rather as the heroes of P. C. Wren's *Beau Geste* novels joined the French Foreign Legion – either because they were hopelessly enamoured of an unattainable lady-love, or because they felt the need to atone for a crime or sin of some kind. What Malory had seen and experienced in France – the deaths in battle of brothers-in-arms, the rapine and plunder of conquering troops, and last but perhaps not least the martyrdom of Joan of Arc – could have left him with a desire to atone for his own sins and those of his compatriots. He may hint at such a state of mind when he makes Sir Lancelot fail to achieve the Grail, and humbly say, with infinite regret, 'I know well I was never the best.' Rallying to the defence of Rhodes had as much spiritual value as going on crusade, and Malory was old enough to have known about Henry V's deathbed regrets at the slaughter of his French wars, his dying regret that he had never reached Jerusalem, and his fears for his immortal soul.

A journey by Malory to Rhodes would explain several curious features of the *Morte Darthur*. There are remarkably accurate details about routes across Europe and evidence of an unusually extensive knowledge of European romantic literature. Malory refers to the threat of heathen invasion and the merits of crusades much more often than his sources do. He also places more emphasis on the loyalty, high ideals and religious seriousness of the Round Table knights, and of the international nature of their brotherhood. He plays down the elaborate digressions on courtly love in the French versions but indulges himself in long descriptions of elaborate cere-monies (ritual feasts were a notable feature of the Order's calendar), as well as giving lengthy blow-by-blow accounts of heroic Christian knights defeating infidel paladins. In 'The Tale of King Arthur', he writes of 40,000 Saracens invading the lands of the kings who rebel against Arthur, burning and slaying 'without mercy' and laying siege to castles and making 'great destruction'. He changes the incident in which Tristram seems to refuse a papal summons to go on crusade. In his version, Tristram rejects the summons (actually sent by his wicked uncle, King Mark) because he knows it is a false one *before* it arrives, rather than afterwards, as his source had it.

Like the Knights of Rhodes serving their six-month stint on the galleys, Lancelot and Galahad 'dwelled within [a] ship half a year, and served God daily and nightly with all their power; and often they arrived in isles far from folk, where there repaired none but wild beasts, and there they found many strange adventures and perilous'. It is also intriguing that Malory drops the 'royals of Rhodes' from a list of the forces of the villainous Emperor Lucius that is otherwise identical to his main source, the English alliterative poem *Morte Arthure*. Dropped too is a reference to a 'Reynald of the Rhodes' whoring in Prussia, a scurrilous slant on the support given by the Hospitallers to the Teutonic Knights in the second half of the four-teenth century.

Finally, on the last page of his book, Malory dramatically alters the usual downbeat final account of 'the dolorous death and departing' of King Arthur by telling us that the survivors of the tragedy, Lancelot's kinsmen Sir Bors, Sir Ector, Sir Blamore and Sir Bleoberis, did not just settle down in their countries as hermits. Instead, they 'went into the Holy Land thereas Jesu Christ was quick and dead, and anon as they had established lands there [as] Lancelot commanded them for to do, ere he passed out of this world. These four knights did many battles upon the miscreants or Turks. And there they died upon a Good Friday for God's sake.' The fact that Malory knew the Turks had taken control of Palestine from the Mamelukes reveals that he was well-informed of the current state of affairs in the Levant.

The year 1435 was, moreover, a good one for an adventurous man to leave England. A truce, perhaps even a peace, was being negotiated with France, and the Earl of Warwick, Richard Beauchamp, now in his fifties, had every reason to hope that his campaigning days were over. Such an absence fits with the records: there is no mention of Thomas Malory in England while the expedition was away, but in 1439, six weeks after a Genoese ship loaded to the gunnels with exotic luxuries acquired in Rhodes by Sir Robert Malory and his companions dropped anchor at Sandwich, Thomas Malory of Newbold Revel witnessed a contract for a Warwickshire cousin, Sir Philip Chetwynd. So although the idea that Thomas Malory accompanied his uncle to Rhodes is pure speculation, there are good reasons for believing that he did so: what follows is a reconstruction of his imagined journey.

Voyage to Rhodes

The summons sent from Rhodes in 1434 by Antonio de Fluvian, Grand Master of the Knights Hospitallers, explained to the European Priors that two formidable enemies were threatening the island. One was the Turkish Sultan Murat II, the other the Mameluke ruler of Egypt, Sultan al Mazer el Dayer. Fluvian asked each of the langues to send the reinforcements to Rhodes by March 1435. As soon as his fellow Hospitaller knights and their entourages had arrived, Sir Robert Malory, now at least fifty years old, prepared to gird himself for war. The royal council provided Sir Robert with a licence to travel on 25 January 1435. It also authorised him to take gold and silver coins and plate with him. Normally this was forbidden, but the council permitted

> *gold and silver coined to the sum of 100 marks sterling, three basins, three ewers, four pots, three silver saucers with covers, three dozen silver cups, eight with covers, four chargers of silver, eight platters of silver and two dozen silver spoons, one silver chalice, one little bell for mass and two phials of silver and other suitable equipment.*

Some of this bullion and plate was for Sir Robert's personal use, but most of it will have been destined for the use of the English langue in Rhodes. Other monies were transferred by letters of exchange. The English Hospitallers favoured the great Florentine banking house of Alberti, which had a branch in London.

Although it was very early in the year for travel, there were attractions to heading south immediately. The winter of 1434–5 was so cold that the Thames froze over. If Sir Robert had succeeded in raising twenty-five fully armed men, each with one or two servants, the cortège may have numbered around seventy. They would have taken arms with them, and horses, four for each knight and two for each servant. Their route ran along Watling Street (now the A2) to Rochester, where Sir Robert presented a candidate to the living of Burgham on 11 February. The chances are that they later paused at Canterbury Cathedral to ask a blessing of St Thomas Becket, whose skull, brains and tonsure were gruesomely exhibited in gilded and bejewelled reliquaries. Having waited at Sandwich until the weather was suitable, they crossed to Calais.

Earlier crusaders headed directly south to the commandery of St Gilles, close to Marseilles, a favourite embarkation point for Hospitallers travelling to Rhodes, but it was safer in these troubled times to take the route which Malory describes the Emperor Lucius's messengers using: 'They took the water and passed into Flanders, Almayn [Germany], and after that over the great mountain that hight [is called] Godarde, and so after through Lombardy and through Tuscany.' This is exactly the route shown in an itinerary tucked into a book owned by an English Hospitaller in the 1380s. The distances between Calais and Bruges, Bruges and Venice and Venice and Rhodes are supplied. Including the ninety-five miles from London to Calais, and the many detours large and small, the journey by land and water was at least 1,800 miles.

How fast did they travel? Express messengers riding long days and frequently changing horses could cover a hundred miles a day. Sir Robert's party were mounted but impeded by substantial amounts of luggage, so they would not have averaged much more than thirty miles a day. Overnight or longer stops could be made at such German Hospitaller priories as Wesel, Cologne, Strasbourg, Heitersheim and Kusnacht. All were wealthy establishments, with excellent libraries, but Heitersheim was especially palatial. It had just been rebuilt as the seat for the Prior of Germany.

Progress through the Alps was even slower. In *The Medieval Traveller*, Norbert Ohler estimates a mere two to three miles a day, 'depending on the weather, the time of year and the traveller's constitution'. Once over the St-Gotthard Pass they headed for Milan, then Asti, the seat of the Prior of Lombardy, and then either Venice or Genoa, where they commissioned ships to take them to Rhodes. Stops during the voyage to top up supplies of food and water were frequent. The Genoese route took them past the Italian Hospitaller bases of Pisa, Messina on Sicily's north-eastern tip, and perhaps Taranto. Speed of sailing depended on fair winds, but the ships were equipped with oars as well as sails. Faced with too relentless a calm, travellers transferred to galleys as they got closer to Rhodes.

Hospitallers from other langues probably joined forces with the English contingent *en route*; it was always safer to travel in company. A favourite way of passing time on journeys was to exchange stories. These weeks spent with companions from different parts of Europe would explain Malory's extensive knowledge of history, legend and romance. One of the Irish brother knights might have recounted a version of the old thirteenth-century French verse romance of 'Sone de Nausay', which is set in the Templars' house in Ireland. 'I cannot tell you whether they played together or whether he talked of love, but they did not make much noise', runs one wry line from it; it closely resembles Malory's gallantly non-committal account of what

Lancelot and Guinevere did when alone: 'And whether they were abed or at other manner of disports, me list not hereof make no mention, for love that time was not as it is now-a-days'.

Sir Robert would have told his nephew a good deal about the splendours of the headquarters of the Order, but nothing can prepare the first-time visitor for its reality: the sheer drama of the city's position on the north-eastern tip of the legendary 'island of roses', and the cosmopolitan bustle of its harbour and streets. Memories of Malory's first sight of Rhodes may be enshrined in his description of the arrival of Beaumains and Dame Linnet at the castle of the Red Knight of the Red Lands:

> And they came to a fair castle . . . with full warlike walls; and there were lodged many great lords nigh the walls; and there was great noise of minstrelsy; and the sea beat upon the one side of the walls, where were many ships and mariners' noise with 'hale and how'.

Rhodes is almost invariably bathed in sunlight, unlike the coast of Turkey which frowns across at it from underneath a thick cap of clouds. The city's massive walls, built out of light and easily workable tufa rock, still exist, over thirty feet thick in places. From the sea, Rhodes was impregnable. On one side of the harbour was a long fortified mole, on which stood a row of windmills that also offered vantage points for archers. On the other side a shorter mole jutted out, ending in the 180-foot-high Naillac Tower. Deep inside was a huge windlass that raised a gigantic iron chain from the seabed which closed the harbour mouth when enemies approached.

The harbour was crowded with shipping – the Hospitallers' own galleys, tubby Greek merchant coggs, gun-carrying European carracks, and graceful lateen-rigged Arab dhows. Rhodes was an entrepôt between East and West, and an infinite variety of merchandise passed through it: saffron, beeswax, pepper, caviar, wheat, olives, soap, woollens, linen and silk fabrics, carpets, pottery, oil, wine, hides, sugar and slaves. Florentine, Venetian and French merchants and bankers all had outposts in the city, and unless there was an imminent threat of war, Turkish merchants were as free to go about their business as Christian ones.

Rhodes has carefully preserved its medieval atmosphere within the wide, towering walls of the original city. The street plan is little changed, and as you wander among its massive but elegant stone buildings, it is easy to imagine the arrival of the Malorys' party, and to follow their probable route. At the dockside to welcome them was the English turcopilier, Sir Thomas Lancelevec. Leaving their servants to unload the ships, the travellers walked through the heavily fortified harbour gate, past the Admiralty and the Hospital, and entered the church of Our Lady of the Castle to offer thanks to God for their safe arrival. Next door to the church was Inn of the English, which Sir Robert had seen begun on his last visit. It was still not finished in 1435, but the new donations Sir Robert had raised would hasten its completion. Coats of arms on the plaque on the façade of the building identify it as the headquarters of the English knights. In the first row, the royal arms of England are carved. Next to them is the escutcheon of the Malorys of Newbold Revel (*ermine, a chevron engrailed gules*). The two shields below show the arms of two later Priors of England, Sir John Weston (1476–89) and Sir John Kendall (1489–1501). The arrangement of the arms suggests that Sir Robert was regarded as the moving spirit in the construction of the building, and made substantial contributions to its cost. It is not unlikely that Thomas, newly come into his inheritance, and perhaps with handsome profits from his war service in France, did the same.

Most of the inns of the other langues open off the steep central spine road still known as the Street of the Knights. It leads from the church of Our Lady of the Castle up to the Palace of the Grand Master and the great church of St John, the spiritual heart of the Order. The street is barer today than it was then; only the stone supports for the balconies that once fronted the houses remain, and there is no longer a forest of banners signalling which knights were at home in the various inns. But the inns themselves are still there, and you can glimpse their courtyards through arched gateways. On the left hand side there are fewer inns and a maze of narrow alleys. The tall flat-fronted houses in these alleys were once the homes of resident Hospitallers. The area was all within the Collachium, the wall of the original Roman walled town. It created a 'city-within-a-city' which offered redoubled security. At a crowded time like this, many knights were quartered in these cool, lime-washed, marble-floored houses, sheltered from the heat of the sun by the houses all around, and with roof gardens looking over the sprawling commercial city beyond the Collachium and to the sea. Several of their portals still display the carved arms of their medieval owners and the cross of the Order of St John.

Once the Malory party had visited the Castellania to add their names to those available for garrison duty, and washed away the dust of their journey in the city's luxurious bathhouse (the Europeans enjoyed the oriental *hammams* as much as the native Rhodians did), they could have strolled around the city. The sound of hammers ringing on metal led them to the Hospitallers' mint, where silver and gold booty was turned into Rhodian ducats. Visiting knights and men-at-arms were provided with a small allowance in these coins, which were worth about a fifth of £1 in the 1430s.

In the cool of the evening, the knights often rode out to dine in the English langue's private garden, which was high on a hill just west of the city. It was planted around a small chapel hewn out of the rock-face and rich with colourful murals, which is still there, dimly lit by votive candles and heavily scented with incense. An earlier visitor described the garden as full of 'beautiful tall trees, mainly cedars and chestnuts, with thickets of bay laurel and orange groves set with ornamental fountains', with fruit 'in luscious profusion'. Rich carpets were spread on the ground, and colourful silk hangings draped over bushes and from trees as canopies. Then low tables were set out in the shade, decorated with garlands of flowers. Well-spiced dishes of venison, boar, goat and all manner of wild fowl were served, and washed down with resinous wines. There was good hunting in Rhodes, on fast Arab ponies and with well-trained hounds, often bred in Afghanistan. Falcons from Rhodes, especially from the Lachania, Apolakkia and Kattavia districts of the island, were much sought after. The Grand Masters sent them as presents to European rulers.

At the time of the Malorys' visit, the Order was as cultured as it was wealthy. The magnificent library of the Grand Master Juan Fernandez de Heredia had been brought to Rhodes as *spolia* from his last home in Avignon after his death in 1396. It held contemporary European chronicles and romances as well as translations of such classics as Plutarch's *Lives*, Thucydides' *Speeches*, a *History of Troy* and much devotional literature. In the 1430s its librarian was Brother Melchior Bandini, who was researching what would be the first history of the Order. Interested as he was in hunting and falconry, Malory would have looked forward to the completion of a French translation of *Hierakosophion*, a treatise on falconry written by Agepetos Kassianos, a Rhodian Greek who was falconer to several Grand Masters. It was heavily influenced by Oriental bird lore and veterinary prescriptions. English translators were also at work in Rhodes; among the books they were working on in the mid-1430s were a new version of Vegetius's military treatise, *De Re Militari*, and a collection of over a hundred Greek poems 'on love and desire'.

All new arrivals attended mass in the great church of St John of the Collachium, high above the rest of the city beside the Palace of the Grand Master. It was a glittering cavern of priceless relics. One of these had particular resonance to Arthurian myth: a spine from the crown of thorns, exquisitely housed in a crystal and silver tabernacle. The spine was reputed to bloom every year on Good Friday for three hours. The staff which Joseph of Arimathea brought with him from the Holy Land to Glastonbury had been made from the same miraculous tree as the crown of thorns; legend had it that the thorn tree that sprang from the staff when Joseph thrust it into the ground on Glastonbury Hill also bloomed on Good Friday.

Once Sir Robert's party had settled in, they toured the island, certainly hunting and hawking, perhaps taking their turn on guard duty in one of the many fortresses around the coast. Some, like Lindos and Kattavia, were substantial castles, others only fortified towers. They were positioned so that a continuous sight-line of beacons could be lit to signal approaching enemies. Geology helped the defenders – the fortresses were built on steep-sided crags that made assaults on them all but impossible. The most dramatic is the aptly-named Monolithos, a five-hundred-foot-high flat-topped pencil of rock which rises almost vertically from sea level. The long haul up the narrow zig-zag track to the top would have exhausted attackers. Much of the fortress has crumbled away, but its small whitewashed chapel is still in use, and its vaulted storage cellars, essential in times of siege, can be explored. There are crenellated battlements to sit on and gaze over the wine-dark sea at the offshore islands shimmering in the mist of the setting sun.

Malory, who shows himself knowledgeable about the ways of boats in his tales, could have taken the opportunity of joining a Hospitaller fleet on a voyage, known as a caravan, to confirm the authority of the Knights of Rhodes in the Dodecanese. All knights had to undertake at least one six-month stint on these seaborne patrols that combined the protection of Christian ships with predatory attacks on infidel vessels. Their fast, well-armed galleys were rowed partly by Muslim slaves and partly by Greek Rhodians. A favourite ploy was to operate in pairs, one galley concealing itself behind a promontory while the other chased a Turkish or Arab merchantman towards its guns, grappling irons and boarders.

The closest destination to Rhodes was the island of Simi, furthest afield was Lemnos, and between them were Kalamos and Kos. The highlight of any voyage was a visit to the Knights' new citadel of St Peter the Liberator, better known as Bodrum. Today it still towers above the coast of mainland Turkey, looking across the straits to Kos at its twin, the great Hospitaller fortress of Andimacchio. The fortress, on a promontory that is almost an island on the Turkish coast opposite Kos, had been captured from the Turks in 1404 to compensate for the loss of Smyrna in 1402. A Hospitaller stronghold on the mainland coast was an essential sanctuary for Christians fleeing overland from Turkish and Mongol persecution.

Sir Robert Malory had helped raise funds for Bodrum twenty-five years earlier, when the then Grand Master, Philbert de Naillac, came to London in 1410 during a pan-European fund-raising tour. Since the Pope had issued a decree in 1409 that all those who assisted in the construction of the new castle, either by donating funds or going there to help build it, would receive an indulgence giving them full remission for all sins they had ever committed, pious Christians rushed to contribute. The arms of the most generous donors were carved on the castle's walls. Above the northern entrance door to Bodrum's south-east or 'English Tower', which was finally completed at just this time, the visitors from England will have inspected the English escutcheons. Twenty-six can still be seen: those of Henry IV and his four sons Prince Hal, Thomas, Duke of Clarence, John, Duke of Bedford and Humfrey, Duke of Gloucester, as well as those of Edward, Duke of York, Richard, Earl of Warwick, Strange of Knockyn, Grey, Zouche, de la Pole, Neville, Percy, Holland, Burleigh, FitzAlan, Montague, Stafford, de Vere and Courtenay. Malorys were probably among the many lesser donors; they too would have received an indulgence like the one granted to Sir William FitzHugh and his wife Dame Margery which is preserved in the Order of St John's Museum at St John's Gate.

The arrival of hundreds of European knights and their supporting forces made the Turkish and Egyptian sultans reconsider their invasion plans and talk of truce: a thankful reprieve as shortly afterwards, in 1437, the Grand Master Fluvian died. An unusually full chapter elected Jean de Lastic as his successor. Some of the European knights stayed on in Rhodes for several more years, but others, Sir Robert among them, requested permission to return home. On 30 November 1437, the Chapter extended his original ten-year tenure of the Priory of England to life, and gave him permission to go back to England and to supplement the manpower of the English langue by admitting twelve new novices (an indication of the shortage of English Hospitaller knights at the time). The Chapter asked him to make a detour into Italy on his homeward journey in order to tell Pope Eugenius IV of the death of Fluvian and the election of de Lastic.

Sir Robert did not leave immediately. He wanted to arrange to exchange the Derbyshire preceptories he had been granted a few months earlier for that of Newland, near Selby in Yorkshire, which had been held by his kinsman John Malory a hundred years earlier. This was agreed by the Chapter in early December. He and the other English visitors also did some shopping. A Genoese carrack loaded with Oriental carpets, silks, bed and table linen, velvets, wine and armour, to be delivered to Sir Robert Malory and Sir Robert Botill, arrived in Sandwich early in 1439.

Sir Robert went home via Pisa in order to go to Ferrara to seek an audience with Pope Eugenius, who was attending a General Council of the Church there. The Pope confirmed de Lastic's appointment, and listened with interest and concern as Sir Robert explained that danger presented by the Turks and Arabs was still very real. His message supported the pleas of the Byzantine Emperor John Paleologus, who was also in Ferrara begging for help from the West against the infidels. They were persuasive enough for Eugenius to declare a crusade in 1439. Sir Robert was still in Italy on 29 May 1438 when the Pope confirmed the extension of his priorate to life.

Crossing over the Alps in high summer was much pleasanter than it had been in early spring, and once the Rhine became navigable, Sir Robert could travel fast and comfortably downstream to Flanders. He may have been back in England by 28 June, when he is named as the patron of a candidate new hospitaller for the preceptory of Salcombe, Devon. He was certainly in London on 8 July, when he signed tenancy agreements at a meeting of the English Hospitallers' Chapter in Clerkenwell. Early in November he asked King Henry VI for a safe-conduct back to Scotland for Sir Andrew Meldrum and five companions – the sixth must have either stayed in Rhodes or died. On 24 February 1439 he attended the royal council and two days later the King asked him to assemble all the English Knights Hospitallers to discuss 'extremely important matters'. It is possible that Sir Robert had inspired his pious monarch to support the papal call for a crusade.

Thomas Malory could have accompanied Sir Robert to Ferrara to see the Pope, and then have returned to Genoa to see the goods they had acquired in Rhodes transferred to a Genoese ship suitable for the voyage around the coast to England. It would make sense if he and some of the other English knights had travelled in the ship, stopping off at Marseilles and Majorca, Lisbon and Cilicia. The voyage of the Hospitallers' Oriental luxuries was a leisurely one. It did not arrive at Sandwich until late March or early April 1439. Its cargo was meticulously listed in a Chancery order to the 'customers' (customs officers)

*to deliver to the Prior of St John of Jerusalem in England
and to Robert Botell his brother, Preceptor of Melchbourne,
or to their deputies without payment of custom or subsidy
eighteen barrels of wine of Rhodes containing six butts of
wine, one valet [i.e. a 'wallet', which at that time could mean
a very large carrying bag as well as a pocket-sized one]
holding Turkey carpets, sheets and napkins, one chest with
armour, and cloths of silk and chamlett [a luxurious, silky-
soft fabric] in a carrack in that port, Anthony Querinus
[being its] master and owner, which were bought and pur-
veyed at Rhodes for the consumption and needs of the Prior's
household, and five cartels of wine of Rhodes containing two
butts, and two chests of cypress in the said carrack likewise
bought etc, for consumption of the Preceptor, as witness has
been borne in chancery.*

Six weeks later, 'Thomas Malory, esquire', described for the first
time in a surviving record as 'of Newbold Revel', emerges in Warwickshire, witness to a settlement made by his first cousin, Sir Philip
Chetwynd, at Grendon on 23 May 1439.

Sir Robert Malory did not enjoy his life tenure as Prior for long.
He was dead by 10 May 1440, when Henry VI wrote to the Grand
Master Jean de Lastic to confirm the English Hospitallers' choice of
Sir Robert Botill as his successor. Malory had been an active Prior,
raising the status of the Lincolnshire Bailiff of Eagle in 1433 so that
its holder, then Sir Richard Paule, was entitled to a seat on the Council
in Rhodes, ordering a list of English Hospitaller estates to be drawn
up by John Stillingfleet in 1434, and quick to react to royal attempts
to curtail Hospitaller privileges. In 1432, he was made a member of
the Tailors' Company of London, and confirmed their status as confraters of the Order. They regularly feasted at Clerkenwell, no doubt
in return for generous donations to Rhodes. There is also an
intriguing 1430s case, in which his lawyer sparred successfully in the
courts against an attorney called Thomas Greswold. This canny
Crown lawyer would prove his nephew Thomas's nemesis in the 1450s.

Whether he went to Rhodes with Sir Robert or not, Malory must have grieved at the loss of a highly influential kinsman and an inspiring mentor. The dignity, idealism and spirituality of the Order are still evident at Sir Robert's first, perhaps favourite, commandery, Temple Balsall in Warwickshire. Thomas is likely to have visited him there as well as at Clerkenwell. Approached from Balsall Common, past a pub called the Saracen's Head, the tiny hamlet is dominated by the magnificent single-naved red sandstone church. Built by the Templars in the thirteenth century, it is proportionately high for its length, and looms like a stranded ark over a little confluence of brooks in the surrounding water meadows. Below its eaves, portrait heads of the knights were carved. Centuries of wind and rain have blurred the few remaining original faces into romantic anonymity; most date from the 1840s when the great Victorian-Gothic architect Giles Gilbert Scott restored the entire building.

The interior is more like a magnificent guildhall than a church. Its medieval glass was destroyed in Puritan times, but Scott substituted romantic replacements illustrating the history of the two crusading orders. Next to the church is the original residence of the preceptor, a fine example of an early timber-framed hall house. I was taken round it by Frederick West, the verger for the charitable foundation that now runs Temple Balsall as a residential home for the elderly. He showed me a massive wooden pillar, blackened with age. 'That's been dated as an oak cut down in 1190 – and grew from an acorn that fell in 780!' The Hospitallers used the hall as their hospital, and added a wing for the preceptor to live in. The cornice in its upstairs parlour is decorated with the coats of arms of former Priors. One shield is Sir Robert's, painted with the red chevron on a black-and-white 'ermine' ground of the Malorys of Newbold Revel.

Did Thomas Malory ride over from Newbold Revel in 1434 in answer to his uncle's appeal, and sit in a great oak chair at the side of the stone fireplace to discuss with him who else to contact, and what he would need in the way of arms, servants and horses? Or did he just come on Sir Robert's return and merely hear about his adventures? Whatever happened, or didn't happen, he is likely to have spent many thoughtful hours at Temple Balsall, drawing parallels between the close-knit international brotherhood of the 'monks of war' and King Arthur's Knights of the Round Table. There is a rich intermingling of elements from French, Italian and German romances as well as English ones in Malory's tales. If he did indeed sail to the defence of Christendom with his uncle, much of his knowledge may have been the fruit of long evenings in the Grand Master's Palace in Rhodes spent listening to the 'great noise of minstrelsy' from the varied talents of the German minnesingers, French and Italian *jongleurs* and troubadours, Spanish *cantantes* and English minstrels.

Battling in Bayonne

*Then Tor alighted off his mare and pulled out his sword,
kneeling, and requiring the king that he would make him
knight, and that he might be a knight of the Table Round.
'As for a knight I will make you', [said King Arthur] and
therewith smote him in the neck with the sword, saying,
'Be ye a good knight, and so I pray to God so ye may be,
and if ye be of prowess and of worthiness ye shall be a
knight of the Table Round'.*

Malory, 'The Tale of King Arthur'

An alternative scenario for Malory's life between 1436 and 1439 would be the renewal of his military service under Beauchamp. Beauchamp had been discharged from his duties as royal mentor in May 1436; Henry VI was after all fourteen years old, officially a man, and well grown 'in stature of his person and also in conceit and knowledge of his high and royal authority and estate'. Now feeling his age, the Earl planned to retreat from national politics and spend more time on his own affairs, but it was not to be. In 1436, the English realm in France came under attack. Its long-term regent, John, Duke of Bedford, died at Rouen in September 1435. Two years earlier, in 1433, Bedford's much-loved wife Anne, the sister of the Duke of Burgundy, had died. Bedford, still heir to the English throne and still childless, had lost no time in remarrying. His second wife, the seventeen-year-old Jacquetta of St-Pol, was a princess of the Burgundian fief of Luxembourg, but Anne's death ended Bedford's close personal alliance with Burgundy.

For thirteen years, ever since his brother Henry V's death in 1422, Bedford had been a highly effective king of England in all but name, without ever threatening his nephew's position. Thanks to his flair for both military campaigns and civil administration, England had acquired far more land in France than Henry V had initially conquered, and Normandy had been under English rule for nearly twenty years. Bedford had even established a university at Caen, complete with a School of Civil and Canon Law. But defending the English conquests was becoming increasingly difficult, especially as the French army was now well-organised and equipped with artillery that could easily demolish city defences. Bedford had tried and failed to make peace with France in August 1435. Six days after his death on 10 September, the French King Charles VII did sign a peace treaty at Arras, but it was with Philip, Duke of Burgundy. The English settlements were now threatened from three sides: Brittany, France and Burgundy. When Henry VI received letters from his 'good uncle' of Burgundy, his former feudal subject, addressing him as mere King of England, he is said to have wept and declared that he feared for the whole future of his dominions in France. The betrayal biased him for ever against alliance with Burgundy.

Simultaneous offensives were quickly launched against English bases by both the French and the Burgundians. By the end of 1435, Dieppe, Crotoy and Harfleur had all fallen. 'And thus Englishmen began to lose little by little in Normandy,' wrote a chronicler. Early in 1436, the Burgundians advanced on Calais. The English were however ready for them. Bedford's death had given his much more militarily aggressive brother, Duke Humfrey of Gloucester, increased influence in the King's council. Over three thousand men had already embarked for Calais in July 1435 and Exchequer expenditure on its garrison's wages soared. The biggest army to leave the shores of England during the 1430s set sail in May 1436. Beauchamp indented with 823 men. The commander-in-chief was officially the nineteen-year-old Richard Duke of York, who was Bedford's successor as Lieutenant in France, but it was the experienced veterans Gloucester and Beauchamp who were really in charge.

Calais was saved, but the Franco-Burgundian alliance made it necessary to appoint a more experienced leader than York. In April 1437, Henry VI asked Beauchamp to return to Normandy as

Lieutenant. Beauchamp, now fifty-five, agreed to do so extremely unwillingly.

> *My going over at this time is full far from the ease of my*
> *years and from the continued labours of my person at sieges*
> *and in daily occupation in the war, seeing the length of time*
> *that I have belaboured in the service of noble kings of good*
> *memory, your grandsire and father and about yourself, as*
> *well in your wars as about your royal person.*

But go he did, sailing from Portsmouth with his wife Isobel and his son Harry and over five thousand men in July 1437. The survival of his London tailor's bill for that year reveals that he was equipped in splendid style. He had ordered heraldic banners, a cloth-of-gold coat for himself and two more economically cut coats of 'demi-gold' for his heralds. He also took substantial provisions, including a herd of cattle which drovers brought from Budbrooke, near Warwick. Beauchamp made an exceptionally detailed will before he left, a natural precaution, but perhaps a sign that he was in poor health. Five abortive attempts to cross the Channel were made in as many weeks, and when they finally did set sail, the entire family spent the journey lashed to the mainmast for safety. On reaching Harfleur, they made a leisurely progress up to Rouen, arriving there in November. Beauchamp did what he could to improve the increasingly desperate military situation, appointing Talbot, released from captivity in 1433, Commander of the army in the field. But what small gains were made over the next year were balanced by losses, and late in 1438 he began negotiations for peace with the French. However, Charles VII was now powerful enough to refuse to agree to anything except the abandonment of the English claims to French territory.

Weary, demoralised and emaciated, Beauchamp died in Rouen on 30 April 1439. In October his body was taken down the Seine and across the Channel to England, where it was 'worshipfully buried in the College of our Lady Church' in Warwick. His will provided funds for the building of a magnificent chantry chapel and tomb, for which the finest artists in northern Europe were commissioned to work; it was finally completed in 1475. Malory could have been with

Beauchamp at his end, or have heard the news of his death after his return from Rhodes. Wherever he was, he had now lost the man who had been his first and most important mentor. Beauchamp's son and heir, Harry, was only fourteen, and lived with his child wife Cecily Neville at Cardiff Castle. Malory would enter his service a little later, but first he wanted to achieve a knighthood. His writings show that he believed it to be the highest honour in the world, and his lands now entitled him to it. His repeated emphasis in the *Morte Darthur* on the importance of being made a knight for 'deeds of great prowess' suggests that he would want to win his spurs in battle. There was now little hope of achieving outstanding military distinction in Normandy. But the English also had a war on their hands in Gascony, and Malory's first cousin Sir Philip Chetwynd was about to set out to fight there.

Malory witnessed a legal document for Sir Philip on 23 May 1439; it described him as 'Thomas Malory esquire'. It assigned Sir Philip's Grendon estates to feoffees because he was going to Gascony in the service of Sir William Bonville. It would have been natural for Sir Philip to suggest to Malory that they became companions-in-arms. He too had served in Beauchamp's retinue; he was part of it in 1427 when he was awarded a silver collar by Henry VI. He was now a member of the élite corps of king's household knights. His other feoffees were William Purefoy of Shirford, the husband of his (and Malory's) aunt, Margaret Chetwynd, Robert Whitgreve of Stafford, and Simon Melbourne, the Rector of Grendon. All three men were stay-at-home types. Malory was not a feoffee but a witness, a role quite compatible with his departing for Gascony himself. The other witnesses were Sir Thomas Erdington, who was also one of the king's household knights, and John Chetwynd esquire, Sir Philip's uncle (though only nine years older than he was). Both had previously fought in France. It could have been at this point that Thomas Malory enfeoffed his own estates to four of his neighbours and kinsmen: Eustace Burneby, Henry Sharp, John Moveley (or Moseley) and Robert Malory, son of Simon Malory.

There is no doubt that Malory knew a remarkable amount about the geography of Gascony, especially in the area in the far south in which Sir Philip was campaigning. Towards the end of his 'Tale of Lancelot and Guinevere', he adds a completely original passage to the source on which he based this part of his story. When Lancelot is banished from Arthur's kingdom because of the undying enmity of Sir Gawaine, a hundred knights loyally follow him, shipping with him at Cardiff to sail to Benwick, his kingdom, 'Some men call it Bayan and some men call it Beawme, where the wine of Beawme is', Malory tells us. He goes on to relate how Lancelot 'stuffed and furnished and garnished all his noble towns and castles', and then called a *parlement* where, with a prophetic eye to his own imminent death, he distributed the lands he was awarded after Arthur's European campaign. He crowned Sir Lionel King of France, Sir Bors King of the conquered Claudas's lands, and Sir Ector de Maris (his younger brother) King of Benwick and all Gascony.

Any educated English gentleman knew of Bayonne, and the regular cargoes of wine that were imported from there and Bordeaux. But Malory then adds a list of the lands that Lancelot (who he describes as King of France) grants to his loyal knights. Sir Blamore is made Duke of Limousin; Sir Bleoberis Duke of Poitiers; Sir Gahalantine Duke of Auverne; Sir Galihodin Duke of Saintonge; Sir Galihud Earl of Perigord; Sir Menaduke Earl of Rouergue; Sir Villiars the Valiant Earl of Béarn; Sir Hebes le Renowne Earl of Comminges; Sir Lavaine Earl of Armagnac; Sir Urré Earl of Astorac; Sir Nerovens Earl of Pardiac; Sir Plenorius Earl of Foix; Sir Selyses of the Dolorous Tower Earl of Marsan; Sir Melias de l'Îsle Earl of Tursan; Sir Bellyngerus le Beuse Earl of the Landes; Sir Palomides Duke of Provence; Sir Saffir Duke of Languedoc; Sir Clegis Earl of Agen; Sir Sadok Earl of Sarlat; Sir Dinas Duke of Anjou; and Sir Clarrus Duke of Normandy. The list includes provinces that the English had never conquered, including an extraordinary number of fiefs in the hinterland of Bayonne, many so small that only someone who had been there (and perhaps enjoyed its wines) would have known their names. They are not mentioned in any of the sources Malory used.

The driving force behind the expedition to Gascony in 1439 was Duke Humfrey, a man of mettle and dash who was likely to have appealed to Malory as a leader. Gloucester more than anyone else on the royal council stood for continuing the struggle against the French and for securing not only Normandy, which his brother Henry V had said in his will should never be abandoned, but Anjou, Maine, Gascony and the Crown of France itself. Humfrey, next in line to the throne, had considerable influence on his nephew the King. He also had extensive estates in Gascony. When word came that a powerful French army led by some of Charles VII's most feared mercenary captains (including Sir Pothon de Saintraille) was ravaging the Médoc and even raiding the suburbs of Bordeaux, he argued vigorously for an expedition to recover Gascony. Henry agreed, and John Holland, Earl of Huntingdon, was appointed as commander-in-chief of the expedition.

Ships for Huntingdon's army were requisitioned from most of the southern ports of England and ordered to be in Plymouth Roads by 1 May. Plenty of armaments were taken on board: 2,000 sheaves of arrows, 8,640 bowstrings, 1,401 quarters of the best sulphur for gunpowder, 400 lances with ironheads and 100 long pavises (huge convex body-shields which pages held in front of knights and archers so they could advance behind a shield wall). Sir William Bonville's retinue, including Chetwynd and his men, mustered there with Huntingdon's other troops on 8 June, and a heavily armed escort delivered £9,000 in cash, three months' wages from that date, from the Exchequer. Raising the money had been difficult, and was only achieved by a last-minute loan of 13,000 marks by Cardinal Beaufort in exchange for his being allowed to buy the valuable royal marcher lordship of Chirk and Chirklands in settlement of the debt. Next year Duke Humfrey would argue that Chirk was worth much more than 13,000 marks, and complain that he had had 'no other remedy' but to agree to the sale rather than see the 'breaking and loss' of Huntingdon's army.

When Huntingdon finally set sail in mid-June, he had 2,310 men: 2 bannerets, 6 knights, 292 men-at-arms and 2,009 archers. The knights were Sir Robert Vere, Sir Edward Grey of Ruthin, Sir Thomas Grey, Sir John Holland (Huntingdon's son), Sir Robert Clifton and Sir Philip Chetwynd – whose wife of a year, Helen, travelled with him. Malory witnessed a document with Sir Edward Grey three years later. He had served with Clifton's father, Sir Gervaise Clifton, under Grey of Codnor in 1417, and in the late 1460s he is linked with Sir Robert's younger brother, another Gervaise Clifton. Huntingdon had originally undertaken to bring sixteen English knights with him, which supports the idea that among the men-at-arms listed were several armigerous squires like Malory and Gervaise Clifton, men who hoped to win the high honour of knighthood for feats of valour during the summer campaign. To make up numbers in the meantime, Huntingdon retained a clutch of Gascon knights ousted from their fiefs as commanders by the French.

The expedition arrived at Bordeaux on 2 August 1439, and quickly began a very successful offensive. They captured La Roquette, a fortress on the Gironde from which English shipping bound for Bordeaux had been harassed, and then began to campaign in the Landes. Part of the deal for those who undertook the campaign was that successful commanders would be rewarded with lordships. Sir Robert Clifton was made Constable of Bordeaux. Huntingdon took Lesparre for himself, making Robert Rokeley its castellan and John Hayward its bailiff. It was a short-sighted policy which triggered the desertion of the Gascons from the English cause.

Some time during the next year Huntingdon himself returned to England and in December 1440 gave up what had originally been a six-year appointment. Humfrey of Gloucester put the blame for this squarely on Beaufort's shoulders, claiming that the wages agreed had not been paid and that 'necessity' forced Huntingdon to return. Chetwynd seems to have withdrawn even earlier. On 7 July 1440, a royal warrant dated at Windsor recognised Sir Philip Chetwynd's 'good and agreeable service' and made him Vicomte of Tartas, a town on the main road to Bayonne just south of St Julien (where really good wines come from).

'A passing good man of arms'

Sir Philip Chetwynd's wife Helen died early in November 1440. But he returned to Gascony for the 1441 campaigning season, in which he was so successful that the King honoured him with the title of Mayor of Bayonne when back in England in the autumn. If Sir Philip went to court to accept the office, it is possible that he took Malory with him, and that, on Chetwynd's warm recommendation that Malory was 'so good of his body and full of prowess as man may be', King Henry VI dubbed him knight. A crusade-like journey to Rhodes would also have earned him respect from the pious young King. All that is certain is that the next surviving record of Malory, dated 8 October 1441, describes him as a knight. It was a grant by the Vicar of Ansley, which is twelve miles from Newbold Revel, of certain lands in the parish to a group of eight gentlemen, among them Sir Edward Grey (who had also been on Chetwynd's expedition) and Sir Thomas Malory.

Malory's puzzling imprisonment in the last three years of his life makes much better sense if he felt a personal loyalty to Henry VI as strong as that which Lancelot felt for King Arthur. Given what he reveals of his feelings on the subject in the *Morte*, such loyalty would certainly have been the case if it was Henry VI who had knighted him. Lancelot repeatedly says that his unshakeable obligation to Arthur is due to the fact that he was 'the noble king that made me knight'. Malory puts the phrase into his mouth especially often in the two last tales, 'Lancelot and Guinevere' and 'The Death of Arthur'. During Arthur's war against him at Joyous Gard, Lancelot bars his cousin Sir Bors from attacking the unhorsed King, and gives Arthur his own horse, saying 'I will never see that most noble king that made me knight neither slain ne shamed'.

If Henry VI did indeed knight Malory, an appropriate day would have been 29 September, the feast of St Michael the Archangel. Knighthoods were often conferred on saints' days or church festivals. The royal palaces in which the King spent the most time were Westminster, Sheen and Windsor, but in late September Henry was residing in

Hertford Castle, which he was renovating and extending, having inherited it from his step-grandmother Joanna of Navarre in 1437. Whenever he was knighted, Malory would have observed a succession of rituals: a vigil beside his arms in a church or chapel the night before, and in the morning a ceremonial bath of purification before being laced into a tight-fitting jacket of chamois leather. Over this he wore a mail shirt and mirror-bright plate armour specially made for the occasion. He was then conducted to the chapel with two sponsors – perhaps Sir Philip Chetwynd and Sir Robert Clifton. After high mass was said, the King dealt the accolade – a blow on the neck with the flat of a sword, and said some such formula as 'I now dub thee knight, in the name of God and St Michael. Be faithful, bold and fortunate.' The sword was then belted around his hips, usually by the officiating cleric, and the much-coveted gilded spurs that only knights were entitled to wear were attached to his heels, often by some high-born lady who wished the knight well.

It would be interesting to know if such a lady presented Malory with his spurs. Early on in the *Morte Darthur*, he goes to some lengths to explain that the unique tie between Lancelot and Guinevere was created at Lancelot's knighting ceremony. It was, Lancelot says, the loss of his sword on the day that he was to be knighted that first created his tie with Guinevere.

> '*For that same day ye made me knight, through my hastiness I lost my sword, and my lady, your queen, found it, and lapped it in her train, and gave me my sword when I had need thereto, and else had I been shamed among all knights; and therefore, my lord Arthur, I promised her at that day ever to be her knight in right outher in wrong.*'

On 28 December 1441 Sir Thomas Malory's name appeared at the top of a list of the parliamentary electors for Northamptonshire. This confirms his local rise in status, and also suggests that his principal residence was then his Northamptonshire manor, Winwick. His widowed mother Philippa was perhaps still alive, and living at Newbold Revel. On 28 June 1442, Philip Chetwynd remarried. His bride was sixteen-year-old Joan Burley, daughter and co-heir of

William Burley of Broncroft, Shropshire, an influential lawyer and experienced parliamentarian. The feoffees who had protected Sir Philip's estates while he was abroad now re-granted them to Sir Philip and Lady Joan. 'Sir Thomas Malorre' was one of the witnesses. Another witness was Sir William Mountfort, who appeared on the Beauchamp Roll with Malory in 1414. His extensive estates made him a very prominent man in the county.

Sir Philip did not have long to enjoy a honeymoon. An aged pilgrim disembarked at Portsmouth with an urgent message from Gascony smuggled in the hem of his gown. It was from two royal envoys who had been sent to Bordeaux in May to open negotiations for the marriage of the nineteen-year-old Henry VI to one of the daughters of Jacques, Count of Armagnac. Henry VI had sent a letter with them asking Count Jacques for pictures of all three of his daughters 'in their kirtles simple, and their visages like as you see their stature, and their beauty and colour of skin, and their countenances with all manner of features' so that he could choose between them. The initiative was Duke Humfrey's, who hoped that such a match would make Armagnac a dependable English ally, a permanent bulwark between France and Gascony, his royal nephew's 'oldest inheritance'. In response, Charles VII had massed one of the best-organised French armies ever known and had swept into Gascony. Tartas had fallen on 2 May, and Charles was now heading towards Bayonne.

A relief force of five hundred men indented to serve for three months under the command of Sir Philip Chetwynd in August 1442. Sir Thomas could just have been among them; there is no record of their names, or of Malory in England between June 1442 and August 1443. They reached Gascony in October to find that Bayonne, loyal to the English for the last four hundred years, had surrendered to the French to save itself from being obliterated by the enormous siege engines with which the French army was equipped. But the main French army had moved on, leaving only a garrison. When the citizens heard that Sir Philip had returned, they rose up against the occupying force and welcomed him as Mayor once again.

Sir Philip was back in England by 3 May 1443 when he and one

William Kerver were buying 400 quarters of wheat in Oxfordshire and Berkshire for the provision of Bayonne. This suggests that he was about to return for another summer's campaigning, but there is no record of him making a third expedition. It could have been simply a response to the council's commissioning notables in every county in March for 'stirring and inducing the people of the said shire by all ways and means that they can ... for aid of men, victuals and ships for the relief and succour of Gascony'. The aids were required to support the biggest force that had been despatched to France from England since 1430. Led by Cardinal Beaufort's nephew John Beaufort, Earl of Somerset, who had at last been ransomed after seventeen years in captivity (he had been captured at Baugé in 1421), 4,500 men were to land at Cherbourg, defeat the French forces that were raiding it on a regular basis, and then head south through Anjou and Maine to defend Gascony.

The expedition turned into a disaster in both political and military terms, offending England's one remaining ally, the Duke of Brittany, by pillaging Breton lands, circling aimlessly in Maine, and then retreating to Rouen. Somerset's commission as Captain-General not just of Aquitaine but also of those lands in France 'in which my Lord of York cometh not' was an insulting infringement of the authority of York, still the official Lieutenant of France, and now a more than competent leader. York and his fellow commanders were also furious that the money and men raised for Beaufort were at the expense of the reinforcements and wages they desperately needed to prevent mutiny in Calais and Normandy. Neither Chetwynd nor Malory appears to have joined Beaufort's army. It may be relevant that Humfrey of Gloucester strongly opposed the venture. All the evidence is that Malory, now knighted and lord of Newbold Revel as well as of Winwick and Swinford, decided that it was time to take up the prominent position in local affairs natural to one 'of his high degree'.

Malory at Home

'He is a noble knight, and a mighty man and well-breathed;
and if he were well-assayed', said Sir Lancelot, 'I would
deem he were good enough for any knight that beareth the
life; and he is a gentle knight, courteous, true and bount-
eous, meek, and mild, and in him is no manner of mal
enginé, but plain, faithful and true'

Malory, 'The Tale of Sir Gareth'

nce Thomas Malory became a knight, he had a prominent position in society. This meant that his name appears much more often than before in written records. The frequency with which he held responsible office – JP, MP and Sheriff – in the 1440s shows that he was energetically engaged in local affairs, and respected across three counties. When he writes of Sir Tristram's contribution to the lore of hunting, it is with the self-confidence of a man with an assured place in society:

> Wherefore, as meseemeth, all gentlemen that bear old arms
> ought of right to honour Sir Tristram for the goodly terms
> that gentlemen have and use, and shall to the day of doom,
> that thereby in a manner all men of worship may dissever a
> gentleman from a yeoman, and from a yeoman a villain. For
> he that gentle is will draw him unto gentle tatches, and to
> follow the customs of noble gentlemen.

At home we can imagine Malory riding around his estates managing the day-to-day affairs of life dressed in a stout fustian doublet, a cloak, comfortable leather boots and a hat with a small, upturned brim with a cockade in summer, furred in winter. If he had an eye to fashion, the doublet and cloak would have been very short 'cutted on the buttock even above the rump', but he was probably a little old for such taradiddles. When he was in service with the Beauchamps, his cloak could have had the Beauchamp badge of the bear and ragged staff, perhaps enamelled and gilded, attached to it, or on a chain around his neck. From his belt hung all sorts of useful items – a purse, a dagger to eat with, a rosary to pray with and a short sword in case he needed to defend himself against cutpurses and similar rogues. Of an evening, he took his ease in a long wool or velvet gown, trimmed with squirrel or sable.

The chances are that he celebrated his knighthood by spending some of his hard-earned profits of war on a showy suit of tournament armour so that he could cut a fine figure at local tournaments at Gosford Green, Warwick, or Kenilworth. Tournament armour was reinforced on the left side, which took most of the blows in the lists, and weighed around 100 lb, compared to the 60 lb of war armour. The 'frog-mouth' helm was again heavier than a war helmet, with an eye slit (the frog's smile) and an elaborate padded topknot, often fashioned into fantastic heraldic forms. To accommodate his helmet, Malory's hair would have been shaven around the lower half of his head and left to grow as thickly as possible above his ears to provide natural padding for the helm – a monastic tonsure in reverse.

For friendly tournaments ('jousts of peace') blunted weapons were used, so that when knights dismounted for combat on foot not too much damage would be done. However, fatal accidents were frequent. Malory may well have been in Smithfield in January 1442 to watch the famous jouster John Astley (a near neighbour in Warwickshire) take up the general challenge issued to the knights of England that year by Philippe de Boyle, a knight of Aragon. Astley was knighted by Henry VI for his triumph in the jousts, and given an annuity of 100 marks for life. We only know of the tournament and Astley's reward because he was a devoted collector of souvenirs of his triumphs and chivalric treatises, binding them together in a handsome vellum 'Great Book' with decorative initials and full-page illustrations, which has happily survived. There were many other jousts, local or national, of which no record remains. Chivalry was far from being in decline. There had been a sharp rise in the number of knights since 1400, and its ethics and practice were more discussed and codified than in any other century.

Malory has been described as a poor knight, but a good case can be made for the idea that he was fairly wealthy and extremely competent at managing his properties and assets. His father John had paid a fine in distraint of knighthood in 1430, so he must then have been worth £40 a year, perhaps considerably more. As we have seen, in 1436 John's widow was assessed for £60, but this referred only to Warwickshire lands. When she died, her son Sir Thomas added her assets to his own, and his income could have been at least three times as much as hers, around £180 a year. His financial acumen is suggested by the efficiency with which he at least twice enfeoffed his properties to protect them, by his surviving many years in prison without ruin, by the lack of evidence of major actions of debt against him, and by the fact that he handed on his estates intact at his death in 1471. There is no record of his borrowing on the security of his estates; on the contrary, early in the 1440s he lent money to his brother-in-law Robert Vincent on the security of Vincent's manor at Swinford, and ended up buying it from him outright – adding to, rather than detracting from, the estates that his heirs inherited. Since there are no records of his seeking funds for a ransom either, it is reasonable to suppose that Malory made profits rather than losses from his years overseas.

If Malory was indeed a wealthy and travelled man with a keen interest in new cultural developments, he would have enjoyed a grander domestic lifestyle than his father and mother. At some point in the fifteenth century, the old manor house of Fenny Newbold, so called because of its low-lying position, was rebuilt and renamed Newbold Revel. Excavations made there suggest that the short wings of the fourteenth-century manor house were later extended into an H-plan. If it was modernised in the 1440s, Newbold Revel's hall windows would have been tall rectangles with stone cinquefoil arches at the top. Its parlour may have been enhanced with a projecting oriel window. Glass was getting cheaper, and square panes

Little is known of Malory's childhood, but the baptism of infants was never too soon at a time when immortal souls could be stolen by evil spirits for the want of a splash of holy water. This stained glass window (*c*.1480) in Holy Trinity Church, Tattershall, Lincs, shows godparents watching as a newborn baby is immersed three times.

Hunting was certainly an important part of Malory's education. Boys were introduced to its complex lore at the age of seven or eight. Malory seems to have been especially fond of the chase, praising Sir Tristram for his prowess and expertise and frequently sending his knights off in pursuit of beasts real and legendary; he may well have owned a manuscript *Book of Game* similar to that shown below.

The Malorys were proud of being 'gentlemen that bear olde arms'. Windows (*above*) in the Leicestershire church of Stanford, adjacent to the Malory manor of Swinford, show (*left*) the husband of a great-granddaughter of Sir Thomas Malory kneeling and (*right*) his Cave arms linked to four variations of the Malory arms.

Little altered since Elizabethan times, the Malory manor of Winwick, Northamptonshire, is the most atmospheric of all Sir Thomas Malory's estates. The photo (*below*) was taken by the author during a motor glider flight over the Malorys' midlands holdings.

Tournaments, great or small, were hugely popular events. They combined the attractions of the race-course (thundering hooves, gay silk liveries, and bookies) with those of the football ground (folk heroes and dazzling technical skills). This manuscript shows Malory's near neighbour Sir John Astley fighting the Aragonese knight Philippe de Boyle at the tournament ground at Smithfield, London, on 30 January 1442; it was commissioned by Astley soon after the event for his *Ordinances of Armoury*.

Malory and his brothers-in-arms were promised 'a country fertile, pleasant and plentiful', with 'rich cities, beautiful towns, innumerable castles' to entice them to cross the Channel in 1414 in service with Henry V's invading forces. He and other members of the Earl of Warwick's retinue will have enjoyed visiting shops in Rouen (*above*) and in Paris; they were also offered generous hospitality by their Burgundian allies as in this feast scene from the Duc de Berry's *Book of Hours* (*left*).

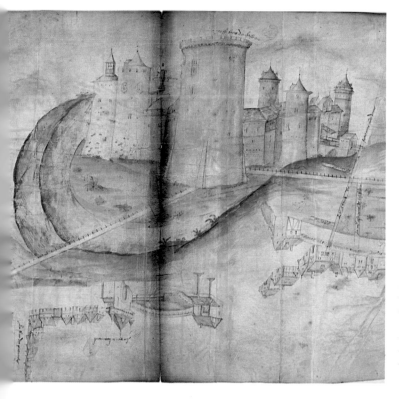

Fifteen years of English triumphs were brought to an abrupt end when a peasant girl called Joan of Arc persuaded the Dauphin to march to the relief of the siege of Orléans in April 1429; the pen and ink sketch of her (*above left*) was made by Clément de Fauquembergue, the secretary of the Parlement of Paris, on 10 May 1429. The famous savant Christine de Pisan (*above*) lauded the Maid's achievements in verse. But Joan was captured and handed over to the English, who immured her in the Bouvreuil tower (*left*), in the citadel of their Rouen headquarters. Malory may have witnessed her trial.

The Malory family had many connections with the Knights Hospitallers. Temple Balsall, Warwickshire (*above*) was the first and favourite preceptory of Malory's uncle, the Knight Hospitaller Prior Sir Robert Malory. When Sir Robert travelled to Rhodes in 1436 to defend it against the Turks, Malory may well have accompanied him. The Pinturrichio fresco (*left*) shows just such a young English Hospitaller praying against a landscape. The city of Rhodes can be seen in the distance.

When European Knights did stints in Rhodes they had to spend six months with the Hospitallers' fleet, which patrolled the eastern Mediterranean, ambushing and attacking Turkish galleys (*opposite*).

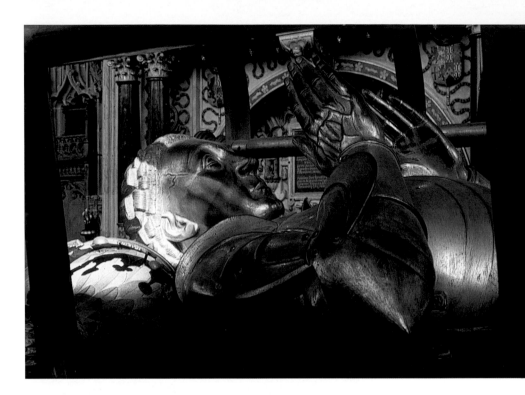

In 1439, Malory's first liege lord, Sir Richard Beauchamp, Earl of Warwick, died; his exquisite tomb survives in St Mary's Church, Warwick.

Between 1439 and 1441, Thomas Malory became a knight. The ritual would have resembled this illustration (*left*) from a 1463 manuscript *Tristram* showing Galahad receiving his sword and spurs before a church altar.

more common, but it was still enough of a luxury for the iron casements in which the glass was set to be made portable, locked into place with iron bolts and protected with an iron grille. These windows could be removed and replaced by shutters during an owner's absence, or taken with him to another residence. Such casements were often heraldic family portraits, proud displays of both ancestry and allegiance.

Malorys liked such memorials. There were armorial panes in the windows of Newbold Revel's parlour. Seven still survived when Sir William Dugdale visited the house on 4 August 1637, and he copied them into his great history of Warwickshire. Some at least date from the 1480s, as three show the coats of arms of the Kingston family:

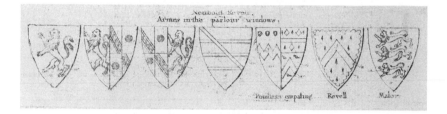

Katherine Kingston was wife of Sir Thomas Malory's grandson Nicholas. But the two on the right were older – the variant of the Revel arms: *ermine a chevron gules engrailed sable* (a red chevron on a ground of ermine tails rather than the original Revel gold ground, bordered with a wavy black line) which was used by Malory's grandfather and father, and the Malory arms used by an earlier ancestor, the thirteenth-century judge Sir Peter Malory of Winwick: *or three lions passant sable* (gold ground, three black running lions, heads facing forward).

Who revived Sir Peter's arms, with their marked implication of loyalty to the King? We can only guess, but it seems very likely to have been Sir Thomas Malory himself. Examples of the Malory arms survive in several Midlands churches. From a window in Monks Kirby Church, Dugdale copied a shield showing the variant of the Revel arms used by Sir John Malory and his son John quartered with Sir Peter's three black lions passant on a gold ground. Whether it was

Sir Thomas Malory, his son or his grandson who combined the two sets of arms in this way, we do not know.

'Go to thy realm, and there take thee a wife, and live with her with joy and bliss'

Malory was certainly married by the 1440s, as his son and heir Robert was born in 1447/8. We also know, from post-mortem records, that his wife's name was Elizabeth, and that she was Robert's mother. What we don't know is whether she was his first or a later wife, or where she came from. Peter Field has proposed that she was a Walsh of Wanlip, a manor a few miles north of Leicester, as the Walsh arms appear in Newbold Revel's parlour window (centre in Dugdale's engraving). I suggested earlier that Malory's connections with the Pulteneys in the 1420s could have stemmed from a marriage, an idea supported by the presence of their arms in the window as well. If Malory was married twice, first to a Pulteney, and secondly to a Walsh, everything would be explained. As Thomas, John and William Walsh became feoffees for Malory in the 1450s, and he had associations with Helen Walsh in the 1460s, it is reasonable to assume that his wife in the 1440s, Elizabeth, was indeed a Walsh.

As to children, we know that Malory had at least two sons: Robert, who was described as 'twenty-three and more' when declared to be his father's heir in 1471, and 'Thomas Malory Junior', who died in the late 1450s. He was described as 'junior' not because he was a child but to distinguish him from his father. There may also have been a third son, John, who became a Knight Hospitaller. He was probably born in the 1430s, or even the 1420s, as he had served at least five years in the headquarters of the Order by January 1468 when he was granted two preceptories. Malory's frequent long absences abroad and a possible period of widowerhood could have meant that his children were widely spaced in age. Other sons could have died besides Thomas, and no doubt he also had daughters. Women lost their name on marriage, and their original family is often not given on pedigrees. But if Malory had daughters who married into the families of his neighbours the Hathwycks of Harbury and the Boughtons of Lawton, it would explain the repeated support both families gave him when he was in prison in the 1450s.

Mention has already been made of the Malorys who appear in the Normandy rolls between 1436 and 1443: a Robert Malory served at Château Gaillard under Talbot in 1436; a John Malory mustered at Portsdown in 1441 in the retinue of Sir John Cressy, part of Somerset's ill-fated expedition to Cherbourg and Maine; and a Richard Malory mustered at Portsdown in 1443 in the retinue of Thomas Wake. John Malory went to France again in 1444, this time in the retinue of John Langton; with him was one John Aleyn, whose name will recur in connection with that of Sir Thomas Malory in 1454. In all probability, these Malorys were close or distant cousins, but if Malory did marry in the 1420s, he could have had sons of fighting age in the 1440s.

Whatever his relationship to these kinsmen, Sir Thomas, as the only knight in the family at this date, was now a figure of great authority in the family. His experiences as brother, cousin, father and uncle may explain his evident interest in kinship relationships in his *Arthur*. Some kinsmen are benevolent, others malign. Lancelot's notably loyal cousins Sir Bors, Sir Ector de Maris, Sir Blamore, Sir Bleoberis and Sir Lionel save his life time and again. But Arthur's sinister half-sisters and the ill-starred sons of King Lot of Orkney bring about the downfall of Camelot.

When a medieval lord referred to his 'family', he did not just mean his kinsfolk. The word still held its Latin meaning of 'household'. An estate the size of Newbold Revel required a hundred or more indoor and outdoor servants, agricultural labourers and tenants. Thanks to a detailed memorandum of the legal charges made against Malory and his accomplices in 1451 naming the accomplices accused with him of attacking the Abbey of Coombe, we know how substantial his household was, and have the names of many of its members in the 1440s. Two were gentlemen: Richard Malory of Radclyffe-on-the-Wreake (who may well have been the man mustered with Thomas Wake at Portsdown), and John Appleby, who was described as Malory's servant. Probably being trained up as a squire, he may have been an Appleby of Appleby Magna, near Bramcote. There was a cook called John Cook, a smith called Robert Smith, a bowmaker called Thomas Marriot, and a groom called John Masshot. The family's tailor John Furness lived in nearby Brinklow. Among the dozen or more yeomen, husbandmen and labourers named was an Irishman called Richard and a Welshman called Griffin; their presence may reflect journeys made by Malory himself to Wales or even Ireland, but they could also have been men he met while serving abroad and brought home with him.

Also listed was 'John Harper lately of Fenny Newbold in the county of Warwick, harper'. Given the warmly enthusiastic way that Malory writes of Sir Tristram's skill at harping, and the musicality of his own writing, it is no surprise that he had his own harper. Nor is it odd that John was pugilistic enough to join in the attack on Coombe. Harpers in medieval times were the highest-ranking minstrels. They were talented reciters, often composers, of romances, legends and histories, using their harps as a dramatic accompaniment to the storytelling. A Norman 'minstrel knight' led the charge against the Saxons at Hastings in 1066, chanting the 'Song of Charlemagne' and twirling his sword like a cheerleader. They were given privileged status – one manuscript illustration shows a harper perched on the table right in front of a king, strumming a lay to him and his court.

Malory uses this tradition to dramatic effect when Sir Dinadan, an Arthurian minstrel knight, suggests a way in which Sir Lancelot can be revenged on King Mark, who has sent poison-pen letters to King Arthur accusing Guinevere of adultery. Dinadan writes a scurrilous ballad about King Mark, and teaches it to 'an harper that hight Eliot'. Eliot teaches it to all the harpers he can find, and finally turns up at King Mark's court and sings it to Tristram.

> *And when Sir Tristram heard it, he said: 'O Lord Jesu, that Dinadan can make wonderly well and ill, thereas it shall be.' 'Sir,' said Eliot, 'dare I sing this song afore King Mark?' 'Yea, on my peril,' said Sir Tristram, 'for I shall be thy warrant.' Then at the meat came in Eliot the harper, and because he was a curious harper men heard him sing the same lay that Dinadan had made, the which spake the most villainy by King Mark of his treason that ever man heard.*
>
> *When the harper had sung his song to the end King Mark was wonderly wroth, and said: 'Thou harper, how durst thou be so bold on thy head to sing this song afore me.' 'Sir,' said Eliot, 'wit you well I am a minstrel, and I must do as I am commanded of these lords that I bear the arms of. And sir, wit ye well that Sir Dinadan, a knight of the Table Round, made this song, and made me to sing it afore you.' 'Thou sayest well,' said King Mark, 'and because thou art a minstrel thou shalt go quit, but I charge thee hie thee fast out of my sight.'*

In Malory's French sources, Eliot simply pleads that he is a fool; the idea that he could claim to be protected by Sir Dinadan because he bore his arms is entirely Malory's.

Besides those martial enough to be making rough music at Coombe Abbey, the Malory household would have had a chaplain, nursemaids, laundrymaids and sewing-women, and a baker and brewer. Humorous asides on the subject of servants in the *Morte Darthur* suggest that Malory was an agreeable master. He produces his own version of the scene in which Tristram and Isolde drink the love potion intended by Isolde's mother for King Mark. Instead of being handed the doctored wine by a servant who has made a mistake, Tristram unearths it, takes a swig and says jokingly to Isolde that their servants must have been keeping this 'noble wine' for themselves.

Mid-fifteenth-century life in a well-built house like Newbold Revel was extremely comfortable. Walls in such important rooms as the hall and the lord's and the lady's chamber were often completely lined with tapestry hangings, which created warmth and deadened sound. These were sometimes exquisite works of art in themselves, woven or painted to illustrate colourful scenes from romances or history. Minstrels used these as visual prompts as they entertained the assembled company at table in the hall. To the north of the hall behind a screen were the service quarters: a pantry and a buttery from which food and drink were dispensed, and a passage leading to the kitchen, in which dishes on their way to the hall could be laid out to be collected by the young servitors. Above the buttery and pantry there was a gallery, in which musicians could play and waits 'whiffle' at Christmas.

The first-floor rooms in the north wing were for the use of visitors and gently-born servants. To the south were the family's quarters and quite possibly a small upstairs room with an altar at its east end: the oratory which we know Malory's grandfather had installed at New-bold Revel. The private chambers or 'retiring rooms' were peaceful spaces away from the bustle of the household, attractive for such occupations as reading, making up accounts and needlework. They contained beds, but these were not only used for sleeping. Before the days of easy chairs, people lounged on beds by day as well as at night. Curtains and canopies provided privacy and warmth, and made them little rooms within rooms. Mattresses were made of canvas stuffed with straw, covered, if you were lucky, with a feather bed, linen sheets and heaps of furs. Bedcovers and curtains were woven with patterns, flowers, birds and beasts and heraldic insignia and, in the grander houses, embroidered with gold or silver thread.

Ceremonial furniture was intricately carved, especially the lord's chair on his dais in the great hall and the dresser or 'cup board' on which the family's plate was displayed on special occasions. The rest was simply and solidly made from elm, ash or oak. Since rooms usually had more than one function, items were often portable: tables made by putting two or three long boards on trestles, chests with carrying handles and locks, truckle beds on wheels for servants and children. Even the great canopied beds were easy to take to pieces.

Downstairs, floors were tiled or flagged, covered with plaited carpets of green-gold rushes, which were cheap to make and hard-wearing, and gave out a wonderful scent of new-mown hay when dampened to refresh them. Carpets, woven from silk or wool, were valuable items, and were spread on tables or thrown over high-backed benches rather than trodden underfoot. Some of the luxurious furnishings from that carrack from Rhodes that the Prior of St John brought duty-free into the country may well have ended up at Newbold Revel if Sir Thomas inherited them from his uncle. We could endow him and Lady Elizabeth with that sweet-smelling cypress chest full of damask sheets and napkins, a fine Turkey carpet to spread on the family's 'high table' in the great hall, and velvet wall-hangings to insulate the outside walls of the great parlour.

Of Books and Libraries

The breadth of reading displayed in the *Morte Darthur* suggests that Malory had privileged access to some fairly grand libraries. But there is no reason why a man with his interests and resources should not have had books of his own, including Arthurian romances, some in French, others in English. If the poverty-stricken Don Quixote could 'furnish his library with books on knight errantry', then so could Malory, even if he too had to sell a few acres to do so. The scarcity of books in wills and inventories has been seen as proof that it was unusual for any but very wealthy families to own them in substantial numbers, but it is just as likely to mean that books, like many valuables, were handed on before death as gifts or inherited entirely off the record. We only hear of them as bequests when an unusual disposal was made, such as Sir Richard Roos willing 'my great book called Saint Grall' to his niece rather than his heir in 1480. Elaborately illuminated books come to mind when we think about medieval reading matter. But such works of art were rare wonders. Their front-ispieces often show them being presented to a royal or noble patron, ornately bound in gilded covers inset with semi-precious stones and metals. Their pecuniary and aesthetic value is the reason that they survived; most medieval books became battered and broken from use (another reason for not including them in wills and inventories), and popular Arthurian romances were especially likely to be 'loved to death'.

Literacy was widespread in the fifteenth century. All over Europe, noble, gentle and wealthy mercantile families were demanding reading matter. Initiative, persistence and cash were all that it took to acquire books. Readers' tastes were diverse: devotional literature (the access-ible prayer books known as primers, or books of hours, were probably the commonest texts of all), Bible stories, riddles, classical literature, poems, prophecies, saints' lives, medical treatises, manuals on farming and the upbringing of children. Stories 'pleasant for to pass the time' that could be read aloud in vernacular English were hugely popular: histories, romance, and lurid moral tales like *The Hermit and the Outlaw, The Adulterous Falmouth Squire* and *How the Merchant did his Wife Betray*. Volumes of chronicles and romances were often among the spoils acquired by veterans of the French wars. Sometimes books were copied at home, but by the fifteenth century there was a brisk trade in copying manuscripts and binding them. Unpretentious everyday reading copies were turned out ten at a time by a squad of scribes taking dictation. All books were highly prized – on a page of a fifteenth-century English romance, *The Adventures of Arthur*, the Essex gentleman who owned it wrote a curt ownership rhyme: 'He that stealeth this book / shall be hanged on hook'. They were only lent to trusted friends.

Much reading matter was ephemeral – a few sheets (quires) of paper folded and sewn together down a fold and placed in a hinged wooden cover for temporary protection if it was being read or circu-lated between neighbours. Dedicated bibliophiles had copies of these oddments made and bound them together into what were called 'Great Books', folio-size miscellanies that reflected their owner's inter-ests. They were often a stimulating mix of prayers, stories, advice, written music and songs and riddles. Mention has already been made of the collection of chivalric treatises and tournament records of Malory's neighbour Sir John Astley. Sir John Paston, who met Astley at Henry VI's court, had Astley's book copied, and added several more items to what he referred to as 'my book of knighthood'. The bill from his scribe, William Ebesham, is a vivid window into the lost world of the scrivener. He charged twopence a sheet for the description of Edward IV's coronation and treatises on knighthood, war, and 'the challenges and acts of arms', but for *De Regimine Principe* asked only 'a penny a leaf', adding 'which it is right well worth'. The whole book, written on paper rather than vellum, and without any lavish illustrations and illuminations, cost £3 3s 5d. Paston was slow to pay up. A later letter beseeches him 'most tenderly to see me somewhat rewarded' as Ebesham is being dunned for the cost of paper and ink; he even asks Paston to send him 'for alms one of your old gowns'.

It would be reasonable to assume that Malory had at least one such miscellany. When Sir Bors and Sir Lancelot finish telling King Arthur about their adventures on the quest for the Grail, Malory comments, 'All this was made in great books, and put up in almeries at Salisbury'. The *Morte Darthur* itself has been seen as a fictional parallel to the collections of chivalric lore made by Astley and Paston. Most of these contained three elements: a treatise on military strategy, one on chivalric ethics, and one on princely statecraft. Malory's 'Tale of King Arthur' shows wise statecraft, his 'Arthur and Lucius' outlines military strategy, and his 'Tale of Sir Tristram' illustrates chivalric ethics. 'The Tale of the Sangreal' examines the relationship between knighthood and Christian virtues, and the final books tell the tragic story of how a combination of the human failings of the knights and an obsession with kinship issues above the loyalty due to a king bring about the downfall of the kingdom.

Although palaces, monasteries and universities might boast dedicated libraries and chained volumes, smaller collections of books were often stored in chests. This was not just for safety; the chests were carried around so that the books could be enjoyed wherever their owner happened to be. An educational tract of 1409 by Jean Gerson gave advice to Louis, Duke of Guienne, on the ideal contents of a basic library which could be 'carried, like a second Ark of the Covenant, through the desert of this world'. The young Duke died at Agincourt, aged only eighteen; if his 'ark' of books was in the plundered French baggage train, it could have ended up on sale in Paternoster Row, then a mecca for bibliophiles. Edward IV's wardrobe accounts include payments of 5d 'for black paper and nails for closing and fastening of divers coffers of fir wherein the King's books were conveyed and carried from the King's great Wardrobe in London unto Eltham.'

In a house like Newbold Revel, the books could have been kept in the chapel, as they were in Sir Thomas Urswick's manor at Marks, or in a small panelled closet or 'cabinet' off a private chamber, above the front porch, or at the top of staircase turrets. Such a 'cabinet' was both a secure place to store books and a peaceful retreat for literary composition. Manuscript illustrations show special chairs used by writers. They have a fixed slope in front of the seat with candleholders on each side of it, a holder for an inkhorn, and a beaded string of lead weights to keep the parchment or paper pages flat. Quills were made from the wing feathers of geese. The size of the feather was tailored to the user, and left-hand wing feathers were used to make right-handed pens, so that the curve swept outwards, balancing the quill for writing and (I am reliably informed) preventing it from tickling your chin. Scribes used the tips of their penknives, held in their spare hands, to steady the parchment and maintain even hand pressure. The knife was used for erasures as well as to sharpen the quill.

Ink was made from lampblack or gall. Lampblack is carbon, which could be made by setting a silver bowl over a candle, scraping off the soot, and mixing it with water and gum. Gall was extracted from oak galls which are formed when the gall wasp stings the twig of the tree to lay its eggs, producing a small apple-like berry. The caustic gall actually etches into the parchment. Naturally colourless, it was mixed with iron salts, lampblack, and other vegetable or mineral pigments. Red lead was usually used to highlight titles and important words, hence the word rubric, from rubeum – red. Parchment (sheep or goatskin) and vellum (calfskin), soaked and bleached, then stretched and scraped, was generally used for legal documents and grand volumes. Paper, made from pulverised cotton or linen rags dried on a wire mould and pressed, was used for more everyday reading matter. It was usually imported from France or Burgundy.

Although manuscript illuminations show authors such as Christine de Pisan doing their own writing, dictation was very common, and scriveners and secretaries were employed in many households. Malory's vigorous, colourful writing, much enlivened by direct speech and dialogue, sounds best spoken aloud, and his book may well have been written down by a listener. The 'William Verdon, scrivener' with whom Malory was associated in 1468 was probably his own employee; perhaps at work even then on the final revision of the *Morte Darthur*.

Friends and Neighbours

Almost everybody associated in legal records with Sir Thomas Malory in the 1440s lived, or had property, within a day's ride of his estates. This shows that he had an extensive network of connections: kinsfolk and friends, neighbours humble and great, well-wishers and enemies. Prominent among Malory's kinsfolk in Warwickshire was his last remaining uncle, Simon Malory of Chilverscoton. Knowledgeable about property matters and the law, he could advise his nephew on how to deal with avaricious overlords and recalcitrant tenants. He evidently also spent time in London; his burial in the church of the Hospitaller Priory at Clerkenwell suggests that he retired there as a corrodian.

Sir Thomas was also on friendly terms with the Malorys of Walton-on-the-Wold, Saddington and Croxton in Leicestershire and Tachbrook Mallory and Botley in Warwickshire. His father John had been a feoffee for the Walton branch of the family, conveying Saddington to the heir, William, and his wife in 1419. William's son John had some land very close to Newbold Revel at Harbury in 1428 and inherited Botley, a pretty hunting lodge in the Forest of Arden which had been his mother's dower, in 1434. Sir Thomas Malory was a witness of its sale in August 1443; so was Sir Thomas Erdington, who was one of Leicestershire's wealthiest knights. There were Malorys, too, at Litchborough and Green Norton. Malory will also have known something of his East Anglian cousins, Sir William Malory of Papworth St Agnes, who died in 1445, and his son and heir Thomas Malory, who took out a distraint of knighthood in 1465 and died four years later. He may even have visited or welcomed as guests such far-flung relatives as the Yorkshire Malorys of Hutton Conyers, near Ripon.

The chance survival of a single year of the accounts of Monks Kirby Priory during the 1440s shows that relations between Newbold Revel and the Priory were then amicable. In 1444–5 it was paying Malory an annuity of £2 a year. Such an amount was a common enough 'douceur' at the time – to ensure good neighbourliness and support against enemies. In the same accounts Malory is recorded as paying the Priory £5 for the tithe-corn (a tenth of his own harvest) of Stretton-under-Fosse. Monks Kirby was a daughter priory of the Carthusian monastery at Axholme, in Lincolnshire. Axholme, which had been founded in 1398 by Thomas Mowbray, Duke of Norfolk, was what was then known as an 'alien house' as it was an offshoot of the Carthusian foundation of St Nicholas of Angers, in France. Monks Kirby had gone into steep decline by the end of the fourteenth century, and only two monks were reported in residence. It may well have made a recovery under the guidance of Axholme, but it is likely that it was a useful source of rents rather than a respectable foundation in its own right.

There is one record of Malory's actions in the 1440s at which modern eyes might look askance. In the Sheriff of Northamptonshire's county court of October 1443, Thomas and his brother-in-law Eustace Burneby were indicted for attacking Thomas Smith of Spratton, a village about six miles south-east of Winwick and equally close to Burneby's manor of Watford. They were said to have insulted, sworn at, wounded, imprisoned and maltreated Smith, taking away £40 worth of his goods and chattels and committing other enormities 'ad grave dampnum' ('to his serious damage/injury') and against the peace. Neither appeared to answer the charge and the Sheriff sent Richard Gey and John Fray to fetch them.

In truth, there was nothing out of the way in the indictment. Such incidents are echoed in hundreds of cases involving medieval gentlefolk and, indeed, nobles. Nor were Malory and Burneby convicted. Either some settlement was made out of court, or the charge was dropped or disproved. But in view of the hail of accusations against Malory (two of them involving a couple called Hugh and Joan Smith) in the next decade, it is thought-provoking. What can we deduce from it? Smith was then as now a very common name, but to have had £40 of goods and chattels suggests that Mr Smith of Spratton was a man of some means. The phrase 'grave dampnum' is very vague in comparison with the usual gruesome details given of gouged-out eyes and lopped-off hands and 'hangers' (as testicles were colloquially known); nor does the indictment end, as a great many did, by saying that Smith's life was 'despaired of'. So any wounds are unlikely to have been serious. If Malory and Eustace Burneby believed that Smith had done wrong, or stolen something, they will have seen themselves as behaving in time-honoured knightly fashion rather than committing an injustice, in which case we could draw the conclusion that Malory was a man who had a hot temper and liked to take independent action. The fact that Thomas Smith bothered to take the matter to court suggests that Sir Thomas and his brother-in-law may have got the wrong man. The Spratton episode was not seen as a serious misdemeanour by Malory's contemporaries, as it did not prevent his acquisition of county offices or election as an MP soon afterwards. In both 1439 and 1448 Eustace Burneby was made Sheriff of Northamptonshire, 'a presentable office' which was held by 'the worshipfullest in the shire'.

The Camelot Years

Largesse engenders familiarity, that is true service; true
service engenders friendship, friendship engenders counsel
and help, by these things is all the world established.

The Governance of Princes (1456)

alory places great emphasis on the importance of having a good lord. 'Sir,' says Tristram, 'I thank you of your good lordship that I have had with you here, and the great goodness my lady ... hath shewed me, ... for in the parts of England it may happen I may do you service at some season, that ye shall be glad that ever ye shewed me your good lordship.' The driving force of politics in this period, says the historian Ian Arthurson, was 'loyalty to a lord and loyalty to his family and blood; and what flowed therefrom: pursuit of his right, revenge, and the demand for justice'.

In the early 1440s, Malory was retained by the most attractive 'good lord' in England: Richard Beauchamp's son Harry, 14th Earl of Warwick. Although a minor, he had considerable power, for he was surrounded by loyal allies. For although his mother had died shortly after his father, Henry VI had allowed her to choose both Harry's guardian and custodians for the Beauchamp lands. The Beauchamps' chaplain and biographer, John Rous, noted 'the early appearance of an heroick disposition' in the boy, describing him as 'a person of extraordinary hopes'. Nicknamed 'Child Warwick', he was a favourite companion of the King, making his first appearance in the royal council in November 1441, when he was only sixteen. When he came of age in 1446 he would be one of the three wealthiest nobles in the country, with an income of more than £7,000 a year. But his attendance at council shows that he was a force to be reckoned with well before then.

Lady Beauchamp's choices show the family's political allies. Passing over the Beaufort faction entirely, she appointed Duke Humfrey of Gloucester as Harry's guardian and Richard Neville, Earl of Salisbury, and Richard, Duke of York, as custodians of his Beauchamp estates. Salisbury was Harry's father-in-law; York's wife, Cecily Neville, was Harry's aunt by marriage. Both were abroad, defending the English territories in northern France; she knew Harry planned to join them. Their stewards provided the young heir with £200 a year; the rest of the profits from the Beauchamp lands went to Duke Humfrey. But Harry had other resources. Lady Beauchamp had enfeoffed her huge Despenser inheritance to her own and Harry's use before her death, and had also persuaded the King to allow her to select the trustees who would do the donkey work of managing this part of her son's inheritance. These men, reliable local gentry like John Beauchamp of Powicke, John Norris, Sir William ap Thomas, John Throckmorton, Thomas Hugford and John Vampage, did not only ensure that Harry was well provided for; they also carried out his orders. Thomas Portaleyn, a cultured book-lover who had been Keeper of the Beauchamps' household since 1436 and was now receiver-general of the Beauchamp estates, paid out over £300 for cloth of gold and other Italian luxuries for his young master.

A list of the young heir's retainers shows that he paid Sir Thomas Malory a retainer of 20 marks (£13 6s 8d) a year. This connection explains both the prestigious county offices that Malory held in the early 1440s, and the fact that he was MP for Warwickshire in 1445. Now probably in his early forties, widely read and full of exciting stories about battles in France and Hospitaller campaigns against the Turks, Malory would have been an attractive and knowledgeable mentor for an idealistic teenage aristocrat like Sir Harry. A contemporary parallel is provided in Oliver La Marche's 1445 description of Sir Jean d'Auxy's contribution to the education of Charles, Count of Charolais, heir to the dukedom of Burgundy:

This knight was a fine man, of good repute, mature and well-spoken, and gladly he told stories of chivalry and states-manship. He was a huntsman and a falconer, expert in all exercises and games; and I have never known a knight more eligible to have the governing of a young prince.

This kind of role may even have been what first prompted Malory to lift his quill (or hire a scribe to take dictation) to embark on the huge labour of translating the Arthurian stories into contemporary English prose. Knowing that these would be read or heard by Harry Beauchamp and his young wife, to say nothing of Harry's sister Anne, her husband Richard Neville and hopefully Henry VI himself, would have been a potent incentive to write them down. 'It offers well to kings and princes to have and get read before them oftimes old ancient noble stories,' advised Sir Gilbert Hay in his *Book of the Governance of Princes* (1456). 'Fashioning a gentleman or noble person in virtuous and gentle discipline should be most plausible and pleas-ing, being coloured with an historical fiction, the which the most part of men delight to read, rather for the variety of matter than for profit of the example,' wrote Edmund Spenser in the preface of his 'prequel' to King Arthur's reign, *The Faerie Queene*, a century and a half later.

Attendance on Sir Harry and his young wife Cecily would have taken Malory to Hanley Castle, their favourite home. It was a small curtain-walled castle, founded and much loved by King John. Comfortable rather than grand, it stood on a hill ten miles north of Tewkesbury and only a mile from the Severn, looking over the game-filled forests of Malvern Chase to the Malvern Hills and beyond into Wales. Walk up to its turf-veiled ruins from the river, and it is easy to understand its charm, although nothing more than the wide ditch that was once its moat marks its site.

When in London the Beauchamps stayed at Warwick Inn, or at their palatial manor in Walthamstow. They attended the Duke of York at Baynard's Castle, his Thameside fortress just south of St Paul's, when he was in England, but his position as Lieutenant-General of the English forces in France meant that he spent most of the early

1440s in Normandy. More frequent visits could be made to the Duke and Duchess of Gloucester at their riverside palace at Greenwich, 'Plaisaunce'. This was a magnet for Italian humanists, Flemish artists and talented English poets and chroniclers, and had hundreds of books in its library. Humfrey's literary interests ranged freely between romance and classical learning: he christened his two illegitimate children Arthur and Antigone. Humfrey was, like Beauchamp, a patron of John Lydgate, poet and chronicler. Both Harry and the young King were intelligent and fond of books. Margaret of Anjou's Clerk of the Signet was another poet, George Ashby, and Harry's arms appear in the front of a copy of John Lydgate's *The Fall of Princes*. It may well have been given to him by Duke Humfrey. Beauchamp gave Duke Humfrey at least one book at about this time, a copy of a French translation of Boccaccio's *Decameron*. Malory's knowledge of chronicles and romances would certainly have been enhanced if he visited Duke Humfrey with the Beauchamps.

The Beauchamps also spent time at Windsor and Westminster in attendance on King Henry VI, now a tall, thin, sensitive young man with fine-boned hands and feet. Rumours that he was 'not steadfast of wit as other kings hath been' were intensifying, but he was much loved for his innocent directness and generosity of spirit. Dominated by his spiritual advisers, he spent more time than most kings reading the Scriptures, and even had his own copy of the Bible in English. He valued education highly, and founded Eton College at Windsor and King's College, Cambridge. His favourite English kings, Alfred the Great, and Edward the Confessor, were noted for their learning, and he tried to get the Pope to canonise them both. Harry Beauchamp also had an interest in learning and a pious side. He contributed to the foundation of Eton, and knew the Psalms of David by heart, 'reciting the whole psalter daily', says Rous, 'when not prevented by greater business'. Pope Nicholas V wrote to him personally to ask him to be 'captain of his wars' in his proposed crusade against the Turks. It is easy to imagine the two idealistic young men listening to Malory telling the story of the quest for the Holy Grail – and identifying firmly with Sir Galahad and Sir Percivale.

Harry was eager to win the lofty status of the King's first knight by showing 'great hardiness and noble prowess in arms' in France. 'Before he accomplished full nineteen years of age,' writes Dugdale, 'he tendered his services for the defence of Aquitaine.' Harry's nineteenth birthday was 22 March 1444. This suggests that he was on the way back from France when he was honoured at Dover by the King in person in the spring of 1444. A charter Henry VI signed there on 2 April created him premier earl of England, with precedence over all other earls and the right to wear a gold circlet. Henry also made Harry one of the small and exclusive band of Knights of the Garter, and by special dispensation allowed him to come into full possession of his inheritance early. These favours made the young Earl a target for resentment. Squabbles over precedence between peers could lead to duels to the death, and there were demands for promotion from other peers, especially those who felt their blood superior to that of the Beauchamps. Foremost among the envious was Humphrey, Earl of Stafford. To placate him, Henry VI made him Duke of Buckingham in September 1444.

'There was a mighty duke . . . that held war against him long time'

Since it was Buckingham whom Sir Thomas Malory will be accused of attempting to murder in January 1450, we need to know more about him. Buckingham's sense of his own importance had some justification. Born in 1402, he was first cousin of the Duke of Suffolk and the Earl of Westmorland. He shared a great-grandfather with the King: Humphrey de Bohun, whose immense inheritance had, through his two daughters, been divided between the house of Lancaster and the Staffords. Buckingham also had royal blood: Edward III, Henry VI's great-great-grandfather, was Buckingham's great-grandfather, as his grandmother Elinor de Bohun had married Edward III's youngest son, Thomas of Woodstock. The Stafford family's biographer, Carole Rawcliffe, calls Buckingham 'an unimaginative and unlikeable man' with a 'harsh and often vindictive disposition' and a selfish dislike of being drawn into other men's quarrels. 'Fat and full of grease', according to a contemporary lampoon, he was ruthlessly single-minded in pursuing his own interests. 'Blatantly partisan' is the judgement of one modern historian. But he was also exceptionally politically adroit, and it was he who turned the Earls of Stafford into premier dukes of the realm.

Barely eighteen when he first went to France in 1420, Buckingham served there off and on for nearly twenty years, holding such offices as Constable of France, Governor of Paris, and Lieutenant-General of Normandy. In 1424 he married Anne Neville, daughter of Ralph, Earl of Westmorland and his second wife Joan Beaufort, and thus a niece of Cardinal Beaufort. He was well rewarded for his efforts in France with the captaincy of Bellême Castle and an income of 800 marks a year as Count of Perché. In 1438, the death of his mother, the Dowager Countess of Stafford, meant that he inherited her huge double jointure (she had been married to both the 3rd and the 5th earls), and her shared claim to the earldoms of Essex, Northampton and Hereford via her Bohun mother. This added another £4,500 a year to Buckingham's existing income of £1,500. A staunch ally of Cardinal Beaufort and the peace party, he went to France in 1439 to negotiate the end of the war. In 1444, he married his son and heir to the daughter of Edmund Beaufort, Duke of Somerset, another descendant of Edward III. In 1445, he would look even higher. After the death of the wife of the French Dauphin Louis (later Louis XI), he was in negotiation with Louis's father Charles VII for a match between Louis and one of his daughters.

In the 1440s Buckingham turned his attention to his English estates. In 1438 he had acquired Maxstoke Castle from the Clintons. Built in the 1350s, it lies in a commanding position eight miles north-west of Coventry at the crossing of Watling Street and Akeman Street, close to Sir William Mountfort's seat at Coleshill. Its quadrangles, polygonal corner turrets and crenellated walls remain remarkably unchanged. In the 1440s it still had a curtain wall for extra defence, a walkway for sentries behind its battlements and a forbidding gatehouse, complete with 'murder holes' from which to drop missiles on intruders and prison cells. Inside it was luxuriously appointed, with a plentiful provision of garderobes. Its banqueting hall was a scaled-down version of the 'great chambers' at Kenilworth and Warwick Castle, with an elaborately traceried west window and a fine crown-post timber roof. Buckingham also held Weedon Bec and Atherstone, east of Maxstoke, both granted to him for life by the Crown in 1438. Another of his strongholds was Rugby Castle, just ten miles from Newbold Revel.

Given his character and ambitions, and his policy of paying generous retainers to tempt traditional Beauchamp supporters into his affinity, it is not in the least surprising that Buckingham and his close ally Sir Edward Grey of Groby soon came into open conflict with both Harry Beauchamp and Malory. But Harry Beauchamp's position in the county was unassailable. The sheriffs from 1444–6 – Sir Robert Harcourt and Sir Thomas Erdington – were both his men. His chaplain John Rous and his retainer Ralph Neville replaced nominees of Buckingham and Grey as Justices of the Peace in 1444. In February 1446 Harry himself became a Justice of the Peace, ousting Buckingham from the bench. Most of the other county offices were also held by Beauchamp supporters. Although Buckingham was asked to serve with the two MPs on the first shire commission to assess taxes, he was replaced in 1446 by John Carpenter, Bishop of Worcester, who was, like Harry, close to the King.

Simmering magnate rivalry, and the fact that Beauchamp's power was in the ascendant, probably explains an incident involving Malory and Sir William Peyto, the man who had galloped into Warwick with a gang of retainers during the 1427 parliamentary elections and substituted his own name as candidate in place of that of Thomas's father. A petition by Lady Katherine Peyto to the Chancellor and Archbishop of Canterbury, John Stafford, claimed that Sir Thomas Malory 'of Fenny Newbold' stole four oxen from her estates around Sibbertoft Castle, a few miles east of Swinford, and threatened to maim or murder the bailiff who tried to stop him. The date of the incident is uncertain, but it could well have been in the mid-1440s.

To justify, or at least make sense of, Sir Thomas's action, we need to know what had been happening to Peyto. As aggressive and disaster-prone as Gawaine, he was now serving in France under the Talbots, who were in dispute with Harry Beauchamp over his inheritance, and the Beauforts, also rivals rather than friends of the Warwick earls. Disaster hit him in 1443 when he was in command of the siege of Dieppe. The English captured the castle, but not the town, and then found themselves besieged when a relief force led by the Dauphin arrived. After ten months the French took the castle; most of the English were put to the sword and Peyto was held to ransom for £500 – far more than he could afford to pay. For the next ten years he was in debt to anyone in the Midlands who would lend him money, and remained mortgaged to the hilt.

Malory and Peyto were old enemies, and will clash again. We have no way of knowing the rights and wrongs of the matter, but we do know that justice was as important to the young Duke of Warwick as it was to Malory. 'Sir Harry', Rous writes, would not allow any 'officer of his to oppress any man' and if it came to his knowledge that they had, 'he would sore punish them and [if] they would not mend thereby they should not serve him'. If the incident did take place in 1445 or 1446, there is a strong possibility that Malory was merely taking goods in lieu of money owed to him or Harry Beauchamp when he rustled the oxen.

Certainly when Lady Peyto petitioned 'my lord of Warwick', whom she described as 'now late being in the countrey [i.e. Warwickshire]', she found she could 'have no remedie'. Nor did she get any satisfaction when she complained about a very similar attack on Peyto's lands further west in Gloucestershire which certainly took place in 1446. That it, too, was carried out by prominent and respectable men who were retained by the stewards of Harry Beauchamp's estates (Thomas Burdet, John Rous and Thomas Throckmorton) suggests that Beauchamp rather than Malory was behind both raids. Lady Peyto must have been hoping that the court of the Chancellor, Archbishop John Stafford, would prove more accommodating to a family now more closely linked with allies of Stafford's kinsman Buckingham than to Beauchamp.

Doves versus Hawks

Acrimony between Buckingham and Harry Beauchamp locally was mirrored by clashes between them at court. The burning political issues of the early 1440s were the war with France and the King's marriage. They were interlinked. England was split between those who were prepared to compromise both on territories held and grandiose claims to the French Crown and make peace with the French, and those who believed that to do so would be a betrayal of all that Henry V had lived and died for. The doves, who dominated the royal council and had been systematically starving the war effort for years, were led by Buckingham, Cardinal Beaufort, the Bishop of Chichester, Adam Moleyns (who was the King's secretary), the Earls of Somerset and Dorset (both Beaufort's nephews), and William de la Pole, Duke of Suffolk. Suffolk was the peace party's most active member in the 1440s. He was close in age to Malory and, like him, a veteran of the French wars. He fought at Harfleur in 1415 and had served under Humfrey of Gloucester in 1417. In the 1420s he was a notably successful commander. Captured by the French in 1430, he is reputed to have said that he would only surrender to Joan of Arc herself, because she was the bravest woman on earth. After he was ransomed in 1431, he stayed in England where he became a key member of the royal council and was given the well-paid position of 'keeper' of Charles of Orléans, still a prisoner of the English fifteen years after Agincourt. It was a congenial duty. Both men had notable chivalric reputations. Suffolk was inspired by Charles's poetry to write French verse himself; Charles experimented with rondels in English. Personal friendship may have led Suffolk to argue for Orléans's release as an ambassador for peace, but there was no doubt that by 1440 he himself favoured the end of hostilities. In 1441, Orléans was finally freed.

The hawks were headed by Harry Beauchamp's two most powerful well-wishers: his guardian Humfrey of Gloucester and Richard, Duke of York. In 1437 Duke Humfrey had commissioned a biography of his brother Henry V that was intended to remind the new generation of all that had been fought for. It may have been on his urging that in

1438 Cardinal Beaufort at last set masons to work on Henry's long-delayed chantry tomb in Westminster Abbey, and his influence that made it an exceptionally triumphalist monument to Henry's French ambitions. Richard of York, Commander-in-Chief in France, was constantly urging more support to maintain the English holdings there. Harry's eagerness to go and prove himself in Aquitaine suggests that he too was committed not just to the defence of the English territories in France but to the recovery of any lost conquests.

But although public opinion was with the hawks, they were no match for the political acumen of their opponents. One by one, they came under devastating attack. The first move was made against Duke Humfrey's one-time mistress, now wife, the charismatic and powerful Elinor of Cobham. She was accused of sorcery in 1441. The charge was fed by the same superstitious fears of necromancy that had made possible the financially very profitable trial and conviction of Henry IV's Queen Joanna of Navarre by Henry V. This time the plan was to destroy the influence of the Duchess on the King, which contemporary chroniclers all agreed was considerable, and also to put into question Gloucester's suitability to inherit the throne. The line between the 'white magic' of alchemy and astrology, in which interest was widespread, and the 'black magic' of witchcraft and sorcery was a fine one. Whether or not the Duchess of Gloucester did ask the astrologer Roger Bolingbroke to cast her horoscope with an eye to finding out if she was going to be Queen of England one day, we do not know, but she admitted to employing Bolingbroke, who had the reputation of being more sorcerer than astrologer. She confessed only to using love potions to persuade Duke Humfrey to marry her and fertility potions to help her bear him a legitimate heir, but the court, which was headed by Buckingham, Suffolk and other peers hostile to the Gloucesters, convicted her of witchcraft, heresy and treason.

Elinor was stripped of all her honours, her marriage was dissolved, and she was condemned to life imprisonment. The bishops, led by Beaufort and Moleyns, who had acted as chief prosecutor, also imposed an immediate and shockingly public penance. Three times in a week she walked barefoot and hoodless through the streets of London to offer candles in atonement for her sins in different churches. It was a devastating humiliation for a proud woman who had hoped to be Queen of England, but she did it, a spectator reported, 'right meekly, so that the most part of the people had on her great compassion'.

Elinor was first imprisoned in Leeds Castle in Kent, but early in January she was taken to Chester Castle under heavy guard. We might imagine that Harry Beauchamp, who must have known his guardian's wife well, was indignant about her fate, but the council had passed a pre-emptive edict forbidding interference with the proceedings. 'A word for me no man durst say' runs a line of the anonymous 'Lament of the Duchess of Gloucester'. Harry Beauchamp may however have used his influence with the King to get Elinor moved to Kenilworth Castle, only a few miles from Warwick, in October 1443. Once there, she was looked after by its constable, Lord Sudeley, one of Harry's feoffees for his Despenser inheritance. Duke Humfrey could at least communicate with her, perhaps even meet her secretly.

'Then there was made a provision for the day of marriage'

The shaming of the Gloucesters made the King's marriage more urgent. Otherwise, after Duke Humfrey's death, it would be hard to better the succession rights of Richard, Duke of York. Martially-minded and brusque of speech, and already the father of three sons and as many daughters, Richard was descended from both Edward III's second son, Lionel of Clarence, and his fifth son, Edmund of Langley. Purists could and later would argue that his claim was in fact stronger than that of the Lancastrian kings, who were the descendants of John of Gaunt, Duke of Lancaster, Edward III's third son.

Who Henry VI chose as a bride mattered enormously. Humfrey of Gloucester's hopes of a match with one of the daughters of the rebellious Count of Armagnac had been dashed. The Beauforts' and Suffolk's preferred candidate was Margaret of Anjou. Her father, René, King of Jerusalem, Hungary, Aragon, Sicily and Majorca, Duke of

Anjou, Maine, Bar and Lorraine, and Marquis of Provence, was a charming and cultured man, though most of his titles were wishful thinking and even Maine was occupied by the English. Twice imprisoned for ransom in the attempt to recover his lost domains, he was also far from wealthy. But his capital Angers, which was far more prosperous and cultured than war-racked Paris, was a famous centre for writers, painters and chivalry. Most important of all, his sister Marie was the Queen of France. The Angevins thus had considerable influence at court, and it was hoped that an alliance with them would make Charles VII improve the terms on which he would agree to peace.

Remembering the effort made by Henry VI to be at Dover to honour Harry Beauchamp in April 1444, it is possible that Child Warwick had just returned from a secret trip to France. Somerset's campaign of 1443 had never reached Aquitaine; it got no further than Maine. Somerset returned unfêted, and died soon afterwards. An English expedition did cross to Harfleur on 15 March, but it was in search of peace, not military glory. The truce signed at Tours in May 1444 was being negotiated and it was a time when a knight with a safe-conduct could cross enemy territory to fight in a tournament – as Sir John Astley had done in 1438, three years before the arrival in England of the Spanish knight errant Sir Philip Boyle for the January 1442 Smithfield challenge.

An incognito trip to Anjou to inspect the prospective Queen, even perhaps entering the lists as a young unknown in one of René's frequent tournaments, would certainly have appealed to the son of the man whom the Emperor Sigismund had praised as 'the father of courtesy'. If Sir Harry did go, there is also no doubt that Malory would have enjoyed accompanying him. King René, then thirty-nine, was the acknowledged European expert on tournaments and loved the Arthurian legends. In 1446 he organised a tournament at Saumur, the fairy-tale château which was the family's favourite residence. Its jousts were fought by knights dressed up as heroes of the Round Table; there was a wooden castle called Joyeuse Garde, in which lions, tigers and unicorns from the royal menagerie roamed. A dwarf dressed as a Turk bore the royal shield, and a glamorous damsel led the King's horse. René wrote the *Manual for the Perfect Organization of Tourneys*, beautifully illustrated with miniatures in its de luxe versions, which became the standard guide to the correct etiquette and procedures for such occasions. Written in the 1440s, it was later translated into almost every European language. It explained how to draw up challenges, how to decorate the town where the tournament was to be held, how to vet the participants for lineage and prowess, and how to display all the banners and crests of the knightly champions for the benefit of their chosen ladies.

René was himself an accomplished poet and artist, and an ancient tradition has it that he was responsible for illustrating as well as writing the hauntingly romantic *Livre de Cueur de L'Amour Epris*. Its characterful heroes and heroines are said to be lifelike portraits of himself, his family and friends. If so, then Hope, who repeatedly saves the day for Cueur, might well be seen as a likeness of his daughter Margaret: she wears a crown and has a flamboyant mane of red-gold hair, and closely resembles the portrait of Margaret on the title page of the chivalric anthology given to her as a wedding present by John Talbot, Earl of Shrewsbury, the greatest soldier of the age.

Margaret was already renowned for her beauty and intelligence. She came from a long line of powerful women. Her paternal grandmother, Queen Yolande of Aragon, had led the Angevin contingent at the Battle of Baugé dressed in silver armour in 1421, and backed the cause of Joan of Arc in 1429. Her mother, Isobel of Lorraine, was equally spirited, leaving her mother-in-law as regent and setting off alone to Naples in 1435 to fight for her imprisoned husband's Italian inheritance until he could arrange parole or ransom. The six-year-old Margaret was left behind in Anjou, where she lived for eight years with Queen Yolande, who held court in style, mainly in the châteaux of Saumur and Baugé, and gave her granddaughter an education fit for a princess.

By the time her parents returned, defeated, from Italy in 1443, Margaret was thirteen, a clever and vivacious young princess who loved reading romances and riding out to hunt. Charles, Duke of Orléans, told the English envoys that 'this woman excels all others, as well in beauty as in wit, and is of stomach and courage more like to a man than to a woman'. She could 'have been formed by heaven to supply to her royal husband the qualities which he required in order to become a great king'. Orléans's twenty-five-year-long captivity in England meant that he knew better than most the qualities that Henry lacked. He had seen the English King grow from a baby to a well-meaning but distinctly malleable young man.

The idea of a peace with France that renounced the English King's right to the throne of France, let alone surrendered land, was still deeply unattractive in England, especially in London, and the Beauforts stood well back from the official negotiations. It was William de la Pole, Duke of Suffolk, who was named as chief ambassador, authorised by Henry VI 'to conclude a peace or truce with our uncle of France' and to negotiate the marriage. Aware that the mission would make him hugely unpopular, he petitioned the King in full council for an absolute indemnity against any future charges brought against him by the King or his heirs on account of anything effected by the embassy. Duke Humfrey sat in sullen silence while it was granted, but it may have been his doing that at the same time over £11,500 was issued in assignments to the Duke of York for the unpaid wages of the Dieppe garrison.

Suffolk and his embassy landed at Harfleur on 15 March 1444. If Harry Beauchamp and Malory had indeed crossed the Channel with him, they could have continued to Saumur for an Angevin tournament, and then returned to England to be at Dover on 2 April. It is, frankly, a fantastical idea but, as with the speculations (see Chapter 9) over the extent of Malory's knowledge and experience of the Knights Hospitallers, it illuminates our understanding of the times to imagine it happening – or at least Sir Harry and Malory wishing that it could have happened.

The negotiations, which had opened in Vendôme on 8 April and continued at Tours on 26 April, took place with ceremonial worthy of the *Morte Darthur*. The English ambassadors reached Tours after a pleasant sail down the Loire from Blois, and the journey was punctuated by feasts with King Charles VII, the Dukes of Brittany and Alençon, and René of Anjou. A month of festivities preceded the signing of the marriage treaty and Margaret's betrothal on 24 May.

There were tournaments, an archery contest between the French King's Scots guards and English archers, battles between giants on camels and a great Maying, at which three hundred knights and squires rode out with the Dauphine, Charles VII's daughter-in-law.

The treaty was remarkably unfavourable to England. Margaret renounced all claims to her father's lands and her dowry was an empty claim to the kingdom of Majorca and 20,000 francs. Though a truce was signed, it was only for twenty-one months. Suffolk returned to England to tell his country to prepare to receive a queen 'of high and noble birth, greatly endowed with gifts of grace and nature'. Duke Humfrey was unimpressed, objecting to Parliament that Margaret was 'not worth ten marks', but he, York and Beauchamp could only accept the King's decision with good grace and consider how best to win the new Queen's favour. Henry VI himself was excited and eager. He distributed largesse gratefully and Suffolk was elevated to a marquisate.

No one was more honoured than Harry Beauchamp. In a dramatic declaration of favour, Henry VI made him Duke of Warwick with, to Buckingham's ill-concealed fury, precedence over all other dukes except those of royal blood. He also made him King of the Isle of Wight and gave him the manor of Bristol and all the royal manors in the Forest of Dean. Finally he awarded him and his male heirs the reversions (i.e. after their present holder Buckingham's death) of the lordship of the Channel Islands and the stewardship in tail male of the enormous Duchy of Lancaster lordship of the Honour of Tutbury and the High Peak. The stewardship gave its holder immense territorial power in Staffordshire and Derbyshire, and in Beauchamp hands would be a formidable threat to Buckingham's influence in the north Midlands. It had never before been granted as an hereditary office. Buckingham must have been incensed with fury.

In November 1444 Harry Beauchamp joined the splendid embassy of peers and peeresses, led by Suffolk who was to act as Henry's proxy, that set out in a fleet of fifty ships to collect Margaret. It was a long-drawn-out expedition, as Charles VII and René of Anjou were making the most of the truce to defend René's territory in Lorraine.

English troops were sent to help them, but even so it was March before the proxy marriage took place in Nancy. Margaret wore a white satin dress embroidered in silver and gold thread with daisies – *marguerites*, her personal emblem. There were eight days of festivities, including jousts. Sir Harry could have participated in them, but the only bout recorded in detail is the show joust between Margaret's personal champion Sir Pierre de Brezé and Suffolk. Then she processed northwards. Making the best of things, Richard of York met her in Paris and presented her with a pretty palfrey caparisoned with crimson and gold velvet sewn with gold roses which had been sent to her by Henry VI. York travelled with her to Harfleur, where a fleet of fifty ships awaited her.

The crossing was a long and stormy one. When Margaret finally arrived at Portchester Castle at the head of Southampton Water on 9 April, she was desperately seasick, and Suffolk had to carry her ashore; they were both soaked to the skin. It took the fifteen-year-old girl over a fortnight to recover. On 23 April, she and Henry were married quietly at Titchfield Abbey by the King's confessor William Ayscough. Ayscough was a domineering killjoy who, it was said, warned the King only to have intercourse with his wife in order to procreate children, not for 'wanton sport'.

Wedding presents flooded in, including a live lion sent by an anonymous admirer. Malorys sported lions on their coats of arms; so too did Beauchamps. Whoever sent it, it was a highly appropriate gift for a girl who matured into a truly lion-hearted queen. Another fine gift was the imposing anthology presented to Margaret by Talbot. Sumptuously illustrated, it contained Arthurian and other romances in French, poems, a document on the Order of the Garter, two important manuals of chivalric warfare, Honoré Bouvet's *Arbre des Batailles* (which included actual battle plans) and Christine de Pisan's *Faits d'armes*, and a book on royal governance, Giles of Rome's *De Regimine Principum*.

It was Humfrey of Gloucester who escorted Margaret to London from Hampshire with a guard of honour of five hundred men, and she spent her first few days in the capital at his Greenwich palace. It was then surrounded with a deer park of 100 acres, and its towered belvederes, one of them on the present site of the Royal Observatory, gave superb views of London. Given her education and interests, she will have admired its library as well as the luxurious furnishings, wall paintings and stained-glass windows.

Margaret's coronation took place in Westminster Abbey on 30 May. As usual there were splendid pageants when she progressed through the City of London from the Tower. Everywhere daisies were sported in her honour and the water conduits ran with 'both white wine and red for all people that would drink'. Every peer in the realm was urged to attend, 'all other things left and excuses ceasing', and there were three days of tournaments and feasting afterwards.

Knight of the Shire

In January 1445 Sir Thomas Malory was chosen to sit in Parliament for the first time. His fellow MP for Warwickshire was Sir William Mountfort, now some sixty-five years old. Sir William had sat in Parliament on no fewer than eight occasions. He had been steward of the Beauchamp household in Sir Richard's time, and the Countess had made him executor of her will and one of the trustees of Harry Beauchamp's estates. But Mountfort's election was not necessarily good for Beauchamp influence: in recent years Sir William had become a trusted retainer to Buckingham.

Parliament first met on 25 February 1445, reconvening after Easter on 29 April, so Malory would have been in London to witness the coronation. Plague broke out in the city in June, and the session was prorogued until 20 October. It was not dissolved until 9 April 1446. One of its first measures was to vote King Henry two fifteenths to pay for bringing Margaret over from France (some £5,000) and the coronation. Parliament also voted Margaret an annual income of 10,000 marks (£6,666 13s 4d), the same as that provided for Henry IV's wife Joanna of Navarre and Henry V's wife Catherine of Valois.

Several important statutes were passed. Elections to the House of Commons were becoming hotly contested, a reflection of Parliament's growing importance. Electing non-resident MPs, often royal courtiers or retainers of influential nobles, in boroughs was now commonplace. As many as two-thirds of the burgesses sent by the towns to Parliament were non-resident. The 1445 Parliament evidently wanted to ensure local representation by preventing the practice from spreading to the shire knights. It enacted that no man should be a knight of the shire unless he was 'a notable knight' of the county he represented, or at least a gentleman of it who was 'able to be a knight'.

Despite the plague, Harry Beauchamp, and perhaps Malory, stayed on in London, assisting with the entertainment of the French ambassadors who arrived to discuss the terms of peace in July. He rode out of London to meet the embassy, which was led by Louis Bourbon, Count of Vendôme, and Jacques Jouvenel des Ursins, the Archbishop of Rheims, one of the principal negotiators, actually lodged with him. He was at their Westminster audience with the King on 15 July 1445. Henry VI welcomed the French ambassadors with effusive enthusiasm, swearing undying friendship for his 'uncle of France', and even offered to go to France to visit him. The French ambassadors came away with the impression that the King would do almost anything to achieve peace, that Suffolk was high in favour with the King, and that Gloucester was not. Worse was to come. When York had returned at the end of his five-year term as Lieutenant in Normandy in the autumn of 1445, he found himself cold-shouldered. There was no move to repay the £38,677 owing to him for his service in France.

Parliament reassembled in London in October 1445. As a retainer of Harry Beauchamp, Malory would have been interested in an acerbic precedency dispute in the Lords. When Henry VI had declared earlier that year that Harry Beauchamp's dukedom would, when he came of age, rank above that of Buckingham, he showed himself remarkably insensitive to the Duke of Buckingham's pride in his royal descent. Buckingham was 'so stomackt' that he raised the matter in Parliament in early December. Beauchamp insisted on his rights. 'The contention and strife moved betwixt them for that pre-eminence' were so great that it was decided that they would hold pride of place turn and turn about. When Harry Beauchamp came of age in April 1446, 'one of the said Dukes should have the pre-eminence and sit above the other an whole year, and then that other above him all the next year after'. Harry was to take precedence the first year.

After a year of marriage, it was becoming clear that Henry VI was deeply in love with his enchanting young French wife and would do anything she asked of him. How completely Margaret gained the King's utter confidence is revealed in an extraordinary survival: a cache of seventy-five letters from Margaret unearthed in 1861 in an attic at Emral, the ancient seat of the Puleston family in Flintshire. They are full of requests for favours for herself and her own servants, marriage-brokerage and attempts to interfere in court cases. They show an intimate knowledge of Privy Seal mandates from Henry, often recommending that these be acted upon in terms that make it clear that the orders were Margaret's idea in the first place. A letter from her to the Parker of Salisbury's great deer park at Ware shows that, like Rider Haggard's 'She', the Queen expected to be obeyed:

> *Well beloved, for as we much as we know verily that our cousin th'erl of Salisbury will be right well content and pleased that, at our resorting unto our castle of Hertford, we take our disport and recreation in his park of Ware; we, embolding us thereof, desire and pray you that the game there be spared, kept, and cherished for the same intent, without suffering any other person there to hunt or shoot, course, or other disport.*

'Almost all the affairs of the realm were conducted according to the queen's will, by fair means or foul, as was said by several people,' wrote the contemporary chronicler Thomas Gascoigne. 'What will be the result of all this, God knows.'

More serious than exercising power at home was Margaret's influence on England's relations with France. Letters written within weeks of her coronation promised her 'dear uncle' the King of France that she would do her utmost to persuade Henry to cede Maine to the person who was in her eyes its rightful ruler, her father, René of Anjou. Although rationalisation of the English holdings in France was urgently necessary, to give away an entire hard-won French province with no assurance of any concession in return was diplomatic lunacy. Even the dove-dominated council was uneasy when it began to realise that Henry had decided to do just that. On 9 April 1446 Parliament was told that the King had decided, 'of his own mind and by divine inspiration, not by the promptings of his council', to cross the Channel in September and discuss peace with his uncle Charles VII face to face. The plan was to meet on the River Seine, between Meulan and Mantes. What no one but Henry, Margaret and the French secretary who wrote the letter then knew was that months before, on 22 December 1445, after much cajoling from his wife Henry had secretly written to Charles VII unconditionally promising to cede Maine to his new Angevin relations as his dear and well-beloved companion the Queen had repeatedly requested him to do.

The early 1440s were in all probability the happiest half-decade of Malory's life, his Camelot years. Retained by the most splendid young duke in Christendom, possessed of three handsome manors and a growing library of books on romance and chivalry, Member of Parliament for his shire, enjoying the presence on the throne of an idealistic young king and a cultured and beautiful queen whose antecedents were as romantic as the most ardent chivalric hero could desire, and with sons growing up to follow his example, there was every reason to be content. This peaceful period, and the influence of a French queen steeped in her father's extensive knowledge of romantic literature, may have encouraged Malory to acquire, or at least borrow and read, a greater variety of books, especially books in French. Careful analysis of his writing in the last two decades has revealed that he had read far more versions of the Arthurian legends than previously realised, and that he accumulated more knowledge as he went along. This explains why there are occasional contradictions in his tales. It also suggests that writing was a lifelong interest rather than something he turned to in the last few years of his life to escape the ennui of imprisonment.

So what exactly had he read? A complete reconstruction is impossible. But by the time he finished his Arthuriad, he had digested or tasted at least one version of *Merlin, Suite de Merlin, Lancelot,*

Perlesvaus, Tristan, La Queste del Saint Graal, Escanor, La Mort le Roi Artu, Le Chevalier de Charette, and *Yvain* (by Chrétien de Troyes). Many of these French romances ran to a thousand pages or more. In English he knew the alliterative *Morte Arthure,* the stanzaic *Le Morte Arthur, Torrent of Portyngale, Lybeaus Desconus, Ipomadon, Syre Gaweyne and the Carle of Carelyle, The Avowing of King Arthur, Ywain and Gawain, Arthour and Merlin, Sir Launfal, The Jest of Sir Gawayne, The Awynters of Arthure* and *Sir Degrevant.* He also appears to have read Chaucer's *Troilus, Knight's Tale* and *Franklin's Tale,* the Duke of York's *Book of Game* and other hunting manuals, John Hardyng's *Chronicle,* Lydgate's *Fall of Princes, Resoun and Sensuality,* 'Complaint of the Black Knight', 'That Now is Hay', *Pageant of Knowledge and Wisdom,* Vegetius's *Art of War,* the devotional writings of Nicholas Love, and the New Testament.

Broad as Malory's reading in English was, his long years in France seem to have produced a passion for French romances, It is clear that he thought that 'the French books', which he cites as his source some seventy times, were much more reliable Arthurian authorities than were English ones. He mentions these only once, and disparagingly at that.

> *And there they all lived in their countries as holy men. And some English books make mention that they went never out of England after the death of Sir Lancelot, but that was but favour of makers. For the French book maketh mention, and is authorised, that Sir Bors, Sir Ector, Sir Blamore, and Sir Bleoberis, went into the Holy Land thereas Jesu Christ was quick and dead.*

The influence of English sources is most marked in the first tales; by the time Malory gets on to 'The Book of Sir Tristan', he is clearly much better read in French romances than he was when he wrote 'The Tale of King Arthur'. Although he frequently shows originality in his writing, there are also long passages which are almost word-for-word translations from the French. It may have been politic to admire French literature, given the well-known interest of the new Queen in high romance, and it is possible that the reason that he tackled the formidable challenge of 'briefly drawing out' the stories into English was to provide an English translation of French Arthurian tales so that Margaret of Anjou could use it as a way of improving her English.

Malory may have experimented at about this time with different forms of writing. There is evidence that, influenced by reading Chaucer, he tried his hand at writing verse: there are a remarkable number of similarities between the *Morte Darthur* and a contemporary verse romance called *The Wedding of Sir Gawaine and Dame Ragnell*. Both feature a character called Sir Gromer Somer Joure – a very unusual name, unknown in any other surviving romance. Both linger over long and expertly described hunting scenes. There are, moreover, a remarkable number of identical commonplace phrases and tricks of speech that suggest one man wrote both texts. *The Wedding* is not great poetry, but it could have been calculated to appeal to a newly-married queen with a liking for romantic reading matter.

These halcyon years would have been an appropriate time for Malory to have worked on his surprisingly long 'Tale of Sir Gareth', the story of how Beaumains, just such a noble young knight as Harry of Warwick was, made his name as a knight of prowess and worship. He could also have worked on 'The Book of Sir Tristram', which contains within it the very similar stories of Alisander Le Orphelin and La Cote Male Taile. The number of new names and subplots that Malory introduces into his version of Sir Tristram's adventures suggests that it would be fertile ground for the techniques used by the literary cryptologist Ethel Seaton. Her subject was Malory's exact contemporary, Sir Richard Roos, for whom she claimed a hundred or more poems previously ascribed to other poets or simply labelled anonymous. With extraordinary ingenuity, she puzzled out anagrams and punning word-plays to reveal a hidden world of court gossip and teasing personal references. Seaton's conclusions are disputed, but her biography of Sir Richard Roos gives a vivid picture of a fun-loving queen, and her ladies-in-waiting and courtiers. Malory could have known Roos well – his Duke de la Rowse may be a tribute to him.

On 11 June 1446 Malory's prospects were brutally shattered. Barely two months after his twenty-first birthday, Harry Beauchamp died suddenly at Hanley Castle. 'This hopeful branch, the only heir male to these great Earls, was cropt in the flower of his youth before the fruits of his heroik disposition could be fully manifested to the world,' mourns Dugdale. No reason for his death is known, and it was evidently seen as suspicious, cited as murder in the long catalogue of crimes of which Suffolk was accused. Suffolk may well have viewed Sir Harry's closeness to the King with distrust, especially when such influential household figures as the Treasurer, Lord Sudeley, and the carver, Sir John Beauchamp of Powicke, had more to gain from Harry's good lordship than his own. The Beauforts were also aware that Harry's martial ambitions would make him oppose their own conciliatory peace policy. But if a murder had been contrived, the prime suspect has to be Buckingham. He had far more to gain from Harry's death than anybody else – both in ducal precedence and in local pre-eminence. Unwilling to lose any of the dignities he felt were his due, and incensed by the King's grant to Harry and his male heirs of the stewardship of the Honour of Tutbury and the High Peak, an office he had long regarded as his family's right, the enmity he felt towards the handsome young man whose future was so bright and whose influence on the King was so great was intense. The fact that Harry replaced him on the Warwickshire bench in February 1446 may have been the last straw.

Even if Buckingham did not engineer the young Duke's untimely death, Sir Thomas Malory may have suspected him of doing so. As he mourned the young man with the traditional prayers, doles and requiem masses, it is easy to imagine the seed of dislike sown by Buckingham's oppression of several of Malory's friends and neighbours growing into an ineradicable, foolhardy hatred.

> *'Alas,' said Sir Lancelot, 'this is the heaviest tidings that ever came to me.' 'Now, fair sirs,' said Sir Lancelot, 'shew me the tomb of Sir Gawaine.' And then certain people of the town brought him into the castle of Dover, and shewed him the tomb. Then Sir Lancelot kneeled down and wept, and prayed heartily for his soul. And that night he made a dole, and all they that would come had as much flesh, fish, wine and ale,*

and every man and woman had twelve pence, come who would. Thus with his own hand dealt he this money, in a mourning gown; and ever he wept, and prayed them to pray for the soul of Sir Gawaine. And on the morn all the priests and clerks that might be gotten in the country were there, and sang mass of Requiem; and there offered first Sir Lancelot, and he offered an hundred pound; and then the seven kings offered forty pound apiece; and also there was a thousand knights, and each of them offered a pound; and the offering dured from morn till night, and Sir Lancelot lay two nights on his tomb in prayers and weeping.

Misrule Doth Rise

In every shire with jakkes and salades clene
Misrule doth rise and maketh neighbours war
The weaker goeth beneath, as oft is seen,
The mightiest his quarrel will prefer . . .
For in your Realm Justice of Peace be none
That dare ought now the cantankerous oppress

John Hardyng, *Chronicle*

here are signs that Henry VI was devastated by Harry Beauchamp's death. From the very next month, there was an ominous change in the nature of the royal records. The detailed council minutes, which had up until now shown a dialogue between the King and his advisers, full of intelligent questions and informed answers, ended abruptly. It is of course possible that Harry Beauchamp had prompted the questions, but given Henry's later history of mental instability, the most obvious cause of the change was some sort of breakdown. Subtle and not so subtle shifts in policy reveal that Suffolk, Buckingham and the Beauforts' influence on Henry VI and his queen was now complete. The disgraced Duchess of Gloucester, Elinor Cobham, was hustled away from Kenilworth to the Isle of Man; if there had been secret meetings between her and her ex-husband, they were at an end. Once the martially-minded young Duke of Warwick was dead, the King's natural inclination for spreading peace and goodwill among men could be exploited to the full by the pro-French party. In November 1446 Bishop Moleyns accused the Duke of York of malpractice in Normandy. He defended himself convincingly, summoning soldiers who testified that Moleyns had offered them bribes to complain of unpaid wages, but was not allowed to continue as Lieutenant-General in France. The peace party were not going to risk his interference in the plans to concede Maine. Instead, in December 1446, Edmund Beaufort, who would be dubbed Duke of Somerset in 1448, was given command. York was pointedly sidelined by being made Lieutenant of Ireland, a challenging enough office, but far from being his chosen theatre of war.

Harry's death altered Malory's position in the county. Apart from sitting with Sir William Mountfort on the July 1446 commission that decided who should be exempted from the taxes imposed by Parliament, the normal consequence of a seat in the Commons as a knight of the shire, he held no local or national office for four years. The Beauchamp inheritance once more fell to a minor, this time a much younger and more helpless one: the young Duke's eighteen-month-old daughter Anne. Her wardship automatically belonged to the King, who gave it, as he gave so much else, to his wife. Queen Margaret began an orgy of dispersals. Over fifty grants of Beauchamp possessions were made in the next month. But since only offices held for life by Harry Beauchamp could legitimately be redistributed, the Beauchamp trustees soon stepped in to stop illicit disposals of lands. A petition to the royal council from Anne Beauchamp's grandfather, the Earl of Salisbury, called the plunder to a halt. On 24 July 1446, the King in council ordained that 'we will that all persons that had wages, fees or offices for term of life of grant of the Duke of Warwick that dead is have letters of confirmation thereof under his great seal during the minor age of Anne, daughter and heir to the said Duke'. Almost all the illegal grants were rescinded, though a few were reserved to their new holders.

Malory was among the many Beauchamp retainers who breathed a sigh of relief when their offices and annuities were restored. By September 1446, the executors of the estate had got round to paying him the eighteen unpaid weeks owing to him. In the absence of any evidence connecting him with another affinity, it is likely that he continued in the service of the Beauchamps. If so, for the next few years he owed indirect allegiance to William de la Pole, Duke of Suffolk, now the most powerful man in the country. For in September Suffolk bought Anne Beauchamp's wardship from the Queen. The tiny child, already officially 15th Countess of Warwick, was the perfect future wife for the Duke's baby son; if both survived to marry, the next Duke of Suffolk would be among the wealthiest peers of the realm.

Anne was placed in the care of Suffolk's wife Alice Chaucer (1404–75), the granddaughter of the famous poet and storyteller Geoffrey Chaucer. She had been a friend of Harry Beauchamp's mother, Isobel; both were 'Garter wives', among the select few of the spouses of Garter knights who were entitled by special privilege to wear the robes of the Order themselves. Like Isobel, Alice was pious as well as learned, and an heiress in her own right. She also had jointures from two previous marriages. An independently-minded woman, she invested much of her wealth in improving her favourite home, Ewelme, in Oxfordshire. Isobel often stayed near by at the Beauchamp manor of Caversham, a convenient staging post between Warwick and London. By the time that little Anne Beauchamp came into her care, Alice had extended Ewelme into a palace. She was now busy overseeing the completion of a new church with a quadrangle of almshouses and a school attached. There were already several children in the household, including her little son John and another of Suffolk's wards, Margaret Beaufort, the three-year-old heiress of the Duke of Somerset.

Did Malory escort the tiny Countess of Warwick and her nurses to Ewelme, happy to have the excuse to meet the granddaughter of England's most renowned poet? If so, a corner of his world survives almost unchanged. The village of Ewelme is virtually as its fifteenth-century builders left it. Pensioners still live in the almshouses, and classes still go on in the medieval school founded by Alice Chaucer. What Malory would not have seen is her magnificent double-decker tomb in the church – she didn't die until 1475. The top effigy shows her astute, ascetic face above her Garter robes; the lower, sheltered by stone arcading, holds an aged, skeletal alabaster corpse, a flimsy shroud barely covering her nakedness. It is all but a twin of the Tewkesbury Abbey tomb commissioned by Isobel Despenser, Harry Beauchamp's mother, though Alice drew the line at the worms that Isobel told the sculptor she wanted to rise from her belly. Such tombs, and the hundreds of masses which Alice, Isobel and their contemporaries ordered to be said for their souls, show the intensity of medieval piety.

Warwickshire Allies and Enemies

The Duke of Suffolk's interest in the county of Warwickshire increased once he acquired the wardship of the Beauchamp heiress. As chief steward of the Duchy of Lancaster, he sat on the Warwickshire commission of JPs, but affairs of state gave him little time to exert much personal influence. Instead he ensured the loyalty of local notables by endowing them with offices in the royal household. Among those now promoted at court were Thomas Walsh and Thomas Burneby, both of whom became queen's squires at about this time. If Malory was indeed married to Elizabeth Walsh, then Thomas Walsh was his nephew. He became a feoffee for Malory in 1462, as did two other members of the Walsh family. Thomas Burneby was the brother of Malory's sister Philippa's husband Eustace. He, Eustace and Malory himself became feoffees for William Malory of Saddington at about this time. Thomas Burneby was a particular favourite of the Queen; at about this time she wrote a wheedling letter to the wealthy widow Lady Jane Carew, suggesting him as a husband. He was also close to Cardinal Beaufort, who left him a silver-gilt cup in his will.

Also high in favour at court was Sir Robert Harcourt (1410–70), who was made a queen's knight in 1446. A Richard Harcourt appeared with Malory on the 1414 Beauchamp Roll of men who served in Calais, and Sir Robert had overseen Malory's election as Member of Parliament in 1445; he was then Sheriff of Warwickshire and Leicestershire. He held the Leicestershire manors of Market Bosworth, between Bramcote and Kirkby Malory, and Gilmerton, which is about six miles from both Swinford and Newbold Revel. His most substantial estates were in Oxfordshire, where he was elected as knight of the shire in 1447 and 1450. His main seat was just west of the city of Oxford at Stanton Harcourt. Another estate bordered on Ewelme, where there is still a Harcourt Hill. Sir Robert was a cousin of Sir

Thomas Erdington, who was his feoffee in 1433, and who witnessed documents with Malory in 1439 and 1443.

The Harcourts were, like the Malorys, a cadet branch of an ancient and distinguished Norman family. The battle helm on Sir Robert's tomb effigy at Stanton Harcourt has a peacock upon it and his feet rest on a lion; he was a hot-headed and active man who had at least one illegitimate son as well as his six children by Lady Margaret. He went to France with Suffolk and Harry Beauchamp to fetch Margaret of Anjou in 1444. He was in high favour with the Queen, receiving generous New Year gifts from her in both 1447 and 1448; in 1453 Margaret gave his infant son a special child-sized Lancastrian livery collar of entwined silver Ss.

Malory was evidently comfortably off at this time. Between September 1448 and August 1449 he bought his brother-in-law Robert Vincent's mortgaged Swinford lands outright. In October 1448 Malory, Sir Robert Harcourt and others sued three obscure Leicestershire men, two smallholders and a miller, for unspecified transgressions. He and Sir Robert were probably taking firm joint action against local villains. In October 1449, Malory and Harcourt again acted together against the offending Leicestershire men. Links between the two families were strengthened in December 1449, when Malory's kinsman Thomas Walsh married the sister of Sir Robert Harcourt's wife, Margaret Byron.

At just this time, Lady Elizabeth Malory gave birth to a son, Robert. Born some time in the twenty-fifth year of Henry VI's reign (between 1 September 1446 and 31 August 1447), he might have been named in memory of his long-dead uncle, the Prior of St John, or for Malory's cousin Robert (who is recorded in Rome in 1448, apparently on pilgrimage), but a child had two godfathers and it was usual to choose a powerful living mentor for one's child. There is a reasonable chance that his godfather was Sir Robert Harcourt.

Malory had enemies as well as friends in the Midlands. Buckingham's actions in Warwickshire became increasingly high-handed. He seized the manor of Bramcote from the Charnells, the family into which Malory's Uncle Thomas had married, and handed it to Joan Burdett. He supported his retainer Thomas Bate's abduction of, and marriage to, the widowed Lady Cockayn, so keeping Malory's comrade-in-arms John Cockayn out of his inheritance for the rest of her lifetime. Buckingham also developed a strong alliance with Edmund Mountfort, youngest but most favoured son of Sir William Mountfort and an up-and-coming man at court, who had contrived to persuade his aged father to disinherit his older sons in Edmund's favour. During the legal battle royal that ensued after Sir William's death in 1452, Buckingham would, 'by might and favour [of Henry VI]', imprison first Sir Baldwin Mountfort and then his oldest son Simon until they agreed to abandon their rights; his reward was to be named heir to Coleshill (conveniently adjacent to his seat at Maxstoke) if Edmund died childless.

On 22 May 1448, a simmering feud over unpaid rents between Sir Robert Harcourt and Buckingham's kinsmen, the Staffords of Grafton, came to a head when the two sides met in Coventry during the Corpus Christi pageant. Anybody who was anybody in the Midlands came to Coventry for the nationally renowned mystery plays mounted there during the Pentecostal feast. A heated argument broke out when Sir Robert Harcourt and Sir Humphrey Stafford and his son Richard met in the street. Suddenly Sir Robert swung at Richard's head with a sword. Richard lunged forward with a dagger, but he stumbled, and one of Sir Robert's men 'smote him in the back with a knife'. Sir Humphrey was knocked from his horse and two of Harcourt's men were killed. It all happened, a Paston Letter records, 'in a Paternoster while' (i.e. faster than a man could say the Lord's Prayer). Sir Robert, a yeoman called John Aleyn, and several others were indicted the same day for Richard's murder, and imprisoned in Chester Castle. Although Aleyn and the other men were outlawed, Harcourt's influence at court produced a writ from the privy seal allowing his release on a technicality. Malory, who lived only seven miles away, might well have been there; five years later we know that Malory was accused of consorting with an outlawed yeoman called John Aleyn who was described as his servant.

'And for I understand they be
murderers of good knights I left their company'

It would not be surprising if Malory was now troubled by the national state of affairs. The royal household had vastly inflated in size and was hugely expensive to run. 'Ye have made the king so poor / That now he beggeth from door to door – / Alas it should be so', ran a critical ballad addressed to the court in 1450. 'Truth and poor men be oppressed, / And mischief is nothing redressed; / The king knoweth not all'. No knight who valued worship and prowess as highly as did Malory could approve of the way the royal household was dominated by powerful churchmen and laymen who were more interested in lining their own pockets and lavishly endowing ecclesiastical foundations to sing masses for their corrupt souls than in preserving the King's French realm, let alone defending Christendom from the Turk.

The prospects for the English territories in France were gloomy. Huge debts were owed to Henry's commanders there, and they were becoming increasingly resentful at the absence of support from England. There was, moreover, little interest from the gentry in enlisting to serve abroad. To make things worse, the French were now much more effectively organised in military terms than the English, with a standing army and technologically innovative artillery. Aware that, thanks to Margaret's influence, Henry VI was determined to achieve peace at any price, Charles VII announced in September 1446 that he wanted Normandy back as well as Maine. Suffolk and the Beauforts knew that there would be outrage all across England at such terms. They hoped that a personal visit to France by Henry VI would make Charles relent. But first they decided to make a pre-emptive attack on the man who would undoubtedly oppose the sacrifice of Henry V's conquests, and who would naturally expect to be Regent of England if the King crossed the Channel: Duke Humfrey of Gloucester.

A skilful propaganda campaign was set into action, the fruit of several autumn meetings of the royal council from which Gloucester and York were absent. Somebody, a bishop, it was rumoured, told Henry VI that Gloucester had told him in the confessional that he was plotting to use the King's absence in France to free his wife Elinor and usurp the throne. Extra troops were mustered to protect the King. In December a new parliament was summoned for February 1447, officially to discuss arrangements for the King's journey but afterwards said to have been 'made only for to slay the Duke of Gloucester'. On 24 January, its venue was suddenly switched from Winchester to Bury St Edmunds, the heart of the Duke of Suffolk's territory. Courtiers leaned heavily on local sheriffs to make sure that the MPs elected were as pliable as possible. Although sons, especially younger sons, were rarely elected to Parliament in the lifetime of their fathers, Edmund Mountfort sat for Warwickshire; the election was conducted by another household man, Thomas Everingham, and the attestors were very small fry; 'leading gentry were notable by their absence', comments Mountfort's biographer, Simon Payling.

Suspecting nothing, the fifty-seven-year-old Gloucester and a mere eighty men arrived at Bury on 18 February. They were told to go straight to their lodgings in St Saviour's, a local hospital. Later that day, a squad of magnates, headed by the Duke of Buckingham and Viscount Beaumont, Steward of England, arrived to tell Duke Humfrey that he had been appealed of treason in front of the King, and was under house arrest until Henry decided what to do with him. Five days later, on 23 February, Duke Humfrey died – 'of heaviness', it was said. Although his corpse was put on view in the Abbey church, rumours were rife that he had been strangled, suffocated, drowned or 'thrust into the bowel with an hot, burning spit'. There seems little doubt that there had been foul play, effected so swiftly that Humfrey had no chance even to see his nephew the King, or any friends he might have had in the Parliament. The Duke of York, his closest political ally, appears not to have arrived until 26 February. Sir Robert Harcourt, who was sitting as MP for Oxfordshire, may have told Malory more than we will ever know about what really happened, including Buckingham's part in the affair. Suspicion of foul play increased when the scramble for Gloucester's estates began. It was discovered that a huge cluster of new grants of his lands and offices, by reversion after his death, had been made in late January – only a month before he died. One of the richest plums granted was Penshurst Castle in Kent. It was given to Buckingham.

Many of Gloucester's retainers were put on trial. Among them were Sir John Cheyne, for whose family Malory witnessed a settlement in 1431, Griffith ap Nicholas of Carmarthen, with whose sons and grandson Malory would be excepted from pardon twenty years later, and Sir Roger Chamberlain, who later posted bail for Malory in London. Eight of them were tried and convicted of plotting to make their master King and free Elinor Cobham, and of marching in force to Bury to overawe Parliament. Condemned to death, they were taken on a humiliating progress around the country and exhibited in market places as traitors. Finally, they were taken back to Tyburn in London and hoisted up on gibbets. They had been taken down, just alive, so that they could feel their intestines being drawn out before they were quartered, when a carefully staged last-minute pardon arrived from the King.

A month or so after Duke Humfrey's death, Cardinal Beaufort, 'haughty in stomach and more noble in blood than in learning, rich above measure but not very liberal', died in his Winchester palace of Wolvesey. He was not, as Shakespeare had it, hag-ridden by visions of his murdered nephew. Instead, aged just three score years and ten, he closed his eyes complacently, confident that his generous benefactions to monasteries and chantry chapels on condition that thousands of masses were said for his soul would ensure him a speedy journey to heaven. His heirs were his nephews, Edmund Beaufort, Marquis of Somerset, and Henry Beaufort, Earl of Dorset. They were now well placed to further the peace policies that the Cardinal had promoted for so long. Their lands in Maine had been exchanged for more tenable estates in Normandy, and Edmund held the vast Chirk estates that the Cardinal had acquired in over-generous settlement for loans to the King in 1441. They also had great expectations closer to home. As long as Henry had no child, the Beauforts could, despite their bastard origins, dream of inheriting the throne – especially if York could be discredited.

In July 1447 the truce signed with France when Henry VI married

Margaret of Anjou was extended to May 1448. Delivery of Maine, under the face-saving pretence that it was being returned to René of Anjou and Henry was still its sovereign, was promised by November. The dukes of Suffolk and Buckingham led negotiations. But the near-mutinous English garrison commanders in Maine refused to surrender. In February 1448 Charles VII surrounded Maine's capital, Le Mans, with 7,000 well-drilled troops, a large artillery train and siege engines. In March the English garrisons, glowering with resentment, marched out. The bulwark of southern Normandy was in enemy hands, and England had gained absolutely nothing in return. Somerset, the new Lieutenant in Normandy, had not even crossed the Channel.

Gloucester's political mantle of defiance against France fell on the thirty-three-year-old Richard, Duke of York. So too did his status as heir presumptive to the throne; he now held precedence before all other dukes. He protested hotly at the surrender of Maine, which he called 'great obloquy' on the estate of princes 'of high and noble blood, honour, prowess, renown and virtue'. But Suffolk and the Beauforts had all but exclusive access to the King and Queen and did not scruple to poison the royal minds against this alarmingly powerful cousin. With heavy heart, York at last crossed to Ireland and took up his lieutenancy. What was Malory's reaction to these momentous events? He is likely to have mourned the demise of 'Good Duke Humfrey', and he had comrades among the returning troops displaced from Maine, many of whom had been settled there long enough to have children for whom France was the only home they knew. He is also likely to have agreed with the short chronicle of his age by John Vale which asserted that Gloucester's death began all the troubles, with the House of York initially merely out to right the wrong done to him. As we shall see, Malory knew Vale, witnessing a document with him in 1469.

A passage in Malory's 'Tale of Sir Tristram' is a striking parallel to the displacement of York and Gloucester from the King's favour by Suffolk, a descendant of a mere merchant, and the Beauforts, stained by bastardy:

Our king had [these two knights] so in charity, that he loved no man nor trusted no man of his blood, nor none other that was about him. And by these two knights our king was governed, and so they ruled him peaceably and his lands, and never would they suffer none of his blood to have no rule with our king. And also he was so free and so gentle, and they so false and deceivable, that they ruled him peaceably; and that espied the lords of our king's blood, and departed from him unto their own livelihood. Then when these two traitors understood that they had driven all the lords of his blood from him, they were not pleased with that rule, but then they thought to have more, as ever it is an old saw: Give a churl rule and thereby he will not be sufficed; for whatsomever he be that is ruled by a villain born, and the lord of the soil to be a gentleman born, the same villain shall destroy all the gentlemen about him: therefore all estates and lords, beware whom ye take about you.

My Lord of Warwick

Eight months later, on 3 June 1449, Anne Beauchamp, just five and a quarter years old, died at Ewelme. She was buried in Reading and many Beauchamp retainers, among them perhaps Malory, attended her requiem mass. He will have mourned her death, but may have been relieved that the Beauchamp inheritance was no longer in the gift of her guardian, Suffolk, the most notoriously avaricious of Henry VI's courtiers. The next heir was an older and wiser Anne Beauchamp, Harry's only sister 'of the whole blood'. Malory had known Anne since her babyhood. Now in her early twenties, she had been married for thirteen years to Sir Richard Neville, son of one of the greatest of England's military commanders in France, the Earl of Salisbury. They came south from the Nevilles' Middleham Castle in Yorkshire as soon as they heard of their little niece's death. On 19 June the twenty-year-old Neville attended Parliament as sixteenth Earl of Warwick – in right of his wife.

It is this Earl of Warwick whose extraordinary future career led Shakespeare to immortalise him in his *Henry VI Part III* as the 'proud plucker down and setter up of kings' – and W. C. Sellar and R. J. Yeatman to ridicule him in *1066 and All That* as the ultimate 'wicked baron', to whom would-be monarchs submit job applications which include their preferred means of death. Opinions of 'Warwick Make-King' have always been mixed, veering from the adulation of his first biography, Thomas Gainsford's *Unmatchable Life and Death of Richard Neville Earl of Warwick in his time the Darling and Favourite of Kings* (1618) and the Victorian novelist Bulwer Lytton's *The Last of the Barons* to a generally unfavourable press in the last hundred years. His most recent biographer Michael Hicks finds more to praise than to condemn.

> *There was nothing Warwick would not attempt and no obstacle that he would not overcome. He was indomitable, never surrendered, and never failed to recover until the very end. For twenty years he shaped events, his own career, and indeed history itself. An underlying strength of will and determination and an intolerance of opposition and vicious-ness towards opponents needs to be set against the charm that cajoled, persuaded and won over men of whatever stand-ing. It was this indefinable popularity that made him so much greater than the greatest of subjects.*

What is beyond doubt is that the new Earl of Warwick was one of the most charismatic figures of the century, a man of great personal magnetism and a strong sense of his own destiny. He had won his spurs defending the Northern Marches against the Scots, and was joint Warden of the Western Marches with his father, Salisbury, when he was only eighteen. Open-handed and generous, he was 'in such favour with all persons, of high and low degree . . . so that they judged him able to do all things, and that without him, nothing to be well done', wrote the chronicler Edward Hall. 'For which cause his auth-ority shortly so fast increased that which way he bowed, that way ran the stream, and what part he advanced, that side got the superiority.'

Warwick was related directly or by marriage to almost every noble house in England. In the 1450s, his father and four of his uncles (Lord Fauconberg, Lord Latimer, Lord Abergavenny and the Bishop of Durham) sat in the House of Lords, as did the four great magnates married to his aunts (Buckingham, Norfolk, York and Northumberland). He was even related – albeit by devious byways and by the half-blood – to Henry VI himself. His grandfather had married Joan Beaufort, daughter of Katherine Swinford and John of Gaunt, Henry's great-grandfather.

As Earl of Warwick and Anne Beauchamp's husband, Richard Neville was Sir Thomas Malory's natural 'good lord'. Malory must have welcomed the prospect of a protector who could act effectively in Warwickshire against Buckingham. Warwick was probably happy to keep in his affinity a knight who had had connections with the Warwick earls for over thirty years. The incompleteness of the records of the new Earl's household means that we don't know for certain that Malory's retainer continued, but in general there was continuity among the earldom's officers and tenants. Warwick retained several of Malory's friends, including his brother-in-law who held the responsible post of Clerk of the Kitchens, Sir Robert Harcourt (who was Steward of Warwick's Oxfordshire estates by 1451), Sir Thomas Erdington, and John Hathwyck of Harbury.

But in 1449, Malory and the new Earl of Warwick did not know each other well. Possibly they never became close. Pride was the keynote of Richard Neville's character, whereas loyalty was paramount to Malory. Although he enjoyed chronicles of noble achievements, Neville did not have the Beauchamps' deep love of art and literature, or Malory's breadth of reading. His brilliant mind was more scientific and pragmatic, more interested in military and naval technology and strategy. The Burgundian ambassadors who visited him in his London Inn in the early 1460s described his way of life as barbarically splendid, not cultured. The only surviving book directly associated with him, a beautifully illuminated Flemish treatise on the nature of true nobility dated 1464, was probably commissioned for him by his wife Anne, to whom he left management of the finer things of life. Its frontispiece may be the only portrait of them in existence. It shows a knight kneeling to 'Lady Imagination' outside a church.

Anne Beauchamp was the epitome of 'Lady Imagination', an approachable and sympathetic companion, liberal 'and in her own person seemly and beauteous'. She was said to be 'good and gracious to all', and intensely loyal: her motto was 'And Ever Shall'. She was also 'ever a full devout lady'. Her signature appears on the flyleaf of a copy of *The Book of Ghostly Grace*, an English translation of the visions and prophecies of the German mystic St Mechtild of Hackeborn, a book remarkable for its colourful imagery. It was Anne who chose the craftsmen who made her father's tomb one of the most splendid chantry chapels of the age, and she was the driving spirit behind the creation of the two beautifully illustrated memorials of her family, the *Beauchamp Pageant* and the *Rous Roll*. The *Rous Roll* frequently dwells on Beauchamp connections with King Arthur. Rous derives the bear badge of the Earls of Warwick from the first syllable of the name of Arthgal, a knight of the Round Table, which means 'bear' in Welsh. Was Anne's interest in Arthurian history inspired by Malory's presence at her father's and brother's courts? If so, she would have been pleased to see him again when she returned to Warwickshire. It would be natural, too, for Malory to have felt that his first loyalty lay to her, the last of the Beauchamps, rather than to her husband.

> *I promise you as I am true knight, that in all places I shall be my lady your daughter's servant and knight in right and in wrong, and I shall never fail her, to do as much as a knight may do.*

Warwick entered into his new inheritance with a decisiveness that suggests that he must have foreseen its likelihood. He was wise to move quickly. Three days after little Anne's death, Thomas Daniel, a notoriously acquisitive courtier who was retained by Suffolk and had a violent record in East Anglia, was appointed steward, receiver, constable and master forester of Abergavenny, part of the Despenser inheritance. But there were few other misappropriations. Warwick had allies close to the King in his Beauchamp feoffees, Lord Sudeley and Lord Beauchamp of Powicke. Travelling with whirlwind energy, the new Earl visited all the relevant estates to such good effect that all the official inquiries into the lands held at death (inquisitions post mortem) returned the same favourable verdict: Anne and Richard were sole heirs, even of Anne's mother's Despenser lands (which should by rights have been shared with her cousin George Neville).

Warwick knew that he had to step warily and avoid making enemies. Opposition to his and his wife's inheritance would come from Richard Beauchamp's three daughters by his first wife, Elizabeth Berkeley. All were women of influence: Margaret was married to John Talbot, Earl of Shrewsbury, Eleanor to Edmund Beaufort, now Duke of Somerset and soon to be the King's most favoured counsellor, and Elizabeth to George Neville, Lord Latimer. Shrewsbury and Somerset were both in France, but Eleanor's and Somerset's daughter was married to the Duke of Buckingham's heir, Humphrey, so Buckingham would undoubtedly want to advance her interest. But Warwick had won approval from the King as early as April 1449, when Henry rewarded him for 'intimate services', perhaps in the border campaigns against Scotland in 1448–9. His inheritance of the hugely valuable Beauchamp estates and dignities transformed him into a major player in national politics. He was entering the limelight at a time of crisis in both domestic and foreign affairs.

Knight Reformer

When lords' will is lands' law
Priests' will treachery, and guile held sooth saw.
Lechery called privy solace,
And robbery is held no trespass –
Then shall the land of Albion
Turn into confusion.

Merlin's Prophecy

y 1449, Henry VI's limp, amiable approach to government meant that money was pouring out of the royal coffers and into the pockets of self-serving and corrupt courtiers. The Exchequer was some £300,000 in debt. Bands of thugs with powerful connections were preying on the weak. Nor was there any confidence that justice would be done in the King's courts, where sophisticated manipulation of the letter of the law was rife. 'As the world goes now,' lamented William of Worcester in 1450, men with a training in law and 'civil matter' are held of more account than gentlemen who had spent 'thirty or forty years in great jeopardy' in the King's wars in France. His *Book of Noblesse* was written to liken the achievements of the 'right noble martyrs' Henry V and his brothers in conquering France, and so increasing 'the common wealth', to the deeds of the great Worthies of the past – foremost among whom was England's own King Arthur. But he praised the triumphs of Henry V in vain. There had been no effective military initiatives in France for eight years. Opinion in England was now out of kilter with that of the English settlers and garrisons in Normandy. Peace was the main objective, though it still had to be peace with honour. The King's marriage to a French princess was one cause of the change in mood.

Sheer weariness, given the long-drawn-out hostilities, and the haemorrhaging cost of the defence of Normandy were others. There was a counter-argument, nurtured by Queen Margaret, Suffolk and the Beauforts, that Henry V himself would, by now, have been aiming for peace so that European Christians could unite against the attacks from Islam.

Normandy was threatened by a three-pronged attack from Charles VII, Burgundy and Brittany. The English garrisons ejected from Maine in December 1448 had moved to deserted castles in the borderland between Brittany and western Normandy. On 24 March 1449 they attacked and occupied the prosperous Breton wool town of Fougères. The attack was authorised by Suffolk on behalf of the King in a misguided attempt to put pressure on Francis, Duke of Brittany, to release his unjustly imprisoned brother Giles, who had been a close friend of Henry VI since their shared childhood. But all it did was alienate Duke Francis and hand Charles VII an excuse to declare war. In May 1449 Pont de l'Arche, a crucial Seine crossing five miles from Rouen, was taken by a ruse, and William Neville, Lord Fauconberg, who had only arrived there the day before on an embassy from the King, was captured. Fauconberg, short, choleric and 'with the heart of a lion', was Warwick's uncle, and had fought with him in the Scottish campaign. Warwick must have been appalled at his capture. So too, in all probability, was Malory. For not only did Fauconberg hold lands and tenements at Litchborough, he also stood bail for Malory ten years later in 1458.

Member for Great Bedwyn

On 23 September 1449, Parliament was summoned, the second to meet that year. Money was urgently needed to launch a major defensive campaign in Normandy. Considerable efforts were made to ensure that Parliament, which was increasingly often being used as a forum for the expression of discontents in the form of personally presented petitions, was malleable. Household men put heavy pressure on the elections in order to minimise criticism of royal policies and maximise taxation. On the day that the election was announced, eighty of the Duke of Buckingham's men assaulted Thomas Ferrers of Groby, in Coleshill, and attempted to force their way into Tamworth Castle itself to get at his father, who was Sheriff of Staffordshire. The terror tactics worked. Two long-standing supporters of Buckingham were elected for Staffordshire: John Hampton, who was sitting for the sixth time, and Richard Whitgreve, a long-term servant of Buckingham. However, powerful critics of court policy also set about establishing influence.

This background is the best explanation for how Malory came to be sitting as an MP, not as a knight of the shire for Warwickshire but as a burgess for Great Bedwyn. He seems to have been aware early on that, although one of the electors for Warwickshire was his cousin and feoffee, Robert Malory, he would not be elected for his own county. It could be that the new Earl of Warwick thought him dangerously independent-minded, but it is more likely that Neville was still unfamiliar with his affinity. For although the MPs who were elected for Warwickshire on 20 October were recognisably a Suffolk dove and a Yorkist hawk, one of them has seemed to posterity to be an extremely surprising choice. The dove was William Catesby, shrewd, legally trained and a King's Sergeant, a safe pair of hands for the Suffolk administration.

The hawk was Robert Arderne, a man whose record of troublemaking makes Malory seem a model citizen. His father had been Sir Ralph Arderne, who had, like Malory, gone to Calais with Beauchamp in 1414; he died fighting in France in 1420. Although Robert had inherited estates with rents of at least £113 a year, he was often heavily in debt, and he had a talent for creating mayhem. On one occasion, he had been accused of being an accessory to murder. Aggressively litigious (perhaps with good reason), he was also hotly pursued by other men's lawyers, including those of William Catesby, Sir Robert Harcourt and his stepbrother Sir Thomas Erdington, whom he accused in court of lying in his teeth. 'Tu mentiris in capud tuum' recorded the indictment in picturesque Latin, adding that Arderne was 'insania et furore repletus' (full of madness and fury). In 1449 he was severely tangled in accusations and counter-accusations of crimes, debts and misappropriation of lands. He was aggressively anti-Suffolk, whom he had sued successfully for the return of one of his wife's properties. Arderne's biographer describes his election as knight of the shire as 'astonishing' and 'beyond convincing explanation'. But it could have been the doing of Warwick himself, impressed by Robert's military record, and seeing only a useful fighting man whose family had a tradition of serving the Warwick earls. Robert himself may have spent more time in France than the records show; one reason for his debts could have been a ransom commitment. He had signed on for service in Aquitaine, perhaps with Malory, in the early 1440s. If he was a veteran, he may have wanted to be in the Commons to criticise the mismanagement of the war. In 1452 he emerges as a vehement supporter of York.

Six days before this oddly assorted pair were elected for Warwickshire, Malory was returned as MP for Great Bedwyn. Great Bedwyn is over eighty miles away from Newbold Revel, just off the main London to Bath road between Marlborough and Newbury. It had earned borough status in the Doomsday Book because it was a prosperous wool town, but by 1449 it was hardly more than a large village. To sit for an obscure borough eighty miles away from his Midlands estates shows that Malory's interest in national affairs was keen. But what took him to Great Bedwyn? Traditionally, its MPs had been local gentry. But in the 1440s, placemen put forward by men of influence began to appear there as in other boroughs. Members of Parliament sitting for Great Bedwyn have been assumed to have connections with Buckingham, who was overlord of the manor, but quite a few were closer to William Waynflete (c.1394–1486), who had held the bishopric of Winchester since the death of Cardinal Beaufort in 1447. Malory's fellow MP for Great Bedwyn in 1449 was Thomas Welles, steward of Waynflete's episcopal estates. In 1450 the MP for Great Bedwyn was William Bridges, who later became Waynflete's bailiff.

Waynflete was one of the most learned and interesting men of the age: headmaster of Winchester College between 1430 and 1442, when Henry VI appointed him as second provost of his new school at Eton, and founder of several schools and colleges. His appointment to the richest bishopric of the realm and the fact that he was one of Henry VI's confessors reflected royal trust in him. He had known Harry Beauchamp, who had interested himself in Eton. He could have met Malory at Windsor in the early 1440s, and admired him, as Archbishop William Zouche had admired his kinsman Anketil Malory in the 1380s, as an 'armiger literatus' of independent spirit and high ideals.

Why would Waynflete use his influence to get Malory into Parliament? There are several intriguing links between Malory and Winchester. The only known manuscript of the *Morte Darthur* surfaced in 1936 in a library safe at Winchester College. Richard Malory of Litchborough went to Winchester in the 1500s, and it has been suggested that he brought the book with him. But perhaps both the manuscript's presence in the library and young Richard's choice of school signal an earlier connection between Sir Thomas Malory himself and Winchester. It is easy to imagine Malory and Waynflete as kindred spirits. In the *Morte Darthur*, Camelot is confidently identified as Winchester, the ancient capital of Wessex. The tournament ground outside Winchester Castle where the last and greatest tournament in the book takes place actually existed in the fifteenth century, and in the castle's great hall hung what Malory and his contemporaries believed to be the original sixth-century Round Table. It was one of the proofs of the real existence of Arthur, listed by William Caxton in the preface to his first printing of Malory in 1485. A magnificent piece of furniture, eighteen feet in diameter and weighing more than a ton, it is still on display.

The Parliament that sat in Blackfriars Hall, Westminster, and finally in Leicester, between 6 November 1449 and 8 June 1450 was one of the most turbulent and eventful of the fifteenth century. When the first session opened, England was reeling from the news that on 29 October the Duke of Somerset had surrendered Rouen, the English capital of Normandy, without a siege (because, it was said, a cannonball had whistled into the ducal nursery, and the Duchess had panicked); he had then retreated to Caen. The majority of the English in Normandy were said to be 'utterly ruined and in a state of beggary'. More bad news from across the Channel arrived every day, and

Gascony was also under attack. Richard, Duke of York, the man whom English public opinion increasing billed as the only man who could save the King's French realm, was far away in Ireland.

Attempts were made to appease the Commons' anger. Gunpowder was immediately sent to Caen and Cherbourg and £5,000 was sent to the Earl of Somerset. The Chancellor, Archbishop Stafford, announced that forces were being raised to defend both Calais and Normandy. But although Sir Thomas Kyriel, an experienced commander, was asked in October to take 4,500 men to the relief of Normandy, and £9,000 was promised in wages, no men of rank would enlist to join him. To make matters worse, the 425 men-at-arms and 2,080 archers he did manage to raise were soon causing havoc around Portsmouth because they had not been paid. On 23 November there was another blow to national pride: Richard the Lionheart's 'jaunty castle' on the Seine, the famously impregnable Château Gaillard, surrendered. Chief among those blamed were Suffolk and Bishop Moleyns, who resigned the Privy Seal on 9 December. Buckingham somehow avoided censure, perhaps because of his unarguably high lineage and immense wealth. But he had been almost as busy in the French negotiations as Moleyns and was as assiduous a signatory of Privy Council papers as Suffolk, witnessing over 75 per cent of royal charters between 1446 and 1449.

Parliament was prorogued for Christmas on 17 December, but there were few festivities. Shortly after Christmas, Harfleur, Henry V's first conquest in France, fell to the French. Demonstrations against anyone associated with royal policy increased in violence. On 9 January 1450 Moleyns arrived in Portsmouth to pay Kyriel's men, but foolishly disputed the amount due 'with boisterous language'. An angry mob of soldiers beat him up, crying that he was the traitor who had sold Normandy; they may also have had in mind his attempt to blacken York's reputation. Moleyns died of his injuries, after making a confession blaming not only himself but also Suffolk and other 'traitors' of the Crown.

Kent, where both gentry and commons had suffered badly from extortion and oppression by court favourites, and which was the first landing place of the disillusioned soldiers expelled from Normandy, was the most anarchic shire of all. Feeling against Buckingham was reflected in an attack on his deer park at Penshurst by a band of a hundred or more armed poachers wearing false beards and faces blacked with charcoal, 'calling themselves servants of the queen of the fairies, intending their names should not be known'. At Eastry two hundred men elected captains with such teasing pseudonyms as 'Robin Hood', 'Jenessay' (je ne sais) and 'Haveybynne' (have I been) under a leader 'feigning himself a hermit yclept Bluebeard'. The uprising was quickly put down and Bluebeard was summarily executed at Canterbury on 9 February.

'Never a knight being a murderer hath worship, nor never shall have'

It was at this time and against this political backdrop that the first serious crime of which Sir Thomas Malory was accused took place. On 4 January 1450, Malory and twenty-six or more men, their names unknown, were said to have ambushed the Duke of Buckingham in Coombe Abbey woods. It was the Christmas recess, and Coombe's woods bordered on Newbold Revel land, so Malory could certainly have been there. He and his men were said to be helmeted and jacketed and armed with swords, spears, longbows and arrows and crossbows. They were accused of lying in ambush in order to kill and murder (the medieval gerund 'murdrum' sounded an ominous roll of thunder through the accusation) the Duke 'ad ipsum cum arcubus & sagittis predictis sagittandum' (by shooting arrows at him with the aforesaid bows and arrows).

Had Sir Thomas Malory decided that it was time to take up arms against Buckingham, just as Sir Gareth did battle with the Knight of the Red Lands?

> 'Trust not, in him is no courtesy, but all goeth to the death or shameful murder, and that is pity, for he is a full likely man, well made of body, and a full noble knight of prowess, and a lord of great lands and possessions.' 'Truly,' said

Beaumains, 'he may well be a good knight, but he useth shameful customs, and it is marvel that he endureth so long that none of the noble knights of my lord Arthur's have not dealt with him.'

It seems desperately unlikely. Assassination would have been a shockingly cowardly way of 'dealing with' an enemy. Malory was a chronicler of chivalric romances who belonged to an ancient family with a proud tradition of honourable behaviour. Nor had any gentlemen of his rank and connections been involved in uprisings against the King's much-hated counsellors at this point. Although it has to remain a possibility that Malory's attack was the first of the violent assaults on members of the King's inner circle that were to come, it is a remote one.

Let us turn the accusation on its head. The person who already had an impressive record for ungallantly attacking local gentry with a mind to forcing them to do his will was Buckingham himself, as Thomas Ferrers already knew and Baldwin Mountfort would soon discover. Always a litigious man, he was unusually legally aggressive between 1449 and 1451, suing over sixty people. His actions were very effective because he had numerous lawyers and crown justices on his personal payroll. In 1451 his retainers included the Sheriff, one MP, the coroner, the escheator and numerous JPs. Suppose that Buckingham had heard that Malory had been at the forefront of the MPs calling for reform and had decided the Christmas recess was a good time to whip him into line. The perfect base for a surprise attack was the Abbey of Coombe, next door to Newbold Revel, and the Abbot, Richard Atherstone, was an old crony of Buckingham, who held mortgages on several of the Abbey's properties. If Malory heard that the Duke was skulking in Coombe with a large force preparing for an attack, in all probability at night, he would certainly take the offensive in order to protect his own home, muttering, as Lancelot did, the 'old saw, that a good man is never in danger but when he is in danger of a coward'.

The accusation later made against Malory produces strong negative evidence to support this. It did not give any reason for the presence of Buckingham in Coombe woods, nor did it claim that anyone was killed, or even injured – an extraordinarily fortunate outcome if Buckingham's entourage was in truth ambushed by two dozen and more heavily armed men carrying crossbows and long-bows. But if the Duke was approaching Newbold Revel by night and found himself challenged by a strongly armed first line of defence, he would have had little option but to retreat, aware that even if he did rout Malory and his men, he had lost the element of surprise and would find Newbold Revel itself well-defended.

Buckingham's kinsman Humphrey Stafford of Grafton and two hundred men-at-arms made just such a surprise attack on Sir Robert Harcourt in his Oxfordshire manor of Stanton Harcourt four months later. Fortunately for Sir Robert and his family, they had time to retreat into the church before the attack began, and it was strong enough to withstand a six-hour siege, even though Stafford's thugs attempted to burn it down. They had to content themselves with looting the house and outbuildings. Another MP, Sir John Gresley, who inherited from his father in 1449 and sat for Staffordshire later in 1450, seems to have been whipped into line more effectively by accusations against him by the Abbot of Burton-on-Trent in May 1450; Gresley had to appear before his 'full doubtful lord' Bucking-ham, when he pleaded that the charges were malicious. He ended up as a retainer of Buckingham.

Oddest of all is the fact that Buckingham made no complaint about this murderous attack for over a year. Malory returned to London to be at Westminster on 22 January 1450 when Parliament reassembled. It was one of the most dramatic sessions of the century. Warwick and Buckingham were in the Lords to hear the Duke of Suffolk defend himself against Moleyns's deathbed confession. It was, he said, a 'great infamy and defamation' which had led to 'odious and horrible language' being used on almost every lip to 'his most heavy dislander'. He reminded them of the faithful service of members of his family, both in the French wars and in England for thirty-five years or more. Unimpressed by his eloquence ('set under sugar he showeth them gall' ran one contemporary lampoon), the Commons demanded Suffolk's arrest and the London mob surged around

Westminster. Rumours revived of his involvement in the deaths of Humfrey of Gloucester, Harry Beauchamp and even John Beaufort, the former Earl of Somerset. The lampoon above continues:

> *Witness of Humfrey, Henry, and John*
> *Which of late were alive and now be they gone.*

Suffolk was placed in the Tower, as much for his own safety as to satisfy the Commons.

On 7 February, the Speaker William Tresham presented the Commons' formal petition against Suffolk. It accused him of selling England out to the King of France and René of Anjou, planning to marry his son to the Beaufort heiress, Margaret, in order to place them on the throne (evidently, after four childless years of marriage, Henry VI was thought unlikely to beget heirs), and fortifying Wallingford Castle in preparation for a French invasion. It also indicted him for 'insatiable covetise', corruption at home and incompetence abroad. John Mowbray, Duke of Norfolk and hereditary Marshal of England, presented a similar petition in the Lords.

Suffolk rejected all the allegations. The Lords suggested that the advice of the judges should be sought, but Henry VI ordered the matter to be 'respited' at his will. This was tantamount to a pardon, though Suffolk remained in the Tower. 'The Duke of Suffolk is pardoned, and hath his men again waiting on him, and is right well at ease and merry, and is in the King's good grace, and in the good conceit of all the Lords, as well as ever he was,' wrote Margaret Paston to her husband John. In the same letter she told him that the French had raided Cromer and Caistor and taken Englishmen for ransom.

The Commons sent in a second petition on 9 March detailing other grievances. Suffolk was moved from the Tower to the King's palace of Westminster, a further sign of royal favour that intensified discontent. On 13 March at a meeting of the Lords in council, he again rejected the accusations, arguing (with some justice) that in all these affairs 'other lords were as privy thereto as he'. He blamed the murdered Moleyns for overreaching his instructions as to Maine, then cagily submitted himself to the King's judgement rather than to the more usual trial by his peers. Henry VI, who knew the truth about the ceding of Maine, judged the Duke 'neither declared nor charged'. The Lords could only make a formal protest, saying that they were not parties to the King's decision. On 17 March Henry declared the Duke banished for five years from 1 May. Suffolk slipped secretly away down the Thames to his Suffolk manor of Wingfield to prepare for departure.

There was widespread fury at his escape. London church doors were papered with accusatory handbills and there were uprisings all over England. Proclamations against riotous meetings 'which claimed to be held for the common weal of the land' were issued. A London wine-drawer was hanged, drawn and quartered for treason at the end of March. His four quarters were hoisted high where riots most threatened: Stamford and Newbury, both York's towns and, interestingly, in view of Malory's Warwickshire home and election for Great Bedwyn, Coventry and Winchester. But the Midlands were regarded as loyal for the most part and when, on 30 March, Parliament was adjourned for Easter, it was told to reassemble on 29 April in Leicester. Its removal from the unruly and turbulent capital was the doing, it was said, of the Queen.

Warwick had returned to Warwick Castle by 21 March. He had been shown high favour by the King, who had made him premier earl of England on 2 March; he could now sport the same golden coronet that Harry Beauchamp had received, and must have hoped that before long he too would be dubbed Duke of Warwick. He may have welcomed Suffolk's downfall, but he was certainly not in favour of mob rule, and he agreed with alacrity to the King's request that he bring a strong force of men-at-arms to Leicester, perhaps for his sovereign's defence, perhaps to take to the defence of France. 'Four hundred men and more' trooped behind him when he arrived to attend the Leicester session of Parliament on 5 May. The chances are that Malory, still MP for Great Bedwyn, was with him.

They found Parliament in a state of shock. On 1 May, Suffolk had taken ship from Ipswich for Calais, which Buckingham, its captain, had probably told to welcome him. But on 2 May he was intercepted by the privateering fleet which supplemented England's official navy and taken on board its flagship, the *Nicholas of the Tower*. Mystery still surrounds what happened next. A mock trial on the same impeachments as those offered by the Commons took place, and Suffolk was found guilty. He was put into a small boat with an execution squad. When it arrived on the shore,

> *One of the lewdest of the ship bade him lay down his head and he should be fair faired with [i.e. honourably treated], and die on a sword, and smote off his head with a rusty sword within half a dozen strokes, and took away his gown of russet and doublet of velvet mailed, and laid his body on the sands of Dover, and some say his head was set on a pole by it.*

The pole was intended as a macabre pun on Suffolk's family name of de la Pole. None of those with Suffolk were harmed. The message was clear: this was justice, not piracy, an execution, not murder.

'The Complaint of the Commons of Kent'

Early in June reports began to reach Leicester, where Henry VI and Margaret were still in residence, of a serious rebellion in Kent. The royal couple must have shuddered. Immediate action was taken. Parliament adjourned on 6 June and the Lords were asked to muster forces to St Albans to aid the King against the rebels. Henry VI asked Warwick to be part of his personal bodyguard; a letter from the Earl, written on 8 June 1450 to William Ferrers of Chartley, asked Ferrers to send as many of his men as he could to Warwick in two days' time so that he could be 'assisting and advanting upon' the King's person. Warwick must have despatched similar letters all around the county, including perhaps to Newbold Revel, where Sir Thomas Malory evidently had a band of 'marvellous good men of their hands'.

The rebellion in Kent was well organised. Its leader Jack Cade was forceful and articulate. His followers included gentlemen, well-to-do farmers, tradesmen, Londoners and thousands of lesser men. A host estimated at 40,000 men had set up a fortified camp at Blackheath, just east of London. After the King had returned to London, lodged for safety in the Hospitallers' well-fortified Priory at Clerkenwell, a delegation from the royal council led by Bishop Waynflete was sent out to the rebels. They were presented with a manifesto, 'the complaint of the commons of Kent'. Its fifteen articles echoed the petitions made to the King by the Commons in February, and are an excellent summary of what was wrong with Henry VI's government. They give us a clear picture of how Malory will have seen the state of things in England.

The King was, it said, surrounded by malicious liars who 'daily and nightly informed him that good was evil and evil was good', telling him that he was above the law, when in fact he had sworn to abide by it at his coronation. Only bribes to these false courtiers brought admission to the King's presence, though everyone ought to have free access to it 'to ask justice or grace as the case required'. They also told him that the people were planning to bring in the Duke of York to be King, when in fact York was his 'very friend'. While 'the good Duke of Gloucester' was impeached by one false traitor and murdered before he came to answer, Suffolk had been spared even a trial. The manifesto also declared as murders the death of Sir Harry, Duke of Warwick and, rather less convincingly, those of Cardinal Beaufort and the previous Dukes of Somerset and Exeter, and demanded that their assailants be found and punished.

It complained that parliamentary elections were not free, as county magnates could dictate the candidates elected. Sheriffs and their underlings extorted and oppressed 'the poor people' by false charges in courts, causing them to travel to distant parts of the county by holding courts far from their homes. False accusations of treason were made in order to grab the lands and goods of the accused, but the King was not allowed any part of such ill-gotten gains. Men were dispossessed of their rightful estates through false legal actions, for 'the true owners dare not hold claim nor pursue their right'. People were not paid for food and other articles taken for the King's household by his purveyors because they wrongly claimed that he was allowed to 'live off his commons'; officials obtained the revenues of the Crown while the people were oppressed with taxes. As a result

His lands are lost, his merchandise is lost, his commons destroyed, the sea is lost, France is lost, himself so poor that he may not pay for his meat or drink; he oweth more than ever did king in England.

The manifesto asked, as the last Parliament had, that the King resume all the lands, liberties and privileges that he had granted away on bad advice and keep them himself 'for his own richness, the war in France and to pay his debts'. Then shall 'our Sovereign lord reign with great worship, love of God and his people ... able with God's help to conquer where he will, and as for us we shall be ready to defend our country from all nations and to go with our Sovereign lord where he will command us'. It also said that it did not blame all lords or all about the King's person, nor all gentlemen, lawyers, bishops and priests. Only those who were found guilty by a 'just and true inquiry by the law' should be punished. Cade was no democrat: his manifesto called on the King to appoint a much more broadly based government headed by the ancient lords of the blood royal: York, Exeter, Buckingham and Norfolk, not 'the false progeny and affinity of the duke of Suffolk'.

The articles were predominantly concerned with the wrongs endured by ordinary Englishmen. It was a reflection of the general loss of enthusiasm for the English domain in France that only one of them concerned France. Referring to rumours that the English losses there were due to treason, it called for a national inquiry to establish if this were the case, and if so, to find the traitors so they could be punished by law 'without any pardon'. The men of Kent repeatedly emphasised their loyalty. There was no question of toppling an anointed king from his throne. Reform did not entail revolution. They were not 'risers and traitors' but true liegemen of the King 'and his best friends with the help of Jesus, to whom we cry daily and nightly, with many thousand more, that God of his righteousness shall take vengeance on the false traitors of his royal realm that have brought us in this mischief and misery'. They also promised that they had no intention of pillaging or plundering. 'These faults amended, we will go home'.

On 18 June, the King rode out to Blackheath at the head of ten thousand men, including Warwick's retinue, in which, we might guess, were Malory and his own household men. But rather than appear in arms against the King, the rebels had fled. Punitive expeditions were sent against them, most notoriously two thousand of the Queen's 'men of Cheshire' who advanced as far as Canterbury, plundering so indiscriminately that several were later tried for breaking the peace. The King did make a small gesture of appeasement, ordering the arrest of the two men most vilified as extortioners by the rebels, James Fiennes, Lord Saye, and William Cromer, former and present sheriffs of Kent. But unrest remained extreme, with widespread murmurings in the King's own army that the rebels were justified in their complaints. Henry VI retreated to the safety of Kenilworth, protectively cordoned by the Earl of Warwick's retinue.

On 24 June, Caen fell. The 4,000 dispirited men who returned with Edmund, Duke of Somerset to England in the next fortnight added to the discontent. Cade returned to the outskirts of London and occupied Southwark. Sympathisers from Essex advanced on Mile End. On 3 July Cade entered London, cutting the ropes of the drawbridge of London Bridge to prevent it being closed against him. Inevitably pillaging took place – especially of the homes of those identified as traitors. Cade then held a commission for trial and punishment in the Guildhall. Fiennes and Cromer were dragged out of prison and executed. All over the home counties there were attacks on those deemed to have betrayed England. Most shocking of all was the murder of the King's confessor Bishop Ayscough, who was dragged from his house at Edginton, in Wiltshire, and 'killed as if he was a wild beast, with cudgels and boar-spears'.

After a week, London's citizens rallied behind royal troops from the Tower led by Lord Scales and Matthew Gough, an experienced veteran of the French wars. The rebels were ousted from the city, leaving London Bridge strewn with bodies, including Gough's, and a truce was declared. Bishop Waynflete and York negotiated with Cade, offering him and his followers a free pardon if they dispersed. They accepted. The roll was soon filled with hundreds of names. Cade was listed as John Mortimer, a troubling sign that he aspired to kinship with the Duke of York, whose mother had been a Mortimer.

Cade's pseudonym showed that he had little faith in his pardon. Hoping to win a refuge, he went on to attack Queenborough Castle on 9 July. Its constable, the same Roger Chamberlain who had so nearly been drawn and quartered as well as hanged after Duke Humfrey's death, now a retainer of the Duke of York, held out successfully. The Exchequer immediately issued writs putting a price of 1,000 marks on Cade's head and announcing that he was a necromancer, a murderer and a French *agent provocateur*. Three days later, on 12 July, Alexander Iden, the new Sheriff of Kent, caught up with Cade at Heathfield in Sussex and captured him, injuring him so severely that Cade died before he could be executed. He was ritually dismembered anyway, and his quarters despatched for display, three to different corners of Kent, one to London Bridge.

Nemesis

*'What,' said Sir Lancelot, 'is he a thief and a knight and
a ravisher of women? He doth shame unto the order of
knighthood, and contrary unto his oath; it is pity that he
liveth.'*
Malory, 'The Tale of Sir Lancelot du Lake'

lthough Cade was dead, Henry VI's troubles were far from
over. The day before Cade died, the formidable Normandy
fortress of Falaise was ceded to Sir Pothon de Saintraille,
now Charles VII's Commander-in-Chief, as part of the price for
safe-conducts for the garrison of Rouen. Malory may have had memories of shivering outside the walls of Falaise during Henry V's five-
month-long siege in 1418 – and of a time when it was Saintraille who
was in captivity. Then the world had revolved around the confident
generalship of Bedford and Richard Beauchamp. Now the English
cause was utterly lost. The French advanced on Cherbourg,
the last English stronghold in Normandy. Despite heroic resistance
by Thomas Gower, it fell on 12 August 1450. 'We have now not a foot
of land in Normandy and men are feared that Calais will be besieged
hastily,' wrote James Gresham to John Paston on 19 August.

At this point Richard of York decided to return from Ireland.
Rumours of his involvement in Cade's uprising made him dread being
declared a traitor. He urgently needed to clear his name. He landed
at Beaumaris, on the Isle of Anglesey, on 7 September, and made
'with great bobaunce' for his castle at Ludlow, brushing off but noting
resentfully attempts by royal officers to waylay him and to capture
his officers. From Ludlow, York sent petitions to Henry VI, denying

any intention of usurping the throne and explaining that he was returning to prove his loyalty and prevent any 'corrupting of his blood'. He knew that on 5 September writs had been issued for a new Parliament to meet in November, and must have dreaded a repeat of Humfrey of Gloucester's summons to the Bury Parliament.

A week later he set out for London, summoning men from his scattered Midlands estates to join the huge retinue he had raised in Ireland and Wales. He travelled by way of Warwickshire, and had talks with his nephew Warwick. He also arranged to meet William Tresham of Sywell, Speaker in the last Parliament, at Northampton. Previously retained by Suffolk, he was in need of a new 'good lord', and his experience of the Commons made him a valuable asset. The meeting never took place. Evidently apprehensive, Tresham crept out at dawn's crack from Sywell, which is five miles from Northampton. But he was ambushed by a gang of 160 men and beaten up. He died of his injuries. Tresham's death signalled the beginning of another ruthless race to get the right men elected to the Commons.

On 27 September York and a three-thousand-strong retinue clattered into London. Benet's *Chronicle* reported that at their first meeting the King received him graciously, and declared that he accepted him as his 'true subject and well-beloved cousin'. York protested at his reception in Beaumaris, where the constable of the castle had told him he had the King's orders not to let him land, and at attempts to kill his chamberlain, Sir William Oldhall, and arrest other officers. Henry replied that his men had only been told to ascertain York's intentions, and countered by a complaint that York's men were interfering with royal rent collections in the Welsh Marches. Their next meeting was less affable. York was furious to see that Somerset, the betrayer of Normandy, was at the King's side. Glaring at him, he pressed the King to do justice on those 'commonly spoken of as traitors', and demanded reforms 'much after the Commons' desire'. Henry fenced, promising the election of a 'sad and substantial council, you to be one' with new powers to effect reforms.

Member for Wareham

York then left London to make a pilgrimage to Walsingham, an understandable piety but also a good excuse to visit Bury St Edmunds to spend time with John Mowbray, Duke of Norfolk, the son of his wife Cecily Neville's sister Katherine. As proud of his ancient blood as York and Warwick, Norfolk also shared their hawkish stance towards France and distrust of Somerset. He has been vilified as a disreputable thug because of the violent attacks carried out by his retainers in Norfolk, but many were in revenge for the illegal acts of Suffolk's hydra-headed affinity. Long excluded from power, he too wanted access to the King's ear; there was as yet no thought of a change of king.

York and Norfolk intended to get enough supporters into Parliament to engineer Somerset's fall. It may seem far-fetched to suggest that Malory was discussed, but it looks as if York at least thought that Malory would be a useful man to have in the House of Commons. Perhaps he had been impressed by the way the bold lord of Newbold Revel had dealt with Buckingham in Coombe woods. Neither he nor Norfolk had enough influence to get him elected in Warwickshire, where Buckingham was backing Sir William Mountfort and Warwick had chosen his own annuitant, Thomas Middleton. But like all great magnates, York had several pocket boroughs at his disposal. His patronage would neatly explain why, when Parliament opened at Westminster on 6 November, Thomas Malory took his seat as MP for Wareham, in Dorset. Wareham had been a prosperous port until the silting up of the Frome river meant that ships could no longer get there from Poole's enormous harbour. But in 1435 it was listed among the 'desolated, wasted, destructed and depopulated' towns in the county, now most noted for its 'gardens for garlic'. The overlord of this least fragrant of rotten boroughs was the Duke of York.

There was evidently some sort of link between Malory, York and Norfolk. It is possible that it concerned the overlordship of Newbold Revel, which was recorded in a post-mortem inquisition of 1434 as one of the fiefs held by Joan of Kent, who had inherited it from her brother, the Earl of Kent, in 1408. York was one of the six heirs of Joan of Kent (her first husband had been Edward Langley, the Duke of York, who had died in 1402). It could have been he who inherited Newbold Revel. However, he had little interest in that part of Warwickshire. But Norfolk, who held the nearby castle of Brinklow and the hunting lodge and great deer park of Caluden, and was patron of both Monk's Kirby Priory and Coombe Abbey, may well have coveted the overlordship of Newbold Revel, and he would certainly have known Malory. York was raising all the money he could at this time. Did he do a deal with Norfolk? All that we know is that, by 1461, Newbold Revel was listed as held by the Duke of Norfolk.

However Malory came to be sitting in Parliament for a Yorkist borough, we need to bear in mind that doing so does not imply that he was an adversary of Henry VI of Lancaster. It would be wildly anachronistic to see sharp divisions between followers of York and Lancastrian loyalists as yet. The Duke of York himself still sought Henry VI's favour and the removal of corrupt royal counsellors by the usual political process of the time. He certainly packed the November 1450 Parliament to some effect. At least twenty-five MPs besides Malory owed their seats to York or his allies. Among them was Sir Robert Harcourt, who sat for Oxfordshire and is recorded as being Warwick's steward in 1451. In addition, many other MPs had relatives in France or were war veterans themselves. York's chamberlain Sir William Oldhall was chosen as Speaker. A fortnight after Parliament opened, York arrived in London at the head of a long cavalcade of liveried men. The next day Norfolk arrived with an equally imposing retinue. The day after that the Earl of Warwick cantered into the city 'with a mighty people arrayed for the war'. It was a carefully orchestrated show of force. On 30 November, there was 'a marvellous and dreadful storming and noise of the commons and of lords' men at Westminster, crying and saying to the lords: "Do justice upon the false traitors or let us be avenged"'. On 1 December a mob attacked the Duke of Somerset at Blackfriars, hoping to lynch him. They looted the friary, but Somerset escaped, smuggled out of the water gate on York's orders, it was said, and taken for safety to the Tower.

Next day, in another showy demonstration of his power, York turned out with his entire retinue and marched through the city, arresting looters. The following day Henry VI himself processed through the city, backed by the united forces of York, Warwick, Salisbury and many other nobles – some ten thousand men. What a noble sight, wrote one chronicler – if only it had taken place in Normandy. Two days later, Henry VI showed his gratitude by recognising Warwick's right, which was being disputed by the Countess of Shrewsbury, to the hereditary Beauchamp chamberlainship of the Exchequer.

In Parliament the Commons petitioned the King to take back his over-generous grants of Crown lands and offices in order to put Crown finances back on an even keel. It also asked for the removal of thirty people from positions of power in his household. First on the list was Somerset, who was accused of betraying the King's cause in France. Next was Suffolk's widow, Alice Chaucer, evidently a woman of influence. Among the lesser fry was the wealthy lawyer Thomas Greswold of Solihull, a self-made man who gained his substantial holdings in Worcestershire and Warwickshire in part by marriage and in part by grants of confiscated estates given to him by Somerset and Buckingham. As a King's Sergeant, Greswold had far-reaching judicial power in Westminster. He was also coroner for Warwickshire, where he often acted for Buckingham. Malory must have known him well. Was it he who asked for Greswold's removal? All we know for certain is that for the rest of his life, Greswold made it his business to pursue Malory through the courts with relentless malevolence.

York was now in perilously deep water. He could and did add a demand for action against Somerset for the loss of Normandy to his original petition for the reconstruction of the King's council. But he could do nothing about the influence on the King of the hugely popular Talbot, the foremost English commander in France since 1429 and still martially redoubtable even in his mid-sixties. Not only were Talbot and Somerset brothers-in-law; their wives were daughters of the former Earl of Warwick, Sir Richard Beauchamp, by his first marriage – Warwick's rivals for the Beauchamp inheritance. When

Talbot returned in December 1450 from the pilgrimage to Rome that had been a condition of his release in exchange for the surrender of Falaise, he backed Somerset to the hilt.

Parliament was prorogued for the Christmas recess on 18 December, and Malory and Warwick returned to their estates. Within a week, Talbot and Somerset had prevailed upon the Queen, and thus the King, to give the custody of the dower of the Duchess of Warwick, who had died on 26 July 1450, to all four Beauchamp sisters – their own wives Margaret and Elinor, Elizabeth, Lady Latimer and Anne, Countess of Warwick. This reversed several previous inquisitions which had found for Anne as sole heir of her mother. The King also cancelled his grant of the chamberlainship to Warwick. Talbot then announced that as the husband of Margaret, the eldest of Beauchamp's daughters, he regarded himself as the rightful Earl of Warwick. Warwick was facing a sustained attack on his inheritance, some of it at least legally justifiable.

When Parliament reassembled on 20 January 1451, there were signs that the King's backbone had stiffened – or been stiffened by the joint efforts of Queen Margaret, Talbot and Somerset. In response to new rumbles of revolt in Kent, he set out in battle array on 28 January with several thousand men, led by Somerset and Henry Holland, Duke of Exeter, a young firebrand but at this point ferociously loyal to his royal cousin. A succession of trials for treason produced a grisly 'harvest of heads', with quarters sent to towns all over England as a ghastly warning of what became of rebels. Warwick and York were loyally supportive of the punitive judicial progress, and both were appointed to trial commissions. Henry returned to Westminster in triumph on 23 February, graciously pardoning a host of 'miscreants' who waited at Blackheath to beg his mercy, and riding 'right royally through the city'. Such displays of regal magnificence and power, always carefully staged, were deliberately intended to make a lasting impression on all who witnessed them. At this time the King was not only the greatest authority in the land, kingship was seen as a God-given appointment. 'No sovereign on earth may be his judge,' observed Sir John Fastolf in 1435. Lords and Commons might propose, but only the King disposed.

Miscreant Knight

In mid-March, Malory received a shock. Fifteen months after the confrontation in Coombe woods, Buckingham had thought of a way of making use of it. A warrant for the arrest of Sir Thomas Malory was issued on 15 March 1451. It also called for the arrest of his servant John Appleby and eighteen other men, some members of his household, others tenants and neighbours, 'on account of diverse felonies, transgressions, insurrections, extortions and oppressions, for which they are indicted'.

Malory's alleged ambush of the Duke of Buckingham would account for the insurrection mentioned. Two later, and similarly retrospective, accusations against him may explain the warrant's reference to 'extortions and oppressions'. Margaret King and William Hales 'of the parish of Monks Kirby' were willing to swear that Malory and his servant John Appleby, gentleman, had 'by threats and oppression' extorted £5 from them on 31 May 1450. The other incident took place on the same day: John Mylner, again of the parish of Monks Kirby, was deprived of 20s on 31 August. Mylner's name may mean he was a miller, or perhaps a miller's son. If his father was 'Robert Mylner, miller', one of the men against whom Malory and Harcourt had gone to law in 1448 and 1449, he could well have had a grievance against Malory. As extortions went, the sums of £5 and £1 were meagre: 40s was the lower limit for suits of debt brought in the court of common pleas. Since both incidents happened on the last day of the month, we might guess that there was a disagreement about rents due.

The man who should have arrested Malory in response to the writ was Sir William Mountfort, as Sheriff. But he took no action, although he was presumably, like Malory, still in London for the next session of Parliament. It could be that the old man, who had known Malory since he was a boy, disapproved of the indictment. Parliament's last session opened on 5 May 1451. The King's party was conciliatory, desperate for a vote of money. Ships and men had been commandeered to send to Bordeaux, one of the few remaining Gascon cities loyal to the English, under the command of Sir Richard Wood-ville, now Lord Rivers. But they were still in Plymouth, threatening to disperse unless their wages arrived. With an exemplary display of authority and diplomacy, Henry VI dealt with the Commons' aud-acious petitions. He refused to condemn the dead Duke of Suffolk, but otherwise he was conciliatory. He accepted in principle the ban-ishment of the thirty members of his entourage indicted as corrupt, but he insisted on excepting any who were peers of the realm (which included bishops) and anyone he was 'accustomed to have about him' (which seems to have included Greswold). Although he accepted the petition for his own resumption of Crown lands, he reserved the right to make exemptions.

On 3 June all attempts at conciliation ended abruptly. The reason was a petition put forward in the Commons by Thomas Young, MP for Bristol and a known placeman of York's. It asked that the Duke of York be recognised as the heir to the throne. Given the King's five childless years of marriage, there could have been no more inflamma-tory demand. The request was well beyond the Commons' remit. Despite the fact that no money had been voted, Parliament was dissolved. Young was taken straight to the Tower of London.

After Parliament was dismissed in June 1451, England remained restless. Local quarrels escalated into private wars, notably in the West Country, where the Earl of Devon besieged Lord Bonville in Taunton in September, and in East Anglia, where 'great riots, extortions, hor-rible wrongs and hurts' were reported. No man of rank felt safe without a retinue to protect him. Henry VI only paid lip service to the demands for change. He ignored his promise to York to take the advice of his 'sad and substantial council', and although he did retrieve many of the lands alienated since 1422 through an Act of Resumption, he confirmed those in royal favour in possession of the rest. York and his Neville relatives were not in favour. York lost Hadleigh Castle, an important fortress on the Thames estuary near Southend, to Queen Margaret. Warwick lost the Channel Isles and his custody on George Neville's half of the Despenser inheritance. Salisbury lost the honour of Richmond. Potentially allies of the King, they were driven into opposition by Somerset's and Talbot's greed.

Each only attended two royal council meetings between 1450 and 1453. Warwick spent most of his time in the Welsh Marches, defiantly occupying parts of his wife's inheritance to which he no longer officially had a right and ignoring royal mandates to surrender. King Henry VI renewed his punitive royal progresses. Councillors, officers and domestics of the Duke of York were arrested. Some were specifically accused of treason and rebellion, others of random felonies.

On 13 July 1451, another warrant was issued for the arrest of Sir Thomas Malory.

> *Know that for a few certain and notable causes set forth in our presence and the presence of our Council we have assigned you to take and arrest Thomas Malory, knight, and John Appleby, servant of the same Thomas Malory, wherever they may be found – as well within liberties as without – and to find sufficient mainpernors [sureties] who will be willing to give mainprise for them under good and sufficient penalty, to be enforced by you according to your reasonable discretion, that they, nor either of them, shall cause no injury or evil to the Prior and convent of the Carthusian Order of the Isle of Axholme or to any of our people, nor shall burn their house, nor shall procure or cause the same in any way, and that the same Thomas Malory, knight, and John Appleby in their persons shall appear in our presence and the presence of the Council aforesaid on the quinzaine of Michaelmas next [c.13–14 October] to answer upon those charges which shall there and then be preferred against them.*

There are several interesting things about this warrant. It was addressed not to the Sheriff, Sir William Mountfort, but to Humphrey, Duke of Buckingham, and Richard Neville, Earl of Warwick. The phrase 'as well within liberties as without' meant that the warrant was not limited to the jurisdiction of the Sheriff of Warwickshire. Malory could also be arrested outside the county, or in Coventry, which was a separate 'liberty' from the county. There was no mention of the eighteen other men referred to in the warrant of March 1451, only of John Appleby. The timing of the new warrant and the mention of Axholme suggests a connection with yet another later accusation: the theft, on Friday 4 June 1451, of seven cows, two calves, 335 sheep worth £22 and a cart (evidently a particularly solid one, as it was worth £4) from Cosford, a hamlet three miles from Newbold Revel. The men accused of rustling the stock were Malory and four of his servants: John Masshot (who was listed with him as a Beauchamp retainer in 1446), William Smith, Geoffrey Gryffyn and John Arnesby (possibly a miswriting for Appleby). The men to whom the stock belonged were William Rowe and William Dowde of Shawell. Rowe, who was described as 'clericus', was probably a monk: Cosford was held of the Priory. Malory had lands at Shawell, and was lord of the neighbouring manor of Swinford. What was going on? Malory's brother-in-law Robert Vincent was Clerk of the Kitchens at Warwick Castle at the time; he could have asked Malory to requisition food for the Earl's retinue, which returned with him from Parliament in May. Or Malory could have commandeered the stock in distraint of unpaid rent or some other form of debt. It is also possible that Monks Kirby Priory had misappropriated the stock in the first place – there were many complaints about its predatory behaviour at around this time.

But Malory's venture into rustling or high-handed distraint is unlikely to have occasioned the warrant, which was issued directly by the King in council. These unusual writs, introduced in the fourteenth century by Edward III, bypassed normal common law procedures. They dealt mainly with counterfeiting, heresy, serious riots, the spreading of rumours against the nobility, and 'cases which held a natural interest for the king' – in other words, top-secret matters. Issued under the privy seal, they were deeply disliked because they gave the defendant no clue to the charges against him. Their bearers were sometimes beaten up to prevent them delivering a writ, or even made to eat the parchment on which it was written. Use of such non-committal warrants was increasing at this time. Complaints against them increased after 1449, and they were challenged in Parliament in 1453. In the end, the Commons acceded to a royal request to allow the writs for another seven years on condition that they were only used in cases of riot.

The date of the warrant is very interesting indeed. The King's spies would later claim that on 20 July 1451 they had heard Sir William Oldhall, York's most trusted councillor, plotting to depose the King. Treasonable letters attempting to rouse the people to support York 'and his false and traitorous purposes' had, they said, been circulated around the country. Buckingham could have engineered the arrest because Malory had made his anti-court opinions loudly known when he sat in Parliament for Wareham, or because he disliked him personally. But it is also possible that Malory, as bonny a writer as he was a fighter, had a sideline in persuasive propaganda that was making him particularly obnoxious to the men of power in the royal council.

The warrant was addressed to the Earl of Warwick as a matter of form – Warwickshire was his county. He may have known nothing about it. When it was issued he was in Wales, busily defending his disputed inheritance. The Duke of Buckingham not only knew about the conciliar warrant; in all probability he initiated it. This time, he took no chances over Malory's capture. He went to fetch Malory himself, rising at dawn on 25 July 1451 and riding out from his manor at Atherstone with no fewer than sixty of his men. To go to such lengths suggests extreme animosity towards Malory.

The day of the arrest was a Sunday – no doubt deliberately chosen to take Malory by surprise and put him at a disadvantage. Sir Thomas was perhaps attending prayers in Newbold Revel's little chapel when the thunder of horses' hoofs heralded the arrival of sixty armed men in the Stafford livery and led by Buckingham himself. They took Malory to Coventry, where he was committed to the custody of the Sheriff, Sir William Mountfort. Mountfort took Malory to his own moated manor house at Coleshill, in the north-east of the county, rather than putting him in Coventry's clink, or allowing Buckingham to imprison him in Maxstoke Castle, a fate that, as we have seen, had been met by more than one Warwickshire gentleman who failed to see eye-to-eye with the Duke.

Coleshill Manor was then a substantial, rambling building with over thirty rooms, seven gables to its façade and wings jutting forward on each side. Its prison was probably a room rather than a dungeon, perhaps the 'inner chamber' containing 'one bedstead, one close stool', listed in a contemporary inventory of the house. Sir William did not live there but at Kingshurst Hall, a few miles to the west. It is likely that after seeing that Malory was safely locked up, he returned to Kingshurst. If he had really wanted to keep his captive secure, that was a mistake. For on the Tuesday after his arrest, 27 July, Malory broke out of his prison at night, swam across the moat and escaped. This was no mean achievement: medieval moats were used for sewage as well as defence. He must moreover have had help. Newbold Revel was nearly thirty miles away, but Malory was back there on Wednesday. Horseback was the only way to travel that fast, and the later indictment did not accuse Malory of stealing a horse, only of breaking out of his prison.

Malory's next actions suggest that he was as 'wild wood' as Lancelot when he was unfairly accused by Guinevere. On the very day of his return, he summoned every available able-bodied man in the neighbourhood. We can imagine the crowded stables and whinnying horses, the hubbub of voices in the great hall, the clash of steel and iron as weapons – swords, lances, ropes, bows and arrows – were issued from the armoury. Wasting absolutely no time, he set out that night with a motley army that included Newbold Revel's cook, smith, groom and bowmaker, as well as his cousin Richard Malory of Radclyffe-on-the-Wreake, John Appleby and dozens of brawny yeomen and husbandmen, 'up to an hundred and more'.

They crossed the Smite Brook, the boundary between Malory's lands and those of Coombe Abbey, and advanced on the Abbey itself. Using 'great baulks of wood' as battering rams they smashed open its gates and doors 'in great destruction and spoliation of the monastery'. It was said that they broke open two chests belonging to the Abbot, and took one bag containing £21 of gold, another with 25 gold and silver marks, and other jewels and valuables worth in total around £40. As light dawned on Thursday 29 July, it was easier to see what was happening. Witnesses again said that over a hundred men were involved in the assault. They 'riotously battered in eighteen doors', insulted the Abbot, the monks and their servants, and broke open another 'three iron chests corded and sealed'. These were not described as the property of the Abbey. The valuables stolen were carefully itemised: three gold rings with precious stones (worth 100s) and two silver signet rings (6s 8d), two silver girdles (30s), three strings of prayer beads, one of coral (5s), one of amber (5s) and one of jet (2s), two bows (5s) and three sheaves of arrows (6s).

Could the attack on Coombe Abbey have been a reflection of the Abbey's own shortcomings? Fifteenth-century abbots were more often determined and bellicose than gentle and saintly, Cora Scofield reminds us in her richly textured life of Edward IV. An abbacy was regarded as a lucrative sinecure as often as a vocation. Richard Atherstone, the Abbot of Coombe, had just as bad a reputation for extortion and maltreatment of tenants as his frequent business associate, Buckingham. John and Joan Shawe, clothiers of Coventry, had gone to law to accuse 'Richard, Abbot of Coombe, with other persons unknown' of breaking into their property 'vi et armis' (by force of arms) while John was away and of taking away two horses, two saddles and bridles, two packs of wool, a cloak, some red silk cloth ('sangweyn taffet') and some green cloth worth 5s. Calls for church reform were flaring up all over the country, and the reliance of the King on clerical advisers, many of them dishonest and avaricious men, had led to numerous attacks on Church property. A very similar attack to that on Coombe took place in 1450 at Ramsay Abbey, near St Ives. Ramsay was then a notoriously corrupt institution – a visitation (an official inspection) had recorded 'drunkenness and surfeit, disobedience and contempt, private aggrandisement and apostasy, drowsiness, sloth and every other thing which is on the downward path to evil and drags men to hell'.

It is, however, unlikely that Malory decided to launch an attack on monastic corruption twenty-four hours after escaping from prison. It is much more probable that there was something at Coombe Abbey that he needed to get hold of without delay and at any cost, and which a large number of his friends and neighbours believed he had every right to possess. What is most striking about the details given of the attack is that, as with his supposed ambush of Buckingham, nobody was killed or badly hurt. Although the Abbot was said to have been 'insultum', a word that could mean assaulted, no details of injury were given. Clearly a very thorough search of the Abbey was made, long enough to last into Thursday morning. But only about £40 was said to have been stolen – a remarkably small sum considering Coombe was the largest and most powerful abbey in Warwickshire.

Contemporary inventories show that every medieval landowner of substance had at least one 'iron chest of evidences'. What was in those 'three iron chests corded and sealed' that were not said to belong to the Abbot? They could of course have been deposited there for safe-keeping by a third party. But it would make excellent sense of the raid if they were stuffed with Malory's own possessions, removed from Newbold Revel by Buckingham when he made his arrest on Sunday and dropped off at Coombe, conveniently close and on the road to Coventry. It was common practice to take away potentially incriminating documents when arresting a suspect. But if delicate matters of state – or much more personal issues – were at stake, Buckingham would have left the chests at Coombe because he wanted to examine them for himself, not hand them over to the Sheriff in Coventry. Now the speed with which Malory acted becomes understandable. He had to get to the Abbey before Buckingham did – and the minute he was known to have escaped, Buckingham would head for Coombe.

If so, what was in the chests? The proceeds of Malory's French campaigns? The title deeds of Newbold Revel? French romances collected while Malory was abroad? The first draft of his history of the reign of King Arthur? Letters from the dukes of York and Norfolk? Letters that he himself had composed arguing York's case? A writer of stirring English prose like Malory would be an enormously useful asset in an age when the most effective propaganda was bills posted on church doors. It is even possible that he was known to have been writing a history of England and France from the point where Froissart had left off in the 1420s – the mysterious *Collectiones Anglicas* tantalisingly listed by John Bale a century later. Such a reminder of past English triumphs would be distinctly unpopular in the new climate of pacifism.

The most convincing explanation for the raid on Coombe Abbey is that by it Sir Thomas Malory saved his own life, recovering not only valuables which would enable him to survive imprisonment but papers that could and would have been used to implicate him in far more serious crimes than those of which he will be accused at Nuneaton. He may not have been able to stop his men looting more than he would himself have wished; he may even have felt that they were justified in doing so. The complete absence of any reference to the raid in the *Register de Cumba* for the year suggests that the monk who recorded significant events throughout this period felt ashamed rather than outraged by it.

Retribution

On 23 August 1451, a special court was held in the fashionable and exclusive Priory of Nuneaton, in Warwickshire. The unusual event caused a flutter of surprise among its inmates, the most aristocratic nuns in the country. Nuneaton was a daughter house of the Abbey of Fontevrault, on the Loire near Saumur, an order founded in the age of Elinor of Aquitaine especially for the benefit of clever and well-born women. The Abbess of the convent, Dame Maud Evering-ham, was just such a woman, a personal friend of King Henry VI and his queen, Margaret of Anjou.

The justices and jurymen who gathered at Nuneaton had been summoned by the Duke of Buckingham. His castle at Maxstoke was only ten miles from Nuneaton, and Atherstone, another of his manors, was even closer. Nuneaton was not normally used for holding judiciary sessions, but Dame Maud was happy to accommodate the whims of her powerful neighbour. Beside him on the bench sat Sir William Birmingham of Birmingham – then little more than a village, but already known for its metalworkers. The other two men were prominent local lawyers: Thomas Bate of Arley, Escheator for War-wickshire, and Thomas Greswold of Solihull, formerly Coroner and King's Sergeant for Warwickshire. They were there to consider 'diverse felonies, trangressions and misdeeds' committed in the county of Warwickshire. Such a session was the first stage in arranging trials, reading out descriptions of the crimes committed before a panel of Justices of the Peace. This 'indictment', which the clerk recorded in

Latin, was then sworn to be true by a jury of fifteen local men. At the top of the agenda was the task of looking into an extensive list of appalling accusations against Sir Thomas Malory of Newbold Revel and his retainers. It is unlikely that any of them were there. No mention is made in the indictment of Malory's re-arrest, or of his presence in court.

First the background to the accusations was explained: Malory's arrest on Sunday 25 July 1451, his imprisonment in Coleshill Manor, his escape and the ransacking of Coombe Abbey. After this dramatic preamble, the clerk itemised the accusations against Sir Thomas in detail, beginning with his supposed ambush of Buckingham himself on 4 January 1450, with twenty-six 'malefactors and breakers of the King's peace unknown ... armed and arrayed in warlike manner'. Next came another, more detailed description of the attack on Coombe Abbey on 27 and 28 July 1451. The clerk then listed the three 'extortions'. Sir Thomas Malory and John Appleby, gentleman, had taken 'by threats and oppression' £5 from Margaret King and William Hales on 31 May 1450, and £1 from John Mylner of Monks Kirby on 31 August 1450.

The next charges were the ones that have most puzzled and shocked admirers of Malory's *Morte Darthur*. It was asserted that on 23 May 1450 Sir Thomas broke into 'the close and house of Hugh Smyth' in Monks Kirby and 'feloniously raped' his wife Joan, 'et cum ea carnaliter concubit'. The Latin verb 'rapere' then usually meant to seize or take away rather than to rape. But the next phrase – 'and lay with her in carnal fashion' – allowed for no ambiguity over what had happened. Moreover, it was claimed that Malory raped Joan Smith again some ten weeks later, on 6 August, in Hugh Smyth's house in Coventry. This time, it was said, he also stole £40 worth of Hugh Smith's goods and chattels and took them away with him to Barwell, in Leicestershire. Finally came the incident at Cosford of 4 June 1451. It was listed as a new inquisition, and fresh jurors were summoned to swear to the fact that on this date Sir Thomas Malory and four other men 'extortionately took seven cows, two calves, a cart worth £4, and 335 sheep worth £22' belonging to William Rowe and William Dowde of Shawell, Leicestershire, and carried them off to Newbold Revel.

Malory's was not the only case to be heard at Nuneaton. On the same day, his friend John Hathwyck of Harbury was indicted for theft by the Malorys' old adversary Sir William Peyto of Chesterton. Chesterton bordered on both Harbury and the lands of Malory's cousins at Tachbrook Malory. Since both estates were well south of Newbold Revel, it was even odder for this case to be heard in Nuneaton. William Smith, Malory's co-defendant in the Cosford stock-rustling affair, was a tenant of Hathwyck. Perhaps the court suspected, but could not prove, that he too had been involved in the raid on Coombe. No further action was taken against Hathwyck and in 1453 a counter-accusation was successfully made. Peyto was convicted of assaulting Hathwyck on 7 June 1451 in Faringdon, London. In 1454 Hathwyck was to put up bail for Sir Thomas.

Malory's arrest and indictment are startling events considered, as they always have been, in isolation. But we need to look at them in the context of national politics. No parliaments were called between June 1451 and March 1453. All over England retribution was being exacted by court favourites for the humiliation they had suffered during the long-drawn-out Parliament of 1450–1. There was a systematic campaign to punish those who had had the temerity to demand reform. It happened most visibly in the judicial progresses which Henry VI made in Surrey, Sussex, Hampshire, Wiltshire and Kent between 22 June and 20 August. The Chief Justice and a small army of lawyers travelled with the King, as did Somerset, Buckingham, Shrewsbury and Salisbury on occasion. In other parts of the country there was more covert retribution. Sir Thomas was not the only MP to be prosecuted. Pretexts were found to imprison, fine or simply assault many of the would-be reformers in the Commons, or to oppress their kinsmen, and the more useful they had been to the opposition, the heavier their punishment. William Tyrell, MP for Weymouth, another pocket borough, John Bellers, MP for Leicester, Ralph Shirley and John Vernon, both related to MPs, were all harassed by lawsuits. The usefulness of the ancient 'appeal' – an accusation by one individual against one or more miscreants at King's Bench in Westminster rather than in local courts – was rediscovered. Not only did this take the accused away from their friends, it meant they were outlawed if they did not appear before the court at the appointed time. There was a sharp rise in both appeals and outlawries in the late 1440s and 1450s.

The proceedings at Nuneaton now appear in a new light. With what has the feel of clever, careful and deliberate malice, the indictment accused Malory of breaking every single element in the oath he had sworn on becoming a knight: to defend the weak, to be merciful, not to do murder or steal and not to ravish women. Nothing could have been more calculated to hurt a man who valued chivalry as highly as he did. The court was outrageously partial. The first accusation against Malory was the attempted murder of the Duke of Buckingham, who presided over it. Of the other three justices, Sir William Birmingham was employed by Buckingham, as was Thomas Bate. Thomas Greswold was married to the daughter of Buckingham's wealthy retainer John Cockayn. None of the four Warwickshire JPs who belonged to Warwick's affinity was present. The jurymen were all from the environs of Buckingham's north Warwickshire manor of Atherstone rather than those of Coombe and Newbold Revel.

If Malory was being persecuted for his reformist views, why didn't York, Warwick or Norfolk defend him? It is likely that they were nervous of crossing the fine line that separated loyal opposition from treason. York was being particularly cautious, with good reason; he had to save his fire to protest at the arbitrary imprisonment of men much more important to him than Malory. Norfolk was finding it much easier to deal with Somerset than with Suffolk and was in fact busily mending fences with Henry, who would make him a Knight of the Garter in 1452. Warwick was more interested in regaining favour (and as much as possible of the Beauchamp and Despenser inheritances) than in protecting a knight whom he personally did not know well.

What of the Countess of Warwick, Anne Beauchamp? She had known Sir Thomas since she was a small girl, and might surely have persuaded her husband to intervene. Warwick was not the henpecked type, but he was feeling especially close to her in the last few weeks of her pregnancy. Or Bishop Waynflete, if he was indeed sympathetic both to Malory's reforming zeal and to his Arthurian idealism? The reason that absolutely nobody of rank and influence seems to have made any attempt to help Sir Thomas must surely lie in the most damning of the accusations made against him at Nuneaton: that not once but on two separate occasions he was guilty of the most shocking crime a knight could commit against a woman – rape.

Ravisher of Women?

Then Peace entered the Parliament Hall
And said that Wrong had wilfully lain with his wife,
And abducted Rose, who was due to marry Reginald
And deflowered Margaret, however hard she struggled

William Langland, *Piers Plowman*

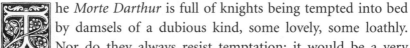he *Morte Darthur* is full of knights being tempted into bed by damsels of a dubious kind, some lovely, some loathly. Nor do they always resist temptation; it would be a very boring book if they did. But there is nothing in the book that condones rape. It is a crime which is singled out as exceptionally evil. When Sir Lancelot hears of the outrages committed by Sir Perys of the Forest Sauvage, he is furious. 'What? Is he a thief and a knight? And a ravisher of women? He does shame upon the order of Knighthood, and contrary to his oath. It is pity that he liveth.' Malory added rape to Sir Perys's crimes himself: originally, he was only a bullying thief. The oath Lancelot refers to is also Malory's addition. It is the one that King Arthur makes his knights swear after the defeat of the Emperor Lucius, and which I compared in Chapter 6 to Henry V's ordinances for Normandy. It also resembles the oath sworn by Knights of the Bath. But Malory's version places more emphasis than either of these on a knight's duties towards women.

> *Then the king established all the knights and gave them riches and lands; and charged them never to do outrage nor murder, and always to flee treason, and to give mercy unto him that asketh mercy, upon pain of forfeiture of their worship and lordship of king Arthur for evermore; and always*

to do ladies, damsels and gentlewomen and widows succour; strengthen them in their rights, and never to enforce them, upon pain of death. Also that no man take no battles in a wrongful quarrel for nor love nor for worldly goods. So unto this were all knights sworn of the Table Round both old and young. And every year so were they sworn at the high feast of Pentecost.

According to Sir Walter Scott, a medieval knight convicted of rape risked being formally degraded from his rank. His spurs were cut off with a cook's cleaver, his arms were basted (debased) and reversed by the hangman, his belt was cut to pieces and his sword broken, and his horse's tail cut off short, close to the rump, and thrown on a dunghill. The death-bell tolled, and the funeral service was said; he was then forced to enter a monastery.

Throughout his book, Malory condemns the unchivalrous treatment of women, however badly they behave, often altering his French sources to make his knights more gallant. In the *Suite de Merlin*, King Pellinore sees an attractive milkmaid, rapes her despite her desperate resistance, and then steals her greyhound for good measure. The girl brings up Tor, the baby she gives birth to, as the son of her cowherd husband Aries, but as he grows older he becomes obsessed with becoming a knight, nagging his parents about it night and day. Aries hears that King Arthur, who has just married Guinevere, has promised to grant all comers any reasonable request. He takes his tall handsome son to court, and explains that though his other thirteen sons are perfectly happy to labour in the fields, Tor is obsessed with the idea of becoming a knight. Impressed by Tor's appearance, Arthur knights him, whereupon Merlin reveals that King Pellinore is his father. Malory makes significant changes. When Tor's mother is summoned before Arthur, she explains that she was not married when she met Pellinore (thus removing any dishonour done to Aries) and that it was only 'half by force' that the 'stern knight' had her maidenhead. Malory adds a romantic gloss on the taking of the greyhound: Pellinore 'said he would keep it for my love'. And he makes Merlin say that Pellinore may 'right well advance' Tor and his mother – he knew that fifteenth-century law required fathers to provide maintenance for their illegitimate children.

The fact that the Nuneaton indictment presented against Sir Thomas Malory of Newbold Revel in August 1451 included two accusations of rape has been a serious stumbling block to accepting him as the author of the *Morte Darthur*. Edward Hicks, who discovered the document in 1926, adopted the ostrich position. 'The charge of "raptus" was doubtless merely incidental,' he wrote in *Sir Thomas Malory: his Turbulent Career*. 'It amounts to little more than a legal fiction.' He saw the offences as no more than rough-handed but temporary removals of 'Goodwife Smith' from her house while it was ransacked for goods which Malory thought were his due. He preferred to see Malory as a ruthless landlord in search of unpaid rent rather than as a rapist. To do so, he glossed over the fact that the indictment specifically said that on both occasions Malory feloniously raped Joan and carnally lay with her ('felonice rapuit & cum ea carnaliter concubit').

But in 1933, A. C. Baugh found another version of the incident in the records for the Court of King's Bench: an appeal by Hugh Smith, Joan's husband, in King's Bench, Westminster 'on the fourth day' of the Michaelmas term – which would be about 14 October 1451. The Coram Rege Roll summary was briefer than that of the Nuneaton inquisition, and did not specify time or place, but it gave a startling new aspect to the affair. Sir Thomas Malory was said to be one of four attackers. The others accused were William Weston, gentleman, 'late of Fenny Newbold', Thomas Potter, husbandman, of Bernangle, and Adam Brown, weaver, of Coventry. Was Malory not just a rapist, but a gang-rapist?

Peter Field's 1983 biography of Malory established beyond reasonable doubt that it was Sir Thomas Malory of Newbold Revel who wrote the *Morte Darthur*. But the Joan Smith case was a hot potato that he was loath to handle. He concluded neutrally that 'the rape charges plainly involve rape in the modern sense rather than (as some have wanted to believe) abduction or assault', though he drew attention to an oddity: when Hugh Smith pressed his charge against Malory and his three companions in the King's Bench, he did so under a rarely used statute of 1382 'whose purpose was to make elopement into rape despite the woman's consent'. He signed off by reminding his readers of the 'gap between the work and the life' of other authors – Chaucer the courtier, Spenser the civil servant and Shakespeare the London businessman. The mention of Chaucer was teasingly apposite – he too had been accused of rape; the woman, Cecily Champaign, agreed to settle out of court.

Critics and later commentators were far from satisfied. Reviewing Field's biography for the *London Review of Books*, Tom Shippey jeered that Malory must be 'the least politically correct author still read'. Charting the 'general discomfiture' since Edward Hicks made his damning discovery, he himself cheerfully accepted that Malory was guilty as charged. It was all a matter of class. 'The historical Malory need see no contradiction between the idealism that lies behind Lancelot's outrage at Sir Perys du Foreste Sauvage's abuse of women and his own rape of the "non-aristocratic Mrs Smith".' Felicity Riddy's literary critique of Malory hazarded that the *Morte Darthur* could be read as 'the legitimisation of a lawless man's fantasies'. Most recently Jonathan Hughes uses the charges of rape and other crimes as evidence that Malory was not only 'a misfit' but 'a violent, adventurous man', who 'admired these qualities in Edward IV' and was paying tribute to the notoriously promiscuous Yorkist King in writing the *Morte Darthur*.

Malory was certainly adventurous, and a great lover of battles, real or on the tournament ground. He was a man who expressed his opinions vigorously and acted with energy and forcefulness. But none of the witnesses to his supposed felonies reported any actual bodily injury to the victims – except to Joan Smith. So was she really violated? If we consider the rape accusations in the context of medieval case law, and then look critically at the wording used, matters become much less cut and dried.

The Medieval Laws of Rape

The original meaning of the verb to rape was simply to seize and take away – hence the title of the famous painting 'The Rape of the Sabine Women', and of Alexander Pope's mock-epic poem about a stolen ringlet, 'The Rape of the Lock'. In the Middle Ages, rape meant abduction just as often as it meant a sexual attack. When there had been an actual sexual attack, an appeal of rape had to be brought by the wronged woman, who was expected to 'raise the hue and cry' immediately, by going to local law officers and showing evidence of the attack (torn clothing, bleeding and injuries). The offender would then be arrested and appealed by his victim either in the county court or before the King's justices, either travelling 'in eyre' or sitting at Westminster. The appeal had to spell out that the perpetrator came 'violently' and 'wickedly', and took the victim's 'maidenhead', thus depriving her of what was defined in law as much a part of her as a limb was. To prevent casually malicious accusations, rapists of married women, lawful concubines, prostitutes and widows could not be appealed; they had to be indicted by a 'jury of presentment': at least twelve men from the locality who agreed that the charge was 'a true bill'. The case would then go to trial at the county court.

By the end of the thirteenth century, only the rape of virgins was punished by death; for other women, punishment on conviction was blinding and castration, carried out in at least one case by the woman herself. But conviction was extremely rare. Almost all appeals were either dismissed on technicalities, or the defendants settled with their accuser out of court, either with financial compensation or marriage. The surprising frequency with which the option of marriage was taken up after supposed rapes reveals various devious uses of the law. Often accusations were made in order to shoehorn unwilling parties into a marriage. A girl could marry the man of her choice against her parents' will by accusing her lover of raping her and so forcing her parents to accept the *fait accompli* – and their marriage. A discarded mistress could attempt to force her lover to marry or at least to compensate her. If the rapist or victim was already married, however, there could be no concord: the punishment had to be 'of blood'.

Two new laws concerning abduction and rape were passed in 1275 and 1285. Known as Statutes of Westminster I and II, they were primarily intended to benefit deserted husbands, the parents of runaway daughters and the guardians of runaway wards, both male and female. The appeal by the victim was still normally used for genuine cases of rape. The first statute confirmed that the 'ravishing', which it defined as taking away by force, of any woman was illegal and allowed the Crown (but not a private party) to prosecute if no appeal was made by the woman within forty days of the offence. The crime was a trespass, not a felony, and penalty was set at two years' imprisonment and a fine. The second statute decreed that if a man took a woman away without her consent, and property was taken with her, the crime was a felony, even if she consented after her abduction. The penalty on conviction after indictment by a jury (but not appeal) was death or castration. This solved the difficulty parents had in getting a conviction if an eloping daughter declared afterwards that she had consented to the rape. Another clause made life difficult for runaway wives: any wife who consented to her abduction automatically forfeited all chattels taken with her and also her dower (unless she was reunited with her husband before his death).

In 1382 a statute supplementing Westminster I and II was passed. The moving spirit behind it was Sir Thomas West, whose daughter Eleanor had eloped a year earlier with Nicholas Clifton, a handsome young soldier who had fought in West's retinue in France. West claimed that Nicholas Clifton and eight accomplices 'made horrible assault' upon Eleanor's mother Alice and her retinue while they were hunting in the New Forest, and had 'feloniously ravished [i.e. abducted] and deflowered' Eleanor. But because Eleanor had consented afterwards, no criminal charges could be brought. In all likelihood, Eleanor had also consented before, tipping off her lover that she and her mother would be hunting that day in a remote part of the forest. They married and settled down happily together. Lady Alice West may have been in on the plot – she was generous to Eleanor and Nicholas in her will. But Sir Thomas was unforgiving. He had had visions of his only daughter marrying into the peerage, not a penniless younger son. He wanted blood if possible, and he didn't want Eleanor and Nicholas to inherit his fortune. He took the case to Parliament, where other landed men with vulnerable, headstrong daughters listened sympathetically. The Commons duly petitioned Richard II that

> *Whereas divers malefactors from day to day do ravish women, ladies, damsels and daughters of the gentle of the realm, to the great dishonour and distress of many of the realm, and for which punishment by life or member is not given by law to any party in cases where the said women agree and consent afterwards; for which it may please to ordain that henceforward, when women, ladies, damsels, or daughters shall in future be ravished, and afterwards consenting, the ravishers and the ravished shall be disabled from having dower, jointure, or inheritance after the death of their barons or ancestors . . . and that the barons of such women if they are married, or their fathers or next of blood if they have no barons living, shall have suit to prosecute the said malefactors and attaint them for life or member, even though the said women have consented after the ravishment. And that no defendant shall be admitted for wager of battle in such case, but that the truth be tried at inquest, considering the great perils and mischiefs involved.*

The novelty of this statute was that a father, husband or next of kin could appeal the 'rape' if the woman or the Crown failed to do so. The penalties on conviction were draconian. Attainder meant loss of all possessions and the legal death of the victim and his family. The abductor could be sentenced to death or castration, and both he and the woman he abducted stood to lose their property. A bonus for cowardly or elderly plaintiffs was that cases brought under this statute could not be settled by single combat ('wager by battle') – a clause no doubt proposed by Sir Thomas West because of the youth and vigour of Nicholas Clifton. Once the statute was passed, Sir Thomas immediately petitioned that it be made retrospective so that he could employ it against Clifton in order to 'attaint him for life and member' and to deprive both him and Eleanor of their inheritances. This was going too far. West's petition was rejected, and a year later the Commons asked that the 1382 statute, which they described as 'too rough and redde [hasty] a law', should be repealed. By then Clifton had been pardoned 'for all felonies and rapes with which he is charged' and he was knighted the following year. The Commons' request was denied, and West's original law remained on the statute books. But it was very rarely used – only one citation, in 1409, is recorded before its use against Malory.

The 1409 case is an interesting parallel. First the defendant's counsel objected to the wording of the accusation: Thomas Vide had been charged with *feloniously* ravishing Thomas Nanteglos's wife, but not of *carnally* ravishing her, 'and if he ravished [i.e. abducted] her and did not know her carnally it is never felony but trespass'. He then objected that Nanteglos admitted that his wife had consented after the ravishment; if she hadn't, use of West's statute was irrelevant and both husband and wife should have made the appeal. Finally came the *coup de grâce*: it emerged that the woman had originally been engaged to Vide, and that it was Nanteglos who had taken her to a church and forced her to marry him against her will. Far from being abducted by Vide, she had gone to him and, 'because of the first contract between them', they had married each other. Flourishing affidavits from doctors of church law, Vide's lawyer argued that the plaintiff had in fact never been legally married, but the justices decided that the woman was *de facto* Nanteglos's wife until the marriage had been annulled. So the statute gave the suit to him even if he was not her legal husband. The case was put on hold until the bishop decided on whether a marriage had ever existed.

Successful indictments or appeals of rape were notoriously rare. Edward Powell's research into gaol delivery cases in the Midlands between 1400 and 1429 reveals that none of 278 trials of those indicted for rape at county sessions of gaol delivery led to a conviction. He concludes that the accusations were a way of penalising promiscuous monks and priests (80 per cent of those accused in Warwickshire were clerics) or notorious adulterers. 'The punishment lay in the inconvenience and humiliation of indictment and arraignment.

Acquittal at the trial itself was "a foregone conclusion". The distinguished American historian of medieval law Henry Ansgar Kelly adds another reason for indictment: resentment against those who had helped wives to escape from unsatisfactory husbands. 'Taking the accusation of abduction of wife and goods on face value as indicating that there was usually substance to the charge will prove very misleading,' he says. In most of the cases Kelly has investigated, there is 'no forcible abduction at all', just 'the wife's voluntary departure from her husband, and the husband's effort either to get her back or receive compensation'. The majority of cases that can be followed in the records turn out to be either willing elopements with a lover if a virgin was involved, or rescues of abducted wards and battered wives by family and friends. In a far from untypical case in 1278, William Hotoft accused a group of men of forcibly taking away his wife Amicia and £10 of his property. It turned out that Amicia had previously been engaged to one of the men, Alexander, and that it was in fact Hotoft who had abducted and raped her, and that she had sent for Alexander and his friends to rescue her.

Women with wealth or good expectations were often tricked into visiting someone they thought could be trusted and then held prisoner until they agreed to marry their captor, or to sign away substantial sums of money to him. Since the woman had gone voluntarily and no rape took place, no offence had been committed. The woman's only way out was to run away – which made anyone who helped her vulnerable to being sued for rape. It may be relevant to Malory's case that in 1453, less than two years after Hugh Smith's appeal, a statute was passed to make it possible for women who were forced into marriage in this way to bring a writ in chancery detailing the untoward pressure on them ('their unreasonable entreating'). If successful, it would void any bonds entered into and open the way for an ecclesiastical annulment of their marriage.

The manor of Newbold Revel, which appears to have been Sir Thomas Malory's favourite home, will have had a gatehouse similar to that of South Wraxall manor (*left*); it also had a small oratory, or chapel, and extensive fish ponds.

This early sixteenth-century sketch (*below*) shows Calais as Malory would first have seen it; today the Riesbank tower in the harbour entrance is capped by a concrete World War II blockhouse. The tallest of the city's medieval towers, the thirteenth-century watchtower also survives, as do portions of the original castle walls.

Illustration drawn for the *c.*1475 Beauchamp Pageant showing heralds inspecting the prizes for the tournament mounted at Calais by Sir Richard Beauchamp, Earl of Warwick, in 1414, the year before Agincourt, and a time when Thomas Malory was recorded as in his service at Calais.

The first king to whom Malory owed allegiance was Henry V (1387–1422); this tomb effigy (*left*) is in his chapel in Westminster Abbey. Henry V's most effective French opponent was the Dauphin, later Charles VII of France (*below left*, 1403–1461). Malory will also have known and respected Henry V's youngest brother, the charismatic and cultured Duke Humfrey of Gloucester (*below right*, 1390–1447).

ARLES VIIE ROY DE FRANCE

The headquarters of the Knights Hospitallers in England was the London priory of Clerkenwell; the modern order is still based there in St John's Gate (*right*). Nearby was a more threatening gatehouse, that of Newgate prison (*below*), where Malory was repeatedly imprisoned in the 1450s and 1460s. But his first experience of prison was in 1451, in the Sheriff of Warwickshire's manor of Coleshill (*below right*); he escaped after two days by swimming its moat.

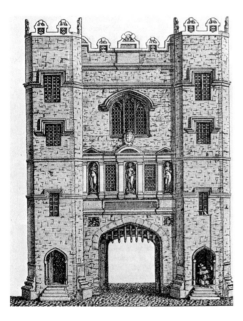

The Malory arms (*top right*: ermine, a chevron gules, and a border engrailed sable) can still be seen on the façade of the Inn of the English, at the foot of the Street of the Knights, in Rhodes. The other shields are the royal arms of England (*top left*), Sir John Weston, Prior of England 1476–1489 (*bottom left*) and Sir John Kendall, Prior of England 1489–1501 (*bottom right*).

In the 1460s Malory's loyalties were torn between the imprisoned Henry VI (*right*, 1421–1471), 'the king who made me knight', and the Yorkist usurper Edward IV (*below left*, 1442–83), through whose triumph he regained his liberty and who kept Arthurian state with his exquisitely beautiful queen Elizabeth (*below right*, *c.*1437–92), daughter of Jacquetta of Luxemburg and Malory's fellow Midlands gentleman Sir Richard Woodville, and formerly the wife of the Lancastrian loyalist Sir John Gray.

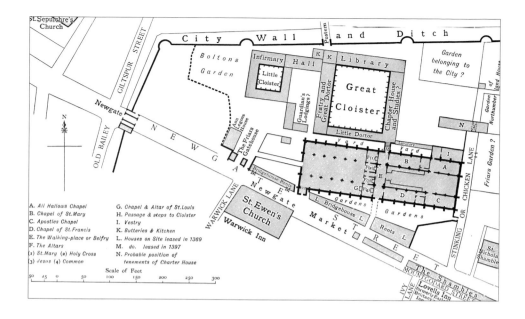

A. All Hallows Chapel
B. Chapel of St.Mary
C. Apostles Chapel
D. Chapel of St.Francis
E. The Walking-place or Belfry
F. The Altars
(1) St.Mary (2) Holy Cross
(3) Jesus (4) Common

G. Chapel & Altar of St.Louis
H. Passage & steps to Cloister
I. Vestry
K. Butteries & Kitchen
L. Houses on Site leased in 1369
M. do. leased in 1397
N. Probable position of
   tenements of Charter House

Scale of Feet

Malory's tomb was recorded as being under the most westerly window of the chapel of St Francis, on the south-west side of the choir of the vast and fashionable church of Greyfriars; its plan was mapped (*above*) for Kingsford's edition of John Stow's Survey of London. The monastery became Christ's Hospital School, but its church burned down during the Great Fire of London in 1666. It was rebuilt by Sir Christopher Wren, using the foundations of the old choir, but was all but destroyed in the Blitz. It is now a peaceful garden where city workers enjoy a lunchtime break. This photograph (*left*) shows the site of Malory's grave. It has no monument – as yet.

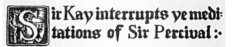

Illustrating the *Morte Darthur*: Wynkyn de Worde's down-to-earth woodcuts (*above*) appeared from the 1490s; Howard Pyle's manly and monumental knights (*right*) at the height of the pre-Raphaelite movement; and Aubrey Beardsley's evil feys (*below*) in the fin-de-siècle world of the 1890s.

The Case against Malory

Hugh Smith's use of West's 'rough and redde' statute against Malory suggests that he had a very knowledgeable legal counsel. The odds are that the same lawyer also worded the Nuneaton indictment. In 1997 Henry Ansgar Kelly published an immensely learned survey of medieval statutes of rape in order to put the charges against Malory into context. He strongly suspects that sophisticated legal chicanery was used to entrap the Warwickshire knight. Given the precedent of the Nanteglos case, he says, 'It is possible, even probable, that carnal knowledge was specified in the indictment because Smith and his lawyers (and Buckingham and the other colluding justices) believed that sexual violation was necessary for the offence to be classified as a felony'.

The wording of the indictments supports Kelly's conclusion. Words were chosen with extreme care in medieval lawsuits. A high percentage of defendants were acquitted because of an irregularity in the wording of the indictment against them; if this was the case, they could demand damages and the accuser could be imprisoned. In Malory's case, the absence of certain words from the accusations is highly significant. There is no mention of force being used against Joan. It was only said that Malory 'carnally lay with her' (*carnaliter concubit*). This was, if true, a sin, since both were married. But adultery was a matter for church courts, not lay justices. The indictment did *not* say, as indictments for actual sexual assault did, that Malory violated Joan bodily (*corporaliter violavit*), or forced her against her will (*afforciavit contra voluntatem*). If Joan herself had objected, then the accusations would have said so explicitly, as it would strengthen the case enormously.

That Malory's 'rape' of Joan was actually a rescue is also implied by a telling detail in the Latin of the second rape accusation in the Nuneaton inquisition.

Ac illam [my emphasis] cum bonis & catallis dicti Hugonis
ad valenciam quadraginta librarum tunc & ibidem inventis

usque Barwell in comitatu Leyc. Felonice furatis fuit cepit &
abduxit contra pacem coronam & dignitatem domini Regis.

The second word in the sentence, the singular female pronoun 'illam'
(her), can only refer to Joan. A literal translation would be:

And her with the goods and chattels of the said Hugh to the
value of forty pounds then and there found towards Barwell
in the county of Leics he feloniously stole, took and carried
away against the peace, crown and dignity of our lord the
King.

Whatever happened on Malory's first visit to Joan Smith in Monks
Kirby in May 1451, there is no doubt from this indictment that what
he and his three companions were accused of doing in Coventry in
August was taking Joan herself away as well as £40 worth of Hugh
Smith's chattels. But the indictment did not say that Joan was kept at
Barwell against her will – again a point always made in genuine cases
of unwelcome abduction.

Further light can be shed on the case by considering what we can
deduce about the Smiths and Malory's three co-defendants, William
Weston, Thomas Potter and Adam Brown. It sounds as if the Smiths
had money. Anyone who went to law needed to be well-heeled – or
to have wealthy friends. They also seem to have had two houses, one
in the parish of Monks Kirby, the other in Coventry. If Joan was in
fact trying to get away from her husband, she would naturally have
taken her own possessions with her: the clothes, jewellery and plate
that made up her dower. If they were really worth £40 or more, she
was a wealthy woman, whose surname may have been much more
aristocratic than Smith. But Hugh need not have been an artisan.
There were Smiths of gentry status in the Midlands. One, Henry
Smith, was an upwardly mobile Coventry grazier who had acquired
substantial estates in the area by the 1420s. His son might have looked
to rise socially by abducting a girl of good family. There was also a
Hugh Smith in Humfrey of Gloucester's retinue at Agincourt; he
may have been the same Hugh Smith to whom John Willoughby of
Middleton left 'twenty shillings and a grey courser' (a fast hound or

horse) for his 'good and faithful service' in France. Dashing a lover as he had been when he was courting Joan, he may have become a violent and cruel husband. If his brother were John Smith, a lawyer in the affinity of Lord Ferrers of Groby, a crony of Buckingham, much would be explained.

What about Malory's companions? They do not sound like wild young tearaways. As a Coventry weaver, Adam Brown could have been a man of substance – Coventry's clothiers were famously wealthy. Thomas Potter, a husbandman from the manor of Bernangle, five miles west of Monks Kirby and Newbold Revel, must have had a small farm. Most interesting of all is the presence of 'William Weston, gentleman'. He was probably a Weston of Weston-under-Witherley, nine miles south of Newbold Revel. The Westons were a family who had just as many Knights Hospitaller connections as the Malorys did. John Weston, who was born in about 1430, was Prior of St John in England from 1476 to 1489. A later William Weston was England's last Hospitaller Prior before the Reformation. Malory's companion could have been John Weston's brother William, who would be knighted by the 1460s. Malory's overlord at Swinford at this time was Thomas Weston, presbyter of the Hospitaller presbytery of Dingley.

Barwell, where Joan Smith was said to have been taken, lay just over the Warwickshire border in Leicestershire. It was only two miles from Kirkby Mallory, and was in all probability then held of Sir Edward Grey (his father, Lord Grey of Ruthin, had held rights of free warren there). Malory had had dealings with Sir Edward Grey in 1441. But it is just possible that it was held of the Knights Hospitallers, to whom the Malorys of Kirkby Mallory had granted part of their estates in 1279.

The final oddity is the fact that the accusations of rape were made over a year after the supposed crimes took place. Malory was supposed to have 'raped' Joan on 23 May 1450 and again on 6 August 1450. The Nuneaton indictment took place on 23 August 1451, and Hugh Smith's appeal in King's Bench was made in early October 1451. It looks very much as if somebody who had heard about Joan Smith's escape persuaded Hugh Smith to go to law, promising not only to advise him but also to foot the bill. It reinforces the picture of a deliberate search for 'ill-wishers' – people with grievances against Sir Thomas Malory of Newbold Revel who could be paid or persuaded to take them to court.

Malory and Women

Under serious scrutiny, the notorious rape case against Sir Thomas Malory collapses like a house of cards. His role in the Joan Smith affair was exactly what we would expect of the author of the *Morte Darthur*: that of a knight chivalrously embarking on the rescue of a damsel in distress, and succeeding after a first, failed, attempt. But how intimately was he involved with Joan? Although any one of his three co-defendants could have been the person with whom Joan wanted to spend the rest of her life, none of my reasoning so far rules out the possibility that Joan and Sir Thomas were having an adulterous affair, that Hugh Smith had got wind of it and began maltreating his errant wife, and that Malory's most chivalrous option was to take her away from him. It was after all in May that he was accused of first bedding Mrs Smith,

> *when every lusty heart beginneth to blossom, and to bring forth fruit; for like as herbs and trees bring forth fruit and flourish in May, in like wise every lusty heart that is in any manner a lover, springeth and flourisheth in lusty deeds. For it giveth unto all lovers courage, that lusty month of May, in something to constrain him to some manner of thing more in that month than in any other month, for divers causes. For then all herbs and trees renew a man and woman, and likewise lovers call again to their mind old gentleness and old service, and many kind deeds that were forgotten by negligence.*

Suppose Joan was a childhood sweetheart, and Malory, passing by her house on one of those magical May mornings, 'called again to mind old gentleness and old service, and many kind deeds', and slipped into bed with her with blossoming heart aglow. The cuckolded

Hugh discovered the two *in flagrante delicto* and took Joan away to Coventry. Malory heard from Adam Brown that she was being harshly treated, found her a refuge with friends in Barwell and rescued her with the help of his neighbour, William Weston, and Thomas Potter, who brought along a spare horse for Joan. All this could have been done on the quiet. Adultery was a sin in the eyes of the Church, but it was far from unknown. Wives had to like it or lump it, and medieval couples frequently included a husband's bastards with legitimate children in their family circle. But when Hugh Smith decided, or was persuaded, to take the drastic and unusual step of an appeal of rape, Sir Thomas Malory's behaviour became the talk of the county, to his 'great disworship'.

Time to turn to a different sort of evidence altogether: that of the *Morte Darthur* itself. Its author may not have been a rapist, but was he an adulterer? There is no doubt that he found women both entrancing and excitingly dangerous. He was the first English author to write at length and in detail about Lancelot and Guinevere's passion for each other. Hardyng's chronicle and the alliterative *Morte Arthure* leave it out altogether, and the stanzaic *Morte* only describes the tragic end of the affair. At the same time, he has no illusions about female shortcomings. Guinevere, Isolde, Elaine, Dame Lyonesse and the rest of his infinitely various feminine cast are vividly characterised, living, breathing women who snap crossly at their rescuers and don't hesitate to use extremely underhand methods of getting their own way.

What about marriage? There is a hint of regret for his bachelor days in a speech Malory gives Lancelot to fend off one of his many amorous admirers:

> *'For to be a wedded man, I think it not; for then I must couch with her, and leave arms and tournaments, battles and adventures.'*

Not all wives were as understanding as Isolde, who urges Tristram to leave their love-nest at Joyous Gard and go to the annual Round Table feast and tournament held at Camelot at Pentecost for all the knights of the Round Table. Unless he did, she says, *'shall I be spoken of with shame among all the queens and ladies of estate; for ye that are called one of the noblest knights of the world, and ye a knight of the Round Table, how may you be missed at that feast? What shall be said among all knights? See how Sir Tristram hunteth, and hawketh, and cowereth within a castle with his lady, and forsaketh us. Alas, some shall say, it is a pity that ever he was made knight, or that ever he should have the love of a lady . . .' 'So God help me,' said Sir Tristram unto La Belle Isolde, 'it is passing well said of you and nobly counselled; and now I well understand that ye love me; and like as you have counselled me I will do a part thereafter.'*

Malory's first book-length biographer Edward Hicks suggests that Sir Thomas's feelings for his wife are reflected in his description of the happy marriage of Tristram's parents, King Meliodas and Queen Elizabeth, whose name Malory changes to that of his own wife from his source's Isobel:

This Meliodas was a likely knight as any was at that time living. And by fortune he wedded King Mark's sister of Cornwall, and she was called Elizabeth, that was called both good and fair . . . within a while she waxed great with child, and she was a full meek lady, and well she loved her lord, and he her again, so that there was great joy between them.

Great joy is all very well, but 'full meek' is not much of a compliment. It does not compare with King Arthur's description of Guinevere as 'the most valiant and fairest I know living'. Nor with Lancelot in exile, looking out every day towards the 'realm of Logris', where King Arthur and Queen Guinevere were. 'And then would he fall upon a-weeping as his heart should to-brast'. If Malory's marriage was a pragmatic arrangement consolidating estates with a Pulteney, a Feilding or a Walsh, his feelings for Lady Elizabeth may have been fond rather than passionate, a situation that would have left him vulnerable to temptation.

What has the *Morte* to say about sex outside marriage? Of the twelve incidents that mention actual 'paramours', only two involve criticism of them. Most of the time Malory is matter of fact over paramours who kill or attempt to kill rivals, and lustful women offering themselves as paramours, King Pelles inviting knights to bring 'wives or paramours' to his tournament and King Arthur asking Sir Gareth if he would like to marry Dame Lyonesse or have her as his paramour. Both extra- and pre-marital affairs were as much everyday lapses among 'sinful man and sinful woman' in Arthur's kingdom as they were in Malory's England.

But knights of the Round Table who attempted spiritual perfection, like Sir Galahad, Sir Percival and Sir Bors, abhorred them. And Malory's two criticisms of adultery are important ones. Both are expressed by Sir Lancelot, the character with whom Malory identifies most completely. Early in his adventures Lancelot rejects an amorous offer from the grateful damsel he has saved from the notorious rapist Sir Perys de Foreste Sauvage with the stern announcement that

> To take my pleasaunce with paramours, that will I refuse in principal for dread of God. For knights that be adulterous, or wanton, shall not be happy nor fortunate unto the wars, for either they shall be overcome with a simpler knight than they be themselves, or else they shall by mishap and their cursedness slay better men than they be themselves. And so who that useth paramours shall be unhappy [unlucky], and all thing is unhappy about them.

Much later in the book, when Elaine of Astolat (Tennyson's Lady of Shallot) asks Lancelot if she can be his wife or his paramour, Lancelot again reacts with revulsion. Nowhere else does Malory transform Lancelot more completely into a fifteenth-century man of property and propriety.

> 'Jesu defend me!' said Sir Lancelot, 'for then I rewarded your father and brother full evil for their great goodness.' 'Alas,' said she, 'then I must die for your love'. 'Ye shall not so', said Sir Lancelot, 'for wit ye well, fair maiden, I might have been married an I would, but I never applied me to be married

*yet; but because, fair damsel, that ye love me as ye say ye do,
I will for your good will and kindness show you some goodness, and that is this, that wheresomever ye will beset your
heart upon some good knight that will wed you, I shall give
you together a thousand pounds yearly to you and to your
heirs.*

This is Malory's own voice, that of an upright and decent fifteenth-
century gentleman. He was a man of the world and had seen plenty
of philandering in his time, but it was not to his own taste. Even
more revealing is a heartfelt digression on how infidelities threaten
marriage in his 'Tale of Lancelot and Guinevere'.

*For like as winter rasure doth alway erase and deface green
summer, so fareth it by unstable love in man and woman.
For in many persons there is no stability; for we may see all
day, for a little blast of winter's rasure, anon we shall deface
and lay apart true love for little or nought, that cost much
thing; this is no wisdom nor stability, but it is feebleness of
nature and great disworship, whosomever useth this. Therefore, like as May month flowereth and flourisheth in many
gardens, so in like wise let every man of worship flourish his
heart in this world, first unto God, and next unto the joy of
them that he promised his faith unto; for there was never
worshipful man or worshipful woman, but they loved one
better than another; and worship in arms may never be
foiled, but first reserve the honour to God, and secondly the
quarrel must come of thy lady: and such love I call virtuous
love.*

*But nowadays men can not love seven night but they
must have all their desires: that love may not endure by
reason; for where they be soon accorded and hasty heat, soon
it cooleth. Right so fareth love nowadays, soon hot soon cold:
this is no stability. But the old love was not so; men and
women could love together seven years, and no licours [lech-
erous] lusts were between them, and then was love, truth,
and faithfulness: and lo, in like wise was used love in King*

Arthur's days. Wherefore I liken love nowadays unto summer and winter; for like as the one is hot and the other cold, so fareth love nowadays; therefore all ye that be lovers call unto your remembrance the month of May, like as did Queen Guinevere, for whom I make here a little mention, that while she lived she was a true lover, and therefore she had a good end.

Malory's vision of chivalry was starkly at odds with that of his French sources, for whom chivalric prowess was merely the background for romantic adventures with beautiful damsels. I think we may safely conclude that although Mrs Smith wanted to escape from her marriage, she was not Malory's paramour. My best guess is that she was in fact once Joan Weston, and that Malory was helping her brother to rescue her.

That is not to say that Malory was a husband who was always faithful in thought, word and deed. In the passage above he draws a clear distinction between paramours and 'true lovers' like Lancelot and Guinevere who 'could love together seven years, and no licours lusts were between them'. This was a totally original interpretation of their relationship, which required Malory to omit entirely the repeated adulteries described in his French sources. Instead, he emphasises again and again that although Lancelot and Guinevere love each other, they also both love Arthur and, because of this, make heroic efforts to resist physical consummation of their affair. As one literary critic points out,

> *Throughout this long book, Malory has carefully and consistently omitted all evidence of any actual adultery between Lancelot and Guinevere, yet many modern readers still assume that Lancelot and the queen are regularly committing adultery, just as they are in Malory's source, the French prose* Tristan.

There is no doubt that Lancelot wants to sleep with Guinevere – he twice has sex with Elaine thinking that she is the Queen. But Malory is careful to emphasise that it is Lancelot's irrepressible love for Guinevere, rather than actual adultery, which makes him fail on the Grail quest. And though when the star-crossed lovers meet again after Lancelot's long absence on the quest, they 'love together more hotter than they did toforehand', Malory deliberately stops short of the *Mort Artu*'s additional declaration that they 'fall in to sin'. He only says they are indiscreet, taking 'many privy draughts together'. Guinevere should be rights have had ladies in attendance. There is still no actual adultery, only much gossip.

As Malory tells the story, the only time that Lancelot and Guinevere do seem to commit adultery is after Meliagaunce ambushes Guinevere and her household when they are a-maying in the woods near Westminster. He severely wounds her ten knights, takes them prisoner, and abducts the Queen as well, hoping no doubt for some carnal concubinage. She manages to send a message by her page to Lancelot at Westminster. As soon as he hears of her plight, he rides his horse across the river and heads full tilt for Meliagaunce's domain. When his horse is mortally wounded after an ambush by thirty of Meliagaunce's archers, he stumbles along on foot in impossibly heavy armour until he can commandeer a woodcart to take him to Meliagaunce's castle; the horse limps after him, 'treading its guts and paunch under its feet'. On arrival, incensed by the giggles of a gaggle of damsels watching from the battlements at the sight of a knight in a cart, he smashes open the gate and smites the porter so hard with his gauntlet that 'his neck brast asunder'. Meliagaunce instantly abases himself to Guinevere, and cunningly persuades her that there will be less gossip if they all quietly disperse. He frees her wounded knights and allows them to sleep in the corridor outside her chamber so that they can afford her some protection and she can nurse them.

Lancelot's sense of humiliation at his unknightly arrival and extreme frustration at not being allowed to exterminate Meliagaunce are only appeased by Guinevere's promise that they can have a quiet talk together through the bars of her window: she laments that he isn't inside the room with her. '"Would ye, madam", said Sir Lancelot, "with your heart that I were with you?"' After all the man she loved has gone through, no one will blame Guinevere for saying 'Yes, truly'. The response gives her champion superhuman powers.

> *'Now shall I prove my might,' said Sir Lancelot, 'for your*
> *love'; and then he set his hands upon the bars of iron, and*
> *he pulled at them with such a might that he brast them clean*
> *out of the stone walls, and therewithal one of the bars of iron*
> *cut the brawn of his hands through to the bone; and then he*
> *leapt into the chamber to the queen. 'Make ye no noise,' said*
> *the queen, 'for my wounded knights lie here fast by me.' So,*
> *to pass upon this tale, Sir Lancelot went up to bed with the*
> *queen, and took nor force of his hurt hand, but took his*
> *pleasaunce and his liking until it was in the dawning of the*
> *day; and wit ye well he slept not but watched, and when he*
> *saw his time that he might tarry no longer he took his leave*
> *and departed at the window, and put it together as well as*
> *he might again, and so departed unto his own chamber.*

Lancelot and Guinevere pay dearly for this (still only implicit) moment of weakness. Meliagaunce, seeing the blood left by his wounded hand on the Queen's sheets, assumes that one of the wounded knights has been in her bed and threatens to lay an accusation against her in front of King Arthur. Lancelot declares that he will champion her, but he is tricked into tumbling into Meliagaunce's *oubliette*. He succeeds in escaping (for the price of kissing the amorous damsel who is his gaoler), and arrives just in time to joust 'à l'outrance' against Meliagaunce, and save Guinevere from the stake.

Why did Malory tone down his sources' references to Lancelot and Guinevere's adultery so much? Beverley Kennedy believes it was 'a matter of patriotism'.

> *If thirteenth-century French aristocratic audiences were not*
> *offended by the portrayal of Arthur as a* roi fainéant *and*
> *hapless cuckold, because he was only a legendary king of a*
> *legendary land (Logris), fifteenth-century Englishmen could*
> *never accept such an unflattering portrayal of the greatest*
> *king in their nation's history.*

But it is more likely that it reflected Malory's own morality. That the idea of committing adultery was both agonising to him and deeply fascinating – not because he had never done it, but because he had, and he knew from personal experience the terrible emotional fallout it involved.

The episode that follows immediately after the rescue of Guinevere from King Meliagaunce is known only in Malory. A damsel comes to court with Sir Urry, whose terrible wounds can only be healed by 'the best knight in the world'. After a hundred and ten knights, including King Arthur, fail the test, Arthur insists that Lancelot should try. Deeply apprehensive, but persuaded by Arthur that he must do so 'for to bear us fellowship, insomuch as ye be a fellow of the Table round', he 'ransacked' Urry's wounds.

> *Forthwith all the wounds fair healed, and seemed as they had been whole a seven year ... Then king Arthur and all the kings and knights kneeled down and gave thankings and lovings unto God and to His Blessed Mother. And ever Sir Lancelot wept as he had been a child that had been beaten.*

So ends one of Malory's most original and sophisticated pieces of storytelling. Through it, he was telling us something both intimate and endearing about himself: that he too loved a woman who was not his wife and was all but unattainable; that she returned his love; that at least once, perhaps only once, they gave way to their passion for each other; that his resulting remorse lasted all his life; that what he hoped for most from the immense labour of telling his Arthurian tales was to teach young men and women to achieve wiser and more worshipful ways of living than he did, as true, not 'mal fait' chevaliers. But the woman whom he loved 'unmeasurably and out of measure long', as Lancelot loved Guinevere, was not, I think, Joan Smith.

'In No Wise Guilty'

*'So God me help,' said the king, 'I may not say but ye did
as a knight should, and it was your part to do for your
quarrel, and to increase your worship as a knight should;
howbeit I may not maintain you in this country with my
worship, unless that I should displease my barons, and my
wife and her kin.'*
Malory, 'The Tale of Sir Tristram'

ut how was Malory to prove his innocence? What happened
next confirms that he was being malevolently persecuted by
some very clever lawyers. On 22 September 1451, Henry VI
and his queen arrived in Warwickshire 'to judge noble peacebreakers'
in Coventry. He and a squad of royal justices remained in the county
for over two weeks, 'hearing and determining' cases. It would have
been natural for Malory to appear before the King, but he was given
no chance to justify himself either to his sovereign or to a jury of
men from his own locality. The point of the hurried August session
at Nuneaton becomes apparent when we discover that on 5 October
1451 a writ *certiorari* was issued, taking Malory's case from Warwickshire to the Court of King's Bench in Westminster. The reason for
the writ was revealed a week later when Hugh Smith appeared in
Westminster at the Court of King's Bench 'in his own person' to
appeal Sir Thomas Malory, William Weston, Adam Brown and
Thomas Potter of the 'rape' of his wife Joan Smith.

Personal appeals took precedence over cases brought by the
Crown. It was Hugh Smith's appeal in King's Bench that took Malory's
entire case to London – well away from the support he might have
hoped for in his home county. The two different accusations of rape

complemented each other to powerful legal effect. An appeal of rape had to be made within a year and a day of the offence. It could only be launched later if a Crown indictment, which could only be made *after* a year and a day had passed with no appeal, was made. The indictment also protected Smith. Normally, if an appeal was dismissed, the defendant could demand damages from the plaintiff. But if the defendant had already been indicted of the crime, he could not opt for trial 'by the body', that is, in single combat (something which would undoubtedly have appealed to Malory), nor could he sue his accuser for damages. Moreover, if there was a conviction, any stolen goods would be restored to the appellant rather than be forfeited to the King. Hugh Smith was not only safe, he could expect a rich reward if his appeal succeeded.

The Court of King's Bench normally operated on a dais at the west end of Westminster Hall, rebuilt during the reign of Richard II, when it was given the magnificent hammerbeam roof that still arches over it today. The Court of Chancery took place close by, and that of Common Pleas against the west wall. It was a hive of activity, and officials marched around the hall to keep order and enforce, not always successfully, the requisite respect for the royal justices. Lawyers usually represented men of Malory's rank in court. But an appeal had to be defended in person, and if the defendant failed to appear, he could be outlawed. Malory and his three co-defendants did fail to appear in Westminster to answer to the charge. Consequently the judge sent an order to the Sheriff of Warwickshire to 'attach' all four of them. Attachment was the confiscation of goods and chattels as sureties for a court appearance. The Sheriff replied that 'they had nothing', a legal device that allowed the judge to order that they be arrested and so forced into court. The date set for the hearing was the 'octave of Hilary' (*c.* 20 January 1452).

Where was Malory? My guess is that he had ridden as rapidly as he could to Warwick Castle to assert his innocence, especially as far as the rape charge was concerned, and to beg for good lordship, in the form of both protection and advice, from the Earl and Countess of Warwick. He is likely to have taken any goods and chattels that he valued (including any chests he had reclaimed from Coombe) to be kept safe in the castle's strongroom. It would also be wise to ensure that his estates were protected from forfeiture. The very lack of evidence of his life up to now shows that he was a clever man, who managed his affairs and his estates so competently that he never had to go to law to defend them (in notable contrast to such contemporaries as the Pastons). His lands had long been protectively enfeoffed, as were those of most Englishmen of property who served in France. But we know that around this time his feoffees changed and were added to. The chances are that, foreseeing trouble ahead, he took immediate action to protect his estates.

The original four feoffees for his Warwickshire estates had been local friends and relations: his nephew Eustace Burneby, Henry Sharp, John Moveley (or Moseley) and his first cousin Robert Malory, son of Simon Malory. The new feoffees, a very well-connected group of eight, were Sir Thomas Walsh (a king's knight), John Walsh, William Walsh, Thomas Pulton, Walter Blount, Ralph Wolseley, Walter Wrottesley and Henry Everingham. If Lady Elizabeth Malory was indeed a Walsh, the Walshes were kinsmen. Walter Blount was doubly related to the Walshes; his mother Margaret was the daughter of Margaret Walsh and Sir Thomas Gresley of Drakelow. Blount was an important Staffordshire figure who sympathised with York and who faced physical as well as legal persecution during the next few years. In 1458 he would offer a retainer to the Richard Malory who had ridden with Sir Thomas to raid Coombe Abbey. He was also Sir Thomas Walsh's brother-in-law: like Walsh and Sir Robert Harcourt (for whom he had stood bail in King's Bench in February 1451), he married a daughter of Sir John Byron. He was close enough to Warwick to be one of the feoffees for his will in 1463. Wolseley had been MP for the pocket borough of Newcastle-upon-Tyne in the 1449–50 Parliament; both he and Wrottesley were right-hand men of the Earl of Warwick. Everingham's overlord was Norfolk, but he had an annuity from Warwick. Responsibility for Malory's estates was now shared among well-wishers with healthily counterbalanced political affiliations.

Although Malory could act to protect his property, he knew that he had to appear in court in person on the appointed date, or suffer outlawry. He decided to face the music. His first recorded appearance in court was on 27 January 1452, when it was said that the sheriffs of London (Matthew Philip and Christopher Warton) brought him to the bar at Westminster to answer to the indictment made at Nuneaton, as demanded by the King's writ. He declared himself 'in no wise guilty', and 'for good or for ill' put himself 'upon his country'. It is an exciting moment for the biographer: the first time that Malory's voice can be heard across the centuries, albeit in reported speech. To put yourself upon your country was every Englishman's right: it meant trial by jurymen from your own neighbourhood. He was handed back to the custody of the city sheriffs until all the accusations could be collected together and jurors summoned from Warwickshire. The date set for the trial was 9 February 1452. At this point, if Malory had found mainpernors, he could have gone free. Richard Malory seems to have done so – he was allowed to take out a pardon later that year.

But four days later, on 31 January 1452, Thomas was confronted with a new accusation. He was summoned before lawyers representing the Duke of Buckingham, John Stafford, Archbishop of Canterbury, and the Duke and Duchess of Norfolk. He was accused of breaking into Caluden deer park on 20 July 1451, stealing six does and doing £500 worth of damage. Caluden was a Mowbray hunting lodge. It sounds as if it was rented by Buckingham and his kinsman the Archbishop; this is why the plea was brought on their behalf as well as the parks' owners, the Norfolks.

There is an echo of the attack on Buckingham's deer park at Penshurst about the case. Malory might well have been enjoying a little sport at the expense of his arch-enemy, and it may be significant that the incident took place just five days before Buckingham's sudden descent on Newbold Revel to arrest him. But it is highly unlikely that a man with Malory's respect for the laws of game and love of hunting would do more than purloin a few deer. Damage to the tune of £500 could only have been accomplished by the ransack, if not the entire destruction, of the handsome hunting lodge of Caluden itself. But if that had happened, it would have been specified in the plaintiffs' bill. Accurate description was a legal essential, and though the plea gave details of the weapons (swords and daggers, but not bows, curiously enough) carried by the malefactors, there was no long list of damaged or stolen property.

There was again cunning legal purpose in the accusation. Poaching was taken so seriously that it was an 'irreplegiable' offence: no bail was allowed, and if convicted Malory would have faced a set prison sentence. The statutory penalty for raiding deer parks was three years' imprisonment and then exile if full reparation was not made. The figure of £500 sounds as if it was plucked out of thin air in order to make it impossible for Malory to make the necessary reparations, and so ensure that he was forced to appear in person to deny the charges or face the perils of outlawry. Again he pleaded not guilty and demanded to be tried by jurors from his own county. Now trapped in prison without option of bail, he returned to the custody of the sheriffs of London. On 2 February 1452, the distraint of all Sir Thomas's goods was ordered, but the court was told that 'he had nothing'. Evidently his possessions were in safe-keeping as well as his lands.

When Malory was brought to court on 9 February, no jurors appeared. The case was deferred until the quindene of Easter – 24–29 April 1452 – and Malory was again taken away by the London sheriffs. A Kafkaesque nightmare now began. It would be eight long years before he disentangled himself from the charges against him altogether. During that time, jurors repeatedly failed to appear, so he was never given a chance to defend himself in open court, or have his side of the case put on record. Instead, he was shunted from prison to prison and court to court in a defiance of common justice that has baffled everyone who has studied his case.

York at Bay

When knitted into national affairs, Malory's experiences become a little more explicable. England was still deeply unsettled. It was becoming clear that the show of household reform in response to Parliament's demands was only superficial. The Duke of Somerset, now high in favour with both Henry VI and, more importantly,

Queen Margaret, was emerging as an energetic leader of Suffolk's old faction. He was made Captain of Calais on 21 September. Across the country, court favourites were re-establishing power and putting down those who opposed them. The barrage of lawsuits against York's supporters intensified. On 6 September, the Talbots seized Berkeley Castle, insisting that it was part of their Beauchamp inheritance and imprisoning Lord Berkeley and his family. On 18 September, Lord Cobham and Sir Hugh Courtney were accused of rousing the towns of Ilminster and Yeovil to support the Duke of York and his 'false and traitorous purpose'. Edward Clare of Stokesby in Norfolk was said to have received treasonable letters from York a few days later. And, at almost exactly the same time as Hugh Smith was appealing Malory, Sir William Oldhall, who was masterminding the Duke's defence of himself around the country with Sir Walter Devereux (York's Seneschal at Radnor and Usk), was cornered in London. He was accused of a string of trumped-up charges in which the vein of truth was his resolute support of York. He escaped custody and took sanctuary in the royal chapel of St Martin's le Grand in London on 23 November. York's attempt to end the private war between feuding families which had broken out in Somerset by the end of September led to his being accused of peace-breaking himself. On 9 January 1452 York sent the King a declaration of loyalty that was almost abject, and invited the Bishop of Hereford and Lord Talbot to come to Ludlow to witness his swearing allegiance to Henry on the Sacrament. But the King was implacable. On 28 January, he ordered Oldhall to be removed from sanctuary. Fortunately for Oldhall, there was a furious protest at this sacrilegious act from the Dean of St Martin's le Grand, and he was returned to sanctuary two days later.

York was now in a terrible quandary. He knew that very few peers would stand up, let alone take up arms, in support of him against his 'enemies, adversaries and evil-wishers' among the King's advisers, the men who had made 'my heavy lord greatly displeased with me'. His only hope was to engineer mass popular protests against Somerset, who he believed, probably rightly, 'laboreth continually about the King's highness for my undoing, and to corrupt my blood, and to disinherit me and my heirs, and such persons as be about me'. He arranged for the distribution of letters that appealed for support from men of influence in towns and counties sympathetic to his cause. Early in February, he began a systematic rallying of his widespread, very numerous and intensely loyal tenantry. From all parts of the country thousands of them made their way to Northampton, from where he sent a herald to warn London of his approach on 22 February.

The King, who had also sent out messengers to rally his supporters, had left the capital a week earlier. By the time Henry VI reached Dunstable, he had assurances of support from most of the lords, including Norfolk and Warwick. London obeyed the royal directive not to allow York into the city, and York was forced to head for Kingston in order to cross into Kent, from which he was hoping for solid support. By the end of February he was encamped with ten thousand men on Blackheath. But the men of Kent had learned their lesson. They did not rally to York but to Henry, who returned to London and advanced on the Duke with an army of, one chronicler claimed, 50,000 men. Elaborately courteous negotiations began at Dartford on 1 March, with Warwick and Norfolk's brother-in-law Thomas Bourgchier, Bishop of Ely, among the go-betweens. York assured Henry of his loyalty, and delivered a formal accusation of treason against Somerset for losing England's lands in France. Such an accusation of a peer by a peer had to be taken seriously, and the King agreed that Somerset would be 'put into ward'.

York had, however, failed to rally enough support among men of rank. The Earl of Devon and Lord Cobham were the only lords who stood at his side, and Henry's army was three times the size of his forces. As he must have realised nervously when he was 'invited' to leave his men and ride at the King's side into the city of London, he was at risk of suffering a suspiciously convenient apoplectic fit in the manner of his mentor Humfrey of Gloucester five years earlier. Three things saved him. First, although his army was smaller than that of Henry, it was no mean threat. Second, he was hugely popular with Londoners. Third, and perhaps most relevant of all, he was the most legitimate heir to the throne – and with a fine crop of children, three of them sons. His virility put Henry to shame: seven years into the King's marriage, Margaret showed absolutely no sign of pregnancy.

Arbiters were appointed to judge the rights and wrongs of the case against Somerset and a general pardon was issued to York's followers. York himself was invited to take a public oath of loyalty to the King in St Paul's. These courtesies were barbed with insults covert and overt. Somerset was never imprisoned, and remained at the King's side during the oath-taking. York found it deeply humiliating to declare in front of the assembled lords and commons that he was 'and ought to be humble subject and liegeman', promising like an erring child not to attempt anything against the King, to inform the King of any such attempt, and to come 'in humble and obeisant wise' when summoned. Henceforth restricted by the King's command to his own estates, York returned to Ludlow at the end of March.

The date of the arbitration was repeatedly postponed. Generous as the general pardon sounded, many of York's followers were excepted. Others were only pardoned at the price of huge bonds for good behaviour or after long-drawn-out proceedings that parallel the endless postponements faced by Malory. Although Oldhall signed up, and paid, for a pardon, he continued to be persecuted. Together with John Sharp of London, Robert Arderne and John Maltman, both Warwickshire men, he was accused of plotting the death of the King on 12 April 1452 – five days after the cut-off date of the general pardon. He escaped capture, but was outlawed and attainted as a traitor, and all his lands were granted to Somerset's supporters. Arderne was captured, taken before the King at Hereford on 10 August, found guilty on four counts of treason and executed on 12 August – the only man of rank actually to lose his life for treason at this time. His estates were given into the custody of Thomas Greswold.

Plans were made for another royal progress. Henry, with the Queen and Somerset at his side, would again tour the country exhibiting the awesome dignity of monarchy. Earlier in the year there had been rumours that the King would go to East Anglia first, but in the event he did not; instead he instructed the Duke of Norfolk to redress the notorious injustices that had occurred there. The Duke was only too pleased to recover control of the county so long dominated by Suffolk and his cronies. Henry's own progress lasted from 30 June until 5 September, visiting Southampton, Poole, Exeter, Bristol, Bath, Gloucester, and the Welsh Marches. When the King reached Hereford, Sir Walter Devereux of Bodenham (like Oldhall, a retainer of Warwick as well as York) was impeached for acts of treason committed on 28 February. The King's route deliberately took him into the lion's den of Ludlow itself, though he did not lodge in the castle but in the house of the Carmelite Friars. Nothing could have been a more potent display of his power than his passing of judgement on York's supporters at a sessions held a stone's throw from one of the Duke's greatest castles. To lessen his humiliation, York had decamped to his Northamptonshire castle, Fotheringhay, before the King arrived. The King and Queen returned via Birmingham and Coventry, and spent the rest of September in their south London palaces at Eltham, Sheen and Greenwich.

Talbot's return to England ensured that the plight of Aquitaine was at last given attention. A secret embassy had arrived from Bordeaux, with an offer of a return to its three-hundred-year-old allegiance to England if an army was sent there. On 2 September 1452 Henry commissioned Talbot to raise a force of a thousand sailors and three thousand men-at-arms and archers. Talbot landed in the Médoc on 17 October. He was in Bordeaux three days later. The winter saw successful consolidation of the reconquest, and reinforcements sent out in the spring of 1453 saw the capture of the key fortress of Fronsac. Hopes of a permanent renaissance of English power in south-west France were high. Henry undertook a third royal progress in October, this time visiting Hertfordshire, Essex, Cambridgeshire, Huntingdonshire, Northamptonshire and Lincolnshire, the principal areas of York's influence south of the Trent. A contemporary London chronicle described how York's tenants 'were compelled to come naked with choking cords around their necks, in the direst frost and snow, to submit to the king because, previously, they had supported their lord against the Duke of Somerset'.

In the Custody of the Marshal

Malory's first experience of captivity in London was custody by the city's sheriffs. Since he was not committed to a specific prison, he was probably lodged in the Sheriff's own house or perhaps in Ludgate Prison, opened in 1378 and mainly used for freemen of the city. Although it seems to have been run down in the 1450s, there was little hardship to imprisonment there for well-off or well-connected prisoners, who could buy themselves most creature comforts. Prisoners could even leave to attend church or for special occasions, as long as they 'came when called'.

It was not unusual for a fifteenth-century gentleman to find himself in prison. John Paston had to cool his heels in the Fleet Prison three times, in 1461, 1464 and 1465. Delays in the legal process were also normal. 'It is most necessary for delays to be made in the process of all actions, so long as they are not too excessive,' wrote Sir John Fortescue in his authoritative treatise on English law, *De Laudibus Legum Angliae* (1471). 'For by such delays the parties, especially the defendants, can often provide themselves with useful defence and counsel, which they would otherwise lack. Nor is danger ever so likely in judgements as when the process is hurried.' Fortescue was Lord Chief Justice of England in the 1450s, the foremost legal authority of the day, and it is interesting that in a few years' time he would make a point of sitting on Malory's case whenever he could. But by even the most conservative estimate, the delays and postponements experienced by Malory were excessive. The crimes of which he was accused may sound dramatic to us today, but in the context of his times they were very minor misdemeanours.

However, Malory's next eight years were not all spent in prison. A careful reading of the haphazard legal records which have survived, especially of the minuscule and abbreviated memoranda inserted between the lines or in the margin, reveals that a bitter struggle took place in the courts between those who wanted the hyperactive Warwickshire knight in prison and those who wanted him free. The court rolls also show that rather than being a helpless victim, Malory was as energetic and valiant in adversity as any of his Arthurian heroes. At a time when many supporters of York languished in dungeons, disappeared without trace or were executed, Malory knew enough about the legal process to get himself freed on bail several times, and on one occasion actually fought his way out of a castle dungeon. He may have made other bids for freedom. Astronomic sums were demanded as guarantees that he would be kept under lock and key; and a mysterious fire in Ludgate Prison and a riot at Newgate coincided with his presence in those jails.

What is most impressive of all is that he stayed financially buoyant. Imprisonment in any sort of comfort was an expensive business in the fifteenth century. As a knight, Sir Thomas had to pay a £3 fee on entering prison and 2s 4d a day for a separate room and the use of a parlour. He had to pay a further 18s 6d a week for food, wine, candles, firewood, washing and so on; in addition, a discharge fee of about £3 was due when he left prison. A man of Malory's rank would also pay for the board and lodging of at least one servant. How did he pay his way? There are no legal records of him selling or mortgaging land. In fact, a land deal completed soon after his arrest in February 1452 shows that though under arrest, Malory was still an active member of the landed community. Although he was sued for debt later in the 1450s, the amount claimed was less than £8 and the suit was, as we shall see, just another attempt to keep him locked up. Either he was a much wealthier man than has been thought, or he had a generous patron. Or did the Knights Hospitallers look after one of their own? Malory was after all the nephew of the revered Sir Robert Malory, and the kinsman, if not the father, of the up-and-coming Hospitaller Knight Sir John Malory. His uncle Simon Malory became a corrodian (pensioner) at Clerkenwell Priory at about this time.

When the sheriffs of London brought Malory to court to face the accusations made in the Nuneaton indictment in the last week of April, he was told that no jurors had appeared, and that his case had been deferred again – this time until the octave of Michaelmas (6–12 October 1452). At this point, Malory was handed over to the custody of the Marshal of the King's Bench. The Marshalsea Prison was in what is now Borough High Street in Southwark, but Sir

Thomas probably had an apartment in the Marshal's own house in its grounds.

Prisoners were allowed to receive friends and family freely. Lady Malory may well have removed to London to be with her husband, as more than one wife did; she or other kinsfolk and friends are likely to have brought Sir Thomas furnishings and distractions, including books and writing materials. Trusted prisoners could make excursions from prison by special arrangement, accompanied by a keeper known as a 'baston'. This cost them a further 10d a day, paid in part to the warden and in part to the Keeper. Perhaps Malory did just this on 26 May 1452, walking or riding across the city to Coleman Street, near Moorgate, where he borrowed £3 from a moneylender called Robert Overton. Coleman Street was known both for its moneylenders and the noisy hammering and sanding of its metal foundries, where candlesticks, chafing dishes, spice mortars and other copper and latten (a mixed metal similar to brass) objects were made. Malory could have been buying home comforts for his new lodgings, and been tempted to make an unexpected purchase.

His sudden need for ready cash could also be connected to the fact that a few days earlier he had a legal breakthrough. On 20 May 1452 arrangements were made for an arbitration by Thomas Bourgchier, Bishop of Ely. It was to rule on 'all the accounts, quarrels, demands and debts pending before the aforesaid duke [i.e. Norfolk] and Malory, and the officials, servants and tenants of the aforesaid duke and Malory from the day of the creation of the world until the day this recognisance was made'.

An arbitration was an out-of-court settlement used to end long-lasting feuds, often over property, enabling both sides to cut their losses without suffering the stigma of defeat. Malorys and Mowbrays may not have been feuding since 'the day of the creation of the world' (then estimated to be *circa* 2000 BC), but their lands adjoined each other and there were apparently other 'accounts, quarrels, demands and debts' to settle as well as the Caluden incident. So had it been a *quid pro quo*? The arbitration was a sign that both sides alleged grievances. The arbiter was the joint choice of the aggrieved parties, and Bourgchier's involvement shows Malory's importance. The

Bishop was Buckingham's half-brother, Norfolk's brother-in-law, and was later to be Archbishop of Canterbury. Bourgchier undertook to make his judgement by Christmas 1452 and Malory agreed to abide by his decision, entering into a bond for 200 marks (around £134), which he would forfeit if he did not stick to his word.

One of the issues under arbitration was certainly Caluden, and since it was usual for an arbitration penalty to be more than the value of what was disputed, it had clearly been conceded already that the £500-worth of damage said to have been done on the poaching raid was a wild exaggeration. But Norfolk also held the advowson of Coombe Abbey and was the patron of Monks Kirby Priory, so the arbitration could have settled some of the other charges made at Nuneaton in so far as they affected the Duke.

It did not clear up all of them, most notably the alleged ambush of Buckingham and Hugh Smith's appeal of rape. For the next five months, long enough to do a good deal of constructive work on his retelling of the Arthurian legends, Malory remained in the custody of the Marshal of the Marshalsea. In the second week of October 1452, he appeared in the Court of King's Bench. But no satisfactory jury turned up, and the case was again deferred, this time until the octave of Hilary 1453 (20–26 January 1453).

'And he that was courteous, true, and faithful, to his friend was that time cherished'

A few days later, however, on 21 October, the court granted Malory bail until 3 February 1453 on his own surety and that of Sir John Baskerville of Eardisley, Herefordshire, William Cecil of London, Thomas Ince of Stanford Rivers, Essex, and John Leventhorpe of Southwark, Surrey. Eardisley was twenty miles from York's marcher stronghold of Ludlow, and Sir John Baskerville's son Sir James was married to the daughter of Sir Walter Devereux; her mother was a Ferrers of Chartley, a Warwickshire family with whom both Malory and the Earl of Warwick had close connections. William Cecil had been in Rome with Robert Malory in 1448. Thomas Ince held his

Essex manor at Stanford Rivers of the Duke of York and joined the Calais garrison when York was its captain. Ince should have returned to Calais in 1453, but his letters of protection were twice cancelled because he lingered in Essex – perhaps in order to help a former companion-in-arms. He would stand bail for Malory again a year later.

The most significant name of all is that of John Leventhorpe. The Leventhorpes held the manor of Newnham Paddox, three miles from Newbold Revel, until at least 1433. In all probability the man who stood surety for Malory was the John Leventhorpe who at this time held the prestigious and lucrative position of Marshal of the Marshalsea of the King's Household, a prison next door to the Marshalsea of King's Bench in which Malory was confined. There is evidence that he was a kindly man. Moreover he had a kinsman, perhaps son, perhaps brother, who was also called John Leventhorpe, whose political career mirrors Malory's closely. This John Leventhorpe was a Hertfordshire esquire who had served in France under Henry V. His father had been one of the warrior King's most trusted servants, and he himself was a Duchy of Lancaster administrator. He was also eager for reform. In 1447, soon after becoming treasurer of Norfolk's household, he blew the whistle on the Duke's corrupt and violent receiver-general, Sir Robert Wingfield. Wingfield was a henchman of Suffolk and a favourite of the Queen; he was among those indicted by Cade's rebels.

Wingfield's reaction was first to try to murder Leventhorpe himself, then to put a price of 500 marks on his head. Although he was hauled into court to answer for this and his misappropriations from Norfolk's estates, Wingfield was given a royal pardon. Norfolk's only hope of recovering his revenues and documents was to take them by force. His raid on Wingfield's manor of Letheringham in the summer of 1448 makes Malory's sortie against Coombe sound like a Sunday-school picnic. According to Wingfield, the Duke, Leventhorpe and numerous others came by night, bringing carts and wagons with cannons and other engines of war, hurled stones, broke walls, towers and chimneys, sawed asunder posts and beams, set the beds on fire and burned crops. They took deer from the park and goods and moneys amounting to some £2,200 and several chests of documents. Wingfield complained to the King's council, and Norfolk was hauled off to the Tower on 28 August. Although released a week later, he was ordered to pay Wingfield 3,500 marks, just about what he claimed to have lost.

Leventhorpe had a hand in the careful preparations made by Norfolk and York for the crucial October 1449 Parliament, going to Chichester to support the election of John Lewknor, half-brother of Norfolk's councillor Thomas Hoo, as MP for Sussex. Although his substantial estates were in Hertfordshire and he was three times an elector for the county, he would sit as MP for the Mowbray pocket borough of Horsham in Sussex in 1453. His kinsman's support of Malory's release on bail suggests that Norfolk, nudged perhaps by York, had settled his differences with Malory by October.

It would be interesting to know the name of the justice who freed Malory. It is possible that Malory deliberately chose to apply for bail when Thomas Greswold and Chief Justice Fortescue were away from Westminster, accompanying the King, the Queen and a substantial number of the peers of the realm on yet another judicial progress, this time in the eastern Midlands. Whoever did agree to his release was evidently nervous about the decision: £2,000 was laid down as the penalty due from the Marshal of the prison if Sir Thomas failed to return. The unusually large penalty, out of all proportion to the offences of which Malory was accused, may have been caused by his escape from Coleshill, but it reinforces the impression of a vendetta against Malory. That the date set for the expiry of Malory's bail was 3 February is also interesting. It shows that he was to be allowed to send an attorney along for the hearing set for 20–26 January rather than returning himself.

Malory may have been over-ebullient when he was released on bail. A legal memorandum four days later noted that:

Thomas Malory of Newbold Revel county Warwick, knight, to William Venner, Bond in £200 payable on the feast of St Simon and St Jude next. Dated 25 Oct 31 HVI [1453] condition that he, Philip Burgh and Thomas Barton shall keep the peace towards William Venner, his servants and them of his household, doing and procuring them no hurt or grievance [no acknowledgement].

William Venner was the Warden of the Fleet Prison, an office held in his family for the last three hundred years. It is just possible that Malory had spent some time in the Fleet and was known to be planning revenge for the way he had been treated, but there is a more likely reason for his threatening behaviour. Venner was also Keeper of Westminster Palace and the courts of justice. Splendid in his mulberry and mustard-yellow livery, he had many duties in and around the law courts and could influence when cases were held and who judged them. He expected to be bribed. At Westminster Hall, 'he that lack'd money might not speed', complained the contemporary satirical ballad, *London Lickpenny*. The odds are that Malory, Barton and Burgh had eloquently expressed their disapproval of Venner's handling of the judicial process and, now that Malory was being released on bail, Venner wanted to make sure there were no recriminations. Malory's bailing out of Thomas Barton is yet another link to the Duke of York. Barton was York's receiver at Wigmore, near Ludlow. Burgh was a common name but if Philip Burgh was a relation of Sir Thomas Burgh, a prominent figure at the Yorkist court in the next decade, he may also have had reformist views. Evidently cases against the supporters of York who had been thrown into prisons on the slightest of pretexts were at last beginning to be heard. It may have been of interest to Malory that John Walsh was among a batch of Yorkist supporters to be delivered from Gloucester Gaol on 28 February 1453.

Malory's triumphant return to Newbold Revel at the end of October was not appreciated by at least one of his accusers. When William Dowde of Cosford eventually appeared in court to bear witness against him he pleaded that in future Malory be kept in prison without the option of bail. Abbot Atherstone had, interestingly, now disappeared from the scene (why, we do not know), but matters between Malory and Coombe were still unresolved, and Malory was evidently angry: as we shall see, in a few months' time the new Abbot,

Robert Hull, asked for protection from him. On 6 December, Sir William Mountfort died. Malory may have hoped that the new Sheriff, Sir Robert Moton, would be more effective in persuading jurors to travel to London to sit on his case. Moton had spent his minority with the senior branch of the Malory family at Castle Bytham and had married Margery, daughter of Sir Anketil Malory. He served in Lord Grey of Codnor's retinue from 1402, going to France with him in 1417. But the seventy-six-year-old Moton was now linked to Buckingham's affinity, and though he was whimsical enough to keep a pet deer, he was unlikely to be energetic on Malory's behalf. He had been far from keen to take office. He said that his 'great age, feebleness and long service' to the Crown both at home and abroad 'to his great and sumptuous charges' meant that he was 'so impoverished in his goods and enfeebled in his person' that he was incapable of exercising the office. His inertia was typical of the times: many eminent and honest men deeply resented being forced to act against friends and neighbours who happened to have fallen foul of interests at court.

While Malory was rejoicing in his freedom from prison, and perhaps canvassing Warwickshire friends to turn up as jurors for him, the royal household returned to London. Back at Eltham Palace by early November, King Henry and Queen Margaret spent Christmas and the first half of January at Greenwich. The King's two Tudor half-brothers were given earldoms, Edmund that of Richmond and Jasper that of Pembroke. They were also granted several manors relinquished by York in the 1451 Act of Resumption. On 8 February 1453, Henry headed out on another progress, this time north-east into East Anglia, returning via Berkhamsted to Reading where a new Parliament opened on 6 March.

It was the first time the Commons had met since May 1451. This time they were tractable, not least because a record number of household men had been elected. They cancelled the reforms passed under the pressure of Cade's rebellion, demanded Oldhall's attainder, and granted the King an annual fifteenth and tenth as well as tonnage and poundage for the rest of his life. Then, with exceptional generosity, they voted three further tenths and fifteenths to pay for 20,000 archers to serve the King 'for the space of half a year'. An army of this size, which required four months' notice of its date and place of muster, could only have been intended as an expeditionary force. Talbot's success in Aquitaine meant that hopes were rising high that Henry V's son might yet regain his father's lost Norman domains as well.

Only Malory's attorneys were in court on the due date for the next hearing at the end of January. But again, no jury appeared, and the case was postponed until the quindene of Easter (16–20 April) 1453. It may have been because of this postponement that Malory did not turn up in the Marshalsea when his bail period ended on 3 February 1453. It appears that the court knew that he was not going to appear: on the day before his deadline, 2 February, they ordered a distraint of his goods.

Malory may have hoped that the distraction of the royal progresses and the summoning of the Reading Parliament would allow him to remain at liberty. But he had not been forgotten. A new warrant for his arrest was issued on 26 March 1453 to Buckingham, Moton and Edward Grey, Lord Ferrers of Groby, instructing them to bring Sir Thomas Malory before the King and council 'to answer certain charges'. Appearing before the King and council was not the same as appearing in the Court of King's Bench. It sounds as if Malory was to be accused of new crimes – perhaps skipping bail, but perhaps something far more serious. But there is no record of any new indictment. Whatever the charges were, they were not going to be made public. This time Buckingham failed to get his man. If Malory had been captured, we would expect the King's Bench record to say when his case came up after Easter that he had been brought to court, as it did on other occasions, and to read of limitations on his liberty. But it did not mention his presence, only that the case was postponed once more for want of jurors, this time until the octave of Michaelmas (6–12 October) 1453. It was an unusually long postponement. My guess is that no one knew where Malory was. There is every reason to assume that he remained free until then.

At War with the Law

*For ever a man of worship and of prowess dreadeth least
always perils, for they ween every man be as they be; but
ever he that fareth with treason putteth oft a man in great
danger.*

Malory, 'The Tale of Lancelot and Guinevere'

arliament's second session began in May 1453. The King's
party was riding high, exhilarated at the news that the Queen
was at last expecting a baby. Margaret's visit to Cecily Neville,
the Duchess of York, at Hitchin in April was probably to confirm –
and boast of – her condition. She also visited Norwich that month,
perhaps to take advice from another experienced Neville matron,
Cecily's sister Katherine, Dowager Duchess of Norfolk. Somerset
began to throw his weight about with more confidence. York was
deprived of the lieutenancy of Ireland. Norfolk's retainers were
arraigned for intimidating electors in Suffolk. Warwick's rival Lord
Abergavenny was licensed to enter Abergavenny and Mereworth, and
Somerset became the guardian of George Neville, Warwick's wife's
co-heir for her Despenser inheritance. By July 1453 most of the
household officers removed in 1451–2 had been restored. Norfolk and
Warwick, previously ostentatiously loyal to their king, had become
almost as deeply disaffected as York. A report reached the council of
'great gatherings congregations and assemblies unlawful' in Cardiff,
with the castle and town of Cowbridge kept with great strength 'as it
were in land of war'. The news made King Henry decide upon another
punitive judicial progress, this time westward. He left Sheen soon
after 21 July 1453.

At this point two hammer blows struck the Lancastrian monarchy. On 17 July the magnificent advance through Aquitaine of the sixty-seven-year-old Earl of Shrewsbury, John Talbot, and his son, Viscount Lisle, came to a terrible end at Châtillon. The English army mounted a heroic but reckless cavalry charge against a French force twice its size and bristling with artillery. Talbot's distinctive white charger was felled by a cannonball, and both the Earl and his heir were killed. A fortnight later, Henry VI collapsed. The thirty-one-year-old King was said to have suffered a 'rash and sudden terror' which sent him into a 'frenzy'. The seizure probably happened at Kingston Lacy, near Wareham, a pretty little manor that belonged to Queen Margaret. Henry was taken to the more substantial royal palace of Clarendon, east of Salisbury, where he remained until early October, when he was removed to Windsor. He was described as completely helpless, unable to feed himself or walk without being supported between two men. 'His wit and reason were withdrawn,' said one observer. Henry's breakdown lasted for the next seventeen months.

What was the 'rash and sudden terror' that sent Henry into his stupor? One possibility was news of the death of the Talbots. But in 1450 Henry had weathered more severe shocks without losing his reason: the loss of his last stronghold in Normandy, Suffolk's murder and Cade's rebellion. A far more likely trigger for the King's dementia would have been the realisation that the baby the Queen was carrying was not his. Margaret was described by contemporaries as a 'great and strong laboured woman' who 'spares no pains' to 'pursue her things to an intent and conclusion to her power'. Rumours that the child was not Henry's were rife at this time. 'When the king was told of the queen's condition he exclaimed, "If she is expecting a child, then it must have been conceived by the Holy Ghost"', the Milanese ambassador told Duke Francesco Sforza. The Milanese ambassador may have misunderstood some pious exclamation of thanksgiving from Henry, but there was no mistaking the general mood of doubt. 'The common people had the opinion that the king was not able to get a child,' wrote the chronicler Holinshed, 'and therefore sticked not to say, that this was not his son, with many slanderous words, greatly sounding to the queen's dishonour; much perchance untruly.' The word 'perchance' hints that Holinshed also thought Henry an unlikely father but was wary even a hundred years later of casting aspersions on a Queen of England. Contemporary chronicles were surer of their facts: the baby was 'no natural son of King Henry,' said Gregory's *English Chronicle*. 'False wedlock [and] false heirs fostered' was said by Fabian to be the 'first cause' of the sickness of the body politic. A 'great wrong' had been done to the Duke of York, recorded Gregory, which pointedly made no reference at all to the birth of Queen Margaret's child.

Certain knowledge that he had been cuckolded, confirmed perhaps by a spy, an anonymous letter or even by the Queen herself, could have resulted in a severe mental breakdown. Margaret may have gambled her life on Henry's evident love for her, arguing with all her notorious forcefulness that it was entirely for his sake that she had found a surrogate father. What she could not have foreseen is that, though she was right in thinking that her husband would never betray her, his mind simply could not cope with the situation. Amnesia is a well-known response to such situations.

The extent of Henry's incapacity was concealed. Queen Margaret and Somerset kept him in complete seclusion at Windsor. Government decisions were postponed as much as possible. When she gave birth to a healthy boy on 13 October 1453, Margaret was in a strong enough position to make the King's illness more public. Despite the whispers, the consensus of opinion was that a Lancastrian heir was exactly what the country needed to unite it – not least because it would make a loyal Englishwoman of Margaret, hitherto seen as dangerously pro-French. The baby, born on the feast of the translation of Edward the Confessor, was baptised Edward, and wrapped after his immersion in a 'crysom' robe heavily embroidered with pearls and precious stones and valued at £554 16s 8d. His godparents were Edmund Beaufort, Duke of Somerset, Cardinal Kemp and Anne Neville, Duchess of Buckingham.

As rumours of Henry's addled wits spread, local feuding increased. Warwick and Abergavenny sparred in the Marches, and the Duke of Exeter and Lord Cromwell in Bedfordshire. In Yorkshire, the Percys and the Nevilles were preparing for war after Thomas Percy and Lord Egremont ambushed a Neville wedding procession at the end of

August. The bitterest quarrel was that between the dukes of York and Somerset. There were speculations in the courts of France, Burgundy and Italy that there would be a new king in England before long. That year Charles of Orléans, who knew more than most about the English, having been imprisoned there for twenty-five years, picked up his pen and composed a roundelay which translates as:

> *Have not the English always betrayed their kings?*
> *Certainly everyone knows of it.*
> *And once again their king is in a precarious position.*
> *Each Englishman pushes himself forward . . .*
> *There is great dispute among them about who will be king.*

In mid-October, a council of great lords met at Westminster to discuss how government should be managed and to 'set rest and union between the lords of this land'. Through arrogance or fear, Somerset did not at first invite York to the Council, a highly insulting omission. But he had gone too far. The council saw to it that a belated letter was sent to the Duke on 23 October, asking him to come 'peaceably and measurably accompanied'. The true feelings of the loyal majority of lords who had once stood solidly behind Somerset because he was the chosen first minister of the King were now emerging. Twenty-five lords attended the Great Council when it finally assembled on 21 November: two archbishops and eight bishops, the dukes of York, Buckingham, Somerset and Norfolk and six earls. In an ominous replay of his petition against Suffolk three years earlier, Norfolk appealed Somerset of treason because of his corrupt mismanagement of the war in France. The lords ruled that he should be arrested and sent to the Tower to await trial by his peers. They also ordered that York's ally the Earl of Devon should be released from Wallingford Castle. York requested that Oldhall's attainder be reversed.

On New Year's Day 1454, Buckingham and Queen Margaret brought Prince Edward to Windsor to present him to Henry.

> *The Duc of Buk took [the baby] in his arms and presented*
> *him to the King in godly wise, beseeching the King to bless*

him; and the king gave no manner answer. Natheless the Duc abode still with the Prince by the King, and when he could no manner answer have, the Queen came in, and took the Prince in her arms, and presented him in like form as the Duc had done, desiring that he should bless it; but all their labour was in vain, for they departed thence without any answer or countenance saving only that once he looked on the Prince and cast down his eyes again, without any more.

There is something heart-breakingly sad about that single glance, and those cast-down eyes.

'God send me good deliverance soon and hastily'

Malory seems to have been living openly either in Lincolnshire or Warwickshire until the autumn of 1453. He witnessed a deed drawn up by the Abbey of Axholme confirming various transactions made by its daughter house, Monks Kirby Priory. Other witnesses included Sir Leonard Hastings, and William Mountfort, Baldwin Mountfort's brother. All the witnesses were more inclined to Warwick and York than to Buckingham. It is possible that the grant was a response to Bishop Bourgchier's arbitration.

However, by early October Thomas had either given himself up or been rearrested by the new Sheriff, the very Sir William Birmingham who had sat at Buckingham's side during the Nuneaton indictment. In the octave of Michaelmas 1453 (6–12 October), 'Thomas Malory, knight' was presented once again at King's Bench by the Marshal to answer to the 'diverse felonies, trangressions, insurrections, extortions and oppressions' of which he was accused. Again no jury appeared. His case was postponed until the octave of Hilary 1454 (20–26 January), and he returned to the Marshalsea. As he left, it must have been some solace to see Sir William Peyto glaring at him across Westminster Hall. Sheriff Moton may have failed to find jurors for Malory's case, but he at least succeeded in bringing Peyto to book for his attack on John Hathwyck in London two years earlier. Peyto was found guilty, and Hathwyck, who had evidently successfully defended himself against Peyto's accusation at Nuneaton, was awarded £60 in damages.

Although back in the custody of the Marshal, Malory's spirits must have soared when Somerset was removed to the Tower and York was restored to the council. If Devon and perhaps Oldhall were to be freed, why shouldn't he be? But York was intent on observing the laws of the land punctiliously. That it was of paramount importance that he was not seen as a law-breaker may explain why he did not put pressure on the judges to release more of his supporters. The mood of Parliament, summoned to meet at Westminster on 14 February 1454, had to be carefully assessed. Oldhall's fate remained unresolved, and Malory spent Christmas in prison. At least, no restrictions were put on him, and discreet excursions, albeit accompanied by bastons, may have started again. Both these and Malory's journeys between the Marshalsea Prison on the south bank of the Thames in Southwark and the Court of King's Bench at Westminster were in all likelihood partly by boat. Countless watermen plied their oars on the Thames, London's quickest, safest and most pleasant highway. Malory's experiences at this time may have added colour and drama to his 'Tale of Sir Lancelot and Guinevere'. When Lancelot hears that Sir Meliagaunce has abducted Guinevere and taken her to his palace, Malory tells us that he 'took the water at Westminster Bridge and made his horse swim over the Thames unto Lambeth' before galloping off 'at a wallop' to rescue the Queen. Malory's contemporaries knew that Westminster 'bridge' was then only a jetty, where a ferry crossed the Thames. But there was a ford there, which could only be crossed at low tide and even then was best negotiated on horseback (hence its name, Horse Ferry). They would also have picked up on the risk that Lancelot was taking: swimming his horse over because he wasn't prepared to wait for the tide to go out.

The general nervousness during these limbo months of eclipsed royal authority was reflected in the annual nomination of sheriffs on 5 November 1453. Although several were as usual members of the royal household, some counties announced that they could not find anyone willing to be sheriff at all. But supporters of York were appointed in Gloucestershire, Yorkshire and, usefully for Malory, in Warwickshire/Leicestershire, where Sir Leonard Hastings, his fellow witness to the Monks Kirby land deal, was elected. After Christmas, London began to fill up with Members of Parliament and lords spiritual and temporal. Buckingham arrived, and ordered two thousand Stafford badges for his men, 'to what intent men may construe as their wits will allow them', John Studley wrote darkly in a January newsletter that teems with vivid details. Malory's mainpernor John Leventhorpe was among Studley's informants. Buckingham was not the only peer to bring a substantial retinue with him. York, Norfolk, Warwick, Richmond, Pembroke and many others were also on their way to the capital, 'everyone of them with a goodly fellowship'. Even Somerset, corralled though he was in the Tower, 'maketh him ready to be as strong as he can make him'. His men had taken all the lodgings around the Tower and his spies 'were going in every Lord's house in the land; some dressed as friars, some as shipmen, and some in other wise, which report unto him all that they can see or hear'.

When Malory's case came to court again in late January, it was postponed once more, this time until the quindene of Easter (8 May 1454). Frustrated and angry, Malory may have made another bid to escape. Or perhaps when he was wandering around town with his bastons he met some old enemies from Warwickshire who had come to London to attend Parliament, and gave them a piece of his mind. For a week after the postponement of his case, on 4 February, the court, 'for the sufficient securing of the peace against Robert Hull, Abbot of Coombe and all the king's subjects', ordered the Marshal to keep Malory securely in his prison. They were not to let him out either on bail or on any terms whatsoever without the express permission of the court, on penalty of £1,000.

The King still showed no signs of recovery. With passionate courage, Queen Margaret proposed that she should herself 'have the whole rule of the land', ruling as regent on behalf of the King and then, if he did not recover, of Prince Edward during his minority. The prospect of the Queen ruling for the next twenty-one years might have seemed normal to Margaret herself; both her mother and her grandmother had ruled their respective husbands' kingdoms on occasion. But it did not appeal in the slightest to the English. The most acceptable constitutional step was to make the tiny Prince of Wales, the official heir to the throne, the ward of a Protector. But who should this be? Somerset had royal blood, but was awaiting trial, nor was he generally popular. York, still humbly reiterating his loyal allegiance to his sovereign lord King Henry, now had the support of the earls of Richmond and Pembroke, the King's Tudor half-brothers, as well as of Norfolk and Warwick. He was the obvious choice. On 27 March 1454, the lords appointed him Protector of the Realm and Chief Councillor. On 2 April, the Earl of Salisbury, Warwick's father, became Chancellor, and so head of the justice system. On 3 April an act of Parliament confirmed York in office.

Adventures in Essex

Salisbury's position as Chancellor meant that at last York could do something for his beleaguered supporters. Oldhall's case was declared erroneous and his trial was adjourned *sine die*, an abbreviation of the legal phrase 'without a day being set', which meant, in practice, for ever. And in the second week of May 1454, Sir Thomas Malory was granted bail for five months on the strength of £200 security, which he offered himself, and £200 offered among no fewer than ten mainpernors. John Leventhorpe and Thomas Ince stood forward once again. There were also two Warwickshire neighbours: John Hathwyck of Harbury, and Sir Thomas Boughton of Lawford, one of the MPs for Warwickshire. Lawford is two miles south of Newbold Revel, and Boughton was married to Simon Malory's wife's niece; he was also Norfolk's steward for Axholme Abbey, which had responsibility for Monks Kirby Priory. Four of the mainpernors, Edmund Fitzwilliam, William Worsop, John Valens, and Ralph Worthington, were from Framlingham, Norfolk's seat in Suffolk. Their presence suggests that Norfolk now wished Malory well.

The most significant of Malory's mainpernors was Sir Roger Chamberlain 'of Queenborough, Kent', the man who had so nearly been executed after Gloucester's death. He was now as close to York as he had been to Humfrey of Gloucester. He may have known Malory for a very long time. He was born in 1406, his brothers' names appear beside Malory's on the 1417 muster roll of Lord Grey of Codnor's troops, and he served in France under Bedford in the 1420s. Like Malory, he sat as a reformer in the 1450 Parliament, knight of the shire for Suffolk.

The reason for the sudden arrival of this small army of friends could have been that Malory's renowned strong arm was needed. Letters of protection frequently saved malefactors who were useful with a sword from going to prison at all; bail was often granted for the same reason. Earlier in May a rebellion had broken out in the North, led by Henry Holland, the impetuous young Duke of Exeter, and his equally hot-headed ally Lord Egremont, a younger son of the great Northumberland family of Percy. On 14 May they had attempted to seize the city of York, an insult which its duke took personally. On 16 May, a week after Malory was released, York assembled as many men as he could at short notice, and rode northwards with 'a great number of men', leaving orders for more to follow him.

Was Malory among the second wave of troops? A man called John Aleyn, 'alias Addelsey, outlaw and yeoman of London', was later accused of breaking into the grounds of the Abbot of Tilty's house at Great Easton on 23 May. He was said to have stolen (he might have called it requisitioned) a grey worth 100s and a bay worth 40s – highly appropriate steeds for a knight and his servant. Tilty Abbey was two miles south of York's castle at Thaxted, a natural place for mustering another band of men to ride northwards. Sir Thomas Malory was accused of knowing about and being an accessory to the felony. John Aleyn is a common name, but an outlawed John Aleyn has appeared in our story before – the yeoman of Stanton Harcourt who was with Sir Robert Harcourt at the time of the 1448 attack on Richard Stafford in Coventry. If this was the same man, Malory might not have regarded him as a criminal but as a potentially useful servant, especially if he turned up with two good horses, and was ready and willing to ride north.

The rebellion successfully quashed, York returned south in mid-June. If Malory and Aleyn returned with him, they could have been at Thaxted in July. For Malory was also accused of harbouring Aleyn and encouraging him in criminal activities at that time. The accusations were made at an inquisition held in Chelmsford on 8 October 1454. John Aleyn was said to have stolen not only the grey and the bay acquired in May, but three more horses from Thomas Bykenen and Thomas Street of Gosfield: a white horse worth £3 6s 8d belonging to Richard Scott, Vicar of Gosfield, on 27 June, a sorrel worth £1 6s 8d and a bay worth £2 on 2 July. Ten days later, on 9 July, it was alleged that Sir Thomas Malory and John Aleyn rode from Waltham Cross in Hertfordshire to Thaxted in Essex on 9 July. There, although he knew of the felonies Aleyn had committed, Malory 'received, favoured and comforted' him overnight. He then rode with him the next day from Thaxted to Braintree, put him up for another night, and helped him to plot 'new felonies'.

The new felonies allegedly involved a plot to rob William Green, William Algore and various other 'faithful subjects of the king' in Gosfield 'while all the Christians in the town were at church'. It was said that, with the advice and consent of Malory, Aleyn and others raided a house belonging to John Green on Sunday 21 July in order to steal William's and his wife's goods and chattels which were stored there. If they had not been interrupted, it was said, they would have stolen coffers and chests of valuables belonging to the Greens. Another indictment, made the same day, accused one John Addesley, described as 'servant of Sir Thomas Malory', of breaking into the close the day before, armed with a longbow and arrows.

We are unlikely ever to know what was really going on at Gosfield. None of the would-be thieves was arrested. 'Addesley' could well have been the John Appleby who had been indicted with Malory in 1451. The Gosford incident may have been an unsuccessful burglary by Appleby and the other men from Newbold Revel who had been outlawed in 1453. Malory's involvement could have been negligible: merely the nobly negative one of refusing to reveal their whereabouts.

It is more probable that Malory had mustered his outlawed men to Thaxted, and told them that they could ride north with him if they found mounts. For York set off for the North again at the end of July on a judicial progress deliberately modelled on those that

Henry VI had used so effectively to display the reality of his authority. The Duke emphasised his status of royal champion by dressing his eighty men in the King's livery. By 3 August, he was in the city of York, hearing indictments against Exeter and Egremont. While he was there, he appointed Salisbury and Warwick as joint wardens of the East March for the next twenty years. He stayed in the north for six weeks, most probably at Sandal Castle. Warwick and Salisbury were based at Middleham Castle and Sheriff Hutton, where York heard more indictments. Early in October he returned to Westminster for the Great Council planned for later that month.

No doubt Malory also intended to return to Westminster in October, in order to appear punctually in front of the justices of King's Bench on the agreed date. He would not have wanted to risk ten good friends forfeiting their bonds. But he didn't make it. There was no sign of him in Westminster Hall on 29 October 1454 when his case came up, this time before the Chief Justice, Sir John Fortescue. Thomas Greswold, who was acting as prosecuting counsel, gloatingly asked for payment of £200 from Malory and £20 from each of his mainpernors. The next step would have been outlawry. That meant all his goods and chattels fell to the King, as did his estates for a year and a day, after which they were given to his overlord. At this point John Leventhorpe and Thomas Ince rose in court to explain that the reason Sir Thomas had not returned was that he had been arrested by the Sheriff of Essex and committed to prison in Colchester Castle on 16 October, accused of aiding and abetting horse thieves and burglars in July. The Constable of Colchester Castle was John Hampton, a notoriously corrupt Staffordshire gentleman – and a retainer of the Duke of Buckingham.

Leventhorpe and Ince knew about Malory's latest misadventure because it occurred in their part of the country – Sawbridgeworth is on the direct route between Waltham Cross and Thaxted, and Stanford Rivers is only ten miles south. He might have been staying with or near them or their families when he was arrested. A fair-minded man, Sir John Fortescue turned down Greswold's request for fines, and next day sent a writ to Colchester to say that proceedings against Malory were to be transferred to Westminster; the Constable was instructed to bring him there to answer to the judges on 18 November. But with typical panache, Malory pre-empted his transfer. Although confined 'forti et dura' (in irons) by Hampton, on 30 October he broke out of Colchester Castle's gaol. It was no mean feat. Colchester Castle still looks formidably massive, and its walls were once twice as high as they are today. He must have had accomplices, as it was said that long swords, short swords and daggers were used 'contrary to the king's peace and the dignity of the crown'. But again, no one was hurt.

Such an escape was, like the attack on Coombe, a desperate course of action. It probably reflected Malory's gloom as to his future prospects. For Henry VI's sanity had returned. At the investiture of the new Archbishop of Canterbury on 22 August 1454, the King had appeared in public to receive his kiss of homage. The Great Council that York had summoned to meet in November, and at which he had hoped to dispose of Somerset for good, was poorly attended. Many peers, including Norfolk, remained in cautious retreat on their own estates. On 3 November, William Barker wrote from Wroxham to Sir John Fastolf that Norfolk 'looked daily for the King to send for him'.

When the Council met on 15 November, it confirmed the legality of York's Protectorate status, praising 'the great nobleness, sadness and wisdom of the Duke of York [and] the sad governaunce and politic rule had in this land'. York had in truth ruled well, quieting the disturbed realm and reducing the vastly inflated numbers of the royal household to an affordable number. But it was decided that there were not enough peers to try Somerset. At least York could argue that there were not enough to let the Duke free on bail either. But it was clear that York's days as Protector were numbered. Significantly, Sir William Oldhall decided to retreat into sanctuary again. The forfeiture of his lands had not yet been reversed.

Malory appeared in front of the justices of the Court of King's Bench on 18 November. The records suggest that it was his main-pernors who brought him to court; they may have had to use all their powers of persuasion. Or perhaps it was Norfolk's fiat. Barker's letter to Fastolf also refers with tantalisingly cryptic brevity to 'the excuse of Sir Thomas etc', conjuring up a picture of a weary Malory kicking his heels in the anteroom of Norfolk's castle at Framlingham, only to be told he must go back to London with Ince and Leventhorpe. Anxious not to risk the King's displeasure, Norfolk would punctiliously avoid any actions that might be deemed illegal. Malory was re-committed to the Marshalsea to await trial on 27 January 1455. His confinement was again close, with an escape penalty of £1,000. When the case came before the court at the end of January, it was yet again dismissed for want of jurors. The same thing happened on the next appointed date, 23 April, when the case was deferred until 8 June. Although he had now been in the Marshalsea for almost five months, no bail was allowed.

Until now Malory's captivity had been intermittent and far from severe. Between 27 January 1452 and 18 November 1454, he had been free on bail or illicitly for seventeen months, and in prison for fifteen months, during most of which time there were no restraints on his going abroad in London. But by breaking out of Colchester Castle he had made it difficult for even the most influential of his friends to justify his release on bail. For the next three years he would be cooped up in an assortment of prisons without any respite at all.

Knight Prisoner

It shall be well understanded, both at the king and at the
queen, and with all men of worship, that I am dead, sick,
other in prison. For all men that know me will say for me
that I am in some evil case an I be not there that day; and
well I wot there is some good knight either of my blood, or
some other that loveth me, that will take my quarrel in
hand.

Lancelot, held secretly a prisoner by King Meliagaunce

alory's three-year imprisonment between November 1454
and October 1457 would have given him plenty of time to
work on his own versions of the Arthurian stories. The
manuscript explicit to the first section of his book, 'The Tale of King
Arthur', runs: 'For this was drawn by a knight prisoner Sir Thomas
Malleorré, that God send him good recover'. Several other explicits
contain prayers for help and deliverance. This was neither the first
nor the last time Malory found himself in prison, but it was easily
the longest uninterrupted stretch of incarceration. There is no need
to wonder which prison library held all of the books he referred to;
it is much more likely that his family and friends supplied him with
both a succession of books and the simple tools he needed: parchment, which could be scraped and reused, for rough drafts, paper for
copying out in neat, penknife, quills and ink, fine sand. He might
have liked the idea of chronicling his own times, but the uncertain
climate of the 1450s was no time for such an enterprise. It was much
safer to embark, perhaps once again, perhaps for the first time, on
'drawing' – a verb then used to describe literary as well as artistic
activity – the Arthurian legends he knew so well and loved so much.

Edmund Spenser, who also lived in a politically tense age, wrote in a letter to Sir Walter Raleigh that

> *I chose the history of King Arthur, as most fit for the excellency of his person, being made famous by many men's former works, and also furthest from the danger of envy and suspicion of present time.*

The way Malory told the history of King Arthur was well-suited to the 1450s. The *Morte* opens in a world in which anarchy threatens: an illegitimate conception, a realm in jeopardy in which 'every lord that was mighty of men made him strong, and many weened to have been king'. It preaches justice, honour and keeping faith – to God, to women and to one's king. Malory's criticism of the bitter envy and mindless loyalty to a family of characters like Sir Palomides, King Mark and the sons of Lot of Orkney will have reminded his first readers of the feuds between families and rivalries between individuals which were becoming such a destructive element of contemporary political life. Of course it was not an exact reflection of Lancastrian England, but many of his asides were veiled messages – comments on the times, personal jokes for friends – and pleas for help.

During his imprisonment, national events proved how much his contemporaries could profit from reflecting on the Arthurian legends. By Christmas 1454, Henry VI seemed to have recovered. 'He said he is in charity with all the world and so he would all the Lords were', Bishop Waynflete told the council after a visit to see him on 7 January 1455. Edmund Clere (of Horning, Norfolk) wrote to John Paston from Greenwich on 9 January describing how

> *the Queen came to him and brought my Lord Prince with her. And then he asked what the Prince's name was, and the Queen told him Edward; and then he held up his hands and thanked God thereof. And he said he never knew til that time, nor wist what was said to him, nor wist where he had been whilst he had been sick until now.*

York's Protectorate was ended. Henry VI was, in theory at least, once more at the helm of the ship of state. But from now on his reputation as a man 'little given to the world and its works' grew. On 5 February Somerset was bailed from the Tower on the condition that he was excluded from the King's presence – as Chancellor, Salisbury was still head of the justice system. But on 4 March Somerset appeared before the King at the Great Council which opened at the Queen's manor, Plaisaunce, at Greenwich. He declared his willingness to 'answer and do all things that a true knight oweth to do according to Law and Knighthood'. The traditional phrase with its capital initial letters shows the equal weight still given to the chivalric code of honour and the law of the land. To answer a challenge according to knighthood was to offer to fight in person, 'body for body'.

The King graciously recognised Somerset as a true and faithful liegeman, welcomed him back to court and restored him to the captaincy of Calais. York's quarrel with him was to be settled by arbitration by 20 June; meanwhile, each promised to keep the peace or forfeit a fortune – 20,000 marks. Salisbury was replaced as Chancellor by Archbishop Bourgchier, a man respected by all sides. But two traditional enemies of the Nevilles, Henry Percy, Earl of Northumberland, and Thomas, Lord Clifford, were summoned to join the Council. Norfolk stayed on his East Anglian estates. Faced by a council dominated by their enemies, York and Warwick withdrew from London.

The First Battle of St Albans

On 16 April 1455, Somerset and his supporters had canvassed enough strength to move against their enemies – but according to law, not knighthood. On 23 April the council, to which York was pointedly not invited, announced that there would be an assembly at Leicester on 21 May 1455 'to provide for the king's safety'. Ominously, it was to have the judicial power of a parliament, with 'commons' as well as lords spiritual and temporal. As real elections would have been run by sheriffs chosen during York's Protectorate, summonses were sent to named men in the shires, carefully chosen for their loyalty to Henry and Margaret. Convinced that the assembly would lose no time in demanding that Parliament attaint them for treason, York and the Nevilles decided to defend themselves 'according to knighthood' from the false traitors who surrounded the King. Malory describes just such a situation in his 'Tale of Sir Tristram', when King Anguish of Ireland is appealed of treason by Sir Blamore.

> *And when the king heard Sir Blamore say his will, he understood well there was none other remedy but for to answer him knightly; for the custom was such in those days, that an any man were appealed of any treason or murder he should fight body for body.*

They mustered their retainers and well-wishers, a few loyal peers and many knights, and marched towards London to confront the King. Some three thousand men had massed at Royston with them by mid-May. Norfolk was said to be on his way. On 19 May Henry VI, then in Westminster, warned them that unless they disbanded they would be proclaimed to be traitors.

On the very same day, the court of King's Bench, also in Westminster, ordered that Sir Thomas Malory be delivered into the custody of the Keeper of the Tower of London 'to be held safely and securely'. There are no records of other prisoners being moved that week to the Tower, which was normally reserved for either high-ranking or politically dangerous prisoners. Had Malory made an attempt to escape again? Or did the powers around the King want to make sure that a knight of his reputation and fighting power was not added to York's supporters?

On 21 May Henry VI headed north to Leicester with thirteen peers, including Buckingham, Somerset, Northumberland, Clifford and Exeter, the Bishop of Carlisle and about two thousand men. They stayed overnight at Watford and then set off very early, hoping to avoid the Yorkists. On riding into the long high street of St Albans at 7 a.m. on Thursday 22 May, they found that they were coralled in a trap. York and his allies had already deployed their forces all around the town. Three hours of negotiations through heralds and letters began, with Buckingham as spokesman for the King. York wanted 'such as we accuse' to be delivered up to him. But such demands were an insult to Henry VI's royal dignity. He refused to be coerced, and Buckingham reminded York that the King's banner was flying: it was treason to attack. But York and Warwick had decided that their only hope was to eliminate Somerset – an undertaking they saw not as treason but as a chivalric imperative. They attacked.

The royal defences were soon breached, as the Yorkists had artillery and archers with them. Warwick's forces found a route through gardens and alleys that brought them out into the market place and into the presence of the King and Buckingham. One accidental arrow almost changed the course of history – it winged the King in the neck. A more determined assault was made on Buckingham, who was wounded in three places. Somerset, Northumberland and Clifford, prime targets, were all cut down in the town's narrow streets. 'And when the said lords were dead, the battle was ceased,' wrote one chronicler. The eventual death toll, about 120 men, was remarkably low.

Divinity still hedged the King, bleeding, battle-scarred and vulnerable though he was. York took Henry into St Albans Abbey for safety until the fighting was over. The victors all kneeled before him and swore that they were his humble liegemen. They had, they thought, accomplished their purpose: a *coup d'état* which restored them to the pre-eminence they deserved, and had enjoyed during Henry's illness. Henry was solemnly presented with his crown three days later in St Paul's, but it was York who handed it to him. Buckingham was released, but only under substantial bonds for good behaviour.

A parliament supportive but very suspicious of York assembled at Westminster on 9 July 1455. It officially exonerated the Duke and his allies by offering a special parliamentary pardon (dated 18 July) for all crimes committed before 9 July; unusually it gave immunity from prosecution by anybody at all, not just the Crown. On 24 July, sixty peers met as a great council during Parliament and swore an oath of loyalty to the King, and solemnly undertook to protect him. On the last day of the session, the King issued his own general pardon; this was limited, as usual, to offences against the Crown. York, Warwick, Salisbury and everybody else involved in the fighting at St Albans signed up for pardons over the next few months. Warwick regained the captaincy of Calais, and his uncle Lord Fauconberg was made Keeper of Windsor Castle, guardian in effect of the King. Other Nevilles were in attendance when the royal family moved to Hertford. York lodged with Salisbury at Ware and Warwick at Hunsdon with Sir William Oldhall. Proper courtesies were observed, but whether the Queen had the heart to disport herself hunting in the great park at Ware, we do not know. Within weeks Oldhall succeeded in getting his indictment overturned in the court of King's Bench, and Sir Walter Devereux and Thomas Young, both now MPs, successfully petitioned for the removal of any stain on their character.

York's victory had no immediate effect on Malory. Thomas Gower, the Keeper of the Tower, had produced him in court on 15 June, but because there were no jurors, his trial was postponed until 13 October, and Malory was again sent back to the Tower. Even if York had wanted him freed, it would have been very difficult for him to speed up the due process of the law for a relatively small fish. He had very limited influence over the royal judges or the Keeper of the Tower, and the new charges brought by the Essex authorities and Malory's armed and violent escape from Colchester Castle complicated the case. It is also possible that this and indeed earlier hearings were held without enough warning for Malory's well-wishers to help him. On 13 October 1455, Sir Thomas was produced in court again, only to find no jurors had turned up – hardly, perhaps, a surprise by then. The case was postponed until 27 January 1456, and he was remitted to the Tower again. This time the judge told the Keeper to hold him under penalty of £2,000 – a vast sum, and double the previous penalty. It sounds as if he had made yet another attempt to escape.

But within weeks, he was given hope. On 12 November 1455, the King, never strong since the confrontation at St Albans, was once more deemed to need guidance and help in the form of a Protector of the Realm, though this time Henry was sane enough to ask to be kept informed about matters 'affecting the honour, surety and worship of his person'. When Parliament reopened on 19 November, it made York Protector, sharing power, as before, with the council. This restored the legitimacy of York's position. Just a week later, on 24 November, Malory was allowed to sign up for the general pardon issued during the July Parliament. Perhaps friends in the newly assembled Parliament helped him to do so; Sir Leonard Hastings was now MP for Leicestershire and his son William Hastings was Sheriff of Warwickshire.

Hope Deferred

When Malory appeared in court on 6 February 1456 he asked for his case to be dismissed because he had been pardoned. He presented the formal 'letters patent' granting it. They recorded that the lord King 'from his own special grace and out of his own certain knowledge' pardoned him 'as far as was assigned by name in the pursuit of his peace which pertained to the King himself towards the same Thomas himself, for the felonies, transgressions, insurrections, extortions, oppressions and other offences' he had committed before 9 July 1455. The graceful words are formulaic pardon phrases, but they reflect the personal nature of government at this time. As one of the select body of men who had sat as knights of the shire, Malory was a known quantity to both the King and his council. The pardon was dated 24 November 1455. Malory also produced six men prepared to stand as sureties for his good behaviour. They were less eminent than on previous occasions. One was a kinsman, Roger Malory of Ruyton, Warwickshire. The others were Londoners: John Benford and William Cliff, both said to be gentlemen, Walter Boys, saddler, and Thomas Pulton and David John, tailors. Thomas Pulton was evidently a successful tailor: he held the manor of Desborough in Northmptonshire and was later one of Malory's feoffees; a man of the same name witnessed the June 1480 inquiry into the death of Malory's wife Lady Elizabeth in 1479.

But Malory could not rejoice in deliverance quite yet. He was sent back into custody, this time to the relative freedom of the Marshalsea, 'until sufficient securities be arranged'. This sounds as if the court wanted someone rather wealthier or more eminent to stand bail for him. Since the securities were to guarantee that Malory would keep the peace towards the Abbot of Coombe and indeed all the King's subjects, they may have once again been dauntingly high. At least there was no penalty attached to his custody, nor limit on his freedom to make use of the Marshal's escorting bastons.

Unfortunately for Malory, before better securities could be organised the political tide turned once again. York had made himself unpopular, not through perfidy but through probity. Pointing out that the King was 'indebted in such outrageous sums as be not easy to be paid', he had pushed for another Act of Resumption cancelling more over-generous grants of royal lands and annuities. He asked that the household granted to the Prince of Wales be reduced and a limit placed on the income of the Queen. The proposal, which would have meant disinheriting the King's Tudor half-brothers, lost York the already tepid support of the lords. Too many of them stood to lose too much. Henry had recovered enough by 25 February to appear in Parliament himself. With its approval, he dismissed York from the Protectorate. The proposed reforms were rejected.

For the next few years, Henry VI was officially said to be in good health. But he was rarely seen abroad, spending his time almost exclusively with his wife and son in Kenilworth and Coventry, a city which became known as 'the queen's secret harbour'. The political landscape was superficially tranquil. York was kept on the royal council, and Warwick, who had shown remarkable flair in the management of the Calais garrison and the keeping of the seas, remained Captain of Calais. But behind the scenes, York's enemies were regrouping and gathering strength. The Queen was understandably fearful for her baby son, aware that only he stood between York and the throne if Henry died. She fortified Kenilworth 'with cannon and other implements of war' and enlarged the loyal Lancastrian retinues attached to her own Duchy of Lancaster lands in the Midlands and the Prince's palatinate of Chester. She remained at the forefront of royal affairs, going alone to the Coventry Corpus Christi plays in May 1457, where she was treated with a ceremony normally reserved for the monarch himself. She accepted gifts from the corporation: three hundred loaves of fine white bread, a pipe of red wine, a dozen capons 'of haut grece', a dozen great fat pikes, a great panier of peascods and another panier full of pippins and oranges and two coffins of comfits and a pot of green ginger. Although he was well enough to attend a dinner given for him by the mayor and corporation on 16 August, Henry did not attend the plays but rode back the same day to Kenilworth 'to his bed'.

Margaret may well have had a hand in dictating the content of a great pageant laid on for the royal couple in Coventry. Instead of the usual Nine Worthies, there were ten: St Margaret was added to the pantheon. All the heroes and prophets emphasised the Queen's right to rule. Jeremiah's opening words were: 'Empress, queen, princess excellent, in one person all three', an acknowledgement that Margaret was currently the most active part of the regal godhead – the anointed, but now frail king, his infant heir and the more-than-capable Queen. Among those who organised the pageant was one 'Malory, Gentleman', no doubt a relation of Sir Thomas's. He could have used his kinsman's knowledge to advise on the coat of armour and 'crest with three grevyves' that the Coventry smiths made for the most important of the worthies, King Arthur, and the wording of King Arthur's speech:

> *Arthur, king crowned and conqueror,*
> *That in this land reigned right royally;*
> *With deeds of arms I slew the Emperor;*
> *The tribute of this rich realm I made down to lie –*
> *Yet unto [you], lady, obey I meekly,*
> *As your sure servant; pleasure to your highness,*
> *For the most pleasant princess mortal that is!*

It was soon to become apparent that the 'male journée' (evil day) of St Albans had left a terrible legacy. 'There was ever more a grouch and wrath had by the heirs of them that were slain'. Somerset's brother Edmund, the new Earl of Somerset, and the young sons of Northumberland and Clifford were intent on vengeance for their fathers' deaths. A blood feud ensued that was as bitter as that between the sons of King Lot of Orkney and Sir Lamorak de Galles and his kin in Malory's *Morte Darthur*.

> *Then Gawaine called privily in council all his brethren, and*
> *to them said thus: 'Fair brethren, here may ye see, whom*

that we hate King Arthur loveth, and whom that we love he
hateth. And wit ye well, my fair brethren, that this Sir Lamo-
rak will never love us, because we slew his father, King
Pellinore, for we deemed that he slew our father, King of
Orkney. And for the despite of Pellinore, Sir Lamorak did us
a shame to our mother, therefore I will be revenged.' 'Sir,'
said Sir Gawaine's brethren, 'let see how ye will or may be
revenged, and ye shall find us ready.' 'Well,' said Gawaine,
'hold you still and we shall espy our time.'

Enmities became open when complaints that York's followers
Devereux and Oldhall had attacked the forces of Jasper Tudor, Earl
of Richmond, in Wales, led to a new royal progress to administer the
King's justice in the Marches. Henry himself summoned justices from
London, and set out with them from Kenilworth. He sat in court in
Hereford for most of April 1457. The law courts reverted to severity
against Yorkist sympathisers unfortunate enough to fall into their
clutches.

The Debtor

Against this background, it is not surprising that Malory seems to
have remained in captivity. Before any wealthy friend could produce
the required extra securities, two brand-new charges, this time of
debt, were slapped down against him in 1456. The amounts were
trivial, but any unpaid debt could keep a man behind bars, nor did
his royal pardon cover a private suit for debt. The first accusation
against him was delivered on 28 June 1456 by Robert Overton, a
London mercer who made a practice of touring the London gaols
and lending money to prisoners at ruinous levels of interest. He
claimed that four years earlier, on 26 May 1452, Malory borrowed £3
from him. Malory, described as 'in custody of the Marshal', came to
court in person and denied it, saying that the signature on the bond
produced by Overton was not his writing. The court ordered the case
to be heard on 18 September, when Malory sent an attorney rather

than appearing himself, but no jury turned up and it was deferred to 31 January 1457.

Overton was an unsavoury character, often accused of false suit of debt. But there may have been deliberate malice in his accusation against Malory. On 15 June, eleven days before Overton's accusation, Sir William Peyto was committed to the Marshalsea to begin what would be three years' imprisonment because he had not paid the £60 damages pronounced as due to Malory's friend John Hathwyck in 1453. Among his Warwickshire associates was a certain William Overton of Brownsover, who could have been related to Robert Overton.

At some point in the summer or autumn of 1456, Malory was sent to Newgate Prison. It may have been more comfortable than the Marshalsea, as it had been rebuilt in the 1420s thanks to the charity of Sir Richard Whittington, the famous Lord Mayor of London. It had two large, well-lit common rooms as well as a chapel. A well-off knight like Sir Thomas Malory would have been housed in well-appointed lodgings, perhaps in the rooms reserved for privileged prisoners above the great gate tower itself, with the privilege of walking on the leads and looking out over the bustling city below. From there there were views north-west towards Clerkenwell and the Hospitallers' Priory of St John, south to the Earl of Warwick's great Inn, or east to the lofty steeple of Greyfriars, London's most fashionable church.

Political dissidents and rebels were often held in Newgate. Among Malory's fellow prisoners were Exeter's younger brother, Robert Holland, and his companion-in-mischief, Lord Egremont. It was also a debtors' prison, but Malory was not there because of Overton's accusation, which had not even come to court yet. Another conciliar writ had been issued 'of our Lord the King', ordering him to be detained until he provided sufficient securities to ensure the keeping of 'our peace and that of all our people and especially the Abbot of Combe and several others of our subjects', and 'for certain other reasons that particularly concern us'. Frustratingly, there is no clue as to what those 'other reasons' could be.

In view of Malory's impressive record of escapes, it is interesting that shortly after he arrived in Newgate, the prisoners attempted a mass breakout. Egremont bribed a warder to smuggle in weapons, something Malory must have done at Colchester. On the night of 13 November 1456, the two noble tearaways attacked the prison Keeper and freed as many other prisoners as possible – just like Malory's Sir Gaheris:

> *Anon withal Sir Gaheris threw the porter unto the ground and took the keys from him, and hastily he opened the prison door, and there he let out all the prisoners, and every man loosed other of their bonds.*

Holland and Egremont made off on the horses they had arranged to have waiting for them. The rest of the prisoners occupied the roof and fought all night before being recaptured. There is good reason to suspect that Malory was among them. Immediately afterwards, the Sheriff in charge of Newgate was removed and Malory himself was moved to Ludgate on the orders of Chief Justice Fortescue 'for more secure custody'. This time his gaoler was made liable to a £1,000 fine if he escaped.

On 24 January 1457 Fortescue, who seems to have now taken over guidance of Malory's case, ordered Malory to be moved from Ludgate, back to the Marshalsea. It is possible that this was an act of mercy. Ludgate, damp and overcrowded, did not get the renovation it desperately needed until 1463. A heartfelt and unusually personal passage in 'The Tale of Sir Tristram' reveals that at some point during his long incarceration, Malory grew seriously ill. 'Sickness is the greatest pain a prisoner may have,' he wrote.

> *For all the while a prisoner may have his health of body he may endure under the mercy of God and in hope of good deliverance; but when sickness toucheth a prisoner's body, then may a prisoner say all wealth is him bereft, and then he hath cause to wail and to weep. Right so did Sir Tristram when sickness had undertaken him, for then he took such sorrow that he had almost slain himself.*

Illness, perhaps following a wound incurred while attempting to escape, would explain why, when the Overton case came to court again on 31 January 1457, Malory sent an attorney rather than appearing in person. It was found that the sheriff had failed even to send a writ to summon jurors, and the case was postponed yet again, this time until 11 May 1457. On this date there were still no jurors and the case seems to have been dismissed.

But Malory's troubles were far from over. It is impossible not to conclude that his enemies were playing cat-and-mouse with him. On the very next day, 12 May 1457, a much tougher adversary than Overton stood up and asked for damages for non-payment of a debt: his old enemy, Thomas Greswold. Greswold claimed that Malory had borrowed £4 9s 8d in Westminster on 3 July 1456. That was just a week after Overton's matter. Perhaps Malory had urgently needed a lawyer to deal with the accusation. The date was not one of the days of the hearings, which suggests that Malory had been able to visit Westminster, perhaps under escort, and discuss his case with lawyers. Greswold said that the debt had been due for repayment at Christmas 1456, but nothing had been paid, 'despite many requests'. Again, it was Fortescue himself who sat on this superficially petty case. Malory admitted the debt, and damages of 3s 4d were awarded to Greswold. He was sent back to Ludgate Prison once again, pending payment of the debt and damages. Soon after Sir John Fortescue had passed sentence on Malory, he set off on a judicial progress to the West Country, where he would spend August passing sentence on the Earl of Devon's turbulent followers.

How altered the England of 1457 was from the triumphant nation of Henry V and the Duke of Bedford was cruelly exposed at the end of the summer. On 28 August 1457 Pierre de Brezé, the French Seneschal of Normandy, attacked the Kent coast port of Sandwich with sixty ships, some French, some Breton. Sixteen hundred men stormed and pillaged the town. De Brezé stayed at anchor in the Downs for several days before returning to Honfleur; the Bretons pillaged Fowey in Cornwall for good measure on their own way home. It was urgently necessary to strengthen the navy, and Warwick, described that year as 'the most courageous and manliest knight living', was the obvious man to do it. Early in October the King's council gave him command of a naval force and in December extended his commission as Keeper of the Seas for the next three years. He was required to recruit several thousand men for the navy and to strengthen Calais by adding three hundred men to its garrison. He returned to London for the Great Council that the King summoned on 12 October 'to set aside such variances as there be betwixt divers lords'.

At some point between May and October, Malory was restored to the relative comfort of the Marshalsea. For it was the Marshal who escorted him back to court on 19 October 1457, so that he could be bailed until St John's Day (28 December) by William Neville, Lord Fauconberg, William Brigham, esquire of Brigham, Yorkshire, and John Clerkson, esquire of Arundel, on sureties of £20 each and on Malory's own surety of £400.

Curiouser and curiouser. Although he had been sent back to prison in July until he settled a debt of less than £4, Malory was suddenly able to provide £400 in sureties – more than enough to satisfy the demands of the Abbot of Coombe and anyone else who was frightened of him. No further mention was made of the 'certain other reasons' that particularly concerned the King. And the man who sprang him from gaol was a renowned warrior: William, Lord Fauconberg, eighth son of the Earl of Westmorland, and so York's brother-in-law and Warwick's uncle. We can imagine the extraordinary scene in the court of King's Bench: the intimidated deputy justices twittering nervously on the dais, Malory, thin and pale between two of the Marshal's sergeants at the bar in front of them. And Fauconberg, resplendent in his baronial robes, and flanked by burly and warlike liveried retainers. After three solid years of imprisonment, three or four months in Newgate, three or four in Ludgate and the rest in the Marshalsea apart from eight months in the Tower, Sir Thomas Malory was a free man.

A Powerful Patron

*At Yule last he . . . gave to me horse and harness, and an
hundred pound in money; and if fortune be my friend, I
doubt not but to be well advanced and holpen by my liege
lord.*

Malory, 'The Tale of King Arthur and the Emperor Lucius'

arwick's need for reinforcements for the Calais garrison is
likely to have been the reason for Malory's release. Lord
Fauconberg was a pugnacious gamecock of a man who had
fought for many years in France until captured in 1449; one of York's
first actions as Protector was to enable him to pay his ransom. He
was now as grizzled with age as Malory and an adventurer after his
own heart. In July 1457 Warwick had asked him to serve as his deputy
in Calais, which Fauconberg agreed to do until December 1458. In
the autumn of 1457 he was looking for men to take with him across
the Channel. If he knew and liked Malory well enough to bail him
out of prison for ten weeks, he may have planned to keep him out
for longer. It would suit him well to hire the services of such a 'passing
good man of his hands', well-seasoned in sea battles, familiar with
Calais, fluent in French, and with known skills in information-
gathering and dissemination. For Malory, service at sea and at Calais
under Fauconberg would be an attractive and exciting alternative
to staying in England dodging his enemies. It would also give him
the opportunity of getting to know the formidable Earl of Warwick
better.

Malory seems to have spent his official freedom at home in
Warwickshire. If so, the Christmas of 1457 was the first he had spent

at Newbold Revel for four years. The Monks Kirby Priory accounts for the thirty-fifth year of Henry VI's reign (September 1457–August 1458) mention the Malory family three times. Sir Thomas himself paid the Priory 6d for the use of Hubbock's Mill, a watermill on the Smite Brook. Lady Elizabeth Malory and Thomas Roche paid the Priory eight shillings rent for some pastureland. The third record is a sad one: the payment of 2d for obsequies for 'Thomas Malory junior'. Obsequies, prayers for the dead, were usually said a week, a month and a year after a death. As only one payment is recorded, it is likely that Sir Thomas's son had died a year earlier. How old he was we can only guess. 'Junior' was used to distinguish adult sons from their fathers as well as for children.

Malory presented himself to the Marshal of the Marshalsea punctually on 28 December 1457. But during the next two years, there is an uncharacteristic silence over his case in the legal records. His whereabouts during 1458 are a complete mystery. He could simply have been immured in the Marshalsea totally incommunicado for two years, except for that short spell of Easter-time freedom. It would certainly have enabled him to write a great deal. But he had already spent at least four of the last six years in prison, ample time to write his Arthurian tales and quite a lot else.

Three developments suggest that Malory was in fact a free man: Fauconberg's interest in him; the death early in 1458 of his most relentless persecutor Thomas Greswold (who may have died of the plague that claimed the life of Buckingham's oldest son that year); and the character of the new Marshal appointed to the Marshalsea in 1457. William Brandon was a Framlingham man, a natural supporter of Norfolk and also known to be bribeable. If Fauconberg or Warwick tipped him the wink (to say nothing of a gold angel or two) he would have given Malory all the freedom he wanted. Brandon set Sir William Peyto free on 10 May 1459, much to the fury of John Hathwyck, who immediately applied for a judgement against Brandon for payment of Peyto's debt to him. Hathwyck's court case is the only reason we know that Brandon freed Peyto. Without Greswold to object, and with Buckingham busy about Queen Margaret's business in the Midlands, Malory could have slipped quietly away.

Suppose Brandon freed Malory early in 1458. He had certainly done so a year later, in April 1459, when there was a complaint, quite possibly by Buckingham, that Malory had been seen in Warwickshire. Brandon was sternly told to keep Malory in custody under penalty of £100 (a remarkably small figure in comparison with earlier penalties) and not to let him go at large at all. But the Controlment Roll did not say, as it normally did, that Malory was present, or whether Brandon succeeded in getting him back into custody. The next reference to Malory says he was transferred from the Marshalsea to Newgate some time in the Hilary term of 1460 (23 January–12 February), to be detained 'safely and securely'. Before then, he could have spent almost two years free as a bird – and have played his part in the dramatic events that put an altogether unexpected new king on the throne of England in 1461. The following narrative will show how he could have fitted into them.

The Calais Station

Fauconberg was said to be 'at Southampton with his navy' in early 1458. The Nevilles' call for sailors for their ships and soldiers for the Calais garrison gained an enthusiastic response. The chronicler Fabyan reported that 'men daily came thick to [the Calais lords] out of diverse parts of England'. The rest of this chapter will assume that Malory was among them, that he joined Fauconberg's navy at Southampton and set sail for Calais 'with great joy, and every'ch knew other; and so the wind arose, and drove them through the sea in a marvellous pace'. In Calais, Sir Thomas would have been delighted to find Warwick's Countess Anne Beauchamp, 'Lady Imagination' herself. The English fleet scoured the Channel to good effect, and raiding parties attacked both the French and the Flemish coast. The prizes and plunder it won helped to pay the garrison's expenses, which were considerable. It was the largest permanent force of English soldiers, ready at a moment's notice to be mobilised for war. The cost of paying their wages, and of victualling and maintaining the fortifications of Calais and its marches, was £20,000 a year. Officially, this was paid by the King, but in fact Warwick, like most lieutenants of Calais before him, footed a considerable part of the bill. He also hired Burgundian gunners to make much-needed improvements in the castle's artillery.

Fauconberg may have wanted Malory in Calais as a negotiator. Calais was more than an English bastion. Lying as it did on the edge of both French and Burgundian territory, it was a thriving trading entrepôt as well as an important forum of European espionage. English, French, Burgundian, Spanish, Scandinavian and Italian couriers passed through it, trading intelligence as energetically and expensively as its merchants dealt in cloth and wool. Its lieutenant was given a special allowance by the Exchequer for employing spies, as were the lieutenants of its satellite castles in the Calais marches, Guines, Mark and Oye.

Politically, England was still deeply unsettled. The Great Council summoned by the King in October 1457 had been poorly attended and had adjourned inconclusively on 29 November. It reassembled on 27 January 1458. Fauconberg stayed in Calais, but Warwick crossed to England with six hundred seasoned troopers, flamboyantly clad in red doublets embroidered with ragged staves. He was not the only lord to bring a threateningly large retinue with him. Exeter, Somerset, Northumberland, Egremont and Clifford had about 2,300 men in all, York and Salisbury 900. The Council was split into two armed camps, between which the few councillors held to be impartial moved to negotiate. Ambushes and brawls were frequent. But by the end of March all grievances had, miraculously, been settled. Those who had fought against the King at St Albans were accepted as faithful subjects. They promised to endow chantries for the souls of those killed and pay their families compensation – as Lancelot offered to do after he accidentally killed Gareth and Gaheris when he rescued Guinevere from the stake. After the council ended, there was a formal 'love day', an optimistic pageant of unity. Sworn enemies processed in symbolic pairings to celebrate mass in St Paul's Cathedral. The Queen walked with the Duke of York, Salisbury with young Somerset, and Warwick with Exeter. Henry VI, saintly peacemaker, crucial pawn, walked alone. Over the next three days, jousts were held near the Tower and at Greenwich. Tristram attempted just such a 'love day' with his uncle King Mark. It was no more successful than this one.

Warwick returned to the business of enhancing the English fleet and strengthening Calais. He was given command of the *Grace Dieu* in April; by then he had at least five ships 'of forecastle', three carvels and four pinnaces under his personal command; others were temporarily commandeered from the Cinque Ports of Kent and the pirate havens of the West Country. We can imagine Malory being involved in the magnificent action undertaken by the Nevilles' Kentish and Cornish privateers against twenty-two Spanish vessels, sixteen of them 'great ships of forecastle', on 28 May 1458. 'There has not been so great a battle upon the sea these forty winters,' wrote one of the mariners, John Jernigan, to a friend. Wildfire, an incendiary mixture of pitch in fiery balls which was hurled by catapults at enemy ships, was used in this action. Malory introduces its use in his 'Tale of Sir Tristram' when he describes King Baldwin's defence against the Saracen fleet.

> *And or it were day he let put wildfire in three of his own ships, and suddenly he pulled up the sail, and with the wind he made those ships to be driven among the navy of the Saracens. And to make short tale, those three ships set on fire all the ships, that none were saved.*

More controversially, Warwick's fleet attacked a fleet of Hanseatic League ships, towing a string of them into Southampton. There would soon be repercussions from this lucrative act of piracy against an English ally.

Malory could have made a most significant acquaintance in Calais. Most of the wool produced in England for export had to pass through the town. Among the London merchants there was William Caxton, who had not yet begun his career as a printer. He was then a successful mercer who spent a good deal of time in Bruges and the Low Countries. Commerce may not have been the only reason for Caxton's journeys. Warwick and York were plotting with such French malcontents as the Duke of Alençon in the hope of recovering Normandy; they also wanted an alliance with Burgundy against France. In May 1458 secret letters were being exchanged between Warwick and Duke

Philip of Burgundy. A safe-conduct to Bruges was issued at just that time to William Caxton and a certain Antoine de la Tour.

The foremost figure in negotiations official and unofficial was Sir John Wenlock, a Bedfordshire knight and a man who thrived on secrets. He had fought in the French wars, and had been at Gisors in 1430, shortly before Malory had held it. He also had family links with Sir Thomas: the niece of his second wife, Agnes Danvers, was married to Malory's nephew, George Burneby. Active in promoting Margaret of Anjou's marriage to Henry VI, and formerly her chamberlain, he was now a king's councillor, officially in Calais to approach Charles VII on behalf of Henry VI to negotiate a triple marriage alliance between three French princesses and Prince Edward, the five-year-old heir to the English throne, Edward, Earl of March, York's sixteen-year-old son and heir, and Henry Beaufort, the new Duke of Somerset, who was twenty-one. However, Wenlock was at this time more Warwick's man than Henry's, and before he approached the French King, he made a detour to Mons, where he met the Duke of Burgundy and offered the same three grooms to a trio of Burgundian brides. It was a proposal unlikely to find favour with Margaret of Anjou.

Malory was certainly involved with Wenlock later, in the 1460s. It would fit the known facts if he was already working for him in Calais – a go-between who was frighteningly easily expendable as his presence was distinctly unofficial. If so, he would have enjoyed meeting Duke Philip 'the Good' of Burgundy. Reputed to be 'trusty as fine gold and whole as an egg', Duke Philip identified strongly with King Arthur, regularly dressing up as the legendary king, and occasionally setting off on a solitary quest or retreating into a forest disguised as a hermit. Warwick visited the Duke at Bruges early in 1459 for a series of lavish banquets, jousts and hunts. He and his retinue admired the magnificent manuscripts in the library of the ducal palace, and passed the evening listening to the Duke's renowned minstrels.

Warwick made several visits to England during 1458 and 1459. In October 1458, he wrote from his Northamptonshire manor of Collyweston to ask the Duke of York if Walter Blount could be loaned to him to serve at Calais for a year. Did Malory prompt him to do so? Walter Blount was one of Sir Thomas's feoffees, and at about this time he took Richard Malory, one of those accused with Sir Thomas of attacking Coombe in 1451, into his service as his squire. Richard may well have travelled with him to Calais.

Rancour and Malice

Despite Warwick's achievements at Calais and at sea, and more amicable relations between the royal council at Westminster and the Nevilles, Queen Margaret remained adamantly hostile to anyone who might be identified as an ally of the hated Duke of York, especially if they were fighting successfully against France. Fauconberg was accused of piracy for the attack on the Spanish fleet in May 1458, and Sir Richard Woodville was appointed to inquire into the Calais fleet's 'piratical attack' on the Hanseatic salt fleet. Warwick returned to London on 9 November 1458 to answer the charges. While he was with the royal council, a riot broke out in Westminster Hall between his followers and members of the Queen's household. Hearing the cries, Warwick returned to the hall, and found himself under attack. Heavily outnumbered, he and his men had to fight for their lives against a rabble of bullying courtiers and brawny cooks armed with roasting spits and grinding pestles. They escaped by barge and returned first to Warwick and then to Calais. The experience shocked the young Earl. He harked back to it repeatedly, convinced it was an assassination attempt and incensed that no one was brought to book. The contemporary chronicler Fabyan recorded that 'the queen's council would have the said earl arrested and committed unto the Tower'. Because of the attack, he continued, 'the old rancour and malice, which never was clearly cured, anon began to break out'.

In February, Warwick's fleet captured three more Spanish warships and a Genoese carrack loaded with silks and spices. Then word came from England that a Great Council had been summoned to meet in Coventry in late June to indict the Yorkists on unspecified, but evidently treasonous crimes. The charges were 'of great rebuke' and made by 'those of right high estate', wrote the Prior of Arbury, near Coventry, in a letter to Salisbury in March 1459. Salisbury, who had hoped to be restored to the Queen's favour and had been using the Prior as an intermediary, expressed horror at the charges: 'I never imagined, thought, or said any such matter or anything like thereunto in my days'. He took the precaution of making a will a month later. Perhaps York's secret approaches to the Burgundians had been discovered. Perhaps the ever-growing rumours that the lively little Prince of Wales was a bastard were being laid at their door. Perhaps York was thought to be preparing another coup. All that was clear was that Queen Margaret had now succeeded in gaining enough political support to act against them.

A chronicler mentions that Fauconberg was in London in April 1459 calming a riot, so it is interesting that it was also during this month that the only sighting of Malory in England between December 1457 and January 1460 occurred. He was said to be in Warwickshire, visiting his family no doubt, but perhaps also gleaning information in Coventry about the intentions of the Queen and her Council. He will have heard that many men had received orders to meet the King at Leicester on 10 May, equipped for two months of military service, and that the garrison of the Tower of London had been enlarged and given extra arms.

Almost all records of the Coventry Council are lost. All we know is that it took place after 24 June 1459, and that York, Warwick, Salisbury, Arundel, Viscount Bourgchier, Archbishop Bourgchier (who had arbitrated on Malory's Caluden case), Bishop Grey of Ely and Warwick's brother, Bishop George Neville of Exeter, were indicted for their non-appearance 'by counsel of the queen'. Buckingham was York's chief accuser. The great Duke was riding high. He had just married his second son Henry to the Beaufort heiress Margaret and the unusually generous dower of £600 had been granted to the young couple. Buckingham pronounced York guilty as charged. But the King 'of his grace' remitted the punishment. In a carefully stage-managed gesture, Buckingham and the lords knelt before Henry and begged that this should be the very last time York was shown clemency. York, Warwick and Salisbury were then summoned before the Council, and solemnly pardoned. Then they swore new oaths of loyalty.

After this public humiliation, York returned to Ludlow, Salisbury to Middleham and Warwick to Calais. They were seething with fury against the Queen and her advisers. Anticipating new charges, they decided that their only hope was to make a representation to the King himself. To gain access to Henry it would be necessary to lobby from strength. Warwick promised to bring six hundred of the crack fighting troops of the Calais garrison men to Ludlow. Always an independent bunch, they took some persuasion. Disloyalty to a sovereign prince was abhorrent, and the captains demanded that Warwick swear on oath that he would not lead them against the King. Warwick left Fauconberg and the Countess Anne in charge of Calais. My guess is that Malory also stayed there, happy both to serve Richard Beauchamp's daughter and to be spared the dilemma of split loyalties that would soon face Warwick's retinue.

Warwick landed at Sandwich, swung through London on 20 September and headed for Warwickshire, hoping to join York and Salisbury there. But Salisbury, who had been advancing from Middleham, in Yorkshire, had been headed off by Henry VI's presence at Nottingham, and forces led by Somerset at Coleshill forced Warwick to continue on to Ludlow. On 23 September, Salisbury was intercepted at Blore Heath, near Newcastle-under-Lyme, by a royal army led by the courtier lords Audley and Dudley. Although outnumbered, the Yorkists won the brief but bloody battle that ensued. After Audley was killed and Dudley taken captive, the royal army retreated.

Soon after the Yorkist forces were united at Ludlow, a royal proclamation was issued from Leominster. Still anxious for reconciliation, Henry VI offered the Yorkist lords six days to take up a general pardon to all who would lay down their arms. However, Salisbury would be excepted from it, because of the deaths at Blore Heath. After this offer was rejected by York and his allies on the grounds that they meant no treason and were only armed in self-defence, the royal army headed for Ludlow.

When the royal standard was sighted, the men of the Calais garrison saw that both the King and the Queen were arrayed against them. The high treason of appearing in arms against their king was no part of their plan, and their captain, Andrew Trollope, led most of them across the lines to take up the offer of pardon. The number of noble banners which waved beside those of Henry, Margaret and Prince Edward, and the thinning ranks of their own men, emphasised the isolation of the lords in opposition. Realising the hopelessness of their situation, York, Warwick and Salisbury ordered their men to disperse as best they could. They left Ludlow to be sacked by the royal troops, and slipped away – York into Wales and then to Dublin, Warwick, Wenlock and Salisbury, and York's son and heir Edward, Earl of March, into Devon, from where they took ship to Calais.

In November 1459, a new parliament, held in Coventry, attainted the fugitive Yorkists. Even now Henry hoped for a reconciliation. There were very few executions after Ludlow: most of the rebels who submitted were indeed pardoned, though fined. The Queen and her faction had to step warily. York's vision of himself as the King's first minister had not been shared by the rest of lords, including his former allies, Norfolk and the Bourgchiers. But he was still free. Warwick was hugely popular in London and Kent, at Calais, and at the Burgundian court. The cause of reform at home and war against France was still attractive, especially among the gentry – knights and esquires eager both to improve justice at home and make their fortunes overseas.

Coup d'état

What of Malory? He will have been extremely uneasy at the idea of rebellion. One of the recurring motifs in the *Morte Darthur* is Lancelot's unswerving loyalty to Arthur, 'the king who made me knight'. Malory will have had the same kind of loyalty to Henry VI. My guess is that he found some sort of pretext to return to England and simply gave himself up to the Marshal of the Marshalsea. William Brandon had been sacked by Norfolk in the autumn of 1460 for allowing prisoners too much freedom. The new Marshal, Thomas Bourgchier, who was Norfolk's nephew, did not relish having such a troublesome prisoner in custody at such an uncertain political time. He hurried Malory straight into court and asked if he could be kept in a more secure prison. The final reference to Malory in the King's Bench records announced that on an unspecified day in the Hilary Term 1460 (23 January–12 February) Malory 'is committed to the custody of the Sheriff of Middlesex to be detained safely and securely' in Newgate Prison. It does not say that he was in the Marshalsea at the time of this committal, as it did on the previous occasion when he was moved to Newgate. 'Therefore the said Marshall is relieved of the responsibility for him here &c', the entry ends. One can almost hear Bourgchier's sigh of relief.

The Yorkist lords decided on the ultimate gamble. In February Warwick sailed from Calais to Waterford to plan future strategy with York, returning to Calais late in May. On 24 June he sent Fauconberg and John Dynham, a bold Devon squire, to secure Sandwich as a bridgehead for invasion, and two days later landed there with two thousand men, his father Salisbury, his uncle Fauconberg and his son Edward of March. As they advanced through Canterbury to London, supporters, including Lord Abergavenny and Lord Cobham, flocked to join them. Their army was said to be 20,000 strong by the time it reached Blackheath. On 1 July they entered London. Lord Scales, Lord Hungerford and their men retreated into the Tower. Warwick established himself in Blackfriars. At this point the London prisons were searched for Yorkist sympathisers. If Malory was still in prison, he could easily have been among those released. Was one of the conditions of their freedom that they should fight with the Neville peers?

> 'We be here twenty knights, prisoners,' said they, 'and some of us have lain here seven year, and some more and some less. Sir, said she, an ye will fight for my lord, ye shall be delivered out of prison, and else ye escape never with the life'.

If so, they must have been reassured to hear the Neville peers and Edward of March swear on the Canterbury Cross, the holiest relic in St Paul's Cathedral, that they were liegemen to King Henry, come to remedy 'misrule and mischief' and to refute in person before the King 'such false accusations laid against them'. Warwick left Wenlock, Salisbury and Fauconberg to lay siege to the Tower of London and headed north with the Earl of March. Malory could have played safe and stayed in London, or he could have ridden north with Warwick, in whose retinue he would certainly be numbered in 1462, for the most momentous battle of the decade.

Warwick later insisted that he had not wanted to resort to arms: all he wanted was to get into the King's presence and negotiate in person. But Buckingham told Warwick's herald that if the Earl approached the King, he would be killed. Battle stations were taken up on a curve of the River Nene. The short sharp struggle on 10 July that was later dignified as the Battle of Northampton was as surgically precise as the carefully controlled affray at St Albans in 1455. Warwick's victory was made the easier by the defection from the King of Lord Grey of Ruthin, who helped Warwick's men over the barriers on the royalist right wing. The chronicles record that Warwick ordered his men not to lay hands on the King or the common people, 'but only on the lords, knights and squires'. Only three hundred men were slain, and the King was respectfully taken into Warwick's safe-keeping. The young Earl of Shrewsbury, John Talbot, Thomas Percy, Lord Egremont, and John, Viscount Beaumont all died – sought out in their tents after the surrender and murdered in cold blood, said one rumour. But the most significant death for Malory's story was that of the Duke of Buckingham; at whose hand he died, history does not relate. For the first but not the last time Warwick, charismatic, daring and the toast of the common people, had England in his gift. Henry VI was treated as if he had been rescued, not captured. The King played along with the charade, comforted by the fact that his wife and son were safe in the North. After funeral rites for the fallen, the victors rode together to London – York's son Edward at the King's side, Warwick in front, holding the King's sword point uppermost.

On 22 July 1460, the Tower fell, and Lord Scales was dragged out and murdered by the mob. It had been without supplies of food for two weeks, but its defenders had firearms and machines to hurl wildfire. Warwick, who had studied the latest European developments in gunnery, had however brought siege artillery and Burgundian gunners over with him from Calais. A chronicle described how

They that were within the Tower cast wildfire to the city and shot in small guns, and burned and hurt men and women and children in the streets. And they of London laid great bombards on the further side of the Thames against the Tower and crased the walls in diverse places.

Malory's description of Mordred's siege of the Tower of London adds similar weapons to the siege engines mentioned in his source: 'And short tale to make, he laid a mighty siege about the Tower and made many assaults, and threw engines unto them and shot great guns'. Malory's addition could have been inspired by his own nightmare experience, whether in prison or free, of watching the 'noble knights of Merry England' bombarding one of their own king's palaces.

The memorandum of Malory's imprisonment in Newgate in the

Section from the King's Bench Controlment roll record of the legal proceedings against Malory (PRO KB29/83 m25d).

Hilary term of 1460 is the final line of the parchment record of his case in the King's Bench Controlment Roll. Early biographers concluded that he simply stayed in Newgate until he died. But newly discovered references to him as a free man early in the 1460s destroy that theory. A more careful look at a much earlier part of the Controlment Roll shows what really happened. Written in a tiny cramped hand between the lines is the Latin phrase that had liberated Sir William Oldhall: 'cartam allocatam sine die' and a date, Hilary 1455. In other words, the pardon Malory had proffered in 1455 had in the end been accepted, and Malory would not be required to appear in court again. The entry, in a new hand and in different ink, must be a later addition and is not dated. But it is evidence that the securities demanded in 1455 by Chief Justice Fortescue had been provided, or dismissed as unnecessary. A clue to when the line was added may lie in the fact that Coombe Abbey itself was called to account in the Michaelmas law term of 1460. All the lands of its abbot, Robert Hull, were distrained and Hull himself was summoned to appear at King's Bench between 20 and 26 January 1461 to answer the King 'concerning certain articles presented against' the Abbey. The case was evidently settled out of court. Had it not been, we might well know a great deal more about the reason that Sir Thomas Malory took his life in his hands and attacked Coombe ten years earlier.

'Well I wot that love is a great mistress'

Ten years of malevolent harassment were over. But what were they really all about? Even if Malory had committed the crimes of which he was accused, other knights had committed far worse misdemeanours, and their trials had been prompt. It was normal practice to convict and fine, not to imprison for indefinite lengths of time. Malory may well have been eager for reform in 1450, but he was not an obvious threat to the status quo. And time would show that, though he had to trim to the prevailing political wind for a while, his loyalty lay with Henry VI, 'the king who made him knight', as unwaveringly as a compass points north.

What really changed things for Malory was not the Yorkists' temporary triumph but the death of Buckingham. Somehow Sir Thomas had succeeded in mortally offending the proud Duke. If the issue had been a matter of property, the most usual bone of contention, there would have been evidence in the courts of claim and counter-claim. The secretive wording of the original writs and the trivial accusations that had been the stuff of the indictment until Malory's arrest incited him to commit the undeniably heinous sin of attacking Coombe Abbey suggest that his enemies had not wanted to reveal their real grievances against him. We know that he sat as an MP in two of the most obstreperous parliaments of Henry VI's reign, and that his writing skills were considerable. This was a time when a memorable rhyme attached to a few dozen carefully chosen church doors or a handbill posted up in market places and fairgrounds could affect public opinion dramatically. Circulating damaging evidence of corruption and malpractice in the royal household would be quite enough to make the court party want to muzzle him.

There is another possibility, also based on what we know of his character. My own inclination, given the fascination with women, especially strong-minded ones of high degree, so evident in the *Morte*, is to look to the lady. Bearing in mind the intensity with which Malory wrote about women, and remembering that the Duke of Buckingham or his cronies were always at the forefront of Malory's persecution, my guess is that Sir Thomas Malory's own personal Guinevere – or Belle Isolde – was Anne Neville, Duchess of Buckingham. He could first have seen her as a young wife in the English court at Rouen, when Buckingham acted so brutally towards Joan of Arc.

> 'It is pity,' said Sir Lamorak, 'that ever any such false knight-coward as King Mark is, should be matched with such a fair lady and good as La Beale Isoud is, for all the world of him speaketh shame, and of her worship that any queen may have.

In a coded version of *The Romance of the Rose* written by Sir Richard Roos for Margaret of Anjou's revels at her Greenwich palace of Pleasaunce, the Duchess of Buckingham's nickname is Dame Gladness. Anne Neville is known to have collected books, and her romantic nature is hinted at in a manuscript of Chaucer's *Troilus and Criseyde* now in the library of Corpus Christi College, Cambridge. 'Never forgetteth Anne Neville' is written in its margin. To whom she gave it we do not know.

If there had been an affair between Malory and Anne Neville, it may have been pure courtly love – the spur for Malory's insatiable fascination with the many and varied Arthurian romances, the reason why he so obviously dislikes the idea of Lancelot actually bedding Guinevere. But perhaps at some point in the second half of the 1440s when Malory came into association with the Duke of Suffolk, and through him, with Buckingham, the relationship with Anne became – or was believed by a suspicious husband to have become – something more. Buckingham's method of coping with such an unmentionable affront can then be seen to be both ruthless and subtle: piling shame upon shame on Malory and topping the accusations with the one which would most horrify his erring wife: the rape of Joan Smith. At some point during his imprisonment, Malory penned a heartfelt passage which could just have been intended as both self-exoneration and in part apology:

> 'And for this cause,' said Palomides: 'mine offence to you is not so great but that we may be friends. All that I have offended is and was for the love of La Beale Isoud. And as for her, I dare say she is peerless above all other ladies, and also I proffered her never no dishonour; and by her I have gotten the most part of my worship. And sithen I offended never as to her own person, and as for the offence that I have done, it was against your own person, and for that offence ye have given me this day many sad strokes, and some I have given you again; and now I dare say I felt never man of your might, nor so well breathed, but if it were Sir Lancelot du Lake; wherefore I require you, my lord, forgive me all that I have offended unto you.'

Being in favour with great ladies rather than great men would explain a good many of Malory's ups and downs. A woman's kinsmen might look sympathetically on a pleading sister, sister-in-law or aunt, especially if she is able to convince them that her unattractive ('fat and full of grease') husband has not in fact been cuckolded. Anne Neville was Fauconberg's sister, York's sister-in-law and Warwick's aunt. Rumours of such an affair would explain why Norfolk, married to Buckingham's sister, was so ambivalent in his support for Malory. But his wife's influence might have been more than countered by that of his mother, Katherine Neville. She was not only Anne's sister, but Dowager Duchess of Norfolk, and her huge jointure made her one of the wealthiest and most powerful women in England. Like the Ladies of the Lake in Malory's tales, the Neville sisters turn up time and again at times of political crisis. Over the next few years, they proved to be an extraordinarily influential cross-party network across the political scene.

This Sun of York

Musing upon the mutability
Of worldly change and great unstableness
& me remembering how great adversity
I have seen fall to men of high nobleness –
First wealth, and then again distress,
Now up, now down, as fortune turneth her wheel

Anon., *c.*1450

Malory was free of his enemies at last, and the cause of the Yorkists, lords of 'old ancestry of great might and strength' and 'the king's true liegemen', seemed to have triumphed. Henry VI was at last separated from his queen, the Yorkists' most dangerous but always necessarily unnamed enemy. For criticism of the Queen was as much treason as criticism of the King. A new parliament was summoned. Its records are incomplete; Malory could once again have sat as an MP. When it opened on 10 October 1460 in Westminster Hall, King Henry VI took pride of place, seated on his throne in full regalia. But then came a development which filled many Englishmen, especially those with as keen a sense of loyalty as Malory, with deep misgivings. York had set out early in September from Ireland and landed near Liverpool. Resplendent in his family livery of blue and silver marked with falcon and fetterlock, he progressed slowly through Chester, with fanfares of trumpets and sword borne before him point uppermost. It was a powerful piece of theatre, to all appearances a royal progress. As he journeyed south-eastwards to London, he engaged retainers in indentures which were not dated by King Henry VI's regnal year and omitted the usual reservation of each man's overriding allegiance to the King.

When the Duke of York arrived in London, the banner carried before him bore the royal arms pure and simple, unquartered, and without a label indicating a cadet line. The King was not there when he strode into Parliament. The fifty-nine-year-old Duke stood beside the empty throne 'and there under the cloth of estate standing, he gave them knowledge that he purposed not to lay down his sword but to challenge his right . . . and purposed that no man should deny the crown from his head'. He was claiming the throne. There was an awkward silence. Archbishop Bourgchier asked York if he wished to see the King. York's reply was ominous: 'I know no man in England who ought not rather come to see me than I go to him.' He took up residence in the royal apartments, and 'took upon him the rule of all manner of offices of that place'. Henry VI was taken to lesser rooms, where York's men guarded him. On Thursday 16 October York formally submitted to the Lords his superior claim to the throne by right of descent from Edward III's third son. 'Wherein all the lords present were greatly dismayed,' reported the chronicler Fabyan. Henry VI asked the peers to rule on the claim; they submitted it to the justices and the royal law officers who prudently declared that such a decision was 'beyond their learning'.

Malory must have been appalled. Reform had become revolution. Warwick and the rest of the Nevilles were equally unhappy about York's presumptuous action. They had only been as successful as they were through frequent repetition of the fact that they were the King's loyal subjects. They could not afford to alienate conservative allies like the Bourgchiers and Norfolk, or lose the respect they had gained from churchmen, essential and influential mouthpieces for launching propaganda campaigns at local level. Chroniclers record a furious argument between York and Warwick, and Margaret Paston wrote of 'great talking in this country of the desire of my lord of York', adding that 'the people report full worshipfully of my lord of Warwick'.

After a fortnight of discussion, Warwick engineered a compromise 'so that his fame is like to be of great memory'. On 31 October, Henry VI, after 'good and sad deliberation and advice had with all his Lords' and 'inspired with the grace of the Holy Ghost and in eschewing the effusion of Christian blood', made an announcement. He would be 'taken and reputed' to be King of England and France and Lord of Ireland during his natural life. But his successor would not be Prince Edward but York or his heirs. York would 'worship and honour' the King and swear not to 'abridge' his life. A week later York was made Protector for life, with authority to suppress rebellion in England (a reference to the armies Queen Margaret and her supporters were known to be gathering in the North) and to raise forces to fight against France and Scotland. The income from the lands of the disinherited Prince of Wales in Wales, Cornwall and Chester were assigned to York and his two oldest sons, Edward, Earl of March, and Edmund, Earl of Rutland.

The procession to St Paul's to mark this Act of Accord was carefully symbolic. Henry VI wore his crown, Warwick held the royal sword upright ahead of him, and the Earl of March carried his train. York rode sullenly alone, seething at the Londoners' shouts of loyalty to 'King Harry' – and their cheers for the Earl of Warwick. But he knew he needed the Nevilles. Salisbury became Lord Chamberlain. Warwick was Warden of the Cinque Ports, Keeper of the Seas and Governor of the Channel Islands as well as Captain of Calais. Of Warwick's brothers, Sir John Neville became steward of the royal household, and Bishop George Neville was Chancellor. Sir John Wenlock became Chief Butler, and Fauconberg and Blount Lieutenant and Treasurer of Calais. Viscount Bourgchier took up the treasurership he had held under York's last Protectorate; he was also made temporary Constable of the Tower. One of Bourgchier's first acts was to appoint Malory's cousin Robert as his lieutenant.

What did Malory think of this compromise? His profound respect for kingship and chivalry is a constant of his history of Arthur: he would certainly have been relieved that Warwick had succeeded in preserving Henry VI on the throne. Rumours that Prince Edward was a bastard made York's succession the more acceptable. If Malory knew them to be true – and his Arthurian tales show an almost obsessive interest in issues of disputed paternity and illegitimacy – it would have made him even more prepared to accept York as heir.

A Sign from God

The battle for England was not yet won. Although Norfolk and Suffolk had thrown in their lot with York and Warwick, Northumberland and the Percys stood solidly with the Queen, as did all York's old enemies. Margaret rallied her forces around the seven-year-old Prince of Wales in the north. Somerset, Exeter and Devon joined her there. On 2 December 1460, York and Salisbury set out to muster their own northern retainers in order to confront them. Edward of March headed for Wales to raise an army from his estates; with him went Wenlock. Warwick and Norfolk remained in London. Malory is best imagined in London, too, just possibly lending a hand in the composition of the flood of propaganda, both handbills and ballads, which was issued to justify the compromise solution. For a decade later we will find him in close association with one John Vale, whose carefully transcribed collection of contemporary letters, tracts and chronicles gives revealing insights into contemporary politics.

Early in January there was dramatic news from the North of a terrible defeat for the Yorkists. York and Salisbury had got no further than the Duke's great castle of Sandal, near Wakefield, by 20 December, when they heard that the Queen and Somerset were near by in Pontefract. Battle was inevitable, but a truce was called for Christmas. It was scarcely over, with many of York's men still on leave, when Somerset and Andrew Trollope advanced on Sandal. Rashly accepting Somerset's challenge despite being pitiably outnumbered, York sortied from the castle to attack. He was caught in a pincer movement 'like a fish in a net or a deer in a buckstall'. He fought, it was said, like a lion, but was killed. Two thousand or so of his men died in battle, including Warwick's brother, Thomas Neville. York's seventeen-year-old son, the Earl of Rutland, was among the dead. Some said he was stabbed as he tried to escape by Lord Clifford, still vengeful for the loss of his father at St Albans, and that as he struck the boy down he swore, 'By God's blood, your father slew mine, and so I thee and all thy kin'. Salisbury was captured and taken to Pontefract, where he was executed. His sixty-year-old head was stuck on a stake with those of the other fallen leaders. York's was mockingly topped with a paper crown. Rutland's apparent murder and the ignominies imposed on the dead leaders stood in stark contrast to the chivalric courtesy shown to worthy enemies in Malory's *Morte Darthur*. The savage blood feuds caused by the killings at St Albans in 1458 were rekindled.

Within a month, the disaster of Wakefield was balanced by news from the Welsh Marches of a great Yorkist victory. York's heir, Edward of March, had been about to head for London with William Herbert when he heard that Jasper Tudor, Earl of Pembroke, and James Ormond, Earl of Wiltshire, had landed in south Wales with a mixed army of Irish, Bretons and French soldiers. He turned south into Herefordshire to outflank them. The two armies met at Mortimer's Cross, near Wigmore, on 3 February 1461. The weather was exceptionally cold. As the sun rose on the morning of the day before the battle, two more blazing orbs appeared, one on each side of it. It was a rare phenomenon caused by ice crystals refracting light in the solar halo, known to scientists as a parhelion. 'The people were aghast' but for Edward it was a moment of epiphany.

> The noble earl Edward then comforted them and said, 'Be thee of good comfort and dreadeth not; this is good sign, for these three suns betoken the Father, Son and Holy Ghost, and therefore let us have good heart, and in the name of Almighty God go we against our enemies'. Anon fresh and manly he took the field against his enemies and put them to flight.

Edward, who now flamboyantly styled himself 'by the grace of God of England, France, and Ireland, true and just heir, Duke of York, Earl of March and Ulster', used a flaming sun as his badge ever after. Hence Shakespeare's famous pun: 'Now is the winter of our discontent / Made glorious summer by this sun of York'.

Three thousand men died at Mortimer's Cross. Jasper Tudor and James Ormond escaped into deepest Wales, but Jasper's father Owen, once the lover of Henry V's French queen Catherine, was executed. Somebody loved him still: the chronicles all mention a 'mad woman' who took his severed head, washed it and combed his hair, and placed it on the top step of the market cross with a hundred candles burning around it.

'Now is this realm wholly mischieved'

Queen Margaret was already advancing on London with 80,000 Welshmen, Scots, French mercenaries and northerners. These 'misruled and outrageous men of the north' were reported to be pillaging and plundering viciously as they headed south down the Great North Road. Grantham, Stamford, Peterborough, Royston and many other towns, monasteries and villages were sacked. Fear of Margaret's wild army did more than anything else to keep the south loyal to Warwick.

Wenlock returned from Edward's army to London. On 8 February, Henry VI made him a Knight of the Garter along with Warwick, Lord Bonville and Sir Thomas Kyriel. The King will have hoped that the oaths they swore would remind them of their duty of loyalty. On 12 February, Warwick and Norfolk led the army out of London and entrenched their forces to the east of St Albans with a formidable line-up of artillery. With them was Henry himself, the essential symbol of their legitimacy. But the Lancastrians arrived unexpectedly soon, reaching St Albans from the west by night on 17 February. They came through the town and attacked Warwick's army on its vulnerable right flank. The desertion of a band of Kentish men increased the confusion, which was made worse by the noise and smoke of the Burgundian guns. Warwick was forced to withdraw – leaving the King as a prize for the victors.

How Henry VI felt at being restored to the bosom of his own intransigent family we do not know. Oddly, he did not take personal command. Instead, he knighted the eight-year-old Prince Edward and announced him to be Commander-in-Chief of the army. Resplendent in a suit of armour covered with purple velvet and 'i-beat with goldsmith's work', the young Prince knighted thirty other stalwarts, including the intrepid Trollope. He then presided over a court which condemned Kyriel and Bonville to death, even though Henry himself had promised them mercy, and watched, at his mother's side, as the two Garter knights were formally degraded, their spurs broken, their coats of arms torn into four, and they were beheaded.

If Margaret had moved decisively at this point, she could have entered London in triumph. But she wavered, perhaps infected by Henry's havering, and also aware that the city would be as ruthlessly pillaged as St Albans had been by her notoriously wild northerner army. Desperate to protect his city, the Mayor of London sent a message promising her money and food and saying that London would be opened to the royal army if guarantees were given that it would not be pillaged. Interestingly, it was women rather than men who carried the message to the Queen, a remarkable trio of high-born dowagers: Jacquetta of Luxembourg, Dowager Duchess of Bedford, Ismania, widow of Lord Scales, and Anne Neville, Dowager Duchess of Buckingham. Margaret agreed. When the Mayor announced that the royal army was coming, there was widespread panic. Cecily Neville, Dowager Duchess of York, who was also in the city, took the precaution of putting her two youngest sons George and Richard on a ship bound for Burgundy. Then came word of another advancing army. Warwick and Edward of York had joined forces in Oxfordshire. Margaret withdrew northwards, taking the King with her. She was right to retreat. Possession of Henry's person was vital to victory, and it would have been foolhardy to risk it in an attempt to take London, whose citizens were known to be determined to defend themselves, when Warwick and York were advancing rapidly from the west.

On 27 February London flung open the city gates to Warwick and Edward of York. They now faced stark choices. Submit to the pardon still promised by their most Christian and ever-forgiving sovereign King, only to be double-crossed by the Queen and Somerset? Flee into exile? Or take the awful step of usurpation that they had firmly rejected when Edward's father Richard had attempted it? Death or life? Was the parhelion – three suns so dazzling that they appeared to be shining through three crowns – a sign from God of Edward's right to the three crowns of England, Ireland and France? After two days of talks, a mass meeting of soldiers, retainers and Londoners was summoned in St John's Fields, Clerkenwell. The Chancellor, George Neville, addressed them and declared that as Henry had reneged on the Act of Accord, Edward was now the rightful King. With 'tumultuary recognition' they agreed, and the captains sped to Baynard's Castle, to ask him to accept the crown.

On 3 March 1461, Archbishop Bourgchier, George Neville and a few other senior clergy, together with Norfolk, Suffolk, Warwick and what lords they could summon, agreed in council that Edward of York should be made king. Next day the tall, leonine nineteen-year-old went to Westminster Hall, seated himself on the throne and explained his title again, to general cheers and acclaim. He was then taken into the Abbey where, in front of huge and enthusiastic crowds, the lords spiritual presented him with the crown and sceptre.

Swept along by the tide of events, Malory had no choice but to cheer as well. He could only have approved of Edward's coronation speech condemning the lawlessness and cruelty 'worse than that shown by the Turks' that had marred the last decade of Henry VI's reign. Edward's words echoed again the orders Malory had heard Henry V issue when he arrived in France and the oath that King Arthur made his knights swear when they joined the fellowship of the Round Table. No person, he commanded, on pain of death, should rob or spoil any church or person of the church, or deflower any woman, whether wife, maiden or widow.

Most of the machinery of government established under York's last Protectorate remained in place, but Chief Justice Fortescue, before whom Malory had so often appeared in court, immediately gave up his post. He, more than anyone, knew that the Yorkists were now on very dubious legal ground. He slipped north to join Henry and Margaret. His departure, and some new appointments of the royal judges, probably made it easier for Malory finally to close the book on his long legal ordeal.

The Battle of Towton

The new King ordered the array of all able-bodied men between sixteen and sixty. In the first week of March Norfolk left London to raise troops in East Anglia and Warwick set off 'with a great puissance' to raise troops in the Midlands. Malory, for all his age, is likely to have been summoned to ride with him; we know he responded to just such a call a year later. Many other older men rallied to their liege lords' banners, and if Malory could raise a hundred men for an attack on Coombe, he could do so again to fight for Warwick and Norfolk. Newbold Revel would have been the scene of frantic activity: burnishing of armour, shoeing of horses, making of arrows and bows. His son Robert was now about twelve, old enough to be a page to his father. But Malory would not have wanted him to risk his life in so doubtful a cause. Although he had no choice but to answer a summons to battle, he is likely to have been sick with regret. One of the most personal and heartfelt passages in the *Morte Darthur* is the rebuke to his own age that he inserts after his description of England's acceptance of Mordred's usurpation of King Arthur's throne.

> *Thus was Sir Arthur depraved, and evil said of. And many there were that King Arthur had made up of nought, and given them lands, might not then say him a good word. Lo ye all Englishmen, see ye not what a mischief here was! for he that was the most king and knight of the world, and most loved the fellowship of noble knights, and by him they were all upholden, now might not these Englishmen hold them content with him. Lo thus was the old custom and usage of this land; and also men say that we of this land have not yet lost nor forgotten that custom and usage. Alas, this is a great default of us Englishmen, for there may no thing please us no term.*

On 11 March Fauconberg left London with the footmen of the army and two days later Edward himself headed north via Cambridge with an ever-growing army, including a Burgundian contingent under the banner of the French Dauphin. His captains continued to recruit all along the way, a task made easier by the devastation wreaked by the passage of Queen Margaret's army. Edward joined forces with Warwick shortly after crossing the Trent. Word came that Norfolk and his men were on their way, but they advanced without waiting for him, reaching Pontefract on the morning of Friday 27 March 1461.

The Lancastrian army, commanded by Somerset, had taken up a position on the plateau between the villages of Towton and Saxton. It was fifteen miles south-west of York, where Henry VI, Queen Margaret and Prince Edward were ensconced in the castle. Warwick advanced with a small band of men and, after a difficult crossing of the River Aire at Ferrybridge (the bridge had been destroyed by the Lancastrians), established a fortified camp. It was attacked at dawn by a large force led by Sir John Clifford. Warwick, wounded in the leg, had to retreat across the river again. He was hauntingly close to Pontefract, where his father had been murdered three months earlier.

Next day Edward also advanced, and the river was crossed successfully. The entire Yorkist force of 36,000 camped just south of Saxton. It was bitterly cold, and food was in short supply. The army they faced in the dark through a blizzard of snow before the dawn of Palm Sunday, 29 March 1461, was 40,000 strong, and headed by a formidable number of knights and peers, among them Somerset, Exeter and the Earls of Northumberland, Shrewsbury, Devon and Wiltshire. With the Yorkists were the Earls of Worcester and Essex, Lord Grey of Ruthin, Lord Scrope of Bolton, Lord Grey of Wilton and Lord Abergavenny. Norfolk was still on the Great North Road.

For four hours the armies confronted each other uneasily. Veterans of the French wars were to the fore. Trollope held the Lancastrian vanguard with Northumberland, the middle was under Lord Dacre and the rear commanded by Exeter and Somerset. Fauconberg commanded the Yorkist vanguard, Warwick the middle ranks and Edward the rear. Also in the Yorkist army were Sir Walter Blount, Sir Walter Devereux, Sir Robert Harcourt and Sir John Wenlock.

The bells of York Minster were still sounding the strokes of nine o'clock in the morning when the wind changed direction. It was a slight but significant advantage, extending the range of the Yorkists' arrows, and Fauconberg ordered his archers forward. Volley after volley was fired into the packed ranks of Lancastrians, whose arrows, fired into the wind, fell short. As Fauconberg's archers advanced they used these arrows as ammunition. Somerset had no choice but to order an advance. The sheer weight of their numbers almost overwhelmed the Yorkist front line, but Warwick himself had made his way to its most strongly attacked point. It held. Edward rode up and down behind the line, dismounting and fighting on foot wherever it faltered. Six foot three in his own right, with his crested helmet, he stood almost eight foot tall, a young giant who seemed the living reincarnation of his great-great-grandfather, the revered Edward III. Legitimate or not, he was a king to win men's hearts and minds, very different from Henry VI, the mild-minded man who put his faith in prayer rather than action and, it was said, sat out the battle in York, sitting under a tree, singing hymns.

As the hours passed, the heaps of bodies rose, ghastly human ramparts that had to be clambered over to maintain the attack. Then came a flank attack by the Lancastrians, the same unconventional manoeuvre that had paid off so handsomely for them at St Albans. A body of mounted lancers careered out of Castle Hill Wood into the left flank of the Yorkist battle line. 'All the while it snew', a chronicle tells us, 'the blood of the slain, mingling with the snow . . . ran down into the furrows and ditches, in a most shocking manner, for a distance of two or three miles.'

At last Norfolk's forces arrived. Fresh and eager, they carved into the Lancastrian flank at the opposite end of the line. Within an hour, as the winter sun slipped below the horizon, the Lancastrian line had broken and their army turned to flee. The right flank had no option but to strike down a lethally steep, slushy slope to the freezing waters of the fast-running Cock Beck. Hundreds of the heavily armoured men were drowned, or trampled to death by those behind pressing to escape. The heaped corpses were so thick that they formed a bridge across the stream. The Cock Beck was not the only obstacle to retreat: the River Wharfe, soon flowing red with blood, claimed just as many if not more lives. More than 28,000 men died at Towton, the largest ever loss of life in a single battle on English soil. The equivalent proportion of today's population would be a death toll of around a million. To this day the battlefield is known as Bloody Meadow.

Towton was easily the most horrific battle to take place in England in Malory's lifetime. When he told the equally terrible tale of the 'Last Battle' between King Arthur and the usurper Mordred, he seems to have had Towton in mind. Although all other sources describe Arthur and Mordred as charging each other on horseback, Malory says they fought on foot.

> Then the king gat his spear in both his hands, and ran toward Sir Mordred, crying: 'Traitor, now is thy death-day come!' And when Sir Mordred heard King Arthur, he ran unto him with his sword drawn in his hand. And there King Arthur smote Sir Mordred under the shield, with a foin of his spear, through out the body, more than a fathom.

At Towton the commanders were also described as dismounting and fighting 'like common soldiers', and the battle lasted, as Malory tells us Arthur's did, from dawn to nightfall.

> And thus they fought all the long day and never stinted till the noble knights were laid to the cold earth, and ever they fought still till it was near night, and by that time was there an hundred thousand laid dead upon the down.

In the aftermath of Arthur's battle, the few survivors hear cries from the battlefield.

> 'Now go thou, Sir Lucan,' said the king, 'and do me to wit what betokens that noise in the field.' So Sir Lucan departed, for he was grievously wounded in many places. And so as he rode, he saw and hearkened by the moonlight how that pillagers and robbers were come into the field to pillage and to rob many a full noble knight of brooches, and bees and of many a good ring, and of many a rich jewel, and who that were not dead all out, there they slew them for their harness and their riches.

The moon was close to being full on the night after the battle of Towton, and chroniclers described the midnight pillaging of the dead and the murder of the wounded that followed it. Archaeologists excavating the site and its environs confirm that the bodies had been ignominiously stripped before being tumbled into mass graves. In both the legendary realm of Arthur and the real one of Malory's England, such cruel plunder was forbidden. Henry V explicitly forbade it when he was on campaign, and in his earlier battle against the Emperor of the Romans, King Arthur had the bodies of the fallen inspected 'and did so bury them that were slain of his retinue, every man according to his estate and degree'.

There are marked differences between the two battles as well as similarities. Malory places the battle on Salisbury Plain and there is no mention of the thick snow that fell at Towton. And most of the Arthurian combatants charged each other on horseback. Malory would of course have seen it as absurd to transpose any of the battles he fought into his Arthurian histories. But it is easy to believe that the slaughter at Towton was etched deep in his memory and surfaced when he came to write of Arthur's nemesis.

'And so anon was the coronation made'

On 27 June 1461, Edward IV was crowned in Westminster Abbey, with marvellous pageants, ovations and joustings. He distributed honours to his followers. His brothers George and Richard were given the dukedoms of Clarence and Gloucester. Many of Malory's friends were rewarded. Walter Blount was made a Knight of the Bath before he returned to Calais. Sir John Wenlock became Lord Wenlock of Someries, and Viscount Bourgchier Earl of Essex. Sir William Hastings, the Warwickshire Sheriff during whose term of office Malory gained his 1455 pardon, became Lord Hastings and was given the key post of King's Chamberlain.

Most generous of all was Edward's treatment of the Nevilles. All were lavishly endowed with estates forfeited by Lancastrians. Fauconberg was made Earl of Kent and Keeper of the King's Falcons. Sir John Neville became Lord Montagu, and George Neville, already Chancellor, would be made Archbishop of York in 1465. Warwick became Lieutenant of the North and Admiral of England. He was given confirmation of all offices he had previously held, including the captaincy of Calais, and full possession of his Beauchamp and Despenser inheritances. He was now the wealthiest man in England, with an annual income of about £12,000.

On 12 August, Edward IV set off to inspire the men of the south with his splendid person. He processed through Kent and Sussex, then westwards to Bristol to review his fleet and watch a gorgeous pageant of St George slaying a dragon. He then headed north to Ludlow by way of Gloucester. On 29 September he processed through Birmingham. At Christmas, he was back in London and on 7 January 1462 he graciously announced a general pardon as a New Year gift to the nation. The pardons were taken out by faithful allies and former enemies alike. Fauconberg bought one on 5 March; the stoutly Lancastrian Sir William Feilding, whose Newnham Paddox manor adjoined Newbold Revel, acquired his in February.

On 24 October 1462 the pardon of Sir Thomas Malory of Newbold Revel for forgiveness of any real or imagined crimes was inscribed on the official roll. He could now begin life again with a clean slate. Confirmation of his restored respectability lies in a chancery record for the Michaelmas term of 1462 (9 October–29 November). It recorded that 'Thomas Malorre, knight', Thomas Walsh (who had evidently abandoned the Lancastrian cause) and Philip Dand (perhaps a lawyer) gave £2 6s 8d 'for licence to agree with Robert, son of Thomas Malorre and Elisabeth his wife, in a plea of covenant of messuages [i.e. houses] and 12.5 virgates [approximately 500 acres] of land, a watermill etc in Winwick'. This is a licence for a final concord, giving formal recognition to such agreed legal arrangements as conveyances, marriage settlements and entails, so that they could be enforced at law.

It sounds as if Malory's fourteen-year-old son Robert was getting married and that his wedding present from his father was the manor of Winwick. Dand and Walsh were feoffees for the Malory estates. The agreement may have been connected with the departure of the novice Knight Hospitaller John Malory, in all likelihood an older son of Sir Thomas, to Rhodes at about this time. Robert was by now the heir to Malory's estates. Any local family would welcome an alliance with him. But all we know about his wife is that her name was, like Lady Malory's, Elizabeth.

On Campaign in the North

A new adventure now faced Malory. Despite the four-month truce with Scotland, which Warwick had negotiated in May 1462, the North was still a distinct threat. Queen Margaret had succeeded in winning the new King of France, Louis XI, as an ally by promising to cede Calais to him if he helped her to restore her husband to the English throne. In mid-October 1462 she returned with a fleet of forty ships and eight hundred French men-at-arms led by Pierre de Brezé. They picked up Henry VI and Somerset from Scotland and landed in Northumberland, supported by Scottish troops and Lancastrian loyalists. Like dominoes, the coastal fortresses of Alnwick, Bamborough, Dunstanborough and Warkworth toppled into their hands. Edward decided to head north with 'a mighty power'. Like Malory's King Arthur, he

> sent letters and writs throughout all England, both in the length and the breadth, for to as summon all his knights. And so unto [him] drew many knights, dukes, and earls, so that he had a great host.

A short chronicle written at Ely ends in late 1462 with a list of the commanders of Edward's army. It was a splendid roll-call. The peers included Warwick, Fauconberg, Wenlock, Grey of Ruthin, Grey of Codnor, Ferrers of Chartley, Sir Walter Blount, and the new Duke of Norfolk, as well as the Duke of Suffolk and the Earls of Arundel, Shrewsbury, Worcester, Westmorland and Essex – and Sir Richard Woodville, now Lord Rivers.

Among the fifty-nine knights listed after the peers were Sir Thomas Malory, his old friend Sir Robert Harcourt and the redoubtable jouster Sir John Astley. All brought squires, archers and men-at-arms. Numbers were further swelled by the fighting men who had never left the north, and others who arrived by sea. Edward IV himself sailed from Kingston-on-Hull and reached Durham by 30 November, only to be ignobly laid low by an attack of measles. Henry VI and Queen Margaret and their French army were in even direr straits.

Caught at sea in a storm, several of their ships were wrecked. Four hundred French soldiers were forced to land at Lindisfarne, to be killed or captured by the locals. The royal family and Brezé were rescued by a fishing boat, which took them to Scotland.

Warwick and his knights established their headquarters at Warkworth Castle, three miles from Alnwick. Norfolk joined them there with supplies and siege artillery, which he had brought from Newcastle. With him were Sir William Pecche and Sir Robert Chamberlain, son of Malory's friend Sir Roger Chamberlain. It was evidently a good opportunity for networking. Young John Paston, who was too insignificant to be listed by the Ely chronicler, but who must have ridden with Norfolk, wrote excitedly home that

> I am well acquainted with my Lord Hastings and my Lord Dacres which be now greatest about the King's person, and also I am well acquainted with the younger Mortimer and Ferrers, Hawte, Harpor, Crowmer and Boswell of the King's house.

Although the Scots were expected to arrive within a week, Paston doubts if they will, and even if they did 'we have people enough here' and 'ordnance enough' for both sieges and a battle in the field. He also wishes his family a merry Christmas. 'Make as merry as you can, for there is no jeopardy yet'. Paston's letter goes on to make it clear that it was not so much Yorkist enthusiasm as self-preservation that brought so many southerners north in the train of the King.

> Yelverton and Jenney are likely to be greatly punished, because they came not hither to the king. They are marked well enough, and so is John Billingforth and Thomas Playter, wherefore I am right sorry. I pray you let them have witting thereof that they may purvey their excuses in haste, so that the King may have knowledge why that they came not to him.

Paston asks for money to be sent to pay his soldiers their wages, as no one is being allowed leave, and anyone who 'steals away' is in danger of being 'sharply punished'.

Evidently, support for Edward IV was not negotiable. Malory's presence in the north did not necessarily mean that he was heart and soul Edward IV's man. 'Then came King Arthur with Sir Gawaine with an huge host, and laid a siege all about Joyous Gard', he wrote in his 'Tale of Lancelot and Guinevere'. That battle too was a confrontation between forces that ought to have been united. It may have been significant that when he describes Lancelot's later burial at Joyous Gard he says that the citadel was one of the much-disputed Northumbrian castles. 'Some men say it was Alnwick, and some men say it was Bamborough'.

King Arthur's siege of Joyous Gard lasted for fifteen weeks before Lancelot unwillingly sallied out to fight. King Edward only had to wait a month for Alnwick, Bamborough and Dunstanborough to capitulate. Queen Margaret and Henry VI escaped to Scotland, but Somerset, Jasper Tudor, Lord Roos and many other Lancastrians were captured. There were few notable Yorkist casualties, but on 9 January Fauconberg died at Durham. We can imagine that Malory would have deeply mourned the man who had been such a trusty friend to him in adversity.

Edward was determined to unite the nation behind him. He used the vast patronage now at his disposal with discrimination, strengthening loyal lords in the regions (Hastings in the east Midlands, Herbert, who was made Earl of Pembroke, in the Welsh Marches, and Howard in East Anglia), but not being over-generous with courtiers and councillors. He tried hard to win Lancastrian hearts and minds. He offered to restore Somerset to his estates if he would swear allegiance to him. Somerset accepted and was pardoned. Edward took him on hunting trips and arranged a tournament at Westminster in March 1463 so that 'he might see some manner sport of chivalry after his great labour and heaviness'. Somerset was nervous at first, wondering no doubt if one of his many enemies would use the opportunity to despatch him, but 'the king prayed him to be merry and sent him a token'. It is not far-fetched to imagine Sir Thomas Malory, if not competing himself, at least looking on. The Lancastrian cause must have seemed utterly lost as he watched Somerset, Henry VI's Commander-in-Chief and closest friend, gallop into the lists 'full justly and merrily', his helm 'a sorry hat of straw'. Tilting helms were topped with magnificent but ephemeral facsimiles of family crests, woven from straw and brightly painted and gilded. Somerset's had evidently received 'many great buffets'.

Although hopeful that he now had Somerset's loyalty, Edward took the precaution of keeping the Duke's brother Edmund Beaufort a prisoner in the Tower. One pound a week for his maintenance was paid to Malory's cousin Robert, still its Lieutenant under the new Constable, John Tiptoft, Earl of Worcester. Robert, who we first came across as a member of the Tower garrison under Sir Richard Woodville in 1425, must now, like his more famous kinsman Sir Thomas, have been about sixty. His long experience was an invaluable asset.

In late May 1463 the North was, however, yet again under threat. Sir Ralph Percy had reneged on his allegiance to Edward and ceded Bamborough and Dunstanborough to the Lancastrians, and Sir Ralph Grey had surrendered Alnwick. Valiant old Sir John Astley was captured and taken to France where he remained a captive for three years. Warwick immediately headed north. There is no record of Malory being with him, but no lists of the royal retinue survive. Edward IV commandeered ships in London and the Cinque Ports to scour the northern seas for French ships bringing aid to the Lancastrians, and set off northwards himself. But before he had even arrived, Warwick and Sir John Neville had frightened off the combined Franco–Scottish–Lancastrian force 'garnished with great artillery' that had set out from Berwick on 26 July. The Nevilles pursued them fifty miles or more into Scotland, wasting the countryside, destroying fortresses and acquiring a great many prisoners. The Scots agreed to treat for peace. Queen Margaret, Prince Edward and a loyal band of followers (including Sir Richard Roos, Sir John Fortescue and Edmund Mountfort) set sail for Flanders, eventually finding sanctuary in the Queen's father's castle of Koeur in Lorraine. On 9 December, Warwick signed a ten-month truce with the Scots and headed south to report to Edward.

But four months later the north rose yet again. Henry VI had remained in Scotland. In March 1464 Somerset abandoned his feigned allegiance, raised troops in north Wales, and headed to meet his sovereign lord, Henry VI, in Northumberland. Sir Ralph Grey, whom Edward had made Commander of Bamborough, did the same. The Nevilles were ready for them. There were two brief and bloody battles, one on 25 April at Hedgeley Moor and one on 15 May near Hexham. Seventeen notable Lancastrians were executed – including Somerset. Edward then watched with satisfaction as his 'great guns', 'Dijon', 'London' and 'Newcastle', made rubble of the walls of Bamborough Castle. After Bamborough surrendered, Sir Ralph Grey was publicly degraded of knighthood and executed, a cruel charade intended to warn other feigned loyalists that dishonour as well as death faced them if they did the same. Henry VI himself eluded the victors. In all probability it was Sir Humphrey Neville, a scion of the senior branch of the Neville family which was as hot for Lancaster as Warwick and his relations were for York, who spirited the once – and future – King from his refuge in Bywell Castle. He left behind only a coroneted headpiece, a 'bycocket' trimmed with 'two crowns of gold and fret with pearls and rich stones'.

Princepleaser

I pray you be wary of your guiding, and in chief of your language, so that from henceforth by your language no man may perceive that you favour any person contrary to the king's pleasure.

John Paston

here are good reasons for thinking that after Malory returned from the North he lived in London rather than the Midlands. His name is almost entirely absent from Warwickshire records. Perhaps there was little there to attract him. Warwick was constantly on the move, and held court only rarely at Warwick Castle. Malory's son Robert and his wife were managing Winwick competently. During the 1450s Lady Elizabeth had got used to running Newbold Revel and Swinford on her own. If a grand passion did lie behind Malory's persecution, she may have preferred him to be away. Did plaintive letters arrive from her, like the one sent to London in 1468 by Jane Topps, a wealthy Norwich widow who was unhappily married to the philandering court poet Sir Richard Roos?

The cause of my writing to you at this time is this marvelling sore that it liketh you neither to come hither nor to send word. For now I know for certain that it is your pleasure to put me to pain and disworship . . . But though it liketh you not to remember me, you might remember the children the which I have borne by you. And whereas you took a displeasure with me that I might not shift you any money on your land when you sent to me, William Paston writeth daily unto me to call upon that livelihood for his debt to see how he may be saved harmless of his jewels. And moreover I am credibly informed that you say sir you have left me sufficient livelihood to live upon and I have taken accounts thereof by advice of council and there remaineth not to me all charges borne from the feast of All Saints last past till Hallowmass next coming but £12 . . . And this is not sufficient to keep all charges as I am put to . . . But to complain to you the which have no pity it is but folly in me. For ye keep your promise whereas you said you would never write unto me more . . . But where as it liketh you not to come nor to send to me yet I will send unto you while I live as God knoweth who ever preserve you and bring you in to a better remembrance. And your daughter Elizabeth recommendeth her unto you and beseecheth you of your blessing.

But we will imagine that matters were less anguished between the Malorys. There is no sign that Thomas lived beyond his means; he may well have had London-based enterprises that meant he could send home a useful contribution for Lady Elizabeth's maintenance. Perhaps he was like Lancelot, who respected but did not love his son Galahad's mother Elaine, even though she loved him 'out of measure'. And perhaps his wife always wished him well, as Elaine did Lancelot, even though she knew her love was unrequited. In this case, her letters would have been more like this no-nonsense epistle sent by Margaret Paston to her own London-based husband, John, in October 1460:

Thomas Bone hath sold all your wool here for 20d a stone, and it is sold right well, after that the wool was, for the most part, right feeble. Item, *there be bought for you 3 horses at the St Faith's fair, and all be trotters, right fair horses . . .* Item, *your mill at Hailsdon is let for 12 marks, and the miller to find the repairs; and Richard Calle hath let all your lands at Caistor; but as for the Maltby lands, they be not let as yet.*

Such separations were common among those who could afford them. There was no divorce in the modern sense at this time, and annulment was a lengthy, expensive and far from certain process which had to be referred to the Pope himself. It was only embarked on for dynastic reasons or when inheritance was an issue. Malory intended his family estates to continue in the legitimate line – he was no William Mountfort to disinherit his first family in favour of a second. But there was nothing to stop him simply jumping the marital ship (as William Shakespeare did a century later) and living most of the time near the love of his life in London, returning home for special occasions – Christmas and Easter, weddings and funerals.

London in the mid-1460s was an exciting place for a man of Malory's spirit and talents. It was 'an ample and magnificent town' wherein there was 'much trafficking with all nations; also much people and many craftsmen, chiefly goldsmiths and clothworkers, and very beautiful women dear in price'. It was also full of his kinsmen and well-wishers. As well as Robert Malory, the Lieutenant of the Tower, there was Anthony Malory, a merchant, and William Malory, who lived in the Knights Hospitaller manor of Sutton-le-Hone, close to the royal palace of Pleasaunce at Greenwich. Simon Malory, now a widower, was a corrodian in the Hospitallers' Priory at Clerkenwell, which was also the London home of the Knight Hospitaller Sir John Malory when he returned to England. Malory could easily have had a London house of his own, but he and his personal servants might well have been attached to the permanent household that the Earl and Countess of Warwick kept at Warwick Inn.

After 1464, Warwick spent less time in the north. Instead, he divided his time between London, Calais and his Midlands estates. Very few Neville records from the 1460s survive, but the size and splendour of Warwick's household were the talk of Europe.

> *The which Earl was ever had in great favour of the commons of this land, by reason of the exceeding household which he daily kept. In all counties wherever he sojourned or lay, and when he came to London, he held such a house that six oxen were eaten at a breakfast, and every tavern was full of his mead, for whoever had any acquaintance in that house should have had as much sodden [boiled meat] and roast as he might carry on a long dagger.*

Edward IV's court, based at Westminster when Parliament was in session there, but otherwise held in whichever of his many palaces he happened to be, was kept so splendidly that a favourite conceit was to compare it to Camelot. Likening the monarch to King Arthur was a favourite English form of flattery, and Edward IV, tall, auburn-haired and astonishingly handsome, enjoyed such comparisons. The mercer Roger Thorney wrote of Edward IV that 'of a more famous knight I never read / Since the time of Arthur's days', and at his funeral a Latin lament described him as 'an Arthur to his enemies'. Undeniably, the role of chivalric high king, especially one who occasionally slipped into bed with paramours, suited Edward IV far better than it had his pious cousin Henry. Edward was a self-conscious Arthurian, deeply interested both in historical precedent, alchemical prophecies and magic. He had a fine collection of chronicles, romances and chivalric literature. Splendidly illustrated, bound in gilded leather or velvet, with laces and tassels of silk, and clasps of copper and gilt, and ornamented with the York rose and the royal arms, many were dedicated to the King personally, urging him to emulate the noble deeds of the Greek heroes and the Roman emperors. Among Edward's books was *Le Chemin de Vaillance ou Songe Doré* – 'The Road to Courage or the Golden Dream', a guide to knightly behaviour told in the form of advice from Lady Courage. The King also had a fine copy in French of Ramon Lull's *Order of Chivalry*, still the most famous guide to knightly etiquette.

Edward IV's other role model was his ancestor and namesake, the great Edward III, who had also interested himself in King Arthur. He ruled England for fifty years and founded the Order of the Garter to create a body of high-born and redoubtable knights as personally loyal to him as the Knights of the Round Table were to Arthur. Under Henry VI and Margaret of Anjou, the Order had degenerated into a political tool, used to honour foreign dignitaries and loyal courtiers, and levels of attendance on St George's Day and Pentecost were low between 1446 and 1461. Edward IV virtually re-founded the Order, returning it to his great-great-grandfather's original vision. When he filled the thirteen seats left empty by the deaths and attainders after the Battle of Towton, he chose predominantly English knights with great chivalric reputations whom he hoped would form an élite cadre of followers as loyal to him as the the original Garter knights had been to Edward III.

Malory knew at least four of Edward's first Garter knights well: Sir William Hastings, Sir Robert Harcourt, Sir William Chamberlain and Sir John Astley. Astley was still a captive in France, negotiating for ransom. Until he returned in 1466, Malory was a useful proxy authority on chivalry. Sir Robert Harcourt was obedient to the Yorkist King, distinguishing himself on the northern campaign. He was given the constableship of Wallingford Castle and remained friendly with his neighbour at Ewelme, the still formidable Duchess of Suffolk, Alice Chaucer – he would later be suspected of contacts with the Lancastrian exiles. Hot-headed when younger, Harcourt had now mellowed into a civilised, well-read man; he became Steward of Oxford University in 1466. Connections with Harcourt could have brought new books to Malory's library.

Malory would also have welcomed Edward IV's revival of the tournament tradition. It had never entirely died out. There had been several notable tournaments in the 1440s, including Sir John Astley's famous encounter with Philippe de Boyle of Aragon at Smithfield in 1442 and the jousts on the occasion of his marriage. But Henry VI had been much more interested in his intellectual foundations, Eton College at Windsor and King's College, Cambridge, and though he had a suit of jousting armour, it was more for show than for use.

Edward IV by contrast liked nothing better than riding in the lists himself. His fast and furious bout at Eltham in April 1467 is described by Sir John Paston:

> *My hand was hurt at the tourney at Eltham upon Wednesday last. I would that you had been there and seen it, for it was the goodliest sight that was seen in England this forty years of so few men. There was upon the one side, within, the king, my Lord Scales, myself and Sellenger; and without my Lord Chamberlain, Sir John Woodville, Sir Thomas Montgomery and John Aparre.*

We only know of this tourney from Paston's letter, but a reply from his brother refers to the 'king's tourneys' as if such jousts were frequent. Paston was obsessed with romance and chivalry. An inventory of his books taken in 1469 included *Gawain and the Green Knight*, *La Belle Dame Sans Merci* and 'a book had off my hostess at the George of the Death of Arthur' – which, besides offering an unexpected vision of a delightfully literate ale-wife, raises the intriguing possibility that Paston was one of the first to read Malory's epic.

The most renowned jousters of the age were the Woodvilles. Sir Richard, now Earl Rivers, had been as active as Astley in keeping the tradition alive, jousting at the Tower of London in 1439 and fighting an individual challenge against Pedro Vasquez de Savaadra at Westminster on 26 November 1440. Woodville invited all comers to a *pas d'armes* near Calais in 1449, and won first prize at the *Pas du Perron Fée* at Bruges in 1453. His son Sir Anthony, who rode as Malory did to the defence of Alnwick in 1462, shared his enthusiasm, and had starred in the jousts mounted to celebrate the reconciliation between Henry VI and York in March 1458.

The May Queen

Edward soon had a much closer link with the Woodvilles than a love of tournaments. On 1 May 1464, a week after Sir John Neville turned an ambush of his troops into a Lancastrian rout at Hedgeley Moor, he married Sir Richard Woodville's widowed daughter Elizabeth. He was twenty-two, she was twenty-seven, with two sons from her marriage to the loyal Lancastrian knight, Sir John Gray, who had died at Towton. On his way north to join Neville, Edward had stopped at Stony Stratford on 30 April. The next day he said he was going hunting and slipped away to Grafton Regis. The ceremony was held in the Woodvilles' private chapel. Witnessed by the bride's mother Jacquetta, still known as the Duchess of Bedford, and a handful of discreet servants, it was kept totally secret. Bride and groom went to bed, then Edward rode to Stony Stratford and headed north to Leicester, where he stayed for ten days. Soon afterwards, he returned to Grafton, staying three or four days with the Woodvilles before continuing north to congratulate Sir John Neville on a second resounding victory at Hexham on 15 May. The marriage stayed secret for three months. Edward was well aware that Warwick was negotiating with Louis XI for the hand of Princess Bona of Savoy, a sister of the French Queen. But Edward did not choose to have his queen selected for him, and he had a shrewd feel for the public mood. Many Englishmen blamed Margaret of Anjou for the civil war, nor would a French marriage alliance further his secret ambition of recovering his lost French domains.

His marriage to Elizabeth has been described as 'the first major blunder of his career', 'the impulsive love-match of an impetuous young man'. Elizabeth and her mother, it is said, took advantage of Edward's 'thoughtlessness and youthful passion'. But this will not do. Edward was not much younger than Henry V had been when he became King in 1413, and no less competent in bed and on the battlefield. The May Day marriage was an elegant gesture, straight out of courtly romance, but it was not a casual impulse. It was three years since Edward had pardoned Lady Woodville and restored her dead husband's lands to their beautiful daughter. Since then he had visited Grafton several times openly, perhaps more often in secret. Undoubtedly 'allured by the lineaments of her body and her wise and womanly demeanour', he had had time to get to know Elizabeth well, and to become more fascinated by her, not less.

> For she was a woman . . . of such beauty and favour that with her sober demeanour, lovely-looking and feminine smiling (neither too wanton nor too humble) beside her tongue so eloquent and her wit so pregnant.

He soon discovered that she had no intention of accepting his offer of 'many gifts and fair rewards' if she would be his 'paramour or concubine', after which 'she might so fortune' to become 'his wife and lawful bedfellow'. This line had gone down well enough before with other English gentlewomen – Elizabeth Lucy was even then tending his two first bastards, Arthur and Elizabeth Plantagenet. Lady Gray had loftier ambitions. Doubtless 'feminine smiling', she said that

As she was for his honour far unable to be his spouse and
bedfellow, so for her own poor honesty, she was too good to
be either his concubine or sovereign lady.

It was the good omen of Sir John Neville's victory at Hedgeley Moor that decided Edward to follow his heart – and perhaps reassure his disaffected subjects that he welcomed former Lancastrian loyalists into the Yorkist fold.

He had one person to placate before he could do so: his mother Cecily, Dowager Duchess of York, one of the redoubtable Neville sisters. It was not an easy task. Hall records a splendidly spirited exchange in which Cecily told her son that Elizabeth, 'though there is nothing in her person to be misliked', was doubly unsuitable. Not only had she been married already, 'a great blemish to the sacred majesty of a prince', but she was 'his subject', rather than 'some noble progeny out of his realm'. 'That she is a widow and hath already children', Edward rapped back, boded well for the succession. 'By God his blessed lady, I am a bachelor and have some too, and each of us hath a proof, that neither of us is like to be barren.' As to her Englishness, he saw that, and her Lancastrian connections, as positive advantages. He 'reckoned the amity of no earthly nation to be so necessary for him as the friendship of his own, which he thought likely to bear him so much the more hearty favour, in that he disdained not to marry with one of his own land'. Foreign matches could be arranged for 'other of his kin', if 'all parties could be contented'. As for himself, 'I marry where it liketh me'. Although marriages 'ought to be made for the respect of God', 'the parties ought to incline to love together [as he trusted it was in his case] rather than for the regard of any temporal advantage . . . For small pleasure taketh a man of all that he ever hath beside, if he be wived against his appetite.' When his mother warned him that his cousin Warwick 'was not like to take it well', he drew himself up, every inch the King, and said:

I am sure that my cousin Warwick neither loveth me so little,
to grudge at that that I love, nor is it so unreasonable, to
look that I should in choice of a wife rather be ruled by his
eye than by my own, as though I were a ward that were

bound to marry by the appointment of a guardian. I would
not be a King with that condition, to forbear my liberty in
choice of mine own marriage. As for the possibility of more
inheritance by new affinity in strange lands, it is oft the
occasion of more trouble than profit. And we have already
title by that means to as much as it sufficeth to get and keep
well in one man's days.

These are not the words of a headstrong boy, but of a thoughtful
young man who had drawn his own conclusions from his country's
recent history – and the miserable arranged marriages of many of his
contemporaries. Edward IV was the most English King since the
Norman Conquest. His determination to marry someone who could
guarantee him not just an heir but a thoroughly English one made
very good sense after England's experience of the half-French (some
said half-mad) Henry VI on the throne.

Elizabeth's unsuitability on account of her birth has been exaggerated. Her lineage was far grander than that of Katherine Swinford,
the humble English mistress that Edward III's son John of Gaunt
made his wife, and from whose belatedly legitimised line the Beauforts
were descended. Her mother, Jacquetta of St-Pol, was a princess of
Luxembourg, and close kin to Philip of Burgundy, Edward's preferred
European ally. Both her sisters were women of influence: one was
Countess of Maine, the other the Dowager Duchess of Brittany. Time
would prove the marriage to be, in personal terms, a notable success.
It lasted nineteen years, and Elizabeth bore Edward twelve children,
including four sons, two of whom grew up into strong young boys.
Edward was, moreover, right in predicting the 'hearty favour' of the
commons. 'I have been in divers places within Norfolk, Suffolk, and
Essex, and have communicated this marriage, to feel how the people
of the country were disposed,' reported Sir John Howard, 'and, in
good faith, they are disposed in the best wise, and glad thereof. Also,
I have been with many divers estates, to feel their hearts; and, in good
faith, I found them all right well disposed.'

Warwick grew to loathe the match, but he escorted Elizabeth into
Reading Abbey for the announcement that she was to be Queen of

England in October 1464. He did not attend her coronation in London in May 1465 because war threatened. Between 11 May and 22 July he was in Calais, preoccupied with persuading King Louis XI of France not to back the Lancastrian rebels at Koeur. But Elizabeth's uncle Jacques, Count of St-Pol, came over for the celebrations, bringing with him three hundred retainers. Knights from Luxembourg and Burgundy as well as England took part in the magnificent tournament after the ceremony. The scale of the two-day event is reflected in the need for twenty-four carpenters on stand-by to repair the lists. Twelve more men were employed to run in and pick up the broken spears and shields during the jousts and mêlées, a terrifying job, akin to being a ballboy at Wimbledon trying to dodge Grand National riders rather than histrionic tennis stars. The first prize, a gigantic ruby set in a ring, went to Thomas, Lord Stanley, husband of Warwick's sister Eleanor. Hopefully Warwick appreciated the compliment to his family.

Courtly-makers

Malory would have fitted well into the glittering new world of the young Sun King. There is no reason to doubt the sixteenth-century literary historian John Bale's statement that 'because of his magnanimous and heroic temper, due largely to the great variety of virtues and talents he possessed, Malory easily outshone the scholars of his time'; certainly, no more impressive contemporary writer exists. Bale also describes Malory as having 'many duties of state'. Were these ceremonial court duties of some kind? The mid-1460s are the most likely time for such commitments. Whatever the cause of his sustained persecution by the Lancastrian authorities in the 1450s, Malory's efforts in the north against Edward's enemies had earned him some sort of reward. If the absence of John Paston's friends Yelverton and Jenney from Norfolk's retinue was 'marked well enough' to require written apologies to the King, Edward is likely to have noticed that Malory, despite his age, was there. For the new King was blessed, it was said, with *a memory so retentive, in all respects, that the names and estates used to recur to him, just as if he had been in the habit of seeing them daily, of nearly all the persons dispersed throughout the counties of the kingdom; and this even if, in the districts where they lived, they held the rank only of mere gentlemen.*

Malory's age was no bar to his having a position at court. Edward IV respected the older generation not just as military commanders but as chroniclers, poets and advisers. When not riding in tournaments himself, he sat enthroned on a grandstand above the lists with twenty or more white-haired advisers around him. 'They resembled senators set there together to counsel their master'. Malory may have been among them, commentating and making notes for his after-dinner description of the day's events. Blow-by-blow descriptions of the skilled, if often lethal, techniques exhibited in encounters in the lists were his speciality:

With that came Sir Lancelot du Lake, and he thrust in with his spear in the thickest of the press, and there he smote down with one spear five knights, and of four of them he brake their backs. And in that throng he smote down the King of Northgalis, and brake his thigh in that fall. All this doing of Sir Lancelot saw the three knights of Arthur's. 'Yonder is a shrewd guest,' said Sir Mador de la Porte, 'therefore have here once at him.' So they encountered, and Sir Lancelot bare him down horse and man, so that his shoulder went out of lith. 'Now befalleth it to me to joust,' said Mordred, 'for Sir Mador hath a sore fall.' Sir Lancelot was ware of him, and gat a great spear in his hand, and met him, and Sir Mordred brake a spear upon him, and Sir Lancelot gave him such a buffet that the arson of his saddle brake, and so he flew over his horse's tail, that his helm butted into the earth a foot and more, that nigh his neck was broken, and there he lay long in a swoon.

Poets and chroniclers were often given jobs in royal households. Chaucer worked in the customs office, and the poets Hoccleve and George Ashby in the offices of the privy seal and the signet. Richard Green's *Poets and Princepleasers* sees a line of 'courtly-makers' stretching unbroken from them through the satirist Lydgate, the chronicler John Hardyng, the printer William Caxton, Sir Thomas More, Thomas Wyatt and Sir Philip Sidney. Malory would fit nicely between Hardyng and Caxton. Now in his mid-sixties, he was more than ready to give up the hurly-burly of military campaigning and turn a lifelong hobby into a full-time occupation.

John Bale (1495–1563) lived closer to Malory's time than any other literary commentator on his writing. 'Malory zealously pursued his study of literature,' he wrote in the 1550s. 'He spent hour after pleasant hour reading historical texts. Some events he would visualize as occurring in their historical context; others he would visualize as occurring in the present – before his very eyes, as it were. Once thoroughly versed in these texts, he collated the many materials written in both French and Latin and painstakingly translated them into our tongue.' This description of how he worked is specific in detail and utterly unlike the usual vague praise. It sounds like total recall, a memory passed on by someone who had actually seen Malory at work on his history of Arthur, which is indeed partly written as history, and partly as dramatic, immediate dialogue. Sophisticated linguistic analysis of the text of the *Morte* has proved Bale right about its author's breadth of reading, and scholars are continually adding to the list of books Malory knew. The most likely time at which Malory was both undertaking 'many duties of state' and finding time to read and collate quantities of books is the mid-1460s. In 1515, John Bale was twenty; one of his contemporaries could easily have talked to an septuagenarian who had known Malory well in the 1460s. Anyone who had done so would certainly have boasted of the fact: 'In our times Malory enjoys an illustrious reputation', Bale's entry in his *Dictionary of Illustrious British Authors* concludes.

A fascinating recent book by Jonathan Hughes draws attention to the extent of Edward IV's interest in Arthurian myth and alchemical prophecies. I don't agree with Hughes's argument that Malory identified Edward with Arthur – or himself with Tristram. But there is no doubt that Edward would have been interested in an English translation of the Arthurian legends. So too would Elizabeth Woodville, who we know had an early-fourteenth-century French collection of Arthurian romances. Other likely enthusiasts for chivalric literature were Thomas and Richard Grey, Elizabeth's sons from her first marriage, and the young Lancastrian wards then in the court. One of these was Lord Maltravers, heir to the earldom of Arundel. Malory adds a gratuitous mention of Arundel in his 'Tale of Alisander Le Orphelin', and he changes the name of the Constable of the castle from Berengere to Bellinger. The Bellinghams were an important Sussex family and Sir Thomas Bellingham had ridden north with Malory in Warwick's retinue in 1462. Was it a coded message of some sort? Alisander's father has been murdered by King Mark, but his mother escapes with him and takes refuge in Arundel Castle. When he is a knight, she tells him, 'he shall have his father's doublet and his shirt with the bloody marks', and avenge his father's death. Also a royal ward was Henry Stafford, Buckingham's son – a welcome audience, perhaps, for his mother's sake. But the boy whom Malory would most have wanted to inspire with the high ideals of chivalry was of course far away. The eleven-year-old Prince Edward was, ironically, then being schooled in constitutional law at Koeur Castle by Sir John Fortescue, the Chief Justice who had sat in on Malory's case so frequently at the King's Bench in the 1450s.

Fortescue himself was writing a book aimed at countering the dangerously despotic French influence of Margaret of Anjou by giving Prince Edward an understanding of the English legal system. His *De Laudibus Legum Angliae* (*In Praise of the Laws of England*) actually features a lively and talkative Prince Edward in dialogue with the author (personified as 'a certain aged knight'), asking and responding to questions about the best way to govern the realm that he confidently expected to inherit. Both Fortescue and Malory were clever, thoughtful men who valued justice above all, though they differed as to by whom, and how, it should be administered. Fortescue wanted to restore the good name of the law. Malory wanted to add ethics and courtesy to his contemporaries' obsession with the dignity of knighthood, and to channel the fierce natures of fighting men for the common good. Both approaches marked them as men of their times, but Malory was more ambitious and less cynical than Fortescue. The Chief Justice merely wanted men's impulses hedged around with prohibitions and policed by penalties. Malory aimed to change the mind-set of the mighty, re-instilling true knightly values in place of haughty pride and selfishness. As different but as complementary as two sides of the same coin, the two men were an ideal combination of mentors for any fifteenth-century king.

On 12 September 1464, Malory took time off from his duties and went down to Warwickshire for the marriage of John, son of William Feilding of Lutterworth (six miles from Newbold Revel) to Helen Walsh. Malory may have been Helen's uncle; he certainly seems to have been her guardian. Her father, Thomas Walsh of Wanlip, had died in 1463. He had initially fled with Queen Margaret to Scotland, but had returned to toe the Yorkist line before his death. Her mother Margery was a Byron, and sister of Lady Robert Harcourt. The Stormsworth lands settled on the young couple adjoined Malory's Swinford estates. The other witnesses to the marriage give us a revealing glimpse of Malory's connections at this time. They show that he kept company with men who had not only once been loyal subjects of Henry VI but would flock to his banner as soon as the opportunity arose.

The Feildings were a very wealthy merchant family who made their money from wool, trained themselves in legal matters and systematically accumulated lands during these troubled times. William's father John had served under the Duke of Bedford in France, and had married Margaret Purefoy, sister of the William Purefoy who had married Malory's aunt, Margaret Chetwynd. His brother Geoffrey Feilding was a London mercer. William himself was granted licence to ship wool free from Ipswich in repayment for loans he had made to the Crown as a merchant of the Calais staple. It was no doubt profits from dealing with wool that enabled William to acquire Newnham Paddox, which bordered on Newbold Revel, from the Leventhorpes in 1433. He sat for Leicestershire in the 1449–50 Parliament, when Malory was sitting for Bedwyn. Staunchly loyal to Henry VI, and probably a member of the royal household, he also sat in the vengeful 1459 Parliament which attainted the Duke of York and the Nevilles, and he sat on commissions to try suspected rebels in 1460. He was exempted from Edward IV's general pardon of March 1461, which suggests that he fought on the Lancastrian side at Towton. However, he was allowed to take up the January 1462 pardon, and did so on 16 February. Elizabeth Woodville may have put in a word for him: he was one of the feoffees for the jointure granted to her on her marriage to Sir John Gray in 1455, and which Edward had restored to her while they were courting. But he stayed away from court, accepting the fact of Edward's accession, but not approving it.

The other witnesses at the wedding were Henry Everingham, Sir Richard Boughton and John Green. Everingham held the manor of Withybrook, which adjoined Newnham Paddox and Newbold Revel to the north-west, and was one of Malory's new feoffees. He was retained by Warwick, but his father had been killed fighting for Henry VI at Towton. Richard Boughton was the son of Thomas Boughton of Lawford, who had stood surety for Malory in 1454. Boughton and Feilding both rallied to the Lancastrian cause in 1470.

If he returned to Newbold Revel for Christmas of 1465, Sir Thomas will have had the pleasure of holding an important new grandson in his arms. Nicholas, son of his own eighteen-year-old son and heir Robert, would eventually inherit all the Malory estates. He could have been named for Nicholas Revel, from whom the Malorys had inherited Newbold Revel, or, if he was born early in December, for the patron saint of children, women and Christmas itself: 6 December is the Feast of St Nicholas. A longer shot would be a naming as a tribute to the great reforming Pope Nicholas V (1447–55), who had resolved the schism in the papacy and tried to rally all the European powers for a crusade against the Turks after the fall of Constantinople in 1453.

For crusading was once more in the air. Tournaments, literature and May Day romancing were dear to Malory's heart. But in the Middle Ages, the minds of men in the last decade of their allotted lifespan of 'three score years and ten' often turned with increased intensity to spiritual things. To Malory, the most promising aspect of

Edward's accession may have been the prospect of a crusade against the infidel. Edward had been born in Rouen, and the alchemists' prophecies that so fascinated him had told of 'a delicate rose of Britain called Edward of Rouen' who would recover not only Jerusalem but the True Cross. Eastern Europe was quailing under the shadow of the 'infidels'. Bosnia was now a Turkish province, and Ragusa (Dubrovnik) and Venice were both under threat. In 1463, Pope Pius II had chided Christians for living for pleasure and spending nothing on the defence of the faith. He preached a crusade, winning Milan, Venice, Hungary, Albania and Burgundy to the cause in a speech which brought tears to the eyes of many in the College of Cardinals. For he had announced that he himself, 'an old man broken by infirmities', would go with the promised fleet to Greece and Asia. 'Unless we arm and go against the foe', he warned them, 'our religion is doomed.'

A truce between France, Burgundy and England was agreed at St-Omer in October 1463, and thousands of would-be crusaders set out from Lubeck, Ghent, Spain and even Scotland. Duke Philip of Burgundy announced that he would lead the crusade. Now was the time for the English to show what they were made of. George Ripley, Edward's personal astrologer and alchemist, and George Neville, Archbishop of York, were both enthusiastic. A crusade would win them all heavenly glory; it might also unite the country behind the new King. Archbishop Neville was all for setting out himself, offering to march at Burgundy's side with three hundred men. The Knights Hospitallers were also sending men, and it is likely that Sir Thomas's kinsman Sir John Malory planned to ride with them.

Edward offered to send a band of English archers to accompany the Duke of Burgundy. But he was displeased when, in the spring of 1464, Pius II announced a levy of a tenth of the income of the clergy of England to support the crusade. Such levies had been forbidden since the passing of the 1393 Statute of Praemunire, and Edward refused to allow such a precedent. Instead he announced that he would himself levy a subsidy for the crusade from the clergy. Nothing came of the venture. Edward discreetly squirrelled away the subsidy in his own treasury.

Good Governance

To do Edward justice, this was no time for either a crusade to the East or an invasion of France. He was a shrewd, competent man who knew that he needed to set the monarchy on a sound financial footing. His household expenditure was already only half that of Henry VI. He was determined, he told Parliament, to 'live of his own' except in time of war. He gained £12,000 for the Crown by slightly devaluing and recoining the English currency – the Crown took a percentage on every new coin made by the Master of the Mint. Instead of distributing largesse indiscriminately, he dedicated it to his own and his queen's glorification.

His court was a smaller and more closely-knit group than Henry's, and he took pains to make it representative of his realm. His household squires were 'of sundry shires, by whom may be known the disposition of the counties'. He also knew he had to woo the merchant community, the most reliable source of loans for the monarchy. He spent much more time than Henry had in London, giving it a generous new charter in 1462 and making five of its most prominent citizens Knights of the Bath on the eve of the coronation of Queen Elizabeth. He gave banquets for city notables, invited them to advise at council meetings, took them on hunting parties in Waltham Forest, and flirted outrageously with their wives (who loved him for it).

He had a sound grasp of economics, and improved trade for English wool merchants and clothiers by limiting foreign imports and exports of wool and cloth. Aware of the huge profits to be made, he launched his own trading ventures, exporting wool, cloth and tin in royal ships on stand-by for England's defence, and even chartering them to other merchants. The royal ships could also be hired to provide protection for wool and fishing fleets. He encouraged merchants to look for new markets, appealing to the Pope against the Portuguese monopoly of the North African market (where two English merchants acquired more lions for the Tower's menagerie in 1465) and royally entertaining such merchant explorers as William Heryot, 'a merchant of wondrous adventures into many and sundry countries, by reason whereof the king had yearly from him notable sums of money from customs, besides other pleasures'.

When the Bohemian jousting champion Leo von Rozmital visited England during his 1466 tour of European courts in search of tournaments, his recorder Gabriel Tetzel wrote that Edward had 'the most splendid court that could be found in all Christendom'. They sat through fifty courses at a dinner given in their honour by the King, and on another occasion watched in amazement as Queen Elizabeth sat alone at table in a priceless gold chair for three hours, eating in complete silence, with 'even the mightiest nobles' kneeling while she did so.

Edward and Elizabeth were well aware of the importance of pageants and processions, visual evidence of regal power. Nothing in Edward's reign evoked the Arthurian mood more than the famous challenge issued in April 1465 by Anthony Woodville, Lord Scales. Woodville was kneeling before his sister the Queen in her palace at Sheen when the ladies of the court fluttered up to him and closed a collar of gold and pearls around his thigh. Hanging from it, richly bejewelled, was 'a noble flower of souvenance enamelled and in manner of an emprise'. They then gave him a letter tied with thread of gold: it said that Woodville would win the emprise by issuing a chivalric challenge to 'a noble man of four lineages' to fight a two-day tournament. Woodville decided to challenge Anthoine, Comte de la Roche, a famous jouster known as the Grand Bastard of Burgundy because he was a much-favoured illegitimate son of Duke Philip of Burgundy. Heralds cantered between London and Bruges, and the contest was finally fought in the Smithfield lists on 11 and 12 June 1467. The old tournament stands were magnificently refurbished. In the royal gallery stood Edward's cloth-of-gold-draped throne, with a canopy above it topped by a golden eagle holding Scales's arms. Crowds thronged to watch, including visitors from all over Europe. No less than four eyewitness accounts survive of the event, more than for most major battles of the century.

The challenge was to be single combat to the death, unless one of the contestants yielded. First came a single course with sharp spears. Both knights missed. Next they charged each other on horseback with swords. Up to thirty-seven strokes could be delivered, with the tourney ending when either party was unhorsed or seriously injured. Again and again they charged each other, swords flailing. But suddenly the Bastard's horse collapsed, fatally wounded, it seems accidentally, by Scales's sword. Two of the eyewitness accounts hint at foul play – an illegitimate spike of steel mounted somewhere on Scales's fearsome destrier. Malory describes a strikingly similar incident in a joust fought between Sir Lancelot and the Saracen knight Sir Palomides.

> *And Sir Palomides rushed unto Sir Lancelot, and thought to have put him to a shame; and with his sword he smote his horse's neck that Sir Lancelot rode upon, and then Sir Lancelot fell to the earth. Then was the cry huge and great: 'See how Sir Palomides the Saracen hath smitten down Sir Lancelot's horse.' Right then were there many knights wroth with Sir Palomides because he had done that deed; therefore many knights held there against that it was unknightly done in a tournament to kill an horse wilfully, but that it had been done in plain battle, life for life.*

Furious with rage, Lancelot warns Palomides that he intends to be avenged – but Palomides pleads for mercy. Attacking Lancelot's horse was his only hope of victory – and his lady's favour. Magnanimous as ever, Lancelot forgives him, saying, 'I understand for whose love ye do it, and well I wot that love is a great mistress'.

Scales and the Bastard then came to blows on foot, slashing and hewing at each other's armour with axes and daggers with as much violence as any of Malory's superheroes. Finally Edward parted them. Honours, it appeared, were even, a politic decision. For the background to the whole event was Edward's hopes of the marriage of his sister Margaret to Charles, Comte de Charolais, heir to the Duchy of Burgundy. For the next few days other would-be champions took to the lists: the earls of Arundel, Shrewsbury and Kent, the Duke of Suffolk and young Buckingham, William Herbert and Stafford of Southwick, Sir Walter Blount and Sir Thomas Montgomery. While they jousted, secret negotiations between Edward and the Burgundians continued. Although only forty-seven, Duke Philip was known to be ailing. On 17 June 1467, news arrived that he had died, and the tournament ended. But there would be a follow-up event. Plans were soon being made for an even more magnificent tournament a year later. It would celebrate Margaret's marriage to the new Duke of Burgundy in Bruges in July 1468.

For nearly four years, Malory watched and even wistfully enjoyed the glorious renaissance of chivalry, culture and romance. As in the early 1440s, there was a young king and a beautiful queen, and gallant knights ready to fight against all comers. But in his eyes, and those of many closet Lancastrians, the new Camelot was a sham. Peace and order had not been restored in the shires. Crime was still rife, and justice as much in rich men's pockets as it ever had been. The Earl of Warwick was not a Beauchamp, but a self-seeking, cold-hearted Neville. Magnificent and all-competent as Edward IV was, he was *de jure* Duke of York, not King of England. The Queen was not a fairy-tale French princess but the cool, calculating daughter of a Northamptonshire knight. There had been no new invasion of France – and no crusade to Jerusalem. Instead of learning the arts of war, the young men of Edward's court were revelling in promiscuity. And if Malory had indeed been in love with Anne Neville, he would not have welcomed her remarriage to his own feoffee, Sir Walter Blount, Lord Mountjoy, now one of Edward IV's most trusted lieutenants. Was this in his mind when he wrote the heartfelt passage about love in his 'Tale of Lancelot and Guinevere'?

> *Nowadays men cannot love seven nights but they must have all their desires. That love may not endure by reason, for where they beeth soon accorded and hastily, heat soon killeth. And right so fareth the love nowadays, soon hot, soon cold. This is no stability. But the old love was not so. For men and women could love together seven years, and no lecherous lusts were betwixt them, and then was love truth and faithfulness.*

In his youth, Malory was probably as ready as any young man to flirt and seduce, but he was now older and sadder – a generation away from clever young courtiers like his kinsman Thomas Danvers. Writing to his friend Sir John Paston ('the best cheser of a gentlewoman that I know') in January 1467, Danvers teased him about his request for a copy of the Roman poet Ovid's still popular guide to love-making, *De Arte Amandi*:

> *I shall send him you this next week, for I have him not now ready. But me thinketh Ovid* De Remedio *were more meet for you, but if [unless] ye purposed to fall hastily in my Lady Anne P's lap, as white as whale's bone.*

Malory's service to the usurping monarchy was already feigned, not heartfelt, when on 24 July 1465 a weary and travel-stained prisoner, his feet tied to his stirrups, was ignominiously led into the city of London. His arrival, I will argue, made all the difference to the rest of Sir Thomas's life. And it explains the second great puzzle of his life: his exception from three general pardons between 1468 and 1470.

The Secret Agent

*By means of books we communicate to friends as well as
foes what we cannot safely entrust to messengers, since the
book is generally allowed access to the chamber of princes,
from which the voice of its author would be excluded.*

Richard de Bury, *Philobiblon* (*c.*1344)

ver since the rout at Hexham in May 1464, Henry VI had
been a fugitive, first in Scotland, then in Cumbria and
Lancashire, sheltered by families brave enough to risk their
lives for the rightful King. In June 1465 he was captured. He had been
sheltered at Waddington Hall, in the depths of the Lancashire forest
of Bowland, by Sir Richard Tempest, whose sister Dionysia was married to Sir William Malory of Hutton Conyers. It was Sir Richard's
brother John Tempest who betrayed Henry's whereabouts. When a
squad of Yorkist soldiers arrived to arrest him, Henry managed to
escape but was caught trying to cross the Ribble at a ford with the
memorable name of Bungerly Hippingstones.

Edward and Elizabeth, who were ambling towards Canterbury on
a summer pilgrimage when they heard the news, ordered a celebratory
Te Deum to be sung in the cathedral on their arrival. Warwick, putter-
up and setter-down of kings, hastened back from Calais to London in
time to meet Henry at the little village of Islington, on 24 July. He formally
arrested him in Edward's name, ordered his gilt spurs to be stripped off,
an unnecessarily cruel humiliation, and had his feet tied to the stirrups
of his horse. Then he led him into London through Newgate and along
Cheapside to the Tower. Warwick had taken the precaution of issuing a
proclamation forbidding any man, on pain of death, to show any mark

of enthusiasm or respect. He tried, it was said, to encourage derision, shouting 'Treason! Behold the traitor!' But the crowds who had gathered to witness the passing of the man who had ruled England for thirty-nine years were largely silent. For many, there was something Christ-like about the one-time King's ignominious entry to London.

In the Tower, Henry was in the custody of Robert Malory. The Exchequer paid only a frugal £2 a week for the keep of 'Henry of Lancaster, late *de facto* and *non de jure* king of England' and that of his attendants – no more than bed and board in the Marshalsea had cost Sir Thomas Malory and his servants ten years before. But Robert Malory, a 'full worshipful, charitable and gentle' gaoler according to another of his charges, John Turner, saw to it that Henry was 'well-beseen'. He purchased fine cloth, blue velvet with a 'violet ingrain', to be made into gowns for him. Wine was acquired for him from the royal cellars, perhaps after a word from Lord Wenlock, the Chief Butler. Somebody also spoke to Edward IV about Henry's chaplain, William Kimberley, who was giving his services for nothing; as an act of mercy, Edward provided 7½ pence a day for him.

Edward believed he had nothing to fear from his apparently docile cousin, who patiently counted out his days and the beads of his rosary in the Tower. 'Every man was suffered to come and speak with him by licence of the keepers,' says Gregory's Chronicle. The confident young ruler may have thought that the contrast between him and Henry was enough to convince anyone who was the better king. But he underestimated both the charisma that surrounds any anointed king and Henry's quiet but potent appeal. A great many Englishmen, especially those who had been knighted by Henry, stayed secretly loyal to him. Later events suggest that Malory was among them. Lancelot repeats the phrase, 'the noble king that made me knight', no less than eight times in the *Morte*'s last two hundred pages, on seven occasions to express abhorrence at fighting Arthur himself, and finally to condemn Mordred's rebellion.

> '*Alas,*' *said Sir Lancelot,* '*that ever I should live to hear that most noble king that made me knight thus to be overset with his subject in his own realm.*'

Yorkist propaganda distorts the truth about Henry. A portrait of him as a young man show that he was tall, with a long, fine-featured face. He was certainly amiable, pious and easily influenced, but the fact that he chose to stay in the land he regarded as his rightful realm rather than simply follow the Queen and Prince to France shows that he was less feeble-minded than rumour claimed. No doubt his breakdowns and hardships reduced him to a pale shadow of his former self, as wounded as Malory's 'Fisher King', but a true knight's allegiance remained unshaken by his liege lord's misfortunes. In fact, visitors reported him as calm and lucid, confident that his God, 'who preserveth them that are true of heart', would protect him, and never shifting from dignified certainty that he was England's King. 'When pressed by some impertinent person to justify his usurpation', wrote his contemporary biographer John Blacman, he answered:

> My father had been king of England, possessing his crown in peace all through his reign; and his father, my grandfather, had been king of the same realm. And I, when a boy in the cradle, had been without any interval crowned in peace and approved as king by the whole realm, and wore the crown for well-nigh forty years, every lord doing royal homage to me, and swearing fealty as they had done to my forefathers.

Since his cousin Robert was Lieutenant of the Tower, Sir Thomas Malory could easily have gained access, openly or in secret, to the King. They would have had many shared memories of Henry's intense friendship with Harry Beauchamp in the 1440s. Malory will have had a chance, perhaps his first, to explain and ask pardon for his extraordinary actions in 1451. He could also have told the King stories about his father, Henry V – about his piety and learning as well as his valour.

But if others were listening, Malory would have performed the office he was best known for – 'passing the time pleasantly' by narrating the old legends that everybody knew and loved: the tales of King Arthur's triumphs over rebels, of his adulterous yet ultimately faithful Queen Guinevere, of Sir Bors and Sir Lamorak, Gawaine and Gareth, Percival and Galahad. Perhaps it was Henry's arrival that led Malory to break off from Lancelot's and Tristram's adventures and work instead on the tale most calculated to appeal to Henry: 'The Quest for the Holy Grail'. For when he finished his final revision, Malory would give this particular story a puzzling dedication:

> *Thus endeth the tale of the Sangreal, that was briefly drawn out of French – which is a tale chronicled for one of the trewest and of the holiest that is in the world – by sir Thomas Malerorré, knight.*
>
> *O, Blessed Jesu help him through His might.*

No one has satisfactorily explained this explicit. But Henry VI would be a prime candidate in any Lancastrian loyalist's eyes for being 'one of the trewest and of the holiest that is in the world'. If this is indeed the explicit's coded meaning, its final prayer for help could refer just as easily to the imprisoned King as to Malory himself.

Visits to poor 'Henry of Lancaster' could have been thought entirely innocent by Edward, who knew Sir Thomas as merely an ageing chronicler and romancer. But they put Malory suspiciously close to the natural hub of a Lancastrian conspiracy, and he may well have been watched – and watched deservedly. For the most plausible interpretation of the startling records of the next three years is that Malory acted as a trusted go-between for Henry VI in the Tower of London and Queen Margaret's court in exile.

Insurrections and Trespasses

On 14 July 1468, in celebration of his sister's marriage to the Duke of Burgundy, Edward IV issued the second general pardon of his reign. It was an amnesty offered to 'all manner of men for all manner of insurrections and trespasses', to be applied for by the coming St John's Day, 27 December. Although the cost of such a pardon varied according to the sins you were known to have committed, it was a generous gesture, inviting those who were wavering in the shadows to enjoy the Yorkist sunshine. It was also politic. Edward wanted to rule a united realm, not a nest of malcontents and rebels. He also wanted to impress Europe with the strength of his position. But as usual, a general pardon was prefaced with exceptions. Edward's grace did not extend to Henry, 'lately king', his wife Margaret and her son Edward in France, or anybody with them there. He also excepted anyone attainted of high treason and everyone in the town and castle of Harlech, the sole remaining Lancastrian citadel in Britain.

Only eleven other individual exceptions were made. The second person named was Sir Thomas Malory. It is a shock to see his name, its first appearance in four years, in such company. For the diatribe of insults laced around the names and the mention of 'damnable, most malicious and hateful deceptions' show beyond any shadow of doubt that the eleven men were seen as active conspirators and secret agents. The list was evidently a hurried addition to a long-planned pardon because of a sudden crisis: the revelation of a far-reaching conspiracy that aimed to topple Edward IV from his throne.

On 20 June 1468, Sir Thomas Cook, a former Mayor of London who had been made a Knight of the Bath by Edward in 1464, was accused of listening to treasonous intrigues and sending valuable woollen cloths to contribute to the cause of the Lancastrians who were doggedly holding out at Harlech Castle. Cook was only the most notable of a whole clutch of eminent Londoners accused of collaboration with the enemy, but he was one of the few who were actually convicted – not, fortunately for his head, of treason, but of the 'misprision' of not reporting the traitors who approached him. He had to pay an enormous fine: over £6,000. While he was in the Tower awaiting trial, his various residences were ransacked by officers of the King, several of them the Queen's Woodville relatives, searching for incriminating evidence. As well as papers, they took gold and silver salt cellars, spoons, platters, spice plates, candelabra, cushions and bed-hangings. The King's mother-in-law Jacquetta was rumoured to have coveted, and gained, Cook's fabulous collection of tapestries showing Nebuchadnezzar, Alexander, the Passion and Last Judgement and the siege of Jerusalem, and valued at £984. Cook later claimed that valuables were lost and damage done to the tune of £15,000.

Because of this pillage, Sir Thomas Cook's troubles appear in most history books as an example of Woodville greed. But if we examine earlier conspiracies and look at who was involved, and what they did later, it is clear that a genuine threat to Edward's throne lay behind the notorious 'Thomas Cook affair'. The King had known for some time that there was a major conspiracy afoot. He was, like all successful rulers at this time, an accomplished spymaster, taking to heart the advice Christine de Pisan gave to rulers in her *Feats of Arms* (one of the books in his library): 'Be curious and diligent to send forth here and there espies subtle . . . to understand the purpose of [your] enemies'. He had a sophisticated network of spies, organised through the county sheriffs, who had been allowed from the autumn of 1466 to keep back up to £300 a year from taxes due to the King to seek out information 'on account of the grave dangers of the troubled times'. His anxieties were confirmed soon afterwards when his men caught 'one called Jon Worby of Mortlond a spy', who confessed he was in the pay of Margaret of Anjou. He said that Lancastrian plans for an invasion of England were well advanced, and offered to turn double agent. He may have proved an effective one. Two couriers carrying letters from Queen Margaret to the garrison at Harlech were captured in Wales by Lord Herbert in October 1467. 'Put to the question' in London, one of them 'made many accusations, and said that there were rumours overseas that the Earl of Warwick himself was beginning to favour the party of Queen Margaret'.

At this point, such an idea was only wishful Lancastrian thinking, although Warwick was certainly cooling in his enthusiasm for Edward, not least because the Nevilles were being beaten at their own nuptial game. Queen Elizabeth had rapidly arranged a large number of ennobling and enriching marriages for her many relatives. Edward summoned Warwick to Westminster. The Earl, haughty as ever, refused to leave Middleham over such a trifle. The King, who enjoyed games of cat and mouse, sent the Lancastrian courier to Middleham so that the Earl could investigate the matter himself. Warwick reported that it had been proved to be a frivolous accusation. Nothing more was heard of the incident, nor were the couriers ever named or charged. But from then on King Edward retained two hundred archers as a personal bodyguard. It is also noticeable that the number of people accused of treasonous activities began to increase, judging from the rising numbers of pardons issued to those who had talked their way out of the accusations. Of the disappeared, lying anonymously in gaols, we know nothing.

Edward spent more money on espionage in 1468 than in any other year of his reign. In January he ordered the sheriffs of counties on the coast to build beacons in case there was an invasion after the truce with France expired in March. In February, men-at-arms were rallied in the Isle of Wight and ships and sailors were commandeered for a royal fleet to defend the Channel. In May, Sir Richard Harcourt of Wytham was granted £20 a year for life 'in consideration of his labour and diligence in resisting the malice of certain traitors in the county of Oxford'. In all, over £2,200 was transferred from the Exchequer to the King's own chamber and spent on 'certain secret matters concerning the defence of the kingdom'. One payment was of £34 to 'a secret person for a great cause we will not be named'.

The King's investments delivered. In the first week of June a man called John Cornelius, travelling as a merchant dealing in shoes, was arrested at Queenborough in Kent. Letters found on him showed that he was a courier in the service of Sir Robert Whittingham, formerly Keeper of the Great Wardrobe to Henry VI and now with Queen Margaret at Koeur. The letters were from Whittingham and the exiled Queen. One was addressed to Malory's kinsman Thomas Danvers, the dashing young lawyer who wrote that teasing letter about Ovid to Sir John Paston. He was promptly arrested and taken to the Tower. Another lawyer, Hugh Mille, whose father and brother had died fighting for the Lancastrian cause in 1460 and 1461, and who had been in the Fleet prison perhaps awaiting the arrival of guarantees for the pardon he had been granted in July 1467, soon joined him. It is possible that Mille had been one of the couriers arrested by Herbert and exonerated by Warwick. Perhaps it was he who implicated Cornelius.

The seriousness with which Edward took the arrest is shown by the fact that Cornelius was tortured. After fire was applied to the soles of his feet, he reeled off a string of names: Peter Alfray, Sir John Plummer, Sir Gervais Clifton, Hugh Pakenham, Nicholas Hussey, Thomas Portaleyn, William Belknap, Robert Knollys, John Fisher of the Temple and John Hawkins, a servant of Lord Wenlock.

Hawkins was next to face torture, this time using the Tower's notorious Brake, a form of rack described as a 'harrow fit to reel men's bodies out like silk'. He claimed that Lord Wenlock himself had been involved in the plotting, which had begun in October 1466 when Hugh Mille, Hawkins and Alfray had made approaches to a number of eminent Londoners, including Sir Thomas Cook. They had asked for financial support to be sent to Sir Richard Tunstall, in command at Harlech. They also told those they approached that Queen Margaret was planning to invade England shortly in order to restore Henry VI, and that Sir Richard would support her by a march from Harlech, gathering forces on the way in Cheshire and Lancashire, both hotbeds of closet Lancastrians.

Hawkins said that support had been given in October 1466 by Hugh Pakenham of Southwark (40s), Thomas Portaleyn (100s), John Shuckburgh (£20) and Sir Thomas Cook (valuable woollen cloths). In addition Alice Paslowe had been persuaded by Peter Alfray on 6 December 1467 to send 10 marks to Harlech by John Norris, a courier of Sir Richard Tunstall. On 20 May 1468, Alfray had persuaded Sir John Plummer to send Tunstall 10 marks, again by John Norris. Finally, it was said that on 10 March 1468, Sir Gervais Clifton, Nicholas Hussey, Robert Knollys and John Fisher had sent Cornelius to Queen Margaret promising their support. Cornelius must have been returning from Koeur, probably via Calais, when he was picked up at Queenborough.

Edward moved very fast indeed. Letters patent for an exceptionally heavyweight commission of oyer and terminer to try the suspects were issued on 20 June. It was headed by his brother George, Duke of Clarence. The other peers who sat on it were Warwick, Sir John Neville (now elevated to Earl of Northumberland), Henry Bourgchier, Earl of Essex, Lord Rivers, Lord Hastings, and four other lords. Thomas Oulgreve, Mayor of London, Sir John Markham, Chief Justice of King's Bench, and five other judges were also appointed to the commission.

Edward IV, who liked to interrogate prisoners personally, may well have found out a good deal more from Cornelius and Hawkins than appeared in the indictments. It was beginning to look as if the

London conspirators were just one element in a potentially devastating plot to co-ordinate Lancastrian risings in different parts of the country – the north and south-west of Wales, the north of England, the West Country, Kent, and perhaps even in London itself. The risings, led by Lancastrian exiles supported by French arms, would prepare the way for the return of Queen Margaret and Prince Edward, now a martially-minded fifteen-year-old who, wrote a Milanese ambassador who met him at Koeur, 'talked of nothing but chopping off heads'. King Louis XI of France had already given Jasper Tudor ships, money and men to launch an invasion, using Harlech as a port of entry. The coup was timed to happen after the departure of hundreds of English notables to Burgundy to accompany Edward's sister, Margaret of York, to Bruges for her marriage to the Duke of Burgundy. The capital would be more vulnerable at such a time. Worse, such an uprising might well shake Duke Charles's confidence in Edward enough to prevent the marriage altogether.

Edward was determined not to let anything get in the way of the departure of his beloved sister. He soothed her anxieties over the arrest of Sir Thomas Cook, an old friend who had put up surety for a tenth of her dowry by freeing him 'for as long as she was in the land'. Margaret set off on 18 June, escorted through the streets of London by her two younger brothers, George of Clarence and Richard of Gloucester and Warwick and their retinues. It was a leisurely journey, a pageant and a pilgrimage as well as a parting. After making an offering at St Paul's, Margaret processed along Cheapside, where she was presented with two great silver-gilt bowls by the Lord Mayor of London. After crossing London Bridge, she and her escort arrived at the Abbey of Stratford, where they spent the night. There Edward IV himself joined her, having impetuously decided that he too would ride with her to the coast. They took three days to get to Margate via Rochester, Sittingbourne and Canterbury, where they stopped to pray at the shrine of Thomas Becket. The message to the ubiquitous eyes and ears of spies and diplomats from the Continent was that England was stable, not in crisis, and that Warwick was with Edward, not against him. Edward was well aware of the danger of rumour, the need to persuade both his enemy, France, and his hard-won European allies Brittany and Burgundy that he was firmly seated on his throne.

The next day Margaret and several hundred nobles, knights and ladies, each with their travelling household, embarked at Margate, sailing in a fleet of sixteen ships. Anthony Woodville, Lord Scales, who shared Margaret's love of books and manuscripts religious and romantic, was her chief presenter and would fight in the tournament as her champion.

As soon as the fleet had set sail, Sir Thomas Cook was taken to the Tower to join the other recently arrested malefactors. The seriousness of the situation intensified a few days later when royal spies in Harfleur sent word that Jasper Tudor had set sail for Harlech on 24 June. On Sunday 3 July Edward commissioned Lord Herbert to array the border counties of Gloucestershire, Herefordshire, Shropshire and the Welsh Marches against Jasper. Next day indictments were read out against John Hawkins, Hugh Mille and Peter Alfray. On Tuesday they were brought before the court. Hawkins denied his guilt, but the jury found him guilty and the judge condemned him to be hanged, drawn and quartered. Hugh Mille produced his July 1467 pardon and it was accepted – perhaps luck, perhaps a sign that he had traded information for his life. Alfray was sentenced to death, but as he mounted the scaffold a pardon sought for him by George Neville, Archbishop of York, arrived to save him.

The jurors were then asked to indict Hugh Pakenham, Thomas Portaleyn and Sir Thomas Cook, who had all been imprisoned in the Tower. But they balked at convicting their neighbours on the strength of confessions extorted from spies under torture, and they refused to allow the charge of giving money and valuables, only that of concealing the conspiracy. A new jury was called, which accepted both charges against the trio, but when they came before the court on Friday, Portaleyn and Pakenham were declared not guilty of active support, though they were kept in the custody of the sheriffs over the issue of concealment. Sir Thomas Cook was also found not guilty of aiding the Lancastrians, but he was convicted of concealment. He was put in the Marshalsea to await notice of what fine would be levied.

In the end, the juries refused to indict nine of the original twenty-four accused. Of the fifteen who were indicted, only six stood trial.

The other nine malefactors vanished from the record. The justices were told on Wednesday 6 July that Cornelius, John Norris, Sir Gervais Clifton, Sir John Plummer, John Fisher, Alice Paslowe, William Tyler, Charles Wynn and Nicholas Hussey could not be brought into court because they could not be found. Proceedings to outlaw them began. Cornelius may well have died in prison. Sir Gervais Clifton and Nicholas Hussey may have sailed for Calais where they had many friends. The others emerged from hiding or sanctuary over the next few months and settled out of court, paying a substantial amount in fines and for pardons.

Because only John Hawkins was condemned to death, the seriousness of the conspiracy has been underrated – a triumph for royal propaganda. But there is confirmation of the treasonous iceberg that lay under the tip of the Thomas Cook affair in Warkworth's Chronicle:

> And in the seventh year of King Edward, Sir Thomas Cook, Sir John Plummer, knights and aldermen of London, and Humphrey Hayford and other aldermen were arrested, and treason surmised upon them, whereof they were acquitted, but they lost great goods to the king, to the value of 40,000 marks or more; and divers times, in divers places of England, men were arrested for treason, and some were put to death and some escaped [my emphasis].

False Traitor Knight

The individuals announced as being excepted from the long-planned general pardon on 14 July, just days after the trials ended, are likely to be the men whom Edward believed were the masterminds and ringleaders of the country-wide conspiracy. Here is the complete list, in original wording and order:

> Humfrey Nevyll, knight
> Thomas Malarie, knight
> Robert Marshal, lately of Culham, Oxon, squire

Hugh Mille, lately of London, gentleman
Gervase Clyfton, lately of London, knight
William Verdon, lately of London, scrivener
Peter Hussey, lately of London, esquire
Morgan ap Thomas ap Griffith, of Carmarthen, gentleman
Henry ap Thomas ap Griffith ap Nicholas, lately of Carmar-
then, squire
Maurice ap Owen ap Griffith, lately of Carmarthen,
gentleman
Thomas Philip, lately of Rea, Gloucestershire, yeoman.

Seven of these men were influential Lancastrians whose loyalty Edward had once hoped to win. The thirty-year-old Sir Humphrey Neville was a particularly resolute and daring military commander. After unfurling the Lancastrian banner at Brancepeth on the day before Edward IV's coronation in June 1461, Neville was arrested by officers of the King stationed in Durham and imprisoned in the Tower of London where, although attainted with other leading Lancastrians in November, he was treated well. In February 1462, he was pardoned, granted his life and restored to his estates on the condition that he would stay in the custody of the Lieutenant of the Tower (Robert Malory) during the King's pleasure. Within months Neville had escaped; he then fled back to the North and began hell-raising again. He helped Henry VI escape from Bywell Castle in 1464. His renewed forays over the border led to more complaints from Durham in April 1465 and he was attainted in January 1466. Neville was the most feared Lancastrian still on the loose. If word had come that Sir Humphrey was once more on the warpath, it would explain why Warwick's brother John, Earl of Northumberland, galloped north as soon as the trials were under way.

The three Welshmen were the son and grandsons of Griffith ap Nicholas of Carmarthen, whom the Welsh had regarded as a national hero, potentially a successor to Owain Glen Dŵr. Since Griffith's death, they had followed Henry VI's half-brother Jasper Tudor, leader of the Lancastrian rebels in Wales. All three had fought with Jasper against Edward at Mortimer's Cross, but been pardoned. They were certainly dangerous: Morgan ap Thomas and Henry ap Thomas would seize Carmarthen and Cardigan castles for Lancaster in the autumn of 1469 – at exactly the same time as Sir Humphrey Neville yet again invaded Northumberland. The fact that they were named in the pardon shows they were not part of the Harlech garrison, which was excepted as a whole. Edward may have discovered that they were raising rebels in south Wales to ride north to join Jasper Tudor's forces. One chronicler estimated that two thousand men joined Jasper after he landed in Barmouth, just south of Harlech.

Sir Gervais Clifton, younger son of a Nottinghamshire family, had married a wealthy widow with estates in Kent and Lincolnshire. Now about fifty-five years old, he too was a feisty soldier who was knighted after his service with the Talbots during the siege of Bordeaux and the disaster of Châtillon in 1453. Experienced in naval warfare, he had been Treasurer of Calais under Henry VI and had defended the Tower of London against Warwick in 1460 before fleeing to join Queen Margaret in the North. He probably fought at Wakefield, as he was one of the twenty-two people excepted from the pardon Edward offered to all adherents of Henry VI in March 1461, but he was allowed to take up a pardon in June 1461. He had been suspected again of treason in 1465 and outlawed. His power base in the turbulent county of Kent made Clifton exceptionally dangerous.

Hugh Mille was another younger son, a lawyer who came from a West Country family with close connections with the Talbots and estates at Duntingbourne Rous and Harescombe, near Gloucester. He has been identified as commissioning a chivalric prose romance translated from the French, which is fascinating additional evidence of the likelihood of his being a close friend of Sir Thomas Malory. Hugh's father died in 1460, possibly in the Lancastrian cause, and his older brother Sir William Mille was fatally wounded fighting for Henry VI at Towton and attainted posthumously. The confiscated Mille estates were given to Thomas Herbert. Mille took out a pardon in September 1462; he was then described as 'of London, gentleman, alias formerly of Harescombe'. He sat on a Middlesex commission of the peace in 1464, and three years later in July 1467 secured another pardon, a precaution that would save his life.

Malory's years in service to the young Duke of Warwick, Harry Beauchamp – seen here (*left*) kneeling in mourning in an initial letter of the prayer roll he commissioned after his father's death – were probably the happiest years of his life. Sir Harry was a close friend of the young king Henry VI, and gallant escapades, such as the one illustrated in René of Anjou's chivalric romance, *Cueur* (*below*), were much to Sir Harry's taste; he seems to have made a covert journey to France just before Henry VI agreed to marry Margaret.

Malory may have visited the romantically craggy promontory of Tintagel (*above*), supposedly the scene of King Arthur's conception, with his cousin, John Chetwynd, who was Constable of Tintagel in the 1440s.

He certainly knew of the existence of what was then believed to be the original sixth-century Round Table, hanging in the great hall of Winchester Castle (*left*), and he describes King Arthur as holding court at Winchester, identifying it with Camelot. The table was later repainted by Henry VIII (whose older brother was christened Arthur, but died aged 23).

In 1453 Malory appeared in front of the Court of King's Bench, illustrated in session in the mid-fifteenth century (*opposite*). It was almost a decade before he extricated himself completely from the clutches of the law.

In the 1450s the Court of King's Bench sat in the north end of Westminster Hall. Malory probably arrrived by boat from the Marshalsea, the south bank prison in which he was first held.

Released on bail, he failed to return because he had been accused of aiding and abetting horse thieves in Essex and had been imprisoned in Colchester Castle (*below*); he escaped but was eventually persuaded to return into the custody of the London sheriffs.

Malory's fortunes were affected by the early stages of the Wars of the Roses in the mid-1450s. He was released to join the forces of the Earl of Warwick's uncle, Lord Fauconberg. When word came of the Yorkist advance on London in 1460, Malory was moved to the city's most secure prison: the Tower. The picture above shows the release from the Tower in 1440 of another famous writer, Charles, Duc d'Orléans, kept hostage since 1415. Malory was finally released after the Yorkist triumph in 1461 at Mortimer's Cross, Herefordshire; the victory was heralded by the spectacular phenomenon of three suns seeming to appear, known as a parhelion (*left*).

Malory's relationship to the Duke of Warwick's successor, Sir Richard Neville, the legendary 'Kingmaker' and Earl of Warwick (portrayed *above left*, behind his father, Sir Ralph, with other members of the immensely influential Neville clan, including his formidable sisters), seems to have been less close than his links to the Beauchamp earls. But in all likelihood he remained intensely loyal to Neville's wife Anne Beauchamp, Sir Harry's sister and the source of his right to the title of Earl of Warwick. She may be portrayed as 'Lady Imagination' in one of the few books known to have been owned by her husband, *Enseignement de la vraie Noblesse* (*above right*).

Phrases in the explicits to the *Morte Darthur* make it seem likely that Malory was writing it for a patron, perhaps in the hope of it influencing his release from prison, perhaps to inspire a future monarch of England. The illustration below shows just such a labour of love being presented in 1448 by Jean Wauquelin to Duke Philip of Burgundy.

Invading Lancastrians attacked
the Tower of London with long-
bows and crossbows, handguns,
cannon and shipborne troops in
October 1470 (*above*); Malory,
imprisoned in about 1469, after
being implicated in conspira
cies in about 1468, was probably
freed after Henry VI regained
his throne and Edward IV went
into exile in Flanders.

Malory's gravestone said that he
died on 14 March 1471. Perhaps
this was just as well; Edward IV
re-invaded England that very
day, and the Lancastrians were
decisively defeated at Barnet,
where Warwick fell, and
Tewkesbury (*right*), where
Henry VI's son Edward of
Lancaster was killed.

Malory's death vigil is likely to have resembled this illustration of a death vigil from a manuscript *Book of Hours* commissioned by Sir William Hastings, and painted in the late 1470s.

Peter Hussey was one of the Sussex Husseys. He had married the widow of John Hampden, a committed Buckinghamshire Lancastrian whose feoffees included three of those implicated in the London plot: Thomas Danvers, Lord Wenlock and Sir John Plummer. He could well have been a relative of Nicholas Hussey, once the Earl of Warwick's victualler in Calais and one of the men whom Hawkins accused.

Thomas Philip of Rea (which is close to Gloucester) had fought for Queen Margaret at Bamborough and had been the ringleader of the Lancastrian risings in Gloucester which had sent Edward racing down in person to superintend a number of executions and beheadings in February 1464. Philip was attainted but escaped to join Queen Margaret's court at Koeur. In 1466 he was pardoned, and said to have become a chapman – the medieval equivalent of a travelling salesman and an ideal disguise for a courier.

All eight of these men were highly likely to have been engaged in fomenting risings to coincide with Jasper Tudor's arrival in Wales. The remaining three, Marshall, Verdon and Malory, were identified as enemies of York for the first time. As far as Marshall and Verdon are concerned, we can only inch forward with guesswork. Marshalls held estates at Kilby, Leicestershire, fifteen miles north-east of Newbold Revel. A Robert Marshall, said to be a gentleman 'of Southwell, Nottinghamshire', escaped from Nottingham Gaol in 1465. Southwell is only fifteen miles from the Cliftons' family seat. The fact that Robert Marshall was 'lately of Culham, Oxfordshire', a well-known sanctuary, suggests he was a fugitive. Culham is not far from the road than runs through Oxford and Gloucester to Wales – or from Thomas Danvers's Oxfordshire manor of Waterstock. Finally, it is intriguing that there was a Robert Marshall among Edward IV's minstrels. Minstrels – along with merchants, lawyers, clerics, doctors and women – were often employed as intelligence agents.

William Verdon was probably the William Vernon who is recorded as a member of the London Scriveners Company in 1464; he could have been a kinsman of the Derbyshire Vernons, who were at this time involved in a blood feud with Lord Grey of Codnor – with the support of Edward IV. He is an interesting person to find in Sir

Thomas Malory's company. We may be staring at the name of the man to whom he dictated his Arthurian tales – or who organised copies of them. He may have known Malory for some time, as he could also have been the William Vernon who stood security for Sir Robert Harcourt after the affray in Coventry in 1448. A master scrivener would also, however, be needed to arrange multiple copies of treasonous and seditious writings. Malory, Vernon and Marshall: a gifted writer, a scrivener and a squire who might have been a minstrel who had close access to Edward IV and could have overheard many unguarded conversations. Are they a significant trio? Was Malory's exception from pardon unjustified, a panic measure taken at a time when any sort of writing might hold encrypted messages? Or were he and his companions in truth key secret agents?

A respectable case can be made for Malory being a go-between for Henry and the conspirators. He had close connections with many of the London plotters. There is more than a hint of a literary circle about them: Hugh Mille translated a French romance and called one of his sons Gawaine, and in the 1450s had helped Bishop Waynflete arrange the endowment of Magdalen College, Oxford. Sir Gervais Clifton and Sir Robert Whittingham were also feoffees of Magdalen. Thomas Danvers's letter to John Paston shows that he was well read; he too was involved in the setting up of Magdalen College, and was the bailiff of Waynflete's Oxfordshire manors. No one ever attempted to implicate Waynflete in the conspiracy, but he was in all probability involved in it. He took out a pardon soon afterwards. So too did Robert Malory; he also seems to have been removed from the lieutenancy of the Tower at around this time.

Malory also had links with Thomas Portaleyn, one of the men indicted with Sir Thomas Cook. Described in 1441 as 'literatus' by the Bishop of Llandaff, Portaleyn had been receiver-general for both Richard Beauchamp and his son Harry, and had made the young Duke generous loans. Books belonging to him survive, and he married a wealthy London widow, both of whose previous husbands had been lawyers. In the 1450s, he remained in the service of Warwick, moving between London and the Midlands, and he was MP for Warwickshire in 1453. But he did not follow Warwick into rebellion against Henry

VI, and lived in London in perhaps deliberate obscurity in the 1460s, until he was implicated by Cornelius in 1468.

The paths of Sir Humphrey Neville and Malory could have crossed when Neville was imprisoned in the Tower between 1461 and 1463. Robert Malory had been his gaoler then; he was named as one of the five-man commission sent north to arrest Neville after he escaped early in 1463. Sir Thomas Malory would have thoroughly approved of Neville's adventurous spirit. John Norris was a younger son of the eminent Lancastrian courtier, John Norris. The still extant fifteenth-century windows of Ockwells, the family manor at Bray in Berkshire, link Norris's arms with those of Harry Beauchamp, Duke of Warwick, Sir John Wenlock, Henry VI and Margaret of Anjou.

Most interesting and suggestive of all are Malory's links to John, Lord Wenlock, who had been his effective overlord at Newbold Revel since 1461. When the Duke of Norfolk died that year, he had acquired the wardship of the young Duke. Much the same age as Malory, Wenlock was an extremely able man, learned and multilingual; he laid the first stone of the chapel of the college founded by Margaret of Anjou at Cambridge. He came late to the Yorkist cause, forced like many others to a point of no return after the death of Richard of York at Wakefield. He fought for Edward at Towton, and in the early 1460s Edward, who was short of good men, loaded him with administrative and diplomatic responsibilities.

Wenlock had close connections with the Earl of Warwick, and was held in high repute by some very eminent Lancastrians. Anne Neville, Dowager Duchess of Buckingham, whom I have suggested was Malory's 'Dame Gladness', had made him steward of her lands in Huntingdonshire, Bedfordshire and Buckinghamshire on 20 February 1462. He had a positive bevy of Lancastrian wards: Eleanor Beaufort, whose father Edmund, Duke of Somerset, had been killed at St Albans in 1458 and whose husband, the Earl of Wiltshire, had been beheaded after the Battle of Hexham in 1461; Eleanor Moleyns, wife of Lord Hungerford, who was also executed after Hexham; and Lady Anne Hampden. Lady Anne's husband Sir Edmund Hampden had been a close associate of Wenlock when they were both in Queen Margaret's household in the 1450s; he was now in exile in Bordeaux. His role as guardian was to prevent them aiding their husbands. But he proved to be an effective protector of their interests.

Wenlock had also been granted the lands of the exiled Chief Justice, Sir John Fortescue. Fortescue knew the lawyers involved in the conspiracy. His writings were included in a fascinating (and incriminating) collection of manuscripts, books and letters expressing criticism of Yorkist claims that were carefully, and probably secretly, preserved in a large folio volume by Sir Thomas Cook's secretary, John Vale. Wenlock too had links with London lawyers. Early in the 1460s, he married Lady Agnes Fray, the widow of a lawyer and former Baron of the Exchequer. Agnes was the sister of the Thomas Danvers to whom Cornelius was bringing that incriminating letter from the court of Margaret of Anjou. Danvers was, as we have seen, linked with Malory. George Burneby's wife Alice was Agnes Danvers's niece. It is not surprising that Burneby took out a pardon early in 1470.

Wenlock was not taken into custody, despite the fact that Hawkins 'had said many things against him'. He was already abroad, in Calais, part of the embassy (which also included William Caxton) chosen to settle the commercial differences between the Flemish and English cloth merchants at a diet which was to be held in Bruges after Margaret's wedding. He was paid £100 on 8 June 1468 as expenses for this embassy and for accompanying the Lady Margaret when she arrived in Bruges. Wenlock remained at Calais for the next fifteen months, playing a perilous double game in which the only consistent strand was loyalty to Lancaster.

The feast of the wedding, and of the jousts at the feast

Since Sir Thomas Malory was not tried with the other conspirators in the first week of July 1468, he too could have slipped abroad. The Latin tag *nuper de* ('lately of') after names on the pardon is significant. It means that the person's recent whereabouts are known – either because they were last seen there, or because that is where they were arrested. The pardon of 14 July does not place either Neville or Malory, though the third knight, Sir Gervais Clifton, was said to be 'lately of

London'. Neville was in Scotland. If Malory had also left England, he could have gone to Calais with Lord Wenlock.

Calais protected England from Europe. But it could also menace the realm. It was from Calais that Warwick and Edward had sailed to take London in 1460. Now agents of Queen Margaret's court at Koeur had joined the international and itinerant throng of merchants, couriers, diplomats and spies who exchanged news there. John Cornelius, John Hawkins, Nicholas Hussey, Sir Gervais Clifton and Thomas Philip all knew Calais well. We have no proof that Malory went there with Wenlock in June 1468, but he would have relished the opportunity of witnessing Margaret's wedding to the Duke of Burgundy. Charles the Bold was a fierce, energetic man, as fascinated by legends, history and chivalric traditions as his father had been. When Margaret's fleet made port at Sluys, in Flanders, on 25 June, Malory had after all not yet been called a traitor by name, and was perhaps not even incriminated until Hugh Mille sang for his life. At least two as yet unexposed members of the conspiracy, Poynings and Alford, did go to Sluys with Margaret.

All manner of legends were revived for the wedding. As London was reputed to have been founded by Brutus as 'New Troy', the ship Margaret sailed in was named the *New Ellen* to signify that Margaret was a second Helen. A set of splendid tapestries made soon after the wedding for the Burgundian ducal palace tell the story of Troy, and show the Greek fleet off Troy looking just like Margaret's wedding fleet in Sluys. Margaret later encouraged William Caxton to publish his translation of a collection of the Trojan legends in English.

Tall and slim, with an oval face and grey eyes, Margaret was not conventionally beautiful, but had 'an air of intelligence and will'. Duke Charles evidently liked what he saw. There was, it was said, a remarkable amount of kissing during and after the formal betrothal. Margaret and he then boarded a barge to Damme, where the actual wedding took place in a private ceremony. From there Margaret travelled alone to Bruges for the traditional 'Joyeuse Entrée'. She sat in a gilded litter draped with crimson cloth of gold, drawn by six white horses caparisoned to match. Nearly two thousand nobles, knights, minstrels and musicians walked beside the litter, undeterred by pouring rain, through city streets carpeted with rugs, hung with tapestries and Burgundian and English banners, and garlanded with flowers. As they passed through the cheering crowds, pageants on nuptial themes were played out: Adam and Eve, the Song of Solomon, the marriage of Moses and Zipporah, Antony and Cleopatra.

Margaret entered the gates of the ducal palace to see red and white wine flowing from the bows of sculpted archers, and ippocras (a mixture of honey and mead) spouting out of the breast of a gilded pelican perched in a bejewelled tree. The staterooms of the palace were hung with brilliantly coloured tapestries woven with gold and silver. On each of the next nine days there was a splendid feast in the great wooden hall of the Order of the Golden Fleece. Huge gold and silver platters in the shapes of unicorns, swans and peacocks presented magnificent arrays of eatables, and between every course there were entertainments: invasions of giants and ogres, a dwarf riding a lion, a wild Saracen on a camel. All sorts of weird and wonderful curiosities were exhibited, including a 41-foot tower crammed with monkeys, wolves and dancing bears.

The days were filled with jousting. The Tournament of the Golden Tree was solemnly opened on the afternoon of the wedding day by Duke Charles, his robes encrusted thickly with jewels. It was declared to have been summoned 'at the bidding of the Lady of the Hidden Isle', who was demanding that three great tasks should be undertaken for her sake: to break one hundred and one spears, or to have them broken; to suffer one hundred and one sword cuts; and to decorate a Golden Tree with the arms of noble champions. As each knight taking part entered, he hung his coat of arms on a Golden Tree at the entrance to the lists. The pages wore harlequin costumes and carried armorial shields. Sir John Paston wrote home excitedly:

> They that jousted . . . have been as richly beseen . . . as cloth
> of gold, and silk and silver, and goldsmith's work might make
> them; for of such gear and gold and pearl and stones, they
> of the Duke's Court, neither gentlemen or gentlewomen, they
> want none; for without that they have it by wishes, by my
> troth, I heard never of so great plenty as there is . . . As for

the Duke's court as of lords, ladies and gentlewomen, knights, squires and gentlemen I heard never of none like it save King Arthur's court. And by my troth, I have no wit nor remembrance to write to you half the worship that is here.

In the best Arthurian tradition, many knights entered in disguise: the Black Knight, the Ancient Knight, legendary heroes. No holds were barred in the jousts, which were fought fast and furiously. Duke Charles himself participated until Margaret begged him to return to her side; the Bastard of Burgundy, who had arranged the entire tournament, broke his leg. In the end Sir Edward Woodville was declared Prince of the Tourney and the Burgundian Lord d'Argueil Prince of the Joust. The festivities ended on 11 July, and the English set off for home the next day.

It is tempting to imagine that Malory went to Bruges, and that he not only witnessed the tournament, but actually took part – perhaps as the Ancient Knight. If so, we could see the fact that Edward waited until 14 July, three days after the festivities ended, to publish the general pardon and its damning exceptions as a merciful gesture towards a knight he respected, even though he was suspected of treasonous intrigues. Edward certainly had spies in Bruges. He will have heard, as Paston did, that 'the Duke of Somerset and all his band departed, well-beseen [i.e. in fine clothes and well-horsed, thanks to Burgundian largesse] out of Bruges a day before that my Lady the Duchess [Margaret of York] came hither, and they say that he is [gone] to Queen Margaret that was, and shall no more come again or be helpen by the duke'.

'For this was drawn by a Knight Prisoner'

Paston and most of the English visitors set off for home on 12 July. Several people were arrested as soon as they returned to England. Some escaped indictment in return for paying stiffish fines. Humphrey Hayford, a sheriff of London who had been thought to be too merciful to his fellow citizens during the Cook affair, had to pay so much that it was said he had 'lost his cloak'. Edward was still taking the danger of a Lancastrian invasion seriously. On 3 August he peremptorily requisitioned every ship in every port of the kingdom. He may have been as concerned to prevent them being taken away by rebels as to use them himself. Despite the taking of Harlech in August by Edward's lieutenant in Wales, Lord Herbert, and the consequent flight of Jasper Tudor, a substantial royal fleet was assembled under the command of Sir Walter Blount and Sir Anthony Woodville in Southampton on 20 September. Its official purpose was to transport the three thousand archers Edward had promised in August to the Duke of Brittany for use against France. Though Brittany signed a truce with France on 10 September, the fleet was still mustered, amid rumours that it was intended for Aquitaine. But it remained in home waters, policing the Channel, until late November.

In September 1468 Sir Robert Botill, the Prior of the Knights Hospitallers, died. The Hospitallers' own candidate as next Prior was Sir John Langstrother, formerly Castellan of Rhodes and now preceptor of Temple Balsall and Bailiff of Eagle. He was a martial man whose Lancastrian sympathies were well known. The Hospitaller headquarters in the London Priory of Clerkenwell would have been an ideal refuge for secret agents. Edward, who will have known much more about what was going on at Clerkenwell than we do, decided to scotch the danger of plotting there and to enrich his wife's family even more lavishly by announcing that the next Prior would be the Queen's brother, Sir John Woodville, who was only eighteen years old and not even a Hospitaller. It was an illegal move that enraged devout opinion. It would have been especially offensive to Malory and his Hospitaller kinsmen.

More arrests were made in October and November. Two were of young Lancastrians, likely leaders of a West Country rising. Henry Courtenay, heir of the Earl of Devon, and Sir Thomas Hungerford, heir of Lord Hungerford, were both taken in Wiltshire, and imprisoned in Salisbury Castle. A distinguished London skinner called Richard Stairs, said to be 'one of the cunningest players of tennis in all England', was charged in the court of chivalry with passing on letters on behalf of Queen Margaret, and Alford and Poynings, both retainers of the Duke of Norfolk, were tried for being in traitorous contact with Lancastrian exiles while they were in Bruges. All three were executed on Tower Hill at the end of November.

Soon afterwards the young Earl of Oxford, whose father and brother had already been executed for treason, was put in the Tower and persuaded to talk. As a result, Sir Thomas Tresham and Sir John Marney, both prominent in Henry VI's reign, were imprisoned. In January 1469 Courtenay and Hungerford were accused of conspiring together on 21 May 1468 and on other occasions, and of plotting, in league with Margaret of Anjou, 'the final death and final destruction ... of the most Christian prince, Edward IV'. The most Christian Prince had the trial delayed so that the royal eye could be on the judges when the verdict was pronounced. Both were found guilty and were executed in Salisbury with the customary exhibitionist cruelty. Many other conspirators escaped scot-free. William Waynflete took out another pardon on 1 February 1469.

Sir Thomas Malory's whereabouts may have been revealed by Oxford, or he may have been arrested earlier in the autumn. For, thanks to a document only discovered in 2000, we now know that on 20 April 1469, he was one of twenty-one men who acted as witnesses in Newgate Gaol to the deathbed declaration of one Thomas Mynton. Since one of the other witnesses was Thomas Philip, and both he and Malory had been excepted from the July pardon, it seems probable that both were, like Mynton, prisoners in Newgate. Several of the other witnesses may have had connections with Calais and the North. John Berton, gentleman, could have been the John Barton of Middleton, Lancashire, gentleman 'lately of Calais', whose name appears on a 1480 pardon. John Dawson, gentleman, could have been the Doncaster man of that name who took up a pardon in 1465. John Lee could have been the yeoman of the King's chamber mentioned in 1461 and still alive in 1475; John Despoy, gentleman, and Peryn Garard, yeoman, sound as if they had French connections. Also intriguing was the presence of 'Dominus John Draper, priest'. Eight years later, in 1477, a John Draper, 'lately chaplain of Draughton, in Northamptonshire [where Malorys had long held land and could still have had the living in their gift] alias John Hawkins, clerk' was pardoned. It was

Lord Wenlock's servant John Hawkins who had originally revealed the conspiracy. If this was the same man, he had evidently succeeded in escaping the gallows, perhaps pleading benefit of clergy, perhaps by betraying his fellow conspirators.

Not all the witnesses were inmates of Newgate. Several were servants or friends of Sir Thomas Cook, for the purpose of the deathbed declaration was that Thomas Mynton was abjuring any claim to certain Colchester tenements owned by Cook. The most interesting person present was John Vale, Cook's trusted private secretary, the man who so carefully copied politically interesting documents into the volume recently published as *John Vale's Book*. Vale himself wrote a short chronicle of his times, ending in 1471. It is frequently reminiscent of Malory's writing, and shows signs of being influenced by his opinions. Vale writes that Henry VI reigned for many years 'in great nobility, worship, wealth and prosperity into the time when he was only conduit, governed and ruled by divers of his counsel such as were not to be comen of the blood royal, but they that were brought up of nought'. It was the 'sinister counsel, envy and prepensed malice' of these men that caused 'the subversion and fall most dolorous of the said King Henry from his most royal and excellent dignity and estate'. Malory also talks of the 'evil counsel' that caused the rift between Lancelot and Arthur. 'But, sir,' says Lancelot, 'liars ye have listened [to], and that hath caused great debate betwixt you and me'. Vale's chronicle dated the decline of the reign of Henry VI from 1447, when the murder of Duke Humfrey of Gloucester at Bury followed the death of Harry Beauchamp the year before. As we have seen, Malory's sorties on the wrong side of the law began very soon after those tragedies. Vale and Malory, in the same room . . . it is not proof, but it is added evidence that both men were as deeply engaged in Lancastrian intrigues as Sir Thomas Cook himself.

Why was there no record in King's Bench of Malory's arrest or imprisonment? If Malory was indeed in the service of Lord Wenlock, to indict him for treason might affect the delicate balance of relations between Edward and his over-mighty subject the Earl of Warwick, and international confidence in Edward himself. Wenlock was after all Warwick's Lieutenant in Calais. But both Edward and Warwick were watching Wenlock with suspicion at this point. He had been Margaret of Anjou's Chamberlain. Where did his real loyalties lie? Arresting Malory might have been a way of finding out. All we know for certain is that at about this time Malory spent at least a year, perhaps longer, in captivity. He was fortunate not to be stripped of his spurs and executed. He must have been aware that his life hung by a thread. He certainly seems to have feared that he would simply be left to rot in prison without trial for ever. He had one last hope. These are the closing words of his *Morte Darthur*, missing in Winchester, which lacks its last eight pages, but fortunately preserved by Caxton:

> *I pray you all gentlemen and gentlewomen that readeth this book of Arthur and his knights, from the beginning to the ending, pray for me while I am alive, that God send me good deliverance, and when I am dead, I pray you all pray for my soul. For this book was ended the ninth year of the reign of King Edward the fourth, by Sir Thomas Maleoré, knight, as Jesu help him for his great might, as he is the servant of Jesu both day and night.*

Edward IV's reign began on 4 March 1461, so the ninth year of his reign was from 4 March 1469 to 3 March 1470. Whether Malory 'ended' his book early or late in the year, we do not know. But at that time there was only one person who could deliver Sir Thomas Malory from prison: Edward IV himself. Did Malory try to placate Edward by offering him his life's work, the book which he had originally intended for the young Prince in exile at Koeur?

Any such direct appeal to the King, supplemented perhaps by appeals to his own feoffee Sir Walter Blount, Lord Mountjoy, or to his veteran contemporary Sir Richard Woodville, Lord Rivers, both of whom were high in favour with Edward, would have been made in Malory's preface to his book. It has not survived. The first eight pages of the Winchester manuscript are, like the last eight, missing. But the explicits preserved by the two scribes who made that copy of Malory's book in the mid-1470s show beyond any shadow of doubt that Malory made repeated appeals for help, mercy and deliverance.

They also suggest that the book was being delivered, one section at a time, to be copied out in an attractive format by scribes, before being presented to someone of importance and influence. Blount? His wife Anne Neville? Edward IV himself? Was Malory, like Scheherazade, spinning stories in a desperate effort to save his own life?

Lancaster's Champion

*Also me seemeth by the oft reading [of Malory] ye shall
greatly desire to accustom yourself in following those gracious knightly deeds . . . faithfully to serve your sovereign
prince.*

Wynkyn de Worde

ll the evidence is that Malory won his longed-for deliverance.
For although he felt himself near death when he wrote the
last words of the *Morte Darthur*, he would live for at least
another year – and see his hopes of Henry VI's restoration to the
throne fulfilled. Relations between Edward IV and Warwick had
worsened. Edward's refusal to agree to the marriage of his brother
Clarence and Warwick's daughter Isobel, his favouring of the Woodvilles and men like Hastings and Blount above the Nevilles, and
the clash between his pro-Burgundian foreign policy and Warwick's
preference for a French alliance all contributed to the rift. Warwick
also resented the fact that Lord Herbert was becoming Edward's chief
counsellor as well as his Lieutenant in Wales and its Marches –
territory where his interests frequently clashed with Warwick's.

A much more personal injury may have been the root cause of
Warwick's 'deep dissimuling' and the 'continual grudge that lurked
in his stomach toward King Edward IV'. Several chronicles repeat the
rumour that Edward 'did attempt a thing in the earl's house which
was much against the earl's honesty'. 'Whether he would have violated
the earl's niece or another damosel in the earl's house all men knew
not, for the king was a man who loved both to see and feel a fair
maiden'. Thomas Carte's 1747 *History of England* went further, saying

that after news of the engagement of Clarence and Isobel 'took air', Edward himself

> *whether it was out of a political view to break the intended match, or by an effect of his amorous complexion, made an attempt to debauch the young lady, without considering the eternal reproach an action of such ingratitude would bring upon himself and the indelible mark of infamy it would fix upon the noble family he deigned to dishonor. A man of Warwick's virtue, magnanimity and honour could never forgive such an attempt on his daughter's virtue; he saw all his services buried in oblivion: and imagining Edward, after acting so dishonourable a part, capable of any other, however shocking, resolved to provide against the worst that could happen.*

Modern historians, obsessed with economic and political motives, ignore this incident. Carte, 250 years closer to Warwick's lifetime than we are, had a better understanding than we do of a fifteenth-century nobleman's prickly sense of honour. Magnanimity then meant not generosity but high-mindedness. If Edward did fondle, or even just flirt with, Isobel or Anne of Warwick, there is no doubt that it would have incensed their proud, blue-blooded father 'out of measure'.

The final insult had come in June 1467 when Edward and Herbert had walked into the Southwark palace of Warwick's brother George, Archbishop of York, and demanded the great seal, in effect sacking him as Chancellor of England. Edward may well have discovered that the Archbishop was making illicit use of his office to further his secret negotiations with Rome for papal permission for his niece's marriage to Clarence (a dispensation was needed because they were cousins). As Edward's brother, Clarence was next in line to the throne; Queen Elizabeth had so far only given birth to daughters.

Warwick watched and waited, Hall tells us, suffering 'all such wrongs and injuries as were to him done, till he might spy a time convenient, and a world after his own appetite, for the setting forth of his enterprise, and accomplishing of his purpose'. On 14 March 1469, the all-important papal dispensation was finally signed in Rome. The next hurdle was a licence from Thomas Bourgchier, the Archbishop of Canterbury, which was obtained on 31 June. Warwick, already in Calais on legitimate business, sent word to Clarence. They met at Sandwich for four days of festivities, and the blessing of Warwick's new flagship, the *Trinity*. They then crossed to Calais where Isobel and Clarence were married by Archbishop Neville on 11 July. Although the ceremony was held safely distant from interference by the King, it was no hole-in-the-corner affair. Several great Neville ladies had come to Sandwich to see them off, including Cicely, Dowager Duchess of York, mother of both the groom and the King, and great-aunt of the bride. Attending the ceremony itself were five Knights of the Garter besides Warwick, 'and many other lords and ladies and worship-ful knights, well accompanied with wise and discreet esquires, in right great number to the laud praising of God, and to the honour and wor-ship of the world'. Among the Garter knights were three friends of Malory: Lord Wenlock (who had been made Warwick's Lieutenant at Calais in May), Sir Walter Wrottesley and Sir Robert Harcourt.

Warwick now had the most threatening weapon possible: a pawn ready and eager for promotion to king. Next day Warwick, Clarence and the Archbishop issued an ominous, all too familiar manifesto. Widely distributed across the south of England by an efficient network of scribes and couriers, it was a declaration of intent to remove the low-born self-interested counsellors who surrounded Edward and prevented him from governing properly. It complained of widespread injustice and peculation, including the theft of revenues meant for the crusades – a reference to Edward's 1464 annexation of the subsidy levied for Pope Pius II's crusade and his outrageous appointment of young Sir John Woodville as Prior of the Knights Hospitallers in September 1468. The manifesto called on 'all true subjects' to array at Canterbury on 16 July where Warwick and his men from Calais would meet them. The manifesto was suspiciously similar to the bills just issued by the leaders of another rebellion against Edward's 'false counsellors' which had broken out a fortnight earlier, on 28 June in Yorkshire, led by a man who called himself Robin of Redesdale. With superficial loyalty, Warwick had written to Coventry to muster men to quell the rebellion shortly before the Calais wedding of Clarence and Isobel. But he was undoubtedly aware that riding with 'Robin' were relatives of his own – his brother-in-law Lord FitzHugh and his cousins Sir Henry Neville and Sir John Conyers.

Kentishmen and mariners flocked to join Warwick and Clarence. Their ever-growing army reached Canterbury on 18 July and a few days later marched triumphantly into London. Warwick needed every available supporter to follow him to the Midlands, and the prisons were searched for men with potential. Malory was a former servant of the house of Warwick. Wrottesley or Harcourt could have suggested his release. Or he could have been freed by Sir John Langstrother or Robert Malory, both of whom rode with Warwick. If they all travelled to Warwickshire together, Malory would have visited Newbold Revel. He could have handed over the master manuscript of his history of King Arthur for his wife and children to enjoy. Perhaps he asked Lady Elizabeth to have another copy of it made. The two scribes who wrote the Winchester manuscript are thought to have come from the Northamptonshire area. Scribes would have charged about 2d a page for such a simply executed book, so the cost of copying its 1,000 pages was perhaps £10 including rubrication of the names of the knights in red, and a plain binding.

At first Edward assumed that the rebellion in the North was led by Lancastrian troublemakers, but by 9 July he was suspicious enough of Warwick's intentions to order Herbert and Stafford to raise reliable troops from his own estates in the West. Meanwhile Robin of Redesdale's Yorkshiremen, 40,000 strong, it was said, had got as far as Banbury by 24 July, where the men hastily mustered by Herbert and Stafford confronted them at Edgecote on 24 July. They were decisively defeated. The Queen's father, Earl Rivers, her younger brother Sir John Woodville and Edward's right-hand man, Lord Herbert, were all captured and executed.

Warwick's and Clarence's perfidy was revealed when, after their deliberately delayed arrival, they joined forces with the northerners. Warwick was showing his strength: he could tilt the balance of power for or against whichever king he chose. For the moment, he chose Edward. The Archbishop of York arrested the shaken Yorkist King at Warwick's manor of Olney, and escorted him to Warwick and Clarence in Coventry. On 28 July, two of his kinsmen were captured at Chepstow and taken to Kenilworth. On 12 August Edward was taken to Coventry to watch their execution. Soon afterwards, in what may have been intended as a preliminary to dissolving Edward's marriage, the Queen's mother Jacquetta, Duchess of Bedford, was accused of sorcery at Warwick assizes by Thomas Wake of Blisworth. Both events have intriguing links with both the Hospitallers and the Malorys. Sir John Langstrother was an eminent Hospitaller and he and Robert Malory were later accused by the Duchess of executing Rivers and Woodville. And Thomas Wake had been a companion-in-arms of Richard Malory in 1443; his son would be a witness of the post-mortem inquiry into the estates of Sir Thomas Malory's wife Elizabeth in 1479.

To eliminate his four most hated enemies and capture Edward with such speed and economy was an astonishing coup by Warwick. All Europe was agog at the extraordinary spectacle of a country with not one but two imprisoned kings. Henry remained in the Tower. Edward was taken north to Warwick's Yorkshire headquarters, Middle-ham Castle. The Milanese ambassador in London sent a bemused report to Duke Galeazzo Sforza of Milan:

> The Earl of Warwick, as astute a man as ever was Ulysses, is at the king's side, and from what they say the king is not at liberty to go where he wishes. The queen is here [i.e. in London] and keeps very scant state. The duke [Clarence] is to come here, and a brother of the earl, Archbishop of York, who was sometime chancellor, and they wish to arrange for a parliament to meet and in that they will arrange the government of the realm. Everyone is of the opinion that it would be better not; God grant it so.

The great offices of the kingdom left empty by the executions were shared out between Warwick and his allies. Warwick himself took command in Wales and the Marches. Sir John Langstrother was recognised as Prior of the English Hospitallers. But difficulties beset Warwick on every hand. Edward was a far more able politician than the meek, trusting Henry VI. The conservative mass of the gentry, many closet Lancastrians, disapproved of such 'wiles and treason'.

Warwick, fearful that there would be riots during the elections, decided not to summon Parliament. Opportunists began to settle long-held personal grudges in vengeful local wars.

The indefatigable Sir Humphrey Neville chose this pivotal moment to invade from Scotland with an army of Scots and Lancastrian exiles. There were also rumours that Henry and Morgan ap Thomas ap Griffith might shortly 'presume or take it upon them to arrive' in south Wales. Both these threats to Edward's throne were led by men barred from pardon with Malory in 1468. Did Malory, whose whereabouts at this point are utterly unknown, help to orchestrate them? As we shall see, he was still regarded as an enemy of the realm in February 1470.

Sir Humphrey Neville's rising was a serious embarrassment to Warwick because when he tried to call up men to go north to fight against him, they refused to recognise his authority. King Edward had to be seen to be free. He was released from the fastness of Middleham, and went first to York and then to Pontefract. As a result, men flocked to Warwick's now regally legalised banner. They soon defeated Sir Humphrey Neville's brave little army. Sir Humphrey and his brother Charles were captured and Edward IV came up from Pontefract to witness their execution in York on 29 September.

Edward then returned to London, where loyal peers hastened to his support. Always at his best in adversity, he considered his next move. The news that Henry and Morgan ap Thomas ap Griffith had now seized Carmarthen and Cardigan castles for Lancaster and that a French fleet of privateers was blockading Sandwich was an urgent reminder of how much Edward needed Warwick, his finest naval commander. Though he now knew that he could not trust the great Earl, he was carefully conciliatory. 'The king hath good language of the Lords of Clarence, of Warwick, and my Lords of York and Oxford, saying they be his best friends; but his household men have other language, so that what shall hastily fall I can not say,' reported John Paston on 7 October 1469. Presciently, Edward strengthened his alliance with Burgundy by bestowing the Order of the Garter on Duke Charles, and accepting the Order of the Golden Fleece in return.

A Great Council was summoned to meet in the parliament

chamber at Westminster early in November. It was an exceptionally full and representative meeting of the magnates of the realm and stayed in session until February. Edward used it to endorse all his decisions and to reassert the royal authority. Warwick lost the commands in Wales he had granted himself, but Sir John Langstrother was accepted as Prior of the Order of St John. Aware that he needed new allies in order to counter Warwick, Edward set about promoting men with traditional Lancastrian loyalties to high office in order to lessen the attractions of rebellion. Langstrother was also made Treasurer of the Realm. Henry Percy was released from the Tower on 27 October, and moves began to restore him to the earldom of Northumberland – at the expense of its present holder, Warwick's brother, Sir John Neville. To prepare the way for this, the King offered a generous consolation prize. His oldest daughter, the four-year-old Elizabeth, was betrothed to Sir John's three-year-old son and heir, who was to become Duke of Bedford. It was a carefully calculated package, firmly curbing Warwick but not punishing him over-harshly. The final flourish was a general pardon to Warwick, Clarence and any of his subjects who had been guilty of insurrections, murders, riots and assemblies before Christmas 1469.

This pardon, issued on 20 February 1470, had an even shorter list of individual exceptions than that of 1468 – only six. The first, and the only knight, was Sir Thomas Malory. Then came Thomas Philip, William Verdon, Robert Marshall and two followers of Sir Humphrey Neville: John Workington and John Manningham. This was quite extraordinary, given that Warwick, Clarence and all their supporters were being forgiven. It suggests strongly that Malory and his three familiars were not seen as followers of Warwick, but as Lancastrian loyalists – and particularly dangerous ones at that. A remarkably gifted writer, a scrivener, a chapman and a man who might have been a minstrel: could the threat they presented have been inciting rebellion by propaganda? Did the Lancastrian manifestos and justifications that were circulating all over the country at just this time originate with them? Were their pens feared as much as rebel swords? If so, John Vale's unique and extensive collection of anti-Yorkist literature contains carefully preserved copies of their word-weapons.

'Turn again, ye commons, and dread your king'

Within a few weeks the wheel of fortune had spun once again. Early in February Sir Robert Welles, Sir Thomas Dymmock and Sir Thomas Delalaunde, all closet Lancastrians, attacked the Lincolnshire home of Edward's Master of Horse, Sir Thomas Burgh. Edward announced on 4 March that he was going to march north himself to quell the disorder. The infuriatingly efficient rumour-mongers had been at work again: bills nailed on church doors warned that the general pardon was not going to be honoured, and that the King's judges 'should sit, and hang and draw a great number of the commons'. Welles and his friends raised local levies, and it was said that tens of thousands of Yorkshiremen were marching to join them. Edward advanced north rapidly, calling on Warwick and Clarence for aid. They hung back, hoping for a repeat of the victory at Edgecote. But Edward convincingly defeated the rebels near Stamford on 12 March. Their flight was so precipitate that the battle was named 'Lose-coat Field'.

Afterwards Edward found, or claimed to have found, evidence in a casket belonging to Sir Robert Welles, and in the confessions of those captured, that Warwick and Clarence were 'partners and chief provokers of all these treasons'. With a vast army at his back, he summoned them to his presence, promising 'indifference and equity' but no sort of safe-conduct. Warwick and Clarence did not respond to the summons. After a failed attempt to raise support in Derbyshire and Lancashire, they rode with frantic haste to the West Country, with Edward in hot pursuit. At Dartmouth they embarked for Calais with their womenfolk, including a heavily pregnant Isobel. Warwick knew from experience that there could be no better place from which to launch a successful invasion of England.

Edward outwitted him. Before pursuing them into the West Country, he sent word to Calais ordering the garrison to keep the port and its castles closed to Warwick. When Warwick's fleet headed into harbour on 17 April, it was shot at by the cannons the Earl himself had installed in the Rysbank Tower and Calais Castle. Anchoring out of range, Warwick asked for a parley, his need made urgent by the premature birth of Isobel's baby – Warwick's first grandchild, a son – potentially a king of England. But Wenlock refused them entry, though he sent two casks of wine for Isobel's relief. He is believed to have also sent a secret message, explaining that the townsfolk and most of the garrison were loyal to Edward, that Calais would prove a trap, that France was a safer refuge, and that great things might yet be done. Isobel's baby died within hours of his birth. Warwick upped anchor and roamed the Channel, doubling the size of his fleet by capturing dozens of Burgundian ships but losing many of them, as well as hundreds of men, in fending off a bold attack by Edward's fleet. Finally he took shelter in the mouth of the Seine at Honfleur on 5 May and sent messengers to King Louis.

Edward rewarded Wenlock for his apparent loyalty by giving him overall command of Calais and the Marches. He also sent his 'faithful bailiffs' there a carefully circumscribed pardon. Dated 3 May 1470, it included all his subjects in Calais and the Marches, but a proviso announced that it did not extend to Queen Margaret and her son Edward, and anybody with them, or Warwick and Clarence and their retinues, or a large number of Calais's civil administrative officials. It was only concerned with the King's subjects in his Calais realm or travelling elsewhere abroad. There was no mention of Henry VI, who was still in the Tower of London, or of anyone known to be in England.

It is therefore fascinating that the Calais pardon did specifically exclude Malory, Marshall, Vernon, Philip, Workington and Manningham from the King's grace. Their appearance on a version of the pardon addressed to the inhabitants of Calais suggests very strongly that they were believed to be there – and that Edward IV feared them much more than other Lancastrian exiles. It confirms the impression of a band of tough, competent and experienced men – spies, messengers and propagandists – who had been travelling regularly between London and Koeur for several years.

Wenlock's refusal to admit Warwick to Calais brought about the most unlikely alliance of the century: that of Warwick and Margaret of Anjou. Wenlock was playing a double, or rather a triple, game.

Although he succeeded in persuading both Warwick and Edward that he was loyal to them, his true allegiance lay with the Lancastrians. Edward, always well-informed, had stopped trusting him nine weeks later, for on 11 June he appointed Sir Anthony Woodville as 'General Governor and Lieutenant' of Calais. But Woodville was at sea challenging Warwick for the all-important control of the Channel and his authority was only nominal. Wenlock's personal grip on Calais was confirmed when the garrison refused to admit a hundred archers sent over by Edward in July to reinforce it against Warwick. In July, the Duke of Burgundy tried to buy Wenlock's loyalty with a pension of 1,000 écus.

Although Louis XI was delighted that the English were once more fighting each other rather than France, he gave Warwick only a qualified welcome. He did not want to find himself at war with Burgundy until he could be sure of having England as an ally. He persuaded Warwick to return the Burgundian prizes, and insisted that their negotiations be kept secret, telling other European ambassadors that he was trying to make Warwick leave France.

As Warwick paced the quayside at Honfleur in baffled fury, he realised that an alliance with the Lancastrians was now his only hope of regaining power in England. He would be supported by Lancastrians all over the country and backed by French ships, money and men as the champion of Henry VI. Late in July Warwick and Queen Margaret met at Angers. King Louis refereed the sessions himself. He was desperate to get these troublesome guests out of France before the Duke of Burgundy made their presence an excuse for war. But he was also fascinated by the possibilities that unrolled if they were successful.

First Warwick asked for pardon from Margaret and Prince Edward for his actions in 1459–61; it was grudgingly granted when he pleaded on bended knee that he had only acted as 'a noble man outraged and dispeired [desperate] ought to have done'. Perhaps he reminded Margaret that he had opposed Richard of York's attempt to snatch the throne, but that by the time York's son Edward had done the same, he had had no option but to support him. It was then agreed that, after Edward IV had been deposed, Warwick was to be 'regent and governor' of England for the 'king and the prince' until Prince

450

Edward came of age. There was tacit acceptance that Henry VI could not rule on his own.

The linchpin of the new alliance was the marriage of Prince Edward and Warwick's younger daughter Anne, which was to take place immediately. Louis XI gained the promise of a thirty-year truce with England, and an offensive alliance against Burgundy once Lancaster was restored to the throne, and the hope that Margaret would make good her agreement to grant him Calais. The treaty was signed on 22 July, and on 25 July Edward and Anne were betrothed in Angers Cathedral.

Malory must have seen the betrothal as some kind of miracle: the granddaughter of his first liege lord Sir Richard Beauchamp would one day be Queen of England. Little as he liked Warwick himself, much could be hoped for from Edward and Anne, both young people who had been taught to hold high ideals. If secret doubts, even secret knowledge, of the true paternity of Prince Edward lay in his breast, he could have comforted himself that some of the finest knights of the Round Table, even King Arthur himself, had been begotten in shady circumstances. Again and again in his tales, actions announce the truly chivalric hero more surely than lineage. A knight proved himself valiant 'by the honour of his hands and the faith of his body'.

A carefully planned propaganda offensive in England supplemented Warwick's well-organised military and naval preparations in France. Four different manifestos, cleverly tailored to persuade different audiences, have survived; copies of them, and of stirring ballads praising Henry VI and Prince Edward and scurrilous slanders against Edward IV and the Woodvilles, were put up on bridge posts, town gates and church doors all over the country. In London, the Lord Mayor, the grocer Richard Lee, complained to Edward IV that they were nailed up in Cheapside, London Bridge and other places faster than he could have them torn down. Again, the only surviving copies of these manifestos are in John Vale's 'Great Book'. Many phrases in them are reminiscent of Malory: Warwick would 'always hold the party and quarrel of King Henry' and would serve him, the Queen and Prince 'as true and faithful subject oweth to serve his sovereign lord'.

451

As Lancaster's champion, Warwick now had the legitimacy that he had previously lacked. How much it strengthened his cause was evident as soon as his forces landed at Exmouth, Dartmouth and Plymouth on 13 September 1470. The troops were led by Clarence, Jasper Tudor, John Vere, Earl of Oxford, Thomas Neville (a bastard son of Lord Fauconberg) and many other Lancastrian exiles. Louis XI had provided ships, a thousand French archers and the sum of £6,000. All over England and Wales, Lancastrians declared themselves for Henry VI and Prince Edward and flocked to join them, even though Queen Margaret had refused to let her son cross the Channel until Warwick had restored Henry VI to his throne.

Edward IV was too far away to do much about the invasion. He was in York, putting down a cleverly timed rising in the North led by Warwick's brother-in-law, Lord FitzHugh. It melted away on his approach. Edward, who thought Warwick was bringing a huge French army with him and would land in Kent, sent frantic letters there calling on his 'true subjects' to array themselves in arms to resist the malice of the traitors and the 'great might and power' of the French. Queen Elizabeth, heavily pregnant, moved into the Tower, 'stuffing and garnishing' it for defence as best she could. But Warwick had bypassed all these preparations by landing in the West Country. By the time he reached Coventry, where Shrewsbury and Stanley joined him, his forces numbered 60,000.

At this point Edward IV's foolishness in depriving his most loyal ally in the North, Sir John Neville, Lord Montagu, of the earldom of Northumberland became glaringly apparent. Instead of joining Edward with the troops supposedly raised on his behalf, Montagu declared for Henry VI and advanced on Edward himself. 'Seeing that almost all his partisans were deserting him and joining up with his enemies, the king could not tell with certainty whom he must guard against [and] . . . judged it most opportune to take flight', wrote the French chronicler Thomas Basin. Edward IV had failed, reflected Warkworth, to deliver the 'great prosperity and rest' he had promised; moreover, it had never been Henry VI who was disliked, only the 'false lords' around him. Edward watched and waited at Nottingham, but when he heard of Montagu's approach, he judged it best to flee.

On 29 September he took ship from King's Lynn, arriving off the coast of Holland on 3 October after narrowly evading some hostile Hanseatic ships. On landing, he was lucky enough to encounter an old friend, the Dutch Governor Lord Gruythuise, a former Burgundian ambassador to England, who took him safely to The Hague, and later entertained the fugitive King royally at his own luxurious palace.

The coalition between Warwick's followers and the Lancastrians, together 'a decided majority of the nation' according to Basin, was regarded in Europe as an extraordinary development. The Duke of Burgundy's agent in Calais, Philippe de Commines, was amazed at the speed with which York's White Rose emblem was replaced by Warwick's Ragged Staff. Men regarded with deep suspicion were now courted assiduously, he said. 'This was the first time that ever I learned how unstable the things of this world are,' he wrote with bemusement.

London, where Edward was hugely popular, and to which he owed a great deal of money, was less quick to turn. His loyal Kentishmen were invited in to strengthen the garrison, but their turbulent presence was soon resented by the citizens. Once news of Edward's flight abroad reached the city, committed Yorkists fled or took sanctuary. Queen Elizabeth left the Tower and took shelter in the Westminster Abbey sanctuary with her three little daughters and her mother, Jacquetta. Her first son, the future Edward V, was born there on 2 November. On 3 October, Bishop Waynflete and Mayor Lee went to the Tower to find King Henry. It was something of a shock. He 'was not so worshipfully arrayed . . . and nought so cleanly kept as should beseem such a Prince', the chronicler Warkworth records. Henry had been treated with less kindness and respect by Robert Malory's successor; he was still wearing the blue velvet gown made for him in 1465, now sadly shabby. But they led him to the luxurious apartments just vacated by the Queen 'and new arrayed him, and did him great reverence'.

On 6 October, Warwick and his allies arrived in London and rode to the Tower to kneel before Henry. Next day, Henry was taken in procession to St Paul's and the crown of England was once more placed on his head. He moved back into the state apartments of the royal palace of Westminster, where 'daily much people and in great number' came to renew their allegiance. 'Return, oh backsliding children!' was the text of Archbishop Neville's speech to the Parliament when it opened at Westminster on 26 November in the presence of Henry VI. After five years in captivity, he was a pathetic figure. Looking on, the Burgundian chronicler Chastellain, a profound admirer of Edward IV, jeeringly described him as a 'stuffed wool sack, a shadow on the wall, victim of a game of blindman's buff, a crowned calf'. Warwick knew that the sooner the martial young Prince Edward could be paraded around England the better. But Margaret was still wary, wanting to see how firmly Warwick held her husband's suddenly reacquired kingdom. Although a splendidly large embassy arrived from the court of the King of France to finalise plans for the promised Anglo-French invasion of Burgundy, she and Prince Edward stayed in Anjou.

Warwick made few immediate changes in the legal and civil administration. But it is another sign of the importance of the 1468 conspiracy that its key figures were immediately rewarded. Sir John Plummer became Keeper of the Great Wardrobe, and Sir Thomas Cook took control of the customs of Southampton. Cook also petitioned Parliament as soon as it met to ask for restoration of the £15,000 of losses he had suffered in 1468. Sir Richard Tunstall, whose valiant defence of Harlech had been sustained by the Londoners' contributions, was made Master of the Royal Mint. Nor were there many reprisals, except against Edward IV's notoriously punitive constable John Tiptoft, Earl of Worcester, who was executed on Tower Hill on 16 October.

The Once and Future King

Henry VI's return to power was formally known as the 'Re-adeption'. The parliament held to acknowledge his return met for only a few weeks, November–December 1470, and January–February 1471. As we know the names of only thirty-nine MPs, we cannot tell whether Sir Thomas Malory was once again an MP, or whether he was in London at all. Election as a knight of the shire in the present circumstances was a perilous honour. On 14 November 1470, Malory's old friend Sir Robert Harcourt, who had boasted that he 'had the good will of the lords coming in', was killed in his own home by a gang of 150 men led by his old enemies, the Staffords of Grafton. It was undoubtedly revenge for the death of Richard Stafford twenty years earlier. But there was a political element in the murder – the Staffords were not made to answer for the murder after Edward IV recovered his throne, despite five years of pertinacity in the law courts by Lady Harcourt.

Dissent soon emerged among Warwick's allies. The treaty he had signed with Margaret of Anjou committed him to restoring all the lands and property which the Lancastrians had lost through attainders and confiscation. This meant that many of his own followers had to surrender property. His brother, Lord Montagu, did not regain the earldom of Northumberland, and lost the West Country lands that Edward IV had given him as compensation for it. The Lancastrian lords welcomed the return of their lands and titles, but they were less happy about the dominant position which the Nevilles now held in government.

Warwick's offensive alliance with France, signed on 16 February, was generally disliked. It committed England to war against Burgundy – a disaster as far as the London merchant community was concerned. Worse, it catapulted Charles the Bold into alliance with Edward IV, whose presence in Holland he had hitherto studiously ignored. Nor was Warwick's original ally, 'false, fleeting, perjur'd Clarence', to be relied upon. Although generously treated, he coveted more authority. He realised the weakness of his position – if his brother Edward was defeated, he would be entirely expendable. It was now clearer than ever that the war was a three-cornered fight between Warwick, Edward and the Lancastrians. Whoever was to hold the mastery would in the end have to defeat two opponents, not one.

On 14 December Queen Margaret and Prince Edward left Amboise for Paris, then headed for Rouen to prepare for their journey to England. The truce with France was signed on 6 February. Troops had already been sent to strengthen Wenlock's Calais garrison, and eight thousand more men would be despatched there to help Louis XI attack Burgundy once the Queen and Prince had reinstated themselves in England. At first Warwick planned to cross over to fetch them himself, but there were rumours that Edward IV had gathered a fleet in Flushing and was about to set sail for England. Instead, he sent an escort led by Sir John Langstrother. A fortnight of storms in the Channel delayed their longed-for homecoming. Then came word that Edward had stolen a march, or rather a voyage, on them. His thirty-six ships were sighted off Cromer in the evening of 12 March 1471.

On 14 March Edward landed at Ravenspur on the Humber. Richard of Gloucester and Anthony Woodville, now Earl Rivers, landed their ships a little further to the north. With them were some two thousand Flemings, Easterlings and Danes. Yorkshire was hostile to his return, but Edward swore that he was now a loyal subject of Henry VI, and had only returned to claim his hereditary title of Duke of York. He was allowed to reach his family castle at Sandal. Crucial to his survival was the fact that the two most powerful men in the north, Montagu and the Earl of Northumberland, decided not to oppose his progress. As Edward approached the Midlands, he was joined by more supporters. On 25 March he reached Leicester, where three thousand more men joined him. Meanwhile Warwick had reached Coventry. Edward advanced to the town of Warwick and offered battle. The Earl refused to leave his strong defensive position within Coventry's high walls. He was waiting for Exeter, Beaumont, Oxford and Clarence. But Edward IV had sent fond messages to his errant brother Clarence, who was at Banbury with four thousand men, wondering which way to jump. He decided that family came first, and the two brothers returned to Coventry and once more invited Warwick out to fight. He again refused, aware that Montagu was on his way to join him. Edward decided to make for London, which he entered unopposed, enthusiastically acclaimed by its citizens, since the earls of Somerset and Devon had just left for the West of England to await the return of Queen Margaret and Prince Edward. 'Henry of Lancaster', now so frail that he had to be led by the hand, welcomed his cousin home. 'I know in your hands my life will not be in danger', he is reported as saying as he was taken back to his old quarters in the Tower. Edward then went to see his queen – and his firstborn son Edward, who had been born while he was in exile. Yorkist supporters from the home counties flocked into London.

On Easter Saturday, 13 April 1471, Edward IV marched out with some ten thousand men against Warwick's advancing Lancastrian army. Now joined by Montagu, Beaumont, Exeter and Oxford, it numbered ten to fifteen thousand. It had taken up a position on a ridge of high ground north of Barnet, on each side of the main road to St Albans. In an unorthodox manoeuvre, Edward ignored the attractions of a quiet night in Barnet and under cover of darkness drew up his forces very close to Warwick's army, but well to the left of it. Warwick's artillery let fly, but the Yorkists were so close that the cannonballs flew harmlessly over their heads. Edward held his own fire, to preserve the element of surprise.

Easter Sunday dawned in thick fog, and the battle began at 4 a.m. Fighting blind, the right flanks of both armies found themselves advancing with virtually no opposition. The Earl of Oxford scythed into the Yorkist left flank, which was led by Hastings, scattering it utterly. The eighteen-year-old Richard of Gloucester failed, however, to overcome the Earl of Exeter, to whom Warwick had sent reserves when he realised what was happening. The Yorkists were in a desperate plight, but then disaster struck for the Lancastrians. Returning from his pursuit of Hastings, Oxford failed to realise how much the lines had swivelled, and attacked his own side: the ranks under Montagu's command. Seeing Oxford's emblem, a star and streams, Montagu took it for Edward's sun and streams, and opened fire. There were shouts of treason, and Oxford's men fled. Panic spread through the Lancastrian lines, and the Yorkists rallied. Exeter was said to be dead, and his forces gave way. One of Oxford's men felled Montagu, for what had appeared to be a treacherous attack. The Lancastrian line wavered and collapsed, and Warwick realised his danger – he had been fighting on foot to encourage his men, and he was now too far from his own lines to get to a horse in time. Luck had finally failed the 'Kingmaker'. Weighed down by his armour, he was quickly overtaken by Yorkist men-at-arms, who thrust a knife through his visor and into his brain and stripped his corpse of its shining carapace of useless steel. He was forty-two years old.

Three thousand men died at Barnet, twice as many Lancastrians as Yorkists. But only two of the Lancastrian leaders, Warwick and Montagu, were killed – the rest succeeded in escaping north to Scotland. Edward treated his dead cousins with respect. Their bodies were put on display for two days in wooden coffins in St Paul's Cathedral, so there could be no doubt that they were indeed dead, but then they were interred in the Neville family vault at Bisham Abbey.

On the very day of the battle, Queen Margaret and Prince Edward, still hopeful of their unlikely champion's victory, landed at Weymouth. With them were the Countess of Warwick, Anne Beauchamp, and her little daughter Anne Neville, now Princess of Wales. As soon as she heard of Warwick's defeat and death, Anne and her daughter took sanctuary in Beaulieu Abbey. But Margaret and Edward, cheered out of their initial despair by Somerset's optimism and solid support from the West Country, headed for the Welsh border, hoping to join up with Jasper Tudor and loyal Lancastrians from the north. Edward marched rapidly to intercept their progress, and succeeded in doing so at Tewkesbury. Both armies numbered around six thousand men when they faced each other just south of the town on 4 May. Somerset attempted the outflanking manoeuvre that had won the day for him at Northampton, but this time it failed – mainly because no advance was made by the Lancastrian vanguard, commanded by Lord Wenlock. Incensed, and assuming that Wenlock had betrayed him, Somerset returned to his lines and smashed an axe into Wenlock's skull. His forces were now in disarray, and among the many casualties was young Prince Edward, hacked down by advancing Yorkists troops, who may well not have known who he was.

Margaret of Anjou, who had been sheltering in a nearby convent, was captured and taken to London, humiliated by having to ride in Edward IV's victory procession. She was imprisoned in the Tower. There was to be no reunion with her husband. Once Prince Edward had been killed, Henry was doomed. There is little doubt that it was Edward IV who ordered his discreetly managed death on the night before he himself entered London in triumph on 22 May 1471. The official verdict was that Henry died, as Richard II had done, 'of pure displeasure and melancholy'. But it was said that blood leaked from his coffin when it was displayed, open as was customary, in St Paul's Cathedral. On 24 June, Hugh Bryce was paid £15 3s 6d to cover the cost of

Wax, linen, spices, and other ordinary expenses incurred for the burial of the said Henry of Windsor, who died within the Tower of London; and for the wages and rewards to divers men carrying torches from the Tower aforesaid to the cathedral church of St Paul's London, and from thence accompanying the body to Chertsey.

It was the cheapest king's funeral ever recorded. At least Henry's mortal remains were given the dignity of a mass in St Paul's before being rowed upstream on a funeral barge to Chertsey-on-Thames, where he was buried uncoffined in the Lady Chapel of Chertsey Abbey. Almost at once secret pilgrimages to his shrine began, images of him in churches were covertly venerated, and an impressive roll-call of miracles was ascribed to his intervention. After Edward IV's death, Richard III had his body reverently re-interred in a handsome coffin and entombed close to that of his royal rival in St George's Chapel, Windsor. Henry VII, who lobbied three successive popes to canonise his uncle, originally intended the fabulous Lady Chapel at the east end of Westminster Abbey as a mausoleum for Henry VI as well as for himself. He never got round to bringing the hallowed remains of 'Holy King Henry' from Windsor to Westminster, and today the tomb of the first of the Tudors rather than the last of the Lancastrians is the centrepiece of the 'Henry VII chapel'.

A Good End

Thou art a monument, without a tomb,
And art alive still, while thy book doth live,
And we have wits to read, and praise to give.

Ben Jonson

hatever Sir Thomas Malory was doing during Henry's brief second reign, he is likely to have heard that Edward was planning to return. The Yorkist King had been negotiating for ships for some months, and he had been in Flushing assembling his fleet since the middle of February. He actually planned to embark on 2 March, but had to wait for fair winds for nine days. London had up-to-date intelligence of these activities, and its citizens knew within two days that Edward was heading for the Humber. On 16 March, Clarence had picked up the rumour in Somerset, writing from Wells to Henry Vernon: 'We be adcertained that it is said about London that king Edward is sailed by the coast of Norfolk towards Humber'. But this time Malory would have no opportunity of riding as Lancaster's champion. He died within a day or two of Edward's landing at Ravenspur on 14 March 1471. Why he died is unknown; all manner of ills assailed medieval septuagenarians, but there were many deaths that year in London from a new epidemic of plague. We can imagine that he died hopeful of the triumph of 'the king who made him knight'. Certainly, he never heard of Edward IV's victories at Barnet and Tewkesbury, the deaths of Warwick and Prince Edward, and the murder of Henry VI.

In a society in which the brevity of mortal life and the terrors or bliss of eternity were constantly being emphasised and no church was without a lurid depiction of Judgement Day, death was life's greatest event: this explains why the 'The Death of Arthur' was the title of so many versions of the life of the legendary king. Planning the manner of one's death was essential. An unprepared death could mean eternal perdition, and crucifixes were fixed in houses, on city walls and at every turn of the highway – spiritual lifebelts to be grasped in an emergency. One of the most popular texts of the age was the manual to seemly dying, *Ars Moriendi*; in 1490 Caxton printed a translation of it, *The Art and Craft to Know Well to Die*. It explained how, in the hour of your death, demons of past sins massed around you. Only compete contrition could save you. A bad life could be redeemed by a 'good end', shriven of all sin and given the last Christian rite of extreme unction with your eyes fixed on a crucifix to remind you that Christ died to save your soul. Funerals, which could affect your fate in the after-life for ever, were far more important occasions than christenings or weddings. Those on the verge of death often dictated their preferred funerary rites in detail, and medieval wills included long and lovingly detailed prescriptions for their management: black cloths to drape the coffin, wax candles to burn throughout the day of death, payment for candles to be burned and masses to be said at the 'month-mind' and the 'year-day' of their death, and sometimes into the indefinite future.

A picture of how Malory might have chosen to die, or at least of the spirit with which he approached death, is offered by the last chapter of the *Morte*. 'While she lived she was a true lover', he wrote of Guinevere, who died surrounded by nuns at Amesbury, 'and therefore she had a good end', winning her 'soul-heal'. Lancelot, who had by then been a priest for a year, was told of her death in a vision the night she died. He rode to Amesbury with his followers to oversee her funeral and her burial by Arthur's side at Glastonbury. When he saw her face, 'he wept not greatly, but sighed', wrote Malory, with masterly understatement. He then gives a detailed picture of the funeral, borrowed from his own age.

And so he did all the observance of the service himself, both the dirige, and on the morn he sang mass. And there was ordained an horse bier; and so with an hundred torches ever burning about the corpse of the queen, Sir Lancelot with his eight fellows went about the horse bier, singing and reading many an holy orison, and frankincense upon the corpse incensed. Thus Sir Lancelot and his eight fellows went on foot from Almesbury unto Glastonbury. And when they were come to the chapel and the hermitage, there she had a dirige, with great devotion. And on the morn the hermit that some-time was Bishop of Canterbury sang the mass of Requiem with great devotion. And Sir Lancelot was the first that offered, and then also his eight fellows. And then she was wrapped in cered [waxed] cloth of Raines [linen made in Rennes], from the top to the toe, in thirtyfold; and after she was put in a web of lead, and then in a coffin of marble. And when she was put in the earth Sir Lancelot swooned, and lay long still.

Over the next six weeks, Lancelot pined away. Hardly eating or drinking at all, 'evermore, day and night, he prayed, but sometime he slumbered a broken sleep; ever he was lying grovelling on the tomb of King Arthur and Queen Guenevere'. Eager for death, he asked for the last rites, and begged his companions to take his body to his best-loved retreat, Joyous Gard, for burial. The very next day, their priest told them he had woken merrier than he had ever been, for he had seen 'angels heave up Sir Lancelot unto heaven, and the gates of heaven opened against him'. Sir Bors and the others went to Lancelot's bedside and 'found him stark dead, and he lay as he had smiled, and the sweetest savour about him that ever they felt'.

The funeral and interment of Sir Thomas Malory took place in Greyfriars Church. It is close to Newgate, and it has previously been assumed that Malory was buried there because he had died a prisoner. It is true that some prisoners who died in Newgate were buried in Greyfriars, but most of those laid to rest in its magnificent interior were not criminals. Malory's presence in London in March 1471 adds to the likelihood of his being known to be a faithful servant of Henry VI, as does his burial in Greyfriars, for it was one of London's grandest and most fashionable places of worship. Just under 300 foot long, 89 foot wide and with a 64-foot-high roof and a tall octagonal steeple, it was second only in size to St Paul's Cathedral, and stood less than two hundred yards north of it. It was founded by the Franciscans, who were known as the Grey Friars from the colour of their habits. They were the followers of St Francis of Assisi, who died in 1226. Known both as Franciscans and Friars Minor, they were originally an itinerant order – 'the wheels of God's chariot' – vowed to perpetual poverty and dedicated to caring for the needy. They soon established convents as settled as those of the Benedictine monks who they had once criticised for their worldliness. Their London convent just inside the city wall by Newgate became immensely wealthy through donations from London's merchants and resident gentry. By the fifteenth century, its church had a soaring gothic choir, famously beautiful stained-glass windows animated with vivid strips telling biblical stories, delicately carved choir-stalls, painted pillars and walls and 'many rich jewels and ornaments'.

Burial in Greyfriars Church was a sought-after honour. The tombs and memorials of four queens, two princesses and 663 'persons of quality' – dukes, earls, countesses, barons, knights, bishops, and merchants – are recorded in a list of its 'sepulchral inscriptions' made after the Dissolution of the Monasteries in 1536. One of the names on the list is that of Sir Thomas Malory. He was interred in the Chapel of St Francis, a place especially holy to Franciscans. It was off the choir rather than off the nave. A position so close to the most sacred part of the church was highly prized; it enabled one's soul to get closer to the King of Kings when the Day of Judgement came.

It seems, then, that Malory, like Guinevere, 'had a good end'. That his family, friends, servants, and a couple of friars were at his side when he heard the last rites, praying for his soul at a domestic altar while his corpse was washed and scented, sewn securely into wrappings of waxed linen cloth, and placed in its open-topped coffin. That they sang requiem hymns as they processed with burning torches behind the horse-bier draped in the Malory arms which carried his coffin to the great church. And that his funeral resembled that of his favourite knight, Sir Lancelot:

There they laid his corpse in the body of the quire, and sang and read many psalters and prayers over him and about him. And ever his visage was laid open and naked, that all folks might behold him. For such was the custom in those days, that all men of worship should so lie with open visage till that they were buried.

As the bells of Greyfriars tolled his death knell, Malory's body was placed in his chosen burial place. The 1536 list of inscriptions records the names of almost seventy people in the Chapel of St Francis, which was on the south-west side of the choir and was about 70 foot long and 25 foot wide. Under its fourth window

> *lies under a stone Sir Thomas Malory,*
> > *a valiant knight,*
> > *who died 14th day of March AD 1471,*
> > *of the parish of Monks Kirby in the county of Warwick.*
> > *[iacet sub lapide Dominus Thomas Mallere,*
> > *valens miles,*
> > *qui obiit 14 die mensis Marcii Anno Domino 147[1],*
> > *de parochia de MonkenKirykby in comitatu Warwici]*

Dominus (Lord) was a courtesy title, often applied to the head of an armigerous family. Malory's tomb was one of the minority distinguished in the list as 'sub lapide'. So it was grander than most, topped with an engraved stone, probably of marble, rather than a mere brass plaque. It may have been in a wall niche: the list specifies 'in plano' when gravestones were on the floor. That Malory was closer to the Lancastrians than to the Earl of Warwick at the time of his death is hinted at by the contrast of his epitaph with that of his feoffee Sir Walter Wrottesley two years later. Warwick had made Wrottesley his lieutenant in Calais in 1471, and Sir Walter held out there until 6 August. He was pardoned, but Edward had no intention of forgiving the Garter knight. The pardon was an expensive one; Wrottesley was quickly accused of debt and imprisoned in the Fleet. He died there two years later on 10 April 1473. Like Sir Thomas, he was buried in the chapel of St Francis at Greyfriars. His epitaph proudly recorded him as 'A knight strenuous in arms with the Earl of Warwick [*cum comite Warwici*]'. Malory's declared no such allegiance. It said only that he was 'of the parish of Monks Kirby in Warwickshire' [*in comitatu Warwici*].

After Sir Thomas's funeral came the customary wake. These 'almost orgiastic' feasts could last for several days. Ralph Stonor's went on for over a week. Thomas Stonor's wake in 1474 cost £74 2s 5d. Two-thirds of that was spent on food: venison, brawn, sirloin and other 'baked meats'. Temporary buildings were set up to accommodate the guests and provide a kitchen. For John Paston's wake in 1466, ninety-four serving-men were hired to wait on the guests. Two men were kept busy for two days flaying beasts for the feast, and eighteen barrels of beer and a large quantity of malted ale and a runlet of red wine were provided.

It is possible that both Malory's funeral and his wake were more austere than those of Stonor and Paston. In the final epilogue to the *Morte Darthur*, written while he was in Newgate, he calls himself 'the servant of Jesu by day and by night', and all three of the preceding explicits call on Jesus and ask for mercy. Newgate had a visiting chaplain from Greyfriars, and constant meditations on the life of Christ with special emphasis on his human nature were the core of the Franciscan approach to prayer. Christ's agonising death, the perfect man shedding his blood to save sinful souls, was the chief concern of such meditations. Devout souls were encouraged to saturate their minds with detailed imaginings of the events of the Passion at intervals throughout the day and the night. Many men, and women, turned to holy orders at Malory's time of life. Perhaps he too had done so: 'dominus' was also a title given to priests. His burial in the chapel of St Francis could simply mean that it was his chosen place of prayer. Wills frequently include a request to be buried 'where as I was wont to sit' or 'afore my seat'.

A thoughtful man like Sir Thomas Malory could also have had an intellectual affinity with Greyfriars. Besides being close to Newgate, it was opposite Warwick Inn, and close to the Hospitallers' Priory at Clerkenwell. Malory could have got to know its self-contained, peaceful world well, both when he was in Newgate and if he was, as I have surmised, living in London in the mid-1460s. The Franciscan friars were recognised as the best preachers of the day; their sermons were witty and outspoken. Many of the foremost medieval philosophers – Roger Bacon, William of Ockham and Duns Scotus – were Franciscans. Cosmopolitan and well travelled both in England and in Europe, they did not hesitate to denounce injustice or moral failings and had strong views on political and social issues. Greyfriars boasted one of the best libraries in the city. It had been embellished by generous donations from London's Mayor, Sir Richard Whittington, in 1421. Within three years the building, which was 129 foot long and 31 foot wide, was panelled with fine wainscoting, equipped with twenty-eight desks and settles, and filled with books worth over £500. No records of what they were survive, but records from other such libraries show a wide range of books. Dugdale grumbled in *Monasticon*, his great survey of the English religious orders, that

> *The friars of all orders, and chiefly the Franciscans, used so diligently to procure Monuments of Literature from all Parts that wise Men looked upon it as an Injury to Lay Men, who therefore found a difficulty to get any Books.*

Visitors were allowed to read the books. 'When I happened to turn aside to towns and places where the mendicants [i.e. friars] had their convents', wrote the insatiable fourteenth-century book collector Richard of Bury, 'I was not slack in visiting their libraries. There, amidst the deepest poverty, I found the most precious riches treasured up.' However, although monastic libraries did include histories and a scattering of romances, their books were predominantly theological works. It is very unlikely that Malory found his numerous sources there. But it is quite possible that he found it an inspiring place in which to work.

One last romantic surmise. To be buried in Greyfriars Church meant not only status but also wealth. Either Malory was deeply respected by the friars or he made a generous donation, perhaps of books, to Greyfriars in his will. Or did someone make a donation for him? The church was especially important to the Blount family; no fewer than eight of them are buried there. Sir Walter, the 1st Lord

Mountjoy, was one of Malory's feoffees. He, or his wife Anne Neville ('never forgetteth . . .'), could have arranged for Malory's funeral and burial in Greyfriars. Sir Walter was buried there himself in 1474.

The convent of the Grey Friars was closed down soon after 1536, when Henry VIII declared that all England's religious houses were to be dissolved. Malory's funerary slab was probably among the 140 marble stones sold off by the Mayor, Sir Martin Bowes, in 1546. The convent was re-founded as Christ's Hospital, a school for orphans. The church was renamed Christ Church, and became the parish church for the area until it burned down in the Great Fire of London in 1666. Sir Christopher Wren built a new, much smaller, church on the site of the original choir, its walls matched to the foundations of the medieval ones. The tower was built over what was once the seventh bay of the choir, and to the west a churchyard covered the seven lost bays of the nave.

The church that Sir Christopher Wren built over the eastern half of the foundations of Greyfriars was blitzed to destruction in the 1939–44 war. Its shell survives, and its interior is a peaceful garden, a sanctuary from the bustle of city traffic. Office workers take their sandwiches there to enjoy its tranquillity. The fourth window of the chapel of St Francis is now the bay in the south-west corner of the skeletal church, beside the tower. It has as yet no memorial of any sort to Sir Thomas Malory.

A Tangled Inheritance

It was routine practice after the death of any landed gentleman for the county escheator to find out whether any fees, wards or reversions of title were due to the King. No records survive of inquiries into Malory's holdings in Warwick and Leicester, which suggests that they were known to be held of feoffees. But an inquisition post mortem for his lands in Northamptonshire was held on 6 November 1471. The jurors reported that Sir Thomas held no lands or houses in chief or in service of the King or of anyone else in Northamptonshire on the day of his death, which was declared to have been 12 March – two days before the date on his gravestone. The anomaly was probably a scribal error (XII and XIV are easily confused), though it could also have been an attempt to prevent a posthumous attainder.

Malory's heir was found to be his son Robert, who was then about twenty-three. It was probably he who took out a pardon on 9 May 1471, as otherwise the inheritance which he expected to come into after his mother's death might have been in doubt. However, Robert died in the autumn of 1479, and Lady Elizabeth died a few weeks later. It was again a year marked by an epidemic of plague. The returns to the writs inquiring into Robert's holdings in Warwickshire and Leicestershire which were sent on 4 November do not survive, but they presumably said that his mother had held all the Malory estates. Now that she too had died, the process started again. In June 1480 writs inquiring into Lady Elizabeth's holdings were sent to Northamptonshire as well as to Warwickshire and Leicestershire; Lady Elizabeth had evidently been living at Winwick on her death. The inquisition past mortem reported that she had died on 30 September or 1 October, holding for life the manors of Newbold Revel in Warwickshire, Winwick in Northamptonshire, Swinford in Leicestershire, and property in the honour of Peverell in chief of the King. Newbold Revel was held of the seven-year-old Anne Mowbray, Duchess of Norfolk and wife of the King's son, Richard, Duke of York, who was just six. Anne Mowbray was a ward of the King, which meant that Newbold Revel was regarded as held of the King. Since the heir to the Malory lands was Robert's son Nicholas, and the boy was only about fourteen, wardship of his person, his lands and his marriage thus fell to the King. In October 1480 this was granted to Margaret Kelem, one of Queen Elizabeth's ladies-in-waiting. She married Thomas Kingston and subsequently married her ward Nicholas to Kingston's daughter Katherine.

These arrangements were soon called into question. In February 1481, Edward IV authorised William Catesby, a prominent local landowner whose father had been a committed Lancastrian, to collect evidence of the Malorys' title to their lands. Catesby, a clever but devious-minded man who admitted in his will to acquiring much land wrongfully, may have suggested the idea himself. The fact that he bothered to do so is confirmation of the attractions of the Malory estates. He duly collected four boxes of papers, examined them himself, and sent them to Margaret Kelem. The fate of the boxes is unknown.

The kaleidoscope of power twisted dramatically in 1483. After ten years of shrewd, merciful and financially competent government that saw England becoming prosperous and relatively peaceful, and that has earned Edward IV the accolade of 'one of the greatest of English kings', Edward fell ill at the end of March, and died two weeks later on 9 April. He was only forty years old. Mystery surrounds his death, 'neither worn out with old age nor yet seized with any known malady'. There was talk of poison, of ague, and of apoplexy (Edward's physical appetites were prodigious). At least he had time to repent of his sins, achieving a better end, said the enjoyably frank, if prim, Croyland Chronicler, than could have been hoped for 'after the manifestation by him of so large a share of the frailties inherent to the lot of mankind'. His thirteen-year-old son succeeded as Edward V, but within three months he and his brother Richard, Duke of York, were dispatched to the Tower by their uncle, Richard, Duke of Gloucester. Gloucester then had himself crowned Richard III, on the shaky ground that Edward's children by Elizabeth Woodville were illegitimate. It was claimed that the former king had entered into a clandestine pre-contract of marriage with Lady Eleanor Talbot before his marriage to Elizabeth Woodville and that their union was invalid as a result.

Queen Elizabeth, now plain Dame Elizabeth Grey, retreated into sanctuary at Westminster. Most of her relations were executed or banished. She may have reflected on the irony of sharing the fate of her former mistress and queenly rival, Margaret of Anjou, who had died just a year before, on 20 August 1482. Elizabeth had done what she could for Margaret in the early 1470s, interceding to have her imprisoned at Windsor instead of in the Tower, and then committed to the gentle custody of Alice Chaucer, Dowager Duchess of Suffolk, at Ewelme. Margaret's father King René, penurious as ever, was unable to pay the 50,000 crowns which Edward IV had demanded for her ransom; to make matters worse, King Louis XI seized Anjou for himself by force in 1474, leaving René no option but to retreat to Aix-en-Provence. In 1475, René signed away his family rights to Provence to the French Crown in exchange for Louis's paying Margaret's ransom and granting her a pension for life, and she too took refuge in Aix. After René's death in 1479, Margaret was allowed to return to Anjou, where she lived in seclusion at the Château de Dampierre, close to the place where she had grown up as a hopeful, romantically-minded girl: her grandmother's great castle of Saumur.

The Malory estates now came under threat. Margaret Kelem had lost her royal patron, and Catesby, a close crony of Richard III, seized Swinford for himself; his justification, if any, for doing so does not survive. But two years later, the wheel of fortune turned again, when news of the deaths of Edward's sons in the Tower of London turned discontent at Richard's usurpation into a climate of continual rebellion. On 7 August, Henry Tudor, son of Henry VI's half-brother Edmund and Margaret Beaufort, who could trace her line back through John of Gaunt to Edward III, landed at Milford Haven in Wales and marched to Staffordshire with an ever-growing army. Richard III confronted him in Leicestershire, near Market Bosworth, with a much larger, but far from loyal, force. When three thousand of his men deserted him for Henry, he charged, 'inflamed with ire', into battle. He was killed 'fighting manfully in the thickest press of his enemies'. Catesby was attainted and executed, and all his lands were forfeited.

Six months into the reign of Henry VII, Ralph Wolseley appeared in Chancery to plead that he was the last surviving feoffee of Sir Thomas Malory's Leicestershire lands, and that the Leicestershire inquisition of 1480 had unjustly deprived him of Swinford and its tenements. Wolseley was granted both Swinford and eight years of retrospective profits on the lands and properties. In 1488 Sir Thomas Malory's grandson Nicholas Malory came of age, and into his impressively complete inheritance.

At the Sign of the Red Pale

Three years earlier we can imagine fifteen-year-old Nicholas turning the pages of a quite different, and much more enduring, legacy with immense pride. For on 31 July 1485, William Caxton finished printing his edition of Sir Thomas Malory's *The Birth, Life and Acts of King Arthur, of his noble Knights of the Round Table, their marvellous Enquests and Adventures; th'Achieving of the Sangreal, and in the end the dolorous Death and Departing out of the World of them All.* Caxton had learned the revolutionary craft of printing with moveable type in Flanders. He printed his own translation into English of a history of Troy in 1474, encouraged, he said, by Edward IV's sister, Margaret, Duchess of Burgundy. He set up his printing workshop in Westminster two years later, and had been successfully printing documents, pamphlets and books ever since. Malory's *Arthur*, both entertaining and morally uplifting, fitted his list very well indeed. There was intense interest in loyalty, service and chivalry in the 1470s and 1480s. They were flourishing themes at a time when England's rulers were intent on restoring stability after decades of political upheaval. Caxton's *Book of Noblesse* displayed a succession of chivalric heroes. The story of Geoffrey of Boulogne, the crusader who won and ruled Jerusalem, was published in 1481. Ramon Lull's *Order of Chivalry* came out in 1484, with an epilogue by Caxton recommending that jousts should be held every year, leading 'gentlemen to resort to the ancient custom of chivalry'. The life of Charlemagne, another of the three Christian kings among the famous 'Nine Worthies', appeared in 1485. Arthur was not only the third Christian worthy, he was English.

Publishing a life of King Arthur was so obviously a good idea that the question that really needs to be answered is: why didn't Caxton print the *Morte Darthur* earlier? The watermarks of the paper of the Winchester manuscript date from between 1475 and 1478. The dim shadows of offsets of type on the Winchester manuscript suggest that it was in Caxton's hands well before 1485, the date of the printed edition. Experts in Caxton's use of typefaces have shown that the marks, made when wet printed sheets were carelessly put down on the manuscript, date from some time during the years 1480–3. So Caxton had the *Morte Darthur* by him for several years before printing it. Why the delay? Why print the two foreign Christian worthies first? One reason could have been that he wanted to work on the manuscript personally, and it was hard for someone as busy as he was to find time to do so. In 1480, he published his own prose version of the *Brut*, which he called *Chronicles of England*. It was so popular that he printed a second edition in 1482. Linguistic analysis has shown that Caxton's history was used as a guide by whoever abbreviated, modernised and altered Malory's 'Tale of King Arthur and the Emperor Lucius'. Caxton also edited the rest of the text with painstaking care. He divided it into twenty-one 'books', and subdivided those into a total of 507 chapters, the content of each of which was briefly described in the preliminary list of the chapters. His divisions followed those of the manuscript very faithfully, almost always either using a capital letter or the double-slash as a cue.

Perhaps it made good sense to drag his feet over the presentation of a history of King Arthur written by a knight whom Edward IV, a man of elephantine memory, had no cause to love. Edward's death and Richard III's usurpation of the throne could have been what made it possible for Caxton to take the manuscript, which he may have edited some time earlier, out of storage. He will have known that it would be one of his most popular titles: the story, written in drivingly exciting and dramatic prose, of the hero of virtually every English pageant of victory mounted in the fifteenth century. Richard III had only been sixteen when Malory was excepted from pardon by Edward IV in 1468. He had, moreover, married Anne, the granddaughter of Sir Richard Beauchamp after the death at Tewkesbury of her first husband, the Lancastrian Prince Edward. Now Queen of England, and with a son, another Prince Edward, who was heir apparent, she would surely have welcomed the printing of Malory's book. So too would her mother, Anne Beauchamp, at last reinstated to high degree after a period of penurious sanctuary in Beaulieu Abbey. The glorious memorial chapel to her renowned father in St Mary's, Warwick, had been completed in the 1470s, and she was busy in 1484 overseeing the making of the *Beauchamp Pageant*, a eulogy of her family which ended with a picture of her daughter Queen Anne, King Richard III and their son Edward of Middleham. The *Beauchamp Pageant* extolled the chivalric virtues of loyalty, courtesy and maintaining the right. Malory's history of King Arthur and his noble and joyous knights did the same. Caxton's preface recommends the book to gentlewomen as well as to gentlemen, something which he tended to do when he was printing a book at the request of a woman.

How did Caxton come by the manuscript? He claims in his preface that he decided to print it because

> *many noble and divers gentlemen of this realm of England came and demanded me many and oft times, wherefore that I have not do made and imprint the noble history of the Saint Greal, and of the most renowned Christian king, first and chief of the three best Christian [of the Nine Worthies] King Arthur, which ought most to be remembered among us Englishmen to-fore all other Christian kings ... considering that he was a man born within this realm, and king and emperor of the same: and that there be in French divers and many noble volumes of his acts, and also of his knights.*

When Caxton told them that many people said Arthur was a mere legend, and that all books about him were 'feigned or fabled',

> *they answered, and one in special said, that in him that should say or think that there was never such a king called Arthur might well be aretted [credited] great folly and blindness. For he said that there were many evidences of the contrary.*

The 'one in special' was remarkably knowledgeable about such evidences, listing all the early chronicles that mentioned Arthur, as well as books in French, Dutch, Italian, Spanish and Greek, and pointing at the material relics of Arthur's reign: his sepulchre at Glastonbury, his seal in St Edward's shrine in Westminster Abbey, Gawaine's skull and Craddock's cloak at Dover Castle, the Round Table at Winchester, Lancelot's sword and 'many other things', including a generous littering of 'great stones and marvellous works of iron lying under the ground, and royal vaults' in Wales. Any member of Sir Thomas Malory's family was likely to be better informed than most on these matters. The simplest explanation of the manuscript's arrival in Caxton's printing works is that one of them provided Caxton with a copy of it. But if Malory did indeed try to win his freedom by presenting his history of Arthur to an influential patron in 1469, it could have been that patron who gave it to Caxton.

The existence of such a manuscript is proved by innumerable small details that suggest that Caxton's typesetters were working from another version of Malory's book. There were certainly other manuscripts of it in circulation at the time, although the only one known today is the manuscript discovered at Winchester in 1936. This is smaller than Caxton's printed folio, and is a sturdy volume for use rather than show; all the names of the characters are highlighted by being in red, and there are 120 decorated capital letters. Its punctuation suggests that it was intended to be read aloud: a combination of double slashes, small capitals and mid-line dots guide the narrator to the appropriate pauses and emphases. Rubricating the characters' names calls attention to the arrival of new characters and the need for a change of voice. When Merlin appears in disguise, he is only referred to as 'M'. You can almost see the storyteller looking round at his audience, a knowing finger on his lips. It must have been wonderful family entertainment.

Whoever put it into Caxton's possession, we can imagine the printer receiving it with enthusiasm, though he did not give any details in his preface on the provenance of the 'copy unto me delivered, which copy Sir Thomas Malory did take out of certain books of French, and reduced it into English', nor did he expand on the merits of the long-dead author. He also removed Malory's by then irrelevant pleas for mercy and deliverance from the text, keeping only the last explicit. By the time the book saw the light of day, there was less need to be reticent on the subject of Sir Thomas Malory. For Caxton finished printing the *Morte Darthur* on 31 July 1485, three weeks before Richard III was killed at the Battle of Bosworth Field on 22 August and Henry VII became king.

The *Morte* could not have appeared at a more appropriate time. Henry VII's propagandists made the most of the example it offered of a lost heir becoming King of England by conquest. They were quick to establish an imaginative bloodline running from the Tudors back to King Arthur through the Welsh King Cadwallader. It was a useful distraction from the shortage of English royal blood in their ancestry. Henry VII's first son was born in September 1486. 'A fair prince and large of bone', he was christened Arthur in Winchester, which Malory had confidently identified as Camelot. In the 1498 pageant series at Coventry, the eleven-year-old Prince was hailed by a 'King Arthur' who greeted him as one chosen by the Court Eternal 'to be equal one to me in might, To spread our name Arthur, and acts to advance'. When Philip the Fair, Archduke of the Netherlands, visited England in 1506, Henry VII arranged for him to see the Round Table hanging at Winchester, and likened their friendship to that between Arthur and his allies; he had earlier told a Milanese ambassador that the Garter was 'the badge and first order of King Arthur'.

Events would prove, however, that Caxton had been wise to play down the Malory connection with the *Morte Darthur*. The whole clan was notably disaffected in the last thirty years of the century. They did not favour Henry VII. Only one claimant to the throne interested them: the young Earl of Warwick, son of Richard III's older brother Clarence and Isobel Neville, who was half a Beauchamp. Aware of the threat presented by his Plantagenet blood, Henry VII had him locked up in the Tower of London as soon as he came to the throne. That didn't prevent a pretended Earl of Warwick, Lambert Simnel, from appearing in Ireland in 1488. Four Northamptonshire Malorys were prominent among his supporters: John Malory of Litchborough, Robert Malory of Fawsley, Giles Malory of Green Norton and William Malory of Stowe. In 1495, Richard Malory of Monks Kirby, who may have been Nicholas's younger brother, was executed for his part in the Perkin Warbeck conspiracy. Also incriminated were John Kendall, Prior of the English Knights Hospitaller, and a good many of the descendants of Sir Thomas Malory's old associates: Sir Simon, Sir Edward and Henry Mountfort, the sons and grandson of Sir Baldwin Mountfort, and Robert Chamberlain of Gedding, son of Sir Roger Chamberlain.

In 1500, weary of the unending conspiracies, Henry VII ordered the execution of Edward, Earl of Warwick, the last male Beauchamp.

We do not know how many *Morte Darthur*s were printed. Although only two copies of that first edition survive, several hundred could have been made. Norman Blake, Caxton's biographer, suggests that he printed 250 copies of the almost equally long *History of Troy*. A history of the English King Arthur, published in London, was likely to be much more popular. Caxton took on more space in the Westminster precincts at this time, and no other major book was printed in 1486. It evidently sold well. In 1498 Caxton's successor, Wynkyn de Worde, published a new edition, this time called *The Book of the Most Noble and Worthy Prince King Arthur*, with woodcuts made especially for it. It was reprinted in 1529.

The Never-ending Story

Prince Arthur died before he could become King Arthur II. But his brother Henry VIII grew up to enjoy what was by then called Malory's *Book of King Arthur*, and remained an enthusiast for Arthurian imagery all his life, ordering the repainting of the Winchester Round Table with a King Arthur in his own rosy, bovine image. He was a formidable jouster, 'daily running at the ring with his companions-in-arms', holding May Day tournaments and entering the lists incognito in 1510. In 1520 his talks with Francis I of France were accompanied by a chivalric sporting extravaganza straight out of Malory's pages: the Field of the Cloth of Gold. A huge statue of King Arthur presided over its banqueting tent. Malory was however frowned upon by the post-Reformation puritans. The Tudor humanist Roger Ascham was shocked that Malory's book of 'open manslaughter and bold bawdry' should have been read in the royal chamber. But John Bale's added information about Malory in the 1559 edition of his biographical dictionary could well have come from contemporary hearsay, old memories aroused by the appearance of William Copland's new edition of Malory, *The Story of the Most Noble and Worthy King Arthur, The Which was the First of the Worthies Christian, and also of his Noble and Valiant Knights of the Round Table*. It was published in 1557, on the eve of the accession of Henry VIII's daughter Queen Elizabeth. 'Gloriana' was happy to be likened by the court poet Edmund Spenser to the Faerie Queene who directed the fortunes of Arthurian heroes. George Gascoigne's entertainment for the Virgin Queen at Kenilworth in 1575 made use of the *Morte Darthur*. John Grinkin compiled a summary of the book at about this time, and a new edition was published by Thomas West in 1578. 'Honest king *Arthure* will never displease a soldier,' wrote Sir Philip Sidney, who liked to have books, especially legends of Arthur, with him on campaign. 'Poetrie is the companion of Camps', he believed. For men 'have found their hearts moved to an excess of courtesy, liberality, and especially courage'. He drew on Malory for episodes in his *Arcadia*.

Ben Jonson also used Malory to inform the Arthurian entertainment he put on at the court of James I. In 1634, William Stansby published a lavishly capitalised 'newly refined' edition of *The Most Ancient and Famous History of the Renowned Prince Arthur King of Britaine, Wherein is Declared his Life and Death, with all his Glorious Battailes against the Saxons, Saracens, and Pagans, which (for the Honour of his Country) He Most Worthily Achieved. As Also, All the Noble Acts, and Heroicke Deeds of his Valiant Knights of the Round Table*. The republication of such a 'prophane and frivolous' book was greeted with horror by the preacher Nathaniel Baxter (*c.* 1550–1635), who deplored 'the horrible acts of those whoremasters, Lancelot du Lake, Tristram de Lionesse, Gareth of Orkney, Merlin, the lady of the Lake, with the vile and stinking story of the Sangreal, of K.Peles, etc'. John Milton must have browsed through it when he was considering an epic poem on Arthur, but in the event he turned from its ambivalent morality and gave the world a very different fallen hero in Lucifer, the dark angel of *Paradise Lost*. The high point of Malory's *Arthur*, the Quest for the Holy Grail, was anathema to seventeenth-century Puritan thinking. But in 1696 William Nicolson's *English Historical Library*, a work which gave 'a short view and character of most of our historians', included 'Thomas Malory, a Welsh gentleman', whose telling of 'King Arthur's story in English' was 'a book that is, in our days, often sold by the ballad-singers, with the like authentic records of Guy of Warwick and Bevis of Southampton'. Unfashionable among the intelligentsia, it was evidently still enchanting those who liked their literature read aloud.

There are no records of new editions of Malory in the eighteenth century. But copies of his book were still circulating. The antiquary William Oldys had certainly read it. In an article on William Caxton in *Biographica Britannica* (1747–66), he assumed that Sir Thomas Malory was not only a Welshman but a priest, an idea he derived from Malory's description of himself as 'the servant of Jesu' in his last explicit. Oldys drily commented that 'As the author has not made his heroes any great commanders of their passions in their amours, nor rigorously confined them to honour or decorum, in point of fidelity and continence, his book became a great favourite with some persons of the highest distinction for a long time'. He dismissed it as 'entertainment [for] the lighter and more insolid readers'. But towards the end of the rumbustious and vice-ridden age of enlightenment, when dark satanic mills spread across England's green and pleasant land, men began recalling the high endeavours of chivalry with wistful nostalgia. Dr Johnson declared himself 'immoderately fond of reading Romances of Chivalry', and referred to Malory's *Arthur* affectionately in a poem, praising

> *. . . the whole sum*
> *Of errant knighthood: with the dames and dwarfs,*
> *The charmed boats, and the enchanted wharves,*
> *The tristrams, lanc'lots, etc.*

In the 1800s, Sir Walter Scott used to read Malory's 'excellent old English' aloud after dinner at Abbotsford, saying the book was 'indisputably the best Prose Romance' and 'breathed a high tone of chivalry'; its spirit was the inspiration for his swashbuckling medieval novels.

During the nineteenth century, a flood of new editions allowed Malory's 'noble and joyous' book to become essential reading in an age of religious revival that found in its ethic of gallantry an attractive alternative to the rampant materialism of the Industrial Revolution. The Holy Grail was seen not as a heresy but as a potent metaphor of purity, capable of inspiring new generations of Christian soldiers to sweep onwards, creating a British Empire on which the sun never set. Queen Victoria's favourite poet Lord Alfred Tennyson used Robert Southey's 1817 edition of Malory to retell the Arthurian legends in verse. His ponderously dignified King Arthur, his bold Sir Lancelot singing 'tirra lirra by the river' in dazzling armour, and his haunted and haunting Lady of Shalott were far removed from Malory's realistic, carefully imperfect characters; 'not so much Morte d'Arthur as Morte d'Albert' was Swinburne's acid judgement on *The Idylls of the King*.

Bowdlerisation afflicted most Victorian versions of Malory. Editors cut out broad swathes of battles and tournaments, and excised all talk of buttocks, 'hangars' and ravishings. Illustrations of his stories by Edward Burne-Jones, Dante Gabriel Rossetti and other artists of the Pre-Raphaelite movement show Malory's strong-minded, characterful women as vapid damsels and malign enchantresses, his knights as impossibly *point devise*. But the popularity of all things medieval was unstoppable. Country houses became towered and battlemented, lined with oak panelling and tapestries endowed with oriel windows. Even suburban houses had inglenook fireplaces, stained-glass lights in their windows and romantic little turrets. William Morris furnishings, textiles and wallpaper turned late-Victorian interiors into fantasy recreations of Malory's age.

The twentieth century found different messages in Malory. The magic and miracles inseparable from his knights' adventures satisfied the romantic patriotism of W. B. Yeats; the failures of his heroes fascinated the austerely intellectual T. S. Eliot. T. E. Lawrence found him strangely relevant to the still medieval world of the Arabian desert; tribal loyalties, he pointed out, were interestingly similar to feudal allegiances. But the two world wars, won not by brigades of cavalry but by tanks and bombers, required a reassessment of what constituted true chivalry. It was T. H. White who shrewdly plucked off the pious shroud which the Victorians had draped over Malory. He was a highly unusual English schoolmaster ('boys in the mass are like haddocks', he once wrote to a friend) who had a passion for hunting and kept hawks. He picked up the *Morte Darthur* one day when he was bored and

*was thrilled and astonished to find that (a) the thing was a
perfect tragedy, with a beginning, a middle and an end
implicit in the beginning and (b) the characters were real
people with recognisable reactions which could be forecast.
Mordred was hateful; Kay a decent chap with an inferiority
complex; Gawaine that rarest of literary productions, a swine
with a streak of solid decency. He was a sterling fellow to his
own clan. Arthur, Lancelot and even Galahad were really
glorious people, not pre-raphaelite prigs.*

T. H. White retold the story of Arthur in four separate novels,
later printed in one volume as *The Once and Future King*. The first,
The Sword in the Stone, is a near perfect book, a description of how
Merlin gave Arthur (the 'Wart') an education that really was an
education. Still much loved by children, it became a very successful
Walt Disney cartoon. *The Queen of Air and Water* is a tragicomic
picture of the dysfunctional home life of King Lot's doomed family.
The Ill-Made Knight describes how an ugly, deeply thoughtful Sir
Lancelot struggles, and fails, to achieve knightly perfection. *The
Candle in the Wind* takes the now realistically middle-aged heroes
through the final downfall of Arthur's kingdom. The whole epic is a
mix of modern thinking and medieval setting which is as imperfect
a great novel as Lancelot is a great knight, and its analysis of why
men go to war is distorted by White's own prejudices. But it is a true
mirror of Malory's genius, and it has sent thousands of readers
straight to the book which inspired it. Many of its most arresting
lines are word-for-word quotes from the *Morte* – sometimes secret,
sometimes acknowledged homages. 'Sir Bors, who did not care for
the Queen, once said to her: "Fie on your weeping, for ye weep never
but when there is no boot"'. When Lancelot finds to his astonishment
that, sinful as he is, he has been allowed to heal Sir Urry, who can
only be healed by the 'best knight in the world', White ends with
Malory's own words: 'And ever Sir Lancelot wept, as he had been a
child that had been beaten'.

White proved that Malory can do more for us than while away
tedium or provide an escape from modern life. The innumerable

works of art, novels, films and games that continue to draw on the great Arthurian themes that Malory defined with such candour show that the *Morte* still has lessons to teach us: lessons about taking personal responsibility, being loyal and tolerant, defending the weak – the 'generosity of spirit' that Sir Walter Scott saw as the essence of chivalry. Scott described Malory as 'the Father of Chivalry'. This biography, necessarily riddled with guesswork, has I hope made the fifteenth-century Warwickshire knight who wrote Britain's greatest epic real enough for us to understand how he came to be worthy of such an accolade. The epitaph would surely have delighted the man who as a boy had ridden to war with Sir Richard Beauchamp, lauded as the 'Father of Courtesy' by the Emperor Sigismund in 1414. The gravestone *envoi* that Malory received from his contemporaries was simply 'knight valiant'. But valiant is a favourite adjective of praise in the *Morte Darthur*. It has, moreover, a directness and simplicity that is well-suited to the honest, impetuous, wise and deeply loyal man that I have imagined Sir Thomas Malory to be.

ABBREVIATIONS

AOM	Archives of Malta
BIHR	*Bulletin of the Institute of Historical Research*
BJRL	*Bulletin of the John Rylands University Library of Manchester*
BL	British Library
Cal. Ch. Rolls	*Calendar of Charter Rolls*, 6 vols, London 1903–27
Cal. Pap. Reg.	*Calendar of Entries in the Papal Registers relating to Great Britain and Ireland.* In progress, London 1916–
CCR	*Calendar of Close Rolls* (Henry III–Henry VIII), 59 vols, London 1902–65
C.E.M.	Dr Charles Moreton (History of Parliament Trust)
CFR	*Calendar of Fine Rolls* (Edward I–Henry VII), 22 vols, London 1911–62
CIPM	*Calendarium Inquisitionum Post Mortem*, London 1806–88
CPR	Calendar of Patent Rolls (Henry III–Henry VII), 54 vols, London 1901–16
CRO	County Record Office
CSPM	Calendar of State Papers of Milan
CUP	Cambridge University Press
D.I.G.	Dr David Grummitt (History of Parliament Trust)
DKPR	Annual Report of the Deputy Keeper of the Public Records
DNB	*The Dictionary of National Biography*
EETS	Early English Text Society
EHR	*English Historical Review*
GEC	G. E. Cockayne, ed., *The Complete Peerage*
HPT	History of Parliament Trust
H.W.K.	Hannes Kleineke (History of Parliament Trust)
IPM	Inquisition post mortem
KB	King's Bench

L.S.C.D.	Linda Clark (History of Parliament Trust)
Malory	When used as source reference for quotations, this refers to the most recent edition of A. W. Pollard's rendering of *The Morte Darthur* (edited by John Matthews, Cassell, 2000).
M.P.D.	Dr Matthew Davies (History of Parliament Trust)
OED	*Oxford English Dictionary*
OUP	Oxford University Press
PRO	Public Record Office, London (now known as the National Archives)
Proc. & *Ord. PC*	*Proceeding and Ordinances of the Privy Council of England*, ed. Sir (Nicholas) Harris Nicolas, 7 vols, 1834–7
RP	Rotuli Parliamentorum, 7 vols (London, 1832)
S.J.P.	Dr Simon Payling (History of Parliament Trust)
Works	*The Works of Sir Thomas Malory*, edited by Eugene Vinaver (Oxford, 1947), revised by P. J. C. Field (Oxford, 1990).

ENDNOTES

INTRODUCTION

PAGE 9 It befell: Malory, I.1. Quotations cited 'Malory' are taken from the *Morte Darthur*, ed. John Matthews (Cassell, 2000). This is a slightly revised version of A. W. Pollard's edition (Medici Society, 1900). Quotations which appear only in the edition of the manuscript of the *Morte Darthur* by Eugene Vinaver, *The Works of Sir Thomas Malory* (Oxford, 1947), are cited 'Works'.

PAGE 10 T. E. Lawrence, *Seven Pillars of Wisdom* (Cape, London, 1926), and Malcolm D. Allen, *The Medievalism of Lawrence of Arabia* (1991).

Lewis: C. S. Lewis, 'The English Prose Morte', in J. A. W. Bennett, *Essays on Malory* (Clarendon Press, Oxford, 1963).

Chandler: personal communication from P. J. C. Field – who also sees the *Morte Darthur* as the key to Gavin Lyall's *Midnight Plus One* (1965).

Comic books: Michael Torregrossa, 'Camelot 3000 and Beyond', *Arthuriana* 9.1 (1999).

'Heroic and magnanimous temperament': John Bale, Bishop of Ossory, *Scriptorum Illustrium Maioris Brytanniae* (Basle, 1557–9), quoted in *Malory: The Critical Heritage*, ed. M. J. Parins (Routledge, 1988).

Identity was uncertain: Bale opines that Malory came from Mailoria, 'a certain region of Wales in the vicinity of the River Dee', by inserting what Leland's *Dictionary of Antiquities* said about that area in his account of Malory. However, although Leland mentions Maelor in the jottings he made while surveying England and Wales between 1535 and 1543 (later published as *The Itinerary of John Leland*, edited by Lucy Toulin Smith, 1906–10, 5 vols, repr. 1964), he makes absolutely no connection between it and the 'Thomas Melorius' he later included in a long list of the Arthurian historians he consulted when writing his *Assertion of King Arthur* (1544). The only Malory mentioned in the *Itinerary* appears to have been encountered at Papworth St Agnes, as his name comes immediately after Leland mentions that village. But Leland does not link this man with either the *Morte Darthur* or Maelor.

Kitteridge: Kitteridge, George Lyman, 'Who was Sir Thomas Malory?' in *Johnson's Universal Encyclopaedia*, v (1894, rev. in *Studies in Notes and Philology*, Boston, 1897).

PAGE 11 1414 list: BL Cotton Roll xiii 7, m.2. Epitaph: BL Cotton Vitellius F.xii, fol. 28 r.

Edward Hicks, *Sir Thomas Malory: His Turbulent Career* (Harvard, 1928; 2nd edn Octagon Books, New York, 1975). The Nuneaton indictment is now in the National Archive at Kew: PRO KB 9/265/78, m.3

Search of other legal records: notably by A. C. Baugh, 'Documenting Sir Thomas Malory', *Speculum* 8 (1933) 3–29. Pardons: PRO C67/46, m.37; PRO C67/47, m.9.

Disappointed admirers: notably William Matthews, *The Ill-Framed Knight: A Skeptical Inquiry into the Identity of Sir Thomas Malory* (University of California Press, Berkeley, 1966), whose theories will be discussed further below, and R. R. Griffith, 'The Authorship Question Reconsidered: A Case for Thomas Malory of Papworth St Agnes, Cambridgeshire', in T. Takamiya and D. Brewer (eds), *Aspects of Malory* (Brewer, Cambridge, 1981), 159–77.

Closer examination: See P. J. C. Field, *The Life and Times of Thomas Malory*, (Brewer, Woodbridge, 1993), 8–10. In addition, Griffith mixes Bale and Leland references with his own surmises in a misleading way, and ignores the fact that if Leland, a keen Arthurian, had heard anything about the author of the *Morte* either in Maelor or Papworth St Agnes, it is very odd indeed that he did not make a note of it – he did digress on John Roos and John Hardying (II, 157, 167). Bale's information about Malory did not, it seems, come from Leland at all, for although he used Leland's lost work *De Scriptoribus Britannicis* for the first edition of his own biographical dictionary, the interesting details he gives about Malory's personality and career only appear ten years later in his own book's second, expanded edition (see below, ch. 22). Moreover, the East Anglian Thomas Malory was not only not a knight but, I discovered on browsing through the History of Parliament Trust's (HPT) records, he positively rejected knighthood: he took out a distraint of knighthood in 1465 (see HPT List of Distraints, Thomas Maulery of Cambridgeshire).

PAGE 12 The 'rug' is now kept in Thurbern's Chantry, Winchester College.
The year 1993: No one living has spent more time studying Malory than Field. His revision of Vinaver's edition of *The Works of Sir Thomas Malory* was published by OUP in 1990; he is now at work on a completely new edition of the Winchester manuscript.

PAGE 13 Too advanced an age: Field, 1993, 64. Field was strongly influenced by Matthews' argument (Matthews, 1966, 73) that 'Fifty-five or so is a mature age to commit rape and attempt assassination, but it is by no means prohibitive. But seventy-five is no age at all to be writing *Le Morte Darthur* in prison. Nothing is impossible; but recalling the ages at which medieval authors normally sank into silence, recalling the vitality, energy, and even occasional gaiety of *Le Morte Darthur* and the long, persistent labour that it represents, one needs hardly to be skeptical to doubt that the work was written by an ancient of seventy-five.'

Despite Field's valiant efforts: See, among many others, M. C. Carpenter's review of Field, 1993, in *Medium Aevum* LXIII; also 'Thomas Malory and Fifteenth-Century Politics', in *BIHR*/53 (1980), 31–43.

PAGE 14 'worship': to be 'of worship' or 'worshipful' was a notable compliment, meaning that you were unusually worthy of praise.
John Gower: '*Cronica Tripertita*', in John Gower, *The Complete Works* (London, 1899–1902).

PAGE 15 John Shirley: John Stow wrote that Shirley 'painfully collected the works of Geoffrey Chaucer, John Lydgate and other learned writers, which works he wrote in sundry volumes to remain for posterity', quoted by M. Connolly, *John Shirley: Book Production and the Noble Household in Fifteenth-Century England* (Ashgate, Aldershot, 1998).
John Hardyng: H. Ellis, *The Chronicle of John Hardyng* (London, 1812).
Sir John Fortescue: S. B. Chrimes (trans.), *Sir John Fortescue: De Laudibus Legum Angliae* (CUP, 1949).
Thomas Dormandy: reviewed by Frances Spalding, *The Independent*, 27 January 2001.

PAGE 16 Violence of the times: A. J. Finch, 'The Nature of Violence in the Middle Ages; an alternative Perspective', *Historical Research* LXX. 173 (October 1997) is a useful summary of the new thinking. Work still in draft at the HPT on the lives of fifteenth-century MPs is set to challenge a great many assumptions about the age (see below, Ch. 7).
'Wars of the Roses': M. C. Carpenter, *The Wars of the Roses* (CUP, 1997); R. L. Storey, *The End of the House of Lancaster* (2nd edn Sutton, Gloucester, 1986).
Campaigns were brief: Andrew W. Boardman, *The Medieval Soldier in the Wars of the Roses* (Sutton, Stroud, 1998) estimates that of the fourteen campaigns that took place during the 35-year-period of hostilities, nine lasted less than three weeks and three less than a fortnight. Except in the major campaigns, that of 1462–4 and that of 1471, the battles tended to involve only small numbers of troops.
Visitors to England: Mrs Henry Cust, *Gentlemen Errant, being the Journeys and Adventures of Four Noblemen in Europe during the Fifteenth and Sixteenth Centuries* (John Murray, London, 1909), 41–5.

PAGE 17 Wealth of country squires: Maurice Keen, *English Society in the Later Middle Ages 1348–1500* (Penguin, London, 1990), 63–5.
Incomes: T. B. Pugh, 'The magnates, knights and gentry', in S. B. Chrimes, C. D. Ross and R. A. Griffiths (eds), *Fifteenth-Century England 1399–1509* (Sutton, Stroud, 1995). Accurate estimates are difficult at a time when incomes could be protected from taxation by such legal contrivances as enfeoffment to use. The figures in this paragraph are abstracted from E. F. Jacob, *The Fifteenth Century 1399–1485* (UP, Oxford/NCW, York, 1961).
Parliament: J. S. Roskell and L. S. Clark, *The House of Commons 1386–1421*, 3 vols (Sutton, Stroud, 1993) (cited as *The Commons*), J. S. Roskell, *Parliament and Politics in Late Medieval England* (Hambledon, London, 1981), vol. 2.

London merchants: J. L. Bolton, *The Medieval English Economy 1150–1500* (Dent, London, 1980).

Religosity: for this and other details see Eamon Duffy, *The Stripping of the Altars: Traditional Religion in England, 1400–1580* (Yale UP, 1992).

PAGE 19 Neither nostalgia nor escape: 'A fifteenth-century knight like Sir Thomas Malory could hardly escape chivalry, which was not one of a series of possible life-styles but a definition of the noble life itself': Larry Benson, *Malory's Morte Darthur* (Harvard UP, 1976). He disagrees, as I do, with Arthur Ferguson's vision of decline (*The Indian Summer of English Chivalry*, Duke UP, Durham, NC, 1960). One of the most detailed and convincing outlines of chivalry was written two hundred years closer to Malory's time by Sir Walter Scott: 'Essay of Chivalry', 1816, reprinted in *Essays on Chivalry, Romance and the Drama* (Frederick Warne, London, 1881). Using Jean Froissart to great effect, he pictures the Hundred Years War as the high point of noble chivalric practice; not a nostalgic attempt to restore an imaginary golden age, but a great improvement on the past.

THE *MORTE DARTHUR* BRIEFLY DRAWN

PAGE 23 All that evening: Mark Twain's setting of this scene in Warwick, into which steps a mysterious stranger who knows all about Arthurian times, is interesting, considering how close it was to Malory's Newbold Revel home. Malory scholars have always dated the first connection between the Warwickshire knight and the author of the *Morte* as Kitteridge, 1894. Warwick was of course a famous medieval town and, since it was close to Shakespeare's home at Stratford-upon-Avon, it would have been on any literary-minded American visitor's itinerary.

PAGE 24 Each subdivided: Recent summaries of theories on how Caxton worked include P. J. C. Field, *Malory: Texts and Sources, Arthurian Studies* XL (Brewer, Cambridge, 1998) and N. F. Blake, 'Caxton at Work: A Reconsideration', in *The Malory Debate*, ed. Bonnie Wheeler et al., *Arthurian Studies* XLVII (Brewer, Cambridge, 2000).

Vinaver's edition: This is now widely used by commentators on Malory, although its accuracy has recently been queried by Helen Cooper in her essay 'Opening Up the Malory Manuscript', in Wheeler, 2000.

PAGE 26 Gave lands and realms: *Malory*, V.12.

Horrible hordes: Malory, V.8. The complete list enriches our understanding of Malory's world picture: Lucius sent messengers to 'Ambage [Albania] and Arrage [Arcadia], to Alexandria, to India, to Armenia, whereas the river of Euphrates runneth into Asia, to Africa, and Europe the Large, to Ertayne [Hyrcania] and Elamye [for the Elams, see Acts 2:9], to Araby, Egypt, and to Damascus, to Damietta and Cayer [Cairo], to Cappodocia, to Tarsus, Turkey, Pontus and Pamphylia, to Syria and Galatia'. (P. J. C. Field, 'The Empire of Lucius Iberius', *Studies in Bibliography* 49 (1996), 106–28.)

PAGE 28 No rehearsal of the third book: That omitting the third book of Sir
Tristram was a deliberate choice is suggested by a later explicit which
owns up frankly to losing the continuation of Lancelot's story. As a result,
he omits the story of Tristram's last days with Isolde and his betrayal and
murder on the instigation of King Mark. He refers to Tristram's death only
in a casual aside in the list of knights present at the healing of Sir Urry
(Malory. 11).

PAGE 32 Ninth year: Events were often dated by regnal year in the fifteenth
century. Edward IV came to the throne on 4 March 1461, so the ninth year of
his reign ran from 4 March 1469 to 3 March 1470.

Read or listen: How effective Malory's *Arthur* sounds when told aloud as a story
has recently been illustrated on an audio CD using medieval pronunciation,
included with Karen Cherewatuk and Joyce Coleman (eds), 'Reading Malory
Aloud', *Arthuriana* 13. 4, Winter 2003. See also Joyce Coleman, *Public Reading
and the Reading Public in Late Medieval England and France* (CUP, 1996).
Malory can also be heard in abridged passages using Pollard's version, either
read by Philip Madoc (Naxos Audiobooks) or Derek Jacobi (High Bridge
Audiobooks).

C. S. Lewis, 'The English Prose *Morte*', in Bennett, 1963, 7–28.

PAGE 35 Stevenson's bold declaration: 'Essay on Charles of Orleans' (Cornhill
magazine, 1881), quoted Hicks, 1928, 90.

Remarkably scholarly: John Bale, *Index Britanniae Scriptorum*, ed. R. L. Poole
and M. Bateson (Brewer, Woodbridge, 1990).

Its marginalia: P. J. C. Field, 'Malory's Own Marginalia', in *Medium Aevum* LXX, 2,
226–39; Helen Cooper, 'Opening up the Malory Manuscript', Wheeler, 2000.

PAGE 36 'Roasted': *Works*, vol. 1, 269.

'And to tell the joys': Malory, IX.17.

'It is nearly always true': Letter to Ero and Chase, Rome, 26 April 1957, in John
Steinbeck, *The Acts of King Arthur and his Noble Knights*, ed. Chase Horton
(Heinemann, London, 1976), 304.

PAGE 37 Malory's hero: C. S. Lewis also prefers Malory's Lancelot to Chretien's
(Lewis, 1963); P. E. Tucker's essay 'Chivalry in the Morte' in Bennett, 1963, has
special emphasis on Lancelot.

The name 'Malory': P. H. Reaney, *The Origins of English Surnames* (Routledge,
London, 1967), ch. 13, sec 3.

CHAPTER 1

PAGE 39 'And as fast': Malory, IX.1

Turn of the fourteenth century: There is no record of Malory's birth year; all we
know is that he died in March 1471. For the purposes of this re-creation of his
christening, I am going to assume that it was in 1399, because he would need
to have been at least fourteen to be, as I believe he was, the Thomas Malory

who went to France with the Earl of Warwick in 1414. But it could have been a few years earlier. It is possible that his parents had not yet inherited Newbold Revel when he was christened, and that the ceremony took place at Swinford or Winwick, other Malory manors. But they were living at Newbold Revel by 1406, when an enfeoffment records John as 'of Newbold' (*A Descriptive Calendar of Ancient Deeds*, 6 vols, London, 1890–1915, iii, 262). Moreover, childbirth was often superintended by senior female members of a family, and Dame Philippa could have been staying in her parents-in-laws' house for her accouchement. I must apologise for illustrating so early that there are many surmises in this story, but could not resist picturing the christening in a church which has a bell that predated Thomas. It is the oldest in the present frame of eight, and weighs a little under 13 cwt (*St Edith's Church, Monks Kirby*, 1977). The church was originally dedicated to the Virgin Mary, and became a place of pilgrimage after the Black Death of 1359. It was renamed St Edith's after the Priory was suppressed (private communication, Dr Benjamin Thompson, Somerville College).

Soon would be: Richard II was certainly dead by February 1400, of, it was said, starvation and petty torture.

Fourth largest: Coventry vied with Norwich for size: the only larger cities were London, easily the largest of all with *c.* 40,000, then York *c.* 15,000, Bristol *c.* 13,000, and Norwich and Coventry *c.* 8000.

PAGE 40 'Green mantle': John Speed, of Warwickshire, *Counties of Britain, A Tudor Atlas* (Thames and Hudson, New York, 1989).

'Sadly lax': The many legal disputes and complaints against Coombe, a Cistercian abbey, are listed in Robin Moore, *History of Coombe Abbey* (Jones-Sands, Coventry, 1983); it too was under the patronage of the Mowbray dukes of Norfolk.

Much-reduced: Monks Kirby Priory was one of the alien priories suppressed by Richard II, and its estates were made over to the new Carthusian monastery which was founded on the Isle of Axholme, Lincolnshire, by Thomas Mowbray, Duke of Norfolk, close to their seat at Epworth, Lincolnshire. Consent to the transfer was dated 1396, but Henry IV reversed the decision in 1399. The suppression was delayed until Henry V's need for cash for his French wars in 1414.

Moated manor house: Excavation would be required to confirm this, but the house's low-lying position, in a natural bowl that had once been a marsh, makes it very likely. Even in the mid fifteenth century, Newbold Revel was still sometimes called Fenny Newbold.

Well-liked: Field, 1993, 46–7 for the few minor disputes. On his visit to Newbold Revel in 1637 the antiquarian and historian Sir William Dugdale saw the deeds and court rolls of the manor and discovered that the manors of Easenhall and Stretton-under-Fosse had originally been part of it (William Dugdale, *History and Antiquities of Warwickshire*, 2 vols (London, 1656), 80–3); Sister M. Stanislaus, *Newbold Revel, A Warwickshire Manor*, St Paul's College of

Education (Rugby, 1976); Philip Styles, 'Sir Simon Clarke', *Birmingham Archaeological Transactions* XLVI (1945–46).

'Grimly throes': Malory, VIII. 1. Main sources for details of christenings and infants' upbringing: Edith Rickert, *Chaucer's World* (CUP, 1948); Nicholas Orme, *Medieval Childhood* (Yale UP, 2001).

'Nourished him with her own pap': Malory, I.3.

PAGE 41 Suckle her own babies: Illustrated in Barbara Hanawalt's *Growing Up in Medieval London* (OUP, 1993), 57: 'As she him took all in her lap. / He took that maiden by the pap. / And took thereof a right good nap [grip]. / And sucked his fill of that licour.' For historic virtues of breast-feeding and also medieval child-rearing, see Christina Hardyment, *Perfect Parents* (OUP, 1993).

'Gentlemen that bear olde arms': Malory uses this expression when praising Tristram's contribution to the lore of hunting: 'Wherefore, as meseemeth, all gentlemen that bear old arms ought of right to honour Sir Tristram for the goodly terms that gentlemen have and use, and shall to the day of doom, that thereby in a manner all men of worship may dissever a gentleman from a yeoman, and from a yeoman a villain. For he that gentle is will draw him until gentle tatches, and to follow the customs of noble gentlemen' (Malory VIII.3). He will no doubt have regarded himself as 'of gentle strain of father's side and mother's side' (Malory, II.1).

Variants on the distinctly Norse name: S. V. Mallory-Smith, *History of the Mallory Family* (Phillimore, Chichester, 1985), 14; Field, 1993, 38.

PAGE 42 This Anschetil: Four-fifths of the four hundred known medieval Malorys can be shown to have descended from this first Anschetil or his immediate ancestor (Field, 1993, 37).

Red, forked-tail lion: Coat of arms: Mallory-Smith, 1985, 126. Branches of the family who remained in France appear in *Grand Armorial de France*, ed. R. de Warren (1947). Stephen Friar, *Heraldry* (Grange, 1997), 195.

Owned by Lord Byron: George Farnham, *Leicestershire Medieval Village Notes* (Leicester, 1919–33), 6 vols, I, 147.

Fairly distant cousin: They were descended from brothers who flourished in the mid-thirteenth century. The fullest pedigrees of the Malory family are given in Mallory-Smith, 1985.

PAGE 44 Feoffee of Tachbrook Mallory: Mallory-Smith 1985, 21.

'Armiger literatus': K. B. McFarlane, *The Nobility of Later Medieval England* (Clarendon Press, Oxford, 1973), 237. He stresses that Zouche was describing an abnormal degree of accomplishment, including a knowledge of Latin, not just literacy.

Royal favourite: Sir Henry Green was the Green of 'Bushy, Bagot and Green', the notorious trio of Richard II's councillors pilloried in Shakespeare's *Richard II*.

Eight branches: Details, necessarily tentative because of the incompleteness of the records, of the several contemporary branches of the family can be found in Mallory-Smith, 1985 (passim, and qualified in later corrigenda sent in personal correspondence) and in Field, 1993, Appendix I.

Part of the neighbouring manor of Swinford: The Malorys were co-tenants at first with the Revels, the Vincents and the Swinfords themselves (Field, 1993, 187; J. G. Nichols, *History and Antiquities of Leicestershire*, 4 vols, (1795–1811; repr. Wakefield, 1971), 362–8; Arthur Mee, 'Swinford', in *King's England: Leicestershire and Rutland* (Hodder & Stoughton, London, 1967)).

PAGE 45 Eminent judge: Though in Scottish eyes notorious for trying William Wallace for treason, and personally supervising his torture (as shown in the film *Braveheart*).

Coat of arms: Erdeswick's Roll for 1295, Mallory-Smith, 1975, 41. In early heraldry, the *lions passant* of both the Malory and the royal arms were called leopards (Friar, *Heraldry*, 1997, 195).

Hugh Revel: Cecil Humphery-Smith, *Hugh Revel* (Phillimore, Chichester, 1994).

When Sir Stephen married Margaret Revel: Signalled by his father Sir Simon's grant to him and Margaret of the manor of Draughton's sale (Mallory-Smith, 1985, 117). Paylington/Pailton came to the Malorys with Newbold Revel. A John de Charnells owned part of a knight's fee there in 1297 (P. R. D. Escheat 25.E.I.n.51). This would be the same family as the Charnells whose widow, Margaret, married a Thomas Malory (whom I will later suggest was our hero's uncle) in 1407.

Sir John Malory: Details from Field, 1993, Appendix I; Mallory-Smith, 1985, and Stanislaus, 1976.

Born soon after 1332: If Sir Simon's grant of Draughton to Sir Stephen and his wife in 1332 signalled their marriage, Sir John must have been born after 1332 to be legitimate (cf Field, 1993, 42, 'about 1325').

Adopted a variant of the Revel arms: Nichols' *Leicestershire*, IV, 368, records John Malory of Winwick as Lord of Stormsworth, and his arms as *or three lions passant gardant*. The original Revel arms had a gold rather than ermine ground. Coats of arms were real property that could be inherited with lands.

PAGE 46 Sir Peter Malory: Field, 1993, 192–3.

Important man in local affairs: Field, 1993, 42. He was on a commission of array to recruit soldiers in 1386 and on a commission to inquire into the lands of Monks Kirby in 1389–90.

'Lord of Newbold Revel': Actually 'dominus de Fenny Newbold' (Field, 1993, 43). For John Malory's life, see Field, 1993, 43–53; *The Commons*, III, 673–4.

Cadency marks: Illustrated Dugdale, *Warwickshire*, 1019, these show crescent (second son), bird (fourth son) and ring (fifth son).

Coleshill: The Malory connections with Coleshill are obscure, but Sir Robert Malory's first Hospitaller estates were at Temple Balshall. Balshall, Bramcote and Chilverscoton were all within ten miles of Coleshill, an important market town. Its manor was held by the Mountforts, whose lives, as we will see, are intricately intertwined with those of the Malorys. The windows may well have been in memory of a respected joint ancestor or in celebration of a connection by marriage. William Mountfort rebuilt the church early in the fifteenth century (*The Commons*, III, 797–9).

His brother Robert: We know that the Hospitaller Robert Malory was a scion of Newbold Revel because he used the Malory Revel arms in his preceptory at Balshall and in Rhodes (see ch. 9). He must have born in 1375 at the very latest. You had to be twenty-one to join the Order, and to have spent at least five years in Rhodes before qualifying to hold Knights Hospitaller estates in England; we know that Robert Malory held the same seniority as Robert Pargenham who cannot have been younger than twenty-six and may well have been much older when he was granted a commandery in 1402 (Greg O'Malley, private communication). Field, who wants to make John rather younger than I do, speculates that John, Robert and Simon were sons rather than brothers of Nicholas. This requires an unconvincing degree of invisibility for Nicholas as an adult and ignores the fact that Robert has to be at least twenty-one by 1397 – in fact, Hospitallers were usually in their thirties or older before they got English estates.

Simon Malory: John Malory and his brother Simon sued the parson of Withybrook (which borders on Newbold Revel) for debt in August 1411 (Field, 1993, 45, citing *CCR* [*1409–13*], 236). Simon married a widow, who was the daughter and heiress of Margaret Sutton (PROC1/6/110, 'Simon Malorie, of co. Warwick, and Margaret his wife, late the wife of Edmond Dalby v. Hugh Dalby, William Peyto, Geoffrey Aldesley, and William Derset, esqrs.: Lands [unspecified] covenanted to be settled on said Margaret, daughter of Margaret Sutton'). Further details, Field, 1993, 78.

PAGE 47 Thomas Malory: This is a convenient point at which to give all the evidence for my speculative 'Uncle Thomas'. He acquired connections early with his Castle Bytham cousin, Sir Anketil Malory, as there is a record of Thomas Malory of Catthorpe being acquitted of stealing something worth £20 from the Prior of Lenton (which is five miles north of Castle Bytham) in 1391; the Prior was said to be 'in mercy for a false claim'. Field, 1993, 58 says it is the Lenton in Notts, but Farnham does not specify which Lenton it is. When Sir Anketil died in 1391, Uncle Thomas could have become a retainer, later the squire, of Anketil's eleven-year-old son. He too was called Thomas Malory, but can be easily distinguished as he was knighted shortly before our hero, little Thomas of Newbold Revel, was born. He is listed as a knight fighting in Scotland with his stepsister's husband Lord Grey of Codnor in 1400 and 1401. With him is another Thomas Malory, who I surmise was 'Uncle Thomas'. It is also likely to have been 'Uncle Thomas' who was commissioned by Robert Braybrooke, Bishop of London, and Sir Gerald Braybrooke to give possession (seizin) of property in Shackerstone, Leicestershire to a purchaser in 1403/4. Braybrooke was a cousin of Newbold Revel's overlord, Thomas Holland, Earl of Kent (Field, 1993, p. 58; K. B. McFarlane, *Lancastrian Kings and Lollard Knights* (OUP, 1972), p. 217; *The Commons*, II, pp. 343–50). He may have still possessed Catthorpe, an extensive manor with 300 acres which was held of the King for fealty and a pair of gloves yearly (Farnham, *Village Notes*, VI, 283). In 1407 it was probably this Thomas Malory who married Margaret, the daughter of Sir Thomas Grendon, a Staffordshire neighbour of Philippa Malory's family, the Chetwynds, and the widow of William Charnells, a family which had long-standing connections with Catthorpe (Farnham, passim). The manor of Bramcote, in north Warwickshire, was settled on the couple, perhaps by Lord Grey of Codnor, who seems to have continued to retain 'Uncle Thomas' (see ch. 6 below). But it is also possible that the Malorys themselves had an interest in it as, in 1411, Thomas Malory and Margaret Charnells are described as 'deforciants' in a plea mounted by Robert Malory, Sir William Bulcote and John Malory (Dugdale, *Warwickshire*, 1122; Carpenter, 1983, 299, n.62; Shakespeare Birthplace Trust, DR37 Box 36, 1409, Fin.lev 8 HIV [1407], Fin. lev oct Mich 13 HIV [1411]). Such suits were often fictitious – collusive actions which were intended to establish title to somewhat unofficial sales or gift settlements.

An image of John Malory: Dugdale, *Warwickshire*, 1105.

In about 1396: Chetwynd ownership of the manor of Grendon and the advowson (the right to nominate the Rector) to its church was only legally confirmed in 1393, after protracted wrangling. The images on the windows must date from soon after 1392, when the Grendons acquired a licence to hold divine service in the chapel in Grendon Manor because the church was being rebuilt. Sir William died in February 1395, and his eldest son Roger in 1397.

The windows showing two Chetwynd sons at a time when the third son John was only about six are likely to have been installed between their deaths. Dugdale also provides drawings of Philippa's widowed mother Alice, Lady Chetwynd, and two rectors of Grendon whose kneeling figures appeared in the small windows on each side of the chancel (choir); below them a ribbon of text asks for prayers for their souls. The fact that one of the rectors died in 1407 has led Field to conclude that the windows must all date from between 1407 and 1412, when Alice died. However, the style in which the priests are drawn is altogether more fluid and expressive than the statically posed figures of the family, and it is quite possible that they were commissioned a decade or more after the windows in the rest of the church. Details from H. E. Chetwynd-Stapleton, *The Chetwynds of Ingestre* (London, 1892), and G. Wrottesley (ed.), 'The Chetwynd Cartulary', *William Salt Archaeological Society Transactions*, old series 12 (1891). The date of the windows is important. Field, deeply affected by William Matthews' scorn at the idea of a seventy-year-old writing the *Morte Darthur*, posits that John was only just of age in 1406, and dates the Grendon window at about 1410. This enables him to suggest *c.* 1415 as Malory's likely birth date. But there are too many references to Thomas Malorys in the 1410s and 1420s for this to be convincing.

The maker of the window at Grendon: William Matthews sees these images differently. He claims that Philippa Malory is 'depicted as a heavy-set, blunt-featured woman' and John as 'an old man of rustic cast, with short beard, hair draped over the forehead, and deep-set eyes'. He also distorts John Malory's distinguished public record as MP, JP and sheriff as the 'unspectacular economic advance' of a 'solid citizen' (Matthews, 1966).

Richard: he was born in 1381 and inherited after his brother Roger died in 1397. As he was only sixteen, he became a ward of the King, who sold the wardship and guardianship of the family's main estates of Ingestre to Richard Scrope, Bishop of Coventry and Lichfield, despite the protests of Lady Alice that these estates were enfeoffed to her use for life. Richard died in 1418. Richard's son by Thomasina (who later became 'fatua et idiota') was the Sir Philip Chetwynd who is associated with Sir Thomas Malory in 1439.

PAGE 49 Feoffee: Enfeoffment to use was a popular way of avoiding feudal obligations. Traditionally, one's lord could charge an entry fee (relief) whenever an heir succeeded, and could take lands back into his own hands temporarily during the minority of an heir or heiress (wardship); he also had a say in the marriage of such a ward. But if the tenant had granted (enfeoffed) his lands to the 'use' of a group of feoffees, they became the owners of the lands in common law. The enfeoffment usually included their undertaking to devote the profits to the use of the grantor, his wife and his heirs, who generally continued to live on the estates. No rights to reliefs or wardship could now arise, because when the owner died, the estate remained the legal property of the trustees and lands. The system also protected the estates of those attainted for treason. The case of Alice Chetwynd shows that kings and powerful magnates sometimes rode roughshod over enfeoffments to use, but, as we shall see, Sir Thomas Malory successfully employed it to protect his estates from confiscation.

About six of the gentry families: among them the Mountforts, the Peytos, the Ardernes and the Lucys (Field, 1993, 49; M. C. Carpenter, *Locality and Polity: a Study of Warwickshire Landed Society 1401–1499* (CUP, 1992), ch. 3, passim).

'Livery of robes': Clothes, especially if trimmed with fur, were valued items, and the 'livery of robes' consisted of two complete outfits a year, often with chains or badges decorated with the lord's insignia. Regimental uniforms are a hangover from this tradition. It also endures in top families: Arthur Inch, a retired butler, showed me a fine collection of buttons, one from each of the very aristocratic families he had worked for as footman and butler, and all sporting coats of arms.

PAGE 50 Cousin of Richard II: In 1360, Edward the Black Prince (the oldest son of Edward III) had married Joan, the younger daughter of Edmund of Woodstock (youngest son of Edward I), and widow of Thomas Holland, Earl of Kent. The Black Prince died just before Edward III did, so his son Richard II came to the throne aged only ten. In 1399 Thomas Holland, Earl of Kent, was thus Joan's grandson and Richard II's cousin (Michael Hicks, *Who's Who in Late Medieval England 1272–1485*, Shepheard-Walwyn, London, 1991).

One [tax assessment] made in 1436: PRO E179/192/59.

PAGE 51 The Christian name of the most important godsib: Some 86 per cent had the same Christian name as the godparent; the custom could lead to children with identical names (Orme, 2001, 37).
A safer choice: Both could have been his godfathers: Richard Beauchamp's godfathers were Richard II and Archbishop Richard Scrope.
And when the child is born: Malory, I. 4

PAGE 53 Miraculous oil: J. H. Ramsay, *Lancaster and York 1399–1485*, 1 (Clarendon Press, Oxford, 1892), 4–5; T. A. Sandquist and M. R. Powicke (eds), 'The holy oil of Thomas of Canterbury', in *Essays in Medieval History presented to Berthe Wilkinson* (Toronto, 1969).
Twelfth Night celebrations: Ramsay, 1892, 1, 20.

PAGE 54 Imprisoned in the Tower: A John Malory is recorded as being taken to the Tower 'and kept in custody until further notice' on 12 February 1400 (CCR 1 HIV Pt 1, 43); it is only surmise that he was John Malory of Newbold Revel, but the idea is endorsed in *The Commons*, III, 673–4. After Thomas Holland's execution, the earldom of Kent passed to his sixteen-year-old brother, Edmund, whose wife was Lucia Visconti of Milan. He remained in Henry IV's custody. By 1408 he had died without having children. His title and estates, including Newbold Revel, were inherited by five co-heirs. Newbold Revel fell to his sister Joan, who in 1400 was the wife of the Duke of York (d. 1407) but had by 1408 married Hugh Willoughby of Eresby and Middleton, Warwickshire. In 1409 she married Henry Scrope of Masham, who was executed in 1415 for conspiring against Henry V (G. E. Cockayne, *Complete Peerage of England, Scotland, Ireland and the United Kingdom*, 13 vols (new edn 1910–59), 1910–40). Joan continued to hold Newbold Revel until her death in 1434 (Field, 1993, Appendix III).
Document at Ruthin: PRO E326/10765.
Released from the Tower: There is no record of the date of John Malory's release, and it is of course possible that he remained incarcerated until next heard of in 1406. But it is unlikely. Henry IV was in a conciliatory mood at this time.

PAGE 55 Sir Giles Malory: Giles sat in the Beauchamp interest as MP for Northamptonshire in 1385, 1388 (Feb.), 1393 and 1394. He was recorded as Warwick's household steward in 1497. He had to sue for pardon after the fall of Thomas Beauchamp, but evidently regained Richard II's confidence. In 1498 a loan to Giles of £24 from the royal favourite Sir Henry Green, husband of his cousin Sir Anketil Malory's daughter, is an example of the links between different branches of the family. He sat for Northamptonshire again in 1401 and 1402, no doubt with the approval of the new Earl of Warwick, Thomas's son Sir Richard Beauchamp. Giles died in 1403 (*The Commons*, III, 671).
13th Earl: to avoid confusion between the two very different Earls of Warwick with whom this story is concerned, Sir Richard Beauchamp the 13th Earl

(b. 1382, d. 1439), famous as the 'Father of Courtesy', and his son-in-law Sir Richard Neville (b. 1428, d. 1471), who was the 16th Earl, and has been aptly nicknamed 'Warwick the Kingmaker', I have generally called the first 'Beauchamp' and the second 'Warwick'.

PAGE 56 'muster rolls': PRO E101/42/40; PRO E101/42/38; Field, 1993, 57. 'Hare-brained Hotspur': *Henry IV Part 1*.

PAGE 57 His banner: pictured in Beauchamp Pageant Cotton MSS Julius E4. 202.
'Well-proportioned': Holinshed's *Chronicle* (1577; repr. Johnson et al., London, 1808), III, 58.

PAGE 58 'Sanctuary . . . at Monks Kirby': J. H. Wylie, *The History of England under Henry IV*, 4 vols (CUP, 1884–98), II.
Stayed loyal: Cynics will point out that Beauchamp was well-rewarded: Henry IV granted him the confiscated Mowbray lordship of Gower, the title of which the Beauchamps had lost to the Mowbrays in 1396.

CHAPTER 2
PAGE 59 Small children: *Medieval Lore from Bartholomeus Anglicus*, ed. Robert Steele (King's Classics, London, 1893), cited as *Bartholomeus*. The English Franciscan Bartholomew wrote his encyclopaedia *De Proprietatis Rebus (Concerning the Properties of Things) c.* 1250; after it was translated into English by John Trevisa in 1397 it became hugely popular.
Four of the . . . battles: Blore Heath, Northampton, Edgecote, Bosworth.
A rider in a hurry: According to Norbert Ohler, *The Medieval Traveller* (Boydell, Woodbridge, 1989), fourteenth-century papal messengers covered sixty miles in twenty-four hours; that was as nothing to the 190 miles covered by fourteenth-century Indian relay runners described by Ibn Battuta or the 235 miles run by the Mongolian relay messengers witnessed by Marco Polo. In *The Pastons and Their England* (CUP, 1968), H. Bennett estimates thirty-five miles a day as a comfortable pace. See also Ann Hyland, *The Horse in the Middle Ages* (Sutton, Stroud, 1999), ch. 10, 'Travel', passim.

PAGE 60 Now speed you: all quotes in this paragraph from Malory, *Works*, 190–1. This passage is not in the Caxton text.
The mansion that occupies its site: Details and diagram from A. Gomme, *Newbold Revel: An Architectural History* (HM Prison Service, n.d.) and author's visit.

PAGE 61 Hidden house: Plan in Gomme, *Newbold Revel*.

PAGE 62 Dugdale copied: Dugdale, *Warwickshire*, I, 83.

PAGE 63 The nurse is glad: *Bartholomeus*, 44. Crooked limbs were actually caused by a vitamin D deficiency, but it was thought that strapping the baby to a cradle board could correct them. This also allowed the baby to be suspended out of reach of household animals, fire and other domestic hazards.

Most medieval parents: Linda Pollock, *Forgotten Children* (CUP, 1983).

All children be: *Bartholomeus*, 45.

PAGE 64 For all the indulgence: Details from Hardyment, 1993; Nicholas Orme, *From Childhood to Chivalry* (Methuen, London, 1984); Rickert, 1948, 102 (quoting *How the Good Wife Taught Her Daughter, c.* 1475); Hanawalt, 1993, 70–1.

Would be taught: Details from Orme, 2001.

PAGE 65 Regularly read aloud: Coleman, 1996, 221 and passim.

'The lord and knight': Stephen Hawes: 'The Comfort of Lovers', II. 106–7, in *The Minor Poems*, ed. Florence W. Gluck and Alice B. Morgan (EETS 271, London, 1974).

Generally held: There were those who disputed his existence, most notably Ralph Higden, whose *Polychronicum* was brought up to date by William Caxton in 1482 (see also below, ch. 25).

Nine Worthies: quotes from Caxton's preface and Malory; the other eight worthies were Hector, Alexander, Julius Caesar, Joshua, David, Judas Maccabeus, Charlemagne and the crusading hero Godfrey of Boulogne.

Morte Arthure: The title is misleading as, like Malory's *Arthur*, it was written in English. There are many variations of the French spelling of this title, all of which signify different versions of the Arthurian story. None is as comprehensive and readable as Malory's telling.

PAGE 66 Own chaplain: 'One would have difficulty in finding a household document which does not mention at least one resident chaplain and numerous "clerici"' (Kate Mertes, *The English Noble Household 1250–1600* (Blackwell, Oxford, 1988), 142).

Lollards: The name was originally an insult, derived from the Dutch *lollen*, to mumble. The name 'Lollebroeders' was given to an unusually pious and humble semi-monastic order who cared for the poor in Holland *c.* 1300; it continued to be applied to all heretics who argued for church poverty.

Heretical views: John of Gaunt had admired Wycliffe, but broke with him over the question of the reality of the Blood Sacrament of communion. Malory is careful to refer in his 'Tale of the Sangreal' to 'God's body in a cup', whereas the Lollards preferred the idea that his presence was metaphorical rather than real. Malory also liked Latin enough to quote Arthur's epitaph in that language rather than in English. Wycliffe's works were banned in 1382; the first Lollard to be burned as a heretic in England was William Sawtry, in 1401. Accusations of Lollardy were frequently made against Ricardian rebels in the first two decades of the century.

The closest that the devout reader: P. J C. Field, *Romance and Chronicle: A Study of Malory's Prose Style* (Barrie & Jenkins, London, 1971), citing Deanesley,

'Vernacular Literature in the Fourteenth and Fifteenth Centuries', *Modern Language Review*, 1920, 354–5.

Spiritual education: Kate Mertes, 'Household as Religious Community', in *People, Politics and Community in the Later Middle Ages* (Sutton, Gloucester, 1987), 129; John Mirk, quoted in Duffy, 1992, 80.

PAGE 67 Echoes of Love's vivid immediacy: Field, 1971, 20–22, 76–7.

Probably also brothers: If one of Thomas's older brothers had the name, as was likely, John, then it would explain the curiously prolific records of a John Malory, described as 'lord of Winwick' in July 1414, and as 'gentleman' (a more lowly rank) of Newbold Revel in 1415 (Field, 1993, 45, citing BL Add. Ch. 21823, 21820–1). Field attributes all such records to John Malory senior, but once his heir was of age, he could easily have been granted/enfeoffed with a set of estates.

PAGE 68 At four year age: Hardying, *Chronicle* 1–2.

'Ah, fie for shame': Malory X.51.

PAGE 69 Rhymes, riddles, word plays: Orme, 2001, ch. 4, passim.

John Catesby: C. M. Woolgar, *The Great Household in Medieval England* (Yale UP, 1999), 103.

Edmund Stoner: Rickert, 1948, 115–16.

Clement Paston: H. S. Bennett, 1968, 1.

Corpus Christi mystery plays: Paul Murray Kendall, *The Yorkist Age: Daily Life in the Wars of the Roses* (Allen & Unwin, London, 1967), 66.

PAGE 70 Racecourse: spectators at tournaments laid bets and studied form just as racegoers do today. Many former tournament grounds are now racecourses.

Loathly Damsel: R. S. Loomis, 'Edward I, Arthurian Enthusiast', *Speculum* 28, 123.

'Not the best in the kingdom'; Froissart, quoted K. Davies, *The First Queen Elizabeth* (Lovat Dickson), 1937.

Practice at the archery butts: Jim Bradbury, *The English Archer* (Boydell, Woodbridge, 1985). The chronicler William of Newburgh wrote that Richard I (the Lionheart) licensed tournaments again in England. He limited them to five grounds, four in the south (Stanford, near Folkestone in Kent, Salisbury, Brackley and Warwick, all in places controlled by nobles loyal to him), and only one north of the Trent, ten miles south of Doncaster between Blythe and Tickhill. The King's writs were hard to enforce in places far removed from London.

PAGE 71 His ancestors: Mallory-Smith, 1985, passim.

In 1306 was a Thomas Malorie: D. J. D. Boulton, *The Knights of the Crown*, Boydell, Woodbridge, 1987, 109–110.

Dunstable tournament: 'Roll of the Arms of the Knights at the Tournament at Dunstable', in 7 Edward III, *Collectanea Topographica & Genealogical* V, Society of Antiquaries, London, 1838, 389. There are two possible, if misspelt, Malorys. The roll also includes members of almost every armigerous family associated with Malory in the fifteenth century: e.g. Greys, Beauchamps, Staffords, Zouches, Astleys, Westons, Blounts, Fauconberg, Wake, ap Griffith, Neville.

Tourneying fraternity: CPR (1343–45), 196, 379. See also Juliet Vale, *Edward III and Chivalry: Chivalric Society and its Context 1270–1350* (Boydell, Woodbridge, 1982).

PAGE 72 'Of the same manner': Hugh E. L. Collins, *The Order of the Garter 1348–1461: Chivalry and Politics in Late Medieval England* (OUP, New York, 2000), 10, citing Jean Froissart, *Chronicles of England, France and Spain*, ed. K. de Lettenhove, 25 vols, 1867–77, IV, 203–6. Froissart was resident in England from 1361 to 1366. Other details from A. Murimuth, *Continuatio Chronicarum*, ed. E. M. Thompson, 1889. Edward may well have had word of the Duke of Normandy's intention of creating a new military order, the Order of the Star. The Earl of Derby and the Earl of Salisbury, who returned in the autumn of 1343 from fighting for King Alfonso XI of Castile, might have brought word of Alfonso's foundation of the Order of the Band of Castile. But those events were more likely to have been parallels than inspirations. It was far from a new idea to associate the flower of British chivalry with King Arthur. Edward I had also done so.

Whitsun-week: Malory always makes much of Arthur's Whitsuntide/Pentecostal feasts.

It has been deduced: By H. M.. Colvin (gen. ed.), *The History of the King's Works*, 4: *1485–1660* (HMSO, London, 1982).

PAGE 73 'About the hour of prime': Holinshed, *Chronicle*.

CHAPTER 3

PAGE 74 The child will not labour: Malory, III.3.

Sir John Fortescue: *De Laudibus*, quoted Michael J. Bennett, 'Education and Advancement', in *Fifteenth-Century Attitudes*, ed. Rosemary Horrox (CUP, 1994), 92–3.

'Sumptuous household': As medieval noblemen went, Beauchamp was fabulously wealthy. A recent article in the *Sunday Times* rated him as eighth in a list of the two hundred richest people in history. Besides being an able soldier, he was a keen jouster (Brindley, 2001, 7). He was also the designated champion of Henry IV's queen, Joanna of Brittany. He stayed friendly with the dowager Queen Joanna all his life – even after she was accused of witchcraft by her stepson Henry V and disgraced.

Beauchamp accounts: Alexandra Sinclair, 'The Beauchamp Earls of Warwick in the Later Middle Ages', London, PhD thesis, 1987.

No names survive: Evidence of the names and numbers of members of Beauchamp's household and retinue is 'extremely rare'; ibid., 249.

PAGE 75 William Mountfort: The Chetwynd pedigree says one of Philippa's sisters married 'a Mountfort' (Chetwynd-Stapleton, 1892, 85) and the diagonally striped red-and-gold shield of the Mountforts was among those on the windows of Grendon Church (Dugdale, *Warwickshire*, 1106). It would make sense of later associations between Malory and William Mountfort if it was William whom she married, dying before he married Margaret Pecche, the earliest wife in his pedigree, who had herself died by 1417. The form of the Mountfort arms at Grendon was that used by one of William's sons. William, who was born *c.* 1380, married his last wife, Joan Alderwich, in 1421 (*The Commons*, III, 797–9). If his eldest son Baldwin was the son of his Chetwynd wife it would make him Malory's first cousin, and explain later associations between Malory, the Mountforts and the Duke of Buckingham.

'Henchmen': Sinclair, 1987, 267.

Reconnaissance: Brindley, 2001, 38.

'Could be palm leaves': The seal is attached to PRO WARD/2/1/3/2; its three additional emblems are a distinct change from his earlier seals (BL Add. Charters 28647 and 21832).

PAGE 76 Thought to date: Although Brindley's *Richard Beauchamp* (2001) suggests the *Pageant* was made earlier, when Beauchamp's memorial chapel was completed *c.* 1475, the portrayal of armour and dress is seen as more typical of the early 1480s by Anne Sutton (private communication, 2004). Alexandra Sinclair, 2003, believes that it was commissioned by Anne Beauchamp, Countess of Warwick, for her grandson, Edward, who was Prince of Wales after the accession of his father Richard III to the throne in 1483, as the last two pages of genealogies include a depiction of Richard as king and an unfinished image of Edward as Prince of Wales. Edward died in 1484.

Palomides: Malory, X.47, XII passim.

PAGE 77 Edward Hall: *Chronicle*, ed. H. Ellis (London, 1809), cited as *Hall's Chronicle*. The description of Prince Hal 'casting iron bars and heavy stones' is interestingly echoed in Malory's description of Sir Gareth 'where there were any masteries done, thereat would he be, and there might none cast bar nor stone to him by two yards' (Malory, VII.2). Such feats of strength still feature in the Scottish Highland Games, e.g. tossing cabers and hurling stones.

Kenilworth: J. H. Wylie and W. T. Waugh, *The Reign of Henry V* (3 vols, CUP, 1914–29), I (cited as Wylie, 1914), I, 315.

PAGE 78 Pleasantmaris: Ibid., III, 270.

Elizabeth: It seems likely that Beauchamp's trusted secretary John Shirley, a noted translator and bibliophile, came to Beauchamp's household with Elizabeth, perhaps as her tutor (Connolly, 1998).

Thomas, Lord Berkeley: He was the patron of the learned cleric John Trevisa and owned translations of Chaucer.

Round Table legends: I. Goldrick, 'The Literary Manuscripts and Literary Patronage of the Beauchamp and Neville Families in the Late Middle Ages *c.* 1390–1500', PhD thesis, Newcastle Polytechnic, 1985

His father had dealings: PRO E326/10765.

Castle Bytham: Henry IV spent some of his childhood here, after the death of his mother, as his aunt was one of the daughters of Lady Alice Malory (by her first marriage). In the early part of the century it was a busy and prosperous estate, conveniently close to the main road from London to the north, and made great profits from its arable lands and its carp-rearing ponds, rated by archaeologists as the sixth most extensive system in the country. It still has a well-preserved chain of fishponds and other pools which were in use at least as early as 1316, when the Great Fishpond and 'fissepolliows, erlesheng and smalwelles' were included in a widow's dower. It remained in the Codnor family, although an unsuccessful claim for both the manor and the castle was made by Sir William Malory of Papworth St Agnes in 1443. It still had 'great walls of buildings' when Leland saw it in 1542, but today there is virtually nothing left of it. But the size of the earthworks on and around its site reveals that it must have been a far grander establishment than Kirkby Malory (Richard Foers, *History of Castle Bytham*, Castle Bytham, 2000, 23). If he had been in service in Castle Bytham as a page, young Thomas Malory could still have enjoyed some foreign travel. In 1413 Henry V sent Codnor to Paris as head of an embassy that included 'lords, knights and clergy to the number of 600 horse . . . richly dressed, and adorned with cloth of gold and silk, with chains and collars of gold set with precious stones, so that the company marvelled greatly at the sight of their luxuries'. They stayed in a palatial residence known as the Temple (presumably the former headquarters of the Knights Templar). 'The French king received them very honourably, and sumptuously banqueted them, shewing them goodly jousts and martial pastimes, by the space of three days together', wrote a contemporary chronicler. In a typically impetuous gesture, the notoriously manic Charles VI insisted on fighting in person 'to show his courage and activity to the Englishmen', and 'manfully broke spears and lustily tourneyed' (Hall, *Chronicle*, from Jehan de Waurin, *Receuil de Croniques . . .*) (cited as Waurin).

PAGE 79 Show the scholars: Quotes on manners from the 'Black Book' of the court of Edward IV (*Household Book of Edward IV: the Black Book and Ordinances of 1478*, ed. A. R. Myers, Manchester, 1959; see also *Early English Meals and Manners*, ed. F. J. Furnival, *EETS*, 1894). Although written *c.* 1473, the *Household Book*'s directives were proudly taken from those specified in Edward III's reign. Tradition was valued more than novelty in the Middle Ages.

PAGE 80 'His own harper': John Harper, 'harper of Fenny Newbold', was among the accomplices accused with Malory of ambushing the Duke of Buckingham in 1450 (Hicks, 1928, Appendix).

As a boy, 'Tristram': Malory, VIII.3.

Good raconteurs: See Coleman, 1996, 82, for quote, and passim.

Lalaing: Michael Foss, *Chivalry* (Michael Joseph, London, 1975), 222, 226.

PAGE 81 Children started practising: Peter Alfonsi, *Disciplina Clericalis*, cited in Orme, 2001.

'By my head': Tale of Cote Male Taille, Malory, IX.4.

Relations between rider and horse: Quoted Peter Earle, *Henry V* (Weidenfeld, London, 1972), 27.

'Horses weep': *Bartholomeus*, 151.

'What is a knight': Malory, X.48.

PAGE 82 Small bows: Orme, 2001, 183.

Long poem: Listed as *Tristram*, no. 4064 in Carlton Brown and R. H. Robbins, *The Index of Middle English Verse*, New York, 1943. Most details of hunting techniques below are from Nicholas Orme, 'Medieval Hunting: Fact and Fancy', in Barbara Hanawalt (ed.), *Chaucer's England: Literature in a Historical Context* (University of Minnesota Press, Minneapolis, 1992), 133–53.

'Glatisant': from glatir, Old French, to howl.

'Wherefore, as me seemeth . . .': *Works*, 375.

The Master of Game, ed. W. A. and F. Baillie-Grohman (London, 1904, 1909).

PAGE 83 Swimming could also be important: 'New chosen knights in summer season shall be taught and used to swim, for they shall not find always ready bridges over rivers and floods': 1408 translation of Vegetius, quoted Nicholas Orme, *Early British Swimming 55 BC–AD 1719* (University of Exeter, 1983); William Horman, *Vulgaria*, 1519, quoted in Orme, 2001, 180. The first English treatise on swimming, *De Arte Natandi*, was written by Sir Everard Digby in the late sixteenth century. William Fitzstephen mentions water-tilting on the Thames in London in the twelfth century (Orme, 2001).

PAGE 84 *Le Petit Jehan de Saintré*: Quoted Foss, 1975, 222.

Ramon Lull: *Book of Knighthood and Chivalry*, translated by William Caxton, rendered into modern English by Brian R. Price (The Chivalry Bookshelf, 2001).

PAGE 85 'Most pleasant jumble': F. J. Furnival, quoted in Parins, 1988, 165.

CHAPTER 4

PAGE 86 'My lord, Sir Lancelot': Malory, XII.9.

Coronation ceremonies: Details Wylie, 1914, I, ch. 1, passim; C. L. Kingsford, *English Historical Literature in the Fifteenth Century* (OUP, 1913), Appendix; *Hall's Chronicle*; Waurin.

PAGE 87 General pardon: Pardons, not just for a particular crime, but for all past crimes known and unknown, were a much-used legal device, essential in a violent age with very little in the way of prison accommodation. They only applied to crimes committed against the King. A general pardon, which anyone in the country, except those specifically excepted by name, also cancelled out any debts to the King, and was hugely popular in an age when

sheriffs and other royal administrators were held personally responsible for any Crown dues
they had failed to collect. Offering a general pardon was not quite such an altruistic act as it appeared. It had to be paid for, and the cost varied according to who was taking it up. But hundreds of people signed up for them when they were issued – usually at the start of a reign, to celebrate a royal marriage, or just before or just after a war or rebellion.

'Gold, scarlet': Wylie, op. cit.

Young Sir William Malory: After young Sir Thomas Malory died (*c.* 1408–12) his daughter Elizabeth inherited most of the family estates. However, his brother William inherited at Sudborough because an entail was made in his favour by his father, who died in 1391. William also inherited estates in Cambridgeshire from the childless Sir William Papworth of Papworth St Agnes and his wife in 1416; the nature of his connection to the Papworths is not known (Sir William Malory, HPT draft biography, L. S. Clark, 2004).

PAGE 88 'Like an angel': This and all subsequent details quoted in Wylie, 1914, I, ch. 1.

Beauchamp's service a year later: see below, Beauchamp retinue roll.

PAGE 89 Spiritual peers: Two archbishops, nineteen bishops and about twenty-four abbots and priors (L. S. Clark, private communication).

Inherited . . . from his mother: In an ingenious but dubious piece of antiquarian research, the French promptly resurrected the ancient 'Salic Law' to exclude women, and therefore Edward III, from succeeding to the throne.

PAGE 90 *Chevauchée*: A looting, pillaging, destructive raiding style of warfare designed to demonstrate that the French King could not protect his subjects. It was risky, but could be hugely profitable.

PAGE 91 'Tranquillity of kingdoms': *Foedera*, IV.ii.107, cited Jacob, 1961, 123.

'Important market': Brabant, unlike Flanders, did not ban the import of English cloth, which entered many European markets via Antwerp. See J. H. A. Munro, *Wool, Cloth and Gold* (Toronto, 1973).

He witnessed a document: John Malory's connection with Grey of Ruthin may have been merely a business one – Ruthin had married Joan Astley, heiress to her family's Warwickshire estates, and John Malory witnessed two earlier documents dealing with the same lands at Bedworth, close to Astley Castle, on 12 and 22 August 1413. He may have been involved in administering the *coup de grâce* against the Welsh rebels if Thomas Burneby, who was made Chamberlain of North Wales in September 1413, was connected to his Northamptonshire neighbours, the Burnebys of Watford. For Thomas Burneby (also spelt Barneby) see Wylie, 1914, I, 108. This man was Treasurer of Harfleur in 1415 (G. L. Harriss, *Cardinal Beaufort: A Study in Lancastrian Ascendancy and Decline*, Clarendon Press, Oxford, 1988, 82).

PAGE 92 If you get Scotland: *Hall's Chronicle*.

PAGE 93 Thirteen-year-old son of Sir John Cornwall: Desmond Seward, *Henry V* (Sidgwick & Jackson, London, 1987), 112. Another example was Sir William Hoo, who was only ten or eleven when he accompanied the Black Prince's expedition to Picardy in 1346/7 (M. Keen, *Nobles, Knights and Men-at-Arms in the Middle Ages* Hambledon, London, 1996), 18.

The *Morte* itself: Malory, *Works*, 233.11, 234.13.

On 3 February 1414: Dugdale, *Warwickshire*, I, 45.

Thomas himself: Bodl. Library MS; Dugdale, *Warwickshire*, 2, 279; Beauchamp Retinue Roll, 1414 BL Harl. 782 f.53, Cotton Roll, xii.7. A crew (French *creu*) was the term used for the most mobile part of a garrison, which was always ready to make a sortie (Anne Curry, 'Isolated or Integrated? The English Soldier in Lancastrian Normandy', ed. Sarah Rees Jones et al., *Courts and Regions in Medieval Europe* (York UP, 2000).

PAGE 94 John Shirley: Connolly, 1998.

PAGE 95 Beauchamp was formally signed up: F. Roll 1 HV, 10; Wylie, 1914, I, 40.

PAGE 96 Notoriously sleepless: Cust, 1909, 31.

Deeper-draught ships: Ian Friel, *The Good Ship: Ships, Shipbuilding and Technology in England 1200–1520* (British Museum Press, London, 1995).

PAGE 98 Pierre de Revel: Jonathan Sumption, *Trial by Battle: The Hundred Years War*, 1 (Faber, London, 1990), 559.

Sir Peter Malory: Mallory-Smith, 1985, 45.

Sir William Lisle: Hicks, 1928, 80. Beauchamp's first wife was a Lisle, and her daughter's son was John, Viscount Lisle (d. 1453).

Service in Calais: *Hall's Chronicle*.

Regnault de Montet: This anecdote appears in R. H. and M. A. Rouse, *Manuscripts and their Makers: Commercial Book Producers in Medieval Paris 1200–1500*, I (Harvey Miller, Turnhout, 2001). I am indebted to Nicholas Barker for this reference.

PAGE 100 Tournament ground outside Guines: The site a hundred years later of Henry VIII's famous tournament of the Field of the Cloth of Gold. The Twelfth Night tournament is additional evidence of the date of the muster roll to the years before Agincourt. Other dates are ruled out by Beauchamp's activities elsewhere, and the death at Agincourt of the French participants Herbaumes and Collard de Fiennes, and the fact that the first joust was said to have taken place on a Tuesday. A full account of the tournament survives in a collection of tournament literature that was copied into Sir John Paston's 'Great Book'; it is reprinted from Lansdowne MS no. 285 xxxvi in F. H. Cripps-Day, *The History of the Tournament in England and in France*, Appendix V, xxxi (Quaritch, London, 1918). It is also illustrated in the *Beauchamp Pageant*.

PAGE 101 When King Agwisance: Malory, *Works*, Bk VII, p. 141, 1.14–10.

'The parallel is so close': Eugène Vinaver, *Malory* (Clarendon Press, Oxford, 1929).

'Tribute to Beauchamp': However, P. J. C. Field ('The Source of Sir Gareth', in *Texts and Sources*) sees Sir Gareth's fair hands as soft and well cared for, and likely to originate in an unknown English folk tale, but he concedes that well-proportioned hands were an attribute of knightliness. The Warden of the Worshipful Company of Barber-Surgeons was engaged to advise on the effigy's anatomical details, and 'it is obvious from the furrowed brow, the blunt nose, an oddly shaped ear and the delicate veining of the hands that Massingham's portrait was intended to be as lifelike as possible' (Sinclair, 2003, 16).

PAGE 102 Including Sir Baldwin Strange: CPR, VI, 354, 361, 457.
The English embassy: DKPR, XLIV, 555–6 – Nov. 1414.
When they arrived in Konstanz: Although issue rolls ordered wages for this trip on 27 October, Beauchamp did not cross until 11 November and then stayed in Calais awaiting a safe-conduct from the French King, only leaving after the tournament (Sinclair, 2003). It is, however, also possible that Beauchamp went to Konstanz in the autumn of 1414 and had returned by Christmas-time.
The Council had been opened: Waurin, 170. *Hall's Chronicle*: 'They were men so well-apparelled and their horses so richly trapped, and all the compagnie so well-furnished, that the Almaines wondered, the Italians gazed, and all other nations were astonied to see such an honourable company come from a country so far distant'. Other details: Sinclair, 1987.

PAGE 103 Edward Gibbon: *Decline and Fall of the Roman Empire* (1766–88), ed. Bury, VII, p. 288; quoted in Martin Scott, *Medieval Europe* (Longman, London, 1975), 363.

CHAPTER 5
PAGE 104 Then there was launching: Malory, XXL.2.
Main sources for this chapter: Anne Curry, *The Battle of Agincourt* (Boydell, Woodbridge, 2000); Wylie, 1914; Rosalind Jarman, *Crispin's Day: The Glory of Agincourt* (Collins, London, 1979); *Gesta Henrici Quinti: The Deeds of Henry the Fifth*, trans. and ed. F. Taylor and J. S. Roskell (OUP, 1975). If Malory was already in service with Codnor, then he would have gone north with him. Codnor held the post of Constable of Berwick until Easter 1417.
Year's service: English contracts specified length of term more often than French ones. They could last for forty days, four months, one or two years, or even 'as it shall please the king'.
Calais: Wylie, 1914, I, 456, refers to Appendix G2 – unfortunately among the sources missing from his book which his death prevented him from completing himself.

PAGE 105 John Chetwynd: Chetwynd-Stapleton, 80.
'Chief port': Waurin, VI, 187. Harfleur is now silted up, hidden behind the huge modern ferry port of Le Havre. The church, in which many of the English who died were buried, is worth a visit.

Already ashore: Wylie, 1914, II, 17.

PAGE 106 The English fleet sailed: Meanwhile, to divert enemy attention, the forces at Calais, under the command of William Misle, carried out a series of increasingly daring raids around Boulogne and as far as Artois.

I am possessed: Quoted Jarman, 1979, 115.

Not a foolhardy commander: given his secret negotiations with Burgundy, he may also have had reason to believe – as the French certainly feared – that the Duke, known to be massing an army, would use it to help him against the French.

PAGE 108 From this day: Shakespeare: *Henry V*, IV, iii.

'I would not': Quoted Wylie, 1914, III, 35. See also C. L. Kingsford, *Chronicles of London* (London, 1905): 'All the royal power of frenchmen came against our king and his little meyne [host].'

Sir Walter Hungerford: Quoted by Jarman, 1979, 144. Hungerford commissioned Henry V's first biography and was the executor of his will.

PAGE 110 No Prince Christian: *Beauchamp Pageant*, quoted Brindley, 2001, 79.

PAGE 111 Sigismund stayed in England: He crossed on 1 May, but was only allowed to disembark after he had formally denied any imperial rights over England to Duke Humfrey of Gloucester, who had ridden his charger 'fetlock-deep' into the surf to demand that he did so. His progress to London was leisurely, stopping at Canterbury, Rochester and Dartford and finally greeted on the outskirts of London by Henry, who was attended by '5000 magnates in their richest array'. Many of Sigismund's retinue returned to defend Hungary, but the Emperor was enjoying himself so much that he stayed nearly four months, lavishly entertained with feasts, tournaments and showers of gifts – jewelled cups, basins of gold coins and splendidly harnessed horses worth thousands of pounds. On 25 May he was made a Knight of the Garter in the chapel of St George at Windsor.

PAGE 112 A westerly wind: The carrack was commanded by Laurent Folieta, and had sixty-two fighting men on board. Most details of the attack and the storm from Dugdale, *Warwickshire*, 409.

PAGE 113 'A grey courser': For Sir Baldwin's will, in which he left Beauchamp 'unum grisium cursorem' (probably in this context his horse, though it could also mean a hunting dog), see *Reg. Chichele*, II, 94, ed. E. F. Jacob (OUP, 1938); PRO Lists and Indexes 9, 158; *DKPR* 44, 555.

Terms for a truce: *Gesta Henrici Quinti*, 169.

CHAPTER 6

PAGE 114 At that parliament: Malory, V.3.

'surfeit-swelled': Shakespeare, *Henry IV Part II*, III, v, 52.

The largest and most elaborately equipped: Kingsford, *Henry V* (Putnam, New York, 1901), 96. Contemporary histories offer *c.* 16,400; muster rolls and

Livius's list suggest 2,300 men-at-arms and 7,400 archers. Henry V's own
retinue was 1,000, and included miners and gunners. Numerous unrecorded
pages and serving men were available as light cavalry for scouting and
foraging.

Muster roll: PRO E101/48/6. Field, 1993, describes this as that of the garrison of
Harfleur because it is bound in a bundle with at least one Harfleur muster
roll. But Grey of Codnor was never part of that garrison; the roll is simply
that of the part of his retinue which moved with him – and Henry V – first to
Caen and later to Argentan.

PAGE 115 After the contract had been fulfilled: English contracts specified length
of term more often than French ones, for forty days, four months, two years,
or 'as it shall please the king'.

A dagger? an arrow?: Anne Sutton prefers the less fanciful idea of a clerical spike,
perhaps the oldest means of temporary filing for papers. But she is, after all,
an archivist. I prefer romance.

John de Brunby: It is just possible that the name is an abbreviation of Burneby,
the Northamptonshire family into which Malory's sister Philippa later
married, but no knight of that name is known. If this Sir John Brunby was
indeed an unrecorded Burneby of Watford, he was a neighbour of the Malorys
of Winwick. A John Burneby, perhaps a kinsman, is listed in Will Swinburne's
retinue in February 1415, and was said to be a clerk at Marck Castle, an
important fortress in the Marches of Calais (HPT records, citing DKPR
xiv.559). A Thomas Burnby [sic] is listed as master of the King's henchmen in
1444 (PRO E403/753, m.10), at a time when Thomas Burneby was a favoured
courtier.

Thomas Malory de Bytham: He could not have been young Sir Thomas Malory
of Castle Bytham, who had died by the time his mother Lady Alice Malory
died in 1412. In her will Alice leaves other lands and possessions to her
granddaughter, Elizabeth, 'daughter of Sir Thomas Malory, knight'. Nothing is
known of this Sir Thomas after 1404. Lady Alice's dower interest in Bytham
passed to her daughter by her first husband, Lady Elizabeth Grey of Codnor.
Thomas Malory and his wife Margaret granted their manor of Bramcote to
feoffees in 1411 (Field, 1993, 59n, from *Warwickshire Feet of Fines*, ed. E. Stokes
et al., Dugdale Society 18 (943) no. 246); this could signal a move to Castle
Bytham.

PAGE 116 Bassinet helmet: No direct evidence, but we know John Malory had
the suit he wears in the window, and armour was certainly handed down – Sir
Anketil Malory left his best suit to his oldest son Thomas and his second-best
suit to his second son William (*Early Lincoln Will*, Lincoln Record Society V,
81914).

An earlier roll records: PRO E101/51/2m.

John Hardyng: E. D. Kennedy, 'Malory's Use of Hardyng's Chronicle', *Notes and
Queries* 214 (1969), 169–70; Field, 1998, 28.

Reinforcements: Back in Warwickshire, Thomas's father John Malory was rallying men, said to be for keeping order locally, but many of whom later turn up in Normandy. CPR HV [1416–22], 10 May 1418, records a commission of array 'for the defence of the realm while the king is in foreign parts for the recovery of the inheritance and rights of the crown' – for Warwickshire. In it were Sir Thomas Burdet, John Cockayn, Sir Edward Doddingselles, —— Malory, Thomas Greville, John de Lee and the Sheriff. The Christian name of Malory has been erased. It is likely to have been John, or a brother of Thomas; it was certainly one of his kinsmen. Cockayn, Burdet and Doddingselles would all serve in France. A Doddingselles married Thomas Malory's sister.

PAGE 117 Vegetius: Christopher Allmand, 'The Fifteenth-Century English Versions of Vegetius', *De Re Militari*, in M. Strickland (ed.), *Armies, Chivalry and Warfare* (Stamford, 1998). Vegetius was made use of by the French woman philosopher Christine de Pisan (1364–*c*.1430) in her *Faits d'Armes*, which was also in the royal library. Christine de Pisan wrote several books for the benefit of the French monarchy, including a life of Charles V, as well as her well-known books promoting women's issues. She was so depressed by the Agincourt campaign that she retired into a convent, only emerging in 1430 to write a paean of praise for Joan of Arc. An interesting case for Malory having read Vegetius is offered in Diane B. Bornstein, 'Military Strategy in Malory and Vegetius', *De Re Militari*, in *Comparative Literature Studies* (University of Illinois), 9 (1972), 123–9.

'Great guns': Dhira B. Mahoney, 'Malory's Great Guns', *Viator* 20, 1989, 296.

PAGE 118 'He got knowledge': Hall, *English Chronicle*, 113.

Philippe de Commines: Ian Arthurson, 'Espionage and Intelligence from the Wars of the Roses to the Reformation', *Nottingham Medieval Studies* XXXV (1991), 134.

Merlin's precautions: Malory I.II.

PAGE 119 The huge fleet: Hall's *Chronicle*, quoted Kingsford, 1901, pp. 211, 191.

PAGE 120 'Then in all haste . . .': Malory, *Works*, 196. Galliard is a lovely word, meaning both gay and valiant. Malory adds the reference to ordnaunce, great carracks, pavilions, ships of forestage (i.e. with turreted forecastles), galleys, galiots and 'spynnesse' (pinnacles). 'Sad' then meant forceful or heavy rather than miserable. The abbreviated passage in Caxton (V. 3) just talks of 'galleys, coggs and dromonds [huge open oar-driven ships]'.

Sweep into the west of Normandy: The tour of Normandy I took following the routes taken by the English brought home the scale of Henry V's achievements over the next few years. Many of the great Norman castles remain, thoughtfully reconstructed. Others have to be sought out. But even where only a few ragged crags of stone on a hilltop remain, it is awesome to realise the number and scale of the obstacles in the path of the English armies.

PAGE 121 Henry settled in: Kingsford, 1913, 66; 1901, 92.

PAGE 122 Volume of French histories: According to the reminiscences of James Butler, 4th Earl of Ormonde.

Capital of a column: It is the only capital to have human rather than vegetable motifs, and many learned papers have been written interpreting it. The latest, by Michel Le Bossé, believes that its hidden meaning is alchemical as well as Arthurian, and is echoed by the figurine-studded façade of a nearby house in the Rue St-Pierre that was once a haunt of three well-known alchemists. There is certainly something magical about the survival of this ancient house, not just through the centuries but also through the 1940s Blitz.

Argentan: Argentan Castle now houses the law courts. Otherwise little is left of the town the English occupied. For Codnor as captain, see *Rotuli Normanniae in Turri Londonensi asservati Johanne et Henrico Quinto Angliae Regibus*, ed. T. D. Hardy (London, 1935), 5 Hen Vm.21, 180.

PAGE 123 Log huts: Wylie, 1914, III, 70. Today the interior of the great keep of Falaise Castle has been imaginatively reconstructed.

Commissioned Humfrey of Gloucester: Keith Vickers, *Humfrey Duke of Gloucester* (OUP, London, 1970), 55–70. Beauchamp was negotiating with the Burgundians on 21 March; his forces invested Domfront on 2 April. An indication that his retinue of usefully experienced men had been distributed among the different fronts lies in a proclamation of 10 April by the Vicomte of Caen, that all the Earl's retinue should rejoin their captain as speedily as possible (Sinclair, 1987).

PAGE 124 Codnor's retinue: *Rotuli Normanniae*, 5 Hen V m23 (182).

'One of the strongest castles': Quoted in Wylie, 1914, III, 108.

Codnor was killed: According to *A Northern Chronicle*, he was at Cherbourg when he died.

Richard, was made bailli: The appointment may have reflected exceptional bravery or have been a compensation for the death of his father. The complete list of captains made during the 1417 campaign was: Sir Grey of Codnor – Argentan; Sir Grey of Codnor – Cherbourg; and, after his decease (1 August 1418), Sir Walter Hungerford (who later had Gisors); Sir John Gray (of Heton) – Tancarville and Harfleur; Sir Richard Beauchamp – Aumarle (Sir William Mountfort was his lieutenant there), Sir Richard 'Erbury' (Merbury) – Conches (Appendix to *Gesta Henrici Quinti*, ed. B. Williams (1850), 265–72). By 1420, the Cherbourg bailli was John Ashton, with attorney John Stokes, and Lt. Walter Charleton (Madeleine de Masson d'Auture, *Cherbourg pendant la guerre de Cent Ans* (Société Nationale de Cherbourg), n.d., 39).

Three thousand men: Vickers, 1970, 64n.

PAGE 125 There before the barrier: Waurin, II, 243.

PAGE 126 Many ordinary Normans: Madeleine de Masson d'Auture, *Henry V*, 218; Drouet, 'Organisation Domestique à Cherbourg 1418–1450', in *Revue des Etudes Normandes* II (1907–8); J. Dupont, *Histoire du Contentin et ses Isles*, 4 vols, 1870–85, II, 515.

PAGE 127 Henry sent Beauchamp . . . to negotiate: Vickers, 1970, 8.

'There may be none hope': H. Ellis, *Original Letters Illustrative of English History*, 2nd series, I, 77.

'Now I shall have the lady Catherine': *Hall's Chronicle*.

PAGE 128 Duke of Burgundy's skull: Earle, 1972, 177.

PAGE 129 'To release us': Malory, *Works*, 246.

PAGE 130 One enterprising investigator: Nellie Slaytor Aurner, 'Thomas Malory – Historian?', *Publications of the Modern Language Association of America* 48 (1933), 362–91.

Henry V's choice of the Knights: See Collins, 2000.

PAGE 131 Our mother-tongue: *A Book of London English 1384–1425*, ed. R. W. Chambers and M. Daunt (OUP, 1931), 139.

CHAPTER 7

PAGE 132 'Pray you': Malory, VII.24

PAGE 133 Benedicta Rowe: 'A Contemporary Account of the Hundred Years War', 41 (1976).

'MPs as a group': See HPT draft biography of Digby, Simon Payling, 2001.

Relatives, friends and neighbours: All the following references were found in the HPT files and draft biographies:

Thomas Beaufort: DKPR.44 606.

Thomas Arderne: His older brother Robert gets into far worse legal scrapes than Malory (see ch. 14 below).

Sir Thomas de Roos: DKPR.48, 275.

Robert Malory: tower garrison: PRO E101/51/121; with Talbot, 1436: BL Add. Ch. 6875m.

John Malory: This John Malory may have been John Malory of Litchborough who had died by 1467, or even the John Malory who was a Knight Hospitaller by 1463, judging by the fact that he was listed as chaplain of Dingley in one muster roll.

Walsh: the family was later linked to the Newbold Revel Malorys by marriage.

Sir John Cressy: PRO E101/53/33m2m; BL Add. Ch. 6875m. Cressy had connections with the Cliftons; in 1441 he married Constance, daughter of Reginald, Lord Grey of Ruthin (d. 1440) and Joan Astley. He was another knight with long and largely invisible service in France – including the captaincies of Rouen (1432) and Gisors (1441–2).

PAGE 134 Thomas Wake: PRO E101/54/5m; see HPT draft biography. In 1422 he was named a feoffee of Elizabeth, Lady Grey of Codnor (Sir Anketil Malory's stepdaughter) for a Huntingdonshire manor. He was MP for Northants (1433, 1437) and Sheriff of Northants in 1446. It is just possible that he was Malory's overlord: he is recorded in a 1465 escheator's account for Warwickshire as holding four knights' fees in Wappenbury, Horningham, Esthorp, Primethorp, Fenny Newbold, Stretton, Easenhall and Pailington (Whitteridge 1973, 258, citing PRO escheator's accounts E357/132, m.6 and E136/224/12; accounts of the escheator of Warwick and Leicester 5–6 Edw.IV). He also had Somerset interests (MP for Somerset, February 1449) and was related to the Hollands. He, like the Malorys of Newbold Revel, held of the Dowager Countess of Kent, Joan Holland, who in 1437 quit-claimed Blisworth and the advowson of its church to him for £100 because of his 'praiseworthy service' to her. His son witnessed the IPM of Sir Thomas Malory's wife in 1479. Wake's loyalties, like those of Malory, were far from clear cut.

In association with men: Pulteneys, Middleham, Cheyne and Chetwynd. See Carpenter, 1983, 82 for identification of knighthood with military service, and Carpenter, 1980, 32–3 for support for the likelihood of Malory having spent time abroad on active service. There is also a ten-year gap in the career of Sir Gervais Clifton, for example, who, like Malory, served in France with Codnor in 1417, and was an MP in 1426. Nothing is then heard of him until 1435 (when he applied for a portable altar), although when he was assessed in 1436 he was one of the richest men in the county. The career of his son, another Gervais, is similarly opaque. In the 1460s, he was a prominent Lancastrian loyalist, and was bracketed with Sir Thomas Malory in 1468, when both were refused pardon.

Memories of Henry V: David Morgan, 'Household Retinue of Henry V and the Ethos of English Public Life', in Curry and Matthew (eds), 2000.

PAGE 135 Pardon in 1417: PRO C67/37 m.33; all other references, Field, 1993, 45–6. To raise a loan: CPR HV (1416–22).

Uncle Thomas: Records of Thomas Malory of Bramcote are scanty. He was sued by another man's executors at Easter 1426 and died by 6 December 1428. He could have been killed in France. He is not mentioned again on the Codnor muster rolls.

Attested the probity: HPT List of Attestors, Simon Malory.

PAGE 136 Preceptor of Balsall: A licence to return home was issued to him in Rhodes on 1 November 1420 (AOM345, f.cxxx [old foliation]/129r [modern]). He had been granted Hogshaw, Buckinghamshire, on 16 October 1420 (AOM345, ff. cxxcii [old foliation]/127r–v modern]), which was probably a sign of special favour (Greg O'Malley, private communication, from research in the cathedral archives in Malta). Sir Robert stayed in England until 1426. See also ch. 9 below, passim.

As young as fourteen: A. Mifsud, *Knights Hospitaller of the Venerable Tongue of England in Malta* (Malta, 1914), 80.

A debate that year: Greg O'Malley, private communication. See also the Order's English Cartulary (BL Cotton Nero E vi f.5v).

Three records: But cf. Field, 1993, 59. He believes they refer to some other Thomas Malory as he envisages Sir Thomas Malory as being born c.1415–18.

A family called Pulteney: *The Commons*, IV, 128–9. There were two other
Pulteney brothers, William, Sir John's heir, who was already a knight, and
Thomas, who had been in the retinue of Thomas, Duke of Clarence and was
perhaps still in France. Thomas Pulteney took out a distraint of knighthood in
1430 (Hertfordshire) and John Pulteney did the same in 1439 (Leicestershire).

Cutting down trees . . . at Edgbaston: Farnham, *Village Notes*, III, 226, citing De
Banco Roll 642, Trinity, 9 Henry V, m272.d.Warr. Edgbaston is near to the
Staffordshire border.

A plea of 'novel disseisin': PRO Just 1/1524/m.30 (renumbered since Field's 1993
reference to it as m.28).

PAGE 137 Sued by another man's executors: Farnham, *Village Notes*, III, 226.

Armorial window: Dugdale, *Warwickshire*, 83. Another connection with the
Feildings occurs in 1433 when John Malory and William Purefoy witness a
grant of the Feilding manor of Newnham Paddox.

William Revel: Possession at Shawell PRO E210/10385. The neighbouring manor
of Cosford, with which both John Malory and Thomas later had dealings, was
probably attached to Shawell.

PAGE 138 'Love is free in himself': Malory, *Works*, 1097. I have not found this in
earlier sources. See Anne Curry, 'Sex and the Soldier in Lancastrian
Normandy, 1415–1450', *Reading Journal of Medieval History* (1988), for
interesting parallel experiences.

'Valorous soul' etc.: From a contemporary French pastoral, quoted Wylie, 1914, I,
159.

Malory's known sisters were married: Field, 1993, 63.

Recently discovered relics: Richard Barber, *The Holy Grail: Imagination and Belief*
(Penguin, London, 2004), 134, citing James P. Carley (ed.), *Glastonbury Abbey
and the Arthurian Tradition* (Brewer, Cambridge, 2001).

PAGE 139 Beauchamp sat in the Lords: He had a female recluse of Winchester
brought to London for three days to be consulted; £2 6s 8d spent on her. She
may have had a reputation as a seer.

PAGE 140 Third expeditionary force: Wylie, 1914, III, 318.

Beauchamp contingent: CPR (21 May 1421), 388.

The three outstanding Dauphinist commanders: J. Pernoud and M.-V. Clin, *Joan
of Arc*, rev./trans. Jeremy du Quesnay Adams (Phoenix, London, 2000), 187;
see also F. Rousseau, *La Hire* (Mont de Mausan, Lacoste, 1969).

PAGE 141 It is fit to speak: Waurin, ii, 365.

Saintraille: Matthews, 1966, 148; Field, 1998, 58–9, 62.

Gratuitously puts his name into the *Morte*: See below, ch. 8.

PAGE 142 Lady Joan Astley: John Malory had dealings with Joan's husband Lord
Grey of Ruthin in 1414. Sir John Astley was a tournament hero whose 'Great
Book' of chivalric treatises and Arthurian romances is discussed below,
ch. 22.

Glamorous fugitive heiress: see R. Putnam, *A Medieval Princess; The Life of Jacqueline of Hainault* (New York, Putnams, 1904).

Stood to inherit Brabant: Philip also hoped to control Jacqueline, and hence Hainault and Holland.

PAGE 143 Horse-drawn litter: Perhaps he recalled reading in an Arthurian romance of Merlin's advice to Uther Pendragon when he too was ill in a time of military crisis: 'Ye may not lie so as ye do, for ye must to the field though ye ride on an horse-litter; for ye shall never have the better of your enemies but if your person be there, and then shall ye have the victory' (Malory, I.4).

20,000 requiem masses: David Morgan, 'Household Retinue of Henry V' (2000).

PAGE 144 Geoffrey of Boulogne: *c.*1060–*c.*1100; one of the legendary heroes known as the Nine Worthies. Caxton lists them in his preface to Malory's *Morte Darthur*. Three were Jews (Joshua, David and Joseph Maccabeus), three 'paynims' (pagans) (Hector of Troy, Alexander the Great and Julius Caesar) and three Christians (Geoffrey of Boulogne, Charlemagne and King Arthur).

Sent spies: J. Webb, 'A Survey of Egypt and Syria, undertaken in the year 1422 by Sir Gilbert Lannoy', *Archaeologia* XXI (1827), 281–444, cited by M. K. Jones in his foreword to Jonathan Hughes, *Arthurian Myths and Alchemy: The Kingship of Edward IV* (Sutton, Stroud, 2002).

The first of the four horses: Waurin.

'Arms . . . of the noble King Arthur': David Starkey, *Arthurian Literature* (1999), believes that these arms were actually those of Edward the Confessor, and signified Henry's lordship, but agrees that what is relevant is that contemporary chroniclers declared them to be Arthur's.

PAGE 145 Yet some men say: Malory, XXI.7.

PAGE 146 Direct parallels: attempted in Nellie Slayton Aurner, 'Sir Thomas Malory – Historian?', *Publications of the Modern Language Association of America* 48 (1933), 362–91.

He often writes like a chronicler: P. J. C. Field, 'Fifteenth-Century History in Malory's *Morte Darthur*', in Field, 1998.

John Bale: See ch. 3 above. In the 1557 edition of Bale, *Collectiones Anglicas* is changed to 'Acta Regis Arthuri – lib 1' and 'De Mensa Rotunda eiusdem – lib 1' (629), which suggests either that Bale was writing from hearsay, and thought the long title of Malory's great work referred to two separate books, or that he may only have had separate parts of his complete work.

Verse romance: P. J. C. Field, 'Malory and *The Wedding of Sir Gawaine and Dame Ragnell*, in Field, 1998, 284–94. Once the long-held but over-facile assumption that Malory only wrote because he was in prison is discarded, more effort could be made to search for other writings by Malory using modern techniques of textual analysis.

PAGE 147 Sir Thomas Gargrave: Connolly, 1998. No muster roll of the men

whose wages John Shirley was given survives. For Beauchamp's campaigns, see
Sinclair, 2003, 37–40.

Bedford . . . gave orders: Waurin, V, III, 60. This passage was copied by
Monstrelet, who recorded this man as Malbery. Later translations convert this
to Merbury because of the well-known family of this name who fought with
Henry V and for Henry VI in France.

PAGE 148 Would become Queen of England: See ch. 21 below. After Henry V's
death, Bedford made Woodville his chamberlain and he was rewarded for his
'grands notables et agréables services' with several confiscated Norman estates
(DNB citing Longnon and Monstrelet).

Robert Malory: Twice mentioned in PRO E101/51/21, which also listed John
Arderne and Thomas Newport – the latter became a Knight Hospitaller.

Gisors: Jean-Paul Basse, *Gisors dans l'Histoire* (L'Age d'Homme, 1998); Escouchy's
chronicle. Today the most atmospheric place in Gisors Castle is a dungeon
tower which is covered with ancient graffiti, drawings and arcane symbols,
many dating back to the Hundred Years War and earlier. I looked hopefully
but in vain for plaintive prayers from English miscreants.

PAGE 149 'In such wise': Malory, V.12.

Verneuil: The Burgundian army was under Lisle-Adam. Alençon and Buchan had
defeated Clarence at Baugé. On 13 October 1424 the Burgundian town of Ham,
on the Somme in Vernandois, was taken by the French, led by Pothon de
Saintraille. John of Luxembourg, whose town it was, recaptured it. Saintraille
escaped, just. Charles VII's son Louis (XI) was born on 3 July 1423. Soon
afterwards the town of Beaumont-sur-Loire was taken by the French –
Bedford sent forces under Lisle-Adam, Lionel de Bournouville and the Bastard
of Thyenne.

Then the king wept: Malory, V.7.

PAGE 150 Personal business: Beauchamp was also worsted in a precedence
dispute with John Mowbray, Duke of Norfolk ('Parliamentary Restoration:
John Mowbray and the Dukedom of Norfolk in 1425', in Rowena E. Archer &
Simon Walker (eds), *Rulers and Ruled in Late Medieval England: Essays
Presented to Gerald Harriss*, Hambledon, London, 1995).

Hanley Castle: J. Toomey, 'A Medieval Woodland Manor: Hanley Castle,
Worcestershire' (unpublished PhD thesis, University of Birmingham, 1997);
notes published in *Worcestershire Historical Society Collections*.

Gave birth to Harry: Sinclair, 2003, 39; Brindley, 2001.

Marriage to Jacquetta: Duke Humfrey went as far as invading Hainault and
challenging the Duke of Burgundy to a duel, but he then deserted Jacqueline
for one of her ladies, Elinor Cobham, of whom more in ch. 13.

He penned a ballad: Brindley, 2001, 110.

PAGE 151 John Lydgate: Kingsford, 1913, 195.

French royal library: Carol Meale, *Manuscripts, Readers and Patrons in Fifteenth
Century England*: 'Sir Thomas Malory and Arthurian Romance', *Arthurian*

Literature (1985), 103, citing Leopold Delisle, *Recherches sur la Librairie de Charles V*, 2 vols (Paris, 1907), I, 142ff. Meale gives Delisle's numbers for all the Arthurian texts – the shabby unillustrated book was 1117; it would be interesting if it was the Tristram and Grai compilation; *La Librairie de Charles V*, catalogue of an exhibition at the Bibliothèque Nationale (Paris, 1968); M. J. Barber, 'The Books and Patronage of Learning of a Fifteenth-Century Prince', *The Book Collector* 12 (1963), 308–15. Charles of Orléans and his brother John of Angoulême acquired several volumes, and took them back to France with them when they were eventually freed in 1440–1. See also Jenny Stratford, *The Bedford Inventories, The Worldly Goods of the Duke of Bedford, Regent of France* (Society of Antiquaries, 1993).

PAGE 152 The Avon navigable: *Warwick Castle and its Earls*, 120.

PAGE 153 Beauchamp mustered men: His force certainly included John Shirley, who was sent from Calais to London with Richard Buckland, the Treasurer of Calais, to seek payment for the garrison on 4 February 1427. He rejoined Beauchamp at Pontorson with, it is to be hoped, the retinue's wages, in April (Connolly, 1998, 23).
Barfleur: The Winchester manuscript follows the alliterative *Morte Arthure* in placing King Arthur's arrival on the Normandy coast at Barflete (Barfleur). Caxton's printed version inserts 'in Flanders', which is of course nowhere near Mont St-Michel
Arthur . . .: Malory, *Works*, 200.

PAGE 154 A queen of England: Edward IV's queen, Elizabeth Woodville's mother, was Jacquetta of Luxembourg, a descendant, legend had it, of Melusine.

CHAPTER 8
PAGE 155 Chastellain: Kervyn de Lettenhove (ed.), *Chroniques des ducs de Bourgogne*, 5 vols (Brussels, 1863–6), quoted in Pernoud and Clin, 2000, 86.
Berkeley estates: Beauchamp's men had forcibly taken possession of Berkeley Castle in 1420; the dispute over the inheritance lasted until 1607, the longest running lawsuit in British legal history.
William Peyto: HPT draft biography, L. S. Clark. A different interpretation is put on this incident by Carpenter, 1992, 385, who plays down Malory's associations with Beauchamp, but it ignores later evidence of the personal feud between the Malorys and the Peytos and the fact that John Malory had sat for Warwickshire four times already without any objection from Beauchamp. Peyto's second wife Katherine was a Gresley, a family with an even worse record than the Peytos for high-handed thuggery. The Under-Sheriff who connived at Peyto's action, Edmund Coleshill, was later accused of conspiring with the Abbot of Coombe, with whom Thomas Malory later had a major feud. By July 1432 Peyto was fighting in France again as an

independent captain, but in little over a decade he and Thomas Malory would cross swords once more.

PAGE 156 He is recorded: Entry in the HPT List of Distraints for 'John Mallory of Warwickshire'. Beauchamp seems to have had no objection; his attorney, John Broun, acted for John Malory in the matter.

Formally appointed: Henry V is said to have asked on his deathbed for Beauchamp to be his son's 'governor' (Brindley, 2001, 105).

PAGE 157 'Examples from history': Storey, 1986, 32, quoting *Proc. & Ord. PC* III, 296–300.

John Somerset: DNB entry.

'Following her appetite': *Hall's Chronicle.*

PAGE 158 Tintagel: In 1998 there was much excitement when University of Glasgow archaeologists led by Professor Christopher Morris discovered a sixth-century slate plaque with a Latin inscription. It read: 'The mark of Paternius, the mark of Coliarus, he made it; the mark of Artognous'. So at least three of Tintagel's inhabitants at that time understood Latin – and one had a name uncannily like Arthur. No doubt there were far more interesting souvenirs to be picked up in the ruined fortress in the fifteenth century. Malory hints that he had a habit of inquiring about Arthur on his travels when he writes, 'Yet some men say in many parts of England that King Arthur is not dead' (XXI.7). By 1478, Tintagel was described as very strong, but in ruins.

PAGE 159 Dressed entirely: Pernoud and Clin, 2000, 58.

PAGE 160 Chartier: Ibid., 71.

PAGE 162 Eight dukes and earls: Norfolk, York, Devon, Arundel, Beauchamp, Stafford, Huntingdon and Ormond.

Sir William Malory: Thomas Carte, *A General History of England* (London, 1975), II, 269; DKPR.XVIII, 275.

Bouvreuil: One of many thirteenth-century fortresses built by the French King Philip Augustus when he conquered the once proudly independent Duchy of Normandy.

'The Maid': Chastellain, quoted in Pernoud and Clin, 2000, 87–8.

PAGE 163 *Livres tournois*: The currency used in Lancastrian Normandy; one English pound was worth four livres tournois.

PAGE 164 *Polychronicon*: A chronicle written up to about 1370 by Ralph Higden and brought up to date by William Caxton in 1480.

PAGE 165 Very different treatment: On 12 August the Beauchamp Household Book for 1430–1 records that 'Pothon prisoner cum 1 scutifero [squire]' sat with Earl (Pernoud and Clin, 2000, 206, citing Marie-Veronique Clin-Meyer, 'Le Registre de Comtes de Richard Beauchamp, Comte de Warwick, 14 Mars 1431–14 Mars 1432', thesis, Ecole des Hautes Etudes en Sciences Sociales, 1981).

This register is the only one of the annual sets of Beauchamp accounts to survive. Had others done so, we would know the facts about Malory's relationship with the Beauchamps.

PAGE 166 Could once more visit England: Beauchamp's Treasurer John Boysham issued special 'prests' to individual soldiers leaving England to join their lord.

The Cheyne family: Field, 1993, 59. Devon CRO MS 1038 M/T4/24. John Cheyne (c.1385–1447) was one of many English captains who served for years in the wars in France, often with Beauchamp's forces. He was made Lord of Haye-des-Puits and La Roche-Tesson, both in Brittany, in 1419. Quainton was part of the dower of his third wife, the much-married Isobel Mortimer. CFR (1420) records the death of Sir John Cheyne on 10 October 1420 and also of William Cheyne, who had even more widespread lands.

French diarist: Bourgeois of Paris, quoted Pernoud and Clin, 2000, 144.

Saintraille: Sinclair, 2003, 44; further details in Sinclair, 1987.

PAGE 168 Real place-names: See also ch. 22.

Courtier poet: Ethel Seaton, *Sir Richard Roos, Lancastrian Poet* (Rupert Hart-Davis, London, 1961).

PAGE 169 Scanty: 'Household retainers who enjoyed daily contact with the lord and lady played an important role in any magnate's following, yet evidence of their names and numbers is extremely rare' (Sinclair, 1987).

Using force: See K. B. McFarlane, *Nobility of Later Medieval England* (OUP, 1973); Carpenter, 1992, passim. Joan also feuded against the Ferrers of Chartley, and left £500 to her heir 'for the defence of the lands'.

Sat on a jury: Field, 1993, 47.

Isobel: She was widowed by the end of the decade, left with a jointure of £10 a year. Carpenter, 1992 describes Edward Doddingselles as a poorish knight who did not take office, but it is equally possible that he prospered in France and avoided taking office at a time when it was risky to do so (CCR [1429–35], 313–14; CPR [1436–41], 343; CPR [1441–6], 438; Dugdale, *Warwickshire*, 902, 1059).

PAGE 170 Philippa ... by 1429: Field, 1993, 63, citing CCR (1429–35), 314.

An assignment of three rents: John Malory 'of Newbold Revel' grants rent of twelve pence and three capons to three Cosford men. Among the witnesses is Eustace Burneby, John's son-in-law. Philippa is recorded as Eustace's widow c.1464 (Field, 1993, 63, citing CFR [1461–71], 137).

Wife of Robert Vincent: Some time before the 1440s, as Vincent mortgaged his Swinford properties to Thomas Malory 'his wife's brother' in 1441 and sold them to him outright in exchange for an annuity in 1449. The sale may have been because of the Vincents' relocation to Warwick Castle.

Robert was Clerk of the Kitchens: *Visitations of Northants 1564 and 1619–19*, ed. W. C. Metcalfe, London, 1887, 149–50.

Or possibly earlier: John Malory's last deal as Lord of Winwick was in 1425, when he witnessed a charter for George Burneby.

She was assessed: PRO E179/192/59. The competent way in which wives and widows could manage their husbands' estates is amply illustrated by the *Paston Letters*.

Conservative guess: Philippa might have shared Newbold Revel with Thomas, however, in which case Newbold Revel itself might have been worth more. Her widowed cousin Thomasina Chetwynd was granted certain rooms in the manor house of Ingestre and some land and rents due from the tenant of a holding called Salt (Chetwynds-Stapleton, 1892, 92). Another death at this time may have had unforeseen consequences in the future: that of the holder of the overlordship of Newbold Revel, Joan Holland: sister of Edmund, Earl of Kent; widow of Edmund Langley, Duke of York (d. 1402), William, Lord Willoughby of Middleton (d. 1409) and Henry, Lord Scrope of Masham (executed 1415); when she died she was married to Sir Henry Bromfleet, later Lord Vessy (d. 1469). Six reversionary heirs could have inherited it after Joan's death on 12 April 1434: her sister Margaret, Duchess of Clarence, her nieces Alice, Countess of Salisbury, and Joyce Lady Tiptoft, her nephew Ralph, Earl of Westmorland, and her great-nephews Richard, Duke of York, and Henry Grey of Tankerville. We have no record of which it was – all we know is that twenty-seven years later Newbold Revel was among the overlordships recorded in the IPM of John Mowbray, Duke of Norfolk. He could have bought it from whoever inherited it from Joan at any time between 1434 and his death in 1461; not only was it conveniently adjacent to his holdings at Brinklow and Caluden but it had been held by the Mowbray family for nearly a hundred years between 1106 and 1200. However, overlordships are not a reliable guide to loyalties at this date.

The Earl of Warwick's main preoccupation: Anne was born in September 1426 (Brindley, 2001, 112). Richard Neville was born 28 November 1428 (Michael Hicks, *Warwick the Kingmaker*, Blackwell, Oxford, 1998, 7). They were married at Beauchamp's Welsh castle, Abergavenny. Negotiations for the espousals could have sent Malory north to the Nevilles' great castle of Middleton, and put him in touch once again with his cousins near Ripon, the Malorys of Hutton Conyers.

CHAPTER 9

PAGE 172 25 January 1435: CPR (1429–36), 452; Field, 1993, 73.

Sir Robert Malory: I am indebted in this chapter to Peter Field for the idea of the importance of the Hospitallers to Malory, first mooted in an article on Sir Robert Malory (P. J. C. Field, 'Sir Robert Malory, Prior of the Hospital of St John of Jerusalem in England (1439–1439/40)', *Journal of Ecclesiastical History* 28:3 (July 1977), slightly revised as ch. 5 of Field, 1993; and to Greg O'Malley for his generosity with his PhD thesis ('English Knights Hospitaller 1460–1522', Cambridge, 1999) and his research (in progress) on the English Hospitallers of the fifteenth century.

PAGE 173 Clerkenwell: Details, Mifsud, 1914, 49. The church's enormous bell tower was blown up in 1548, but its Gothic crypt and chancel survive. The much-restored medieval remnant of St John's Gate now houses a museum and library and is still the London base of the Order, which has a close association with the work of St John Ambulance Service.

PAGE 174 Like any great medieval household: As a result of the virtual invisibility of Hospitallers and their households and tenants in local taxation records, and the fact that members of the Order were frequently not shown on family trees (like anyone who went into a religious order of any kind, they were deemed dead to the world), the nature and extent of Hospitaller influence on both political and religious affairs has been underestimated. One reason for the scantiness of Malory's records is that he held Swinford of the Hospitallers.

'Of gentle strain on both father's side and mother's side', Malory, *Works*, 62.

PAGE 175 Hugh Revel: Humphrey-Smith, 1994. Hugh Revel became a brother of the Order in 1214, and held offices at Buckby and at Chippenham before taking passage for the Holy Land. He was Castellan of Krak des Chevaliers in 1243, and Lieutenant Master of the Hospital from 1248. In 1256 he was Grand Commander of Acre and became Grand Master in 1258.

The only Englishman: The only other is Andrew Bertie, who is Grand Master at the time of writing.

Granted the commanderies: Greg O'Malley, PhD thesis.

Buried in the Priory church: John Stow, *Survey of London* (Clarendon Press, Oxford, 1908).

PAGE 176 Sir Robert Botill: also spelt Bootle.

Sir Andrew Meldrum: Henry VI extended the safe-conduct of Sir Andrew Meldrum, bailiff of Torpichen, and six companions from Scotland, there already on chapter business (Rymer (ed.), *Foedera* V.i.8.)

Two Scropes of Bolton: The French rolls (48th Reprint DKPR, 301) say that John, Lord le Scrope, went as one of the ambassadors to the Grand Master and that he was licensed to take with him 500 marks and Henry, Lord le Scrope of Bolton.

Early medieval romances: Helen Nicholson, *Love, War and the Grail* (Brill, 2000).

'I know well': Malory, XIII.5.

PAGE 177 40,000 Saracens invading, Malory, *Works*, 37, 40. The word Saracen had no necessary Oriental connotation – it simply meant non-Christian, and could mean a pagan Saxon as easily as a Muslim Turk.

'Dwelled within [a] ship': Malory, XVII.13.

Malory drops the 'royals of Rhodes': He keeps in the King of Cyprus and the Greeks (cf. *Works*, 193, and Map 13).

'Reynald of the Rhodes': *Morte Arthure*, ed. Valerie Krishna (Burt Franklin, New York, 1976), 116, l.2785.

PAGE 178 'Went into the Holy Land': Malory, XXI.13.

Witnessed a contract: CCR (1435–41), 268; Wrottesley, 1891, 316–17. Malory is described as an esquire; Sir Philip Chetwynd was his mother's nephew (see ch. 10 below).

PAGE 179 'gold and silver': CPR (1429–36), 452.

Great Florentine banking house: G. A. Holmes, 'Florentine Merchants in England 1346–1436', Economic History Review, 2nd series, 13 (1960), 193–208. On p. 197 Holmes notes (from *Rotuli Parliamentorum* V, 13) that two bishops and Robert Malory petition the King in November 1439 on account of £2,000 which the Alberti owed them.

The winter of 1434–5: Mary-Ann Hookham, *The Life and Times of Margaret of Anjou* (Tinsley, London, 1872), 438. Departure could have been any time between early 1435 and the autumn: details from Field, 1993, 72–6 and correspondence with Greg O'Malley. Sir Robert's first surviving letters of attorney authorising a deputy to act for him are dated 3 March. However, he could have left earlier – later letters of attorney are dated 21 May 1436, a time when he was definitely in Rhodes. Field notes a candidate presented by the Prior to Burgham, Rochester, in February 1435 – the Prior might have been on his way to Sandwich. But another one was presented to Kilmersdon, Somerset, on 13 October 1435 (John Stafford, Register, *Somerset Record Society* 31–2 (1915–6), 129, 136). It is possible that some time may have elapsed between presentation and record of it. Sir Robert was summoned to Parliament in July 1435 for the October session, but that was probably automatic. A similar summons was sent to him on 29 October for the January Parliament, but he was in Rhodes during both these months.

Arms . . . and horses: Mifsud, 1914, 79.

A blessing of St Thomas Becket: Cusp, 1909, 33.

An itinerary: For this and other details, see R. J. Mitchell, *The Spring Voyage: The Jerusalem Pilgrimage in 1458* (John Murray, London, 1965).

PAGE 180 'Sone de Nausay': Helen Nicholson, 'Knights and Lovers: The Military Orders in the Romantic Literature of the thirteenth century', in Malcolm Barber (ed.), *The Military Orders: Fighting for the Faith and Caring for the Sick* (Variorum, London, 1994).

PAGE 181 'And whether they were abed . . .': Malory, XX.3.

And they came to a fair castle: Malory, VII.15.

PAGE 182 Moving spirit: No arms record the Priors between Malory and Weston.

PAGE 183 An earlier visitor: Pero Tafur, *Travels and Adventures*, trans. and ed. M. Letts (London, 1926), quoted in Mitchell, 1965, 80–1.

PAGE 184 Vegetius's military treatise: now in the Bodleian Library (MS Cannon. Class.Lit.174) see also E. Kollias, *Medieval City of Rhodes* (Athens, 1998).

Over a hundred Greek poems: BL Add. MS 8241; Anthony Luttrell, *Latin Greece: The Hospitallers and the Crusades 1291–1440* (Veriorum, London, 1982), 146.
Crown of thorns: Mitchell, 1965, 81.

PAGE 185 Caravan: H. J. A. Sire, *The Knights of Malta* (Yale UP, 1994), 85.
Bodrum: See A. T. Luttrell, 'English Contributions to the Hospitaller castle at Bodrum', in *The Military Orders*, II, ed. H. Nicholson, c.1999; and idem, 'The Military Orders 1312–1798', in J. Riley-Smith (ed.), *Oxford Illustrated History of the Crusades* (1997). The name Bodrum comes from the Greek Petrounion. The German architect Heinrich Schlegelholt supervised construction of the castle, which began in 1407, and incorporated the latest in castle design. The French had developed the art of cannon foundry by this time, so gun embrasures were built along the top of the castle's walls, especially those facing landward. These walls were made thicker than those facing the sea; the Hospitallers had a powerful fleet, so they had little fear of marine attack. Two outer rings of defences were also constructed on the landward side, resulting in a complicated moat system. It was twenty-seven years before the outer walls were finally completed. Castle construction continued throughout the fifteenth century. The chapel (which still stands in its original place inside the castle) was one of the first completed structures. The knights also built a watchtower overlooking the bay from a hill opposite the castle. Many fugitives from the Mongols and the Turks fled to Bodrum over the next eighty years, and special tracker dogs were trained, St Bernard style, to seek them out and rescue them. The size of the visiting parties and their many servants in 1435 and 1436 is reflected by discussion in 1437 over who should be given free hospitality and who should pay (Mifsud, 1914, 91).

PAGE 186 An unusually full chapter elected: Field, 1993, 74–5; CCR (1435–41), 238; *Proc. & Ord. PC*, v 108, PRO E28/59/51.

PAGE 187 Listened with interest and concern: Some surmise by me of causes of events. See also Field, 1993, 74.

PAGE 188 'To deliver to': CCR 17, Henry VI Membrane 10, 25 April [1439]. Spelling a little modernised.
An active Prior: Field, 1993, 70–6.
Tailors' company: C. Clode, *Memorials of the Guild of Merchant Taylors* (London, 1875), 619, 49–50.
Thomas Greswold: Gervers, 'Essex Cartulary' of 1444. Thomas Greswold was acting for the king-in-person in a (failed) claim for the tenement of Odewell in Gestingthorpe.

PAGE 189 Perhaps favourite, commandery: The estate was much improved and enlarged during his tenure of it, and in a debate as to who should hold Balsall and Grafton after the death of its occupant Sir Peter Holt which took place in Rhodes on 12 June 1415, Sir Robert argued successfully that he should as it was 'situated in his country [in partibus suis] and among his friends and kin [inter amicos et cognates]' (private communication from Greg O'Malley, citing AOM339 Liber Bullarum 1409–16). For more details, see Eileen Gooder, *Temple Balsall* (Phillimore, Chichester, 1999).

Saracen's Head: Legend has it that no heathen could go closer than this to the Christian Templar estate.

Upstairs parlour: It has been repainted since the fifteenth century, but the coats of arms are correct for the holders of the preceptory.

PAGE 190 A rich intermingling: There is great scholarly interest in Malory's sources. Relevant recent books include Elizabeth Archibald and A. S. G. Edwards (eds), *A Companion to Malory* (*Arthurian Studies* XXXVII, Brewer, Woodbridge, 1996); P. J. C. Field (ed.), *Malory: Texts and Sources* (Brewer, Cambridge, 1998); D. Thomas Hanks Jr and Jessica G. Brogdon (eds), *The Social and Literary Contexts of Malory's Morte Darthur* (*Arthurian Studies* XLIII, Brewer, Cambridge, 2000); Bonnie Wheeler (ed.), *Arthurian Studies in Honour of P. J. C. Field* (*Arthurian Studies* LVII, Brewer, Cambridge, 2004).

CHAPTER 10

PAGE 191 Then Tor alighted: Malory, Bk III.3.

'in stature of his person': PPC, IV, 1436; CPR (1429–36), 589.

'conceit and knowledge': See Bertram Wolffe's *Henry VI*, 80, for the 'motions and stirrings' that arose a year earlier when Henry VI, then only thirteen, seems to have decided that he was going to assert himself against his council.

PAGE 192 He is said to have wept: Wolffe, 1981, 82–3. Twenty years later, in 1456, the fact that Duke Philip had 'abandoned him in his boyhood' still rankled, and he remained eager to make war on Burgundy.

Simultaneous offensives: R. A. Griffiths, *The Reign of Henry VI* (Benn, London, 1981), 200–5

PAGE 193 My going over: Stevenson, 1861–4, vol II, pt. 1, lxvi; also quoted in Dugdale, *Warwickshire*. This is a fascinating document, tantamount to a conversation. Warwick asked particularly for Willoughby, John Viscount Beaumont and Sir John Burgh to go. He was only given Willoughby.

PAGE 194 Sir William Bonville: *The Commons*, II, 834–6.

It would have been natural: Following Field, 1993, 86, though he suggests Malory went after he was knighted. But I think he would then have been recorded. Sir Philip was in the retinue of Richard Beauchamp, Earl of Warwick when he received a silver collar of king's livery at court at Christmas 1427 (Field, 1993, 66, citing PRO E28/50/22). So too were his (and Malory's) uncle William Purefoy and William Mountfort (who may well also have been their uncle: see ch. 3).

A member of the élite corps: Carpenter, 1992, 409, n.31; PPC, V.121, 160–1; CPR

(1441–46), 205, 244, 175; (1436–41), 136. John Chetwynd indented for service in Gascony or France just before Agincourt (73).

Robert Whitgreve: *The Commons*, IV, 834–6.

Sir Thomas Erdington: Carpenter, 1992, 409.

It could have been at this point: We do not know when, only that those men enfeoffed the estates to eight other men some time before 1461, from evidence offered in a lawsuit raised by one of the second set of feoffees in 1486 (Field, 1993, 127–8, 133–4) in order to protect the interests of Malory's grandson and heir.

PAGE 195 'Beawme': Malory, *Works*, 1204. Vinaver adds the option of Beaune, but that is not a place to which one can sail from Britain, though its wines were far better known in Vinaver's day than the wines of the south-west.

In the hinterland: The relevant fiefs are Agen, Armagnac, Astorac, Comminges, Foix, Landes, Languedoc, Marsan, Pardiac, Perigueux, Rouergue, Saintonge, Sarlat, and Tursan. 'Neither the *Mort Artu* nor the English poem offers any parallel to this passage', Vinaver, Commentary, *Works*, p. 1625, p. 1626 (map). Of course, Saintraille could have contributed their names during his imprisonment in Warwick.

PAGE 196 Charles VII's most feared mercenary captains: Wolffe, 1981, 155.

Huntingdon's army: Details from Malcolm Vale, *English Gascony: 1399–1453* (OUP, 1970), 110.

When Huntingdon finally set sail: PRO E101/53/22.

Sir Robert Clifton: He died in office as Constable of Bordeaux on 22 September 1442.

Helen Chetwynd: Widow of Edmund, Lord Ferrers of Chartley, and daughter and heiress of Thomas de la Roche.

PAGE 197 Under Grey of Codnor in 1417: See ch. 7. Clifton was Treasurer of Calais between June 1451 and December 1460, and garrison captain in Guyenne in 1452–3 (Vale, 1970, 240). An alternative possibility is that Malory was in Sir Edward Grey's retinue; as we shall see, associations between the two recur later on. But perhaps those exist just because they both went to Bayonne. The Pulteneys are also associated with the Greys (Carpenter, 1980, Farnham *Village Notes* iii, 226; Warwickshire CRO, Ward-Boughton-Leigh papers, CR 162/227).

Gascon knights: Louis Despoy, Pierre Durant, Picot de la Rivière and Perrot de Bordeaux.

A royal warrant: PPC v. *c.*150.

Vicomte of Tartas: Chetwynd had taken the town. Its hereditary lord, the Sieur d'Albret, had declared allegiance to Charles VII.

PAGE 198 Mayor of Bayonne: Chetwynd-Stapleton, 1892. Bayonne was important strategically as well as as a port; it commanded both the River Adour and the road to the Spanish frontier.

'So good of his body': Malory, IV.18.

King Henry VI dubbed him knight: At this time the honour was usually
   bestowed either by the King, or a member of the royal family.
Grant by the Vicar: On 8 October 1441, the Vicar of Ansley, which is twelve miles
   from Newbold Revel, granted rights in land in his parish to a group of eight
   gentlemen (PRO E326/10717). Two of them were knights: Sir Edward Grey of
   Ruthin and Sir Thomas Malory, three squires (Robert Grey, Henry Fillongley
   and John Payne) and two gentlemen (William Tandy and William Brett). The
   witnesses were six Ansley men (Field, 1993, 84, from Vinaver, *Malory*, 121;
   William Burton, *History and Description of Leicestershire* (London, 1777) 279;
   and Nichols, *Leicestershire*, IV, 361).
Westminster, Sheen and Windsor: Wolffe, 1981, 363.

PAGE 199 Hertford Castle: Ibid., 94.
Whenever he was knighted: Sir Walter Scott, 1816.
'For that same day': Malory, VIII.7.
Parliamentary electors: PRO C219/15 Pt 1. The very large number (88) of electors
   suggests some dispute. The MPs elected were William Tresham (Speaker in
   the 1449 Parliament, murdered in 1450) and William Vaux.
Philip Chetwynd remarried: Field, 1993, 36; Wrottesley, 1891, 316–17.

PAGE 200 William Burley: *The Commons*, II, 432–5.
William Mountfort: see ch. 3 above. The other witnesses were squires, Hugh
   Erdeswyk, Thomas Standley and Ralph Egerton ('Chetwynd Cartulary', 316–17;
   for Erdeswyk, see *The Commons*, II, 29–31).
Henry VI had sent a letter: Thomas G. Williams (ed.), *Memorials of the Reign of
   Henry VI: the official correspondence of Thomas Bekynton* (London, 1872).
Best-organised French armies: Ordinances for a fixed tax to pay for a
   professional, well-organised standing army to replace the dreaded 'Free
   Lances' or *ecorcheurs* had been passed by the Estates General in October 1439
   (Ramsay, 1892, II, 18). Among the commanders of Charles VII's army in
   Gascony was Sir Pothon de Saintraille.
A relief force: Vale, 1970, 122–6; PPC V, 414.

PAGE 201 William Kerver: Royal official, and a member of the Mercer's
   Company (Anne Sutton, private communication).

CHAPTER 11
PAGE 202 'He is a noble knight': Malory, XVIII.18.
Wherefore, as meseemeth: Malory, VIII.3.

PAGE 203 'Cutted on the buttock': Peter Idley, *c*.1445, quoted in 'Fashion and
   Morality in the Late Middle Ages', in D. Williams (ed.), *England in the
   Fifteenth Century* (Proceedings of the 1986 Harlaxton Symposium,
   Woodbridge, 1987), 266.
Monastic tonsure: The analogy is made by T. H. White in *The Candle in the
   Wind*.

Astley's 'Great Book': G. A. Lester (ed.), *Sir John Paston's 'Grete Book'* (Brewer, Cambridge, 1984).

PAGE 204 Far from being in decline: See Beverley Kennedy, *Knighthood in the Morte Darthur* (Brewer, Cambridge, 1985), passim; J. Stratford (ed.), *The Lancastrian Court* (Proceedings of the 18th Harlaxton Symposium, Collins, 2000); Diana Dunn, 'Margaret of Anjou, Chivalry and the Order of the Garter', in *St George's Chapel, Windsor*, ed. C. Richmond and E. Scarfe (Windsor, 2001), 53.

Poor knight: Carpenter, 1980, 1992; Field, 1993. Inquiries on the death of Lady Elizabeth Malory in 1479 assessed her income at only about £30. Assuming this to be Malory's total income, Field, 1993, deduced that he suffered from financial insecurities and Carpenter, 1980, 1992, assumes him to be a 'poor knight'. However, IPM valuations were notoriously low, and the £30 was most likely to be merely Elizabeth Malory's visible dower. Enfeoffed assets would not show up though they will have been enjoyed by feoffees and/or the guardians of Sir Thomas's grandson Nicholas (whose father Robert died before his grandmother in the 1470s).

Assessed for £60: PRO E179/192/59 (see ch. 8 above).

Major actions of debt: The money demanded in the two suits mounted against him in the late 1450s was in total less than £8.

Lent money to his brother-in-law: Field, 1993, 84.

Buying it from him outright: See ch. 13 below. The loan to Helen and Robert Vincent could also have reflected the death of his mother, Lady Philippa, and his inheritance of her jointure. Burton gives two dates for Thomas Mallory in his pedigree, 19 H VI – i.e. 1 September 1440–31 August 1441 – and 27 H VI – i.e. 1 September 1448–9 – after which Malory took over Swinford in exchange for an annuity to Vincent and Helen – perhaps because Vincent was going to live at Warwick Castle, where he is found as Clerk of the Kitchens in the 1450s.

Fenny Newbold: The manor continued to be known by both this name and that of Newbold Revel until well into the middle of the fifteenth century (Field, 1993, 6, citing J. E. B. Gover (ed.), *The Place-Names of Warwickshire*, English Place-Name Society, 13, Cambridge, 1936), 120.

Rebuilt: Margaret Wood's *The English Medieval House* provides a cornucopia of options as to the original form of Newbold Revel, but only archaeological investigation will provide definite answers. Now that most scholars agree that Sir Thomas Malory of Newbold Revel was indeed the author of the *Morte Darthur*, perhaps a campaign should be mounted to persuade HM Prison Service to allow such an investigation to take place.

PAGE 205 Armorial panes: Dugdale, 83. A similar window made for Malory's contemporary John Norris survives at Ockwells Manor in Berkshire; it includes the arms of Henry, Duke of Warwick, and Sir John Wenlock as well as of Henry VI and his queen, Margaret of Anjou (Everard Green, 'Identification of the Eighteen Worthies commemorated . . . [at] Ockwells

[Berkshire]', *Archaeologia* 56 (1899), 323–9). See chs 12 and 23 below for connections between Malory and the Norris family.

Sir Peter Malory: His arms were originally described as three leopards, but heraldic terminology was updated and such leopards were described as *lions passant*.

Several Midlands churches: Monks Kirby, Coleshill, Stanford, Chilverscoton and Temple Balsall.

PAGE 206 His wife's name was Elizabeth: There is no mention of an Elizabeth of the right age in the Walsh pedigree, but there are other inaccuracies in it. If she were indeed Sir Thomas's wife, one would expect to see their arms impaled or quartered together somewhere. But the only near-contemporary quartering of the Malory of Newbold Revel's black-bordered ermine and red chevron is the one in Monks Kirby Church with the three black *lions passant* on a gold ground, the arms of Sir Peter Malory of Swinford and Winwick. Since the Revel arms are in the husband's position – first and third quarters – this could be a signal that Malory's wife was in fact a Malory herself – from a line distant enough not to require a papal dispensation. It is more likely that Malory was simply uniting two coats of arms that he himself was entitled to use. However, a woman who was not the family heiress did not necessarily have the right to use the family arms. Note that Lady Elizabeth could have been Thomas's only wife. If she was born in about 1405, she was not too old to have given birth to Robert, the son who survived to inherit, in 1447/8. Although incessant childbearing broke the health of many women, others thrived upon it, and gave birth to fifteen or more healthy children. There may have been fifteenth-century parallels to Elizabeth Mott, whose 1720 memorial in Monks Kirby Church records that she was married for forty-four years and had forty-two children. For female longevity, see also Rowena Archer's memorable article, 'Rich Old Ladies: The Problem of Late Medieval Dowagers', in A. J. Pollard, *Property and Politics* (Sutton, Stroud, 1984). Since the arms of whoever Sir Thomas's son and heir, Robert, married might also be expected to feature in the window, we might also settle for the idea that between them father and son married a Pulteney and a Walsh.

PAGE 207 To distinguish him: If he was indeed an adult, he could have been the Thomas Malory listed in the Lichfield register as Rector of Holcot, Northamptonshire, in 1452. A new rector was appointed there in 1458, which was the year Thomas Malory Junior died. However, although the episcopal register records Thomas as rector 1452–8, when I went to Holcot, a list of rectors in the church cites a John Malory as rector for that period. Maybe a local historian could solve this puzzle. A future Knight Hospitaller could easily have been a rector.

Daughters: One (later) pedigree records Philippa Malory as the daughter, rather than sister, of Thomas Malory (*Visitation of Warwickshire*, 1619, PRO Ward 2/1/32, C67/47m5, cited Field, 1993, 85).

Mention has already been made: See ch. 7 above.

PAGE 208 Detailed memorandum: PRO KB 9/265/78, m.3 (see ch. 15 below).
Richard Mallory of Radcliffe-on-the-Wreake: Richard was evidently a fighting
    man. He was pardoned in 1452 (PRO 67/40.30.31 Henry VI), and later entered
    the service of the Greys of Codnor (which reinforces my suggestion that
    Thomas once did so too); ties to the Grey family continued throughout his
    life.
Bowmaker called Thomas Marriot: Like Malory, Marriot was recorded as
    retained by Henry, Duke of Warwick in 1446.
Harpers in medieval times: See J. A. Burrow, 'Bards, minstrels and men of
    letters', in David Daiches and Anthony Thorlby (eds), *The Medieval World*
    (Aldus, London, 1973).
One manuscript illustration: BL Add. MS 10, 292, f. 200 (depicted in Edward L.
    Cutts, *Scenes and Characters of the Middle Ages* (Simpkin, Marshall, London,
    1926), 280). In this thesaurus of serendipitous medieval reference, Cutts calls
    minstrels 'The most dignified of the minstrel craft, the reciter, and often the
    composer, of heroic legend and historical tale, of wild romance and amorous
    song' (271).

PAGE 209 'An harper that hight Eliot': Malory, X.27.
And when Sir Tristram: Malory, X.31.
Entirely Malory's: See Vinaver's commentary on 627, ll 3–5, Malory, *Works*, 1484.

PAGE 210 Exquisite works of art: Thomas Wright, *History of Domestic Manners
    and Sentiments* (Chapman & Hall, London, 1862), 372, citing Bibliothèque
    Nationale no. 6748, a French *Lancelot* of this period which has an illustration
    showing a damsel taking her guests to admire the Arthurian tableaux in the
    hangings that line her chamber.
Feather bed: Still made today, these are deliciously soft and warm to sleep on, or
    rather in. You sink down into them, as if swaddled in a cloud.

PAGE 211 Rushes: Hardwick Hall in Derbyshire is still carpeted in a matting
    woven from rushes from Oulton Broad, Suffolk; its caretaker told me that
    they are incredibly hard-wearing and last for years; refreshed occasionally by a
    sprinkling of water, they have the scent of new-cut hay.
Books of his own: Over-elaborate theories have been put forward to explain how
    Malory got hold of the many different romances and histories that he used for
    his Arthuriad. Edward Hicks, who pictures Malory imprisoned continuously
    in London for twenty years, suggested that he used the library next door to
    Newgate at Greyfriars (see below, ch. 25, for a fuller exploration of this
    possibility). William Matthews, who proposed a Yorkshire Sir Thomas who
    has been proved to be imaginary, opined that Malory had the use of the
    Count of Armagnac's library while he was imprisoned in his castle at
    Castelnau in the late 1460s, but the discovery of a reference to Malory in
    Newgate in 1469 destroys this theory. R. R. Griffith, who plumps for the
    Papworth Thomas Malory as author, guesses that Anthony Woodville

inherited the Duke of Bedford's books, including those he had acquired from the French royal library, via his mother, Jacquetta, Bedford's widow. But there is no evidence of this. The person who did gain a great many of them was Cardinal Beaufort (Harriss, 1988, 364); Bedford sold off many others (Stratford, 1993). Apparently the celebrated bibliophile Charles of Orléans, a prisoner in England for twenty-five years, wept when he saw books from his grandfather's library on sale in Cheapside (Peter Field, private communication). He may well have reacquired many of them, as they now repose in the Bibliothèque Nationale. An example of an average-sized gentleman's library is that possessed by the London lawyer and chief baron of the Exchequer, Sir Thomas Urswick, in his Essex home of Marks when he died in 1479. It included Froissart's *Chronicles*, St Edmund Rich's *Speculum Ecclesiae*, Mandeville's *Travels* and a handsome copy of Chaucer's *Canterbury Tales* valued at £7 18s 11d (HPT draft biography of Urswick, 2004, 21). Urswick was certainly wealthier than Malory, but such a collection could easily have been afforded by a middling-well-off knight with literary interests.

Sir Richard Roos: Karen Cherewatuk, '"Gentyl" Audiences and "Greate Bookes": Chivalric Manuals and the *Morte Darthur*', *Arthurian Literature* (1997).

PAGE 212 Literacy was widespread: According to Charles Kingsford, 'far from being an age of illiteracy, the fifteenth century was one of marked educational progress . . . No person of any rank or station above mere labourer seems to have been wholly illiterate. Wives and sisters of country gentlemen could often write as well as their husbands and brothers and both they and their servants could and did keep regular household accounts' ('English Letters and the Intellectual Ferment', in C. L. Kingsford, *Prejudice and Promise in Fifteenth-Century England*, Frank Cass, London, 1962, 34–5).

Initiative, persistence and cash: Anne Sutton and Livia Visser-Fuchs, 'Choosing a Book in Late Fifteenth Century England and Burgundy', in Caroline Barron & Nigel Saul (eds), *England and the Low Countries in the Late Middle Ages* (Sutton, Stroud, 1995), 72.

The commonest texts of all: 'ateliers in Ghent and Bruges had a profitable line in mass-producing cheap books of hours for foreign markets, including, and perhaps especially, England': ibid., 79; for books of hours see also Duffy, 210–25.

Chronicles and romances: 'A number of romance miscellanies include historical writings [providing] evidence of the congruence of interests in Arthurian fiction and a partisan view of history' (Felicity Riddy, *Sir Thomas Malory*, Leiden, 1987, 14–24). Riddy summarises their didactic emphasis as 'good manners, right conduct, claims for the next world and the British past'.

PAGE 213 Had Astley's book copied: Lester, 1984, 61; A. I. Doyle, 'William Ebesham', BIHR, 1956–7.

'Almeries': Malory, XVII.23.

The *Morte Darthur* itself has been seen: Cherewatuk, 'Gentyl Audiences', 1997, using the categories in 1985.

Wherever their owner happened to be: Describing the plainness of a transcription of a collection of chivalric texts made by the Scottish knight Sir Gilbert Hay for William Sinclair, Earl of Orkney in the 1450s, Cherewatuk (ibid.) writes: 'One gets the clear sense that Hay's volume might well have been carried into battle by the Chancellor Earl'.

PAGE 214 Edward IV's wardrobe accounts: Richard Firth Green, *Poets and Princepleasers* (Toronto UP, 1980), 91, 94.

Special chairs: Christopher de Hamel, *Scribes and Illuminators* (British Museum Press, London, 1992).

Lead weights: If you read folio books in Oxford's Duke Humfrey's Library, you are still provided with just such weights.

Tickling your chin: Peter Field, private communication.

Ink: De Hamel, *Scribes and Illuminators*.

PAGE 215 Botley: Field, 87 SBT MS DR 37 Box 50/2938; other witnesses were Sir Thomas Erdington (who was also a witness for Philip Chetwynd with Malory, and would later be, like Malory, a member of the 1445 Parliament).

PAGE 216 Litchborough: Virtually nothing is known of this branch of the family between 1403, when Giles Malory was county Sheriff, and 1467, when the widow of John Malory of Litchborough sued for restitution of documents from feoffees. Some of the Malorys in France are likely to be from Litchborough.

East Anglian cousins: As explained in endnotes to the Introduction, Field, 1993, 8–10, convincingly refutes R. R. Griffiths's case for Thomas Malory of Papworth St Agnes as the author of the *Morte*.

Distraint of knighthood in 1465: HPT list of distraints, Thomas Maulery of Cambridgeshire. This new discovery is arguably conclusive elimination of the East Anglian candidate.

Annuity: Malory received part of the Stretton tithes from Axholme Abbey, which owned the Priory of Monks Kirby and acted as lord of the parish of the same name, in which Newbold Revel lay. According to Carpenter, 1992, 178, 'he was quite literally reaping the rewards of a political connection, as the abbey fed him.' Tithes were valued enough commodities to be sources of conflict.

Gey: *Sic* – though it could be a misprint by a scribe for Grey.

PAGE 217 'A presentable office': John Skynner to Sir William Stonor, Eric Acheson, *A Gentry Community: Leicestershire in the Fifteenth Century, c.1422–c.1485* (CUP, 1992), 110. Eustace's brother Thomas Burneby was in high favour at court at exactly the time of the fracas with Smith: he was granted an annuity of 20 marks from Henry VI only a month later, in November 1443 (CPR [1441–6], 221). Smith was a very common name, so it is probably not significant that in June 1451, a Thomas Smith was accused of being one of the murderers of William de la Pole, Duke of Suffolk. Or that he was examined by the Duke of Buckingham and then freed without punishment. Buckingham was one of the commissioners examining him, in Kent (Carol Rawcliffe, *The Staffords, Carls of Stafford and Dukes of Buckingham 1394–1521* (CUP, 1978, 78; Roger Virgoe, 'The Death of Suffolk', BJL XLVII (Manchester, 1965), 501–2).

CHAPTER 12

PAGE 218 Largesse engenders: Quoted Green, 1980, 12.

The driving force: Ian Arthurson, *The Perkin Warbeck Conspiracy 1491–1499* (Sutton, Stroud, 1994), 2.

Harry, 14th Earl of Warwick: and 1st (and only) Duke of Warwick: b. 22 March 1425; succeeded to title 30 April 1439; of age, March 1426; d. June 1446. I have used Michael Hicks, 'The Beauchamp Interregnum 1439–1449', BIHR 72 (1999); also 'The Beauchamp Trust 1439–87', BIHR 54.30 (November 1981); John Watts, *Henry VI and the Politics of Kingship* (CUP, 1996, 1999) and Bertram Wolffe, *Henry VI* (1981), to inform this chapter, but I have gone much further than such authorities in extrapolating from the facts the view which follows on Harry Beauchamp's personality and importance.

'A person of extraordinary hopes': This and all Rous quotes below from Charles Ross (ed.), *The Rous Roll, John Rous* (Sutton, Gloucester, 1980). Salisbury paid 4,700 marks, the largest marriage portion of the century, for his daughter Cecily's marriage to Harry Beauchamp (Brindley, 2001, 32).

Favourite companion: Carpenter, 1992, 413 n.53, for grants and presence at royal council meetings. Sir William Mountfort and Sir Thomas Erdington, whose names recur in connection with Malory, were prominent members of both Harry's household and that of the King.

PAGE 219 Force to be reckoned with: Griffiths, 1981, 298, 315; Watts, 1966, 1999, 196–7; H. R. Castor (OUP, 2000), *The King, the Crown and the Duchy of Lancaster*, 266.

Thomas Portaleyn: HPT draft biography, Simon Payling, 2001.

Attractive and knowledgeable mentor: Few details of Harry's household survive, but Malory's name appears in a list of retainers who continued to be paid until his death.

Oliver La Marche: Green, 1980, 74–5.

PAGE 220 Translating the Arthurian stories: Although well-educated young nobles could of course read in French, it was increasingly seen as both fashionable and patriotic to speak and read English.

Sir Gilbert Hay: Quoted Coleman, 1996, 211.

Hanley Castle: Toomey, 1997.

PAGE 221 Magnet for Italian humanists: 'Duke Humfrey and English Humanism', catalogue of an exhibition, Oxford, 1970.

Illegitimate children: Edward IV also had an illegitimate son called Arthur. Henry VII went further – he called his first legitimate heir Arthur.

The Fall of Princes: On the borders of folio one are the arms of Cecily Neville and her next husband, John Tiptoft, but in the centre are the arms of her first husband, Henry Beauchamp.

Fine-boned: A pair of Henry VI's remarkably small boots and his gloves were preserved as relics by a Cumbrian family, the Pudseys (Hookham, 1872, 205).

'Reciting the whole psalter': Committing the 150 psalms to memory might seem unlikely, and the cynical will assume that 'greater business' did often prevent it. But the pious normally attended several religious services a day, and learning by heart was a standard juvenile accomplishment right up to the twentieth century. Equally impressive feats of memory were claimed for the prodigiously bright daughter of Fanny Thrale in the late eighteenth century.

Crusade against the Turks: Ross, 1980. See Field, 1993, 80–2, for Malory's fondness for crusading references.

PAGE 222 A charter Henry VI signed: Hicks, 1999, 38.

One of the small and exclusive band: In 1445 the Angevin ambassador Antoine de la Salle called the English 'the most ceremonious people in matters of decorum that I have ever seen'. Green, 1980, 18.

Duke of Buckingham: Griffiths, 1981, 358. In May 1447 he was given precedence over all other dukes except York.

Mighty duke: Malory, I.1. I have omitted the words 'of Cornwall'.

'Fat and full of grease': Quoted in Rawcliffe, 1978.

'Blatantly partisan': Helen R. Castor, 'The Duchy of Lancaster in the Lancastrian Polity, 1399–1461', unpublished PhD thesis, Cambridge; Castor, 1993, 265.

PAGE 223 Maxstoke Castle: Buckingham exchanged two of his Northamptonshire manors (Whiston and Woodford) for the Clintons' Maxstoke; Sir William Mountfort's mother was a Clinton. Since 1599 Maxstoke has been in the possession of the Dilke family. They also acquired Kirkby Mallory from the Abbey of Leicester after the Dissolution of the Monasteries. Details: C. B. and M. C. Fetherston-Dilke, *A Short History of Maxstoke Castle and its Owners* (privately published, n.d., *c.*1980); Geoffrey Tyack, *Warwickshire Country Houses* (Phillimore, Chichester, 1994): 125–9; engraving of east front, 125; drawing of exterior of banqueting hall, 126.

PAGE 224 Atherstone: The Abbot of Coombe, Richard Atherstone, may have had connections with Atherstone.

Open conflict: One incident parallels one of Malory's misdemeanours: just after the death of Richard Beauchamp, Grey presided over the indictment of Beauchamp retainer John Cotes who had, until then, got away with grabbing compensation in the form of a flock of sheep from Richard Hotoft, who had been holding back his inheritance from him; Hotoft was retained by both Buckingham and Grey. The Duke of Buckingham held the manor of Atherstone from 1438 but it was 'resumed by Act of Parliament 1451'. Staffordshire CRO D.641/1/2/273m.2; commission to assess tax (CFR

[1445–62], 36). Carpenter's favour with the King is reflected by the fact that he was one of the first bishops to be consecrated in the new chapel of Eton College.

The sheriffs from 1444–6: Carpenter, 1980, 404, for the seduction of Beauchamp supporters.

Petition: PRO C1/15/78, printed in Baugh, 1933, 19. The date is discussed in Field, 1993, 91–3. Alternatives are the second half of 1449 or between July 1452 and March 1454. If the incident took place before June 1446, 'my lord of Warwick' would have been Harry Beauchamp; if after July 1449, it would have been the new Earl of Warwick, Richard Neville. Field argues that the Malory attack could have taken place in 1452, but Sir Thomas was then so beleaguered with other accusations that this seems unlikely. Archbishop John Stafford died in 1452. Although the two petitions from Lady Peyto are on separate pieces of parchment, the handwriting is identical and the form of address to the Chancellor is exactly the same – except that in the petition against Malory and accomplices she describes herself as 'your bedeswoman': a conventional phrase, used either to importune a favour of the Chancellor, or offering to pray for his soul. Lady Peyto's petition to the Archbishop refers to the bailiff assaulted by Malory as 'your man' at Sibbertoft. It was natural for her to mount the action as Sibbertoft was a Stafford manor she held in dower from her first husband and after her death it would revert into the Stafford family.

Peyto: *The Commons*, IV, 67–8.

PAGE 225 Will clash again: In 1454 Peyto was brought to book and jailed for beating up Thomas Hathwyck (who will emerge as one of Malory's most faithful friends) in 1451.

'Sore punish them': E.g. the violent measures taken by Thomas Portaleyn and other members of Beauchamp's affinity to oust the Prior of the alien Priory of Goldcliff, the advowson of which had been granted to the Abbot of Tewkesbury by Henry VI in furtherance of Harry's mother's will. This incident echoes Malory's attack on Peyto and foreshadows his reported aggression towards the alien Priory of Monks Kirby (see ch. 15 below). Interesting too, at this time, as a parallel to the later rape accusations against Malory, is the abduction in Highgate of Portaleyn's wife-to-be by one William Gargrave in September 1445 (all details from HPT draft, Portaleyn).

Very similar attack: Carpenter, 1980, 35.

Thomas Burdet, John Rous and Thomas Throckmorton: They were all well-established with the Beauchamps and guardians of the estates.

Archbishop Stafford: Only a distant kinsman of Buckingham, but family mattered in the fifteenth century, and he was close enough to the Duke to share the hunting rights to Caluden with him. The outcome of the case is not known, but later incidents (see ch. 20 below) suggest that the feud was an enduring one. Peyto's service in France in 1443 in company with a Richard Malory (PRO E101 54/5 17 July 21 HVI) may be related to the incident.

PAGE 226 Duke of Suffolk: 1396–1450. Details from C. L. Kingsford, 'Policy and Fall of Suffolk', in Kingsford, 1962.

Commissioned a biography: *Tito Livio Foro-Iulensis Vita Henrici Quinti*, ed. T. Hearne, Oxford, 1716.

PAGE 227 Triumphalist monument: The chapel's statuary includes Saint Denis, patron saint of France, and the imperial crown.

Accused of sorcery: The case against the Gloucesters was the more damning in that they were known to be good friends of Joanna of Navarre (Vickers, 1907; R. R. Griffith, 'The Trial of Elinor Cobham', Bulletin of the John Rylands Library LI (1969). Gloucester had insisted on freeing her chaplain Randulph, despite the fact that he was supposed to be a sorcerer.

Interest was widespread: See Hughes, 2002, passim, and 34 for Elinor Cobham.

PAGE 228 Devastating humiliation: Shakespeare makes the most of it in *Henry VI Part II*, although his play is a wonderful historical muddle, keeping the 13th Earl of Warwick, Richard Beauchamp, who died in 1439, alive throughout and making Queen Margaret of Anjou, who only came to England in 1445, the instigator of Elinor's fall.

'Then there was made': Malory, VII.34.

Margaret of Anjou: My sources include Mary Ann Hookham, *The Life and Times of Margaret of Anjou* (London, 1872); J. J. Bagley, *The Ardent Queen: Margaret of Anjou, Queen of England* (Peter Davies, London, 1948); Helen E. Maurer, *Margaret of Anjou: Queenship and Power in Late Medieval England* (Boydell, Woodbridge, 2003); Patricia-Ann Lee, 'Reflections of Power: Margaret of Anjou and the Dark Side of Queenship', *Renaissance Quarterly* 39 (1986), 183–217.

PAGE 229 Maine: The return of Maine to Margaret's father René, who had been its count before it was conquered, was already being quietly discussed, and the Beauforts soon traded their lands there for more secure estates in Normandy.

Somerset returned unfêted: Somerset's death (27 May 1444) was a little mysterious, although he was said to have been in poor health. Suicide was rumoured, but the only cause on record is that he was gored by a bull (N. H. Nicolas, *A Chronicle of London 1189–1483* (London, 1827).

Sir John Astley: Astley was a kinsman of the Astleys of Wolvey Astley, ten miles from Newbold Revel. He was married to Sir Robert Harcourt's sister Elizabeth and was the most famous jouster of his generation, fighting exhibition bouts against Pierre de Massy in Paris in 1438 and Philip Boyle of Aragon at Smithfield in 1442. He acted as an arbitrating authority at jousts and tournaments on several occasions in the 1440s and 1450s (Dugdale, *Warwickshire*, I, 106–7).

Acknowledged European expert: R. Rudorff, *The Knights and Their World* (Cassell, London, 1974), 223–4.

PAGE 230 *Livre de Cueur*: The story of Cueur was written in about 1457, and illustrated in the 1460s, at a time when Margaret had returned to her father's domain and taken refuge at his Lorraine castle of Koeur. It would have been an appropriate present for his daughter, and its illustrations are believed to portray her and other members of René's family and affinity (F. Unterkircher (ed.), *Le Livre de Cueur d'Amours Espris* (Thames & Hudson, London, 1975).

PAGE 231 Unpaid wages: Sadly for the needy Sir William Peyto, it was ten years before these grants were fully honoured.
The negotiations: Watts, 1999, 222; Wolffe, 1981, 183.

PAGE 232 Royal blood: Somerset had precedence over Norfolk on account of his blood relationship with the King in 1443; for the same reason, Holland had precedence in January 1444 over all except York.
Isle of Wight: *Warwick Castle and its Earls*, 134, which also says Henry VI made Beauchamp Warden of the Forest of West Brere, Ranger of Wychwood Forest, Captain of the Forces of the States of the Church (perhaps a reference to the crusade idea) and Lieutenant-General in the Duchy of Aquitaine. If this last was true, it would explain Dugdale's reference, but I have found no other mention of it.
High Peak: The Winwick lands held in fee of Peveril might have been acquired by Malory from Duke Harry. Peveril was held by Sir William Hastings in the 1460s.
Immense territorial power: 'Such a step – the hereditary grant of a major Duchy office – was absolutely unprecedented . . . It is inconceivable that Buckingham could have been expected lightly to accept the alienation of [the Staffords'] stewardship to a 19-year-old rival' (Castor, 1993, 267). See also H. R. Castor, 'New Evidence on the Grant of the Duchy of Lancaster Office to Henry Beauchamp, Earl of Warwick, in 1444', *Historical Research* 68, 1995.

PAGE 233 Richard of York met her in Paris: Holinshed, *Chronicle*, 207.
William Ayscough: Griffiths, 1981, 256.
Imposing anthology: BL Royal MS 15 E VI. One coroneted young figure in its frontispiece could be a portrait of Harry Beauchamp. For signatures of owners in it, see Anne Sutton and Livia Visser-Fuchs, 'A most beautiful queen', *The Ricardian* 10 (1994–6), 228–30. See, further, André de Mondach, 'L'anthologie chevaleresque de Marguerite d'Anjou', *Actes des Vie Congrès International de Societé Rencesvals pour l'étude des épopées romances* (Aix-en-Provence, 1974).

PAGE 234 'Excuses ceasing': *Brut*, 489, quoted Bagley, 1948, 47.
Retainer to Buckingham: Mountfort had stood surety for John Malory in 1413, and either he or a son of the same name was listed as a squire on the 1414 Calais muster roll on which Thomas's name appears. But he was now more attached to Buckingham's affinity. The cause of this changed loyalty was a family quarrel. Sir William had five sons and several daughters, but he was determined to disinherit his oldest son, Baldwin, in favour of his two younger brothers, Robert and more particularly Edmund, the son of his second marriage, who was a rising star in the King's household. Buckingham obligingly imprisoned Baldwin in the dungeons of his castle at Maxstoke until he agreed

to sign away all his claims to inheritance as oldest son. In exchange, Mountfort left his estates to Edmund and his heirs, with the reversion to Buckingham if Edmund had no heirs. Buckingham continued the *quid pro quos* by proposing Mountfort (unsuccessfully) as a Knight of the Garter in 1450.

One of its first measures: Hookham, 1872, 243.

PAGE 235 It enacted: *Statues of the Realm*, ii, 342 (23 H VI c14); P. J. C. Field, 'Sir Thomas Malory, M.P', IHR 47 (1974), 27. An earlier instance of an attempt to influence an election occurs in 1441, when Malory was one of no less than eighty-eight electors who met to decide on the MP for Northamptonshire (PRO C219/15 Pt 1 and see ch. 10 above).

Assisting with the entertainment: *Warwick Castle and its Earls*, 134.

PAGE 236 'Well beloved': Cecil Monro (ed.), *Letters of Queen Margaret of Anjou* (Camden Society, 1858), 90–1.

PAGE 237 Secretly written: Wolffe, 1981, 185.

Greater variety of books: For further details of Malory's sources, see Vinaver's commentary, *Works*, 1262–3. Terence McCarthy writes that 'Malory was an expert linguist, and we must not imagine that he plodded laboriously through the *Lancelot-Graal*. On the contrary, he was in control of his materials and fully equipped to move around freely in the vast folios of Old French finding material suitable for his own vision of Arthurian history [at a time when] there were no translations, grammars, dictionaries or cribs of any kind for him to use' ('Malory and His Sources', Archibald and Edwards, eds, 1996). See also E. D. Kennedy, 'Malory and his English Sources', in *Aspects of Malory*, ed. T. Takamiya and D. S. Brewer (Brewer, Cambridge, 1981); Riddy, 1987; R. Barber, '*Vera Historia*', in *Arthurian Literature*.

PAGE 238 More reliable: P. J. C. Field, 'Malory's Minor Sources', in Field, 1998. It has been suggested that it was Malory himself, rather than Caxton, who made the late revisions to his text which drastically reduced 'The Tale of King Arthur and the Emperor Lucius' from the sixty pages of the Winchester manuscript to the twenty printed by Caxton, thus cutting down its heavy debt to the English alliterative *Morte Arthure*. Intense debate continues on Malory's sources and the relation between the Caxton and Winchester texts: see Field, 1998, passim.

'Favour of makers': Malory, XXI.13.

PAGE 239 Malory may have experimented: P. J. C. Field, 'Malory and *The Wedding of Sir Gawaine and Dame Ragnell*', in Field, 1998. Even more convincing evidence of joint authorship are numerous lines in both bemoaning the long imprisonment of the author.

Word-plays: It is probably going too far to point out that two of Malory's villains, the ruthless rapist Sir Breuce Sans Pitié and Sir Pynelle le Sauvage, the poisoner of Sir Patrice, share enough letters of their names with Buckingham and Peyto for them to be identified with them according to Seaton's methods.

But cryptological study of medieval texts would be worth undertaking: see Arthurson, 1991, for the extent of interest in codes and ciphers.

PAGE 240 Prime suspect: 'The young courtier Warwick was being promoted largely at the expense of Buckingham, who seven years earlier had received a life grant of the Tutbury offices ... It is inconceivable that Buckingham could have been expected lightly to accept the alienation of [the] stewardship to a nineteen-year-old rival' (Castor, 1993, 267). Carpenter also believes that Buckingham protested strongly at being replaced by Beauchamp (Carpenter, 1997, 414).

Harry replaced him: CPR (1441–6), 480.

'Alas,' said Sir Lancelot: Malory, XXI.8.

CHAPTER 13

PAGE 242 The main sources for this chapter are Griffiths, 1981; Vickers, 1907; Hicks, *Warwick the Kingmaker*; Paul Murray Kendall, *Warwick the Kingmaker* (Allen & Unwin, London, 1957); Wolffe, 1981; Watts, 1999.

'Jakkes and salades clene': Jackets (padded doublets) and helmets; 'clene' may mean they bore no identifying crest; 'ought': anything.

'Ended abruptly': See *Proc. & Ord.* PC, volume VI, 40 onwards.

Some sort of breakdown: A treason trial in 1447 centred on a disparaging reference to the King's mental state.

PAGE 243 Annuities were restored: PRO E368/220/107–8.

PAGE 244 Placed in the care: Hicks, 1998, 32.

Alice Chaucer: Previously married to (1) Sir John Philip, who died when she was only eleven; (2) the great military commander Thomas Montacute, Earl of Salisbury, who was killed during the 1429 siege of Orléans.

Ewelme: Alice inherited it through her mother Matilda Burghersh after her father Thomas Chaucer's death in 1434. It is also possible that another of Suffolk's wards was growing up at Ewelme, the three-year-old Margaret Beaufort, heir of John, Duke of Somerset, and eventually grandmother of Henry VII.

As its fifteenth-century builders left it: A licence to build the almshouses was given to William de la Pole on 3 July 1437; their style suggests that workmen came from the Duke's chief manor of Wingfield, Suffolk. The foundations were also laid of a grammar school to teach local children 'freely without exaction of any school hire'; it is still a school today. *Guide to Ewelme Church*, 17. See also J. A. A. Goodall, *God's House at Ewelme: Life, Devotion and Architecture in a Fifteenth Century Almshouse* (privately printed, Aldershot, 2001).

Tewkesbury Abbey tomb: Only the shell of the exquisite chantry chapel survives. The style of Isobel's tomb was specified in her will and is described by antiquaries.

PAGE 245 Warwickshire commission of JPs: Carpenter, 1992, 408: CPR
(1436–41), 592; (1441–46), 480. Thomas Burneby was given lands in Chartres
by the Duke of Bedford in 1421, a time when Wenlock was Constable of Vexin
(Massey, *Land Settlement in Lancastrian Normandy*). For Jane Carew, see
Monro, 1863, 96–7 – Burneby went to Scotland with the Queen in 1461 and
died in 1463.

Sir Robert Harcourt: Details here and below from HPT draft biography, L. S.
Clark, 1995. The Queen's Knights were an élite chosen by Margaret herself;
Guinevere had a similar band.

PAGE 246 Sir Thomas Erdington: See chs 10 and 11 above.

Swinford lands: Field, 1993, 84. The Vincents held in their own right at Swinford
– this acquisition could mark an increase in size of Malory's original Swinford
estates. Lawsuit: PRO KB27/750 m.48d, Field, 1993, 94. The accused failed to
appear in court, and a year later, on 9 October 1449, Harcourt and Malory
repeated the suit, again with no known result. Walsh/Byron marriage: CFR
(1447–54), 108.

Born some time in the twenty-fifth year: Sir Thomas Malory's IMP (PRO C140/
36/12) says Robert was '23 and more' on 6 November 1471.

Robert . . . in Rome: PRO e135/6/53, 'Admission of William Cecil, Margaret his
wife and Robert Mallorre to the confraternity of the hospital of Holy Trinity
and St Thomas the Martyr, Rome 1448'.

In Warwickshire: Castor, 1993, confirms that Buckingham had lost interest in
Staffordshire. His purchase of Maxstoke was probably the start of a shift of
focus. See also Carpenter, 1980, 1992, passim.

PAGE 247 Might well have been there: One of the men named as involved in the
fray was 'John Aleyn, yeoman, of Stanton Harcourt'; it is a common name,
but a John Aleyn went to France with John Malory in 1444 (see ch. 11 above)
and a John Aleyn was linked with Malory in 1453. The court records say that
Harcourt was committed to the Marshalsea after his outlawry was annulled in
1452, but he was in fact free. This supports my belief that Malory's
imprisonment during the next decade may have been less continuous than has
been thought. One of the men who stood bail for Harcourt, Walter Blount,
was a feoffee for Malory; another, William Vernon, may have been the man of
that name excepted from pardon with Malory in 1468.

PAGE 248 'And for I understand': Malory, X.58.

Critical ballad: 'Advice to the Court', 1450, BL Cotton Rolls ii, 23, printed in
Historical Poems of the XIV and XV Centuries, ed. R. H. Robbins, Columbia
UP, NY, 1959, 203–4.

PAGE 249 In the confessional: Referred to in the contemporary poem 'Examples
of Mutability' (Bodleian Library MS Rawlinson C.813, Robbins, 185).

Edmund Mountfort: HPT draft biography, Simon Payling, 2004.

Rumours: Watts, 1999, 231; Isobel Harvey, *Jack Cade's Rebellion of 1450*
(Clarendon Press, Oxford, 1991, citing KB 9/256, m.13).

Duke of York: There is no record of York being at Bury before 26 February. Gloucester was arrested on 18 February and was dead by 23 February. He was still at Fotheringhay until 26 January at least. Duke Humfrey's chantry chapel survives, albeit without his effigy, in St Albans Cathedral.

Cluster of new grants: R. A. Jackson, *Duke Richard of York 1411–1460* (Clarendon Press, Oxford, 1988).

PAGE 250 Sir John Cheyne: Field, 1993, 159; see also *The Commons.*

Cardinal Beaufort: Harriss, 1988.

Great expectations: Their dreams were fulfilled, though probably not in the way they most hoped for. Their older brother John's daughter Margaret Beaufort was first in line, but she was a vulnerable child. In fact, she proved astonishingly resilient, surviving childbirth at the age of no more than fourteen – when she gave birth to Henry Tudor, the future Henry VII.

PAGE 251 Short chronicle: M. L. Kekewich, Colin Richmond, Anne F. Sutton, Livia Visser-Fuchs, John L. Watts (eds), *The Politics of Fifteenth-Century England: John Vale's Book* (Alan Sutton for Richard III and Yorkist History Trust, 1995), 115.

Malory knew Vale: Anne F. Sutton, 'Malory in Newgate: A New Document', *The Library*, 7th series, I.3, September 2000. See ch. 23 below for Malory's sympathies with Vale and his attitudes. See also Raluca Radulescu, '*John Vale's Book* and Sir Thomas Malory's *Morte Darthur.* A Political Agenda', *Arthuriana*, 9:4 (1999), 69–80.

A mere merchant: De la Pole, a wealthy Hull merchant, was ennobled by Edward III, but memories for lineage were long.

PAGE 252 Our king: Malory, X.61.

Attended her requiem mass: As did Anne's mother Cecily, pregnant by then with Tiptoft's child. Cecily herself died in childbed a year later; the child also died. Heartbroken, Tiptoft soon left the country to make a pilgrimage to Jerusalem (vividly described in Mitchell, 1965); he did not remarry for seventeen years.

Sir Richard Neville: Warwick's father was also called Richard Neville; he became Earl of Salisbury in 1429 in right of his wife.

PAGE 253 'There was nothing': Hicks, 1998, 6.

'In such favour': And following quotes: *Hall's Chronicle.*

PAGE 254 Incompleteness of the records: Anne F. Sutton and Livia Visser-Fuchs, *Richard III's Books* (Sutton, Stroud, 1997), 30.

Continuity: Hicks, 1998, 49. The fact that Warwick was called on to arrest Malory in 1450 and in 1451 but did not do so on either occasion may be a hint that he was, if not his good lord, his well-wisher.

Pride was the keynote: Geoffrey Richardson, *The Lordly Ones: A History of the Neville Family and their Part in the Wars of the Roses* (Baildon, Shipley, 1998), passim. It is an indication of the importance Warwick attached to his family's honour that in 1461 he asked Parliament to revoke the condemnation of his great-grandfather John Montagu, 3rd Earl of Salisbury, for treason against Henry IV (Montagu had supported Richard II).

Enjoyed chronicles: Sinclair, 2003, 14.

Barbarically splendid: Kendall, 1957, 187.

Flemish treatise: See Sutton and Visser-Fuchs, 1997.

PAGE 255 'I promise you': Malory, VIII.12. See also Radulescu, *'John Vale's Book'*.

PAGE 256 By rights: George Neville was son of Elizabeth, Lady Abergavenny, Elizabeth Despenser's daughter by her first husband, Richard Earl of Worcester.

Henry rewarded him: Hicks, 1998, 29, citing CPR (1446–52).

CHAPTER 14

PAGE 57 When lords' will: Trinity College, Dublin MS 516, f. 115r, printed in Robbins, 1959, 121 (modernised by me). The main new narrative source for this chapter is Harvey, 1991.

'As the world goes': William of Worcester, *The Boke of Noblesse*, ed. J. G. Nichols, Roxburghe Club, London, 1860, cited by Keen, 1996, 183. Churchmen had much less to lose from reform than the nobles on whom Henry VI had over-generously bestowed lands he should have kept for his own needs. See also Sutton and Fisser-Fuchs, 1997.

PAGE 258 'Heart of a lion': Kendall, 1957; see also GEC, 282 ff.

Money was urgently needed: In 1449 the king's debts and forward commitments amounted to the horrendous sum of £372,000. To make matters worse, the Hanse fleet and the Duke of Burgundy threatened to ban English cloth from markets under their control. The court knew that they needed all the friends in parliament they could muster in order for generous taxes to be voted to the King (Harvey, 1991, 59; Ramsay, 1892, II, 102).

A forum for the expression: See Peter Booth, 'Men Behaving Badly', in Linda Clark (ed.), *Fifteenth Century, 3: Authority and Subversion* (Boydell, Woodbridge, 2003), 96. Writs were sent out on 23 September 1449 for a November assembly (Carpenter, 1992, 265: 'knights of the shire were elected by acclamation in the shire court, and to be able to control this gathering was an acid test of a magnate's local influence').

PAGE 259 Thomas Ferrers: Sheriff, 1447–9. He was much wealthier than Carpenter, 1992 (which describes him as a loser) allows for, and ended up as a Yorkist (Acheson, 1992).

William Catesby: He was related to Talbot, Earl of Shrewsbury, and was his executor in 1453. Knighted by the King in 1452; he did become close to Warwick but not until the 1460s, it seems. His son chased after Malory papers in the 1480s (Carpenter, 1992, passim; Field, 1993, 128, 135–6).

Robert Arderne: HPT draft biography, Simon Payling, 2002. It is possible that

Arderne had more right on his side than he has been credited with; his guardian had been the ruthless Joan, Lady Abergavenny, and much of his property may indeed have been illegally disposed of during his minority. He makes an interesting parallel to Malory; he too seems to have had powerful enemies.

PAGE 260 Great Bedwyn: a village twenty-five miles north of Winchester. It was a convenient halfway house on the road to Oxford, where Waynflete founded Magdalen College and its school.

William Waynflete: Waynflete's influence on borough elections: Virginia Davis, 'William Wayneflete and the Wars of the Roses', *Southern Review* 11 (1989), 6.

Thomas Welles: of Twyford, Hampshire (HPT draft biography, Linda Clark, 1994). Note that according to R. R. Griffith, the MP for Great Bedwyn was not Sir Thomas Malory of Newbold Revel but his Cambridgeshire namesake and distant cousin Thomas Malory of Papworth St Agnes, who held some of his lands of Buckingham and who served as a mainpernor in 1451 with a previous incumbent of the Great Bedwyn seat, Thomas Humfrey. But Field, 1993, 95–6, thinks this is unlikely. It is true that Malory's knightly status is not mentioned, but such omissions did occur when placemen were planted in pocket boroughs; e.g. Sir Henry Ilcombe represented Cornwall in 1388 and 1395, and then sat as a burgess for Lostwithiel in 1402 and 1407. In 1402 he was called 'dominus Henricus Evelcombe, miles' on the return, but in 1407 his rank was omitted (*The Commons*, III, 472–4). I am indebted to Linda Clark for this reference.

PAGE 261 Richard Malory: He went on to study at Oxford. Malory follows French and English Arthuriads and folk legend in locating Camelot at Winchester. John Hardyng is the earliest written source to locate Camelot at Winchester: 'The round table at Winchester began, / And there it ended, and there it hangest yet' (quoted by Hughes, 2002, 168). The fact that the Round Table hung there in the fifteenth century suggests that the identification of Winchester with Camelot was by then an accepted piece of folklore. The table remains there to this day. There is some dispute over its actual age. The archaeologist Martin Biddle, author of *King Arthur's Round Table* (Boydell, Woodbridge, 2000), believes that it was made for the great Arthurian tournament which Edward I held at Winchester in 1290 to celebrate the marriage of three of his children. Six months were spent preparing the castle for the occasion. A special tournament field was created outside it, and the castle hall was extensively renovated. However, radiocarbon dating tests (which Biddle argues may not be reliable) say that it dates from the reign of Edward III. Edward III certainly planned to re-found the famous Arthurian chivalric Order of the Round Table in the 1340s, but it eventually took shape as the Order of the Garter. In 1486 Waynflete baptised Henry VII's first son Arthur in Winchester Cathedral, in a font surrounded by tapestries woven with stories of the Knights of the Round Table. In 1468 both Waynflete and

Malory were implicated in the Lancastrian conspiracy which led to Malory's second spell of imprisonment.

'Utterly ruined': Anne Curry, 'The Loss of Lancastrian Normandy', in D. Grummitt, *The English Experience in France 1450–1558* (Ashgate, Aldershot, 2002), 4. The Duke of York also lost vast estates (see M. K. Jones, 'Somerset, York and the Wars of the Roses', *EHR* 104, 1989), 285–307. Other details below from Harvey, 1991.

PAGE 262 Bishop Moleyns: There had been widespread rumours that Moleyns had been bribed by the French to agree to the surrender of Maine when he was negotiating the King's marriage in 1445. Everybody knew that he had gone to France in 1448 to oversee the unwilling withdrawal of the English garrisons from Maine.

Over 75 per cent: My calculation from *Proc. & Ord. PC* Vol. VI passim.

PAGE 263 Armed poachers: Harvey, 1991, 121.

'Never a knight': Malory, X.2.

They were accused: PRO KB 9/265/78; reprinted Hicks, 1928, Appendix, 104. See also A. C. Baugh, 'Documenting Sir Thomas Malory', *Speculum* 8 (1933), 3–6. The warrant issued for Malory's arrest in March 1451 probably concerned this ambush; it extended to Appleby and eighteen others (unnamed).

'Trust not': Malory, VI.25.

PAGE 264 Thomas Ferrers: Helen Castor, *The King, The Crown, and the Duchy of Lancaster* (OUP, Oxford, 2000), 281.

Legally aggressive: Rawcliffe, 1978, passim. Forty-two were poachers and six were debtors.

Old crony: Rawcliffe, 1978, passim. Buckingham held the manor of Atherstone from 1438 but 'resumed by Act of Parliament 1451' (Staffordshire CRO D/164/ 1/2/273 m.2).

PAGE 265 Strong enough: Churches had long been built with the dual purpose of house of worship and village fortress – their towers were lookouts and vantage points for archers and their stone buildings more easily defended than most people's houses. For general lawlessness and abuse of the law, see Griffiths, 1981, 128–53. Gresley was a close friend of William Blount, soon to be a prominent Yorkist (E. Madan, *The Gresleys of Drakelow*, Oxford, 1898).

Contemporary lampoon: Bagley, 1948, 65.

PAGE 266 Placed in the Tower: Rumour had it that it was the Queen's idea to house Suffolk in the Tower for his own protection; it is significant that scurrilous criticism of Margaret was now frequently being voiced (Bagley, 1948, quoting Escouchy, I, 303–4).

French invasion: An interesting sidelight on the importance of river travel; Wallingford is on the Thames 90 miles upstream of London.

'The Duke of Suffolk is pardoned': *Paston Letters*, ed. J. Gairdner (Edinburgh, 1910), 4 vols, I, 115.

PAGE 267 Uprisings all over England: Waynflete's palace was plundered in Winchester, although the Bishop was not one of the King's advisers condemned as corrupt; rebels were probably undiscriminating after a few hogsheads of wine.

Golden coronet: Hicks, 1998, 44.

Arrived to attend: *Paston Letters*, I, 127.

PAGE 268 One of the lewdest: Quoted J. R. Lander, *Wars of the Roses*, 39 (Sutton, Stroud, 1990), ed. Gairdner.

A letter from the Earl: *Notes and Queries* (128, V, May 1919), 120.

'Marvellous good men of their hands': Abilities of Thomas Malory's men deduced from names and occupations in the 1451 Nuneaton indictment (Baugh, 1933).

PAGE 269 Manifesto: BL Cotton Roll IV 50, printed Harvey, 1991, Appendix A.

'Who daily and nightly': A striking echo of the last lines of Sir Thomas Malory's 'noble and joyous book of King Arthur', when he declares himself 'the servant of Jesu both day and night' and begs him to help him 'for his great might'.

PAGE 271 'Men of Cheshire': Harvey, 1991, 84.

Dispirited men: 'rendered aimless and disaffected by what they saw as a gross mismanagement of affairs in France . . . were a blight which brought the loss of France home to inhabitants of the south of England in a very immediate fashion' (Harvey, 1991, 131).

Cade was listed: His pardon was said to have been granted at the request of the Queen, interesting confirmation of Margaret's political influence – and guile.

CHAPTER 15

PAGE 273 'What,' said Sir Lancelot: Malory, VI. 10.

Charles VII's Commander-in-Chief: In 1449 Saintraille had entered Rouen at Charles VII's side and carrying his sword in 1449 (*Paston Letters*, I, ed. Gairdner, 139). The Rouen garrison included Somerset and Talbot.

Return from Ireland: York had written to his brother-in-law the Earl of Salisbury in June saying that he would have to return because so few supplies had been sent to him that 'my power cannot stretch to keep it in the king's obeisance, and very necessity will compel me to come into England, to live there on my poor livelihood. For I had liefer be dead than that any inconvenience should fall thereto by my default.' Poor livelihood was over-modest from the richest noble in the country, though it was a timely if unsubtle reminder that the Exchequer still owed him thousands of pounds for his efforts in France. Quotes and details here and below from Paul Jackson, *Duke Richard of York 1411–1460* (Clarendon Press, Oxford, 1988).

PAGE 274 William Tresham: Roskell, 1981, III, 150. Edmund, Lord Grey's men were said to be behind the attack. It was paralleled in another attack, licensed by Buckingham, on Walter Blount's Derbyshire manor of Elveston in 1454,

when it was alleged that 'Walter Blount has gone to serve traitors' and his coat
of arms was symbolically torn into four quarters.
York protested: Wolffe, 1981, 243; Johnson, 1988, 85.

PAGE 275 John Mowbray: Lucy Ellen Moye, 'The Estates and Finances of the
Mowbray Family, 1401–1476', DPhil thesis, Duke University, Durham, NC,
1985; J. R. Lander, *Government and Community 1450–1509* (Edward Arnold,
London, 1980).

Thomas Malory took his seat: His knightly status was omitted in the electoral
return, as it had been at Bedwyn. For reasons why it is again unlikely that
Thomas Malory of Papworth St Agnes was the candidate; see Field, 1993, 95–6
and 98–9.

Overlord . . . was the Duke of York: Johnson, 1988, 87.

PAGE 276 One of the six heirs of Joan of Kent: PRO C139/66/43.

'Listed as held by the Duke of Norfolk': CIPM, IV, 316. But it is possible that
Norfolk was already Malory's overlord, and simply directed him to support
York. In 1438 Cardinal Beaufort and Sir Simon Felbrigg, the only surviving
feoffees of Mowbray's father, recovered lands which reverted to him on the
death of Constance Holland, which could have included Newbold Revel. The
lands were not made over to the new Duke, who had come of age in 1436,
until June 1445 (Harriss, 1988, 363, citing CCR [1435–41], 149; CPR, 223; CPR
[1429–36], 603; PRO C140/5; IPM return for John, Duke of Norfolk, 1461).

York arrived: This and other details from *Six Town Chronicles of England*, ed.
R. Flenley (Clarendon Press, Oxford, 1911), 137.

PAGE 277 Chamberlainship of the Exchequer: Wolffe, 1981, 244.

Thomas Greswold: He married Christiana, daughter and co-heir of William
Hore of Solihull; his son John married Margaret, daughter of Henry Bromley
and Christiana's sister and co-heir, Alice; there also seems to have been a
Thomas Greswold of Kenilworth who was one of his feoffees. He had holdings
in Worcester and London but primarily in Warwickshire. For Sir Robert
Malory's dispute with Greswold ('Essex Cartulary', 1444), see ch. 9 above.

Relentless malevolence: See below, chs 17–20, passim. It was only after
Greswold's death in 1458 ('Political Society in Warwickshire *c*.1401–72', PhD
thesis, Cambridge, M. C. Carpenter, 1976, Appendix) that Malory succeeded in
extricating himself from his eight-year-stint in and out of London prisons.

PAGE 278 Custody of the dower: Hicks, 1998, 47, 77.

Henry returned to Westminster in triumph: Kingsford, 1905, 162–3.

'No sovereign' on earth: Quoted Watts, 1999, 60.

PAGE 279 'A warrant for the arrest: Baugh, 1933, 6–7, citing PRO KB 29/83 m.3;
Field, 1993, 99.

Two later . . . accusations: See Nuneaton indictment below.

PAGE 280 West Country: Ramsay, 1892, II, 146.

East Anglia: *Paston Letters*, ed. Gairdner, vol. 1, no. 173.

Potentially allies of the King: Hicks, 1998, 76.

Another warrant: Baugh, 1933, 6, citing Controlment Roll, Michaelmas, 1451.

PAGE 282 William Smith: A man of this (very common) name was a tenant of John Hathwyck of Herberbury at Oxhill (SC 12/16/37 – pedigree of Hathwycks and rents for Oxhill).

In distraint of unpaid rent: Unproveable, but it is interesting that CCR (1429–35), 314, reveals that in December 1433 John Malory 'of Newbold Revel' granted rent of twelve pence and three capons to three Cosford men. It may also be relevant that Dugdale records that Herberbury was a manor co-owned by Coombe Abbey and the Malorys and that John Malory 'of Co. Leics' (possibly a kinsman from the Tachbrook Malory branch of the family) held a manor there of the fourth part of a knight's fee (CPR.10 Henry VI (1432)). For John Hathwyck's indictment of Nuneaton on the same day as Malory, see below.

Complaints about its predatory behaviour: Hicks, 1928, 49–51.

Unusual writs: Henry V had been asked to include the cause of the summons in the writs but had refused. Their vagueness was what made them so effective. Then, as now, the law was dense with technicalities. Failure to observe absolutely correct procedure in the serving of an ordinary writ, or making assertions that could easily be disproved, was the ruin of many a promising case for the prosecution.

Complaints about them increased: Whittick, 'Role of the Criminal Appeal'.

Another seven years: Despite the expiry of the statutory period, the use of these potent writs continued under Edward IV, 'by which time they were such an essential part of government that the king could not do without them' (John Bellamy, *Crime and Public Order in England in the Later Middle Ages*, Routledge, Toronto, 1973).

PAGE 283 Maxstoke Castle: In the 1450s, Buckingham kept Sir Baldwin Mountfort incarcerated there until he signed away his rights to the Mountfort inheritance.

Coleshill Manor: A Tudor house was built on the site of the old one, within the same moat. Colin Hayfield and Andrew Watkins (*Coleshill and the Digbys: 500 Years of Manorial Lordship*, Arley, Warwickshire, 1995) give medieval details and mention local dislike of Edmund Mountfort after he grabbed the manor in 1452.

PAGE 284 'Wild wood': 'And when Sir Lancelot awoke of his swoon, he leapt out at a bay window into a garden, and there with thorns he was all to-scratched in his visage and his body; and so he ran forth he wist not whither, and was wild wood as ever was man.' Malory, XI.8.

'Great baulks of wood': This and other details from Nuneaton indictment PRO KB 9/265/78, m.3; Hicks, 1928, 93–7. Although the indictment seems to refer to two separate attacks on Coombe Abbey, the first is in the preamble to the full catalogue of Malory's offences, and the second is in fact just a fuller account of the incident, though described as happening on the next day. In all likelihood, only one attack took place, starting late at night on Wednesday, 28 July and ending at dawn the next morning. The need for recording it as two accusations may have been the result of testimonies describing the same incidents being suspiciously different.

PAGE 285 The Abbey's own shortcomings: KB 27/756 for complaints against the monks of Coombe.

Richly textured life: Cora L. Scofield, *The Life and Reign of Edward IV*, 2 vols (Longmans, Green, London, 1923).

As bad a reputation: John Whalley of Coventry complained that he had entered into a tenancy with a 'comoigne' (lay brother) of Coombe, only to have his property raided and valuables removed a year later when the Abbot claimed he was not the lawful tenant, and tenants of the Queen of Brinklow (which bordered on Newbold Revel) complained in Chancery that the Abbot refused to pay his share of the royal taxes due on lands they held in common with the Abbey. The records show Coombe frequently in dispute with its neighbours: the Astleys of Wolvey Astley, the Starkeys of Stretton-on-Dunsmore, and William Purefoy of Shelford, who was either Malory's uncle or his first cousin. Richard Hotoft of Wolston complained that on 4 June 1440 the Abbot, six monks and other men broke into his property and did damage and stole goods worth £40.

Gone to law: With disastrous consequences: a warrant of sub-poena was issued to summon Atherstone to Coventry, but the Abbot did not turn up; instead he and his lawyer ran a counter-suit against Joan in the Court of Arches without her knowledge. It led to her being imprisoned for sixteen days. Pluckily, the Shaws then petitioned Chancery against the Abbot for defamation of Joan's good name. The result is indecipherable, but since the Chancellor was Archbishop Stafford, a kinsman and known associate of Buckingham, their success is doubtful.

Ramsay Abbey: Visitation in 1439 by Bishop Alnwick; see Hicks, 1928, 48.

PAGE 286 Potentially incriminating documents: The reason the fascinating Lisle Letters survived to give us a rich social picture of the 1530s is that they were confiscated in an indiscriminate mass when the authorities were hoping to prove treason and adultery against Arthur Plantagenet, Lord Lisle, in 1540. The Stonor Letters were probably also confiscated, when Sir William Stonor was attainted in 1484. *Lisle Letters*, ed. Muriel St Clare Byrne, Secker & Warburg, London, 1983; Kingsford, 1913, 208–9; see also C. L. Kingsford, *Stonor Letters and Papers*, 2 vols (Camden Society, 3rd Series, 29–30, London, 1919).

John Bale: See ch. 7 above for description of Malory as an eminent historian.

PAGE 287 *Register de Cumba:* Hicks, 1928, 47. It may be significant too that Richard Atherstone was replaced in 1454. But we are unlikely ever to know the truth. When the Abbey, like almost all other monasteries in England, was closed down in the 1530s, its records and monuments were dispersed or destroyed. Its buildings were adapted into a spacious house by the Craven family, and a Palladian façade was added at the end of the eighteenth century. Elements of its great medieval heritage remain. Like Newbold Revel, it still has a medieval kernel; also preserved are the cloisters through which Malory and his turbulent retinue once tramped, and its moat. Today Coombe Abbey is a country house hotel with a real pride in its history. Medieval banquets are regularly held there, so you can quaff mead and eat 'marinated ribs of swine' at 'the Baron's Borde' while damsels dance, minstrels warble and hooded monks loom in the shadows.

Personal friend: Margaret of Anjou had suggested to the Priory a few years earlier that they should choose 'our right wellbeloved' Dame Maud Everingham as their new prioress; her brother was a King's Knight. Nuneaton had no courthouse and I have found only one other record of a court being held there. Hicks, 1928, suggests that the chapter house of the Priory was the most likely place for the court; Michael Hicks (private communication) suggests the main hall or the refectory. Alternatives would have been the Priory church itself, the parish church of St Nicholas, the manor house or the market hall. The Queen's letter still exists, one of many that show how quickly Margaret had understood the power she could wield by patronage (Monro, 1863, 163–4).

'Indictment': PRO KB 9/265/78, m.3.

PAGE 288 His presence in court: Malory's defiant protests are on record when he appeared in court in London.

Twenty-six 'malefactors': Baugh, 1933, gives a detailed description of the men accused with Malory and follows up their fates. They were not in court at Nuneaton: most were tried in 1452 in absentia and outlawed for failing to appear. Their names and occupations give a window into the realities of Malory's world which I have used passim and especially in ch. 11 above.

PAGE 289 John Hathwyck: Baugh, 1933, 20; Carpenter, 1976, 198, 293, Appendix, 151; Carpenter, 1980, passim; J. C. Wedgwood History of Parliament: Biographies, 1936, 235.

William Smith: PRO SC 12/16/37.

Systematic campaign: See Carpenter, 1992, 272: 'The rise in status of the commission may indicate a growth, obscured from us, in the use of indictment and removal to King's Bench in the course of litigation . . . The commission was changing . . . from a professional administrative gathering to a body with real political muscle.' Anxious to prevent vindictiveness against his supporters, York offered to sit on judicial commissions himself, but was told tartly, 'When need demands, or necessity compels, we will invoke your aid.'

More covert retribution: Christopher Whittick, 'The Role of the Criminal Appeal in the Fifteenth Century', in Law and Social Change in British History, ed. J. A. Guy and H. G. Beale (Royal Historical Society, London, 1984).

Harassed by lawsuits: Examples include William Tyrell who fought in France for the Duke of York, and was MP for Weymouth, a York pocket borough, in 1450. He was accused of involvement in Cade's rebellion, but gained a pardon at the Queen's request in July 1450. He was indicted again in 1452 for assembling during the rebellion, and it was alleged that 'he would be captain in Essex' and had called for the deaths of lords close to the King. He said the claims were 'malicious' and surrendered himself to the Marshalsea Prison in June 1454. He was bailed by his brother, and was acquitted a few weeks later during York's Protectorate (HPT draft biography, CEM, 2001); John Bellers, MP for Leicester, an exact contemporary of Malory, a feoffee of his neighbours the Fieldings, and a veteran of the French wars, was sued 'with surprising frequency for a man of his status' in the late 1440s and early 1450s for incidents very similar to those of which Malory was accused. The family was a cadet branch of the Mowbrays; like Malory, Bellers was not favoured by Henry VI's household, but was at heart loyal to the King, lying low under Edward IV, suing for pardon in 1468 and taking office when Henry VI returned in 1470. He was removed again after Edward IV's restoration. Ralph Shirley's manor was attacked by the Longfords in 1450; his kinsman Hugh Shirley sat as MP for Leominster in 1450 (HPT draft biography, Simon Payling, 1996); John Vernon was aggressively pursued by the Exchequer to account for his father's term as Treasurer of Calais, and the Duke of Buckingham acquired the principal part of a manor he claimed, 'effectively ending Vernon's claim'; on 4 November 1452 Vernon offered surety for the good behaviour of a squire implicated in York's February rising (HPT draft biography, William Vernon); Baldwin Mountfort, soon to be estranged from his father Sir William, was imprisoned by Buckingham at Maxstoke to force him to surrender his right to inherit, and was feed by York (Rawcliffe, 1978, 78).

PAGE 290 Appeals and outlawries: Baugh, 1933, 18. For corrupt commissions, see Carpenter, 1992, 264: 'a commission [of JPs] could be suborned either to make untrue indictments or to refuse to entertain indictments for crimes that had undoubtedly incurred'.

Knight of the Garter: On 26 May 1452 Henry VI, perhaps prompted by the Queen, gave the Duke of Norfolk £200 and a gold cup in recognition of his 'good services'. R. L. Storey, *The End of the House of Lancaster* (2nd edn, Sutton, Gloucester, 103, citing PRO R404/68 no. 109).

CHAPTER 16

PAGE 292 Then Peace entered: Langford (*c.*1330–*c.*1400), quoted in Henry Ansgar Kelly, 'Statutes of Rapes and Alleged Ravishers of Wives: a Context for the charges against Thomas Malory, knight', *Viator* 8 (1997). Kelly is an important source in this chapter; other sources are the Latin text of the Nuneaton indictment (PRO KB 9/265/78, m.3); its abbreviated English translation in Hicks, 1928, Appendix; the Latin texts of most of the other accusations against Malory, printed in Baugh, 1933, 3–29; J. B. Post, 'Sir Thomas West and 1382 Statute of Rapes', BIHR 53, 1980; Kelly, 1997; Whittick, 1984; John Bellamy, *The Criminal Trial in Later Medieval England* (Sutton, Stroud, 1998); Corinne Saunders, *Rape and Ravishment in Medieval England* (Brewer, Cambridge, 2001).

'Then the king': Malory, *Works*, 119–120.

PAGE 293 Upon pain of death: The mention of the death penalty echoes the 1419 regulations issued in France by Henry V to his troops.

According to Sir Walter Scott: 'Essay on Chivalry', 1816. Whether such an extreme punishment was often meted out may be doubted.

PAGE 294 'The charge of "raptus"': Hicks, 1928, 53.

Another version: KB 27/762, m.52d (Baugh, 1933, 6).

PAGE 295 Tom Shippey: 'Dark Knight', review of P. J. C. Field's *Life and Times of Sir Thomas Malory, London Review of Books*, 24 February 1994, 22–4.

Felicity Riddy's literary critique: *Sir Thomas Malory* (Leiden, 1987).

'A violent, adventurous man': Hughes, 2002.

PAGE 296 Carried out . . . by the woman herself: A Kent 'eyre' of 1314 decreed that the victim should tear out her attacker's eyes and 'coupe ses botons'.

PAGE 299 Knighted the following year: He was wealthy enough to do so because he had, ironically, inherited a substantial amount of property as his older brother died without issue.

One citation, in 1409: Kelly, 1997, 1410, citing Yearbook of 11 Henry IV Michaelmas Term (1409).

Research into gaol delivery: Edward Powell Kingship, *Law and Society: Criminal Justice in the Reign of Henry V* (Oxford, 1989).

PAGE 300 1453 . . . statute: Kelly, 1997, 374–5.

PAGE 301 'It is possible': Kelly, 1997, 361–419. Carnal knowledge is not explicitly spelt out in his appeal, nor is the word felonious included. Indeed, since there is no specific date for the record either, it could even have been referring to a third incident. No companions are mentioned in the second incident in the Nuneaton indictment, which is distinctly odd.

PAGE 302 Smiths of gentry status: John Malory had dealings with the Smiths of Yelvertoft in the 1410s (PRO E40/6084: 'Grant by William Smyth of Yelvertoft, to John Mallory of Neubold, John Atteyate, rector of the church of Cleycotes, Stephen de Waldegrave, and Thomas Smyth of Yelvertoft, clerk, of all his messuages and lands &c. in Yelvertoft, and of all his goods. N'ham Wednesday before Holy Cross', CPR.7 Henry IV). For other Smiths, see Carpenter, 1992, 274, 666, 694. John Smith, Coventry lawyer, was a JP in 1459; he or his son were later in the affinity of Grey of Groby.

'Twenty shillings': Armstrong, 1983, 70. A Hugh Smith witnessed Gerard

Braybrooke proving his age at Bedford in 1415; the Thomas Malory who was probably our hero's uncle was associated with Braybrooke in 1403 (Field, 1993, 58). By 1501, Easenhall, a manor recorded earlier as belonging to the Malorys (Dugdale, *Warwickshire*, I, 55), was the home of a John Smith.

PAGE 303 Bernangle: Now Barnacle. Richard Recheles of Bernangle held commission to collect taxes in 1446. The Vincents held at Barnake (Bridges and Whelley, 1791). William Weston came from the Lincolnshire branch of the family, who were living in Boston by the late fifteenth century (*Visitations of Surrey*, Harleian Society, 43, 7). William Weston was a Winchester scholar until 1412, when he left to become a scholar of New College (T. Kirby, *Winchester Scholars* (London, 1888)). A Knight Hospitaller by 1460 and Commander of Ansty in Wiltshire from 1470, he died in the mid 1480s. He is buried in Ansty Church. A Thomas Weston was preceptor of Dingley in 1420–1, where he stayed until the mid-1450s.

Barwell: Acheson, 1992, 181 refers to Lord Gray of Ruthin having free warren at Barwell, and Alan Moton (the Motons held at Stapleton-juxta-Barwell, as well as at Peckleton, a few miles to the north-west) helping himself to £20 worth of game from it (Farnham, *Village Notes*, I, 140).

Had granted part of their estates: Mallory-Smith, 1958, 3, citing Nichols; defined as 4 virgates of land (*c.* 120 acres in Farnham, *Village Notes*, I, 147).

PAGE 304 'Ill-wishers': Buckingham repeated his dubious legal manoeuvre at Nuneaton against Simon Mountfort in 1456. Simon was indicted for an abduction allegedly perpetrated the previous May. The sessions were presided over by Buckingham, Birmingham, Bate, Boughton and Littleton. It was after this that Simon and his father Baldwin were incarcerated until they agreed to give back the lands they had just got back from Edmund during York's Protectorate. The court's decision was later reversed.

When every lusty heart: Malory, XVIII.25.

PAGE 305 'For to be a wedded man': Malory, VI.10.

PAGE 306 'Shall I be spoken of': Malory, XII.11.
'This Meliodas': Malory, VIII.1.

PAGE 307 To take my pleasaunce: Malory, V.10.
'Shall not be happy': The idea that promiscuity hampers success in the field was not universally held in Malory's age. The great French general Marshal Boucicault asked, 'Who can be brave without love? Indeed, no one. Love banishes fear and instils bravery, making one forget all pain and willingly perform the labours that he undertakes for the one he loves ... Thus one reads of Lancelot, of Tristan, and of many others whom love brought to the attainment of goodness and renown. Likewise, living in our own time there are many such nobles in France and elsewhere whom we have seen and yet see; thus one speaks of Othe de Granson, of the good Constable of Sancerre, and of many others whom it would be long to name, and whom the service of

love made valiant and virtuous' (*The Book of the Deeds of Marshall Boucicault*, quoted in Benson, 1976, 154).

'Jesu defend me!': Lancelot's condescension considerably outranks in insensitivity Eugene Onegin's notorious admonition to the lovestruck Tatayana: 'Learn to show some self-restraint'. And off he goes, pleased with himself for his generosity, no doubt. When he next sees Elaine, she is dead, lying in a richly caparisoned barge that has made its ritual journey from Guildford, near Astolat, to Westminster, where Arthur's court is meeting. In an ironic twist, Guinevere, normally intensely jealous of any woman who loves Lancelot, reproaches him for not treating her more kindly.

PAGE 308 For like as winter: Malory, XVIII.25.

PAGE 309 One literary critic: Kennedy, 'Adultery in Malory', 1997, 78–99.

PAGE 310 'Many privy draughts': Compare this usage to the reference to Guinevere's wounded knights being laid on beds 'within draughts' around her room (Malory, XIX.6). Kennedy, 1997, argues that draughts mean corridors or paths. But Field says it is a false word division; Winchester has 'in wythdraughts', i.e. in 'withdrawings' or recesses.

PAGE 311 'Now shall I prove my might': Malory, XIX.6.
'If thirteenth-century French': Kennedy, 'Adultery in Malory' (1997).

PAGE 312 After a hundred and ten knights: At this point Malory gives us a magnificent march-past of almost the entire cast of his book, plus enough new characters to fill an equally long one: 'Sir Degrave Saunce Velany [without villainy] that fought with the giant of the black lowe [hill] . . . Sir Lamiel of Cardiff that was a great lover . . . Sir Marrock the good knight that was betrayed by his wife, for she made him seven year a werewolf'.
Forthwith all the wounds: Malory, XIX.12.

CHAPTER 17
PAGE 313 'So God me help': Malory, VIII.12.
'To judge noble peacebrokers': Wolffe, 1981, 251–2.
Writ *certiorari*: A writ issued from a superior court because a party has complained that he has not received justice in an inferior court. 'The use of a chancery writ indicates that the plaintiff was responsible for removal, and was eager to lift the indictment out of a local context to Westminster, where an adversary's influence would be more expensive and difficult to exert': Whittick, 1984.

PAGE 315 The original four feoffees: Field, 1993, 127, citing Nichols' *Leicestershire*, IV, 362; PRO KB 27/900 Rex rot.5–7. Henry Sharp was a canon lawyer (Anne Sutton, private communication). The change in feoffees (referred to in KB 27/900 rot.5–7) could have been made any time up until 1461 when Blount was knighted.

Or suffer outlawry: Fifteen of Malory's men, including Appleby, the three Sherd brothers, his harper and his cook, who failed to give themselves up, were in fact outlawed at the Warwick sessions on 21 August 1452.

PAGE 316 He declared himself: 'He said he was not in any wise guilty thereof, and for good or for ill he puts himself upon his country' (Hicks, 1928, 107). This was a plea of innocence, a standard move, even in cases of obvious guilt. But Malory had the legal right to refuse to plead at all, in which case he could not be tried. However, if he did not plead the justices could keep him in prison as long as they liked. Unfortunately, as we shall see, they intended to do that anyway: he was handed back to the sheriffs for safe custody 'quosque &tc una cum causis &tc'.

Richard Malory . . . a pardon: PRO C67/40 30–31 HenVI [1452].

Caluden: Frank Roden's *Coventry: Echoes of the Past* (Coventry, 2001) says it went to the Berkeleys after the Lancastrians took over, and that they restored it. If so, it could have been brought to the Beauchamps during Countess Isobel's lifetime, i.e. until 1439.

Rented by Buckingham: The arbitration refers to Norfolk and his servants and tenants. Malory may have had a habit of hunting there. See Barbara Hanawalt, 'Men's Games, King's Deer; Poaching in Medieval England', *Journal of Medieval and Renaissance Studies* 18 (1988), 175–93.

Would have been specified: Details were perhaps being saved for the trial, but the fact that the case was settled out of court with a much lower surety penalty confirms that the accusation was an exaggerated one.

PAGE 317 Cunning legal purpose: The plea was of contempt and transgression against the form of the first statute of Westminster concerning malefactors in parks and ponds. This and other legal details from Ralph Pugh, *Imprisonment in Medieval England* (CUP, 1968).

Distraint: 'Ordered that Thomas Malory be distrained of all his goods' (Hicks, 1928, 107, citing Coram Rege Roll, 2 February 30 Henry VI).

PAGE 318 Sir William Oldhall: He was accused by Walter Burgh, a knight in the King's household, of organising the robbery of Somerset's goods at Blackfriars in November 1451; he would later be accused of plotting the death of the King on several occasions.

Private war . . . in Somerset: Between the Earl of Devon and Sir William Bonville; details Johnson, 1988; Griffiths, 1981.

Terrible quandary: Quotes from Storey, 1986, 95.

PAGE 319 Formal accusation: It concerned Somerset's misgovernment of the war itself and misappropriations of the £70,000 granted as compensation for those who lost lands in Anjou and Maine.

PAGE 320 Robert Arderne: HPT draft biography, L.S.C. (1994). Arderne was involved in a rising in Kent led by a Warwickshire man called Wilkins, a saddler from Stratford-on-Avon. Malory might well have sympathised with

Arderne; he had served in France with his father, and was probably only about nine years older than Robert.

PAGE 321 Hopes . . . were high: Wolffe, 1981, 262–3.

'Were compelled': Keith Dockray, *Henry VI, Margaret of Anjou and the Wars of the Roses: A Source Book* (Sutton, 2000), 61.

PAGE 322 Perhaps in Ludgate Prison: Custody by the Sheriff normally meant confinement in such city prisons as Ludgate or the Compter. As Malory was accused of felony, it is a little surprising that he was not imprisoned in Newgate. Ludgate, London's oldest gate, just south of Newgate and a stone's throw from the west front of St Paul's, was decorated with images of King Lud, the Celtic King for whom the city was named. It only became a prison in 1382, and was for debtors rather than felons and traitors. Ordinances for its management were issued in 1439. It may have been at a low ebb in the 1450s, as 'of pitie for the poor prisoners' it was much improved and enlarged in 1463, thanks to a bequest from a wealthy London widow, Dame Agnes Forster (Stow, 1603, passim).

Little hardship: He would not, for example, have been in chains. The 'ironing' of freemen was forbidden in 1431 (Margery Bassett, 'Newgate Prison in the Middle Ages', *Speculum XVIII*, 1943).

Well-connected prisoners: The well-wishers who stood surety for him were eminent men. They included not only Warwickshire neighbours but also former companions-in-arms from the French wars, fellow parliamentarians, wealthy Londoners and distinguished supporters of York, Norfolk and Warwick. Thomas Burneby, a Queen's Squire, may also have brought influence to bear.

'It is most necessary': Chrimes, 1942, ch. 53.

Minor misdemeanours: See Maurice Keen, *English Society in the Late Middle Ages 1348–1500* (Penguin, London, 1990), ch. 8, 'Aristocratic violence: from Civil Strife to Forcible Entry' for the ordinariness and frequent untruth of such accusations.

PAGE 323 Malory knew enough: 'When Malory depicts the law, he depicts historically sound legal practice . . . [justifying] legal punishment by inserting statements not in his source and by specifying appropriate punishment' (Edward C. York, 'Legal punishment in Malory's *Le Morte Darthur*', *English Language Notes*, September 1973, 14–21).

Mysterious fire: *c.* 1453–4 (Pugh, 1968, 109).

Riot at Newgate: See below.

Financially buoyant: His heirs inherited the same estates as he did.

Imprisonment in any sort of comfort: See Bellamy, 1973, and Bassett, 1943–4.

Land deal: It involved his brothers-in-law Thomas and Eustace Burneby. Together with Malory and three others, they were feoffees for William Malory of Saddington; the new deal granted some of William's property to John Pulteney, Thomas Cotes of Honingham and Simon Broke, Clerk (Leicestershire CRO DE2242/6/6).

Sheriffs of London: Stow, 1603, II, 174. 'The King's Bench Marshalsea seems originally to have been a form of custody rather than a place' (Pugh, 1968). There was another Marshalsea Prison, pertaining to the Marshal of the King's Household, a hereditary office held by the Duke of Norfolk. They were 'distinct institutions, although they were side-by-side in what is now Borough High Street in Southwark' (Field, 1993, 107). The Marshal of King's Bench at this time was John Gargrave, a king's squire who had been indicted for corruption by Cade's rebels in 1450. Another 'Gargrave in the Tower' appears in Kingsford, 1913, 365. Gargrave was later imprisoned in Ludlow Castle by York, which suggests that he would have had a deputy to do his work as marshal for him.

PAGE 324 Robert Overton: Baugh, 1933, 26–7.

Coleman Street: Stow, 1603, I, 277.

Arbitration: PRO KB 27/764 m.; between 52d and 54d. Sixty shillings happens to be the exact amount required of a prisoner as a quittance fee – something which Malory may not have been prepared for when the good news of the arbitration was announced.

Thomas Bourgchier: He and Warwick had been among those who negotiated between York and the King at Dartford in February 1452. He was also one of the nine arbiters chosen to settle the quarrel between York and Somerset. Bourgchier and his brother would support York and Warwick once the die of rebellion was cast. He rose to eminence in the Protectorate and became Archbishop of Canterbury after the death of Cardinal Kemp in March 1454. Bourgchier was later among the arbiters who settled the Mountfort dispute in favour of Sir Baldwin rather than his brother Edmund, who was backed by Buckingham.

PAGE 325 Judgement by Christmas 1452: There is no record of the decision of the arbitration, nor do we know that it was actually delivered at Christmas.

Advowson: Benjamin Thompson, a historian of medieval religion, confirms that holding the advowson would make Norfolk personally concerned with the attack on Coombe. It is worth noticing that after Norfolk dies in 1461, Malory reappears free. It is even possible that a dispute over the overlordship of Newbold Revel was behind Malory's attack on Coombe.

'And he that was courteous': Malory, XXIII.24.

The court granted Malory bail: Carpenter, 1992, passim; NB: letter from Warwick to his 'entirely well-beloved cousin, Ferrers', thanking him for sending men to support the King against the Kentish rebels in 1450 (*Notes and Queries*, May 1919, 120). Thomas Ferrers had enough faith in York to make him his feoffee in November 1452 (CPR44 [1454–61], 324).

Thomas Ince: CPR (1452–61), 196: 33 HVI pt 1 memb 18 (1454), and ibid., 205: 33 HVI pt 1 memb 12, item 8 (1455). The sister of Lady Baskerville was married to Sir William Herbert, a royal lieutenant of York.

William Cecil . . . in Rome: PRO E135/6/53. See above, ch. 13.

PAGE 326 The Leventhorpes: See their HPT draft biographies, L.S.C. (2002).

Marshal of the Marshalsea: As hereditary Earl Marshal of the household, Norfolk chose the Marshal of its Marshalsea (prison).

Kindly man: L.S.C. (op. cit.) tells the story of how Leventhorpe prevented a 'false priest' called Robert Colynson, perhaps a paedophile, from assaulting a boy in a tavern.

PAGE 327 Hearing set for 20–26 January: the Controlment Roll says that on that date in January, when we know Malory wasn't there, the case was postponed until quindene of Easter, then to octave of Michaelmas, when he did turn up.

Bond in £200: 31 HVI 1452, in CCR (1447–54), 396; Field, 1993, 109.

PAGE 328 No acknowledgement: Most have one on the same day.

Also Keeper of Westminster Palace: Margery Bassett, 'The Fleet Prison in the Middle Ages', *University of Toronto Law Journal* 5 (1943–4), 383–402.

Thomas Barton: SC11/818. He was probably not the Lyme Regis MP and Household man of the same name (HPT draft biography, M.P.D., 1998).

Sir Thomas Burgh: He was Anne Neville, Duchess of Buckingham's surveyor after Buckingham's death, a time when most of her councillors were prominent Yorkists because her new husband was Walter Blount.

John Walsh: CPR (1452–61).

PAGE 329 Buckingham's affinity: Moton's cousin Archbishop Stafford and Edward Grey, a reliable crony, were both Moton's feoffees. One cause of the interminable delays and postponements of Malory's case may have lain in the personnel of any juries who did make the long journey from Warwickshire to Westminster. When Malory denied the crimes he was accused of, the process of the law required that '24 good and lawful men of the neighbourhood of the vill where the deed was done, who are related to the accused by no affinity, and each of whom has a hundred shillings of land or rents, to certify to the judges as to the truth of that crime'. Any one of the twelve good men and true could be objected to by either defendant or prosecutor. In addition, the jurors had to have incomes of at least 40s a year and four of them had to be from the hundred where the offence had taken place. Fortescue explains that if jurors were found to have made a false oath, a defendant could take out a writ of attaint against them. If it was proved, they were imprisoned, their 'lands confiscated, possessions seized, houses and buildings demolished, woods cut down, meadows ploughed up and they themselves henceforth be infamous, and their testimony to the truth shall nowhere be accepted and the party who failed shall be restored to all he lost' (John Fortescue, *De Laudibus Legum Angliae* in T. Fortescu (ed.), *John Fortescu, Knight . . .* , 2 vols (London, 1869), 'How Juries ought to be chosen and sworn'). He concludes: 'I should, indeed, prefer twenty guilty men to escape death through mercy than one innocent to be condemned unjustly.' His book also reveals how justices lived: they only sat for three hours each day from 8 to 11 a.m.; the rest of the day was spent 'studying laws, reading Holy Scriptures, and otherwise in contemplation at their pleasure, so that their lives seem more contemplative than active. They thus led a quiet life, free of all worry and worldly cares. Nor was it found that any of them was corrupted with gifts or bribes.'

Tractable: Wolffe, 1981, 165–6.

Granted the King: For the Lancastrian tax system see Griffiths, 1981, 107–22.

PAGE 330 New warrant: CPR (1452–69), 61.

CHAPTER 18

PAGE 331 For ever a man: Malory, XIX.7.

'Great gatherings': Quoted Storey, 1986, 135.

PAGE 332 Bristling with artillery: A notable new development was the French army's use of Jean and Jasper Bureau's cleverly engineered small portable cannons.

Henry VI collapsed: There had been surmise that Henry VI's mental disorder was genetic, inherited from his grandfather, Charles VI of France. But the Valois King's madness took a different form: furious, manic rages and wild highs of loose-living. Some form of depressive stupor is now thought more likely (Wolffe, 1981, 270–1).

The Talbots: Tragic though their deaths were, neither the defeats in Aquitaine nor the loss of Normandy were regarded as the final chapters in the story of the English conquest of France.

'Great and strong laboured': Letter to Sir John Fastolf, 6 February 1456 (*Paston Letters*, vol I, no. 275).

Rumours that the child: *Milanese State Papers* (cited Mitchell, 1965); Holinshed's *Chronicle*, 3rd edn 1586, III, ed. Johnson et al. (London, 1808), 236. Holinshed did a good deal of original research, improving on the objectivity of *Hall's Chronicle*; Ramsay, 1892, II, 166.

PAGE 333 'No natural son of King Henry': J. S. Davies (ed.), *English Chronicle of the Reigns of Richard II and Henry VI* (Camden Society 1st, series, 1856).

'False heirs': R. Fabyan (d. 1513), *New Chronicles of England and France* (London, 1811), 628; *Hall's Chronicle*, 230; Chastellain (quoted T. Basin, 1412–1491), *Histoire de Règnes de Charles VII et Louis XI*, ed. J. J. Quicherat (Societé de l'Histoire de France, 4 vols, Paris, 1855).

'Great wrong': 'Gregory's Chronicle', in J. Gairdner (ed.), *Collections of a London Citizen* (Camden Society, London, 1876), 198. It is simplistic to reject all such statements as Yorkist propaganda. There was a remarkable absence of contemporary enthusiasm for the pregnancy. The only reference I have found is an aside to a mention of Richard Tunstall in the parliamentary rolls two years later in 1455 (RP xxxiii Hen VI, 318). They record that Henry was overjoyed when his 'groom of the body' Richard Tunstall brought him 'the first comfortable relation and notice, that our most entirely beloved wife the Queen was with child, to our most singular consolation, and to all our true liege people great joy and comfort', and that Tunstall was rewarded with a £40 annuity for life. The point of the anecdote was to justify the exception of the lands granted to Tunstall to provide this annuity from the Act of Resumption. They do not say *when* he told Henry, or when the patents were granted. It is not impossible that the grant was a piece of window-dressing, made in Henry's name while he was out of his mind.

Exeter: Henry Holland (1430–1475), Duke of Exeter was more closely and legitimately next of kin to Henry VI than the Beauforts, after the baby Prince of Wales. Elizabeth his grandmother was full sister to Henry IV. He was a great favourite at court. He believed that he, rather than the Duke of York, should be Protector of the Realm while Henry was ill, and may well have been backed up by the Queen after her own claim to be made regent had been loftily ignored by the council. He was no friend of Somerset, who had lost France and with it the vast French Holland estates. Exeter hated York, who in 1443 had virtually bought him, aged fourteen, from his dissolute and spendthrift father as a husband for his daughter Anne (their notoriously unsuccessful marriage ended in divorce in the 1460s). After Exeter's father's death in 1447, York acquired his wardship from the King. Exeter regained his estates in 1450, but they were saddled with the dower due to his stepmother, and the little that had been paid of his wife's dowry had been spent by his father. Despite his grand hereditary titles – Duke of Exeter, Admiral of England and Constable of the Tower of London – he was far from rich. In 1451 he decided to make the most of eleven Northamptonshire manors he inherited from a cousin, building up a powerful retinue of equally hot-headed young men. In June 1452 he concocted a bogus title and seized one of the finest estates in England, the manor and castle of Ampthill, just south of Bedford. The fact that its legal owner, the immensely wealthy Crown servant Ralph, Lord Cromwell, was kept out of possession for over two years was another example of the general breakdown of justice in the early 1450s.

PAGE 334 Orléans . . . composed a roundelay: V. J. Scattergood, *Politics and Poetry in the Fifteenth Century* (Blandford, London, 1971), 172.

The Duc of Buk: *Paston Letters*, I, ed. Gairdner, no. 195.

PAGE 335 'God send me': Adaptation of the explicit to Malory's 'Tale of Sir Gareth'. I have substituted 'me' for 'him'.

He witnessed a deed: Lichfield JRO MS B/A/11, fol. 54 r-v. It is an oddity that the Bishop's note of his role in the transaction is dated 'penultimate day of August 1454', but the diocesan record is dated 13 October 1453, when Malory was back in prison. The date may just be that of the entry in the record. See Field, 1993, 109, citing Bodl. MS Dugdale 9, 335. Field surmises that this document was wrongly dated as William Mountfort was also on it, but it is more likely that it was his son who signed it – no knightly rank given. Carpenter, 1992, 473, suggests William was a mistake for Edmund or Baldwin, but there were five other Mountfort sons – one was very likely to be called William.

Peyto was found guilty: KB 27/762 m.30d. He had escaped earlier judgement because he had been in the service of Somerset at Calais; his attorney presented letters of protection (CPR [1452–61], 231). 'Numerous entries on the rolls' (Baugh, 1933, 20) tell us that he (*aet.c.* fifty-seven) and his men had beaten up John Hathwyck (whose manor of Harbury bordered on Chesterton). Despite a royal pardon in 1455, Peyto was committed to the Marshalsea on 15 June 1456, where he remained until 10 May 1459. He did not pay up. Harbury, a tenacious and competent operator, won a judgement against the Marshal, and the debt was satisfied in 1463. Peyto died in 1464, aged about seventy.

PAGE 336 May have added colour: I am indebted to Field, 1993, for this idea.

Made his horse swim over: The ford is mentioned by the Romans. A recent speech made by Lord Gladwin when the Lords were discussing Thames-side tourist attractions (Hansard, 30 October 1997) reveals that a tall man can still cross there at low tide: 'Some will recall the remarkable exploit of the late Lord Noel-Buxton, who, in 1952, walked at low tide across the river bed just here without getting his head wet, to the general admiration of his fellow parliamentarians assembled on the Terrace, in order to prove that there had once been a ford. If any very tall Member of this House would like to follow in his steps, I have no doubt that it would be an excellent tourist draw.'

PAGE 337 January newsletter: *Paston Letters*, I, ed. Gairdner, no. 195.

PAGE 338 Mainpernors: For Boughton, see Carpenter, 1976, 118, 121; Dugdale, *Warwickshire*, I, 69–70. Worsop is mentioned in a letter from John Bocking to John Paston, 8 October 1456; interestingly, he writes, 'And as to Sir Thomas's matter, I write unto you and him jointly what hath be done therein at this time' (written at Southwark, *Paston Letters*, ed. Gairdner, vol. I, no. 295).

Sir Roger Chamberlain: details, HPT draft biography, C.E.M. In 1442 Sir Roger Chamberlain was confirmed by Henry VI as Constable of Queenborough Castle, an office originally granted to him for life by Humfrey of Gloucester. Pardoned after his near execution, he was restored to Queenborough, but not to his estates, which were confiscated by the Crown. Queenborough, which overlooks the Medway from the Isle of Sheppey, was home port to the privateering fleet of Sir Robert Wennington, widely regarded by Flemish and German merchants as a pirate, but authorised in 1449 as an official Keeper of the Seas. There has been surmise that ships from this fleet were responsible for Suffolk's capture, mock trial and execution in 1450. Chamberlain held the castle against Jack Cade in 1450. By 1452, he was steward of York's manor of Swanscombe, near Dartford, and under York's Protectorate, he successfully petitioned Parliament for the return of his estates and the overturning of his indictment for treason because the jurors had acted in 'fear and dread of great menaces'. Chamberlain took out a general pardon in 1455 – as did Thomas

Malory – and sat as MP for Norfolk in 1455. He spent some time in Calais in the late 1450s and died in 1464.

PAGE 339 Earlier in May: York had summoned Holland to appear at Westminster to answer to Cromwell's complaints. For details of the northern campaign, see Benet's *Chronicle*, quoted in Dockray, 1999, 66; Wolffe, 1981, 284.

Appropriate steeds: 'Sir, said the squire, here I have brought you all your arms save your helm and your sword, and therefore by mine assent now may ye take this knight's helm and his sword: and so he did. And when he was clean armed he took Sir Lancelot's horse, for he was better than his; and so departed they from the cross' (Malory, XIII.18).

PAGE 340 Waltham Cross in Hertfordshire: Thus the legal record, but there is a chance that an ignorant legal clerk added the Hertfordshire location – there is also a Waltham's Cross equidistant from Thaxted, Braintree and Gosfield.

John Addesley: Field, 1993, suggests that Aleyn and Addesley were one and the same, but it is unlikely, as the indictments were made at the same place and the same time. It is more likely that Addesley was a misreading for Appleby; to add to the confusion, a John Arnesby, husbandman of Tyrlington, was also among those accused of the raid on Coombe Abbey and afterwards outlawed.

PAGE 341 Early in October: Quite when York returned is unknown. The first record of him in London is 7 November, but as the Great Council was summoned for 21 October he is likely to have been there by then.

On 16 October: Baugh, 1933, 11–13, citing Controlment Roll 84, 32 Hen.VI, m.26 dorso. The delay in the inquisition into the offences until 8 October, and the fact that Malory was not actually arrested and put into Colchester Castle's prison until 16 October, supports the idea that he had been away from Essex for some months. Some of the men who sat as justices at Colchester to indict Malory had connections with the Duke of York, but they had much stronger ones with the Earl of Oxford and the Earl of Wiltshire, who were both opposed to York at this point. Another interpretation of the puzzling events in Essex would be that Malory was illegally imprisoned somewhere in the area (the Earl of Oxford's seat at Hedingham Castle would have been a suitable local stronghold), and that Aleyn had stolen horses in order to free him, but that he had been recaptured.

PAGE 342 Formidably massive: It was also very dilapidated at this time: in 1454, the year after Malory escaped, the roof fell in and all the prisoners escaped.

Henry VI's sanity had returned: Recovery may well have been on the way by early November (Wolffe, 1981, 284).

'Looked daily': *Paston Letters*, no. 221. Norfolk's absence from Westminster over the next few months was so marked that there is speculation that he had gone on pilgrimage.

Cryptic brevity: Which 'Sir Thomas' Barker was referred to is not known. But elsewhere in the letter he reports that he had managed to prevent the double outlawry of John Porter, a servant of Fastolf's who afterwards went into Norfolk's household. Like Malory's confinement in Colchester, the attempt to outlaw Porter was an example of the oppression that the court-dominated justice system was still able to exert on York's supporters.

PAGE 343 No bail was allowed: Baugh, 1933, 12, n5. Whether there were no jurors, or whether Malory repeatedly refused to accept them as suitable because they were 'in great fear of menaces' or 'had malice in their hearts', as typical contemporary protests against jurors claimed, we do not know.

CHAPTER 19

PAGE 344 It shall be well: Malory, XIX.8.

Malory's three-year imprisonment: See KB 29/83 (record to Hilary 1456); PRO C67/41, m.15 (granted pardon 1455); KB 29/87 (committed to Newgate 1457); KB 9/87, m.17 (this is only a brief summary of the long succession of Malory's court appearances. It includes his release on bail 1457; return from bail 1457; transfer to Newgate, 1460).

Plenty of time: Although Caxton's printed version of the *Morte* says the book was finished in 1469–70, the variety of sources Malory used makes it unlikely that it was all written in the immediately preceding years. Careful analysis of the differences between Caxton and Winchester suggests that there was at least one earlier 'original' version, and possibly more. The first eight and last eight pages of the Winchester manuscript were missing – probably fallen away after decades of over-enthusiastic reading. For the explicits in the Winchester manuscript, see summary above, 'Malory's *Morte Darthur* Briefly Drawn', passim.

PAGE 345 Edmund Spenser: *The Faerie Queene*, 1590.

PAGE 346 'Little given to the world': John Rous, *Historia Regum Angliae*, ed. T. Hearne, 2nd edn (Oxford, 1745).

As Chancellor, Salisbury: Hicks, 1998, 112.

'According to Law and Knighthood': For the changing balance of law and chivalry, see Watts, 1999, 32.

Summonses were sent to named men in the shires: Such an assembly was surely of doubtful legality. York declared with some justice that this 'of common presumption implieth a mistrust for some persons' (Storey, 1986, 61).

PAGE 347 False traitors: For the enmity noted between York and Buckingham at this time see Benet's *Chronicle*, 213.

'And when the king heard': Malory, VIII.20.

Proclaimed to be traitors: Carpenter, 1980, 40, from C. A. J. Armstrong, 'Politics and the Battle of St Albans', BIHR xxxiii (1960).

Tower of London: Although the most secure prison in London, the Tower could offer comfortable, even luxurious lodgings to men of rank who could pay for them. Malory could have found himself in reasonably comfortable lodgings in the fourteenth-century Beauchamp Tower. The graffiti there, some of which date from the fifteenth century, show how many errant gentlemen spent time in its cells reconsidering their position and rehearsing requests for pardon. A Ralph Malory carved his name there in 1558.

Long high street: For details of the battle, see Armstrong, 1960.

PAGE 348 York took Henry into St Albans Abbey: Hicks, 1998, 119.

Special parliamentary pardon: Only three people were excepted – Somerset, Thorpe and William Joseph, the King's secretary. The pardon heaped especial blame on the dead Clifford and Percy, and on Thorpe, which 'many a man grudged full sore now that it is passed' (*Paston Letters*, I, ed. Gairdner, no. 253, 19 July 1455). The pardon (*Rotuli Parliamentorum* V, 280–2) gave immunity from prosecution to the Yorkist army and their sympathisers (defined as 'assisters, helpers, stirrers, comforters, counsellors') throughout the country 'for anything that happened the said xxii day [of May] to fall or be done at the town of St Albans'. It was signed by the King's own hand, and then passed by Parliament. Details: Griffiths, 1981, 748; Armstrong, 1960, 71–2.

General pardon: PRO C67/41; Malory's name appears on m.15 of the pardon roll as 'Thomas Malory, late of Fanny Newbold, Warks, knight, alias Thomas Mallore, late of London, knight'. Other people who signed up include Malory connections past and future: Walter Blount, Thomas Broughton, Roger Chamberlain, Gervais Clifton, William Coton, Henry Everingham, John Framingham, Thomas Gower, Richard Harcourt, John Leventhorpe, William Oldhall, Thomas Portaleyn, Robert Roos, Sir William Vernon, Thomas Wake.

PAGE 349 Produced in court: KB 29/83; proceedings transcribed in Baugh, 1933, 13. The Tower's Deputy Keeper was a powerful man. Gower had been appointed by Exeter, the hereditary Constable of the Tower. He was not likely to kow-tow to York, who had no formal authority at this time.

Malory was allowed to sign: Field, 1993, 116; PRO C67/41m15; KB 778 Rex, 34 Hil 34 HVI (Hicks, 1928), 100. William Coton, William Hastings's deputy, is mentioned in the Controlment Roll in association with Malory's case. For Leonard Hastings, see Acheson, 1992, 41. For background on William Hastings, see W. H. Dunham, 'Lord Hastings' indentured retainers, 1461–1483', *Transactions of the Connecticut Academy of Arts and Sciences*, 39 (1955).

PAGE 350 6 February 1456: Field says 30 January but the document says the Friday *after* the quindene of Hilary.

Pardon phrases: Hicks, 1928, 99.

Inquiry into the death: Field, 1993, 127.

PAGE 351 Kenilworth and Coventry: Wolffe, 1981, 370–1.

Fortified Kenilworth: Wolffe, 1981, 302. P. J. C. Field, 'Fifteenth-Century History in Malory's *Morte Darthur*', in F. H. M. Le Saux (ed.), *The Formation of Culture in Medieval Britain* (1995), draws a parallel between the Queen's white swan badge for her own knights and that of Guinevere's 'white shield on green ground'. Details: Coventry Leet Book EETS, 135, II, 300–1.

Treated with a ceremony: J. L. Laynesmith, 'Constructing Queenship at Coventry: Pageantry and Politics at Margaret's "Secret Harbour"', in Linda Clark (ed.), *The Fifteenth Century*, 3: *Authority and Subversion* (Woodbridge, Boydell, 2003).

PAGE 362 'Malory, Gentleman': *Coventry Leet Book*, 135.I, 285. This Malory is listed among those attending the city council to prepare for the pageant to welcome Queen Margaret to the city. There was also a Thomas Broun, weaver, a Guy Weston, a John Straunge and a John Arderne. A John Appleby was appointed as one of the collectors of monies for the pageant. The wording of the speeches was 'an extraordinary reversal of roles and celebration of queenship' (Laynesmith, 2003).

Grevyves: Perhaps griffins (cf. an azure shield with three golden crowns said to be Arthur's arms at Henry V's funeral).

'Ever more a grouch': *Brut*, quoted Storey, 1986, 177.

Then Gawaine called privily: Malory, X.21.

PAGE 353 Seems to have remained in captivity: Matthews, 1966, 25; Field, 1993, 108; Baugh, 1933, 15–19. Although Malory was still in the Marshal's custody for the first hearing of Overton's action for debt, he may have obtained his securities and been released soon afterwards. Debtors were put in prison on conviction until they paid their fines, not before. Overton used attorneys later in the hearings, and though Malory appeared in person on the first occasion, when he denied that the promissory note was in his handwriting, he too sent an attorney afterwards. Overton could have already raised this case in the court of common pleas (cf. the later Greswold debt, below). Overton had two men, Hugh More and Ralph Law, 'plegii de prosequendo', as sureties that he would pursue his case. The Latin of the accusation is far from clear but an odd little phrase in the Controlment Roll suggests that other matters of which Malory was accused may have arisen: 'And he defended [his] force and injury when &c.' There is no mention of force and injury in this accusation, but 'vim et iniuriam' are in the accusative – they are what he denies.

PAGE 354 Unsavoury character: Personal communication from Anne Sutton.

Often accused: E.g. soon afterwards William Hall appealed to the Chancellor, saying that 'out of malice' Overton had sued to remove a debt he claimed was outstanding from Hall's dead wife Joan to the Mayor's court, bringing 'divers actions of trespass' against him and the friends who had stood as sureties for him, vexing them and causing Hall to be at great cost 'coming and going to save my sureties harmless'. Overton may have been a kinsman of William Overton of Brownsover, who was an associate of William Peyto.

Peyto was committed: Sir William's experiences seem to have paralleled Malory's. He too tried pleading his 1455 pardon, but the court said it did not cover debt – a clue to why Malory was so promptly accused of owing money.

Sent to Newgate: Malory's change of prison is recorded in the retrospective summary of his case on the Controlment Roll (KB 9/87, m.17). We know he was there by November 1456, as in January 1457 it was said that he had been committed to a Sheriff of Middlesex who was replaced in November; it may also be significant that during the case's second hearing, on 18 September 1456, his name did not have its usual tag 'in custodia Marescalli', but this could just mean that he sent an attorney – or was ill.

Conciliar writ: Baugh, 1933, 29; Hicks, 1928, 42.

PAGE 355 Anon withal: Malory, VI.9. Malory's description of this incident is much more convincingly detailed than that of his source.

'For all the while': Malory, IX.37.

PAGE 356 Sheriff had failed: The Sheriff of Warwickshire was now Thomas Walsh (September 1456/7), a close associate of Malory. But the sheriffs of London would have been responsible for assembling, or failing to assemble, a jury for this local debt.

Thomas Greswold: Baugh, 1933, 28–9. When Fortescue had moved Malory to Ludgate for more secure custody, he had mentioned that there were still 'diverse causes still pending' to be discussed, and that Malory also stood condemned of a debt to Thomas Greswold.

Sent back to Ludgate: KB 9/87, m.17.

Pierre de Brezé: Ramsay, 1892, ii, 202.

'Manliest knight': Hicks, 1991, 132.

PAGE 357 Bailed until St John's Day: KB 9/87, m.17. The case was heard at the beginning of the Michaelmas law term on 19 October.

William Brigham: A member of the Calais garrison, he drew annuity from a village near Calais in 1461 (Matthews, 1966, 30).

John Clerkson: I have not found any records of this Sussex squire.

CHAPTER 20

PAGE 358 At Yule last: Malory, V.10.

Likely to have been the reason: In 1454, Somerset was Captain of Calais and had used his influence to get the hot-headed Sir William Peyto, another 'passing good man of his hands' (Malory, II.1), released from the Marshalsea so that he could join his garrison.

Pugnacious gamecock: Short of stature but fiery-tempered, Fauconberg had been a captain under Bedford, York and Talbot and was one of the first patrons of Caen University. In 1439, he was captured after the fall of Pont-de-l'Arche in 1449. Because the Exchequer withheld thousands of pounds of back pay he was owed as Keeper of Roxburgh Castle, he had been unable to pay his ransom, and had been a prisoner in France for the last four years. One of York's first actions after he took over the reins of power in November 1453 had been to make the Exchequer pay Fauconberg's wages in full, and he returned to England early in 1454. Generally popular, he was the lord chosen to visit the King and report on his condition, and was one of those who suggested that

Margaret's baby son be made Prince of Wales on 15 March 1454. He was at King Henry's side at St Albans. Fauconberg had given similar pledges for Edmund Arblaster, judging by a record absolving him of responsibility for his ransom (PPC, vi, 208). It is not mere whim to place Malory at Calais rather than in a dozen other possible sanctuaries. An extraordinary number of men who were stationed at Calais at this time are associated with Malory later in the 1460s: John Cornelius, John Hawkins, Thomas Philip, Sir Gervaise Clifton and Nicholas Hussey. Philip and Clifton were excepted from pardon with Malory in 1468. Sir William Pecche was also there (Newhall, 1940): either he or his father was on the Beauchamp retinue roll of 1414.

PAGE 359 Priory accounts: Field, 1993, 121, citing PRO SC6/1107/7, nos. 5, 3, 4 (i.e. all early in the accounting year).

Silence over his case: There is no court record of Malory until April 1459, when there was a complaint that he had been seen at large in Warwickshire (KB 9/87, m.17). The next we hear of him is in the Hilary term of 1460 (23 January–12 February).

William Brandon: Field, 1993, 122.

PAGE 360 Fabyan reported: Fabyan.1811, 634; no official records of the Calais sailors' adventurous jaunt survive.

'With great joy': Malory, XVII.2. The *Morte Darthur* is peppered with knowledgeable nautical lore and convincing descriptions of voyages.

Anne Beauchamp: She went to Calais with her husband in May 1457. Between May 1457 and May 1459, Warwick spent much of his time winning the hearts of the garrison of Calais (Kendall, 1957, 42).

PAGE 361 Calais: Main sources include David Grummit, 'One of the mooste principall treasours belongyng to his Realme of Englande: Calais and the Crown, *c.* 1450–1558', in D. Grummitt (ed.), *The English Experience in France, c.1480–1558* (Ashgate, Aldershot, 2002); Arthurson, 'Espionage and Intelligence' (1991), 135; Armstrong, 1983, 109; Ramsay, 1892, II, 202, 265; *Calendar of Milanese State Papers*, passim.

Gareth and Gaheris: Malory, XXI.9. The incident also parallels Tristram's love day with his uncle King Mark (Malory, X.22).

PAGE 362 John Jernigan: *Paston Letters*, I, ed. Gairdner, no. 317.

'And or it were day': Malory, X.32.

More controversially: See T. H. Lloyd, *England and the German Hanse 1157–1611* (CUP, 1991); Marie-Rose Thielemans, *Bourgogne et Angleterre . . . 1435–67* (Bruxelles, 1966).

Plotting with . . . Alençon: Hicks, 1998, 139. Only hindsight ends the Hundred Years War in 1453. Dreams of re-invasion did not end until Queen Mary I's loss of Calais a hundred years later. The English kept their title to the French throne until the eighteenth century. Alençon was later arrested and tried for treason on charges of inviting English intervention in 1458. Later in the year, a Burgundian–Yorkist alliance was established.

PAGE 363 Sir John Wenlock: Sir John Wenlock of Someries (*c.* 1400–71): see Roskell, 1981, essay on Wenlock. He fought in the French wars: he was Constable of Vernon-on-Seine in 1422 and is recorded at Gisors in 1430 (Jean-Paul Besse, *Gisors dans l'Histoire*, Age d'Homme, Lausanne, 1998). See ch. 8 above for Thomas Malory and Gisors.

Agnes Danvers: Her brother Thomas was a servant of Bishop Waynflete; a later chapter of this book will see Thomas Danvers and Malory accused in the same 1468 conspiracy (Field, 1993, 140–4).

Active in promoting: Wenlock took a leading part in embassies negotiating the royal marriage in the 1440s. By 1448 he was Chamberlain of the Duchy of Lancaster for Queen Margaret and a King's Knight.

Triple marriage alliance: Hicks, 1998, 153–4.

More Warwick's man: Wenlock's sympathy for York's cause began early. In July 1453, he was discharged from this office by Henry VI himself (in what may be the last letter the King wrote before losing his mind) 'because in the untrue troublous time ye favoured the duc of Y[ork] and such as longed to him as O[ldhall] and other' (*John Vale's Book*, Kekewich et al., 1995, 173). The letter's final 'and other' is tantalising – could it have been a reference to Malory? The frequent references to secret matters that were only to be discussed before the King in council in Malory's court records prove beyond doubt that Henry VI had been told of his apparent misdemeanours. But Wenlock remained in office during Henry's illness (which raises an interesting question as to whether anyone except him knew about the letter) and was 'sore hurt' defending King Henry during the affray of St Albans. He was Speaker of the Commons in the July 1455 Parliament, i.e. during York's Protectorate.

'Whole as an egg': Cyastellain, quoted in Kendall, 1957, 47. Other details, ibid.

One of Sir Thomas's feoffees: Appointed some time before 1461 (KB 27/900 rot.5–7).

PAGE 364 Took Richard Malory ... into his service: *Calendar of Ancient Deeds* VI, PRO C6815: Grant by Walter Blount Esq to 'Richard Malorre', esquire, for his good counsel and service, of a yearly rent of 13s 4d for life, charged on his manor of Elveston, 22 July 36 Henry VI (1458). Much later, in 1473, Richard Malory and Blount are linked in a Derby property deal (Field, 1993, 129; *Ancient Deeds* (6 vols, London, 1890–1915), VI, 391, PRO C146/10341).

More amicable relations: Watts, 1999, 346; Fabyan, 1811, 634. Most details from Hicks, 1998, 152–6.

Queen Margaret remained adamantly hostile: Watts, 1999, passim. She wanted to take away Warwick's captaincy of Calais, but Warwick haughtily (but wrongly) insisted that only Parliament could rescind it. Henry was still intent on concord.

In February: *Calendar of Milanese State Papers*, 1, 19.

Prior of Arbury: Hicks, 1998, 155. See ibid., 193, for attainder being a relatively novel and much disapproved of idea, which went against the sanctity of inheritance.

PAGE 365 Prince of Wales was a bastard: Implied by 'such matters as concern specially our honour and worship', Watts, 1999, 347.

To act against them: On 26 April East Anglian squires were summoned to meet at Leicester on 10 May 'defensibly arrayed' and prepared for two months' service. On 7 May, three thousand bow staves and sheaves of arrows were ordered for the Tower 'considering the enemies on every side approaching us, as well upon the sea as on the land'.

A riot: Benet's *Chronicle*, 223. It was between 'men of Fleet St' (presumably supporters of York) and members of the Queen's household. See also Watts, 1999, 350.

Coventry Council: Hicks, 1998, 157.

Unusually generous dower: Cf. the Duke of Warwick's £200 allowance. Somerset, who had been given the sop of the captaincy of Guines, had little voluntary support by contrast.

PAGE 366 Men of the Calais garrison: Trollope's men included many 'old soldiers' (Gregory's *English Chronicle*, Johnson, 1988, 189).

PAGE 367 Simply gave himself up: A more conservative but rather duller alternative take on this period would be that Malory was made an offer by the Neville lords but turned it down, disliking the way things were going – and did in fact remain quietly in the Marshalsea between January 1458 and 1460.

PAGE 368 'To be detained safely and securely': Baugh, 1933, 9; Hicks, 1928, 101. The record continues: 'And later, namely at the term-day of St Hilary in the 38th year of the reign of the said King the aforesaid Thomas Malory was committed to the custody of the sheriff of Middlesex for the aforementioned reasons, in the prison of our lord the King, to be detained safe and sound until such time as &c. Therefore the said Marshall is relieved of the responsibility for him here &c'. Further reference to Malory in the custody of the sheriffs of Middlesex could yet emerge in the still incompletely explored Middlesex county records.

'We be here twenty knights': Malory, IV.7.

PAGE 369 Battle of Northampton: Hicks, 1998, 179; R. I. Jack, 'A Quincentenary: The Battle of Northampton, July 11th 1460', *Northamptonshire Past and Present* III (1960), 21–5.

PAGE 370 They that were within: Gregory's *English Chronicle*, quoted in 'Malory's Great Guns', Dhira B. Mahoney, *Viator* 20 (1989), 299, a very useful account of mid-fifteenth-century weapons of war.

Mordred's siege: Idea from Field, 1993. Mahoney, 1989, argues, unconvincingly, that these 'guns' were just the missiles hurled by the siege engines.

'And short tale . . .': *Works*, 1227. The *Mort Artu* and *Le Morte Arthur* (of which a manuscript copy made in the 1460s has survived) have only a vague reference to 'other kynnes gynne', which might merely have meant 'other kinds of stratagem'. But Malory uses the specific phrase 'great guns', an expression by then generally used of cannon, especially if allied to the verb 'shot'. Cannon were used at the Battle of Crécy in 1347, but were at first far from effective. Better cast and more accurate heavy artillery, developed first by the Burgundians and then by the French, was in general use by 1460. Christine de Pisan recommended a range of specific models of cannon in her *Faits d'Armes* (see above, ch. 6). This was translated and printed by Caxton four years after he published Malory's *Morte Darthur*.

Memorandum: Coram Rege Roll 763 Crown side m. 3.

PAGE 371 'Sine die': 'Many accused appeared ... in King's Bench to plead their pardons and to be excused "sine die"' (Michael Hicks, 'Lawmakers and Lawbreakers', in C. Given-Wilson, *Late Medieval England*, Manchester UP, 1996).

PAGE 372 Called to account: Moore, 1983.

PAGE 373 'It is pity': Malory, X.7.

Dame Gladness: Seaton, 1952, 250; Meale, 'Manuscripts, Readers and Patrons' (1985), 24. See M. B. Parkes and E. Salter (eds), *Troius and Criseyde* (facsimile), Brewer, Cambridge, 1978, 23, n30, for a list of other MSS owned by Anne Neville. This conceit could have been worse – I toyed with the wild surmise that it was the Queen herself who had Malory's heart and he hers, to the extent of fathering the Prince of Wales and being turned into a 'man in the iron mask' figure hidden away in London prisons. But though it would be splendid stuff for any film version of his life (*Malory in Love?*), I regretfully rejected it as too fantastical – though Malory did just happen to have been free at the time Margaret's child was conceived ...

PAGE 374 'And for this cause': Malory, XII.14.

The Neville sisters: As far as I know, no study of them as a group has been undertaken. It deserves to be.

CHAPTER 21

PAGE 376 Musing upon the mutability: Kingsford, 1913, 395.

Cause of the Yorkists: Hicks, 1998, 187–90. Besides Hicks, the main sources for this chapter include Charles Ross, *Edward IV* (Eyre Methuen, 1974); Scofield, 1923.

PAGE 377 'And there under the cloth of estate': Johnson, 1988, 216.

Equally unhappy: Hicks, 1998, 190. Letters from the papal legate Coppini to Pius II also show that Warwick opposed York.

PAGE 378 Temporary Constable: Pending the return of John Tiptoft, Earl of Worcester.

Prince Edward: As early as July 1460 it was rumoured that 'they will make a son of the Duke of York king and that they will pass over the king's son, as they are beginning to say he is not the king's son' (Hicks, 1998, 211, citing CSPM i, 27). The *Milanese State Papers*, however, are full of highly dubious rumours.

PAGE 379 Close association: Anne F. Sutton, 'Malory in Newgate' (2000).
John Vale: Kekewich et al., 1995.
'By God's blood': Keen, 1990, 194.

PAGE 380 Mortimer's Cross: Additional details from Geoffrey Hodges, *Ludford Bridge and Mortimer's Cross* (Logaston Press, Almeley, 1989); Scofield, 1923, I, 138; Hughes, 2002, 81.
'Now is the winter': First line of *Richard III*.

PAGE 381 'Now is this realm': Malory, XX.1.

PAGE 382 Ruthlessly pillaged: The Abbot of St Albans begged Henry to prevent the town and Abbey from being ransacked, but the soldiers ignored the King's command, saying that Queen Margaret had told them that instead of wages they could seize anything they could lay their hands on south of the Trent.

PAGE 383 What lords they could summon: They included Ferrers of Chartley, FitzWalter, Herbert, and Devereux.

PAGE 384 Thus was Sir Arthur depraved: Malory, XXI.1.

PAGE 385 Towton: Additional details from A. W. Boardman, *The Battle of Towton* (Sutton, Far Thrupp, 1994); Christopher Gravett, *Towton, 1461* (Osprey, 2003).

PAGE 386 Almost eight foot tall: Edward's skeleton measured 6ft 3in when his tomb was opened in 1796 (Ramsay, 1892, II 269); his crested helmet would have added at least a foot to his height.
Norfolk's forces: P. A. Haigh, *Military Campaign of the Wars of the Roses* (Stroud, Sutton, 1995). Hall says the Duke himself was absent as he was ill, but Hearne's fragment says he was there and Bishop George Neville mentions his great deeds that day in a letter to the papal legate.

PAGE 387 Then the king gat (and following quotes): Malory, XXI.4.
Bees: Rings, usually gold torques, for necks or arms.
Cruel plunder was forbidden: Aurner, 'Sir Thomas Malory' (1933), 372; Field, 'Malory and the Battle of Towton', in D. T. Hanks Jr and J. G. Brogdon, *The Social and Literary Contexts of Malory's Morte Darthur* (Brewer, Cambridge, 2000).

PAGE 388 Lord Hastings: The constableships of both Leicester Castle and Castle Donington and his marriage to Warwick's widowed sister Katherine Bonville soon made him the wealthiest and most powerful magnate in Leicestershire.

PAGE 389 General pardon: Hardyng, *Chronicle*, 437.
Inscribed on the official roll: PRO C67/45 m.14. Field says that this pardon will be why Malory was freed, but the marginal note in the Controlment Roll was placed beside the record of the 1455 pardon. Legal records of this period are

frustratingly incomplete, and often no date was given of the freeing of men who were evidently out of prison later on. Interestingly, on the same date Lord Wenlock was in London receiving a commission to travel to Bruges in order to treat with the Duke of Burgundy. Their repeated propinquity may be a clue to Malory's hidden life as a secret agent.

The agreement: Farnham, *Village Notes*, 141. We could conclude that Sir Thomas originally had at least three sons: Thomas, who might have expected to inherit, but who died in 1457; John, who became a Knight Hospitaller; and Robert, born *c*.1449, who did in fact inherit. John Malory must have been older than Robert, as he had served at least five years in the headquarters of the Order by January 1468 when he was granted two preceptories. For the identity of Robert's bride, see the analysis of the Newbold Revel armorial window in ch. 11 above.

PAGE 390 Pierre de Brezé: Warkworth's chronicle, quoted A. Rose, *Kings in the North*, Weidenfeld, 2002, p. 438. Margaret had granted him the Channel Islands, of which he was already part conqueror. He held part of Jersey and kept it for the next seven years.

'Sent letters': Malory, XX.10.

Splendid roll-call: Brief Notes, in Gairdner, *Three Fifteenth-Century Chronicles* (Camden Society, new series 18, 1880).

New Duke of Norfolk: John Mowbray had died in 1461, when Newbold Revel was listed among lands of which he was overlord (CIPM, IV, 316).

Sir John Astley: See also ch. 12, note. He had a fine collection of chivalric and heraldic treatises. He was a kinsman of the Astleys of Wolvey Astley, a few miles from Newbold Revel, and also held at Patshull, Staffordshire, and Nailston, Leicestershire (Dugdale, *Warwickshire*). Nailston is only six miles east of Appleby Magna, and Sir John Astley's sister Joan was married to Thomas Appleby, who is likely to have been related to John Appleby, Malory's co-defendant at Nuneaton in 1451.

PAGE 391 William Pecche: The surname Pecche, with an indecipherable Christian name, appears on the 1414 Beauchamp retinue roll that lists Thomas Malory.

John Paston: Quotes from *Paston Letters*, II, ed. Gairdner, no. 464.

PAGE 392 May have been significant: Field points out that Malory could have got this idea from Hardyng's *Chronicle*, in which he describes a 'Mount Dolorous' as being Bamborough. Lancelot's Joyous Gard was originally known as Dolorous Gard ('Malory's Minor Sources', in Field, 1998). But Hardyng's reference is in a non-Arthurian context, and it does not explain Malory's mention of Alnwick as well.

PAGE 393 'Many great buffets': Malory, X.78.

Astley was captured: Warkworth, 38.

Frightened off: Wolffe, 1981, 335.

CHAPTER 22

PAGE 395 I pray you: Horrox, 1994, citing N. Davis (ed.), *Paston Letters* (OUP, 1971–6), 2 vols, I, 263. Main sources for this chapter are Scofield, 1923; Ross, 1974; Green, 1980; Sutton and Visser-Fuchs, 1997; 'Malory's *Morte Darthur* and Court Culture under Edward IV', in J. P. Carley and F. Riddy (eds), *Arthurian Literature* XII (Brewer, Cambridge, 1993).

The cause of my writing: *Paston Letters*, quoted in Seaton, 1952.

PAGE 396 Thomas Bone: *Paston Letters*, quoted in Keen, 1990, 182.

PAGE 397 'Ample and magnificent town': Cust, 1909, 34. Cust has a memorable turn of phrase and firm opinions: she describes Edward IV as 'picknicking in temporary security on the disputed throne of England' (35).

Full of his kinsmen: Derived from Mallory-Smith, 1958; Field, 1993, passim; Stow, 1908, II, 85; PRO and HPT records.

The which Earl: *Great Chronicle of London*, ed. A. H. Thomas and I. D. Thornley (privately printed, London, 1938), 207, quoted Hicks, 1928, 228.

PAGE 398 Fine collection: Sutton and Visser-Fuchs, 1997; Scofield, 1923, II, Appendix: 'Miscellanea'.

Order of the Garter: Collins, 2000.

PAGE 399 Sir Robert Harcourt: He also sat on commissions of array in central southern England; fellow commissioners included Lord Grey of Ruthin, Lord Berners and Lord Wenlock.

Suit of jousting armour: Sir Samuel Rush Meynck, *A Critical Inquiry into Antient Arms from the Norman Conquest to the Reign of Charles II* (London, 1824).

PAGE 400 'Hostess at the George': *Paston Letters*, ed. J. Gairdner (London, 1904), VI, 65.

Sir Thomas Gray: He was the son of Sir Edward Grey, with whom Malory was associated in 1441 (see ch.10 above).

PAGE 401 'Major blunder': Critics include Ross, 1974, 86; Scofield, 1923, I, 343. For Elizabeth Woodville see Katherine Davies, *The First Queen Elizabeth* (Lovat Dickson, 1937); David Baldwin, *Elizabeth Woodville*: *Mother of the Princes in the Tower* (Sutton, Stroud, 2002).

'For she was a woman': This and subsequent quotes are from Hall's *Chronicle*. Purists will object that they are novelettish stuff by a biased sixteenth-century historian, but it is an enjoyable vivid story, even if it must be taken with a fistful of salt.

Other English gentlewomen: It was later claimed that Edward had entered into a pre-contract of marriage with Lady Eleanor Talbot, daughter of the military hero John Talbot, and Margaret Beauchamp, oldest daughter of Sir Richard Beauchamp. She married Thomas, Lord Butler in 1450, and soon after he was killed in 1461, probably fighting for Lancaster, Eleanor had to appeal to

Edward IV for his confiscated manors. This is when the pre-contract was said to have taken place (*The Ricardian* XI, December 1997).

PAGE 403 Her lineage: Davies, 1937, 54.

Escorted Elizabeth: Warwick also presided at the feast for the churching of Elizabeth after the birth of her first daughter, and stood as the child's godfather.

PAGE 404 No reason to doubt: Bale certainly got some things wrong, but there is no reason to disbelieve him unless we can prove his errors. R. R. Griffith points out that anything written by a man who lived so close to Malory's time, and who is authoritative on so many other authors, 'deserves a respectful hearing' rather than being dismissed as 'an antiquarian's guess or fiction' (Griffith, 1981, 160). But he misleads by describing only the first edition of Bale, ignoring the added information on Malory which Bale provided in his second edition (see Parins, 1988, 54–5). For Bale, see also ch. 3 above.

PAGE 405 A memory so retentive: Crowland Chronicler, cited J. R. Lander, *Wars of the Roses* (Sutton, Stroud, 1990), 168.

'Resembled senators': Olivier de la Marche, quoted Kendall, 1967, 172.

With that came Sir Lancelot: Malory, VI.7.

PAGE 406 Quantities of books: ch. 12 above.

One of his contemporaries: Bale's vagueness about Malory's dates in the first (1548) edition of his *Dictionary of Illustrious British Authors* suggests that he met his new source between 1548 and 1557, when the edition appeared from which the quoted description comes. He might have contacted Bale in order to correct him.

A fascinating recent book: Jonathan Hughes, *Arthurian Myths and Alchemy: the Kingship of Edward IV*, 2002.

PAGE 407 Arthurian romances: Elizabeth Woodville's signature on the flyleaf of BL Royal MS 14 E.III is in her maiden name, before either marriage (Orme, 2001, 282).

A gratuitous mention of Arundel: See D. Starkey, 'King Henry and King Arthur', in J. P. Carley and F. Riddy (eds), *Arthurian Literature* XVI (1998), 174–5.

Would most have wanted to inspire: Cf. George Ashby, whose *Active Policy of a Prince* (c. 1470) advised young Prince Edward to 'read in chronicles the ruin / Of high estates and translation (II, 155–6, cited Coleman, 1996). If Malory had Prince Edward in mind as his most important reader, it would explain the nature of the marginalia in the Winchester manuscript. P. J. C. Field ('Malory's Own Marginalia', 2001, 226–239) suggests that the eighty or so pointers to the content of the text were Malory's own work, faithfully transcribed by the scribes who made the Winchester copy of his tales (but cf. Helen Cooper, 2000). Interestingly the marginalia do not draw attention to the moral lessons that Caxton assured his readers could be learned from reading the *Morte*. Instead they concentrate overwhelmingly on deaths, murders, suicides, particularly bloody combats, and prophecies. Invisible knights, sorceress's tricks and the conjuring up of devils are also noted. Such things were highly to appeal to the bloodthirsty and vengeful young Lancastrian heir in exile at Koeur.

Sir John Fortescue: See T. Fortescue, Lord Clement (ed.), *Sir John Fortescue, Knight, his Life, Works and Family History*, 2 vols (London, 1869).

PAGE 408 Any fifteenth-century king: Fortescue's book was finished in 1471. He managed to make his peace with Edward IV by recanting on his long and careful denial that the Yorkists had a legitimate claim to the throne. He lived to the age of ninety.

Thomas Walsh: His brother John, also a feoffee of Malory, had once been an auditor of the Queen's Duchy of Lancaster estates.

As soon as the opportunity arose: K. B. McFarlane, *England in the Fifteenth Century* (Hambledon, London, 1981), 246–7: 'Outward conformity may have covered strong attachments to lost causes . . . to speak of a Yorkist or a Lancastrian family, apart from the royal houses themselves, is almost impossible when successive generations changed sides with so much freedom' – and were intermarried, he could have added. 'Lancastrian loyalism exerted a stronger and more subtle influence in the late fifteenth century than historians have allowed . . . traditional Lancastrian clients maintained their ties at a deep personal level, but also accepted the need to find alternative patrons who could protect their interests under the new regime. When the tide of events favoured the Lancastrians in 1469–71, past loyalties and in some cases grudges against the Yorkists prompted many to risk supporting the Re-adeption. It happened again in 1483 and 1485.'

William himself: For marriage, see Field, 1993, 130, citing Nichols, *Leicestershire*, IV, 368. See also HPT draft biography, Simon Payling. In May 1463, Feilding demised the disputed property to Helen for the term of her life. In 1465, he would buy the manor of Shirford from Malory's cousin William Purefoy; he also acquired lands in Ely and Haddenham. He was at first refused a pardon (CCR [1461–8], 55) but later pardoned (KB 27/802 just.rot.20d). Feilding's future held a return to his loyalty to Henry VI; he was Sheriff and MP in the 1470–1 Re-adeption and he was killed fighting for Lancaster at Tewkesbury in 1471. An alabaster tomb in Lutterworth Church is probably his. See also Dugdale's drawings of Feilding tombs in Monks Kirby church.

PAGE 409 Henry Everingham: HPT draft biography.

John Green: Nichols, *Leicestershire*, 368. Carpenter, 1992, says he was a friend and relative of William Catesby.

Named for Nicholas Revel: 6 December is St Nicholas's Day. Robert is described as '14 and more' in the Northants IPM of his grandmother Elizabeth, and '13 and more' in the Warwickshire and Leicestershire IPMs, so it is just possible he was born in 1466 rather than 1465.

PAGE 410 Pope Pius II: R. J. Mitchell, *The Laurels and the Tiara: Pope Pius II 1458–1464* (Harvill, London, 1862), 257–9. Pius II did eventually set out at the head of a crusading army; he died at Ancona in 1464.

PAGE 411 Devaluing and recoining: Ramsay, 1892, II, 313.
Five of its most prominent citizens: The last time a London citizen had been knighted was 1439, and only eleven had ever been thus honoured. Edward knighted eighteen in the first decade of his reign. One of the citizens' wives, Elizabeth (aka Jane) Shore, became his favourite mistress.
Trading ventures: Scofield, 1923; Ramsay, II, 1892.

PAGE 412 Famous challenge: Cust, 1909; Green, 1980; Scofield, 1923.

PAGE 413 And Sir Palomides rushed: Malory, X.70.
Would-be champions: *Excerpta Historica*, ed. S. Bentley (London, 1833), 205, 210. There was not a Neville among them – or at the Parliament which opened in June.

PAGE 414 Nowadays men cannot love: Malory, *Works*, 25.11, 1119–20.
His kinsman: Danvers was the uncle of the wife of Malory's nephew George Burneby.
'Best cheser': *Paston Letters*, ed. David, II, 379, quoted R. Barber, 'Malory's *Morte Darthur* and Court Culture under Edward IV', in Carley and Roddy, *Arthurian Literature* XII (1993), 153.

PAGE 415 *De Arte Amandi* ('*The Art of Love-making*'): In AD 17 the Emperor Augustus exiled Ovid for writing this notorious manual for seducers, which had sections for women to read as well as for men. *De Remedio* was the refutation of it which Ovid wrote to obtain Augustus's forgiveness.

CHAPTER 23
PAGE 416 *Philobiblon* Trans. E. C. Thomas (Birmingham, 1946). Richard Bury (1281–1345) was Bishop of Durham. His paean of praise for books could easily have been enjoyed by Malory, as it was still in circulation in manuscript in his lifetime. It was printed in 1473. Main sources for this chapter: as ch. 20 plus specialist articles on the Thomas Cook affair, including M. Hicks, 'The Case of Sir Thomas Cook, 1468', EHR, 93 (1978), Anne F. Sutton, 'Sir Thomas Cook and his Troubles, An Investigation', *Guildhall Studies in London History*, April 1978; P. Holland, 'Cook's Case in History and in Myth', BIHR 61 (1988), 21–35. On transmission of news, see Charles Ross, 'Rumour, propaganda and popular opinion during the Wars of the Roses', in R. A. Griffiths (ed.), *Patronage, the Crown and the Provinces* (Sutton, Gloucester, 1981); C. A. J. Armstrong, 'Some Examples of the Distribution and Speed of News in England at the Time of the Wars of the Roses', *Medieval History* 1.2, Headstart History (1991);

Arthurson, 1991; Edward Meek, 'The Practice of English Diplomacy in France 1461–71', in Grummitt, 2002.

Dionysia: The Hutton Conyers Malorys were fervent Lancastrians; Sir William was about Malory's own age.

PAGE 417 John Turner: Once Abbot of Furness. He was condemned to the Tower in 1462 at the age of 'sixty or more' through an enemy's 'wrongful and sinister informations'. Gout-ridden, deprived of his pension and 'full of great sickness and unheart's-ease', Turner 'had nothing to help himself with'. But Robert Malory 'succoured him with meat and drink, which he is not bound to do, but of his own charity, free will and gentleness doth it' (Scofield, 1923, II, 401). Other details Scofield, 1923, I, 380–3.

PAGE 418 Portrait . . . as a young man: National Portrait Gallery.

My father: Ramsay, 1892, ii, 31.

PAGE 419 'Thus endeth the tale': Malory, XVII.23. It could be argued that it was the story of the Grail rather than the person it was written for that was 'one of the truest and holiest in the world'. But there would have been no need to have included the words 'a tale chronicled for' at all if that had been the sense, nor does the OED, which offers 'to chronicle' as a transitive verb, give any examples of it meaning 'to be said to be'.

Second general pardon: PRO C67/46 m.39. Thirty-seven membranes, each listing up to a hundred names, show that between 3,000 and 4,000 people took up pardons – which at a fee of about £1 each (Bellamy, 1998, 144) meant an attractive inflow of revenue as well as an increase of goodwill. Five examples of the copies of their entry which were retained by the individual who applied for a pardon have survived. They show that the pardon was taken up both by groups and by individuals. One was acquired almost instantly on 14 July by William Paston, husband of Anne Beaufort; another on 4 August by the executors of Thomas Beckington, Bishop of Bath and Wells; another on 1 November by the town and burgesses of Nottingham; another on 1 December by the Dean and Chapter of Wells Cathedral; and the last by Thomas Glegg of Gayton, Cheshire (PRO/Chester 2/141, m.9). General pardons only covered crimes committed against the King before a specified date. They did not result in the mass release of criminals. See ch. 4 above.

PAGE 421 An accomplished spymaster: Ian Arthurson, 'Espionage and Intelligence from the Wars of the Roses to the Reformation', Nottingham Medieval Studies XXXV (1991), passim.

'Jon Worby': Arthurson, 1991, p. 153.

Captured in Wales: For Herbert's 'silent assiduity and serpentine methods' see H. T. Evans, Wales and the Wars of the Roses (1915; repr. Sutton, Stroud, 1998), 94.

Edward invented a system of stationing messengers at twenty-mile intervals along the main north–south route, so that letters could travel at the rate of a hundred miles a day (Crowland Continuation). He also had female spies (Philippe de Commines, Memoires, ed. Joseph Calmette, Paris, 1552, I, 99). There were rival spy systems – the Knights Hospitallers were particularly well-organised (*Cely Papers*, ed. H. E. Malden (Camden Society, 1900), 32, 55, 104 (cited Armstrong, 1991)).

Warwick was certainly cooling: Hicks, 1998, 264–5. Time would prove that Warwick's involvement was not as far-fetched as it might seem. The Milanese ambassador was reporting 'a very great division' between Edward and Warwick as early as February 1465, and said that Queen Margaret was very hopeful of a split. He also wrote in May 1467 that there was talk in the French court of getting Warwick to restore Henry VI. But by 1471 he wrote in despair that 'I wish the country and people were sunk in the sea . . . I feel like one going to the torture, when I write about them, and no one ever hears twice alike about English affairs' (CSPM, I, 154).

PAGE 422 'More money on espionage in 1468': Arthurson, 1991, 138.

Sir Richard Harcourt: The Harcourts may well have been double agents. Sir Robert went on a diplomatic mission to France on 28 May 1467 with Warwick, and was rewarded on his return. He was given Duchy of Lancaster stewardship in 1468 (a time when Warwick and his Neville relations were increasingly out of favour) and a royal annuity from Cookham and Bray. However, after Warwick and Clarence had fled to France and Lancastrian invasion threatened, there were rumours that he had had 'the good will of the lords [i.e. the returning Lancastrians] after their coming in'. Richard, Sir Robert's brother, wrote a note in 1470 saying he had no leisure at all, owing to 'the busyness that I have about the King's matters at this time' (HPT draft biography, L. S. Clark, 1995). It may be significant that he was bailiff of Bishop Waynflete's manorial holdings in Oxfordshire.

Over £2,200: Arthurson, 1991, 138.

Thomas Danvers: He was arrested by one of Queen Elizabeth's younger brothers, Sir Richard Woodville. He was neither indicted nor pardoned. Was he simply released without charge? He had connections with Waynflete (who took out a pardon at this time) and Pakenham. He had implicated Cornelius, perhaps in exchange for that 'aforegiven' pardon he produced in July 1468. He was pardoned on 10 December 1471, some time after the final defeat of the Lancastrians.

Cornelius was tortured: See Bellamy, 1973, for the rarity of this.

PAGE 423 Brake: Robert Browning, 'Childe Roland'.

Sir Richard Tunstall: Tunstall had been with Henry VI at Waddington Hall in 1465, and had tried to prevent his capture (Scofield, 1923, I, 381).

John Norris: Son or nephew of the very eminent Lancastrian John Norris of Bray. The latter's first wife was granddaughter of William Mountfort of Codbarrow, Warwickshire (and so a kinswoman of Sir William Mountfort) and he asked Lord Wenlock to be the overseer of his will. His very wealthy widow (and third wife), the daughter of Sir John Chedworth, married Sir John Howard, a loyal Yorkist who became Duke of Norfolk five months after Norris's death (Sutton, 1978; HPT draft biography of John Norris).

PAGE 424 Arrest of Thomas Cook: A. H. Thomas and I. D. Thornley (eds), *Great Chronicle of London* (1938), 204.

Danger of rumour: The superstitious Edward would not have liked the contemporary prophecy of a Welsh bard that a 'brave long-haired invader will come with a fleet, and will hover round the north Wales coast after the Feast and that there will be disturbances in Kent before harvest time and the world will be in a turmoil'.

PAGE 425 Jasper Tudor: Evans, 1915, citing CPR (1467–72), 103, 127. Mille: 'joined the king's enemies in Wales in a few months' (HPT draft biography of Hugh Mille, M.P.D., 1997).

PAGE 426 Warkworth's *Chronicle*, 5.

PAGE 427 Sir Humphrey Neville: Born in Slingsby, Yorkshire, in 1439, he was from the senior, solidly Lancastrian, branch of the Neville clan, nephew of Ralph, Earl of Westmorland. His seat was Brancepeth, near Durham, but he also had properties in Lincolnshire and Ripon (as did the Yorkshire Malorys).

Began hell-raising again: A warrant for Neville's arrest was issued on 7 April 1463 and he was recaptured by Robert Malory (evidently sent north after him), the Hospitaller knight Sir John Langstrother, Geoffrey Middleton, the Mayor of York and Sir James Strangeways. Again Edward was merciful, pardoning him in June on the same conditions. During the winter he escaped again and joined his friends and King Henry VI at Bamborough where Somerset, also out on parole, followed in January. He narrowly escaped capture after a daring ambush of Sir John Neville at Hedgeley Moor in April 1464. He then defended Bamborough with Sir Ralph Gray against the Earl of Warwick and Edward IV. Its walls crumbled under fire from Edward's mighty iron guns, and after one of them collapsed on Sir Ralph Gray and defeat was a certainty, Neville offered to surrender in exchange for pardons for all except Sir Ralph, who he thought was dead. Edward agreed. Neville slipped away, no man knew where; he will have heard later that Gray survived to be executed. According to Ramsay, 1892, II, 344, Neville was in concealment on the Derwent after 1464. He could well have been with Henry VI when the King was captured.

Galloped north: A warrant for £200 was issued to Sir John Neville (now Earl of Northumberland) on 30 July 1468 for his expenses 'in keeping of our great days of truce at our borders three times, as in subduing and repressing our rebels and traitors, Sir Humphrey Neville, Archibald Ridley and other within the county of Northumberland'. The payment was evidently a retrospective one, as Ridley had since been pardoned, but it showed what a menace Neville still was (CPR, I, 343; Scofield, 1923, I, 423).

Griffith ap Nicholas: He had been in Humfrey of Gloucester's retinue at Bury, and one of the indictments against the Duke had been that he 'would raise the Welshmen for to distress Suffolk and destroy him' (Evans, 1915, 25, 113 and 99 n19).

PAGE 428 Sir Gervais Clifton: In 1457 he had commanded the fleet against

Brezé's invasion of the Channel Islands (Colin Richmond, 'English Naval Power in the Fifteenth Century', *History* III, 1967).

Hugh Mille: HPT draft biography, M.P.D, 1997; *Turpine's Story* (E.E.T.S, 2004).

PAGE 429 Ideal disguise for a courier: Suggested by Field, 1993, 141. He could also have been related to the Sir Matthew Philip, a London alderman, who was made a Knight of the Bath with Sir Thomas Cook.

Kilby: Acheson, 1992, 70n.

Minstrels: A trade profitable enough to win country estates might also leave a man with enough leisure to pursue other interests. For Edward IV's minstrel called Marshall, see CPR. 3 Edward IV–Part II Jan 18 1464 (p. 297). Others included a London leather seller called Robert Marshall, who made his will on 19 July 1468; he was either a dying man or a frightened one. A wealthy London tradesman could have had country estates and have held the rank of a squire, or have had a son who did so.

PAGE 430 Seditious writings: 'Nearly every rebel leader of the period had his scribe or secretary and a messenger service' (Harvey, 1991, 75). Danvers was regarded with suspicion in the early 1460s (HPT draft biography, L.S.C., 2001; F. M. MacNamara, *Memorials of the Danvers Family*, Hardy & Co., London, 1985).

In all probability involved in it: According to Leland, Waynflete 'was in great dedignation with Edward IV' in 1468, and 'fled for fear of [him] into secret corners' (*Itinerary*, II, 31). He took out two pardons in rapid succession (Michael Hicks, private communication 5 October 2003).

Thomas Portaleyn: See ch. 12 above; HPT draft biography, Simon Payling, 2001.

Wealthy London widow: Alice (née Domenyk) Dyster's premarital tribulations put Joan Smith's in the shade: just before the wedding she was abducted by a rival suitor, William Gargrave, who 'menaced her hideously to die' until she surrendered to him. A relation of Malory's gaoler at the Marshalsea ten years later, Gargrave gathered forty notorious felons from the prison to help him seize her. Portaleyn got her back and the couple successfully filed a bill of rape against Gargrave. Portaleyn was JP for Middlesex during the Readeption; he probably died either at Barnet or Tewkesbury, and was certainly dead by 1472.

PAGE 431 Windows of Ockwells: See ch. 22 above.

College founded: Margaret of Anjou's foundation was adopted by Edward's queen, Elizabeth Woodville; its two royal patrons are both recognised in its later name of 'The Queens' College'.

Bevy of Lancastrian wards: McFarlane, 1981, 253.

PAGE 432 Sister of the Thomas Danvers: After the death of Sir Robert Danvers of Culworth, Northamptonshire (which borders on Thorpe Mandeville) in 1462, Wenlock became the guardian of his three daughters (Roskell, 1981, ch. 10). The executors were Sir Robert's sister Agnes, his brother Richard Danvers, and his son-in-law George Burneby, who was listed as 'of Sutton-le-Hone'. A

William Malory also lived at Sutton-le-Hone, which was held of the Knights Hospitallers.

The feast of the wedding: Malory, VII.35.

PAGE 433 All manner of legends: Christine Weightman, *Margaret of York: Duchess of Burgundy 1446–1503* (Sutton, Stroud, 1989); Caxton, introduction to *The Troy Book*.

PAGE 434 They that jousted: *Paston Letters*, II, ed. Davis, 318.

PAGE 435 'Well-beseen': ibid.

PAGE 436 Stairs (aka Steers): Ramsay, 1892, II, 335, citing *Rotuli Parliamentorum*, VI, 292. Stairs was also accused of plotting the murder of the Earl of Warwick in 1460. He was tried in the court of chivalry (Michael Hicks, personal communication).

PAGE 437 Persuaded to talk: Scofield, 1923, I, 480. On his way home from Bruges, Oxford had written to John Paston from Canterbury on 18 July, asking him to buy him three sets of horse armour 'as it were for yourself'. He signed off by adding: 'I trust to God we shall do right well, who preserve you'. With conspirators as careless as this among his acquaintance, it is easy to see why William Paston had taken the precaution of signing up for the general pardon only a day earlier.

'Final death': Ross, 1974, 123.

Arrested earlier: Deduced from his presence in Newgate at this time. It is unlikely that he would have been living in London as a free man when he was part of a tiny but evidently notorious élite of *personae non gratae*. He could have been imprisoned any time after the wedding of his niece in Warwickshire in September 1464, but it would have been an extraordinary thing for a knight to be incarcerated for so long in the relatively peaceful mid-1460s without somebody, somewhere, objecting or making an attempt to purloin his estates. In 1468, the situation was quite different. Arrests were frequent and unrecorded.

Document only discovered: Sutton, 'Malory in Newgate' (2000). Anne Sutton, the historian of the Mercer's Company, is editor of *The Ricardian*, and co-author of much fascinating work on fifteenth-century literature. She was examining a volume of copies of title deeds and other evidences of ownership of the properties which John Colet, a London mercer and Dean of St Paul's Cathedral 1504–19, had given to endow his foundation of St Paul's School in 1510. Some of these concerned properties in Colchester bought by Colet from the Cook family. One of them was a document that revealed Malory's presence in Newgate. Its date falls squarely between that of the two pardons from which he was specifically exempted – July 1468 and February 1470.

'Draughton': See Mallory-Smith, 1958, 39–40.

PAGE 438 Vale writes: *John Vale's Book*, Kekewich et al., 1995, 178.

'But, sir': Malory, *Works*, 1197, quoted in Radulescu, 1999.

PAGE 439 'I pray you': Malory, XXI.13.

CHAPTER 24

PAGE 441 'Also me seemeth': Preface to Wynken's 1529 edition of Malory: *The Book of the Most Noble and Worthy Prince King Arthur Sometime King of Great Britain Now Called England, which Treateth of His Noble Acts and Feats of Arms of Chivalry, and of His Noble Knights and Table Round and this Volume is Divided into XXI Books.* Main sources for this chapter are Hicks, 1998; Ramsay, 1892; Ross, 1974.

Marriage of . . . Isobel: Much has been written of the many profitable marriages made by the Woodvilles, but Warwick's Neville brothers and sisters were just as numerous, and almost as successful in the marriage market (Richardson, 1998, 11).

'Did attempt a thing': Hall, 1809, 265–9. Hall's source was probably the continuation of John Hardyng's *Chronicle* which said that the real cause of Warwick's grudge was an attempt by Edward on the honour of one of his womenfolk (pp. 438–9).

PAGE 443 Among the Garter knights: For Wenlock and Wrottesley, see Michael Hicks, *False, Fleeting, Perjur'd Clarence: George, Duke Clarence 1449–78* (Sutton, Gloucester, 1980), 45.

Wenlock . . . lieutenant at Calais: Roskell, 1981, 263.

Sir Robert Harcourt: see HPT draft biography, L.S.C., 1995.

Bills just issued: They confirm the length of contemporary political memory by referring to evils that occurred when such kings as Edward II, Richard II, and Henry VI 'estranged the great lords of their blood from their secret council' (*John Vale's Book*, Kekewich et al., 1995, 212–13).

PAGE 444 Master manuscript: Speculation on the early history of the Malory manuscript has been extensive. See Wheeler et al., 2000, and ch. 25 below.

Captured and executed: Hicks, 1980, 49.

PAGE 445 'The Earl of Warwick': CSPM, I, 131.

PAGE 446 Vengeful local wars: The Duke of Norfolk refused to abandon his siege of the Pastons in Caistor Castle despite missives from the council and the Duke of Clarence, saying, 'He will not spare to do as he is purposed for no Duke in England'.

'Presume or take it upon them': Scofield, 1923, I, 503.

Witness their execution: Scofield, 1923, I, 503.

Great Council: Hicks, 1980, 55.

PAGE 447 A general pardon: PRO 67/47,m.9. John Wirkington (or Wrightington) nuper de Cawood, Yorkshire, gentleman, and John Manningham nuper of Rothwell in the same country were both Sir Humphrey Neville's men (Hicks, personal communication). The other eleven men listed in 1468 were no longer excepted, despite the ap Griffith escapade in the autumn; some may have been dead, others forgiven. Thomas ap Griffith was in trouble again in 1473 (Evans, 195, 117).

PAGE 448 'Turn again': Contemporary ballad.
Vast army: Two dukes, four earls and ten barons, all with substantial retinues of knights, men-at-arms and archers. 'It was said that were never seen in England so many goodly men and so well-arrayed in the field' (*Paston Letters*, II, no. 638).

PAGE 449 Warwick upped anchor: At some point the Neville women were landed, to be safely lodged at Valognes, in the Cotentin.
Circumscribed pardon: PRO C76/56/154, m.4, 3 May 1470.

PAGE 450 King Louis refereed: Lander, 1990, 125; Ramsay, 1892, II, 358.

PAGE 455 'False, fleeting, perjur'd Clarence': Shakespeare, *Richard III*: the words are uttered by Warwick's ghost when he appears to Clarence in a nightmare.

PAGE 458 Bisham Abbey: The abbey and the Neville vault were destroyed after the Dissolution of the Monasteries by Henry VIII in the 1430s.
Official verdict: A. J. Pollard, *Richard III and the Princes in the Tower* (Sutton, Stroud, 1997), 54–5. There is no evidence for Thomas More's later claim that Richard of Gloucester murdered Henry VI without the permission of Edward IV, or for Shakespeare's vision of him stabbing the frail, mazed king and crying, 'Down, down to hell, and say I sent thee there'.
Blood leaked: Exhumation of Henry's remains in 1910 confirmed his violent death: his hair was matted with blood (W. J. White, 'The Death and Burial of Henry VI', *The Ricardian* VI, 1982).

PAGE 459 Hugh Bryce: Ibid.

CHAPTER 25
PAGE 460 'Thou art a monument': Jonson's poem 'To the Memory of My Beloved, the Author, Mr William Shakespeare' opens: 'My Shakespeare rise'.
'We be adcertained': Armstrong, 1991, 80.

PAGE 461 'And so he did' and subsequent quotes: Malory, XXI.11. The Dirige was one of the three funeral services; the first, a Vespers, was said the night before, the second, the Dirige (which began 'Dirige, domine, Deus meus . . .') was a Matins, said in theory after midnight, but usually much later in the morning, only slightly preceding the final service, the Mass for the Dead.

PAGE 462 Grandest and most fashionable: C. L. Kingsford, *The Grey Friars of London* (Aberdeen UP, 1915).

PAGE 463 Stained-glass windows: 'Lo! how men wryten in fenestres at the freres' (Langland, *Piers Plowman*, quoted Kingsford, 1914).
Recorded in a list: BL Cotton Vitellius, F xii, f.284r.

PAGE 464 'There they laid . . .': Malory, XXI.12.

'His visage was laid open': It was still the custom to do this in Malory's day. At John Paston's funeral in 1466, the Dirige was sung by friars of all four orders, thirty-eight priests, thirty-nine boys in surplices and twenty-six clerks. A local prioress, her maid, and an anchorite and twenty-three sisters from a nearby convent hospital were also in attendance (Bennett, 1968, 197).

14th day of March AD 1471: The record actually says 14 March 1470, but that was by modern reckoning 14 March 1471: in the fifteenth century, the year began on 25 March, the feast of the Annunciation. Just to confuse matters, the date of Malory's death in the inquiry into his landholdings issued in November was given as 12 March. Later copies of this list made by John Stow (*Survey of London*) and J. G. Nichols do not include the manuscript's 'sub lapide' (Field, 1993, 133).

Dominus: It was also used as a title by priests and professed monks. There remains a possibility that when Malory called himself 'the servant of Jesu by day and by night' in the very last line of the *Morte* (*Works*, 1260, 128), he was revealing that he had taken holy orders of some kind. It was fairly common for the elderly to do so, and as we have seen, Malory makes Lancelot become a monk.

A mere brass plaque: Such plaques were popular by the 1460s (Duffy, 1992, 332).

Sir Walter Wrottesley: Wedgwood, 1936, 975.

PAGE 465 'Almost orgiastic': Mertes, 1988, 156–7.

Chosen place of prayer: Duffy, 1992, 332. Malory's burial in London rather than in Warwickshire might also be evidence that he was somewhat estranged from his wife. In more settled times, he might however have been taken home. In 1466, John Paston died in London, and his body, escorted by twelve black-robed mourners, went in solemn procession to Bromholm, Norfolk. The journey took six days (Margaret Aston, 'Death', in Horrox (ed.), 1994, 222).

PAGE 466 One of the best libraries: Kingsford, 1915. The Greyfriars library survived until c.1827.

Richard of Bury: *Philobiblon*, 1344, trans. E. C. Thomas (Birmingham, 1946).

Predominantly theological works: Matthews, 1966, 52–6.

Perhaps of books: A much less distinguished figure, the London clothier Thomas of Wallington, willed that 'my library, existing in two volumes, one Catholicon [a Latin dictionary] and one book called Sydrac [a medieval scientific treatise] . . . be sold and the money given to poor scholars to pray for my soul' (Rickert, 1948, 421).

Blount family: Anne herself died in 1480. She chose to be buried in the tomb of her first husband, the Duke of Buckingham, a piety worthy of Guinevere, and no doubt expected of her by her Stafford kin.

PAGE 467 Its shell survives: Christchurch Passage, the alley beside the tower, was once the 'walking place' across the middle of the medieval church, leading to the chapter house, studies and library (Kingsford, 1915, 38–42; a plan on p. 37

shows the location of the chapel of St Francis on the south-west side of the choir).

Inquisition post mortem: PRO C140/36/12; Field, 1993, 133–7; Whitteridge, 1973, 264–5.

PAGE 468 Then about twenty-three: Proof of age: PRO C140/36/12.

Took out a pardon: Whitteridge, 1973, 265, citing Supplementary Patent Roll, PRO C67/46.

The inquisition post mortem reported: C140/75/46 (printed in Hicks, 1928, Appendix). The Malory lands were given to Kelem by letters patent 'for services to the king and Elizabeth his consort' (CPR (1476–85), 220). Kingston was summoned to be knighted at the proposed coronation of Edward V (Field, 1993, citing *Grants Etc. from the Crown during the Reign of Edward IV*, ed. J. G. Nichols (Camden Society, 60, 1854), 69–71).

Authorised William Catesby: The copy of the indenture Catesby signed with the courier survives (PRO E40/14705).

PAGE 469 'One of the greatest of English kings': Carpenter, 1997.

Pre-contract: For Isobel Butler, see endnote, ch. 22 above. Lady Eleanor had died some time before 1483.

Margaret of Anjou: Details from Hookham, 1872.

PAGE 470 Close crony: Catesby was the 'cat' of the doggerel rhyme 'the cat, the rat [Sir Richard Ratcliffe] and Lovell the dog [Viscount Lovell] / ruleth all England under the hog [Richard III]'. A contemporary said of him, 'Indeed you would not wish that a man of so much wit should be of so little faith' (Hicks, 1991).

'Fighting manfully' and other quotes: Lander, 1990.

Ralph Wolseley: KB 27/900 rot.5–7; Field, 1993, 127, 133–7, puts a slightly different interpretation on the records.

PAGE 471 William Caxton finished printing: Analysis and comparison of the Winchester manuscript and Caxton's edited text are a fascinating pursuit, but are too technical a subject to cover in this biography. Experts who have analysed the text include Field, passim, especially 1998, ch. 1: 'The Earliest Texts of Malory's *Morte Darthur*' and ch. 2: 'The Choice of Texts for Malory's *Morte Darthur*'; Ingrid Tieken-Boon van Ostade, *The Two Versions of Malory's* Morte Darthur: *Multiple Negation and the Editing of the Text* (*Arthurian Studies* 35, Brewer, Cambridge, 1995); N. F. Blake, 'Caxton at Work: A Reconsideration', in B. Wheeler et al. (eds), 2000; Wheeler (ed.), 2004.

PAGE 473 Edward of Middleham: The boy's death in 1484 led the scribe who created the *Beauchamp Pageant* to set down his pen and brushes and leave the illustration of the young Prince and his parents unfinished.

Tended to do: See the preface to *Blanchardine and Eglantine*, a romance which Caxton printed at the request of Lady Margaret Beaufort in 1489.

PAGE 474 Arrival in Caxton's printing works: See authorities cited above. The fact that a tear in one of Winchester's pages was mended with a scrap of an indulgence printed by Caxton in 1489 shows that it remained in Caxton's workshop for some time.

Another version: see Takako Kato.

See the storyteller: See Coleman, 1996, for fascinating evidence of reading texts aloud all through the fifteenth century; Cherewatuk and Coleman includes an audio CD of extracts read with fifteenth-century accents.

PAGE 475 'A fair prince': Stowe's Memoranda, in Gairdner, 1880, 104.

Arranged for him to see: Starkey, 1998.

Plantagenet blood: Clarence was descended from Edward III. The Beauchamps continued to be cursed by this link to Plantagenet. Margaret, younger daughter of Isobel and Clarence, was accepted at first by the Tudors, but when rebellions arose after Henry VIII's divorce from Catherine of Aragon and Rome, Henry executed first her son, Henry de la Pole, then Margaret herself – aged seventy-three.

In 1495, Richard Malory: Arthurson, 1994, passim. Nicholas Malory did however become Sheriff of Warwickshire and Leicestershire in 1502. He was the last male Malory of Newbold Revel. He had two daughters, both of whom married into the Cave family. The estate was sold to the Pope family in 1538 (Mallory-Smith, 1958, 28). For details of his descendants and other Malorys, see Field, 1993, Appendix 1; Malory-Smith, 1958, passim.

PAGE 476 New edition: Parins, 1988, 40–6 gives a complete list of the printings.

Henry VIII grew up to enjoy: Deduced from Ascham, *Toxophilis* (see below); Starkey, 'The Age of the Household: Politics, Society and the Arts, *c*.1350–*c*.1550', in S. Medcalf (ed.), *The Later Middle Ages*, Methuen, 1981, mentions the interesting fact that William Blount, Lord Mountjoy, was 'the companion of Henry [VIII]'s studies'. It seems very possible that the Blounts had a copy of Malory's book; young William could even have had stories of Sir Thomas himself handed down to him.

Frowned upon: Ascham wrote in his *Toxophilis* (1545) that 'in our fathers' time nothing was read but books of fained chivalry, wherein a man by reading should be led to none other end but only to manslaughter and bawdry'. The same sentiments were repeated in Ascham's *The Scholemaster* (*c*.1563, published 1570): 'In our forefathers' time . . . few books were read in our tongue save certain books of Chivalry . . . God's Bible was banished from the Court, and Morte Arthure received into the Princes' chamber' (Parins, 1988, 57).

PAGE 477 Nathaniel Baxter (*c*.1550–1635): Parins, 1988, 58. Baxter clearly had not read it, or he would have substituted Gawaine for Gareth.

PAGE 480 Was thrilled and astonished: Gallix (ed.), 1984, 86.

BIBLIOGRAPHY

Acheson, Eric, *A Gentry Community: Leicestershire in the Fifteenth Century c.1442–c.1485* (CUP, 1992)

Adam of Usk, *Chronicle*, edited by E. M. Thompson (1904; reprinted Llanerch, 1990)

Alban, J. and Allmand, C. T., 'Spies and Spying in the Fourteenth Century', in Diana Dunn (ed.), *War and Society in Early Modern Britain* (Liverpool UP, 2000)

Archer, Rowena E. and Walker, Simon (eds), *Rulers and Ruled in Late Medieval England: Essays Presented to Gerald Harriss* (Hambledon, London, 1995)

Archibald, Elizabeth and Edwards, A. S. G. (eds), *A Companion to Malory* (Arthurian Studies XXXVII, Brewer, Woodbridge, 1996). This has a useful select bibliography of Malory studies.

Armstrong, C. A. J., 'Politics and the Battle of St Albans', *BIHR*, XXXIII (1960)

Armstrong, C. A. J., *England, France and Burgundy in the Fifteenth Century*, (Hambledon, London, 1983)

Armstrong, C. A. J., 'Some Examples of the Distribution and Speed of News in England at the Time of the Wars of the Roses', *Medieval History*, 1.2, Headstart History (1991)

Arthurson, Ian, 'Espionage and Intelligence from the Wars of the Roses to the Reformation', *Nottingham Medieval Studies* XXXV (1991)

Arthurson, Ian, *The Perkin Warbeck Conspiracy* (Sutton, Stroud, 1994)

Aurner, Nellie Slayton, 'Sir Thomas Malory – Historian?', *Publications of the Modern Language Association of America* 48 (1933), 362–91

Bagley, J. J., *The Ardent Queen: Margaret of Anjou, Queen of England* (London, 1948)

Baldwin, David, *Elizabeth Woodville: Mother of the Princes in the Tower* (Sutton, Stroud, 2002)

Bale, John, *Scriptorum Illustrium Maioris Brytanniae* (Basle, 1557–9)

Barber, Malcolm J. (ed.), *The Military Orders: Fighting for the Faith and Caring for the Sick* (Variorum, 1994)

Barber, R., 'Malory's *Morte Darthur* and Court Culture under Edward IV', in J. P. Carley and F. Riddy (eds), *Arthurian Literature* XII (Brewer, 1993)

Barron, Caroline and Saul, Nigel (eds), *England and the Low Countries in the Late Middle Ages* (Sutton, Stroud, 1995)

Barron, W. R. J. (ed.), *The Arthur of the English: The Arthurian Legend in Medieval English Life and Literature* (University of Wales Press, Cardiff, 2001)

Bartolomew, Glanville, extracts collected in *Medieval Love from Bartholomeus Anglicus*, ed. Robert Steele (King's Classics, London, 1893)

Bassett, Margery, 'Newgate Prison in the Middle Ages', *Speculum* XVIII (1943)

Bassett, Margery, 'The Fleet Prison in the Middle Ages', *University of Toronto Law Journal* 5 (1943–4)

Batt, Catherine, 'Malory and Rape', *Arthuriana* 7.3 (1997), 78–99

Baugh, A. C., 'Documenting Sir Thomas Malory', *Speculum* 8 (1933), 3–29

Beauchamp Pageant: British Library Cotton MS Julius E IV, article 6

Bellamy, John, *Crime and Public Order in England in the Later Middle Ages* (Routledge, Toronto, 1973)

Bellamy, John, *The Criminal Trial in Later Medieval England* (Sutton, Stroud, 1998)

Benet's *Chronicle*: 'John Benet's chronicle for the years 1400–1462', in *Camden Miscellany*, XXIV (Camden Society, 4th series, IX, 1972), 151–252

Bennett, H. S., *The Pastons and Their England* (CUP, 1968)

Bennett, J. A. W., *Essays on Malory* (Clarendon Press, Oxford, 1963)

Benson, Larry, *Malory's Morte Darthur* (Harvard UP, Cambridge, MA, 1976)

Bentley, Samuel (ed.), *Excerpta Historica*: Illustrations of English History (London, 1833)

Biddle, Martin, *King Arthur's Round Table* (Boydell, Woodbridge, 2000)

Blake, N. F., 'Caxton at Work: A Reconsideration', in *The Malory Debate*, ed. Bonnie Wheeler, Robert L. Kindrick and Michael N. Salda, *Arthurian Studies* XLVII (Brewer, Cambridge, 2000)

Blake, N. F., *Caxton: England's First Publisher* (Osprey, London, 1976)

Boardman, A. W., *The Battle of Towton* (Sutton, Stroud, 1994)

Boardman, A. W., *The Medieval Soldier in the Wars of the Roses* (Sutton, Stroud, 1998)

Bornstein, Diane D., 'Military Strategy in Malory and Vegetius', *De Re Militari*, in *Comparative Literature Studies* (University of Illinois), 9 (1972)

Boulton, D. J. D., *The Knights of the Crown: The Monarchical Order of Knighthood in Later Medieval Europe 1325–1520* (Boydell, Woodbridge, 1987)

Bradbury, Jim, *The Medieval Archer* (Boydell, Woodbridge, 1985)

Bridges, J. and Whalley, P., *The History of Northamptonshire*, 2 vols (Oxford, 1791)

Brindley, David, *Richard Beauchamp: Medieval England's Greatest Knight* (Tempus, 2001)

Brown, C. F. and Robbins, R. H., *The Index of Middle English Verse* (Columbia UP, New York, 1943)

Burton, William, *History and Description of Leicestershire* (London, 1777)

Calendar of State Papers and Manuscripts relating to English Affairs, existing in the Archives and Collections of Milan, I, 1385–1618, ed. A. B. Hinds (1913)

Carew, Richard, *Survey of Cornwall*, 1602 (reprinted Melrose, London, 1953)

Carpenter, Mary Christine, 'Political Society in Warwickshire, c.1401–72', PhD thesis, Cambridge, 1976

Carpenter, Mary Christine, 'Thomas Malory and Fifteenth-Century Politics', *IHR* 53 (1980), 31–43

Carpenter, Christine, *Locality and Polity: a Study of Warwickshire Landed Society 1401–1499* (CUP, 1992)

Carpenter, Mary Christine, *The Wars of the Roses* (CUP, 1997)

Carte, Thomas, *A General History of England* (London, 1775)

Cartellieri, O., *The Court of Burgundy: Studies in the History of Civilisation* (1904; repr. Kegan, Paul, London, 1972)

Castor, Helen R., 'New Evidence on the Grant of the Duchy of Lancaster Office to Henry Beauchamp, Earl of Warwick, in 1444', *Historical Research* 68 (1995), 225–8

Castor, Helen R., 'The Duchy of Lancaster in the Lancastrian Polity, 1399–1461', unpublished PhD thesis, Cambridge, 1993

Castor, Helen R., *The King, the Crown, and the Duchy of Lancaster* (OUP, Oxford, 2000)

Cely Papers, ed. H. E. Malden (Camden Society, 1900)

Cessoles, Jacques de, *The Game and Play of Chess*, trans. and printed by William Caxton, *c*.1483, reprinted (ed. N. F. Blake) London, 1976

Cheney, C. R., *A Handbook of Dates*, new edn, rev. Michael Jones (CUP, 2000)

Cherewatuk, Karen, '"Gentyl" Audiences and "Greate Bookes": Chivalric Manuals and the *Morte Darthur*', *Arthurian Literature* (1997)

Chetwynd-Stapleton, H. E., *The Chetwynds of Ingestre* (London, 1892)

Chrimes, S. B. (trans.), *Sir John Fortescue: De Laudibus Legum Angoiae* (CUP, 1949)

Chrimes, S. B., Ross, C. D. and Griffiths, R. A. (eds), *Fifteenth-Century England 1399–1509* (Sutton, Stroud, 1995)

Clark, Linda S. (ed.), *The Fifteenth Century, 3: Authority and Subversion* (Boydell, Woodbridge, 2003)

Coleman, Joyce, *Public Reading and the Reading Public in Late Medieval England and France* (CUP, 1996)

Collins, Hugh E. L., *The Order of the Garter 1348–1461: Chivalry and Politics in Late Medieval England* (OUP, New York, 2000)

Colvin, H. M. (gen. ed.), *The History of the King's Works, 4: 1485–1660* (HMSO, London, 1982)

Commines, Philippe de, *Memoires de Messire Philippe de Commines*, ed. Joseph Calmette (Paris, 1552)

Complete Peerage of England, Scotland, Ireland and the United Kingdom, ed. G. E. Cockayne, 13 vols (new edn 1910–59)

Connolly, Margaret, *John Shirley: Book Production and the Noble Household in Fifteenth-Century England* (Ashgate, Aldershot, 1998)

Cooper, Helen, 'Opening up the Malory Manuscript', in *The Malory Debate*, ed. Bonnie Wheeler et al. (2000)

Cripps-Day, F. H., *The History of the Tournament in England and in France* (Quaritch, London, 1918)

Crouch, David, *The Beaumont Twins: The Roots and Branches of Power in the Twelfth Century* (CUP, 1986)

Crowland Chronicle Continuations, 1459–1486, The, ed. N. Pronny and J. Cox (Alan Sutton, Stroud, for Richard III and Yorkist History Trust, 1986)

Curry, Anne E., 'The First English Standing Army? Military Organization in Lancastrian Normandy, 1420–1450', in Charles Ross (ed.), *Patronage, Pedigree and Power in Later Medieval England* (Sutton, Stroud, 1979), 193–214

Curry, Anne E., 'Sex and the Soldier in Lancastrian Normandy, 1415–1450', *Reading Journal of Medieval History* (1988)

Curry, Anne E., *The Battle of Agincourt* (Boydell, Woodbridge, 2000)

Curry, Anne E., 'Isolated or Integrated? The English Soldier in Lancastrian Normandy', in Sarah Rees Jones, Richard Marks and A. J. Minnis (eds), *Courts and Regions in Medieval Europe* (York Medieval Press, Woodbridge, 2000)

Curry, Anne E., 'The Organization of Field Armies in Lancastrian Normandy', in M. Strickland (ed.), *Armies, Chivalry and Warfare in Medieval Britain and France* (Stamford, 1998)

Curry, Anne E., 'The Loss of Lancastrian Normandy: An Administrative Nightmare?', in D. Grummitt (ed.), *The English Experience in France 1450–1558* (Ashgate, Aldershot, 2002)

Cust, Mrs Henry, *Gentlemen Errant, being the Journeys and Adventures of Four Noblemen in Europe during the Fifteenth and Sixteenth Centuries* (John Murray, London, 1909)

Cutts, Edward L., *Scenes and Characters of the Middle Ages* (Simpkin, Marshall, London, 1926)

Daiches, David and Thorlby, Anthony (eds), *The Medieval World* (Aldus, London, 1973)

Davies, J. S. (ed.), *English Chronicles of the Reigns of Richard II–Henry VI* (Camden Society 1st series 64, 1856)

Davies, Katherine, *The First Queen Elizabeth* (Lovat-Dickson, London, 1937)

Davies, R. R., *The Revolt of Owain Glyn Dŵr* (Oxford University Press, 1995)

Davis, Virginia, 'William Waynflete and the Wars of the Roses', *Southern Review* II (1989), 1–22

Dockray, Keith, *Henry VI, Margaret of Anjou and the Wars of Roses: A Source Book* (Sutton, Stroud, 2000)

Duffy, Eamon, *The Stripping of the Altars: Traditional Religion in England 1400–1580* (Yale UP, New Haven, CT, 1992)

Dugdale, William, *History and Antiquities of Warwickshire*, 2 vols (London, 1656)

Earle, Peter, *Henry V* (Weidenfeld, London, 1972)

Edward, Duke of York, *The Master of Game*, ed. W. A. and F. Baillie-Grohman (London, 1904, 1909)

Ellis, H., *Original Letters Illustrative of English History* (Camden Society, 2nd series I (1827)

Escouchy, Mathieu de, *Chronique de Mathieu d'Escouchy*, ed. G. L. E. du F. de Beaucourt, 3 vols (Paris, 1863–4)

Evans, H. T., *Wales and the Wars of the Roses* (1915; repr. Sutton, Stroud, 1998)

Fabyan, R. (d. 1513), *New Chronicles of England and France* (London, 1811)

Farnham, George, *Leicestershire Medieval Pedigrees* (Leicester, 1925)

Farnham, George, *Leicestershire Medieval Village Notes* (Leicester, 1929–33), 6 vols

Ferguson, Arthur, *The Indian Summer of English Chivalry: Studies in the Decline of Chivalric Idealism* (Duke UP, Durham, NC, 1960)

Field, P. J. C., *Romance and Chronicle: A Study of Malory's Prose Style* (Barrie & Jenkins, London, 1971)

Field, P. J. C., 'Sir Thomas Malory, MP', IHR 47 (1974)

Field, P. J. C., 'Sir Robert Malory, Prior of the Hospital of St John of Jerusalem in England (1439–1439/40)', *Journal of Ecclesiastical History* 28.3 (July 1977)

Field, P. J. C., 'Last Years of Sir Thomas Malory', in BJRL 64 (1981–2)

Field, P. J. C., *The Life and Times of Sir Thomas Malory* (Brewer, Cambridge, 1993)

Field, P. J. C., 'Fifteenth-Century History in Malory's *Morte Darthur*', in Françoise H. M. Le Saux (ed.), *The Formation of Culture in Medieval Britain* (Lewiston, NY/Edwin Mellen, Lampeter, 1995), 39–70

Field, P. J. C., *Malory: Texts and Sources, Arthurian Studies* XL (Brewer, Cambridge, 1998)

Field, P. J. C., 'Malory and *The Wedding of Sir Gawaine and Dame Ragnald*', in *Texts and Sources*, ed. Field (1998), 284–94

Field, P. J. C., 'Malory's Minor Sources', in *Texts and Sources*, ed. Field (1998)

Field, P. J. C., 'Malory's Own Marginalia', *Medium Aevum* 70.2 (2001), 226–39

Flenley, R. (ed.), *Six Town Chronicles of England* (Clarendon Press, Oxford, 1911)

Foers, Richard, *History of Castle Bytham* (Castle Bytham, 2000)

Fortescue, John, *De Laudibus Legum Angliae*, in T. Fortescue, Lord Clermont (ed.), *Sir John Fortescue, Knight, His Life, Works and Family History*, 2 vols (London, 1869)

Foss, Michael, *Chivalry* (Michael Joseph, London, 1975)

Fox, Dorothy, *The History of the Church and Parish of Kirkby Mallory* (Cleveland, 2001)

Warwick Castle and its Earls, Frances Evelyn (Daisy), Countess of Warwick (London, 1903)

Friel, Ian, *The Good Ship: Ships, Shipbuilding and Technology in England 1200–1520* (British Museum Press, London, 1995)

Froissart, Jean, *The Chronicles of England, France and Spain*, ed. K. de Lettenhove, 25 vols (1867–77)

Furnival, F. J., *Early English Meals and Manners* (EETS, 1894)

Gairdner, J. M. (ed.), *Three Fifteenth-Century Chronicles* (Camden Society, new series 18, 1880)

Gallix, François (ed.), *Letters to a Friend: The Correspondence between T. H. White and L. J. Potts* (Sutton, Stroud, 1984)

Gesta Henrici Quinti: The Deeds of Henry the Fifth, trans. and ed. F. Taylor and J. S. Roskell (OUP, 1975)

Given-Wilson, C., *The Royal Household and the King's Affinity 1360–1413* (Yale UP, New Haven, CT, 1986)

Goldrick, I., 'The Literary Manuscripts and Literary Patronage of the Beauchamp and Neville Families in the Late Middle Ages c.1390–1500', PhD thesis, Newcastle Polytechnic, 1985

Gomme, A., *Newbold Revel: An Architectural History*, HM Prison Service, n.d.

Goodall, J. A. A., *God's House at Ewelme: Life, Devotion and Architecture in a Fifteenth-Century Almshouse* (privately printed, Aldershot, 2001)

Gooder, Eileen, *Temple Balsall* (Phillimore, Chichester, 1999)

Graves, Robert, introduction to *Sir Thomas Malory's Morte Darthur: King Arthur and the Legends of the Round Table*, rewritten (somewhat pompously) by Keith Baines, illus. Enrico Arno (Harrap, 1963)

Great Chronicle of London, The, ed. A. H. Thomas and I. D. Thornley (privately printed, London, 1938)

Green, Richard Firth, *Poets and Princepleasers: Literature and the English Court in the Late Middle Ages* (Toronto UP, 1980)

Griffith, R. R., 'The Political Bias of Malory's *Morte Darthur*', *Viator* 5 (1974), 365–86

Griffith, R. R., 'The Authorship Question Reconsidered: A Case for Thomas Malory of Papworth St Agnes, Cambridgeshire', in Takamiya, T. and Brewer, D., *Aspects of Malory* (Brewer, Cambridge, 1981), 159–77

Griffiths, Ralph Allen and Thomas, R. S. (eds), *The Making of the Tudor Dynasty* (St Martin's Press, New York, 1985)

Griffiths, Ralph Allen and Sherborne, James, *Kings and Nobles in the Later Middle Ages* (Sutton, Stroud, 1986)

Griffiths, Ralph Allen, *The Reign of King Henry VI: The Exercise of Royal Authority 1422–1461* (Benn, London, 1981)

Grummitt, David (ed.), *The English Experience in France c. 1450–1588: War, Diplomacy and Cultural Exchange* (Ashgate, Aldershot, 2002)

Hall, Edward, *Chronicle*, ed. H. Ellis (London, 1809)

Hanawalt, Barbara, *Growing Up in Medieval London* (OUP, 1993)

Hanks Jr, D. Thomas and Brogdon, Jessica G. (eds), *The Social and Literary Context of Malory's Morte Darthur* (Arthurian Studies XLII, Brewer, Cambridge, 2000)

Hardyment, Christina, *Perfect Parents* (OUP, 1993)

Hardyng, John, *Chronicle*, ed. H. Ellis (London, 1812)

Harris, M. (ed.), Account Book of the Great Household of Humphrey, *Camden Miscellany 28*, 4th series, 29 (London, Royal Historical Society, 1984)

Harriss, G. L., *Cardinal Beaufort: A Study of Lancastrian Ascendancy and Decline* (Oxford, Clarendon Press, 1988)

Harvey, Isobel, *Jack Cade's Rebellion of 1450* (Clarendon Press, Oxford, 1991)

Hawes, R., *History of Framlingham* (1798)

Hayfield, Colin and Watkins, Andrew, *Coleshill and the Digbys: 500 Years of Manorial Lordship* (Arley, Warwickshire, 1995)

Hicks, Edward, *Sir Thomas Malory: His Turbulent Career* (Harvard UP, Cambridge, MA, 1928, 2nd edn Octagon Books, New York, 1975)

Hicks, Michael, 'The Case of Sir Thomas Cook, 1468', EHR 93 (1978)

Hicks, Michael, *False, Fleeting, Perjur'd Clarence: George, Duke of Clarence 1449–78* (Sutton, Gloucester, 1980)

Hicks, Michael, 'The Beauchamp Trust 1439–1487', BIHR 54.30 (1981)

Hicks, Michael, *Who's Who in Late Medieval England 1272–1485* (Shepheard-Walwyn, London, 1991)

Hicks, Michael, 'Lawmakers and Lawbreakers', in C. Given-Wilson, *Late Medieval England* (Manchester UP, 1996)

Hicks, Michael, *Warwick the Kingmaker* (Blackwell, Oxford, 1998)

Hicks, Michael, 'The Beauchamp Interregnun 1439–1449', BIHR 72 (1999)

Hodges, Geoffrey, *Ludford Bridge and Mortimer's Cross* (Logaston Press, Almeley, 1989)

Holinshed, *Chronicle* (15/7; 3rd edn 1586; repr. Johnson et al., London, 1808)

Holland, P., 'Cook's Case in History and in Myth', BIHR 61 (1988)

Hookham, Mary-Ann, *The Life and Times of Margaret of Anjou* (Tinsley, London, 1872)

Horrox, R. (ed.), *Fifteenth-Century Attitudes* (CUP, 1994)

Hughes, Jonathan, *Arthurian Myths and Alchemy: The Kingship of Edward IV* (Sutton, Stroud, 2002)

Humphery-Smith, Cecil R., *Hugh Revel* (Phillimore, Chichester, 1994)

Hyland, Ann, *The Horse in Middle Ages* (Sutton, Stroud, 1999)

Information for Pilgrims unto the Holy Land, printed by William de Worde in 1493, ed. Gordon Duff (Lawrence & Bullen, London, 1893)

Jacob, E. F., *The Fifteenth Century 1399–1485* (OUP, Oxford/New York, 1961)

James, M. R., *Henry the Sixth, A Reprint of John Blacmun's Memoir* (CUP, 1919)

Jarman, Rosalind, *Crispin's Day: The Glory of Agincourt* (Collins, London, 1979)

Johnson, P. A., *Duke Richard of York 1411–1460* (Clarendon Press, Oxford, 1988)

Jones, M. K., 'Somerset, York, and the Wars of the Roses', *EHR* 104 (1989)

Kato, Takako, *Caxton's Morte Darthur: the printing process and the authenticity of the text*, Medium Aevum Monographs, new series 22 (Oxford: The Society for the Study of Medieval Language and Litearature, 2002)

Keen, Maurice, *English Society in the Later Middle Ages 1348–1500* (Penguin, London, 1990)

Keen, Maurice, *Nobles, Knights and Men-at-Arms in the Middle Ages* (Hambledon, London, 1996)

Kekewich, M. L., Richmond, Colin, Sutton, Anne F., Visser-Fuchs, Livia, Watts, John L. (eds), *The Politics of Fifteenth-Century England: John Vale's Book* (Alan Sutton for Richard III and Yorkist History Trust, 1995)

Kelly, Henry Ansgar, 'Statues of Rapes and Alleged Ravishers of Wives: a Context for the Charges against Thomas Malory, knight', *Viator* 8 (1997)

Kendall, Paul Murray, *Warwick the Kingmaker* (Allen & Unwin, London, 1957)

Kendall, Paul Murray, *The Yorkist Age: Daily Life in the Wars of the Roses* (Allen & Unwin, London, 1967)

Kennedy, Beverley, *Knighthood in the Morte Darthur* (Brewer, Cambridge, 1985)

Kennedy, Beverley, 'Adultery in Malory', *Arthuriana* 7.3 (Fall 1997), 78–99

Kingsford, Charles Lethbridge (ed.), *Chronicles of London* (Oxford, 1905)

Kingsford, Charles Lethbridge, *English Historical Literature in the Fifteenth Century* (OUP, 1913)

Kingsford, Charles Lethbridge, *The Grey Friars of London* (Aberdeen UP, 1915)

Kingsford, Charles Lethbridge, *Stonor Letters and Papers*, 2 vols (Camden Society, 3rd series, 29 & 30, London, 1919)

Kingsford, Charles Lethbridge, *Prejudice and Promise in Fifteenth-Century England* (Frank Cass, London, 1962)

Kingsford, Charles Lethbridge (ed.), *Henry V* (Putnam, New York, 1901)

Kitteridge, George Lyman, 'Who was Sir Thomas Malory?', in *Johnson's Universal Encyclopaedia* V (1894; revised in *Studies in Notes and Philology*, Boston, MA, 1897)

Kleineke, Hannes, 'Why the West was Wild: Law and Disorder in Fifteenth-Century Cornwall and Devon', in L. S. Clark (ed.), *The Fifteenth Century* vol. 3 (2003)

Krishna, Valerie (ed.), *Morte Arthure* (Burt Franklin, New York, 1976)

Lander, J. R., *Conflict and Stability in Fifteenth-Century England* (Hutchinson, London, 1969)

Lander, J. R., *Government and Community 1450–1509* (Edward Arnold, London, 1980)

Lander, J. R., *Wars of the Roses* (Sutton, Stroud, 1990)

Lawrence, T. E., *Seven Pillars of Wisdom* (Jonathan Cape, London, 1926)

Laynesmith, J. L., 'Constructing Queenship at Coventry: Pageantry and Politics at Margaret of Anjou's "Secret Harbour"', in L. S. Clark (ed.), *The Fifteenth Century*, vol. 3 (2003)

Leland, John, *The Itinerary*, ed. Lucy Toulin Smith, 5 vols (1906–10; repr. 1964)

Lester, G. A. (ed.), *Sir John Paston's 'Grete Book'* (Brewer, Cambridge, 1984)

Lewis, C. S., 'The English Prose Morte', in J. A. W. Bennett, *Essays on Malory* (Clarendon Press, Oxford, 1963)

Loyd, L. C., *The Origins of Some Anglo Norman-Families*, ed. Charles Travis, Harleian Society Publications 103 (1951), 56

Lull, Ramon, *Book of Knighthood and Chivalry*, trans. William Caxton, rendered into modern English by Brian R. Price (The Chivalry Bookshelf, 2001)

MacGibbon, David, *Elizabeth Woodville (1437–1492): Her Life and Times* (London, 1938)

MacNamara, F. N., *Memorials of the Danvers Family* (Hardy & Co., London, 1895)

Mallory-Smith, Sheila V., *A History of the Mallory Family* (Phillimore, Chichester, 1985)

Marin, Jean-Yves, *La Normandie dans la guerre de Cent Ans* (Skitor/ Musée de Normandie, Milan/Caen, 1999)

Marks, Richard and Williamson, Paul, *Gothic: Art for England 1400–1547* (V & A, 2004)

Matthews, William, *The Ill-framed Knight: A Skeptical Inquiry into the Identity of Sir Thomas Mallory* (University of California Press, Berkeley, CA, 1966)

McCarthy, Terence, 'Malory and His Sources', in *A Companion to Malory*, ed. E. Archibald and A. S. F. Edwards (Brewer, Woodbridge, 1996)

McCarthy, Terence, *An Introduction to Malory* (Brewer, Woodbridge, 1998)

McFarlane, K. B., *Lancastrian Kings and Lollard Knights* (OUP, 1972)

McFarlane, K. B., *England in the Fifteenth Century* (Hambledon, London, 1981)

Meale, Carol, 'Manuscripts, Readers and Patrons in Fifteenth-Century England: Sir Thomas Malory and Arthurian Romance', *Arthurian Literature* 4 (1985)

Mee, Arthur, *King's England: Northamptonshire* (Hodder & Stoughton, London, 1945)

Mee, Arthur, *King's England: Warwickshire* (Hodder & Stoughton, London, 1966)

Mee, Arthur, *King's England: Leicestershire and Rutland* (Hodder & Stoughton, London, 1967)

Mertes, Kate, 'Household as Religious Community', in Colin

Richmond and Joel Rosenthal (eds), *People, Politics and Community in the Later Middle Ages* (Sutton, Gloucester, 1987)

Mertes, Kate, *The English Noble Household 1250–1600* (Blackwell, Oxford, 1988)

Mifsud, A., *Knights Hospitaller of the Venerable Tongue of England in Malta* (Malta, 1914)

Mitchell, R. J., *John Free: From Bristol to Rome in the Fifteenth Century* (Longmans, Green, London, 1955)

Mitchell, R. J., *The Laurels and the Tiara: Pope Pius II 1458–1464* (Harvill, London, 1962)

Mitchell, R. J., *The Spring Voyage: The Jerusalem Pilgrimage in 1458* (John Murray, London, 1965)

Monro, C. (ed.), *The Letters of Margaret of Anjou* (Camden Society, old series, 86, London, 1863)

Monstrelet, Enguerrand, *Chroniques . . . 1400–1444*, ed. L. Douet-D'Arcq, 6 vols (1857–62)

Moore, Robin, *History of Coombe Abbey* (Jones-Sands, Coventry, 1983)

Moorman, Charles, *Kings and Captains: Variations on a Heroic Theme* (Kentucky UP, 1971)

Morgan, D. A. L., 'The Household Retinue of Henry V and the Ethos of English Public Life', in Anne Curry and Elizabeth Matthew (eds), *Concepts and Patterns of Service in the Later Middle Ages* (Boydell, Woodbridge, 2000), 64–79

Moye, Lucy Ellen, 'The Estates and Finances of the Mowbray Family, 1401–1476', DPhil thesis (Duke University, Durham, NC, 1985)

Munro, J. H. A., *Wool, Cloth and Gold: The Struggle for Bullion in Anglo-Burgundian Trade 1340–1478* (Toronto, 1973)

Murimuth, A., *Continuatio Chronicarum*, ed. E. M. Thompson (1889)

Myers, A. R., 'The Household of Margaret of Anjou', BJRL 40 (1957–8)

Myers, A. R. (ed.), *The Household Book of Edward IV: The Black Book and Ordinances of 1478* (Manchester UP, 1959)

Newhall, R. A., *The English Conquest of Normandy 1416–1424* (New Haven, CT, 1924)

Newhall, R. A., *Muster and Review: A Problem of English Administration 1420–1440* (Cambridge, MA, 1940)

Nichols, J. G., *History and Antiquities of Leicestershire*, 4 vols (1795–1811; repr. Wakefield, 1971)

Nichols, J. G. (ed.), *The Boke of Noblesse* (Roxburghe Club, London, 1860)

Nicolas, N. H., *History of the Battle of Agincourt* (1824)

Nicolas, N. H. (ed.), *A Journal by One of the Suite of Thomas Beckington* (London, 1828)

Nicolas, N. H. (ed.), *Proceedings and Ordinances of the Privy Council of England*, 7 vols, Record Com (*Proc. & Ord. P.C.*) (London, 1834–7)

Nicolas, N. H. (ed.), *A Chronicle of London 1189–1483* (London, 1827)

Notes and Queries (London, 1850 etc.)

Ohler, Norbert, *Medieval Traveller* (Boydell, Woodbridge, 1989)

O'Malley, Greg, 'English Knights Hospitaller 1460–1522', PhD thesis, Cambridge, 1999

Orme, Nicholas, *Early British Swimming 55 B.C.–A.D. 1710* (University of Exeter, 1983)

Orme, Nicholas, *From Childhood to Chivalry: The Education of the English Kings and Aristocracy 1100–1530* (Mcthuen, London, 1984)

Orme, Nicholas, 'Medieval Hunting: Fact and Fancy', in Barbara Hanawalt (ed.), *Chaucer's England: Literature in Historical Context* (University of Minnesota Press, Minneapolis, 1992)

Orme, Nicholas, *Medieval Childhood* (Yale UP, New Haven, CT, 2001)

Parini, Jay, *John Steinbeck: A Biography* (Henry Holt, New York, 1995)

Parins, M. J. (ed.), *Malory: The Critical Heritage* (Routledge, London, 1988)

Paston Letters, ed. J. Gairdner, 4 vols (Edinburgh, 1910)

Paston Letters, ed. Norman Davis, 2 vols (OUP, 1971–6)

Pavlidis, Vangelis, *Rhodes 1306–1522: a Story*, transl. John Pavlidis (Rodos Image, Rhodes, 1999)

Pernoud, Jean and Clin, Marie-Veronique, *Joan of Arc: Her Story*, rev. and trans. Jeremy du Quesnay Adams (Phoenix, London, 2000)

Pollard, A. J., 'Elizabeth Woodville and Her Historians', in *Traditions and Transformations in Late Medieval England* (Leiden, 2001), 145–58

Post, J. B., 'Sir Thomas West and the 1382 Statute of Rapes', IHR 53 (1980)

Powell, Edward, *Kingship, Law and Society* (Oxford, 1989)

Pugh, Ralph, *Imprisonment in Medieval England* (CUP, 1968)

Pugh, T. B., 'The magnates, knights and gentry', in S. B. Chrimes, C. D. Ross and R. A. Griffiths (eds), 1995

Putnam, R., *A Medieval Princess: The Life of Jacqueline of Hainault* (Putnam, New York, 1904)

Radulescu, Raluca, '*John Vale's Book* and Sir Thomas Malory's *Morte Darthur*: A Political Agenda', *Arthuriana* 9:4 (1999), 69–80

Radulescu, Raluca, 'Sir Thomas Malory and Fifteenth-century Political Ideas', *Arthuriana* 13.3 (2003), 36–51

Ramsay, Sir James H., *Lancaster and York 1399–1485*, 2 vols (Clarendon Press, Oxford, 1892)

Ramsay, Nigel, 'Scriveners and Notaries as Legal Intermediaries in Later Medieval England', in J. Kermode (ed.), *Enterprise and Individuals in Fifteenth-Century England* (Sutton, Stroud, 1991), 118–31

Rawcliffe, Carol, *The Staffords, Earls of Stafford and Dukes of Buckingham 1394–1521* (CUP, 1978)

Reeves, Compton, *Pleasures and Pastimes in Medieval England* (Sutton, Stroud, 1995)

Richard of Bury, *Philobiblon*, 1344, transl. E. C. Thomas (Birmingham, 1946)

Richardson, Geoffrey, *The Lordly Ones: A History of the Neville Family and their Part in the Wars of the Roses* (Baildon, Shipley, 1998)

Richmond, Colin, 'English Naval Power in the Fifteenth Century', *History* LII (1967)

Richmond, Colin, 'Thomas Malory and the Pastors', in C. M. Meale (ed.), *Readings in Medieval Romance* (Brewer, Cambridge, 1994), 195–208

Richmond, Colin and Rosenthal, Joel (eds), *People, Politics and Community* (Sutton, Stroud, 1987)

Rickert, Edith, *Chaucer's World* (CUP, 1948)

Riddy, Felicity, *Sir Thomas Malory* (Leiden, 1987)

Riley, H. T. (ed.), *Ingulph, Chronicle of the Abbey of Crowland* (London, 1854)

Riley-Smith, Jonathan, *Hospitallers: The History of the Order of St John* (Hambledon, London, 1999)

Robbins, R. H., *Historical Poems of the XIV and XV Centuries* (Columbia UP, NY, 1959)

Robertson, Craig A., 'Local Government and the King's "Affinity" in fifteenth century Leicestershire and Warwickshire', *Transactions of the Leicestershire Archaeological and Historical Society* LII (1976–7), 37–45

Roskell, J. S. and Clark, L. S., *The History of Parliament: The House of Commons 1386–1421*, 3 vols (Sutton, Stroud, 1993) (cited as *The Commons*)

Roskell, J. S., *Parliament and Politics in Late Medieval England*, (Hambledon, London, 1981), vol. 2.

Ross, C. D., 'Rumour, Propaganda and Public Opinion during the Wars of the Roses', in R. A. Griffiths (ed.), *Patronage, the Crown and the Provinces* (Sutton, Gloucester, 1981), 15–32

Ross, Charles, *Edward IV* (Eyre Methuen, London, 1974)

Ross, Charles (ed.), *The Rous Roll: John Rous* (Sutton, Gloucester, 1980)

Ross, Janet, *Lives of the Early Medici as Told in Their Correspondence* (Chatto & Windus, London, 1910)

Rotuli Normanniae in Turri Londoniensi asservati: Johane et Henrico Quinto Angliae Regibus, ed. T. D. Hardy (London, 1835)

Rotuli Parliamentorum, ed. J. Strachey et al., 6 vols (London, 1767–7)

Rous, John, *Historia Regum Angliae*, ed. T. Hearne, 2nd edn (Oxford, 1745)

Rouse, R. H. and M. A., *Manuscripts and their Makers: Commercial Book Producers in Medieval Paris 1200–1500*, I (Harvey Miller, Turnhout, 2001)

Rudorff, R., *The Knights and Their World* (Cassell, London, 1974)

Rymer, Thomas (ed.), *Foedera . . . 1066–1333* (London, 1816–69)

Sandquist, T. A. and Powicke, M. R. (eds), 'The Holy Oil of Thomas of Canterbury', in *Essays in Medieval History presented to Bertie Wilkinson* (University of Toronto Press, 1969)

Saunders, Corinne, *Rape and Ravishment in Medieval England* (Brewer, Cambridge, 2001)

Scattergood, V. J., *Politics and Poetry in the Fifteenth Century* (Blandford, London, 1971)

Scattergood, V. J. and Sherborne, J. W. (eds), *English Court Culture in the Later Middle Ages* (Duckworth, London, 1983)

Scattergood, V. J., 'Fashion and Morality in the Late Middle Ages', in D. Williams (ed.), *England in the Fifteenth Century* (Proceedings of the 1986 Harlaxton Symposium, Woodbridge, 1987)

Scofield, Cora L., 'Early Life of John de Vere', EHR (April 1914)

Scofield, Cora L., *The Life and Reign of Edward IV*, 2 vols (Longmans, Green, London, 1923)

Scott, Sir Walter, 'Essay on Chivalry', 1816, reprinted in *Essays on Chivalry, Romance and the Drama* (Frederick Warne, London, 1881)

Scudder, Vida D., *Le Morte D'Arthur of Sir Thomas Malory: A Study of the Book and its Sources* (Dent, London, 1971)

Seaton, Ethel, *Sir Richard Roos, Lancastrian Poet* (Rupert Hart-Davis, London, 1961)

Seward, D., *Henry V* (Sidgwick & Jackson, London, 1987)

Seward, D., *The Monks of War: The Military Religious Orders* (Penguin, London, 1972)

Shaner, M. E., 'Instruction and delight: medieval romance as children's literature', *Poetics Today* 13 (1992)

Sinclair, Alexandra, *The Beauchamp Earls of Warwick in the Later Middle Ages*, PhD thesis, London, 1987

Sinclair, Alexandra, *The Beauchamp Pageant* (Richard III and Yorkist History Society, 2003)

Sire, H. J. A., *The Knights of Malta* (Yale UP, New Haven, CT, 1994)

Skipwith, Fulwar, *A Brief Account of the Skipwiths* (W. Bracket, Tunbridge Wells, 1867)

Somerville, R., *History of the Duchy of Lancaster*, I: 1265–1603 (London, The Chancellor and Council of the Duchy of Lancaster, 1953)

St Edith's Church, Monks Kirby 1077–1977 (anon.) (John Abbott, Lutterworth, 1977)

Stanislaus, Sister M., *Newbold Revel, A Warwickshire Manor*, St Paul's College of Education, Rugby (1976)

Starkey, David, 'The Age of the Household: Politics, Society and the Arts, *c.*1350–*c.*1550', in S. Medcalf (ed.), *The Later Middle Ages* (Methuen, London, 1981)

Starkey, David, 'King Henry and King Arthur', in J. P. Carley and F. Riddy (eds), *Arthurian Literature* XVI (1998)

Steinbeck, Elaine and Wallstein, Robert (eds), *Steinbeck: A Life in Letters* (Heinemann, London, 1975)

Steinbeck, John, *The Acts of King Arthur and his Noble Knights*, ed. Chase Horton (Heinemann, London, 1975)

Stevenson, J. (ed.), *Letters and Papers Illustrative of the Wars of the English in France during the Reign of Henry VI*, 2 vols in 3, Rolls Series (London, 1861–4)

Stevenson, R. L. S., 'Charles of Orléans', *Cornhill Magazine* (July 1881)

Storey, R. L., *The End of the House of Lancaster* (2nd edn, Sutton, Gloucester, 1986)

Stow, John, *Survey of London, 1603*, introduction and notes by C. L. Kingsford (Clarendon Press, Oxford, 1908)

Stratford, Jenny, *The Bedford Inventories: The Worldly Goods of John, Duke of Bedford, Regent of France* (Society of Antiquaries, 1993)

Stratford, Jenny (ed.), *The Lancastrian Court* (Proceedings of the 2001 Harlaxton Symposium, Donington, 2003)

Strickland, Matthew, *Armies, Chivalry and Warfare in Medieval Britain and France* (Proceedings of the 1995 Harlaxton Symposium, Stamford, 1998)

Sumption, Jonathan, *Trial by Battle: The Hundred Years War* vol. 1 (Faber, 1990)

Sutton, Anne F., 'Choosing a Book in Late Fifteenth-Century England and Burgundy', in Caroline Barron and Nigel Saul (eds), *England and the Low Countries in the Late Middle Ages* (1995)

Sutton, Anne F. and Visser-Fuchs, Livia, *Richard III's Books* (Sutton, Stroud, 1997)

Sutton, Anne F., 'Malory in Newgate: A New Document', in *The Library*, 7th series, I.3, September 2000

Sutton, Anne F., 'Sir Thomas Cook and his Troubles, an Investigation', *Guildhall Studies in London History*, April 1978

Tieken-Boon van Ostade, Ingrid, *The Two Versions of Malory's* Morte Darthur: *Multiple Negation and the Editing of the Text* (Arthurian Studies 35, Brewer, Cambridge, 1995)

Titi Livii Foro-juliensis Vita Henrici Quinti, ed. Thomas Hearne (Oxford, 1716)

Toomey, J., 'A Medieval Woodland Manor: Hanley Castle, Worcestershire' (unpublished PhD thesis, University of Birmingham, 1997); notes published in Worcester Historical Society Collections (n.s. vol. 18, 2001)

Twain, Mark, *A Connecticut Yankee in King Arthur's Court* (1889; facsimile ed. S. F. Fishkin, K. Vonnegut Jr and L. J. Budd (OUP, New York/Oxford, 1996)

Unterkircher, F. (ed.), *Le Livre de Cueur d'Amours Espris* (Thames & Hudson, London, 1975)

Vale, Juliet, *Edward III and Chivalry: Chivalric Society and its Context 1270–1350* (Boydell, Woodbridge, 1982)

Vale, Malcolm, *English Gascony: 1399–1453* (OUP, 1970)

Vickers, K., *Humfrey Duke of Gloucester* (OUP, London, 1970)

Vinaver, Eugène, *Malory* (Oxford, 1929)

Vinaver, Eugène, *The Works of Sir Thomas Malory*, 3 vols (Clarendon Press, Oxford, 1947, rev. P. F. C. Field 1990)

Virgoe, Roger, *East Anglian Society and the Political Community of Late Medieval England*, ed. Caroline Barron, Carole Rawcliffe and T. Rosenthal (University of East Anglia, 1997)

Wagner, A. R., *Historic Heraldry* (1939)

Warkworth, John, *Chronicle*, ed. J. O. Halliwell (Camden Society, 1839)

Watts, John, *Henry VI and the Politics of Kingship* (CUP, 1996, 1999)

Waurin, Jehan de, *Recueil de Croniques et Aunchiennes Istories de la Grand Bretagne . . . par Jehan de Waurin*, ed. W. Hardy and E. L. C. P. Hardy, 5 vols, Rolls Series (London, 1864–91)

Wedgwood, J. C., History of Parliament: Biographies of Members of the House of Commons 1439–1509 (HMSO, London, 1936)

Weightman, Christine, *Margaret of York: Duchess of Burgundy 1446–1503* (Sutton, Stroud, 1989)

Wey, William, *Itineraries*, ed. G. Williams (Roxburghe Club, 1857).

Wheeler, Bonnie (ed.), *Arthurian Studies in Honour of P. J. C. Field* (*Arthurian Studies* LVII, Brewer, Cambridge, 2004)

Wheeler, Bonnie, Kindrick, Robert L. and Salda, Michael N. (eds), *The Malory Debate* (*Arthurian Studies* XLVII, Brewer, Cambridge, 2000)

White, T. H., *The Once and Future King* (Collins, London, 1958)

Whitteridge, Gwyneth, 'The Identity of Sir Thomas Malory, Knight-prisoner' (R.E.S. n.s. 24 (1973), 257–65)

Whittick, Christopher, 'The Role of the Criminal Appeal in the Fifteenth Century', in *Law and Social Change in Medieval England*, ed. J. A. Guy and H. G. Beale (London, 1984)

Williams, B. (ed.), *Gesta Henrici Quinti* (English Historical Society, 1850)

Wilson, Stephen, *The Magical Universe: Everyday Ritual and Magic in Pre-Modern Europe* (Hambledon, London, 2000)

Wolffe, Bertram, *Henry VI* (Eyre Methuen, London, 1981)

Wood, Margaret, *The English Medieval House* (Ferndale, London, 1981)

Woolgar, C. M., *The Great Household in Medieval England* (Yale UP, New Haven, CT, 1999)

Wrottesley, G. (ed.), 'The Chetwynd Cartulary', *William Salt Archaeological Society Transactions*, old series 12 (1891)

Wylie, J. H. and Waugh, W. T., *The Reign of Henry V*, 3 vols (CUP, 1914–29)

Wylie, J. H., *The History of England under Henry IV*, 4 vols (CUP 1884–98)

York, Edward C., 'Legal Punishment in Malory's *Morte Darthur*', in *English Language Notes* (September 1973)

LIST OF ILLUSTRATIONS

FIRST COLOUR PLATE SECTION

Stained glass window in Holy Trinity Church, Tattershall, Lincs (*Keith Barley*)
'Stag Hunting' from a book by Gaston Phebus de Foix (*Bibliothèque Nationale, Paris/Bridgeman Art Library*)

Windows in the Leicestershire church of Stanford (*Christina Hardyment*)
The Malory manor of Winwick, Northamptonshire (*Christina Hardyment*)

Sir John Astley fighting Philippe de Boyle from 'Ordinances of Armoury, Jousting, Sword and Axe Combat, and Chivalry' ([M.775 f.277v.] *© 2005 Photo Pierpont Morgan Library/Art Resource/Scala, Florence*)

Fifteenth-century shopping (Illustration from French manuscript [1452–57], *The Art Archive/Bibliothèque Municipale de Rouen/Dagli Orti*)
Feast scene from the Duc de Berry's Book of Hours (January: Banquet Scene. Ms 65/1284 f.1v. by Limbourg Brothers [fl.1400–1416], *Musée Condé, Chantilly, France/Giraudon/Bridgeman Art Library*)

Joan of Arc by Clément de Fauquembergue (*The Art Archive/Joan of Arc Birthplace Domremy, France/Dagli Orti*)
Christine de Pisan (Harl. 4431 f.4. *British Library/Bridgeman Art Library*)
Bouvreuil Tower from Jacques le Lieur 'Le Livre des Fontaines'(MS g3, Planche de gaalor – Château de Philippe Auguste. *Collections Bibliothèque Municipale de Rouen, photography by Thierry Ascencio-Parvy*)

Temple Balsall, Warwickshire (*courtesy of The Temple Balsall Foundation*)
Niccolo Arringhieri by Pinturicchio (*Siena, Duomo, Opera Metropolitana Siena/ Scala, Florence*)

The Hospitallers' fleet from the Book of Hours of Pierre de Bosredon (Battle of the Knights of Rhodes against the Turks, France, c.1465. G.55 fol. 140v. *New York, Pierpont Morgan Library © 2005 Photo Pierpont Morgan Library/Art Resource/ Scala, Florence*)

Sir Richard Beauchamp's tomb, St Mary's Church, Warwick (*© Alan Griffin*)
1463 manuscript *Tristram* (Ms. Fr 99 f.561 by French School, *Bibliothèque Nationale, Paris/Bridgeman Art Library*)

BLACK AND WHITE PLATE SECTION

South Wraxall manor (Country Life *Picture Library*)

Calais from *The Chronicles of the White Rose of York* (*Published by James Bohn, pub. 1845*)

Illustration drawn for the Beauchamp Pageant *c.*1475 (XXVii f.14. *British Library*)

Henry V's tomb effigy, Westminster Abbey (*Bridgeman Art Library*)

The Dauphin, later Charles VII of France (*The Art Archive/Musée du Château de Versailles/Dagli Orti*)

Duke Humfrey of Gloucester (*Bibliothèque Municipale, Arras/Bridgeman Art Library*)

St John's Gate (© *Eric Nathan/Alamy*)

Early engraving of Newgate prison from *Sir Thomas Malory* by Edward Hicks (*pub. 1929*)

Coleshill Manor from Thomas Ward's *Collection for a History of Warwickshire* (*British Library* BL Add. MS 29265–5)

The Malory arms on the Inn of the English, Rhodes (*Christina Hardyment*)

Henry VI by an unknown artist (*National Portrait Gallery, London, NPG 546*)

Edward IV by an unknown artist (*National Portrait Gallery, London, NPG 3542*)

Queen Elizabeth (*by kind permission of The President and Fellows of Queens' College, Cambridge*)

Plan of Greyfriars from *The Grey Friars of London* by Charles Lethbridge Kingsford (*The University Press, Aberdeen, 1915*)

Photograph of the site of Malory's grave (*Christina Hardyment*)

Wynkyn de Worde woodcut (© *Bettmann/CORBIS*)

Howard Pyle's 'Sir Kay interrupts ye meditations of Sir Percival' (litho) (© *Delaware Art Museum, Wilmington, USA/Bridgeman Art Library*)

Aubrey Beardsley's 'La Beale Isoud at Joyous Gard' from *Le Morte d'Arthur* (*pub. 1894, Private Collection, The Stapleton Collection/Bridgeman Art Library*)

SECOND COLOUR PLATE SECTION

Harry Beauchamp kneeling in mourning (© *Museum Catharijneconvent, Utrecht*)

'Cueur' by René of Anjou (*Private Collection/The Stapleton Collection/Bridgeman Art Library*)

Tintagel (© *Skyscan Balloon Photography/English Heritage Photo Library*)

Round Table, Winchester Castle Hall (© *R. Rainford/Alamy Images*)

The Court of King's Bench (*c.*1460, vellum by English School, *Inner Temple* © *Bridgeman Art Library*)

Westminster Hall (© *Adam Woolfitt/Corbis*)

Colchester Castle (© *Philippe Hays/Rex Features*)

The release from the Tower of London of Charles, Duc d'Orléans, from 'Poems of Charles d'Orléans' (BL, MS Roy 16 F11, f73r, *photo © British Library Picture Library*)

Parhelion (© *Doug Allan/Naturepl.com*)

The Neville clan, including Sir Richard Neville from the 'Heures de Neville' by Pol De Limbourg (Paris, BN MS Lat. 1158, fol. 27r, *Bibliothèque Nationale, Paris/ Bridgeman Art Library*)

'Lady Imagination' from 'Enseignement de la vraie Noblesse' by Richard Neville (MS fr.166, *Bibliothèque publique et universitaire, Geneva*)

Jean Wauquelin with Duke Philip of Burgundy (MS 4292 fol 1r. © *Bibliothèque Royale de Belgique*)

Attack on the Tower of London (Roy. 14E iv, fol 23. *British Library*)

Battle of Tewkesbury (Ghent MS 236, fol 5r. *Universiteit Gent*)

Death vigil from William, Lord Hastings' Book of Hours (fol 223 v. [Inv. 15503] *Fundación Lázaro Galdiano, Madrid*)

INTEGRATED ILLUSTRATIONS	Page
Map of English conquests in Normandy (*Leslie Robinson*)	xxviii-xix
Map of South of England from R. Gough's *British Topography*	xx
Dugdale's engraving of memorial window of Chetwynd family in Grendon Church from *The Antiquities of Warwickshire* by Sir William Dugdale, 1730 edition (*courtesy of the London Library, photography by Alex Saunderson*)	48
Plan of Newbold Revel from *Newbold Revel* by A. Gomme (*H.M. Prison Service*)	61
Second plan of Newbold Revel (*from Gomme as above*)	62
Dugdale's engravings of the fifteenth-century coats of arms in the windows of the parlour of Newbold Revel (*from Dugdale as above*)	205
Single coat of arms of the Malorys (Harleian MS 6163, fol.56b. *British Library*)	206
Controlment roll (*National Archives* KB29/83 m25d)	370–1

ENDPAPERS

Map of Malory's part of Warwickshire, the Knighton Hundred, from *The Antiquities of Warwickshire* by Sir William Dugdale, 1730 edition (*courtesy of the London Library, photography by Alex Saunderson*)

While every effort has been made to trace the owners of copyright material reproduced herein, the publishers would like to apologise for any omissions and will be pleased to incorporate missing acknowledgements in any future editions.

Abergavenny, Joan, Lady, 169
Abergavenny, Edward Neville, Baron, 331, 333, 368, 385
Aberystwyth, siege of, 58
Addesley, John, 340
Adam of Usk, 169
Africa, North, 411
Agincourt, battle of, 13–14, 18, 107–9, 114, 149, 214
  prisoners, 106, 107, 110, 158
Agravaine, Sir, 25, 27, 30, 34
Alençon, Duke of, 149, 231, 362
Alençon, 123
Aleyn, John, 207, 247, 339–40
Alford (Lancastrian conspirator), 433, 436–7
Alfray, Peter, 422, 423, 425
Alfred the Great, King, 221
Algore, William, 340
Alisander le Orphelin, 68, 130, 239, 407
Alnwick, 390, 392, 393
Amesbury, 31, 461, 462
Andimacchio (Kos), 185
Angers, 229, 450, 451
Anjou, 90, 105, 123, 139, 147, 150, 152, 196, 201, 229, 470
Anne, Queen (Princess of Wales, later wife of Richard III), 442, 451, 458, 472, 473
Anne of Bohemia, Queen (wife of Richard II), 55
Anne of Luxembourg (wife of John, Duke of Bedford), 150, 191
Appleby, John, 208, 279, 281, 282, 284, 288, 340
Appleby Magna, 208
Aquitaine, 18, 19, 53, 89, 90, 132, 201, 227, 229, 321, 332, 436
Arderne, Sir Ralph, 94, 133, 259
Arderne, Robert, 259–60, 320
Arderne, Thomas, 133
Argentan, 122–3

Aristotle, 67
Armagnac, Jacques, Count of, 91, 200, 228
army, 56, 93, 99–100, 129, 329–30
  equipment, 117–18, 121, 369–70
  French, 100, 106, 107, 110, 139, 140, 200, 248
  English, in France, 95–6, 100, 104–5, 106, 107, 116, 123, 125–6, 139, 166, 196–7, 200, 201, 248, 330
  muster rolls, 94, 95, 114–16, 124, 133, 200, 207, 245
  wages, 201, 262
Arnesby, John, 282
Arras, Treaty of, 128
Art and Craft to Know Well to Die, The, 461
Arthur, King, 10, 24–7, 65, 68, 307, 363, 384, 471, 473
  battles, 120, 149, 153, 177, 386–7, 392, 417, 418
  childhood, 9, 30–2, 145, 177
  court, 12, 30–2, 119, 207–8
  death, 9, 30–2, 65, 145, 177
  and Guinevere, 138, 195, 306, 309, 461
  and knights, 125, 128–9, 198, 292–3, 367, 398, 438, 477, 479–80
  as an English Worthy, 65, 352, 476
  as an example, 363, 398, 471
  as history, 9, 20, 35, 71, 109, 118, 130, 255, 261, 345, 474, 475
Arthur, Prince (son of Henry VII), 9, 12, 82, 475, 476
Arthurson, Ian, 218
Arundel, Earl of, 365, 390, 413
Arundel Castle, 407
Ascham, Roger, 476
Ashby, George, 221, 406
Astley family, 78, 135
Astley, Lady Joan, 142, 158
Astley, Sir John, 203, 213, 229, 390, 393, 399
Atherstone, Richard, 264, 285, 328

Audley, Lord, 366
Auxerre, 158
Auxy, Sir Jean d', 219
Avignon, 72, 102
Avon, River, 44, 152
Avranches, 152, 153
Axholme: Carthusian monastery, 216, 281, 282, 335, 338
Ayscough, William, 233, 271

Baginton, 135
Bale, John, 79, 146, 286, 404, 406, 476
Balsall and Grafton, 136, 173, 189
Bamborough Castle, 390, 392, 393, 394, 429
Bandini, Melchior, 184
Barfleur, 153
Barker, William, 342
Barnet, battle of, 457–8, 460
Barton, John, 437
Barton, Thomas, 327, 328
Barwell, 303
Basin, Thomas, 452, 453
Baskerville, Sir James, 325
Baskerville, Sir John, 325
Bassett family, 42, 71
Bassett, Alice, 42
Bassett, Peter, 132–3
Bassett, Sir Ralph, 73
Bate, Thomas, 246–7, 287, 290
Baugé, 139, 159, 201, 230
Baugh, A. C., 11, 294
Baxter, Nathaniel, 477
Bayeux, 122
Bayonne, 36, 195, 198, 200, 201
Beauchamp family 42, 49, 55, 78, 87, 169, 170–1, 219, 473, 475
  badge, 203, 233, 255
Beauchamp, Anne see Warwick, Anne Beauchamp, 15th Countess of
Beauchamp, Anne see Warwick, Anne Beauchamp, Countess of (sister of 14th and wife of 16th Earl)
Beauchamp, Sir Guy, 78
Beauchamp, Harry, 150, 157, 162, 165, 170, 171
Beauchamp, Sir John, of Powicke, 94, 219, 240, 255
Beauchamp, Sir Richard see Warwick, Richard Beauchamp, 13th Earl of
Beauchamp, Thomas see Warwick,

Thomas Beauchamp, 11th or 12th Earl of
Beaufort family 34, 91, 219, 225, 231, 240, 242, 250, 251, 258, 403
Beaufort, Edmund, 393
Beaufort, Edmund see also Somerset, Edmund Beaufort, Duke of
Beaufort, Eleanor, 431
Beaufort, Henry, Cardinal, 84, 142, 161, 197, 223, 227, 245
  Chancellor, 89, 91–2, 104
  and council of regency, 143, 146, 166, 226
  death, 250, 269
  wealth, 99, 139, 196
Beaufort, Henry (nephew) see Dorset, Henry Beaufort, Earl of
Beaufort, Joan see Buckingham, Joan Beaufort, Duchess of
Beaufort, John see Somerset, John Beaufort, Earl of
Beaufort, Margaret, 244, 266, 365, 470
Beaufort, Thomas see Exeter, Thomas Beaufort, Duke of
Beaumains see Gareth, Sir
Beaumaris, 273, 274
Beaumont family, 41
Beaumont, John, Viscount, 369, 456, 457
Beaune, 195
Beauvais, 165
Becket, St Thomas, 179, 424
Bede, 65, 160
Bedivere, Sir, 30, 31
Belknap, William, 422
Bellers, John, 289
Bellingham family, 407
Bellingham, Sir Thomas, 407
Benedict XIII, Pope, 102, 103
Benford, John, 350
Berkeley family, 150, 155
Berkeley, Elizabeth (wife of 13th Earl of Warwick), 78, 150, 256
Berkeley, Thomas, 157
Berkeley, Thomas, Lord, 78, 117, 318
Berkeley Castle, 318
Berry, Duke of, 91, 98
Berton, John, 437
Beverley, 69
Bible, 18, 66, 221, 238
Birmingham, Sir William, 287, 290, 335
Birmingham, 50, 287

Bisham Abbey, 458
Bishopstone, Sir William, 94
Blacman, John, 418
Blake, Norman, 476
Blamore, Sir, 31, 177–8, 207, 238, 347
Bleoberis, Sir, 31, 42, 141, 177–8, 207, 238
Blois, 90, 231
Blore Heath, battle of, 366
Blount, Sir John, 124–5
Blount, Sir Walter (later 1st Earl
    Mountjoy), 315, 363–4, 378, 385, 388,
    390, 413, 414, 436, 439, 440, 441,
    466–7
Boccaccio, Giovanni: *Decameron*, 221
Bodrum, 185–6
Boethius: *Consolations of Philosophy*, 98
Bohun family, 222, 223
Bolingbroke, Henry *see* Hereford, Henry
    Bolingbroke, Duke of
Bolingbroke, Roger, 226
Bona, Princess of Savoy, 401
Bonaventura, St: *Meditations on the Life of
    Christ*, 66
Bonneville Castle, 120, 121
Bonville, Lord, 381–2
Bonville, Sir William, 194, 196
books, 78, 98–9, 122, 167, 211–15, 398, 416
    in English, 145, 151, 212
    French royal library, 151–2
    Hospitallers' library, 184
    manuscripts, 208, 211–12, 213, 214–15,
        233, 363
    monastic libraries, 466
    see also literature
Bordeaux, 90, 105, 158, 195, 197, 279–80,
    321
Bordesley Abbey, 78
Bors, Sir, 12, 29, 31, 58, 129, 177–8, 195, 198,
    207, 238, 307, 418, 462, 480
Boscherville, Beatrice de, 45
Bosnia, 410
Bosworth Field, battle of, 470, 474
Botill, Sir Robert, 176, 187, 188, 436
Botley, Warwickshire, 215
Boughton family, 207
Boughton, Sir Richard, 409
Boughton, Sir Thomas, 338, 409
Boulogne, 110, 120
Bourgchier, Henry, Viscount *see* Essex,
    Henry Bourgchier, Earl of
Bourgchier, Thomas (Bishop of Ely,

Archbishop of Canterbury), 319,
    324–5, 335, 342, 346, 365, 377, 383,
    442–3
Bourgchier, Thomas, 367–8
Bourges, 158
Bouvet, Honoré, 233
Boyle, Sir Philippe de, 203, 229, 399
Boys, Walter, 350
Brabant, 91, 142
Bracebridge, Ralph (son of Sir Ralph), 157
Bracebridge, Sir Ralph, 94
Bramcote, 135, 246
Brampton, 133–4
Brandon, William, 359–60, 367
Brecon, 57
Bretigny, Treaty of, 90
Breuse sans Pitié, Sir, 28, 33
Brezé, Pierre de, 356, 390, 391
Bridges, William, 260
Bridlington, 18, 138
Brigham, William, 357
Brinklow, 276
Brittany, 71, 89, 123, 152, 153, 258, 436
Brittany, Duchess of, 153, 403
Brittany, Francis, Duke of, 152, 258
Brittany, John, Duke of, 153, 201, 231
Brown, Adam, 294, 302, 303, 313
Bruges, 363, 432, 433–4, 471
Brunby, Sir John de, 115, 116
Brut, 65, 145, 472
Bryce, Hugh, 459
Buchan, Earl of, 149
Buckingham, Anne Neville, Duchess of,
    223, 333, 373–4, 382, 414, 431, 440, 467
Buckingham, Humphrey Stafford, Duke
    of, 73, 94, 222–3, 249, 270, 283, 286,
    334, 360, 374
    attacked, 11, 263, 264, 288
    children, 223, 359, 365, 407
    death, 369, 372
    and Edward IV, 334–5
    estates, 223–4, 250, 287
    in France, 223, 267
    and Henry VI, 347, 348
    influence, 242, 246–7
    and Joan of Arc, 163, 373
    lawsuits, 264, 279, 283, 287, 289, 290,
        316, 325, 330
    marriages, 223
    offices, 232
    peace efforts, 226, 251, 262

Buckingham, Humphrey Stafford, Duke
  of – *cont.*
  power, 163, 222–3, 224, 359
  supporters, 225, 234, 259, 260, 264, 265,
    285, 329, 337
  and Warwick, 235–6, 240, 281, 283, 348,
    369
  and Yorkists, 347, 348, 365, 369
  wealth, 223
Buckingham, Joan Beaufort, Duchess of,
  223
Burdett, Joan, 246
Burgh, Philip, 327, 328
Burgh, Sir Thomas, 328, 448
Burgundy, 89, 91, 92, 107, 110, 117, 124, 140,
  142, 192, 258, 449, 450, 454, 455
  allied with England, 128, 143, 149, 150,
    162, 191, 192, 361, 362, 365, 384, 410,
    446
Burgundy, Charles the Bold, Duke of, 413,
  414, 424, 433, 434, 435, 446, 450, 455
Burgundy, John the Fearless, Duke of, 91,
  92, 97, 99, 108, 109, 111, 113, 126
Burgundy, Margaret, Duchess of (sister of
  Edward IV), 413, 414, 419, 424, 432,
  433–4, 435, 471
Burgundy, Philip the Good, Duke of, 127,
  128, 142, 143, 161, 163, 192, 363, 403,
  410, 412, 413–14
Burleigh family, 186
Burley, William, 200
Burneby family, 170
Burneby, Eustace, 170, 194, 215–16, 245, 315
Burneby, George, 170, 363, 432
Burneby, Thomas, 245
Burne-Jones, Edward, 479
Bury St Edmunds, 249
Butler, Sir Ralph, 140
Bykenen, Thomas, 340
Byron, George Gordon, Lord, 42
Byron, Sir John, 315
Bywell Castle, 394, 427

Cade, Jack, 268, 270, 271, 272, 273, 326,
  329, 332
Caen, 121–2, 192, 261, 262, 271
Calais, 97, 100, 144, 162, 318, 361, 362, 390,
  433, 443, 448–9, 451, 455
  attacked, 192, 201, 262, 273
  as base in war, 11, 13, 104, 105, 106, 109,
    111–12, 120, 140, 162, 267

embassy, 432
  English occupation, 89, 93, 94, 95, 97,
    132
  fleet, 364
  garrison, 97–8, 110, 112, 326, 351, 358,
    360, 366, 449
  marches, 92, 97, 110, 140, 360
  staple, 362, 408
Caluden, 70, 276, 316, 324–5, 365
Cambridge, 431
  King's College, 221, 399
Camelot, 10, 34, 35, 208, 261, 398, 414, 475
Canterbury, 18, 97, 167, 271, 416
  Cathedral, 179, 416, 424
Capgrave, John, 77
Cardiff, 331
Carentan, 124
Carew, Jane, Lady, 245
Carlisle, 59
Carpenter, John, 224
Carte, Thomas: *History of England*, 441–2
Castle Bytham, Lincolnshire, 42, 51, 78, 115
Catesby, John, 69
Catesby, William, 259, 468–9, 470
Catherine, Queen (wife of Henry V), 92,
  126, 127, 128, 129, 138, 139, 142, 144,
  148, 157, 234, 380
Catthorpe, Leicestershire, 44
Caudebec, 125
Cave family, 175
Caxton, William, 80, 84, 362, 363, 406,
  432, 461
  Book of Noblesse, 471
  Chronicles of England, 472
  History of Troy, 433, 471
  and *Morte Darthur*, 3, 9, 24, 26, 34, 130,
    261, 471–2, 473, 474, 476
  Polychronicon, 164
Cecil, William, 325
Cely, George, 138
Cely, Richard, 138
Cessole, Jacques de: *The Game and Play of
  Chess*, 80
Chamberlain, Sir Robert, 391, 475
Chamberlain, Sir Roger, 250, 272, 338–9,
  475
Chamberlain, Sir William, 399
Chandler, Raymond, 10
Charles V, King of France, 151
Charles VI, King of France, 56, 91, 108,
  110, 119, 122, 127, 128, 142, 151

Charles VII, King of France, 161, 165, 192, 193, 196, 200, 223, 229, 231, 232, 236, 237, 248, 363
  coronation, 159, 160
  as Dauphin, 106, 122, 127, 128, 139, 140, 142, 143, 149, 152
  and Joan of Arc, 159, 160, 161, 163
Charnells family, 246
Charnells, Margaret (née Grendon), 47, 175
Charolais, Charles, Count of, 219
Chartier, Alain, 160–1
Chartres, 140
Chastellain (chronicler), 454
Château Gaillard, 126, 128, 133, 207, 262
Châtillon, 14, 132, 332
Chaucer, Alice see Suffolk, Alice Chaucer, Duchess of
Chaucer, Geoffrey, 10, 44, 48, 94, 244, 295, 406
  Canterbury Tales, 16, 238
  Troilus and Criseyde, 238, 373
Cherbourg, 123, 124, 201, 262, 273
Chertsey Abbey, 459
Chetwynd family, 47, 48, 52, 75
Chetwynd, Helen (wife of Sir Philip), 196, 198
Chetwynd, Helena, 48
Chetwynd, Joan (née Burley), 199–200
Chetwynd, John, 105, 158, 194
Chetwynd, Margaret, 137, 194
Chetwynd, Sir Philip, 134, 178, 188, 194, 196, 197, 198, 199, 200–1
Chetwynd, Richard, 47
Chetwynd, Roger, 47
Chetwynd, Rose, 158
Chetwynd, Thomasina, 48
Chetwynd, Sir William, 48
chevauchée, 90, 105, 106
Cheyne family, 166
Cheyne, Sir John, 250
Chilverscoton, Warwickshire, 46–7, 135, 175
Chirk, 196, 250
chivalry, 19, 20, 28, 33, 65, 71, 73, 84–5, 90, 100, 101, 161, 204, 471, 479, 481
  in books, 213, 398, 473
Chrétien de Troyes, 238
Christendom, 172, 190, 258
Christianity, 28, 33, 161, 410, 461
Christine de Pisan, 160, 215, 233, 421
Clare, Edward, 318

Clarence, Duke of see George, Duke of Clarence
Clarence, Isobel Neville, Duchess of, 441, 442, 443, 448, 449
Clarendon, 332
Clarkson, John, 357
Clere, Edmund, 345
Cliff, William, 350
Clifford, Sir John, 385
Clifford, Thomas, Lord, 346, 347, 348, 352, 361, 379
Clifton, Eleanor, 297, 298, 299
Clifton, Gervaise, 197
Clifton, Sir Gervais, 197, 422, 423, 426, 427, 428, 430, 432–3
Clifton, Nicholas, 297–9
Clifton, Sir Robert, 196, 197, 199
Clodeshall, Richard, 136, 143
Cobham, Lord, 318, 319, 368
Cockayn, John, 247, 290
Codnor see Grey of Codnor
Colchester Castle, 341, 342, 349
Coleshill, Edmund, 156
Coleshill, 46, 78, 223, 247, 283–4, 288
Commines, Philippe de, 118, 453
Compiègne, 142, 147, 149
Constantinople, 102, 409
Conyers, Sir John, 444
Cook, John, 208
Cook, Sir Thomas, 420–1, 423, 424, 425, 430, 432, 435, 438, 454
Coombe Abbey, 11, 40, 60, 69, 70, 208, 209, 263, 276, 279, 325, 372
  attacked, 284–7, 288, 315, 328–9, 342, 350, 354, 364, 372
Copland, William, 476–7
Corbie, 107
Cornelius, John, 422, 423, 426, 431, 432, 433
Cornwall, Sir John, 93, 121
Cosford, 170, 282, 288
Cosne-sur-Loire, 143
Cotentin Peninsula, 122, 123
Courtenay, Henry, 436, 437
Courtenay, Richard, 98–9
Courtney, Sir Hugh, 318
Coventry, 39, 50, 57, 59, 66, 69–70, 138, 267, 281, 303, 351, 364, 456
  Great Council, 364, 365
  mystery plays, 69, 247, 351–2
  pageants, 352, 475
  and Queen Margaret, 352, 365

Crécy, battle of, 89, 149
Cressing, Essex, 173
Cressy, Sir John, 133, 207
Cromer, William, 271
Cromwell, Lord, 333
Crosier, William, 88
Croxton, 215
crusades, 110, 161, 172, 177, 187, 409–10, 443
Culham, Oxfordshire, 429

Dand, Philip, 389
Daniel, Thomas, 255
Danvers, Agnes, 432
Danvers, Thomas, 414–15, 422, 429, 430, 432
Dauphin see Charles VII, King of France
Dawgeny, Robert, 136
Dawson, John, 437
death, 462
Death of Arthur, The, 151, 461
Delalaunde, Sir Thomas, 448
Despenser, Isobel see Warwick, Isobel Despenser, Countess of
Despoy, John, 437
Devereux, Sir Walter, 318, 321, 325, 349, 353, 385
Devon, Earl of, 280, 319, 336, 356, 379, 385, 456
Dieppe, 120, 166, 192, 225. 231
Digby, Sir Everard, 84
Dinadan, Sir, 28, 209
Doddingselles, Edward, 169–70
Doddingselles, Sir Edward, 169
Dodmerton, Dorset, 45
Domfront, 124
Dormandy, Thomas: Old Masters, 15
Dorset, Henry Beaufort, Earl of, 226, 250
Dowde, William, 282, 288, 328
Draper, John, 437
Draughton, Northamptonshire, 44
Dreux, 123
Dryby family, 71
Dudley, Katherine, 137
Dudley, Lord, 366
Dugdale, Sir William, 62, 94–5
    History of Warwickshire, 93–5, 137, 205, 206, 240
    Monasticon, 466
Dunstable, 71
Dunstanborough, 390, 392, 393

Dymmock, Sir Thomas, 448
Dymock, Sir John, 88
Dynham, John, 368

Easenhall, 40, 45, 170
East Anglia, 280, 320
Ebesham, William, 213
Ector, Sir, 31, 51, 68, 177–8, 207, 238
Edgecote, battle of, 444, 448
Edward I, King, 70
Edward II, King, 42, 71
Edward III, King, 70, 71, 72, 89–90, 97, 98, 129, 222, 223, 228, 282, 386, 398, 470
Edward IV, King, 15, 34, 285, 295, 380, 404–5, 439, 440, 451
    advisers, 443
    appearance, 386, 398
    army, 384, 385, 386, 390, 391, 448, 452, 457–8
    arrested, 444–5
    attacked, 452
    badge, 380, 453
    battles, 380, 384–6
    bodyguard, 421
    books, 398
    and Brittany, 436
    and Burgundy, 413, 424, 425, 441, 446, 455
    children, 401, 403, 447, 456–7, 469, 470
    compared to Arthur, 35, 398, 407
    coronation, 213, 388, 427
    court, 398, 411, 412
    and crusade, 410, 411, 443
    death, 16, 437, 469, 472
    deposed, 450
    and Earl of Warwick, 421, 438, 441–2, 443, 444, 445, 446, 447, 448, 450, 457
    fleet, 456, 460
    flight to Holland, 452, 455
    and France, 11, 401, 403, 411, 422, 424
    general pardons, 389, 409, 419–20, 422, 426–7, 428, 435, 447, 449
    heirs, 443
    and Henry VI, 417, 449, 456, 458, 459
    household, 79, 214, 429, 430
    imprisoned, 445
    interest in Arthurian myth, 406, 412
    knights, 398–9
    and Lancastrians, 402, 419, 424, 427, 431, 436, 447, 457

and London, 382, 411, 433, 446–7, 453, 456, 460
and Margaret, Duchess of Burgundy, 424
marriage, 400–2, 445, 469
in the north, 390, 391–2, 393, 427, 444, 446, 448, 452, 456
patronage, 388, 392
return from Holland, 456, 460
revenue, 410, 411, 422, 443
royal progresses, 389, 412
threatened by conspiracy, 420, 421–4, 425–6, 436
takes throne, 19, 382–3, 409, 414, 450
tournaments, 399–400, 405, 412, 413
Edward V, King, 453, 469, 470
Edward the Confessor, King, 221
Edward, Duke of York, 82, 186, 192, 201
Edward, Prince (the Black Prince, son of Edward III), 89–90, 158
Edward, Prince (son of Richard III), 472, 473
Edward, Prince of Wales (son of Henry VI), 20, 345, 351, 378, 379, 385, 472
birth, 333
death, 458, 460
exile, 393, 407, 420, 424, 439, 449, 452, 454
knights, 381–2
and regency, 337–8, 450–1
return to England, 455, 456, 458
Egremont, Lord, 333, 339, 341, 354, 355, 361, 369
Egypt, 173, 174, 178
Elaine, 28, 33, 307, 309, 396, 479
Eleanor of Aquitaine, Queen, 19, 89
Elinor of Cobham, Duchess of Gloucester, 227–8, 242, 249, 250
Eliot, T. S., 479
Elizabeth I, Queen, 477
Elizabeth, Queen (née Woodville, wife of Edward IV), 148, 400, 401–4, 412, 414, 421, 445, 452, 453
books owned, 407
children, 442, 453, 457, 469
coronation, 404, 411
Lancastrian connections, 402
as widow, 469
Eltham, 399
Elyot, Sir Thomas, 84
England, 15–17, 56, 144, 286, 390, 445

allies in France, 142, 152
ambassadors, 98, 99, 102
and Burgundy, 455
civil war, 345, 390, 393, 401, 450, 455
defence, 104, 422
genealogy of kings, 151
Great Council, 334, 361, 446–7
peace treaties, 110, 126–7, 178, 193, 223, 226, 229, 231, 232, 237, 251, 257–8, 410, 422
French raids, 111
invasions, 422, 424, 436, 446, 450
rebellion, 268–72, 278, 280, 339, 367, 444
reform, 289, 367, 377
territories in France, 89, 90, 161, 192, 193, 226, 236–7, 266, 270
treason trials, 278, 423–4, 425–6
truce with France, 455
unsettled, 317, 361, 414, 453
wars in France, 71, 72, 89, 90–1, 92, 99, 104–9, 110, 112–13, 125–6, 129, 138, 139, 146–7, 161, 166, 194, 195, 226
wealth, 17, 139
English Channel, 89, 106, 449, 450
English language, 9, 16, 19, 130–1, 151, 212
Erdington, Sir Thomas, 194, 216, 224, 246, 254, 259
Essex, Henry Bourgchier, Earl of, 365, 378, 385, 388, 390, 423
Eton College, 221, 260, 261, 399
Eugenius IV, Pope, 186, 187
Everingham, Henry, 315, 409
Everingham, Maud, 286
Everingham, Thomas, 249
Ewelme, 244, 245
Exeter, Henry Holland, Duke of, 278, 333, 338, 339, 341, 347, 361, 379, 385, 456, 457
Exeter, John Holland, Duke of, 55, 125
Exeter, Thomas Beaufort, Duke of, 133, 269, 270

Fabian, R., 333, 360, 364, 377
Falaise, 14, 123, 273
Fastolf, Sir John, 114, 132, 278, 342
Fauconberg, William Neville, Lord, 254, 258, 348–9, 357, 358, 359, 360, 361, 364, 365, 366, 368, 378, 384, 385, 388, 389, 390, 392
Feilding family, 137, 408

Feilding, Geoffrey, 408
Feilding, John, 408
Feilding, Sir William, 389, 408–9
Fenin, Pierre, 126
Fenny Newbold, 45, 204
Ferguson, Anne-Marie, 3
Fernandez de Heredia, Juan, 184
Ferrara: Church Council, 187
Ferrers family, 325
Ferrers, Edward Grey of Groby, Lord 303,
    330, 390
Ferrers, Thomas, 259, 264
Ferrers, William, 268
Field, Peter, 15, 146, 206
    *The Life and Times of Sir Thomas
    Malory*, 12–13, 15, 294, 295
Field of the Cloth of Gold, 9, 476
Fiennes, Lord Collard de, 100, 108
Fisher, John, 422, 423, 426
Fitzhugh, Henry, Lord, 14, 444, 452
Fitzhugh, Margery, 186
Fitzhugh, Sir William, 186
Fitzwilliam, Edmund, 338
Fluvian, Antonio de, 178, 186
Foljambe, Sir Edward, 116
Fontevrault, 287
Fortescue, Sir John, 15, 74, 322, 327, 341,
    355, 356, 372, 383, 407, 408, 432
Fosse Way, 39, 44
Fougères, 258
Fowey, 356
Framlingham, 338
France, 13, 14, 16, 18, 30, 98, 140, 144, 192
    and Burgundy, 450, 454
    champions, 100, 101, 125–6
    civil wars, 91, 126
    as English kingdom, 151, 161, 195, 196,
        231
    English territories, 132, 192, 227, 236,
        248, 257, 266, 270, 273, 319, 321
    and Lancastrians, 391, 393, 446, 450,
        452
    occupation, 90, 113, 116, 120–3, 132, 154
    peace treaties, 110, 126–7, 178, 192, 193,
        223, 226, 229, 231, 232, 237, 248, 251,
        257, 410, 436, 451
    and Scotland, 139, 147, 149, 232, 393
    war with England, 71, 72, 89, 90–1, 92,
        99, 100, 104–9, 111, 113, 127–8, 129,
        138, 139, 146–7, 161, 226
Francis I, King of France, 9, 476

Franciscans, 463, 465–6
Froissart, Jean, 67, 71, 99, 124, 141, 286
Fronsac, 321
Furness, John, 208
Fusoris, Jean, 99
Gaheris, Sir, 25, 27, 30, 34, 355, 361
Gainsford, Thomas, 253
Galahad, Sir, 10, 28, 29, 33, 98, 177, 221,
    307, 396, 418, 480
Gamaches, 140, 141, 142
Garard, Peryn, 437
Gareth, Sir (Beaumains), 25, 27, 28, 30,
    34, 67, 68, 101, 130, 181, 263, 307, 361,
    418
Gargrave, Sir Thomas, 147
Gascoigne, George, 477
Gascoigne, Thomas, 236
Gascony, 140, 194–5, 196, 197, 198, 200,
    201, 262
Gawain and the Green Knight, 400
Gawaine, Sir, 10, 25, 27, 28, 29, 30, 33, 34,
    68, 90, 93, 129, 130, 146, 195, 240, 241,
    352–3, 392, 418, 473
Genestaille, Bertrand de, 167
Genoa, 187–8
Geoffrey of Boulogne, 144, 172, 471
Geoffrey of Monmouth, 65
George, St, 103, 110
George, Duke of Clarence (brother of
    Edward IV), 382, 423, 424, 441, 442,
    443, 444, 445, 447, 448, 449, 452, 455,
    456, 460, 475
Gerson, Jean, 213
Gibbon, Edward: *Decline and Fall*, 103
Giles (son of Duke of Brittany), 157,
    258
Giles of Rome, 233
Gilmerton, 245
Gisors, 126, 128, 147–8, 363
Glanville, Bartholomew, 59, 81
Glastonbury, 10, 65, 138–9, 145, 184, 461,
    462, 473
Gloucester, 429
Glyn Dŵr, Owain, 55, 56, 57, 117, 427
Gosfield, 340
Gosford Green, 70, 71, 72–3, 169, 203
Gough, Matthew, 271
Gower, John, 14–15
Gower, Thomas, 273, 349
Grafton Regis, 148, 400, 401
Grail, 151

Great Bedwyn, 259, 260, 267, 408
Great Mongeham, 96
Green, Sir Henry, 44
Green, John, 340, 409
Green, Ralph, 94
Green, Richard: *Poets and Princepleasers*, 406
Green, William, 340
Greenwich, 221, 233–4, 373
Gregory XII, Pope, 102, 103
Gregory: *English Chronicle*, 333, 417
Grendon, Sir Walter, 136, 175
Grendon, Warwickshire, 46, 78, 194
    All Saints, 47, 48, 55, 116
Gresham, John, 273
Gresley family, 156
Gresley, Sir John, 265
Gresley, Sir Thomas, 315
Greswold, Thomas, 188, 277, 280, 287, 290, 320, 327, 341, 356, 359
Grey family, 42, 49, 71, 186
Grey (Bishop of Ely), 365
Grey, Sir Edward, of Groby, 224
Grey, Sir Edward, of Ruthin, 196, 303
Grey, Elizabeth *see* Elizabeth, Queen (wife of Edward IV)
Grey, Sir John, 400, 409
Grey, Lord, of Wilton, 385
Grey, Sir Ralph, 393, 394
Grey, Richard, 407
Grey, Thomas, 407
Grey, Sir Thomas, 196
Grey of Codnor, John de, 105, 115, 124
Grey of Codnor, Richard, Lord, 56, 57, 73, 78, 86, 92, 104, 114–16
    as army commander, 123–4, 153, 197
Grey of Codnor, Richard (the younger), 124
Grey of Ruthin, Reginald, Lord, 54, 78, 91, 369, 385, 390
Griffith, Maurice ap Owen ap, 427
Griffith, Morgan ap Thomas ap, 427, 428, 446
Grinkin, John, 477
Gruythuise, Lord, 453
Gryffyn, Geoffrey, 282
Guienne, 72, 158
Guines, 97, 100, 109, 361
Guinevere, 83, 373, 461–2
    and Arthur, 25, 30, 31, 65, 138, 209, 293, 306, 418, 461, 462

and Lancelot, 10, 27, 29, 30, 33, 122, 181, 199, 284, 305, 306, 308–11, 312, 336, 361, 373, 461–2

Hadleigh Castle, 280
Hainault, 142
Hal, Prince *see* Henry V, King
Hales, William, 279, 288
Hall, Edward, 77, 253, 402, 442
Halsham, Richard, 94
Hampden, Lady Anne, 431
Hampden, Sir Edmund, 431
Hampton, John, 259, 341, 342
Hampton Court, 174
Hanley Castle, 150, 152, 220
Hanseatic League, 362, 364
Hanson, Christopher, 132–3
Harcourt family, 246
Harcourt, Jacques d', 140
Harcourt, Richard, 94, 245, 422
Harcourt, Lady Robert, 408
Harcourt, Sir Robert, 224, 245–6, 247, 254, 259, 265, 276, 279, 315, 339, 385, 390, 399, 430, 443, 444, 455
Harcourt, Thomas, 94
Hardy, Thomas, 15
Hardyng, John: *Chronicle*, 15, 65, 67–8, 83, 116, 145, 238, 242, 305, 406
Harfleur, 18, 105–6, 110, 111, 112, 114, 115, 117, 120, 142, 192, 262
Harlech, 420, 424, 428
    Castle, 420, 421, 423, 436, 454
Harper, John, 208–9
Harrington, William, 157
Hastings, Sir Leonard, 335, 350
Hastings, Sir William, 350, 388, 391, 399, 441, 423, 457
Hastings, battle of, 41, 208
Hathwyck family, 207
Hathwyck, John, 254, 289, 335–6, 338, 354, 359
Hawes, Stephen, 65
Hawkins, John, 422–3, 425, 429, 432, 433, 437–8
Hay, Sir Gilbert, 218, 220
Hayford, Humphrey, 435–6
Hayward, John, 197
Hedgeley Moor, 394, 400
Heitersheim, Germany, 180
Hem (near Tournai), 70
Henry II, King, 89

Henry II, King of France *see* Henry VI, King

Henry III, King, 42, 89

Henry IV, King, 15, 16, 39, 51, 53, 54, 55, 56–7, 58, 72, 73, 75, 77, 78, 81, 86, 90, 186

Henry V, King (formerly Prince Hal), 16, 18, 57, 58, 75, 77, 78, 82, 86, 131, 134, 153, 186, 248
  and Agincourt, 14, 109, 111
  army, 96, 387
  biography, 226
  books, 167
  in Calais, 111–12
  challenge to Dauphin, 106
  compared to Arthur, 34, 138, 144, 145–6
  coronation, 86–8
  council, 280
  death, 143–5, 191
  invasion of Normandy, 114, 117, 119–26, 130, 192
  marriage, 126–7, 128, 138, 139, 147–8
  posthumous reputation, 145–6, 418
  and prisoners of war, 106, 107
  tomb, 227
  truce with France, 113, 127
  war with France, 89, 90–1, 92, 94, 99–100, 104–5, 106–7, 108, 109, 127–8, 130, 138, 139, 142, 143–4, 149, 176, 227, 257

Henry VI, King, 15, 16, 19, 20, 165, 167, 187, 198–9, 222, 254, 256, 273, 278, 383, 399, 408, 430, 431
  advisers, 276, 277, 280, 285, 317, 318, 363, 438
  arrested, 416
  authority, 278, 348, 417
  birth, 142
  burial, 459
  character, 221, 231, 418
  compared to Arthur, 34
  coronations, 161, 165, 166, 348, 453
  councils, 218, 242, 346, 349, 357, 361, 363, 364, 365
  deposed, 377–8, 420, 438
  and France, 192, 248, 249, 258, 330, 332, 450
  as fugitive, 392, 393–4, 416, 427
  general pardons, 348, 350, 366, 382
  guardian, 156–8, 191
  half-brothers, 329, 351, 470
  heirs, 196, 227, 250, 251, 266, 274, 275, 280, 319–20, 334, 378
  household, 194, 240, 248, 269, 329, 331, 373
  imprisoned, 415, 416–18, 419, 445, 449
  judicial progresses, 289, 313, 320–1, 327, 329, 331, 341, 353
  knights, 198–9, 203, 221, 381, 417
  and Lancastrians, 382, 390, 394, 418, 419
  marriage, 19, 200, 226, 228, 231–4, 236, 250–1, 257
  mental instability, 242, 332, 333, 337, 403, 418
  murdered, 458–9, 460
  and Parliament, 279, 280, 376
  patronage, 221, 235, 266–7
  peace plans, 231, 236–7, 242, 250–1
  and rebellion, 268–9, 271, 277, 278
  recovery of health, 342, 345–6, 349, 351–2
  regents, 143, 191
  restoration, 390, 423, 441, 451, 452, 453–4, 456
  revenue, 257, 269–70, 277, 279, 329, 351
  and Richard, Duke of York, 273–4, 276, 318, 319, 320, 345, 347–8, 349, 351, 376–7, 400
  separated from Queen Margaret, 376
  son considered illegitimate, 332–3, 334–5, 365, 378, 451
  supporters, 319, 331, 365
  and Yorkists, 347, 366, 367, 368, 369, 381, 385, 386

Henry VII, King, 9, 20, 82, 157, 459, 470, 474, 475

Henry VIII, King, 9, 18, 467, 476

Henry of Grosmont, Duke of Lancaster, 71, 73

Herbaumes, Sir Gerald, 100, 108

Herbert, Thomas, 428

Herbert, William, Lord, 380, 413, 421, 425, 436, 441, 442, 444

Hereford, Henry Bolingbroke, Duke of, 72

Hertford Castle, 199, 236

Heryot, William, 411–12

Hexham, 394, 401, 416, 431

Hicks, Edward, 11, 37, 294, 295, 306

High Cross, Warwickshire, 39

Hilton, Walter: *Mixed Life*, 66

Hoccleve, Thomas, 406

Holinshed, Raphael: *Chronicle*, 73, 332–3

Holland family, 55, 186
Holland, John *see* Exeter, John Holland, Duke of
Holland, John *see* Huntingdon, John Holland, Earl of
Holland, Sir John (son of the Earl of Huntingdon), 196
Holland, Robert, 354, 355
Holland, Thomas *see* Kent, Thomas Holland, Earl of
Holland (Netherlands), 453
Holy Grail, 10, 25, 28–9, 33, 98, 139, 151, 221, 477, 478–9
Holy Land, 31, 53, 145, 172, 178
Honfleur, 120, 125
Horman, William, 83–4
Hotoft, William, 300
Howard family, 392
Howard, Sir John, 403
Hugford, Thomas, 219
Hughes, Jonathan, 295, 406
Hull, Robert, 329, 337, 372
Humfrey, Duke of Gloucester (son of Henry IV), 18, 84, 86, 113, 142, 186, 200, 226–7, 232
    as army commander, 104, 109, 119, 122, 123, 124, 126, 192, 195–6, 197, 201, 231
    death, 249–50, 251, 266, 269, 319, 438
    estates, 249–50
    marriages, 150, 226–7, 242
    library, 94, 151, 221
    literary interests, 221
    Protector of England, 143, 146, 150, 248
Hundred Years War, 89
Hungerford, Lord, 431, 436
Hungerford, Sir Thomas, 436, 437
Hungerford, Sir Walter, 108, 121, 124
hunting, 80, 82, 183, 184
Huntingdon, John Holland, Earl of, 86, 196, 197
Hussey, Nicholas, 422, 423, 426, 429, 433
Hussey, Peter, 427, 429

Iden, Alexander, 272
Ince, Thomas, 325–6, 338, 341
Ireland, 243, 251
Isabel, Queen (wife of Richard II), 56, 89
Isabella (mother of Edward III), 89
Islam, 172, 258
Isle of Wight, 111
Isobel, Queen of France, 91, 110, 127, 142

Isobel of Lorraine, 230
Isolde, 10, 33, 36, 167, 209, 305, 373
Ivry-la-Chaussie, 126, 149

Jacquetta of St-Pol (wife of John, Duke of Bedford), 191, 382, 400, 401, 403, 420, 445, 453
James I, King of Scotland, 104, 147
Jernigan, John, 362
Jerusalem, 69, 75, 76, 144, 145, 172, 176, 471
Joan of Arc, 18, 155, 159–61, 162–4, 165, 176, 226, 373
Joanna of Navarre (stepmother of Henry V), 88, 153, 199, 227, 234
John, King, 89, 121, 220
John II, King of France, 89, 90
John XXIII, Pope, 102
John, Bastard of Orléans, 158
John, Duke of Bedford (son of Henry IV), 81, 86, 111, 142, 151, 186
    army commander, 146, 149, 192, 273
    books, 167
    death, 191
    marriages, 150, 191
    regent, 104, 119, 139, 143, 149, 191–2
John, Duke of Brabant, 142
John of Gaunt, Duke of Lancaster, 48, 73, 77, 91, 228, 254, 403, 470
John of Luxembourg, 140–1, 165
John, David, 350
John Paleologus, Emperor, 187
Johnson, Samuel, 478
Jonson, Ben, 460, 477
Joseph of Arimathea, 139, 184
Joyous Gard, 30, 198, 392, 462

Kassianos, Agepetos, 184
Kay, Sir, 12, 88, 480
Kelem, Margaret, 468, 469, 470
Kelly, Henry Ansgar, 300, 301
Kendall, Sir John, 182, 475
Kenilworth, Warwickshire, 57, 59, 77–8, 138, 167, 203, 228, 351, 477
Kennedy, Beverley: *Knighthood in the Morte Darthur*, 68, 311
Kent, Thomas Holland, Earl of, 50, 51, 53, 413
Kent, 262–3, 268, 269, 270, 271, 278, 319, 428, 452
Kerver, William, 201
Kimberley, William, 417

King, Margaret, 279, 288
Kingston family, 205, 468
Kingston, Thomas, 468
Kingston Lacy, 332
Kirkby Mallory, 42, 51
Kitteridge, G. K., 10
knights, 20, 32–3, 34, 68, 70, 72, 81, 100,
    141, 156, 194, 204
  allegiance, 418
  Christian, 177
  duties towards women, 292–3
  minstrel, 208–9
  rituals, 198–9
  Teutonic, 177
  training, 79–81, 84–5
Knights Hospitallers, 18, 66, 148, 172–5,
    176, 186, 410, 445
  English, 45, 46, 136, 140, 176, 179, 182,
    183, 186, 187, 303, 436, 475
  estates, 44, 50, 133–4, 136, 172, 173, 180,
    185, 186, 187, 188
  fleet, 173, 177, 180, 185
  langues, 172, 173, 175–6, 178, 179, 180, 182
  library, 184
  London property, 173–4, 397
  mint, 183
  priors, 172, 173, 182, 186, 436, 445, 447,
    475
  see also Rhodes
Knights of the Bath, 71, 86
Knights of the Garter, 72, 75, 111, 130, 145,
    233, 244, 381, 398–9, 443, 475
Knights of the Round Table, 20, 23, 25, 26,
    29, 31–2, 72, 125–6, 130, 141, 145, 151,
    177, 190, 229, 292–3, 305–6, 383, 398
Knights Templars, 148, 172, 176, 180, 189
Knollys, Robert, 422, 423
Koeur Castle (Lorraine), 393, 404, 423
Konstanz: Church Council, 102–3, 104
Kyriel, Sir Thomas, 262, 381–2

La Cote Male Taile, Sir, 130, 141, 239
La Hire see Vignolles, Etienne de
Le Mans, 251
La Marche, Oliver, 219–20
La Roche, Anthoine, Comte de (Grand
    Bastard of Burgundy), 412, 413, 435
La Roche Guyon, 126
La Roquette, 197
Ladvenu, Martin, 164
Laguen, Bastard of Arly, 124–5

Lalaing, Sir Jacques de, 80
Lamorak, Sir, 12, 28, 81, 130, 352, 353, 373,
    418
Lancaster, Dukes of, 53
  see also Henry of Grosmont; John of
    Gaunt
Lancastrians, 13, 15, 16, 34, 53, 276, 351,
    394, 402, 404, 414, 424, 436, 444, 445,
    449, 450, 452, 455
  army, 366, 379, 381, 385, 386, 390–1, 392,
    393, 457, 458
  conspiracy, 419, 421, 423, 425–6, 427,
    429, 433
  estates, 73
  kings, 90, 228, 332
  plans for invasion, 421, 423, 424, 450
  propaganda, 430, 447, 448, 451
  wards of court, 407, 431
Lancelevec, Sir Thomas, 182
Lancelot, Sir, 10, 12, 21, 24, 25, 26–7, 28,
    33, 36, 37, 58, 68, 90, 138, 149, 176, 177,
    178, 207, 209, 240–1, 264, 292, 295,
    305, 306, 307–8, 344, 374, 396, 405,
    413, 473, 479, 480
  and Guinevere, 10, 27, 29–30, 31, 83, 122,
    181, 195, 199, 284, 308–11, 312, 336, 361,
    461–2, 463
  death, 145, 238, 392, 463–4
  loyalty to Arthur, 198, 367, 417, 438
Lancelot du Lac, 37, 98, 151, 167
Langland, William, 64, 292
Langstrother, Sir John, 436, 444, 445, 447,
    456
Langstrother, Sir William, 176
Langton, John, 134, 207
Lastic, Jean de, 186, 187
Laval, Guy de, 159
Latimer, Elizabeth Beauchamp, Lady, 256,
    278
Latimer, George Neville, Lord, 256, 280,
    331
Laval, 158
law, 407
  appeals (King's Bench), 289–90, 313–14
  arbitration 324–5
  delays, 322, 328
  general pardon, 87, 320
  indictments, 287–8, 301
  and rape, 295, 296–300
  used to punish reformers, 20, 289
  writs in council, 282

Lawney, Lord Hugh de, 100
Lawrence, T. E., 10, 479
Le Crotoy, 120, 140, 142, 192
Le Mans, 158
Lee, John, 437
Lee, Richard, 451, 453
Leicester, Earls of, 41–2
Leicester, Simon de Montfort, Earl of, 42
Leicester, 42, 59, 267, 268, 365
Leparmentier, Maugier, 164
Letheringham, 326–7
Leventhorpe, John (1), 325, 326
Leventhorpe, John (2), 326, 327, 337, 338, 341
Lewis, C. S., 10, 32
Libelle of English Policy, 145
Limbourg, Pol and Hennequin de, 98
Lisieux, 121
Lisle, Viscount, 332
Lisle, Sir William, 98
literacy, 19, 64, 212
literature, 19, 64–5, 66, 94, 177
    Arthurian romances, 44, 54, 78, 151, 212, 233, 237, 238, 373, 407
    chronicles, 65, 184, 221, 398
    classical, 184
    French romances, 20, 23, 35, 78, 122, 134, 151, 167, 177, 180, 233, 238, 286, 407, 428
    history, 65, 80
    mystery plays, 69
    romances, 19, 80, 99, 176, 177, 184, 190, 212, 221, 398
    translated, 184, 221
Loire, River, 154, 158, 160, 231
Lollards, 18, 57, 66
London, 17, 65, 87, 319, 397, 411, 433
    aldermen, 17, 426
    Baynard's Castle, 220, 383
    Blackfriars, 276
    Brewers' Company, 131
    Christ Church, 467
    Christ's Hospital, 467
    Coleman Street, 324
    Fleet Prison, 322, 328
    Greyfriars Church, 11, 354, 462–7
    guilds, 17
    and Lancastrians, 382, 423–4, 426, 428, 429, 430, 451
    London Bridge, 271
    Ludgate Prison, 322, 323, 355
Marshalsea Prison, 323–4, 325, 326, 336, 343, 353, 354, 359, 368
merchants, 17, 50, 91, 118, 411, 455
Newgate Prison, 61, 323, 354, 368, 437, 462, 465
pageants, 109, 145–6, 167, 234, 361, 424
Paternoster Row, 214
Priory of St John, Clerkenwell, 172, 173–4, 175, 186, 187, 269, 397, 436, 465
prisons, 444
Public Record Office, 11
St John's Fields, 382
St John's Wood, 174
St Martin's le Grand, 318
St Paul's Cathedral, 53, 87, 144, 167, 368, 378, 459
Smithfield, 167, 203, 412
Tower, 16, 20, 54, 86, 148, 337, 347, 349, 365, 368, 369–70, 393, 411, 417, 423, 452, 453
Warwick Inn, 87, 152, 167, 220, 397, 465
Westminster, 198, 328, 336, 453
Westminster Abbey, 87, 129, 144, 227, 234, 383, 453, 459
Westminster Bridge, 336
Westminster Hall, 87–8, 314, 328, 364, 383
    and Yorkists, 368, 382–3, 453
Lorraine, 232–3
Louis IX (St Louis), King of France, 151
Louis XI, King of France, 223, 390, 401, 404, 424, 449, 450, 452, 455, 470
Louis, Duke of Guienne, 213–14
Louth, John, 118
Louviers, 165, 166
Love, Nicholas: *Mirror of the Blessed Life of Jesu Christ*, 66–7, 238
Lucy, Elizabeth, 401
Ludlow, 320, 321, 365, 366, 367
Lull, Ramon: *Order of Chivalry*, 84–5, 398, 471
Lushon, 168
Lutterworth, 18, 66
Lydgate, John, 94, 151, 221, 238, 406
    The Fall of Princes, 221, 238
    'On the English Title to the Crown of France', 151
    Troy Book and Siege of Thebes, 145
Lytton, Edward Bulwer, 253

Maine, 14, 147, 150, 152, 158, 196, 201, 229, 236, 237, 243, 248, 250, 251, 258, 266–7

Mallory Park, 42
'Malorie, Thomas', 42
Malory family, 11–12, 17, 19, 39, 40, 41–6,
    49, 50, 52, 59, 66, 71, 75, 78, 87, 133,
    138, 148, 215–16, 352, 363, 474
  coats of arms, 182, 205–6, 233
  and Knights Hospitallers, 175, 182, 215
Malory, Agnes, 46
Malory, Alice, 46
Malory, Sir Anketil, 41, 42–4, 116, 261, 329
Malory, Anthony, 41
Malory, Anthony (mid-1460s), 397
Malory, Aschetil, 42
Malory, Elizabeth (wife of Robert), 389
Malory, Elizabeth (née Walsh, wife of Sir
    Thomas), 206, 211, 245, 246, 306, 315,
    324, 350, 359, 389, 395, 396, 444, 445,
    468
Malory, Giles (of Green Norton), 475
Malory, Sir Giles, 55, 57
Malory, Helen (sister, later Vincent), 67,
    138, 170
Malory, Isobel (sister, later
    Doddingselles), 67, 138, 169
Malory, John (father), 40, 46, 47, 48–9,
    50, 53–4, 55–6, 57, 62, 71, 75, 87, 89,
    116, 135, 143
  death, 169, 170
  declines knighthood, 156
  as MP, 91, 135, 138, 155–6
  as Sheriff, 135
  in Wales, 91
Malory, Sir John (grandfather), 45–6, 48,
    66, 71, 156, 205, 210
Malory, John (possibly son of Sir
    Thomas), 207, 323, 389, 397
Malory, John, 133, 175, 186, 207, 410
Malory, John (of Litchborough), 475
Malory, John (of Welton), 87
Malory, Katherine (née Kingston), 205,
    468
Malory, Nicholas (grandson), 46, 47, 175,
    205, 409, 468–9, 470, 471, 475
Malory, Sir Peter, 45, 46, 98, 205
Malory, Philippa (mother), 40–1, 47–8,
    49, 50, 62, 169, 170, 199
Malory, Philippa (sister, later Burneby),
    67, 138, 170
Malory, Sir Ralph, 42
Malory, Richard, 42, 134, 207, 208, 284,
    315, 316, 364, 445

Malory, Richard (of Monks Kirby), 475
Malory, Robert (cousin), 42, 133, 148, 194,
    207, 315, 378, 393, 397, 417, 418, 427,
    430, 431, 444, 445
Malory, Robert (son), 206, 207, 246, 384,
    389, 395, 409, 468
Malory, Robert (of Fawsley), 475
Malory, Sir Robert (uncle), 18, 46, 47, 68,
    69, 135, 136, 172, 173, 174, 176, 178–9,
    182, 185, 186–7, 188–9, 246, 323
Malory, Sir Roger, 45, 350
Malory, Simon (uncle), 46–7, 68, 69,
    135–6, 169, 175, 194, 215, 323, 338, 397
Malory, Sir Simon, 45, 148
Malory, Sir Stephen, 45
Malory, Sir Thomas, 37, 41, 85, 155, 383
  absences, 178, 200, 207, 359, 446
  accounts of life, 1–2, 10–11, 12, 18–19, 79
  accused of crimes, 224–5, 263–4, 279,
    281, 282–3, 287–9, 290, 316, 339–40,
    372
  accused of poaching, 316–17
  accused of rape, 15, 288, 290, 291, 294,
    295, 301–4, 313, 374
  and adultery, 304–5, 311–12
  age, 13–14, 15, 94, 136, 152, 219
  appearance, 77
  arbitration, 324–5
  arrested, 279, 281, 283, 288, 314, 437, 438
  attacks Coombe Abbey, 284–7, 288, 384
  bail, 289, 323, 325, 326, 327, 330, 335, 338,
    357
  baptism, 39, 40, 41, 50, 51–3
  and Beauchamp family, 93, 116, 128, 151,
    162, 165, 169, 171, 178, 191, 193–4, 203,
    219, 220, 221, 231, 237, 239, 240, 243,
    254, 255, 271, 451
  birth, 39, 40, 41
  books owned or read, 211, 237–8, 344,
    399, 406
  burial, 462, 463, 464, 465
  in Calais, 93–5, 98, 104, 110, 112, 113, 362,
    363, 366, 433
  character, 35–7, 152, 217, 295, 308, 404
  childhood, 57, 61, 62–4, 67–8
  children, 175, 206, 207, 246, 389
  and chivalry, 161, 290, 304, 309, 378, 399
  at court, 19, 235, 283, 404, 405
  criminal record, 11, 13, 15
  death, 11, 31, 76, 441, 460, 461, 463,
    467–8

debts, 323, 353–4, 356, 357
denied pardon, 15, 250, 415, 420, 426–7,
   430, 432, 446, 447, 449, 472
and Duke of Buckingham, 163, 222, 224,
   240, 279, 283, 286, 288, 290, 316, 325,
   330, 360, 372, 373, 374
and Duke of Norfolk, 342–3, 374,
   384
and Duke of York, 336, 347, 349, 368,
   372, 383
and Earl of Warwick, 358, 369, 384, 393,
   397, 444, 451, 464
education, 64–7, 69–70, 74
epitaph, 464, 465, 481
escape from prison, 284, 337, 341–2, 343,
   349, 354–5
in Essex, 341–2, 349
estates, 194, 198, 199, 201, 204, 237, 246,
   282, 315, 324, 397, 467, 468, 470
'evidences', 286–7
in France (beyond Calais), 102, 105, 114,
   116, 121, 124, 129, 130, 132, 133, 138, 147,
   148, 149, 150, 151, 152, 163, 176, 194–5,
   231
free again, 368, 371, 376, 383, 444
and French language and literature, 134,
   151, 167, 177, 237, 238, 358
friends, 339, 399, 428, 430, 431
general pardon, 349–50, 371, 389
godparents, 50–1, 52
grandchildren, 175, 205, 206, 409
as hero, 130
as historian, 146, 180, 286, 406
historical records, 93–4, 114, 135, 136,
   166, 169, 202
household, 208, 209, 211, 279, 340
as hunter, 82
illness, 355
imprisonment, 11, 12, 13, 15, 25, 26, 27,
   28, 29, 32, 60, 61, 83, 198, 204, 207,
   258, 288, 317, 322–4, 335, 336, 337, 343,
   344, 347, 349, 350–1, 357, 358, 359,
   360, 367–8, 371, 437, 438, 439, 465
and Joan of Arc, 163, 165
as Justice of the Peace, 202
and kinsfolk, 207, 215
and knighthood, 156, 194, 197, 198, 199,
   203, 290, 407–8
and Knights Hospitallers, 172, 174–5,
   176–7, 178, 185, 187, 188–90, 198, 207,
   231, 323, 436

and Lancastrians, 404, 419, 429, 438,
   447, 451, 461, 464
later life, 69, 404, 406, 409, 414
lawsuits, 132, 136–7, 143, 149, 216–17,
   263, 279, 322, 324–5
legal records, 19, 20, 85, 188, 208, 215,
   216, 246, 247, 250, 251, 294, 316, 322,
   330, 367–8, 370–1, 389
in London, 169, 235, 250, 313, 322, 337,
   343, 370, 379, 395, 397, 462, 465–6
loyalty to Henry VI, 198, 255, 367, 372,
   376, 378, 408, 415, 418–19, 460, 462,
   472
marriage, 137, 138, 206, 245, 305, 306,
   395, 396
as Member of Parliament, 11, 19, 202,
   219, 234, 243, 245, 259, 261, 264, 265,
   267, 275, 278, 372, 376, 408, 454
military service, 11, 13–14, 18–19, 68–9,
   83, 93, 114, 116, 119, 121, 124, 128, 129,
   134, 138, 140, 147, 149, 150, 153, 165,
   176, 191, 196–7, 200, 201, 358, 360
and music, 208
mysteries, 94, 132, 134
and neighbours, 215, 338, 408, 409
in Northamptonshire, 199, 444, 467
patrons, 20, 51, 86, 87, 218, 251, 254, 314,
   338, 474
reformist views, 290, 372, 377
and religion, 176, 409, 465
reputation, 1–2, 10, 130, 404
and Saintraille, 141–2, 167, 168
as sheriff, 202
siblings, 67, 138
social position, 202–3, 324
spying, 358, 430
swordsman, 80–1
tomb, 11, 464, 467
and tournaments, 399, 405, 435
training in chivalry, 74, 78, 79–80, 383
travel, 69, 75, 102, 134, 177, 204
and treason, 13, 99, 426, 430, 435, 438
trials, 315–16, 325, 335, 337, 341, 342, 349
and Wales, 54, 477, 478
in Warwickshire, 156, 169, 178, 188, 201,
   215, 219, 243, 281, 287, 290, 315, 358–9,
   365, 395, 408, 444, 465
wealth, 152, 156, 182, 204, 246, 323, 396,
   466
and Winchester, 261
and women, 373

Malory, Sir Thomas – *cont.*
  as writer, 11, 12, 13, 15, 19–20, 32, 76, 93,
    94, 116, 130, 146, 151, 152, 177, 180, 215,
    237, 239, 283, 286, 344, 359, 372–3,
    404, 406, 430
  and Yorkist army, 390, 392
  see also *Morte Darthur*
Malory, Sir Thomas (of Kirkby Mallory),
    51, 56, 57, 115
Malory, Thomas (son of Sir Thomas),
    207, 359
Malory, Thomas (uncle), 56, 57, 68, 115,
    116, 124, 135, 246
Malory, Thomas (of Catthorpe and
    Bramcote), 47, 175
Malory, Thomas (of Hutton Conyers),
    11–12
Malory, Thomas (of Papworth St Agnes),
    11–12, 216
Malory, William (of Hutton Conyers), 87,
    416
Malory, Sir William (of Papworth
    St Agnes), 87, 162, 216
Malory, William (of Saddington), 245
Malory, William (of Sutton-le-Hone), 397
Malory, Sir William (of Walton-in-the-
    Wold and Tachbrook Mallory), 87,
    133, 135
Maltman, John, 320
Maltravers, Lord, 407
Manningham, John, 447, 449
March, Edmund Mortimer, Earl of, 86,
    122
March, Edward, Earl of, *see* Edward IV,
    King
Margaret of Anjou, Queen (wife of Henry
    VI), 221, 230–1, 238, 239, 334–5, 345,
    349, 351, 363, 373, 385, 423, 431, 437,
    451
  allies, 390, 435
  army, 378, 379, 381, 382, 384, 390–1
  and Beauchamps, 243
  character, 332
  and Coventry, 351–2, 365
  death, 469
  and Earl of Warwick, 449, 450, 452, 458
  in exile, 392, 419, 420, 421, 433, 436, 449,
    470
  favourites, 245, 246, 251, 318, 361
  flight to France, 393
  imprisoned, 458, 469

  income, 351
  influence, 236, 237, 248, 258, 267, 278,
    333, 351, 352, 365, 401, 407
  marriage, 228, 229, 232–4, 236
  pregnancy, 320, 331, 332–3
  ransom, 470
  as regent, 337–8, 352
  retinue, 364
  return, 424, 428, 429, 454, 455, 456, 458
  and Richard, Duke of York, 363, 364,
    378
  and Yorkists, 366, 376, 382
Margawse, Queen, 25, 27, 34, 91, 118–19
Marie of Anjou (wife of Charles VII of
    France), 159, 229
Mark, King, 28, 68, 80, 177, 209, 210, 345,
    362, 373, 407
Market Bosworth, 245
Markham, Sir John, 423
Marney, Sir John, 437
Marriott, Thomas, 208
Marseilles, 179
Marshall, Robert, 426, 429, 447, 449
Martin V, Pope, 103
Masshot, John, 208, 282
Massingham, John, 101
Master of Game, The, 82–3
Matthews, John, 3
Maxstoke Castle, 223–4, 283, 287
Meaux, 142, 143
Mechtild, St: *The Book of Ghostly Grace*,
    255
Melbourne, Simon, 194
Melcombe, Dorset, 45
Meldrum, Sir Andrew, 176, 187
Meliagaunce, Sir, 29, 83, 122, 310, 311, 312,
    336, 344
Melun, 128
Merbury, Nicholas, 118
Merlin, 25, 51, 118, 160, 257, 293, 474
Merlin, 151
Metz, 102
Meung, 158
Mézières, Philippe de, 90
Middleham Castle, 366, 445
Middlemore, Thomas, 136
Middleton, Sir Hugh, 176
Middleton, Thomas, 275
Mille, Hugh, 422, 423, 425, 427, 428, 430,
    435
Mille, Sir William, 428

Milton, John, 10, 477
Mirk, John: *Festial*, 66
Misterton, Leicestershire, 136, 166
Moleyns, Adam, 226, 227, 242, 262, 265, 266
Moleyns, Eleanor, 431
Monks Kirby, 60, 279, 465
  Priory, 39, 40, 58, 216, 276, 282, 325, 335, 338, 359
Mont St-Michel, 126, 153
Montagu, Lord *see* Neville, Sir John
Montagu, Thomas *see* Salisbury, Thomas Montagu, Earl of
Montargis, 154, 158
Montgomery, Sir Thomas, 413
Montvilliers, 125
Mordred, 25, 28, 30, 34, 35, 81, 370, 384, 386–7, 405, 417, 480
More, Sir Thomas, 406
Morgan le Fay, 24, 25, 68, 154
Morris, William, 10, 479
Morte Arthur, Le, 37, 238, 305
Morte Arthure, 65, 120, 177, 238, 305
Morte Darthur, 9, 19, 23–37, 71, 85, 134, 141, 146, 215, 378, 476
  adultery, 307, 308, 311
  author confirmed, 294
  battles, 13, 23, 25, 26, 29, 30, 141
  blood feuds, 352
  ceremonies, 177
  composition, 13, 220, 239, 312, 344, 418–19
  copied or dictated, 430, 440, 444
  dedication, 29, 419, 439
  divisions, 24
  editions, 1, 476–9
  ending, 32, 439, 474
  epilogue, 465
  'explicits', 12, 24, 25, 26–7, 28–9, 30, 31–2, 344, 419, 439, 465, 478
  friends mentioned, 141, 168
  hermits, 66, 178
  horses, 81
  illustrations, 476, 479
  influence, 9–10, 20–1, 438, 477, 479, 480–1
  inspiration, 85, 130, 145, 158
  interpretation, 14, 213, 295, 345
  kinship, 207–8, 213
  knighthood, 194, 451
  Ladies of the Lake, 374

language, 130, 406, 451, 480, 481
last chapter, 461–2
loyalty, 49, 68, 213, 367, 417
manuscript (Winchester), 12, 20, 24, 26, 35–6, 41, 101, 130, 261, 439, 444, 471, 472, 474
message, 20–1, 24, 27, 31, 32–5, 145, 479
music, 208, 209
names of characters, 168, 306
paramours, 306–7
place-names, 168
printing, 3, 12, 24, 26, 34, 84, 130, 261, 471–2, 474–5, 476
readers, 20, 312, 400, 441, 476
and religion, 66
servants, 209–10
sorceresses, 154
sources, 20, 23–4, 26, 28, 30, 32, 35, 37, 54, 65, 76, 78, 116, 120, 122, 129, 168, 177, 180, 190, 195, 209, 237–8, 305, 309, 406
and spying, 118–19
style, 19–20, 32, 35, 66, 75, 80, 133, 146, 208
themes, 33, 177, 475
tournaments, 54, 80–1, 261, 405, 413
as translation, 14, 23, 25, 29, 151, 152, 220, 239, 407, 474
uncles and nephews, 68, 91
Welsh links, 54
women, 31, 32, 36, 292–3, 305–6, 307, 373
'worship', 130
'The Book of Sir Tristram of Lyonesse', 27–8, 34, 68, 72, 76–7, 80, 82, 167–8, 202, 213, 238, 239
'The Last Battle', 384, 386–7, 388
'The Table or Rubrics', 24
'The Tale of Alisander le Orphelin', 407
'The Tale of Beaumains', 132, 181, 264
'The Tale of how Arthur became Emperor of Rome', 26, 59–60, 65, 102, 120, 125–6, 128–30, 177, 179, 213
'The Tale of Isolde the Fair', 86, 305
'The Tale of King Arthur', 9, 24–5, 39, 51, 114, 177, 191, 213, 238, 344
'The Tale of King Arthur and the Emperor Lucius', 146, 149, 358
'The Tale of Lancelot and Guinevere', 29–30, 83, 181, 195, 198, 209, 305, 308–9, 311, 312, 331, 336, 392, 414

Morte Darthur – cont.
  'The Tale of Sir Gareth of Orkney', 27,
    101, 202, 239
  'The Tale of Sir Lancelot du Lake', 27,
    37, 138, 145, 199, 273
  'The Tale of Sir Tor', 74
  'The Tale of Sir Tristram', 251–2, 313,
    347, 355, 362
  the tale of the giant of Mont St-Michel,
    153
  'The Tale of the Morte Arthur', 30–2,
    104, 145, 177, 198
  'The Tale of the Sangreall', 213, 419
Mortimer family, 86, 272
Mortimer, Edmund, Earl of March *see*
    March, Edmund Mortimer, Earl of
Mortimer, Sir Edmund, 56
'Mortimer, John' *see* Cade, Jack
Mortimer, Roger, 86
Mortimer's Cross, 380, 427
Moseley, John, 194, 315
Moton, Sir Robert, 116, 329, 330, 335–6
Mountfort family, 78
Mountfort, Sir Baldwin, 247, 264, 475
Mountfort, Edmund, 247, 249
Mountfort, Sir Edward, 475
Mountfort, Henry, 475
Mountfort, Simon, 247
Mountfort, Sir Simon, 475
Mountfort, Sir William, 75, 94, 156, 200,
    223, 234, 247, 275, 279, 283, 284, 329,
    335, 397
Mountjoy, Lord *see* Blount, Sir Walter
Moveley, John, 194, 315
Mowbray family, 49, 70, 324
Mowbray, Anne, Duchess of Norfolk, 468
Mowbray, Thomas, 58
Multon, Robert, 175
Murat II, Sultan of Turkey, 178
music, 79–80, 208–9
Mylner, John, 279, 288
Mylner, Robert, 279
Mynton, Thomas, 437, 438

Naillac, Philbert de, 136, 185
Nanteglos, Thomas, 299, 301
navy, 16, 92, 105–6, 111, 119–20, 436
  French or Breton, 111, 356
  strengthened, 356, 360, 362, 422
Neaufles, 148
Neville family, 34, 171, 186, 280, 333, 346,
    347, 349, 368, 374–5, 388, 393, 394,
    421, 455, 458
Neville, Anne *see* Anne, Queen
Neville, Anne *see* Buckingham, Anne
    Neville, Duchess of
Neville, Cecily (wife of Harry, 14th Earl of
    Warwick), 170, 171, 194, 220
Neville, Cecily (wife of Richard, Duke of
    York), 331, 443
Neville, Charles, 446
Neville, George (Archbishop of York), 365,
    378, 382, 383, 383, 388, 410, 425, 442,
    443, 444, 445
Neville, George *see also* Latimer, George
    Neville, Lord
Neville, Sir Henry, 444
Neville, Sir Humphrey, 394, 426, 427, 428,
    431, 432, 433, 446, 447
Neville, Sir John (later Earl of
    Northumberland, then Lord
    Montagu), 378, 388, 393, 400, 423,
    427, 447, 452, 455, 456, 457, 458
Neville, Ralph, 224
Neville, Ralph *see* Westmorland, Ralph
    Neville, Earl of
Neville, Richard (son of the Earl of
    Salisbury), 170, 171
Neville, Richard *see* Salisbury, Richard
    Neville, Earl of
Neville, Sir Richard *see* Warwick, Richard
    Neville, 16th Earl of
Neville, Thomas, 379, 452
Newbold Revel, Warwickshire, 10, 40, 44,
    45, 46, 48–9, 50, 59, 60–2, 137, 170,
    284, 384, 395, 409, 468
  attacked, 265
  chapel, 41, 66, 210, 214
  coats of arms, 205–6
  furnishing, 210–11
  overlord, 275–6
  as Prison Service college, 60–1
  servants, 208
  windows, 204–5, 206
Newbury, 267
Newnham Paddox, 389, 408
Nicholas V, Pope, 221, 409
Nicholas, Griffith ap, 250, 427
Nicholas, Henry ap Thomas ap Griffith,
    427, 428, 446
Nicolson, William, 477–8
Nicopolis, 102

Nine Worthies, 65, 146, 352, 471
Norfolk, John Howard, Duke of, 390, 391
Norfolk, Mowbray Dukes of, 49, 70, 270
Norfolk, John Mowbray, 3rd Duke of, 275,
    276, 290, 315, 316, 320, 325, 327, 334,
    374
  death, 431
  and Great Council, 338, 342, 346
  household, 326–7
  retinue, 337
  and Yorkists, 379, 383, 384, 386
Norfolk, Katherine Neville, Dowager
    Duchess of, 331, 374
Norfolk, Thomas, Duke of, 72–3
Normandy, 14, 18, 19, 53, 83, 89, 105, 140,
    147, 148, 196, 248, 250, 251, 257, 258,
    261–2, 273, 277, 332, 362
  occupation, 114, 117–26, 130, 132, 133,
    146, 149, 150, 152, 154, 192, 258
Normandy, John, Duke of, 72
Normandy, Rollo, Duke of, 41
Norris, John, 219, 423, 426, 431
Northampton, battle of, 369, 458
Northamptonshire, 45, 46, 55, 468
Northumberland, Henry Percy, Earl of,
    346, 347, 348, 352, 379, 385, 447, 456
  see also Neville, Sir John
Nuneaton, 11, 13, 287, 289, 313
  Priory, 287

Oakeshott, Walter, 12
Ockwells (Bray), 431
Ohler, Norbert: The Medieval Traveller,
    180
Oldhall, Sir William, 274, 276, 283, 318,
    320, 329, 336, 338, 342, 349, 353, 371
Oldys, William, 478
Order of the Garter see Knights of the
    Garter
Order of St John of Jerusalem see Knights
    Hospitallers
Orléans, Charles, Duke of, 91, 108, 158,
    226, 230–1, 334
Orléans, Louis, Duke of, 127
Orléans, 143, 158–9
Oulgreve, Sir Thomas, 423
Overton, Robert, 353, 354, 355, 356
Overton, William, 354
Ovid, 99, 415
Oxford, John Vere, Earl of, 437, 452, 456,
    457

Oxford, 422
  All Souls College, 109
  Bodleian Library, 94–5
  Magdalen College, 430
  University, 399

Pageant of the Birth, Life and Death of
    Richard Beauchamp, Earl of Warwick,
    75–6, 100, 473
Pailton, 40, 45, 170
Pakenham, Hugh, 422, 423, 425
Palomides, Sir, 28, 76–7, 141, 345, 374,
    413
Paris, 98, 105, 122, 125, 140, 142, 166
  Hôtel des Tournelles, 150
  Hôtel Jean de la Haye, 150
  Louvre, 142, 151
  Notre-Dame, 151, 166
  Palais Royal, 166
  royal library, 151–2
Parliament, 19, 42, 113, 157, 234, 261–2, 265,
    268, 274, 289, 348
  attacked, 276
  elections, 346–7
  general pardon, 348, 349–50
  and Henry VI, 279, 280, 347,
  House of Commons, 17, 89, 139, 265,
    266, 269, 277
  House of Lords, 17, 89, 139, 235–6, 265,
    266, 267, 268, 334, 348, 377
  meeting-places, 57–9, 91, 249, 261, 267
  Members, 17, 133, 234–5, 249, 258–9,
    260, 269, 274, 276, 454
  and reforms, 289, 329
Paslowe, Alice, 423, 426
Paston family, 247, 315
Paston, Clement, 69
Paston, John, 137, 266, 273, 322, 345, 391,
    395, 396, 404, 446, 465
Paston, Sir John, 213, 399–400, 414, 430,
    434–5
Paston, Margaret, 266, 377, 396
Paston, William, 395
Patay, battle of, 160
Pattishall, 148
Paule, Sir Richard, 188
Payling, Simon, 249
Pecche, Sir William, 391
Pelham, Sir John, 88
Pelles (Fisher King), 25, 28, 307
Pellinore, King, 33, 82, 293, 353

Pembroke, Jasper Tudor, Earl of, 329, 337, 338, 380, 392, 424, 425, 427, 428, 429, 436, 452, 458
Penshurst Castle, 250, 263, 316
Percival, Sir, 10, 29, 33, 68, 71, 105, 221, 307, 418
Percy family, 56, 186, 333, 339, 379
Percy, Harry ('Hotspur'), 56, 57
Percy, Sir Ralph, 393
Percy, Thomas, 333, 369
Peronne, 107
Perys, Sir, 292, 295, 307
Peyto, Katherine, Lady, 224, 225
Peyto, Sir William, 135, 155–6, 224–5, 289, 335–6, 354, 359
Philip II, King of France, 89
Philip IV, King of France, 89
Philip VI, King of France, 72
Philip the Fair, Archduke of the Netherlands, 475
Philip, Matthew, 316
Philip, Thomas, 427, 429, 433, 437, 447, 449
Picardy, 89, 95, 97, 100, 140
Pierre, Isambart de, 164
piracy, 112–13, 185, 362, 364
Pius II, Pope, 410, 443
plague, 17, 64, 69, 359, 460
Plantagenet, Arthur, 401
Plantagenet, Elizabeth, 401
Plummer, Sir John, 422, 426, 429, 454
Poitiers, 72
    battle of, 89, 149
Pole, William de la *see* Suffolk, William de la Pole, 1st Duke of
Pollard, A. W., 3
Pont de l'Arche, 258
Pontefract, 379, 384, 385
Pontorson, 152–3, 154
Pope, Alexander, 296
Portaleyn, Thomas, 219, 422, 423, 425, 430–1
Portland, Dorset, 111
Potter, Thomas, 294, 302, 303, 313
Poynings (Lancastrian conspirator), 433, 436–7
Pre-Raphaelites, 21, 479, 480
Pulteney family, 136, 137, 206
Pulteney, John, 136, 137, 140
Pulteney, Sir John, 136, 137, 143
Pulteney, Thomas, 137, 139, 149, 166
Pulton, Thomas, 315, 350

Purefoy, Margaret (née Chetwynd), 47–8, 137, 194, 408
Purefoy, William, 47, 75, 137, 194, 408

Queenborough Castle, 272

Ragusa, 410
Ramsay Abbey, 285
Rawcliffe, Carole, 222
Reading Abbey, 403
Regnault de Montet, 98–9
Reims, 159, 160, 166
    Abbey of Saint-Rémi, 160, 165
René, King of Jerusalem, Duke of Anjou, 228–30, 231, 232, 236, 469–70
Revel family, 45, 46, 47, 52, 66, 98, 175, 205
Revel, Hugh, 45, 175
Revel, Margaret, 45
Revel, Nicholas, 409
Revel, Pierre de, 98
Revel, William, 45, 137
Rhodes, 18, 69, 136, 172–3, 174, 176, 177, 178, 181–5, 188, 190
Richard II, King, 16, 39, 44, 50, 51, 53, 54, 55, 72, 90, 458
Richard III, King, 16, 34, 157, 382, 388, 424, 456, 457, 459, 469, 470, 472, 473, 474
Richard, Duke of Gloucester *see* Richard III, King
Richard, Duke of York (father of Edward IV and Richard III), 34, 133, 219, 249, 250, 270, 271, 277, 278, 290, 331, 365, 367
    attainted, 409
    and councils, 334, 342, 351, 365
    death, 379, 380, 431
    enemies, 347, 351, 365, 379
    estates, 275, 280, 329, 365, 366
    and France, 220–1, 226, 227, 231, 242–3, 251, 262
    as heir to the throne, 228, 251, 269, 280, 283, 319, 333, 334, 351, 377, 378, 380, 382, 450
    and Henry VI, 320, 365, 376, 377, 400
    household, 272, 281
    in the north, 339, 340–1
    pardoned, 365
    patronage, 275, 276
    as Protector, 338, 342, 345, 346, 348, 351, 378
    retinue, 337, 339, 341, 347, 361, 376, 379

return from Ireland, 273–5
revenue, 378
and (Duke of) Somerset, 334, 346
supporters, 276, 318–19, 320, 321, 325–6,
    328, 335, 336, 338, 348–9, 353, 364, 368
Richard, Duke of York (son of Edward
    IV), 468, 469, 470
Richard de Bury: *Philobiblon*, 416, 466
Richemont, Arthur de, 152
Richmond, Edmund Tudor, Earl of, 329,
    337, 338, 353
Riddy, Felicity, 295
Ripley, George, 410
Rivers, Richard Woodville, Earl, 133, 148,
    280, 364, 390, 400, 423, 439, 444, 445
Robin of Redesdale, 443, 444
Rochester, 179
Rokely, Robert, 197
Roman Catholic Church, 17–18, 20, 66, 84,
    102–3, 285, 377
  indulgences, 185, 186
  pilgrimage, 18, 69, 75
romances *see* literature
Roos, Lord, 392
Roos, Sir Richard, 168, 211, 239, 373, 395
Roos, Sir Thomas de, 133, 162
Rossetti, Dante Gabriel, 479
Rotuli Normaniae, 121
Rouen, 124, 125, 144, 150, 154, 158, 162, 163,
    164, 165, 193, 261, 273
  Bouvreuil Castle, 162, 163, 165
Round Table, 10, 25, 151, 261, 473, 475,
    476
Rous, John, 218, 221, 224, 225, 255
Rous Roll, 255
Rowe, Benedicta, 133
Rowe, William, 282, 288
Rozmital, Leo von, 412
Rugby Castle, 224
Ruthin Castle, 54
Rutland, Edmund, Earl of (son of
    Richard, Duke of York), 378, 379, 380

Saddington, 135, 215
St Albans, battles of, 347–8, 349, 352, 361,
    379, 380, 381, 431
St-Pol, Jacques, Count of, 404
St Riquier, 140
St-Vaast-la-Hougue, 122
Saintraille, Sir Pothon de, 140, 141–2, 160,
    165, 166, 167, 168, 196, 273

Salisbury, Richard Neville, Earl of, 236,
    243, 277, 289, 348, 361, 364–5
  children, 170, 171, 252, 253
  execution, 379–80
  in Normandy, 121, 125
  offices, 280, 338, 341, 346, 378
  and Yorkists, 366, 367, 368, 379
Salisbury, Thomas Montagu, Earl of, 139,
    146, 158
Salisbury Plain, 30, 388
Sandal, 379, 456
Sandford, Oxfordshire, 173
Sandwich, 59, 60, 95–6, 120, 129, 187–8,
    356, 366, 368, 443, 446
Saumur, 229, 230, 470
Saye, James Fiennes, Lord, 271
Scales, Ismania, Lady, 382
Scales, Anthony Woodville, Lord, 167, 271,
    369, 412–13, 425
Scofield, Cora, 285
Scotland, 55, 56, 90, 91, 92, 104, 147, 390, 393
  allied with France, 149
  and Lancastrians, 390, 391, 393, 446
Scott, Giles Gilbert, 189
Scott, Richard, 340
Scott, Sir Walter, 21, 293, 478, 481
Scrope family, 176
Scrope, Henry, 176
Scrope, John, 176
Scrope, Lord, of Bolton, 385
Scrope, Richard, 55, 58, 75, 77
Seaton, Ethel, 239
Seine, River, 106, 110, 111, 117, 120, 125
Sellar, W. C., 253
Shakespeare, William, 10, 295, 397
  history plays, 16, 56, 73, 108, 114, 250, 380
Sharp, Henry, 194
Sharp, John, 320
Shawe, John and Joan, 285
Shawell, Leicestershire, 44, 45, 136, 137, 138,
    170, 282
Sheen, 198, 412
Shippey, Tom, 295
Shirley, John, 15, 94, 95, 102
Shirley, Ralph, 289
Shrewsbury, John Talbot, 1st Earl of, 230,
    233, 256, 277–8, 289
  army commander, 14, 112, 133, 146–7,
    158, 193, 321
  death, 332
  as prisoner, 160, 162, 165, 167

Shrewsbury, John, 2nd Earl of, 369, 385, 390, 413, 452

Shrewsbury, Margaret Beauchamp, Countess of, 256, 277, 278

Shrewsbury, 57

Shuckburgh, John, 423

Sidney, Sir Philip, 406, 477

Sigismund, King of Bohemia and Holy Roman Emperor, 102, 103, 110–11, 229, 481

Simnel, Lambert, 475

Sluys, Flanders, 433

Smite Brook, 60, 70, 284

Smith, Henry, 302

Smith, Hugh, 217, 288, 294–5, 300, 301, 302–3, 304–5, 313–14, 318, 325

Smith, Joan, 217, 288, 294, 295, 301–2, 304–5, 309, 312, 313, 374

Smith, John, 303

Smith, Robert, 208

Smith, Thomas, 216, 217

Smith, William, 282, 289

Soissons, 102

Somerset, Edmund Beaufort, Duke of, 223, 244, 250, 256, 289, 317–18, 346
  army commander, 243, 251, 261, 262, 271, 274
  arrested, 334
  attacked, 275, 276, 319, 320
  death, 348, 431
  protector, 338
  and Queen Margaret, 331, 333
  retinue, 337
  and Richard, Duke of York, 334, 342, 347, 348

Somerset, Elinor Beauchamp, Countess of, 256, 277, 278

Somerset, Henry Beaufort, Earl of Somerset, 352, 361, 363, 366, 379, 385, 390, 392, 392–3, 393–4, 435, 456, 458

Somerset, John, 157

Somerset, John Beaufort, Earl of, 201, 226, 229, 266, 269, 277, 278, 280

Somerset, 10, 318

Somme, River, 107, 142

Southampton, 111, 114, 119

Spenser, Edmund, 9–10, 220, 295, 345, 477

Spratton, 216, 217

spying, 99, 118–19, 361, 421

squires, 80, 84, 85, 94, 115

Stafford family, 222, 247, 413, 455

Stafford, Dowager Countess of, 223

Stafford, Earls of, 49, 223

Stafford, Henry (son of the Duke of Buckingham), 365, 407, 444

Stafford, Humphrey (of Grafton), 265

Stafford, Sir Humphrey (son of Duke of Buckingham), 247, 256

Stafford, Sir Humphrey see also Buckingham, Humphrey Stafford, Duke of

Stafford, John, Archbishop of Canterbury, 224, 225, 262, 316

Stafford, Richard, 247, 339, 455

Stairs, Richard, 436–7

Stamford, 267
  battle of, 448

Stanley, Thomas, Lord, 404, 452

Stansby, William, 477

Stanton Harcourt, 245, 246, 265

Steinbeck, John, 10, 36–7

Stonor, Sir Edmund, 69

Stonor, Ralph, 465

Stonor, Thomas, 465

Stormsworth, Leicestershire, 44, 408

Stour, River, 96

Strange, Sir Baldwin, 75, 94, 95, 102, 104, 112, 113, 186

Stretton-under-Fosse, 40, 45, 170

Studleu, John, 337

Styrrup, Nottinghamshire, 71

Sudeley, Lord, 228, 240, 255

Suffolk, Alice Chaucer, Duchess of, 244–5, 277, 399, 469

Suffolk, Humphrey, Earl of, 154, 163

Suffolk, John de la Pole, 2nd Duke of, 379, 390

Suffolk, William de la Pole, 1st Duke of, 222, 226, 231, 232, 233, 242, 243–4, 245, 248, 249, 251, 258, 262, 373
  arrest and execution, 265–8, 269, 280, 332
  attacked, 240, 270, 275, 321

Surluse, 76, 81

Sutton family, 46, 175

Sutton, Margaret, 135

Sutton-le-Hone, 174, 397

Swinford, Katherine, 91, 254, 403

Swinford, Leicestershire, 44, 50, 59, 135, 136, 170, 175, 176, 204, 246, 282, 303, 395, 408, 468, 470

Tachbrook Mallory, 44, 87, 215
Tailors' Company, 188
Talbot family, 224, 428
Talbot, Lady Eleanor, 469
Talbot, John see Shrewsbury, John Talbot, Earl of
Talbot, Lady Margaret, 162, 165
Tartas, 197, 200
Tempest, John, 416
Tempest, Sir Richard, 416
Temple Balsall, 189
Tennyson, Alfred, Lord, 10, 21, 29, 307, 479
Tessancourt, 41, 148
Tetzel, Gabriel, 412
Tewdwr, Owen ap Maredudd ap, 157
Tewkesbury
    Abbey, 244
    battle of, 14, 458, 460
Thaxted, 339, 340
Thames, River, 95, 157, 167, 336
Thomas, Duke of Clarence (son of Henry IV), 86, 90, 92, 104, 119, 121, 125, 139, 186
Thomas, Sir William ap, 219
Thorney, Roger, 398
Tilty Abbey, 339
Tintagel, 10, 24, 158
Tiptoft, Sir John see Worcester, John Tiptoft, Earl of
Topps, Jane, 395
Tor, Sir, 33, 74, 191, 293–4
Touques, 120, 121
Touraine, Duc de, 143
tournaments, 70–3, 167, 203, 229–30, 392–3, 399, 404, 476
    armour, 203
    Golden Tree, 434–5
    international, 71, 75–6, 124–5, 412–14
    Twelfth Night, 100–1
Tours, 229, 231
Towton, battle of, 385–6, 387–8, 409, 428, 431
travel, 59–60, 177, 179–80
Tres Riches Heures du Duc de Berry, 98
Tresham, Sir Thomas, 437
Tresham, William, 266, 274
Trinity Royal, 119, 120
Tristan, 99
Tristram (poem), 82, 151, 167
Tristram, Sir, 10, 24, 25, 27–8, 36, 68, 76,
77, 82, 130, 151, 167–8, 177, 202, 209, 210, 218, 305–6, 355, 362, 407
Trollope, Andrew, 366, 379, 381, 385
Troyes, 128
Troyes, Treaty of, 128
Tudor dynasty, 16, 157, 351, 459, 470, 475
Tudor, Owen, 380–1
Tunstall, Sir Richard, 423, 454
Turkey, 173, 174, 178, 181, 410
Turks, 102, 110, 136, 145, 161, 178, 409
Turner, John, 417
Twain, Mark, 23
Twelfth Night plot, 53, 54
Tyler, William, 426
Tyrell, Sir William, 289

Umfraville, Sir Gilbert, 112
Urry, Sir, 33, 312, 480
Urswick, Sir Thomas, 214
Uther Pendragon, King, 24–5, 51

Vale, John, 251, 432, 438, 447, 451
Valens, John, 338
Vampage, John, 219
Vegetius: De Re Militari, 83, 117, 118, 184, 238
Venice, 410
Venner, William, 327–8
Verdon, William, 427, 429, 447
Vere, Sir Robert, 196
Verneuil, battle of, 149
Vernon, John, 289
Vernon, William, 429–30, 449
Vexin, 147, 148
Vide, Thomas, 299
Vignolles, Etienne de ('La Hire'), 140, 158, 160
Vinaver, Eugène, 24, 37, 101
Vincennes, 142, 143
Vincent, Richard, 170
Vincent, Robert, 170, 204, 246, 254, 282
Voyennes, 107

Wagner, Richard, 27
Wake, Thomas, 134, 207, 208, 445
Wakefield (Sandal), 379, 380, 428, 431
Wales, 54, 55, 56, 57, 58, 91, 117, 274, 281, 283, 379, 427–8, 429, 441, 445, 446, 447, 474
    Marches, 353, 380, 441, 445
Wallingford Castle, 266, 399

Walsh family, 206, 245, 315
Walsh, Helen, 408
Walsh, John, 133, 315, 328
Walsh, Margery (née Byron), 408
Walsh, Thomas, 245, 246, 315, 389, 408
Walsh, William, 315
Walsingham, Thomas, 90
Walsingham, 18, 138, 274
Walthamstow, 167, 220
Walton-on-the-Wold, 215
Warbeck, Perkin, 475
Ware, 349
Wareham, 275, 283
Warkworth, John, 426, 452
Warkworth, 390, 391
Wars of the Roses, 13, 16, 19, 34, 59
    see also Lancastrians; Yorkists
Warton, Christopher, 316
Warwick, Earls of, 55, 255
Warwick, Anne Beauchamp, 15th
    Countess of Warwick, 243–4, 245,
    252, 278
Warwick, Anne Beauchamp, Countess
    (wife of 16th Earl), 76, 162, 170, 220,
    252, 254–5, 156, 278, 290, 314, 331, 360,
    366, 472–3
Warwick, Edward, 17th Earl of, 475, 476
Warwick, Harry Beauchamp, 14th Earl of
    (later Duke), 218–19, 225, 228, 261,
    430, 431
    and Buckingham, 224, 225, 226, 234,
        235–6, 240, 243
    death, 239–40, 242, 266, 269, 438
    estates, 232, 240, 243
    in France, 193, 229
    and Henry VI, 222, 229, 232, 240, 242,
        243, 418
    household, 219, 234
    as knight, 221, 222
    marriage, 194
    military service, 221–2, 227, 229
    patronage, 221, 234
    power in Warwickshire, 224, 225
    rivals, 224, 225
    in royal council, 218, 219
Warwick, Isobel Despenser, Countess of,
    150, 152, 162, 167, 193, 218, 219, 244,
    255, 256, 280
Warwick, Richard Beauchamp, 13th Earl
    of, 18, 55, 57, 58, 73, 77, 86, 96, 139,
    186, 430, 451, 481

as ambassador, 102, 103, 111, 125, 127, 151
as army commander, 104, 110, 112, 113,
    114–15, 116, 119, 126, 128, 140, 142, 146,
    147, 150, 152, 154, 165, 178, 192–3, 273
banners, 154, 193
at Calais, 93, 94, 95, 98, 104, 105, 109,
    110, 111
children, 150, 155, 157, 162, 170–1, 256,
    277
death, 193–4
estates, 126, 152, 155
guardian of Henry VI, 155, 156–8, 166,
    167, 169, 191
household, 74–5, 76, 95, 113, 150, 158,
    162, 163, 166
and Joan of Arc, 163
jousting, 100–1, 103, 108
knighted, 55, 111
library, 167
local power, 49, 55, 169
marriages, 78, 150, 155
pilgrimage, 75, 76
Pageant of the Birth, Life and Death,
    75–6, 100, 255, 473
and prisoners of war, 135, 152
and Regency Council, 150, 157, 169, 191
at Rouen, 158, 165, 166
as Steward of England, 88, 129
tomb, 101, 193, 255
wealth, 152, 169, 193
Warwick, Richard Neville, 16th Earl of
    (Kingmaker), 13, 252–6, 259, 277, 278,
    281, 283, 314, 319, 331, 333, 338, 346,
    367, 414
    and Act of Accord, 377–8, 383
    allies, 377, 452, 455
    attacked, 364
    badge, 453
    and Calais, 358, 360–1, 362, 364, 366,
        397, 404, 433, 443, 448–9, 450
    daughters, 441, 442, 451, 475
    death, 457, 458, 460
    and Duke of Clarence, 443, 444, 448,
        449, 456
    and Edward IV, 382, 384, 401, 402, 403,
        421, 424, 433, 438, 441–2, 443, 444–5,
        446, 447, 456
    estates, 280, 395, 397
    and France, 441, 449, 452, 455
    and Henry VI, 267, 268, 369, 377, 381,
        416–17, 430–1, 445, 453

household, 282, 397
and Lancastrians, 421, 423, 445, 447, 450, 452, 453, 455, 456
and Margaret of Anjou, 449, 450, 452, 455
memorial, 472
as military commander, 360–1, 362, 364, 366, 368, 384, 385, 393, 445, 446, 452
offices, 341, 348, 351, 356–7, 378, 381, 388
pardoned, 348, 365
as regent, 450–1, 454
retinue, 290, 337, 361, 364, 366
and royal council, 357, 364, 365
supporters, 315, 335, 348, 359, 363, 368–9, 381
wealth, 388
and Yorkists, 377, 379, 390, 391, 393, 394
Warwick, Thomas Beauchamp, 11th Earl of, 98
Warwick, Thomas Beauchamp, 12th Earl of, 55
Warwick, 193, 203
   Castle, 55, 57, 74, 78, 152, 170, 314, 395
   St Mary's, 472
Warwickshire, 39 40, 49, 57, 135, 224, 259, 468
Watford, Northamptonshire, 170, 216
Watling Street, 39, 60, 95, 179
Waurin, Jehan de, 112, 125, 141, 144, 146
Waynflete, William, 260–1, 269, 271, 290, 345, 430, 453
Wedding of Sir Gawaine and Dame Ragnell, The, 146, 239
Welles, Sir Robert, 448
Welles, Thomas, 260
Wenlock, Sir John, 14, 363, 367, 368, 378, 379, 381, 385, 388, 390, 417, 423, 427, 431–2, 433, 438, 439, 443, 449–50, 458
West, Alice, Lady, 297
West, Frederick, 189
West, Thomas, 477
West, Sir Thomas, 112, 113, 297–9
West Country, 280, 362, 436, 452
West Haddon, Northamptonshire, 45
Westmorland, Ralph Neville, Earl of, 91, 170, 222, 223, 390
Weston family, 303
Weston, John, 182, 303
Weston, Thomas, 303

Weston, William 294, 302, 303, 313
White, T. H., 1, 10, 479–80
Whitgreve, Richard, 259
Whitgreve, Robert, 194
Whittingham, Sir Robert, 422, 430
Whittington, Sir Richard, 354, 466
William I, the Conqueror, King, 41, 121, 123, 148
William of Worcester, 257
Willoughby, John, 302–3
Willoughby, Lord, 115
Wiltshire, James Ormond, Earl of, 380, 385, 431
Winchester, 10, 168, 250, 261, 267, 473, 475
   Castle, 261
   Cathedral, 12
   College, 12, 260, 261
Windsor Castle, 71–2, 198, 332, 349
   St George's chapel, 111, 459
Wingfield, Sir Robert, 326–7
Winwick, Northamptonshire, 45, 50, 59, 118, 170, 199, 389, 395, 468
witchcraft, 153–4, 159, 164, 227
Wolseley, Ralph, 315, 470
Women, 70, 84
   and adultery, 305
   forced into marriage, 300
   and rape, 291, 292, 296–300
Woodville family, 400, 401, 420, 421, 441, 451
Woodville, Sir Anthony (later Lord Rivers), 400, 436, 450, 456
Woodville, Sir Edward, 435
Woodville, Sir John, 436, 443, 444, 445
Woodville, Sir Richard see Rivers, Richard Woodville, Lord
Woodville, Thomas, 148
Worby, Jon, 421
Worcester, John Tiptoft, Earl of, 132, 385, 390, 393, 454
Workington, John, 447, 449
Worsop, William, 338
Worthington, Ralph, 338
Wren, Sir Christopher, 467
Wren, P. C.: Beau Geste, 176
Wrottesley, Sir Walter, 315, 443, 444, 464–5
Wyatt, Thomas, 406
Wycliffe, John, 18, 66
Wynkyn de Worde, 441, 476
Wynn, Charles, 426

Yeatman, R. J., 253
Yeats, W. B., 15, 479
Yelvertoft, 135
Yolande of Aragon, Queen, 159, 230
York, Cicely Neville, Duchess of (wife of
    Richard, Duke of York), 34, 219, 382, 402
York, 339, 341, 385, 386
Yorkists, 13, 15, 16, 34, 251, 276, 347–8, 368,
    376, 379, 380, 381, 431

army, 348, 366, 367, 379, 383–4, 385–6,
    391, 392, 457
attainted, 367
propaganda, 418, 443
Yorkshire, 333, 443
Young, Thomas, 280, 349

Zouche family, 42, 71, 186
Zouche, William de la, 44, 73, 261